מעלי תפילות

On
Wings
of Awe

A Machzor for Rosh Hashanah and Yom Kipp

On Wings of Awe

מעגלי תפילות

A Machzor for Rosh Hashanah and Yom Kippur

Edited and Translated by
Rabbi Richard N. Levy

B'nai B'rith Hillel Foundations
Washington, D.C.

Library of Congress Cataloging in Publication Data
Mahzor. High Holidays (Reform, Levy)
  On wings of awe = [Ma'ale tefilot].

  English and Hebrew.
  1. High Holidays—Liturgy—Texts. 2. Mahzorim—Texts
3. Reform Judaism—Liturgy—Texts. I. Levy, Richard N.
II. B'nai B'rith Hillel Foundations. III. Title RV. Title: Ma'ale
tefilot.
BM 675.H5Z6643 1985   296.4'31   85-12804

MANUFACTURED IN THE UNITED STATES OF AMERICA

CONTENTS

וִיהִי רָצוֹן מִלְּפָנֶיךָ יְיָ, אֱלֹהֵי אַבְרָהָם יִצְחָק וְיַעֲקֹב,
אֱלֹהֵי שָׂרָה רִבְקָה רָחֵל וְלֵאָה, הָאֵל הַגָּדוֹל הַגִּבּוֹר
וְהַנּוֹרָא, אֵל עֶלְיוֹן, אֶהְיֶה אֲשֶׁר אֶהְיֶה, שֶׁכָּל
הַמַּלְאָכִים שֶׁהֵם מַעֲלֵי תְפִלּוֹת יָבִיאוּ תְפִלָּתִי לִפְנֵי
כִסֵּא כְבוֹדֶךָ, וְיַצִּיגוּ אוֹתָהּ לְפָנֶיךָ, בַּעֲבוּר כָּל
הַצַּדִּיקִים וְהַחֲסִידִים, הַתְּמִימִים וְהַיְשָׁרִים, וּבַעֲבוּר
כְּבוֹד שִׁמְךָ הַגָּדוֹל וְהַנּוֹרָא, כִּי אַתָּה שׁוֹמֵעַ
תְּפִלַּת עַמְּךָ יִשְׂרָאֵל בְּרַחֲמִים. בָּרוּךְ אַתָּה שׁוֹמֵעַ
תְּפִלָּה.

May it be Your will
That the angels who raise up prayers to heaven on their wings
Bring in each one of our prayers before Your glorious throne
And offer them before You
For the sake of all the just and upright people who have come
  before us
And for the sake of Your great and awesome Name.

(*Hineni*, page 296)

FOREWORD

This Machzor has emerged out of many years, helped by many hands. It represents an approach to the Days of Awe which tries to be faithful to the philosophy of the B'nai B'rith Hillel Foundations at their best, respecting the diversity of the various movements in Judaism, but affirming common strands of faith amid all our divergences. Trying to emulate the understanding nature of the sage from whom we take our name, Hillel has long striven to enable Jews of many backgrounds to praise as one community the God who formed our faith. For that reason, it is hoped that congregations of various religious perspectives will also find this Machzor appropriate for their encounters with the Yamim Noraim.

As an example, this Machzor offers not only varied English renderings of traditional Hebrew prayers, but varied Hebrew possibilities as well: a Musaf Amidah, certain Reform variants to traditional texts, and the option to praise the Eternal not only as *Elohey Avoteynu,* the God of our Fathers, but as *Elohey Imoteynu,* the God of our Mothers, as well.

The initial text on which the Machzor was based had fewer options. It arose at UCLA Hillel out of a "creative" service which originally reflected the magic, troubled world of the late 1960's but which grew and changed through the years in a more traditional direction along with its congregation of students, faculty and community friends.

The service originated as an alternative to the traditional High Holyday service at UCLA Hillel, conducted by my good friend and former colleague Rabbi David M. Berner, now a resident of Israel. The traditional service for many years davened with a machzor prepared by Rabbi Berner and our colleague Rabbi Moshe Adler, later Hillel director at the University of Minnesota, and Dr. Rachel Adler, on whose remarkable translation we have drawn extensively in this Machzor. In 1977 Rabbi Dan Dorfman, Hillel director at the California State University at Northridge, and Rabbi Laura

Geller, Hillel director at the University of Southern California, helped enlarge the original "creative" machzor, enhancing its suitability for a more traditional congregation. It was then introduced to these campus congregations, as well as to Hillel at the University of California at Santa Barbara and to several Hillel Extension campuses. We were greatly aided in the musical selections for that endeavor by Dr. Marnin Kligfeld, now of San Francisco, long-time *chazzan* for the UCLA Hillel alternative service.

Rabbi Dorfman and Rabbi Geller have continued their association with this text by reading the manuscript and offering many helpful suggestions, as has Jonathan Omer-Man, a scholar of Jewish mysticism and director of the Religious Outreach Program for the Los Angeles Hillel Council. Several other Hillel colleagues, meeting at the 1982 Hillel Directors Conference, offered invaluable counsel. A debt is owed to Rabbi Robert Saks, Hillel director at the University of Maryland, for his initial urging that the Los Angeles machzor should be published, a proposal which was generously supported by the Board of the Los Angeles Hillel Council under two presidents, Michael Rappaport and Mark C. Levy.

But publication would not have occurred without the support and encouragement of Rabbi Samuel Z. Fishman, associate international director of the B'nai B'rith Hillel Foundations, who has ably and cheerfully managed the finances and distribution of the book, nor without the wonderfully patient and helpful nature of Bernard Scharfstein of Ktav, who has shepherded the manuscript through the press with much care and enthusiasm.

Burrowing through weeks and pages of illegible typescript, my secretary Sarah Kalevitch produced an immaculate manuscript with the consummate skill and loving devotion which have marked her many years with Los Angeles Hillel Council. This book could not have reached print without her.

It is a particular pleasure to acknowledge the aid of our daughter Sarah Miriam Levy, now 5, in the pasting up of the manuscript, and the forebearance of her sister, Elizabeth Mauree Levy, now 2, while she was doing it. In our children's second names are reflected my late parents, Miriam and Mauree

Levy, under whose wings I first encountered the Days of Awe. *Zichronam livracha*—their presence continues in this world, full of blessing.

It is also appropriate here to acknowledge a loving debt to my teacher and friend, Dr. Eugene Mihaly of the Hebrew Union College, whose exultant love of midrash fathered my own desire to study and write in that genre, and with whose encouragement I first began to create and translate prayers. His Torah is an enduring gift.

A month after the original version of this Machzor was first used, I met Carol Kretzer, who in the years of our journey from the chuppah has taught me much about love and covenants, sacrifice and preparedness, the resilience and fragility of women and men, the holiness which is a family. Chana, heroine of the haftarah for the first day of Rosh Hashanah, sings:

Because of God my heart exults,
Because of God my self respect has been restored.

To my companion Chana Rissa, whose song has uplifted the life we share, I would add: and because of you.

Ribono shel olam, grant blessings in abundance to all these gracious people, to all whose names have inadvertently been omitted, and to all who will open this book in search of You. Let the day dawn soon when all of us shall meet upon Your mountain, as a single community whose diversity may help reveal to all humanity the myriad gleaming facets of Your throne.

Richard N. Levy

Erev Shabbat Ki Tissa 5743
In which Moses gains atonement for his people

ACKNOWLEDGMENTS

The following publishers and authors have generously granted permission to print excerpts from the works indicated, for which we are most grateful. (Revised) indicates that the selection has been somewhat revised by the editor. Every effort has been made to locate copyright holders of original material. Omissions and errors will be corrected in forthcoming editions.

Rabbi Moshe Adler and *Dr. Rachel Adler:* Translations of Maariv Aravim (revised), Ya-aleh V'Yavo, Psalm 130, second and third paragraphs of the Sh'ma, major portions of the traditional silent Amidah (revised), major portions of the Musaf Amidah (revised), major portions of the Avodah and Eyleh Ezkerah Service. From a High Holy Day Machzor originally prepared for UCLA Hillel Council and Los Angeles Valley College Hillel Council, 1972. Used by permission.

Dr. Rachel Adler. "The Kabbalists tell us," derived from her service, "A Spark (A Service on Mystical Themes)," in *Bridges to a Holy Time,* © 1973 by Alfred Jospe and Richard N. Levy. Used by permission of the co-editor.

Central Conference of American Rabbis. "Adoration" (revised), from *Union Prayerbook,* volume II, copyright © 1945 by the Central Conference of American Rabbis; Hebrew text of Avodah prayer (evening and morning Amidah); and English version of "All the World Shall Come to Serve Thee," adapted from Israel Zangwill's translation (revised), from *Gates of Repentance,* copyright © 1978 by Central Conference of American Rabbis and the Union of Liberal and Progressive Synagogues; "It is hard to sing of oneness," by Rabbi Richard N. Levy, from *Gates of Prayer,* © 1975 by the Central Conference of American Rabbis and the Union of Liberal and Progressive Synagogues. Reprinted by permission of Central Conference of American Rabbis.

Rabbi Dan Dorfman. "Interpretation of Biyshiva Shel Ma-alah," by Rabbis Dan Dorfman and Neil Comess-Daniels. Used by permission of Rabbi Dan Dorfman.

Zev Falk. "All the Vows," by Dr. Zev Falk, translated by Rabbi Stanley Schachter. Used by permission of Dr. Falk.

Rabbi Laura Geller. "Adonay, our people have called you." Used by permission.

Farrar, Straus and Giroux, Inc. "God Means," and "Time is the border of eternity." Reprinted by permission of Farrar, Straus and Giroux, Inc. Selection adapted from *Man Is Not Alone* by Abraham Joshua Heschel. Copyright 1951 by Abraham Joshua Heschel. Copyright © 1979 by Sylvia Heschel.

Rabbi Emanuel Goldsmith. For "Praise me, says God," by Aaron Zeitlin, translated by Emanuel Goldsmith, from *New Prayers for the High Holy Days,* edited by Rabbi Jack Riemer, copyright © 1970, 1971 Media Judaica, Inc. Permission requested from Rabbi Goldsmith.

Alfred A. Knopf, Inc. "Your joy is your sorrow unmasked," reprinted from *The Prophet,* by Kahlil Gibran, by permission of Alfred A. Knopf, Inc. Copyright 1923 by Kahlil Gibran and renewed 1951 by Administrators C.T.A. of Kahlil Gibran Estate, and Mary G. Gibran.

Koren Publishers Jerusalem. The Hebrew text of the Bible chapters is taken from the Bible edition of Koren Publishers Jerusalem, with their permission.

Harold S. Kushner. "Life is not fair," from *When Bad Things Happen to Good People,* by Harold S. Kushner. Copyright © 1981 by Harold S. Kushner, published by Schocken Books. Used by permission of Harold S. Kushner.

Charles Scribner's Sons. Introduction to Eyleh Ezkerah: The
Ten Martyrs is adapted and condensed from *Man's Quest for
God* by Abraham Joshua Heschel with the permission of
Charles Scribner's Sons. Copyright 1954 Abraham Joshua
Heschel; copyright renewed 1982 Sylvia Heschel and Hannah
Susannah Heschel.

St. Martin's Press. "The same stream . . ." from Gitanjali
(Song Offerings) by Rabindranath Tagore, first published 1949
in London by Macmillan & Co. Ltd. and in New York by St.
Martin's Press. Reprinted 1962. Used by permission of St.
Martin's Press.

Ruth Whitman. "Night Song," from the *Selected Poems of
Jacob Glatstein* (October House, 1972) © 1972 by Ruth Whitman. Reprinted by permission of the translator.

INTRODUCTION

1. The Language of Awe

Elul—the sixth month of the Hebrew calendar—ends, like every other month, in darkness. But when the darkness parts before the golden thread of Tishri's moon, the herald of the seventh month, a time is revealed like no other in the Jewish calendar: the *Yamim Nora-im.* Often translated as the High Holydays, the Hebrew literally means the Awesome Days, days of *yir'ah,* days in which a world newly conceived shows us its two sides: full of wonder, majesty, beauty, capable of infinite fruitfulness; but capable also of infinite danger, destructiveness, even death. To stand on the crest of a high mountain is to confront both realities of *yir'ah*: the majesty of all that awaits our gaze, and the peril that awaits our fall. Sensing the presence of both, we are filled with awe.

To such a place have we come to spend the Days of Awe. Now is the majesty of God made manifest: that God is the proper sovereign of all nations, all peoples, is a recurrent theme of these days. But God is a sovereign like no other: God is *Avinu Malkeynu,* a sovereign who is also our father, our mother. We are the child of God, begotten, carried, and nurtured of the Being who created the universe—who conceives it anew each Rosh Hashanah. However lonely, however unworthy, any of us may feel, the Awesome Days remind us that in God's love we are never alone; because God is our ultimate parent we come of the worthiest stock there can be.

Yet the perilous side of these days is there as well. These are the Judgment Days, after all: on Rosh Hashanah, tradition has it, the decision is made as to whether we shall be inscribed in the Book of Life; on Yom Kippur the decision is sealed. As the Unetaneh Tokef reminds us, our whole life passes in judgment at this season—we cling to the mountain peak by a slender thread. But the Tishri moon is just as slender now, and its light

shows the way to our endurance: *tzedaka,* generosity and good deeds; *tefila,* serious prayer; and *teshuva,* penitent turning away from wrongdoing along with earnest efforts to make good our mistakes. Most of us find it easier to embrace the wonder of these days than to heed their warning—yet to enter upon the Awesome Days without the belief that we stand in judgment is to ignore the ancient Jewish belief that our actions matter in the world, that just as our deeds can help end others' suffering, save others from hunger, and bring a bit more *shalom* into the world, so our thoughtlessness, our cruelty, and our selfishness drive the world that much further away from harmony, that much closer to chaos. Whatever each one of us does affects the world, this season reminds us. Because God cares for us, whatever we do is noticed, for good or ill, and remembered.

This Machzor is intended to help us whose world seems so mired in chaos to rise up from its ordinariness, its enmities, its senseless pain, and find our way to awe, its intimate majesty and its compassionate judgment, and return again to earth ennobled by our stay.

Our journey is heralded by the sound of the Shofar, which has been blown in synagogues all through the month of Elul. In the Days of Awe we listen to it first during the Torah service on Rosh Hashanah, and the sound remains with us until the final call at the very end of Yom Kippur. We are commanded not to blow the Shofar but to listen to it; it is as though even the stalwart shofar blower is not the creator of the sound but merely the one who disperses it; the origin of the sound comes from a far greater distance than that person's lips, which is why the listening is so important. At a time of so many words, it is remarkable that the primary sound to which we are commanded is one without any words at all, immediately understood by a child who knows not a single word, a sound that unites all peoples who have been dispersed from each other since the separation of language at Babel. Maimonides heard it as a call to all who live in a moral drowse to awake, take account of our deeds, and remember who created us.

Yet, as in any service, the way to awe lies primarily through

words, through a kind of praying that sometimes seems closer to chaos than to harmony. It is called davening (from the Yiddish *davenen*), and it requires that we not sit ramrod-like in our chairs, reading prayers in decorous conformity with everyone else, but that we give over our whole body to the encounter with God, and that we offer up our prayers, each at our own pace, as a song. A davener is someone who takes seriously the psalm verse quoted in the morning Nishmat prayer, "All my bones shall say: Who is like You?", praying with our head, shoulders, arms, fingers, chest, as many inner organs as we can feel, our legs and our feet—and above all, with the breath that God breathed into us when we were created. A davener is a mover and shaker, who gestures, cries out, argues, exults, cries, demands, appreciates, and sinks into deep silence without necessarily saying a word. If you are to use this machzor with the greatest intensity, you will try to become a davener too. However creaky your voice, you will offer it up to God, chanting where it seems appropriate, reading at your own pace where that seems appropriate, joining in a majestic chorus of reading or singing where that seems right. As a davener, you know that you can sing even when you are reading, and if you use your hands and your body and your tallis to emphasize your feelings, you will find yourself in the middle of an animated conversation with God in which both your body and your *anima*—your *neshama,* your soul—are fully engaged.

Part of this conversation is an acknowledgement of where we have fallen short of what we are meant to be, and a plea that both God and the people we have wronged might forgive us.

Jewish tradition holds that we were created with two inclinations, two *y'tzarim:* a *yetzer tov,* an inclination to do good, to emulate the divine in whose image we were formed; and a *yetzer ha-ra,* an inclination to act contrary to the will of God, to give vent to the passions which may suit our animal form, but not the divine spark God breathed into us. Properly our *yetzer tov* should turn the natural passions of our *yetzer ha-ra* into doing the will of God with a passionate enthusiasm; like the normal human beings we are, too often the reverse happens, and our

yetzer ha-ra subverts the intelligence and cleverness present in our *yetzer tov* into doing schemes that end up being only hurtful and selfish, giving us but a momentary pleasure that soon turns to dross. The days preparing us for Yom Kippur offer us the opportunity to get our *yetzer ha-ra* back into the service of our *yetzer tov*—to remind ourselves that we are not bad people, not doomed forever to be manipulated by our *yetzer ha-ra*, but people created in God's image, whose animal needs can all be turned to the benefit of humanity and the service of God, if we will but work at it, if we will but turn away from our aberrations, our strayings off the path of good into the dangerous borders of chaos. It is from the path that all our images of Yom Kippur come: sin, transgression, crookedness, wrong, are all translations of Hebrew expressions for straying away; *tshuvah*, the proper activity for this season, means returning. But even after we do teshuvah and return to the path of God, we note that our original straying has left its mark. And so we ask God to obliterate the trace of our misdeeds, to cover them over (*kapparah, kippur*), to blot them out (*slicha, mechila*). The mark of our straying creates a gulf between us and God, a sense of alienation from the Source of good and harmony in the world, and hence an alienation from the source of good in ourselves. In ancient days, our people offered animals and grains at the Temple altar as a means of bridging the gulf between themselves and God. With the Temple destroyed, it was decreed that the words and acts of prayer and confession were the means to bridge the gulf—acts demonstrating our intention to behave differently, words of apology that give voice to that intention; acts demonstrating we wish to come closer to God, or struggle harder to understand where God is in our life, and words of apology, the Confessions (Ashamnu and Al Cheyt) which give voice to the changes we have already started to make.

Many of us wince at the word "sin"—the Hebrew *cheyt*, which means missing the mark, seems less condemnatory. But *cheyt* as well calls our attention to the mark we have missed: the image of God in which we were created, the image of a being of judgment, compassion, and creativity that is our proper goal.

To let our *yetzer ha-ra* lead us astray from that mark diminishes the image of God in the world and undermines God's sovereignty over the forces of chaos.

Thus the words that we say, the Al Cheyts we intone for sins that any Jew anywhere in the world may have committed, are words of restoration of the Rule of God.

For all these reasons then, the language in which we daven has a great impact on the quality of our encounters with God.

This Machzor reflects the belief that both men and women responded at Sinai to the *mitzvot,* the commands of God, and hence that the prayers offered up to God should be in language that men and women, in their differences and in their equality, can say with equal appropriateness. Because Jewish tradition has held that God in the divine totality comprises both male and female characteristics, we have used words like Ruler, Sovereign, and Monarch, which embrace both male and female majesty, while at other times we have emphasized particular male and female characteristics of the divine.

Occasionally we have left certain words untranslated, like Adonay, believing that that traditional Hebrew substitute for the four-letter name of God, YHVH, is more all-encompassing than its usual (masculine) translation, "Lord."

Indeed, because the Hebrew text has such depth, and because it admits us to something of the fullness of the Jewish encounter with God through time, we have chosen not to alter the traditional Hebrew text of individual prayers. To do so would close off the possibility of any relationship to the original, forcing us into total dependence upon translation, rather than enabling a dialogue between the ancient speaker and the modern ear. We have preferred to alternate between translating literally, thus preserving some of the original ambiguities, and paraphrasing the original, thus hoping to reveal behind the classic idiom a language with which we may speak as intimately as possible with God.

Some of the English passages in this Machzor are attempts at faithful translations of the accompanying Hebrew prayers; others are paraphrases suggested by themes in the Hebrew.

Sometimes the same Hebrew prayer is translated differently in different services, exposing varying facets of its meaning. Daveners familiar with Hebrew will be able to tell where we have departed from the original; if you are not yet familiar with the Hebrew, it is important that you offer up the prayer as your own, in the spirit of all those prayers written in the Talmudic period which were inspired by the same theme or closing sentence, but which differed considerably in wording or interpretation (the evening Ahavat Olam and the morning Ahavah Rabba are examples of this process). By learning Hebrew, however, you too can participate in the ongoing dialogue of the generations between word and meaning.

But while Hebrew is the language through which God and Israel have come to know each other most intimately, it is important to remember that if the Torah was given at Sinai in all the 70 languages spoken in the world, English was one of those languages. Since God created language and oversaw our scattering to the lands where languages like English are spoken, it is appropriate for us to believe that God's *kedushah,* God's holiness, dwells in English words and sentences as well as in Hebrew, though it may be harder to discern. When Hebrew is opaque for us, English must be the tongue in which we approach our ancient lover. God knows what we are saying. It is up to us to speak, to pray, to daven, with the intention of knowing what God is saying to us.

2. How to Use this Machzor

To accommodate those congregations which observe both days of Rosh Hashanah, alternative versions of prayers and readings have been suggested so that the service of the two days may explore different understandings of the New Year. You may also wish to make selections from the psalms (Pesukey d'Zimra) in the morning services or from the readings in each of the three parts of the Rosh Hashanah Shofar service. Concluding prayers to the Rosh Hashanah morning service have been designed as complements to the introductory readings, though

it is not necessary that they be used in that manner. Other opportunities for creative use of this Machzor are the following:

1. *Introductions.* At the start of the service, daveners might be urged to introduce themselves to those sitting around them, not only out of neighborliness, but as a way of getting to know more personally those on whom much of the quality of everyone's davening will depend. Daveners might thus be encouraged to pray with earnestness not only to approach God more intensely themselves, but to help inspire others to greater intensity as well. In the same vein, if people must share books, they should be encouraged to see this not as bringing an intruder into their praying, but a davening partner. The sharing can be an opportunity to strengthen their own davening by the force of their partner's prayer, and to feel an obligation—to their partner if not to God—to pray in earnest that they may help strengthen their partner's involvement in the service.

2. *English davening.* Encouraging daveners to use melodies for the English prayers in this book, particularly those in poetic form, similar to the chants they might use for Hebrew prayers, can help introduce them to those non-verbal associations which traditional melodies bring to prayers, and give them more independence in praying than a unison reading offers. The reader should give a sample of a davening melody, and show, with another reader, that everyone can daven the words at a different pace, emphasizing some more and others less.

3. *Antiphonal reading.* Another way of varying unison reading is by asking different sides of the room to read alternative paragraphs or stanzas, thus becoming aware of others in the congregation and responding to others' prayers.

4. *Reading psalms in cadence.* Psalms 146, 148, and 150 in the Rosh Hashanah morning service may be read in English in unison in cadence (e.g., *Hal*-le-lu-*yah!* Sing *hal*-lel to *Ya! Praise* A-do-*nay O* my *be*-ing!), evoking the grand manner in which psalms were intoned by the Levitical choirs on the Temple steps. If appropriate, a *tof* may be used to help keep

the tempo, though the voice of a strong leader is sufficient.

5. *Readers.* In addition to the leader of the service, individual daveners might be asked in advance to stand at their seats and read particular passages, especially the prose introductory readings or selections from Jewish tradition, such as those on Tshuvah on Yom Kippur evening. In the section "In Praise of Praise" (page 76), a different reader might rise to speak each of the sentences preceded by a dash. If long texts, like the Avodah, Eyleh Ezkerah, or Jonah are being read by all the daveners, the leader might ask each person sitting on an aisle to read a paragraph, beginning with the back row, then the aisle person in the next row, etc.

6. *Variations in the Amidah.* While each service has its own modified form of the Amidah or the Tefilah, inserted between the Rosh Hashanah and Yom Kippur services will be found a complete traditional silent Amidah in Hebrew and English, which daveners may use instead of the version in each service. Beginning on page 176, the Musaf Amidah for Rosh Hashanah and Yom Kippur will be found, for quiet davening and for the Reader's repetition. The use of asterisks (*) makes it possible for daveners to use the Reform version of certain prayers (e. g., in the Avot, *ge-ulah* (redemption) may be substituted for *go-eyl* (redeemer); in the Gevurot, *mechayey ha-kol* (Reviver of all) may be substituted for *mechayey meytim* (Reviver of the dead); and the Reform version of R'tzey will be found, eliminating the prayer for the restoration of the Temple and its offerings. In addition, those wishing to acknowledge Adonay in the Avot as God of our Mothers (*Elohey imoteynu*) as well as of our fathers (*Elohey avoteynu*) will find this version in parentheses. Many of these options are also included in the versions of the Amidah found in the individual services.

7. *Expressions from the daveners: Judgment and hopes.* In the evening service for Rosh Hashanah, some of us have found it significant to invite daveners to rise to express either a judgment on some aspect of the current situation in the world or in Jewry, or to share a hope for the New Year. (A suitable

place to do this is at page 41, after the Elohai N'tzor, or page 42, after the Kaddish Shalem, particularly if a sermon follows the sharing. Daveners might be alerted before the Amidah begins, to think about judgments and hopes during the silent period that might follow the Amidah.) The leader might briefly explain what is meant by a "judgment" and a "hope," even giving examples, and then encourage people to overcome their shyness and rise. Patience during the periods of silence is important, for generally after a short while more participants will join in. The leader will sense when enough of a silent period has passed to end this part of the service, which can be done by expressing the wish that all the judgments may be heeded and all the worthy hopes fulfilled, both the voiced and the unvoiced.

Prayers for the sick. The Torah reading for the first day of Rosh Hashanah reminds us how God answered Abraham and Sarah's prayers for an end to her barrenness. In that spirit a Mi-she-berach (a prayer that the God who blessed our ancestors might bless our own loved ones with health and well-being) might be offered in the midst of the Rosh Hashanah (or even Yom Kippur) Torah readings on behalf of all those beloved of the congregation who are ill. Daveners may be invited to rise and call out the name of someone who is ill, and at the conclusion, the leader may offer a Mi-she-berach on behalf of them all.

Yizkor. To carry forth the message of the days of remembrance, it can be very moving to invite daveners to share not only the names of those they are recalling at the Yizkor (Memorial) service, but something of their lives as well. Before the names are read, the leader may invite anyone who wishes to share such a brief memorial, with the leader giving an example both of brevity and kind of memories appropriate to share in public. After the names submitted in advance have been read, daveners may be asked to call out additional names, with the leader beginning El Maley Rachamim after an appropriate number of names has been voiced. The leader should prepare daveners at the beginning

of the Yizkor service that both of these sharings will take place, so that daveners have a chance to organize their thoughts.

8. *Study sessions.* Before or after the *Torah readings,* the leader might make some observations on the portion, proffer some questions (or hand them out), and encourage daveners to turn their chairs around to form groups of 8 to 10 to discuss the questions. *Another possibility* for study is to hand out a text appropriate to the day (e.g., a selection from Maimonides' *Hilchot Tshuvah,* the Laws of Repentance, from the Mishneh Torah; from Rabbeinu Yona of Gerona's *Gates of Repentance;* or the chapter on repentance from Luzzatto's *Mesilat Yesharim,* the Path of the Just). Appended to the selection might be a series of questions, and the leader might ask one person in each group to convene the discussion and keep it going. Such discussions might also precede or follow the readings in the *Afternoon Service,* the Avodah, Eyleh Ezkerah, and the Book of Jonah. The Avodah in this Machzor is surrounded by readings which attempt to suggest the purposes and original emotions that may have attended the service of the High Kohen (High Priest) in the Temple, and they too lend themselves to discussion about the nature of the "material" religiosity of animal and grain offerings that preceded and inspired our service of "spiritual" prayers. The readings surrounding the Eyleh Ezkerah raise many questions about the role of God in the tragedies which have befallen the people Israel, as well as the role of human wrongdoing. To include passages whose theology presents difficulties for contemporary Jews can help us learn more about what beliefs are important to us, an opportunity that is lost when such passages are excised from the Machzor. In a smaller congregation, particularly where the daveners know each other well, it may be possible for each group to study the *Al Chets* together, with the convener encouraging people to explore the degree to which each wrong reflects something in their lives they would like to extirpate, and to explore as well how each person could forgive someone who has done that wrong to them.

9. *Music.* Be it a cantor's solo *chazzanut* or congregational singing, good music can offer many uplifting moments throughout the davening. It is often helpful for the *chazzan* (cantor) or song leader to teach some of the music at the beginning of the service, before or after everyone introduces themselves. It may not feel appropriate to do this at the Yom Kippur services, although the teaching and singing of suitable music may serve as fitting punctuation between the readings and discussion of the Afternoon Service. Some years ago at our Kol Nidrey service, each davener was given an unlit candle to symbolize a soul deadened by a year's immersion in the wrongs of the world. When the service ended, the two candles lit at the start of the service were used to kindle one davener's candle, which then ignited another which ignited another, until the room was filled with glowing candles and, it is hoped, revived and glowing souls. We then went outside (though everyone might also remain in the room) and lifting up our newly-kindled light to the dark sky as encouragement to the tentative moon of Tishri, we began to sing. Since there are obvious problems of *halacha* (traditional Jewish law) in this suggestion, it will not be applicable to every group of daveners.

While these suggestions may all increase the creative possibilities for more intense davening, the greatest creativity must inevitably flow from the manner in which each davener appropriates the words of the Machzor, whether in Hebrew or in English, whether silently or aloud, whether in a chanting voice or in unison reading with your neighbor. The ultimate source of creativity cannot be a book, but the openness of each human soul to the voice of the Creator, speaking in the unique way God has chosen for each one of us.

May the prayers in this book inspire you with longing for the God who dwells wherever there is breath, and may their words fly from the page into your heart, lifting your prayers high above the highest mountain, carrying your soul to the embrace of the God who loves you, on wings of awe.

ROSH HASHANAH

EVENING SERVICE
FOR ROSH HASHANAH

THOUGHTS FOR THE NEW YEAR

Our noisy year has now descended with the sun beyond our sight, and in the silence of our praying place, we close the door upon the hectic joys and fears, the accomplishments and anguish, of the year that we have left behind. What was but moments ago the substance of our life has now become its memory, and what we did must now be woven into what we are. On this day we shall not do, but be: we are to walk the outer limits of our humanity, no longer ride unseeing through a world we only vaguely sense beneath our cushioned wheels. On this day, heat and warmth and light must come from deep within ourselves; no longer can we tear apart the world to make our fire. On this day, but a breath away from our creation, we are to breathe in a world from which we may no longer feel apart, but as close as eye to blossom, and ear to the singing in the night.

We are here, on this Rosh Hashanah Eve, poised somewhere between what we have been and what we wish to be. We are here at the start of the ten days of *tshuvah,* of turning, of returning to the self we have covered up behind the roles and masks with which we have learned to protect ourselves. We are here in celebration and in search, in judgment and embrace, ready to confront ourselves and the world in which we find ourselves this night. We seek to open wide the windows behind which we have hidden, and to send forth hand and soul to learn where we have come, what we have become, and what we hope to be.

*　　*　　*

I

To everything there is a season,
And an appointed time for every purpose
Under heaven.

Now is the time for turning.

The leaves are beginning to turn
From green to red and orange.

The birds are beginning to turn
And are heading once more towards the South.

The animals are beginning to turn
To storing their food for the winter.

For leaves, birds, and animals
Turning comes instinctively.
But for us turning does not come so simply.

It takes an act of will
For us to make a turn.

It means breaking with old habits.
It means admitting that we have been wrong;
And this is never easy.

It means losing face;
It means starting all over again;
And this is always painful.

It means saying: "I am sorry."
It means admitting that we have the ability to change;
And this is always embarrassing.

These things are terribly hard to do.
But unless we turn, we will be trapped forever
In yesterday's ways.

God, help us turn—

From callousness to sensitivity,
From hostility to love,

From pettiness to purpose,
From envy to contentment,

From carelessness to discipline,
From fear to faith.

> Turn us around, Adonay, and bring us back towards
> You.
> Revive our lives, as at the beginning.

And turn us towards each other, God.
For in isolation there is no life.

*   *   *

We come here to seek other values than the ones which too
often move the world in which we live; we come here to
build into our lives the acts which must respond more to
the will of God, however we understand it, than to the will
of the authorities of our daily world. We come determined
to find values that will restore just rule to an unjust world.

This is the season of God the Ruler. We celebrate the ultimate rule of the divine, the coherence of all the disparate
parts of the universe in one related cosmos, a realm in
which the power of God could relate all people to each
other, and every person to every corner of the natural
world. Not for us the rule of lesser powers, who govern by
keeping many people out rather than drawing all people in.
This day we renew our vision of how the world should be
governed, and though too often we are tempted to withdraw from concern, at this New Year we determine: we
shall help bring that ideal governance about. We shall help
relate our own corner of the world to a rule that is divine.

To do that—to help to change the world we know—we
need to change ourselves as well. To renew ourselves, we
need be conscious of our faults, the hurts we do to others,
the hurts we do ourselves. We need be conscious of the
mitzvot—the deeds our people has believed that God
desires—which are open to us though we have been closed
to them. And so in this judgment season we shall look
critically into ourselves, as we look critically at the world,

that we may sharpen all our faculties for the job of renewal
ahead.

Hayom harat olam—at this moment is the universe conceived. At this moment all things are possible, and all our
dreams, all the best and strong and loving corners of ourselves, shall rule.

פִּתְחוּ־לִי שַׁעֲרֵי־צֶדֶק אָבֹא־בָם אוֹדֶה יָהּ

Pit'chu li sha-arey tzedek
Avo vam, odeh Yah.

Open to me the gates of justice
That I may enter into them and give thanks to God.

BLESSING OVER CANDLES

The night is dark that cloaks this year we have begun
tonight. Yet the heavens have revealed their new moon to
us, a tiny sliver in the Tishri sky that announces more
triumphantly than the noon's bright sun that a new year
has come, a new time has dawned, a new chance has
opened to us to help create the world for which we yearn.

> But that slim moon cannot dispel the darkness. What
> kind of world awaits us? Shall we find the strength for
> its demands? How many uncertainties shroud our
> steps into the future!

The beacon through the night lies not alone in heaven. We
must encourage the new year's fragile light with this torch
we light on earth. These candle flames we trim tonight
remind us that we need not merely wait for time to reveal
her will, but we ourselves can help bring forth from the
darkness the world we want, the kind of life we wish to live
beneath the many new moons of this new year.

> This year can be a partnership of the light we find and
> the light we make. Let us revel in the darkness, that
> we may gaze upon the lights we find in heaven with

awe, with wonder, with joy at all that has been created for each one of us. But when the lights of heaven
are obscured or powerless before the darkness that
confounds our life, then let us remember all the candles that are ours to kindle, all the bright flames we
have it in our power to trim, so we can burn away the
clouds from heaven's light and bring that light—and
with it truth and caring and hope—to earth once
more.

בָּרוּךְ אַתָּה יְיָ אֱלֹהֵינוּ מֶלֶךְ הָעוֹלָם אֲשֶׁר קִדְּשָׁנוּ
בְּמִצְוֹתָיו וְצִוָּנוּ לְהַדְלִיק נֵר שֶׁל [שַׁבָּת וְשֶׁל] יוֹם טוֹב:

*Baruch atta Adonay Eloheynu melech ha-olam, asher kid-
shanu b'mitzvotav vitzivanu l'hadlik ner shel (Shabbat v'shel)
yom tov.*

בָּרוּךְ אַתָּה יְיָ אֱלֹהֵינוּ מֶלֶךְ הָעוֹלָם שֶׁהֶחֱיָנוּ וְקִיְּמָנוּ
וְהִגִּיעָנוּ לַזְּמַן הַזֶּה:

*Baruch atta Adonay Eloheynu melech ha-olam, shehehiyanu
v'kiymanu v'higianu lazman hazeh.*

You are praised, Adonay our God, Majesty of the universe, who
has commanded us to light these candles, through which we
touch the holiness of (Shabbat and) the New Year. Praised be
the One who has kept us in life through this joyous day, enabling
us to share the miracle of our people's life through light.

Psalm 92 (On Shabbat)

מִזְמוֹר שִׁיר לְיוֹם הַשַּׁבָּת: טוֹב לְהֹדוֹת לַיהוָה וּלְזַמֵּר
לְשִׁמְךָ עֶלְיוֹן: לְהַגִּיד בַּבֹּקֶר חַסְדֶּךָ וֶאֱמוּנָתְךָ בַּלֵּילוֹת:
עֲלֵי־עָשׂוֹר וַעֲלֵי־נָבֶל עֲלֵי הִגָּיוֹן בְּכִנּוֹר: כִּי שִׂמַּחְתַּנִי
יְהוָה בְּפָעֳלֶךָ בְּמַעֲשֵׂי יָדֶיךָ אֲרַנֵּן: מַה־גָּדְלוּ מַעֲשֶׂיךָ
יְהוָה מְאֹד עָמְקוּ מַחְשְׁבֹתֶיךָ: אִישׁ־בַּעַר לֹא יֵדָע
וּכְסִיל לֹא־יָבִין אֶת־זֹאת: בִּפְרֹחַ רְשָׁעִים כְּמוֹ עֵשֶׂב

וַיִּצִיצוּ כָּל־פֹּעֲלֵי אָוֶן לְהִשָּׁמְדָם עֲדֵי־עַד: וְאַתָּה מָרוֹם
לְעֹלָם יְהֹוָה: כִּי הִנֵּה אֹיְבֶיךָ יְהֹוָה כִּי־הִנֵּה אֹיְבֶיךָ
יֹאבֵדוּ יִתְפָּרְדוּ כָּל־פֹּעֲלֵי אָוֶן: וַתָּרֶם כִּרְאֵים קַרְנִי
בַּלֹּתִי בְּשֶׁמֶן רַעֲנָן: וַתַּבֵּט עֵינִי בְּשׁוּרָי בַּקָּמִים עָלַי
מְרֵעִים תִּשְׁמַעְנָה אָזְנָי: צַדִּיק כַּתָּמָר יִפְרָח כְּאֶרֶז
בַּלְּבָנוֹן יִשְׂגֶּה: שְׁתוּלִים בְּבֵית יְהֹוָה בְּחַצְרוֹת אֱלֹהֵינוּ
יַפְרִיחוּ: עוֹד יְנוּבוּן בְּשֵׂיבָה דְּשֵׁנִים וְרַעֲנַנִּים יִהְיוּ:
לְהַגִּיד כִּי־יָשָׁר יְהֹוָה צוּרִי וְלֹא־עַוְלָתָה בּוֹ:

A Song by the Sabbath Day (Interpreting Psalm 92)

With the week completed
God looks upon the world and once again proclaims it
"Very good!"
We can embrace its good
By acknowledging God in every part of world we touch.
It is good to acknowledge God
With the good we acknowledge God
And sing to Your Name, dweller on the heights!
With our ten-string, our six-string, pulling out every
    instrument we know
Chanting tales of Your love the moment we wake up
Reminiscing of Your faithfulness before we go to sleep
How joyful have You made us through your deeds!
If only I could sing an anthem worthy of Your handwork!

    How grand are Your actions, Adonay!
    How profound Your designs!

So many boorish men there are who do not know,
So many foolish women who do not understand!
Wicked people seem to be springing up like grass, more
    each year,

Their cruel and callous actions blossoming like bitter
  flowers,
Yet ultimately they face destruction
So long as You rule on high.

On the seventh day I can survey Your creation
And believe that all the enemies of good, of harmony,
Will be blown away like flowers gone to seed
And You will raise up my head
Like a stag whose antlers graze the sky
Like a woman emerging caressed by oils from her bath,
When I can see myself like them
I will know You have heard my cry.

Let righteous people sprout up tall as palm trees,
As strong as fragrant cedars in the Lebanon!
Planted firmly in God's house
Their sweet blossoms shall crowd out the bitter from the
  courts where God is found,
However old they grow
They will still bring forth lush fruit,
They will forever chant their tales of God's uprightness
To my flawless Rock they will sing and sing
And sing.

Tzadik katamar yifrach
K'erez ba-l'vanon yisgeh
Sh'tulim b'veyt Adonay
B'chatzrot Eloheynu yafrichu
Od y'nuvun b'seyvah
D'sheynim v'ra-ananim yihyu
L'hagid ki yashar Adonay
Tzuri v'lo avlatah bo.

Y'did Nefesh (On Shabbat)

יְדִיד נֶפֶשׁ אָב הָרַחֲמָן. מְשׁוֹךְ עַבְדְּךָ אֶל רְצוֹנֶךָ.
יָרוּץ עַבְדְּךָ כְּמוֹ אַיָּל. יִשְׁתַּחֲוֶה אֶל מוּל הֲדָרֶךָ.
תֶּעֱרַב לוֹ יְדִידוּתֶךָ. מִנֹּפֶת צוּף וְכָל טָעַם:

הָדוּר נָאֶה זִיו הָעוֹלָם. נַפְשִׁי חוֹלַת אַהֲבָתֶךָ.
אָנָּא אֵל נָא רְפָא נָא לָהּ. בְּהַרְאוֹת לָהּ נְעַם זִיוֶךְ.
אָז תִּתְחַזֵּק וְתִתְרַפֵּא. וְהָיְתָה לָהּ שִׂמְחַת עוֹלָם:

וָתִיק יֶהֱמוּ נָא רַחֲמֶיךָ. וְחוּסָה נָא עַל בֵּן אֲהוּבֶךָ.
כִּי זֶה כַּמָּה נִכְסוֹף נִכְסַפְתִּי. לִרְאוֹת בְּתִפְאֶרֶת עֻזֶּךָ.
אֵלֶּה חָמְדָה לִבִּי. חוּסָה נָא וְאַל תִּתְעַלָּם:

הִגָּלֵה נָא וּפְרוֹשׂ חֲבִיבִי עָלַי אֶת סֻכַּת שְׁלוֹמֶךָ.
תָּאִיר אֶרֶץ מִכְּבוֹדֶךָ. נָגִילָה וְנִשְׂמְחָה בָּךְ.
מַהֵר אָהוּב כִּי בָא מוֹעֵד. וְחָנֵּנוּ כִּימֵי עוֹלָם:

Y'did nefesh av ha-rachaman, m'shoch av-d'cha el
r'tzon-echa,
Yarutz av-d'cha k'mo ayal, yish-tachaveh el mul
ha-darecha
Te-erav lo y'didu-techa, mi-nofet tzuf v'chol ta-am.

Ha-dur na-eh ziv ha-olam, naf-shi cholat ahava-techa,
Ana Eyl na r'fo-na la, b'ha-rot la no-am ziv-echa,
Az tit-chazeyk v'tit-rapey, v'ha-y'ta la sim-chat olam.

Vatik yehemu na racha-mecha, v'chusa na al beyn
ahu-vecha,
Ki zeh kama nich-sof nich-saf-ti, lirot b'tif-eret u-zecha,
Ey-leh cham-da libi, chu-sa na v'al tit-alam.

Hi-ga-leh na uf-ros cha-vivi alai et sukat sh'lo-mecha,
Ta-ir eretz mi-kvod-echa, nagila v'nis-m'cha vach,
Maher ahuv ki va mo-eyd, v'chaw-neynu ki-mey olam.

You who love my soul, Compassion's gentle source,
Take my disposition and shape it to Your will.
Like a darting deer I will flee to You.
Before Your glorious Presence humbly do I bow
Let Your sweet love delight me with its thrill,
Because no other dainty will my hunger still.

How splendid is Your light which worlds do reflect!
My soul is worn from craving for Your love's delight.
Please, good God, do heal her and show to her Your face,
So my soul can see You and bathe in your grace.
There she will find strength and healing in this sight,
Her joy will be complete, then Eternal her delight.

What pity stirs in You since days of old, my God!
Be kind to me, Your own child, begotten by Your love,
For long and longing hours I yearned for Your embrace,
To see my light in Your light, basking in Your grace.
My heart's desire is to harmonize with Yours,
Do not conceal Your pity, hide not that light of Yours.

Help, my Lover, spread Your sukkah of peace,
Enfold all human beings, give all pain surcease.
Your presence on this earth do make known to us
And we shall respond then with song and with dance.
Rush, my love, be quick, the time for love is now,
Let Your gentle favor grace us as of old.

In Praise of Another Year

In heaven and on earth,
In a clap of thunder, in a whisper of the soul,
In praise on yellowed parchment in an ancient tongue,
In yearnings of the heart, in a child not yet born,
                                        Praised be God.

    In the taste of tears and wine, sight of starry skies,
    Old people's voices warping the chant, children sing-
       ing,
    Scientists finding, artists searching,
                                        Praised be God.

All the web of creation shining in holy sunlight.
The dew that has gathered in darkness
Transfixes the light of day.
                                        Praised be God.

I am afraid of my suffering, and ashamed,
But God made it. May I be worthy of these bitter,
   holy, gifts.
Who but the living can know their agonies?
Children extinguished, futures lost as broken
   promises.

Praised be God.

To have lived one moment is that much glory.
God's warm sun, God's soul-searing fire,
And moments when our only pride
Is that we have turned away from nothing.

Praised be God.

Strengthen us God, Creator, with self-knowledge,
One and together;
Strengthen us with the hunger for peace
Between nations and between each other.

Grant us another year in the Book of Life.
With its peril and injustice
And the good daylight.

Amen, Amen.

THE SHMA AND ITS BLESSINGS

בָּרְכוּ אֶת יְיָ הַמְבֹרָךְ:

Barchu et Adonay hamvorach:
Praise Adonay to whom all praise is due!

בָּרוּךְ יְיָ הַמְבֹרָךְ לְעוֹלָם וָעֶד:

Baruch Adonay hamvorach l'olam vaed:
Praised be Adonay, to whom all praise is due forever and ever!

Maariv Aravim (In Praise of the Evening-Bringer)

בָּרוּךְ אַתָּה יְיָ אֱלֹהֵינוּ מֶלֶךְ הָעוֹלָם אֲשֶׁר בִּדְבָרוֹ
מַעֲרִיב עֲרָבִים בְּחָכְמָה פּוֹתֵחַ שְׁעָרִים וּבִתְבוּנָה
מְשַׁנֶּה עִתִּים וּמַחֲלִיף אֶת־הַזְּמַנִּים וּמְסַדֵּר אֶת־
הַכּוֹכָבִים בְּמִשְׁמְרוֹתֵיהֶם בָּרָקִיעַ כִּרְצוֹנוֹ. בּוֹרֵא יוֹם
וָלַיְלָה גּוֹלֵל אוֹר מִפְּנֵי חֹשֶׁךְ וְחֹשֶׁךְ מִפְּנֵי אוֹר וּמַעֲבִיר
יוֹם וּמֵבִיא לָיְלָה וּמַבְדִּיל בֵּין יוֹם וּבֵין לָיְלָה יְיָ צְבָאוֹת
שְׁמוֹ. אֵל חַי וְקַיָּם תָּמִיד יִמְלוֹךְ עָלֵינוּ לְעוֹלָם וָעֶד.
בָּרוּךְ אַתָּה יְיָ הַמַּעֲרִיב עֲרָבִים:

You are praised, Adonay
Author of time and space
Who brings on evening with a word,
Opens heaven's gates with wisdom,
Adjusts the ages with sensitive judgment,
Varies the seasons,
And orders the orbits of a sky full of stars.

You create each day and each night afresh,
Roll light in front of darkness
And darkness in front of light
So gently
That no moment is quite like the one before
Or after.

Second by second
You make day pass into night
And You alone know the boundary point
Dividing one from the other.
Unifier of all beings is Your name.

Timeless God,
Rule forever.

You who brings the evening in
Are praised.

* * *

Alternative Maariv Aravim

Alone
I marvel at the evening sky
Gold caressing blue, blue caressing dark.

Here in prayer
I need to see Your hand behind the sky
Your creative words once more forming light in darkness
I need to see the care with which You carved the moon, the
    stars
Which make of fearful darkness
Nurturing night.

The mixture that brings evening forth from day
Morning from night
Has been shaped, like Adam from the earth,
By You.

You who mixes in the evening,
You are praised.

Ahavat Olam (In Praise of the Torah-Giver)

אַהֲבַת עוֹלָם בֵּית יִשְׂרָאֵל עַמְּךָ אָהָבְתָּ. תּוֹרָה וּמִצְוֹת
חֻקִּים וּמִשְׁפָּטִים אוֹתָנוּ לִמַּדְתָּ. עַל כֵּן יְיָ אֱלֹהֵינוּ
בְּשָׁכְבֵּנוּ וּבְקוּמֵנוּ נָשִׂיחַ בְּחֻקֶּיךָ. וְנִשְׂמַח בְּדִבְרֵי
תוֹרָתֶךָ וּבְמִצְוֹתֶיךָ לְעוֹלָם וָעֶד. כִּי הֵם חַיֵּינוּ וְאֹרֶךְ
יָמֵינוּ וּבָהֶם נֶהְגֶּה יוֹמָם וָלָיְלָה. וְאַהֲבָתְךָ אַל תָּסִיר
מִמֶּנּוּ לְעוֹלָמִים. בָּרוּךְ אַתָּה יְיָ אוֹהֵב עַמּוֹ יִשְׂרָאֵל:

You were God
And we were Israel,
Your shy, untutored lover,
Long ago.

You loved us a great love
And you taught us
How to respond to You

Through Torah
Mitzvot
Statutes
Judgments

We go to sleep with them
And with them we awake.

We shall enjoy them forever.

They give us life
They prolong our days
We form our words around them
At nighttime,
In daytime.

Now,
Long after long ago,
Do not withdraw Your love from us.

Lover of Israel,
You are praised.

Alternative Ahavat Olam

You have loved the house of Israel eternally,
A single, unifying love.
You revealed it
In the love notes You left us in Your Torah,
Your mitzvot,
Your ancient statutes, Your modern judgments.

As we speak aloud Your many words
Help us hear in them the single message You intended.
For the secret of our life is there, and the length of our
  days.
If only we could pour over Your letters all the day,
  throughout the night!

As we accept more and more of Your Torah,
Open us to accept more and more of Your love
Do not withhold it from us as we search.

You are praised in our words, Adonay,
As we are loved in Yours.

The Shma: First Paragraph (V'ahavta)

שְׁמַע יִשְׂרָאֵל יְהֹוָה אֱלֹהֵינוּ יְהֹוָה אֶחָד:

Shma Yisrael Adonay Eloheynu Adonay echad:

Hear, Israel, and understand: Adonay is our God, Adonay
is one!

בָּרוּךְ שֵׁם כְּבוֹד מַלְכוּתוֹ לְעוֹלָם וָעֶד:

Baruch sheym kvod malchuto l'olam vaed:

Praised be the Name whose realm reflects glory throughout all time and space!

וְאָהַבְתָּ אֵת יְהֹוָה אֱלֹהֶיךָ בְּכָל־לְבָבְךָ וּבְכָל־נַפְשְׁךָ
וּבְכָל־מְאֹדֶךָ: וְהָיוּ הַדְּבָרִים הָאֵלֶּה אֲשֶׁר אָנֹכִי מְצַוְּךָ
הַיּוֹם עַל־לְבָבֶךָ: וְשִׁנַּנְתָּם לְבָנֶיךָ וְדִבַּרְתָּ בָּם בְּשִׁבְתְּךָ
בְּבֵיתֶךָ וּבְלֶכְתְּךָ בַדֶּרֶךְ וּבְשָׁכְבְּךָ וּבְקוּמֶךָ: וּקְשַׁרְתָּם
לְאוֹת עַל־יָדֶךָ וְהָיוּ לְטֹטָפֹת בֵּין עֵינֶיךָ: וּכְתַבְתָּם עַל־
מְזֻזוֹת בֵּיתֶךָ וּבִשְׁעָרֶיךָ:

Hear, Israel—in whatever language you can understand, in whatever melodies you need to understand, but hear: the single unifying power whom Israel now struggles to know will be known by us and by all peoples in the world to come.

> That powerful name alone deserves our submission; no human government, no human authority. We can fully trust no authority but God's.

Yet how shall we know that authority? If we love the forces which unify the world with all our intellect and all our passion; that is, if we love with all our heart;

> If we are devoted to unifying the world enough to give our life that God's name may be sanctified; that is, if we can love with all our soul;

If we are devoted to unifying the world enough to give up all our possessions for its sake; that is, if we can love with all our might;

> Then these words commanded us today shall be upon our heart, and the Shma shall issue from our lips with all the fire of our intellect and all the fervor of our passion.

We shall then by our example teach them to our children and interweave them in our speech, through intimate conversation of lovers in the house, and the public words of business on the way.

> We shall speak them ere we sleep and when we rise to greet the dawn, the evening Shma our benediction for the day now ended, the morning Shma an overture to the day now opening before us.

Some of us bind them as a sign upon our hand and for frontlets between our eyes; perhaps soon all of us, both men and women, shall have the courage so to bind ourselves to the unification of the world.

Yet even now we can write them as a mezuzah upon the
doorpost of our house, that our door might be a gate for
love to enter in and for the hope of oneness one day to
issue forth.

The Shma: Second Paragraph (V'haya im Shamo'a)

וְהָיָה אִם־שָׁמֹעַ תִּשְׁמְעוּ אֶל־מִצְוֹתַי אֲשֶׁר אָנֹכִי מְצַוֶּה
אֶתְכֶם הַיּוֹם לְאַהֲבָה אֶת־יְהֹוָה אֱלֹהֵיכֶם וּלְעָבְדוֹ
בְּכָל־לְבַבְכֶם וּבְכָל־נַפְשְׁכֶם: וְנָתַתִּי מְטַר־אַרְצְכֶם
בְּעִתּוֹ יוֹרֶה וּמַלְקוֹשׁ וְאָסַפְתָּ דְגָנֶךָ וְתִירֹשְׁךָ וְיִצְהָרֶךָ:
וְנָתַתִּי עֵשֶׂב בְּשָׂדְךָ לִבְהֶמְתֶּךָ וְאָכַלְתָּ וְשָׂבָעְתָּ: הִשָּׁמְרוּ
לָכֶם פֶּן־יִפְתֶּה לְבַבְכֶם וְסַרְתֶּם וַעֲבַדְתֶּם אֱלֹהִים
אֲחֵרִים וְהִשְׁתַּחֲוִיתֶם לָהֶם: וְחָרָה אַף־יְהֹוָה בָּכֶם
וְעָצַר אֶת־הַשָּׁמַיִם וְלֹא־יִהְיֶה מָטָר וְהָאֲדָמָה לֹא תִתֵּן
אֶת־יְבוּלָהּ וַאֲבַדְתֶּם מְהֵרָה מֵעַל הָאָרֶץ הַטֹּבָה אֲשֶׁר
יְהֹוָה נֹתֵן לָכֶם: וְשַׂמְתֶּם אֶת־דְּבָרַי אֵלֶּה עַל־לְבַבְכֶם
וְעַל־נַפְשְׁכֶם וּקְשַׁרְתֶּם אֹתָם לְאוֹת עַל־יֶדְכֶם וְהָיוּ
לְטוֹטָפֹת בֵּין עֵינֵיכֶם: וְלִמַּדְתֶּם אֹתָם אֶת־בְּנֵיכֶם
לְדַבֵּר בָּם בְּשִׁבְתְּךָ בְּבֵיתֶךָ וּבְלֶכְתְּךָ בַדֶּרֶךְ וּבְשָׁכְבְּךָ
וּבְקוּמֶךָ: וּכְתַבְתָּם עַל־מְזוּזוֹת בֵּיתֶךָ וּבִשְׁעָרֶיךָ: לְמַעַן
יִרְבּוּ יְמֵיכֶם וִימֵי בְנֵיכֶם עַל הָאֲדָמָה אֲשֶׁר נִשְׁבַּע יְהֹוָה
לַאֲבֹתֵיכֶם לָתֵת לָהֶם כִּימֵי הַשָּׁמַיִם עַל־הָאָרֶץ:

If we can hear the words from Sinai
Then love will flow from us
And we shall serve all that is holy
With all our intellect and all our passion
And all our life.

If we can serve all that is holy
We shall be doing all that humans can
To help the rains to flow
The grasses to be green
The grains to grow up golden like the sun
And the rivers to be filled with life once more.
All the children of God shall eat
And there will be enough.
But if we turn from Sinai's words
And serve only what is common and profane
Making gods of our own comfort or our power
Then the holiness of life will contract for us
Our world will grow inhospitable
To rains from heaven
And the produce of the earth will not be ours.
Or worse
It will be ours unjustly
And our acts shall isolate us
From the flowing waves of green and gold.
Let us therefore
Lace these words
Into our passion and our intellect
And bind them, all of us,
As a sign upon our hands and our eyes,
Writing them in mezuzot for our doors and gates,
Teaching them to our children,
Listening to our children teaching us.
That our generations may be as numerous
As the stars of heaven and the dust of earth,
As faithful as the living waters
That unite them all.

The Shma: Third Paragraph (Vayomer)

נַיֹּאמֶר יְהוָה אֶל־מֹשֶׁה לֵּאמֹר: דַּבֵּר אֶל־בְּנֵי יִשְׂרָאֵל
וְאָמַרְתָּ אֲלֵהֶם וְעָשׂוּ לָהֶם צִיצִת עַל־כַּנְפֵי בִגְדֵיהֶם

לְדֹרֹתָם וְנָתְנוּ עַל־צִיצִת הַכָּנָף פְּתִיל תְּכֵלֶת: וְהָיָה
לָכֶם לְצִיצִת וּרְאִיתֶם אֹתוֹ וּזְכַרְתֶּם אֶת־כָּל־מִצְוֹת
יְהֹוָה וַעֲשִׂיתֶם אֹתָם וְלֹא תָתוּרוּ אַחֲרֵי לְבַבְכֶם וְאַחֲרֵי
עֵינֵיכֶם אֲשֶׁר־אַתֶּם זֹנִים אַחֲרֵיהֶם: לְמַעַן תִּזְכְּרוּ
וַעֲשִׂיתֶם אֶת־כָּל־מִצְוֹתָי וִהְיִיתֶם קְדֹשִׁים לֵאלֹהֵיכֶם:
אֲנִי יְהֹוָה אֱלֹהֵיכֶם אֲשֶׁר הוֹצֵאתִי אֶתְכֶם מֵאֶרֶץ
מִצְרַיִם לִהְיוֹת לָכֶם לֵאלֹהִים אֲנִי יְהֹוָה אֱלֹהֵיכֶם:

God said to Moses:
Let Israel throughout her generations make tzitzit
Fringes, with a thread of blue,
On the corners of her garments
To look at and remember all the mitzvot of God
And do them.

Otherwise
All of you will follow only what your eyes see
And your hearts desire,
Forgetting that everything you see
And whatever you desire
Are signs of My presence in the world.

But looking at the knotted fringes
You will remember as a knot around the finger
That everything you see
And whatever you desire
Can be seen and done
As one of My mitzvot.

Thus will you share the holiness of God
Who saw you as slaves in Egypt
And desired you
To become a people of God.

I am Adonay your God.

Geulah (A Prayer for Redemption)

אֱמֶת וֶאֱמוּנָה כָּל זֹאת, וְקַיָּם עָלֵינוּ כִּי הוּא יְיָ אֱלֹהֵינוּ
וְאֵין זוּלָתוֹ, וַאֲנַחְנוּ יִשְׂרָאֵל עַמּוֹ. הַפּוֹדֵנוּ מִיַּד מְלָכִים,
מַלְכֵּנוּ הַגּוֹאֲלֵנוּ מִכַּף כָּל הֶעָרִיצִים; הָאֵל הַנִּפְרָע לָנוּ
מִצָּרֵינוּ, וְהַמְשַׁלֵּם גְּמוּל לְכָל אֹיְבֵי נַפְשֵׁנוּ; הָעֹשֶׂה
גְדֹלוֹת עַד אֵין חֵקֶר, וְנִפְלָאוֹת עַד אֵין מִסְפָּר; הַשָּׂם
נַפְשֵׁנוּ בַּחַיִּים, וְלֹא נָתַן לַמּוֹט רַגְלֵנוּ; הַמַּדְרִיכֵנוּ עַל
בָּמוֹת אֹיְבֵינוּ, וַיָּרֶם קַרְנֵנוּ עַל כָּל שׂנְאֵינוּ; הָעֹשֶׂה לָנוּ
נִסִּים וּנְקָמָה בְּפַרְעֹה, אוֹתוֹת וּמוֹפְתִים בְּאַדְמַת בְּנֵי
חָם; הַמַּכֶּה בְעֶבְרָתוֹ כָּל בְּכוֹרֵי מִצְרָיִם, וַיּוֹצֵא אֶת
עַמּוֹ יִשְׂרָאֵל מִתּוֹכָם לְחֵרוּת עוֹלָם. הַמַּעֲבִיר בָּנָיו בֵּין
גִּזְרֵי יַם סוּף; אֶת רוֹדְפֵיהֶם וְאֶת שׂוֹנְאֵיהֶם בִּתְהֹמוֹת
טִבַּע. וְרָאוּ בָנָיו גְּבוּרָתוֹ; שִׁבְּחוּ וְהוֹדוּ לִשְׁמוֹ,
וּמַלְכוּתוֹ בְּרָצוֹן קִבְּלוּ עֲלֵיהֶם. מֹשֶׁה וּבְנֵי יִשְׂרָאֵל לְךָ
עָנוּ שִׁירָה בְּשִׂמְחָה רַבָּה, וְאָמְרוּ כֻלָּם:

True and faithful is all that we have spoken: no one beside You, Adonay, is God, and we, Israel, are Your people.

The truth of Your Torah echoes in Your faithfulness through the ages: how often have You rescued us from wicked kings and pharaohs, popes and caliphs, from enemies too numerous to recall!

However cruel their power, ultimately You carried us to safety past their schemes and plots, preserving us in dignity when others would hurtle us to disgrace.

Because so many have raged against us, we sometimes think all peoples are against us; behind well-meaning criticism, we sometimes see the schemes of evil-doers.

As You have saved us from real conspirators, so may You also save us from the conspiracies we imagine, helping us distinguish between adversaries opposed to Your designs and others of Your children who merely seek to do Your will.

May we not through fear turn friends to enemies; rather may we, through faith in You, turn enemies into friends.

True redemption will arrive when enemies understand the humanity common to us all, when the praises sung by Israel can be sung by all peoples, forever rescued from their fears and hates, their cowardice and cruelty.

As our forebears sang Your praises all alone by the Red Sea, so we sing Your praises here, in the hopes that soon, in our days, we may be joined by the great chorus of all the nations of the world.

(Continue with Mi Chamocha on page 21)

On Redeeming Sparks (A Variation on the Prayer for Redemption)

The Kabbalists tell us that God
In creating the world
Took some of its fresh new light
And poured it into each of the vessels of the spheres of the
   universe.

But such powerful light was stronger than the vessels,
And so they weakened and cracked,
While the precious light spilled out, falling down and down
Through all the worlds
Until they reached into the lowest world,
Our own.

As the sparks of light fell down,
They took on forms, and embedded themselves
In physical things—
Wood and water,

Plants and paper and living creatures.
Always since that time
The sparks yearn to return to the source of all light,
The single, holy light from which they fell.

And so
When we do a mitzvah with food or plants or paper or
    another human being,
When we thank the Creator for having formed this beauti-
    ful and strong and fragrant thing,
We awaken the spark of light within,
And suddenly its fire starts to grow,
And it rises, flaming higher and higher and higher,
Soon to be reunited with its source.

As we have the power, through each mitzvah we do,
To redeem the sparks of light from the tyranny of matter,
In just such a way
God redeems us.
Embedded by the tyranny of the Egyptians,
We awoke to Adonay long centuries ago
To rise to our higher destiny
Of reunion with the divine.

And as each generation
Is embedded in its time's own tyranny,
So do we look toward the redemption
Of the holy spark in each of us,
Ready, each of us,
When our redemption time shall come
To soar further upward to the light from which we sprang
And from which our beings draw their breath.

As we sing the song of the redeemed, standing jubilant
upon the Red Sea's shore, we tune our mind, our body, our
every sense to each song, each prayer, each gesture that we
form, that we too may awaken every spark whose time it is
to soar.

מִי כָמְכָה בָּאֵלִם יְיָ מִי כָּמְכָה נֶאְדָּר בַּקֹּדֶשׁ נוֹרָא
תְהִלֹּת עֹשֵׂה פֶלֶא:

Mi cha-mo-chah ba-e-lim A-do-nay:
Mi ka-mo-chah ne-e-dar ba-ko-desh:
No-ra t'hi-lot, o-seh fe-leh.

Who is like You, Adonay, compared to the powers
humans worship?
Who is like You, majestic in holiness, awesome in praises,
doing wonders?

מַלְכוּתְךָ רָאוּ בָנֶיךָ בּוֹקֵעַ יָם לִפְנֵי מֹשֶׁה זֶה אֵלִי עָנוּ
וְאָמְרוּ:

Mal-chu-t'cha ra-u va-ne-cha
Bo-ke-a yam lif-ney Mo-sheh
Zeh e-li, a-nu v'am'ru:

Your children beheld Your rule
When You split the sea before Moses.
"This is My God!" they responded, and said:
"Adonay will reign forever and ever!"
And it was said that Adonay ransomed Jacob and
redeemed us from a hand stronger than our own.

יְיָ יִמְלֹךְ לְעֹלָם וָעֶד:

A-do-nay yim-loch l'o-lam va-ed.

וְנֶאֱמַר כִּי פָדָה יְיָ אֶת יַעֲקֹב וּגְאָלוֹ מִיַּד חָזָק מִמֶּנּוּ.
בָּרוּךְ אַתָּה יְיָ גָּאַל יִשְׂרָאֵל:

V'ne-e-mar ki fa-dah A-do-nay et Ya-a-kov, ug-a-lo mi-yad
cha-zak mi-me-nu. Ba-ruch a-tah A-do-nay ga-al Yis-ra-el.

You are praised, Adonay, who has redeemed Israel.

Hashkivenu (Night Prayer)

הַשְׁכִּיבֵנוּ יְיָ אֱלֹהֵינוּ לְשָׁלוֹם וְהַעֲמִידֵנוּ מַלְכֵּנוּ לְחַיִּים.
וּפְרוֹשׂ עָלֵינוּ סֻכַּת שְׁלוֹמֶךָ וְתַקְּנֵנוּ בְּעֵצָה טוֹבָה
מִלְּפָנֶיךָ וְהוֹשִׁיעֵנוּ לְמַעַן שְׁמֶךָ. וְהָגֵן בַּעֲדֵנוּ וְהָסֵר

מֵעָלֵינוּ אוֹיֵב דֶּבֶר וְחֶרֶב וְרָעָב וְיָגוֹן וְהָסֵר שָׂטָן
מִלְּפָנֵינוּ וּמֵאַחֲרֵינוּ וּבְצֵל כְּנָפֶיךָ תַּסְתִּירֵנוּ. כִּי אֵל
שׁוֹמְרֵנוּ וּמַצִּילֵנוּ אָתָּה כִּי אֵל מֶלֶךְ חַנּוּן וְרַחוּם אָתָּה.
וּשְׁמוֹר צֵאתֵנוּ וּבוֹאֵנוּ לְחַיִּים וּלְשָׁלוֹם מֵעַתָּה וְעַד
עוֹלָם. וּפְרוֹשׂ עָלֵינוּ סֻכַּת שְׁלוֹמֶךָ. בָּרוּךְ אַתָּה יְיָ
הַפּוֹרֵשׂ סֻכַּת שָׁלוֹם עָלֵינוּ וְעַל כָּל־עַמּוֹ יִשְׂרָאֵל וְעַל
יְרוּשָׁלָיִם:

Give us a place to rest, Adonay, our God.
And peace.
Help us, O Majesty, to stand up to life.

Spread over us Your peace-filled sukkah
That through Your good counsel
We might be repaired.

Liberate us from the place we are
That we might effect Your name.

Shield us from enmity
From slaughter
From hunger of the body and the soul
From unexpected sorrow
From those who would accuse us of being merely human.

Bring us into shelter
In the soft, long evening shadows
Of Your truth,
For with You is protection and safekeeping
And in Your presence is royal acceptance and gentle love.

Watch over us as we go forth.
Prepare for us as we return
A peaceful welcome
Life
A future
And now.

Spread over us Your peace-filled sukkah
And over all we love
Over our Jerusalem
And Yours.

Go with us.

Uf'ros aleynu sukat shlomecha.
(Spread over us Your peace-filled sukkah.)

(On Shabbat)

וְשָׁמְרוּ בְנֵי יִשְׂרָאֵל אֶת הַשַּׁבָּת, לַעֲשׂוֹת אֶת הַשַּׁבָּת
לְדֹרֹתָם בְּרִית עוֹלָם. בֵּינִי וּבֵין בְּנֵי יִשְׂרָאֵל אוֹת הִיא
לְעֹלָם, כִּי שֵׁשֶׁת יָמִים עָשָׂה יְיָ אֶת הַשָּׁמַיִם וְאֶת
הָאָרֶץ, וּבַיּוֹם הַשְּׁבִיעִי שָׁבַת וַיִּנָּפַשׁ.

V'shamru v'ney Yisrael et ha-shabbat
La-asot et ha-shabbat l-dorotam brit olam
Beynee uveyn b'ney Yisrael
ot hee l'olam.
Kee shey-shet yamim asah Adonay
et ha-shamay-im v'et ha-aretz
uva-yom ha-sh'vee-ee shavat va-yi-nafash.

For the children of Israel shall keep Shabbat,
Doing what is fitting
Through all their generations
To make Shabbat an eternal covenant
Between Me and the children of Israel,
A sign throughout all time and space.
For Adonay did the work of heaven and earth
Six days,
And on the seventh day God ceased work,
Rested,
And breathed a new soul into the world.

Tik'u Ba-Chodesh

תִּקְעוּ בַחֹֽדֶשׁ שׁוֹפָר, בַּכֶּֽסֶה לְיוֹם חַגֵּֽנוּ. כִּי חֹק
לְיִשְׂרָאֵל הוּא, מִשְׁפָּט לֵאלֹהֵי יַעֲקֹב:

Sound *tkiyah* on the shofar on the New Moon of
Tishri, at the dark of the moon, the time of our holy
day. For it is a law for Israel, a judgment by the God
of Jacob.

*Reader's Kaddish (Praise Concluding the Shma and Its Bless-
ings)*

Reader:

יִתְגַּדַּל וְיִתְקַדַּשׁ שְׁמֵהּ רַבָּא בְּעָלְמָא דִי בְרָא כִרְעוּתֵהּ;
וְיַמְלִיךְ מַלְכוּתֵהּ בְּחַיֵּיכוֹן וּבְיוֹמֵיכוֹן,וּבְחַיֵּי דְכָל בֵּית
יִשְׂרָאֵל, בַּעֲגָלָא וּבִזְמַן קָרִיב, וְאִמְרוּ אָמֵן:

Congregation and Reader:

יְהֵא שְׁמֵהּ רַבָּא מְבָרַךְ לְעָלַם וּלְעָלְמֵי עָלְמַיָּא.

Reader:

יִתְבָּרַךְ וְיִשְׁתַּבַּח, וְיִתְפָּאַר וְיִתְרוֹמַם, וְיִתְנַשֵּׂא
וְיִתְהַדָּר, וְיִתְעַלֶּה וְיִתְהַלָּל שְׁמֵהּ דְּקֻדְשָׁא, בְּרִיךְ הוּא,
לְעֵֽלָּא לְעֵֽלָּא מִן כָּל בִּרְכָתָא וְשִׁירָתָא, תֻּשְׁבְּחָתָא
וְנֶחֱמָתָא, דַּאֲמִירָן בְּעָלְמָא, וְאִמְרוּ אָמֵן.

May God's great Name be magnified and sanctified in the
world created according to the holy will, and may God's
rule be known in your lifetime, in your own days, and in
the life of the house of Israel, speedily, in a time close at
hand.

May the Name of the blessed Holy One be praised and
extolled far beyond all praises and blessings we can ever
say in the world. Amen.

Preparation for the Amidah (the Great Prayer)

Listening comes hard to us.
We can sing and read and look
Taste and smell and touch,
But listening comes hard to us.

Other people's joy and tragedy
Enter our minds,
But listening to the person behind the joy,
Letting in the person underneath the tragedy,
That takes hard concentration,
And a strong will.

But the New Year is to be listened for.

The world looks the same,
The people all around us look the same,
But underneath the ordinary day that is today
Is a special quiet which we cannot see.

We have to listen for it.

God is like that too.

God is a word:
Adonay
Eternal
Savior
Monarch

And all the rest.
They are all words.

The reality lies beneath the words:
In no word
In a soundless name which is
Being

Existence
Life
That special, electric quality
Which makes the samelooking world
The samelooking people
Extraordinary souls.

The reality behind the names of God
Is to be listened for.

It's hard.

It's there.

AMIDAH (THE GREAT PRAYER)

*(The full traditional silent Amidah in Hebrew and English
is found on pp. 156–171)*

אֲדֹנָי שְׂפָתַי תִּפְתָּח וּפִי יַגִּיד תְּהִלָּתֶךָ:

Adonay, open up my lips
That my mouth might tell
Your Praise.

Avot (God of all generations)

בָּרוּךְ אַתָּה, יְיָ אֱלֹהֵינוּ וֵאלֹהֵי אֲבוֹתֵינוּ (וְאלֹהֵי
אִמּוֹתֵינוּ), אֱלֹהֵי אַבְרָהָם, אֱלֹהֵי יִצְחָק, וֵאלֹהֵי יַעֲקֹב,
(אֱלֹהֵי שָׂרָה, אֱלֹהֵי רִבְקָה, אֱלֹהֵי רָחֵל, וֵאלֹהֵי לֵאָה,)
הָאֵל הַגָּדוֹל הַגִּבּוֹר וְהַנּוֹרָא, אֵל עֶלְיוֹן, גּוֹמֵל חֲסָדִים
טוֹבִים, וְקֹנֵה הַכֹּל, וְזוֹכֵר חַסְדֵי אָבוֹת (וְאִמָּהוֹת),
וּמֵבִיא גוֹאֵל* לִבְנֵי בְנֵיהֶם לְמַעַן שְׁמוֹ בְּאַהֲבָה.
זָכְרֵנוּ לְחַיִּים, מֶלֶךְ חָפֵץ בַּחַיִּים, וְכָתְבֵנוּ בְּסֵפֶר
הַחַיִּים, לְמַעַנְךָ אֱלֹהִים חַיִּים: מֶלֶךְ עוֹזֵר וּמוֹשִׁיעַ
וּמָגֵן. בָּרוּךְ אַתָּה יְיָ, מָגֵן אַבְרָהָם (וְשָׂרָה).

*גְּאוּלָה ,In the Reform tradition

You are praised, Adonay,
God to each of us
God to our grandfathers,
To the grandmothers of their grandmothers,
God to Abraham, to Isaac
To Sarah, to Rebecca
To Jacob, to Rachel, to Leah,
God.
Great and mighty, awesome,
Higher than our minds can climb,
Ancient source of kindness
Warming
The new cold corners of our life.

Their faded deeds have not turned cold
For You.
For You
Abraham and Isaac walked this morning,
Sarah is laughing in fulfillment
Even as we pray.
For their sake You are bringing closer
Someone who will round the corners
Of our too-narrow lives
To break the chains that keep us
From a Godly love.

As You remember them,
Remember us as well.

Joyful monarch
For whom life is Your delight
Say l'chaim to us.
Inscribe us in the book for life
God who is the life of life.

Protector of Sarah,
Shield of Abraham,
Shield us not from life.

Yet
As we search Your way
In life's cold treachery
And ice indifference.
God of our grandmothers,
Keep us warm.

V'zocher chasdey avot umeyvee go-eyl livney v'neyhem l'ma-an sh'mo b'ahava.

Gevurot (God's Power)

אַתָּה גִבּוֹר לְעוֹלָם אֲדֹנָי מְחַיֵּה מֵתִים* אַתָּה רַב
לְהוֹשִׁיעַ. מְכַלְכֵּל חַיִּים בְּחֶסֶד מְחַיֵּה מֵתִים* בְּרַחֲמִים
רַבִּים. סוֹמֵךְ נוֹפְלִים וְרוֹפֵא חוֹלִים וּמַתִּיר אֲסוּרִים
וּמְקַיֵּם אֱמוּנָתוֹ לִישֵׁנֵי עָפָר. מִי כָמוֹךָ בַּעַל גְּבוּרוֹת
וּמִי דוֹמֶה לָךְ. מֶלֶךְ מֵמִית וּמְחַיֵּה וּמַצְמִיחַ יְשׁוּעָה: מִי
כָמוֹךָ אַב הָרַחֲמִים זוֹכֵר יְצוּרָיו לְחַיִּים בְּרַחֲמִים:
וְנֶאֱמָן אַתָּה לְהַחֲיוֹת מֵתִים*: בָּרוּךְ אַתָּה יְיָ מְחַיֵּה
הַמֵּתִים*:

*הַכֹּל, In the Reform tradition,

We pray we might encounter
The Power whose gift is life,
Who quickens those who have forgotten
How to live on earth.

We pray for love that will encompass us
For no reason save that we are human,

For the love through which defeated souls may blossom
Into persons able to determine their own lives.

We pray to stand upright, we fallen
To be healed, we sufferers of the sickness of our kind;
We pray that we might break the bonds that keep us from
    ourselves.

We pray that we might walk within the garden of a life of
    purpose
Touched by the Power of the world,
Touching the meaning of the earth.

Praised be the God whose gift is life,
Who quickens those who have forgotten how to live
    on earth.

Atta Kadosh/Uv'chen (Sanctifying God the Ruler)

אַתָּה קָדוֹשׁ וְשִׁמְךָ קָדוֹשׁ וּקְדוֹשִׁים בְּכָל יוֹם יְהַלְלוּךָ
סֶּלָה:

וּבְכֵן תֵּן פַּחְדְּךָ יְיָ אֱלֹהֵינוּ עַל כָּל מַעֲשֶׂיךָ וְאֵימָתְךָ עַל־
כָּל מַה שֶׁבָּרָאתָ. וְיִירָאוּךָ כָּל הַמַּעֲשִׂים וְיִשְׁתַּחֲווּ
לְפָנֶיךָ כָּל הַבְּרוּאִים. וְיֵעָשׂוּ כֻלָּם אֲגֻדָּה אַחַת לַעֲשׂוֹת
רְצוֹנְךָ בְּלֵבָב שָׁלֵם. כְּמוֹ שֶׁיָּדַעְנוּ יְיָ אֱלֹהֵינוּ שֶׁהַשִּׁלְטוֹן
לְפָנֶיךָ עֹז בְּיָדְךָ וּגְבוּרָה בִּימִינֶךָ וְשִׁמְךָ נוֹרָא עַל כָּל
מַה שֶׁבָּרָאתָ:

וּבְכֵן תֵּן כָּבוֹד יְיָ לְעַמֶּךָ תְּהִלָּה לִירֵאֶיךָ וְתִקְוָה
לְדוֹרְשֶׁיךָ וּפִתְחוֹן פֶּה לַמְיַחֲלִים לָךְ. שִׂמְחָה לְאַרְצֶךָ
וְשָׂשׂוֹן לְעִירֶךָ וּצְמִיחַת קֶרֶן לְדָוִד עַבְדֶּךָ וַעֲרִיכַת נֵר
לְבֶן־יִשַׁי מְשִׁיחֶךָ בִּמְהֵרָה בְיָמֵינוּ:

וּבְכֵן צַדִּיקִים יִרְאוּ וְיִשְׂמָחוּ וִישָׁרִים יַעֲלֹזוּ וַחֲסִידִים
בְּרִנָּה יָגִילוּ. וְעוֹלָתָה תִּקְפָּץ־פִּיהָ וְכָל הָרִשְׁעָה כֻּלָּהּ
כְּעָשָׁן תִּכְלֶה כִּי תַעֲבִיר מֶמְשֶׁלֶת זָדוֹן מִן הָאָרֶץ:

וְתִמְלוֹךְ אַתָּה יְיָ לְבַדֶּךָ עַל כָּל מַעֲשֶׂיךָ בְּהַר צִיּוֹן
מִשְׁכַּן כְּבוֹדֶךָ וּבִירוּשָׁלַיִם עִיר קָדְשֶׁךָ. כַּכָּתוּב בְּדִבְרֵי
קָדְשֶׁךָ. יִמְלֹךְ יְיָ לְעוֹלָם אֱלֹהַיִךְ צִיּוֹן לְדֹר וָדֹר
הַלְלוּיָהּ:

קָדוֹשׁ אַתָּה וְנוֹרָא שְׁמֶךָ וְאֵין אֱלוֹהַּ מִבַּלְעָדֶיךָ
כַּכָּתוּב. וַיִּגְבַּהּ יְיָ צְבָאוֹת בַּמִּשְׁפָּט וְהָאֵל הַקָּדוֹשׁ
נִקְדַּשׁ בִּצְדָקָה. בָּרוּךְ אַתָּה יְיָ הַמֶּלֶךְ הַקָּדוֹשׁ:

Teach us how to be afraid.

Help us fear Your creatures who would do us harm
That we might reach into our power
And emerge
Ourselves unscathed
Having helped our enemies become secure enough
Not to harm again.

Help us stand in awe of all Your creatures
That even in a face of thoughtless words
We might read the holy thought
From which they grew.

Help us stand in awe of You
And gently place that awe
On all Your creatures
That as one harmonious community
We might do Your awesome will
With one united heart,

Thereby knowing that all power
Can only come from You
And so
The power of those who come against us
And the power residing in ourselves
Shall no longer be an object for our fear.

Help us stand in glory
As a people whose deeds bespeak our awe
And bring us hope in Your promise,
Joy in our land, both here and there.
And delight in Your city, Jerusalem and our own.
Raise up the horn of that fortunate creature
One day to be revealed as Your Messiah
And may we each be worthy speedily
Of the blessings the Anointed One will bring.

Then Your power
Will be the only one we know
And holiness will rule in every mount and town.
Adonay will reign forever,
God will rule in every generation.
Hallelujah!

Holy, awesome Majesty,
Exalted through justice justly done,
You are praised.

Atta V'chartanu/Vatiten lanu

אַתָּה בְחַרְתָּנוּ מִכָּל הָעַמִּים. אָהַבְתָּ אוֹתָנוּ. וְרָצִיתָ
בָּנוּ. וְרוֹמַמְתָּנוּ מִכָּל הַלְּשׁוֹנוֹת. וְקִדַּשְׁתָּנוּ בְּמִצְוֹתֶיךָ.
וְקֵרַבְתָּנוּ מַלְכֵּנוּ לַעֲבוֹדָתֶךָ. וְשִׁמְךָ הַגָּדוֹל וְהַקָּדוֹשׁ
עָלֵינוּ קָרָאתָ:

וַתִּתֶּן־לָנוּ יְיָ אֱלֹהֵינוּ בְּאַהֲבָה אֶת־יוֹם [הַשַּׁבָּת הַזֶּה
וְאֶת־יוֹם] הַזִּכָּרוֹן הַזֶּה יוֹם [זִכְרוֹן] תְּרוּעָה [בְּאַהֲבָה]
מִקְרָא קֹדֶשׁ. זֵכֶר לִיצִיאַת מִצְרָיִם:

Ya'aleh V'Yavo (For the Ascent of Our Thoughts)

אֱלֹהֵינוּ וֵאלֹהֵי אֲבוֹתֵינוּ (וֵאלֹהֵי אִמוֹתֵינוּ) יַעֲלֶה וְיָבֹא
וְיַגִּיעַ וְיֵרָאֶה וְיֵרָצֶה וְיִשָּׁמַע וְיִפָּקֵד וְיִזָּכֵר זִכְרוֹנֵנוּ
וּפִקְדוֹנֵנוּ וְזִכְרוֹן אֲבוֹתֵינוּ (וְזִכְרוֹן אִמוֹתֵינוּ) וְזִכְרוֹן
מָשִׁיחַ בֶּן־דָּוִד עַבְדֶּךְ וְזִכְרוֹן יְרוּשָׁלַיִם עִיר קָדְשֶׁךְ
וְזִכְרוֹן כָּל עַמְּךְ בֵּית יִשְׂרָאֵל לְפָנֶיךְ. לִפְלֵיטָה וּלְטוֹבָה
לְחֵן וּלְחֶסֶד וּלְרַחֲמִים לְחַיִּים וּלְשָׁלוֹם בְּיוֹם הַזִּכָּרוֹן
הַזֶּה. זָכְרֵנוּ יְיָ אֱלֹהֵינוּ בּוֹ לְטוֹבָה. וּפָקְדֵנוּ בוֹ לִבְרָכָה.
וְהוֹשִׁיעֵנוּ בוֹ לְחַיִּים: וּבִדְבַר יְשׁוּעָה וְרַחֲמִים חוּס
וְחָנֵּנוּ וְרַחֵם עָלֵינוּ וְהוֹשִׁיעֵנוּ כִּי אֵלֶיךְ עֵינֵינוּ. כִּי אֵל
מֶלֶךְ חַנּוּן וְרַחוּם אָתָּה:

Our God and God of our ancestors,
May the thought of us
Our fathers and mothers long before us
The Messiah You have promised from the seed of David
Jerusalem, holy city,
Israel, a chosen people

May the thought of all these
Ascend and come before Your presence,
And reach You
And be noticed by You
And be pleasing to You

For liberation
For good
For graciousness
For covenant love
For motherlove
For life
For peace.

It's Rosh Hashanah.
Remember us this day

For life.

M'loch (Sanctifying Rosh Hashanah)

אֱלֹהֵינוּ וֵאלֹהֵי אֲבוֹתֵינוּ (וֵאלֹהֵי אִמּוֹתֵינוּ). מְלוֹךְ עַל
כָּל הָעוֹלָם כֻּלּוֹ בִּכְבוֹדֶךָ וְהִנָּשֵׂא עַל כָּל הָאָרֶץ בִּיקָרֶךָ
וְהוֹפַע בַּהֲדַר גְּאוֹן עֻזֶּךָ עַל כָּל יוֹשְׁבֵי תֵבֵל אַרְצֶךָ.
וְיֵדַע כָּל פָּעוּל כִּי אַתָּה פְעַלְתּוֹ וְיָבִין כָּל יָצוּר כִּי אַתָּה
יְצַרְתּוֹ וְיֹאמַר כֹּל אֲשֶׁר נְשָׁמָה בְּאַפּוֹ יְיָ אֱלֹהֵי יִשְׂרָאֵל
מֶלֶךְ וּמַלְכוּתוֹ בַּכֹּל מָשָׁלָה: אֱלֹהֵינוּ וֵאלֹהֵי אֲבוֹתֵינוּ
(וֵאלֹהֵי אִמּוֹתֵינוּ) [רְצֵה בִמְנוּחָתֵנוּ] קַדְּשֵׁנוּ בְּמִצְוֹתֶיךָ
וְתֵן חֶלְקֵנוּ בְּתוֹרָתֶךָ שַׂבְּעֵנוּ מִטּוּבֶךָ וְשַׂמְּחֵנוּ
בִּישׁוּעָתֶךָ: [וְהַנְחִילֵנוּ יְיָ אֱלֹהֵינוּ בְּאַהֲבָה וּבְרָצוֹן
שַׁבַּת קָדְשֶׁךָ וְיָנוּחוּ בָהּ יִשְׂרָאֵל מְקַדְּשֵׁי שְׁמֶךָ] וְטַהֵר
לִבֵּנוּ לְעָבְדְּךָ בֶּאֱמֶת. כִּי אַתָּה אֱלֹהִים אֱמֶת וּדְבָרְךָ
אֱמֶת וְקַיָּם לָעַד. בָּרוּךְ אַתָּה יְיָ מֶלֶךְ עַל כָּל הָאָרֶץ
מְקַדֵּשׁ [הַשַּׁבָּת וְ] יִשְׂרָאֵל וְיוֹם הַזִּכָּרוֹן:

Adonay,
Our people have called You Monarch of the universe.
Help us who live without a monarch on a throne
To perceive Your sovereignty
In the royal splendor that pervades the universe,
In the holy power that creates of all creatures
A single royal household.

Because You are our Monarch
The whole universe is intertwined,
Each part responsible for every other part.

We too are responsible for the whole world
Because You are our Monarch.

* * *

Adonay our God,
Let this holy time lift us to Your presence
In life,
In peace,
In leaping joy.
You have promised us it will.
Find rest in our rest,
Holiness in our peformance of mitzvot,
Help us find our being in Your Torah.
Feed us from your store of good,
Bring us joy in Your victory over evil.
Wash clean our hearts
That we may serve You and Your creatures honestly.
Dower us with love and acceptance,
Joyous delight,
Shabbat and holy festivals,
That we who represent Your holiness
May know joy.
Through (Shabbat and) this Day of Remembrance, may
We
Your people Israel
Find You.

Rtzey: Acceptance of Our Prayer (Traditional Version)

רְצֵה יְיָ אֱלֹהֵינוּ בְּעַמְּךָ יִשְׂרָאֵל וּבִתְפִלָּתָם. וְהָשֵׁב אֶת
הָעֲבוֹדָה לִדְבִיר בֵּיתֶךָ וְאִשֵּׁי יִשְׂרָאֵל וּתְפִלָּתָם
בְּאַהֲבָה תְקַבֵּל בְּרָצוֹן. וּתְהִי לְרָצוֹן תָּמִיד עֲבוֹדַת
יִשְׂרָאֵל עַמֶּךָ. וְתֶחֱזֶינָה עֵינֵינוּ בְּשׁוּבְךָ לְצִיוֹן בְּרַחֲמִים.
בָּרוּךְ אַתָּה יְיָ הַמַּחֲזִיר שְׁכִינָתוֹ לְצִיּוֹן:

Rtzey (Reform Version)

רְצֵה יְיָ אֱלֹהֵינוּ בְּעַמְּךָ יִשְׂרָאֵל, וּתְפִלָּתָם בְּאַהֲבָה
תְקַבֵּל, וּתְהִי לְרָצוֹן תָּמִיד עֲבוֹדַת יִשְׂרָאֵל עַמֶּךָ. אֵל
קָרוֹב לְכָל־קוֹרְאָיו, פְּנֵה אֶל עֲבָדֶיךָ וְחָנֵּנוּ; שְׁפוֹךְ
רוּחֲךָ עָלֵינוּ, וְתֶחֱזֶינָה עֵינֵינוּ בְּשׁוּבְךָ לְצִיּוֹן בְּרַחֲמִים.
בָּרוּךְ אַתָּה יְיָ הַמַּחֲזִיר שְׁכִינָתוֹ לְצִיּוֹן:

*   *   *

Accept us, Your people, Adonay our God.
Help us fashion the service You desire,
Receive our prayers as though they ascended from the fire
    on the ancient altar,
Speed the descent of Your compassionate presence
To Zion,
To us.

Restorer of holy intimacy to Zion,
You are praised.

Modim (Thanks)

מוֹדִים אֲנַחְנוּ לָךְ שָׁאַתָּה הוּא יְיָ אֱלֹהֵינוּ וֵאלֹהֵי
אֲבוֹתֵינוּ (וֵאלֹהֵי אִמּוֹתֵינוּ) לְעוֹלָם וָעֶד. צוּר חַיֵּינוּ
מָגֵן יִשְׁעֵנוּ אַתָּה הוּא לְדוֹר וָדוֹר. נוֹדֶה לְךָ וּנְסַפֵּר
תְּהִלָּתֶךָ עַל חַיֵּינוּ הַמְּסוּרִים בְּיָדֶךָ וְעַל נִשְׁמוֹתֵינוּ
הַפְּקוּדוֹת לָךְ וְעַל נִסֶּיךָ שֶׁבְּכָל־יוֹם עִמָּנוּ וְעַל
נִפְלְאוֹתֶיךָ וְטוֹבוֹתֶיךָ שֶׁבְּכָל־עֵת עֶרֶב וָבֹקֶר וְצָהֳרָיִם.
הַטּוֹב כִּי לֹא כָלוּ רַחֲמֶיךָ וְהַמְרַחֵם כִּי לֹא תַמּוּ חֲסָדֶיךָ
מֵעוֹלָם קִוִּינוּ לָךְ:

וְעַל כֻּלָּם יִתְבָּרַךְ וְיִתְרוֹמַם שִׁמְךָ מַלְכֵּנוּ תָּמִיד לְעוֹלָם
וָעֶד:

וּכְתֹב לְחַיִּים טוֹבִים כָּל־בְּנֵי בְרִיתֶךָ:

וְכֹל הַחַיִּים יוֹדוּךָ סֶּלָה וִיהַלְלוּ אֶת שִׁמְךָ בֶּאֱמֶת הָאֵל
יְשׁוּעָתֵנוּ וְעֶזְרָתֵנוּ סֶּלָה. בָּרוּךְ אַתָּה יְיָ הַטּוֹב שִׁמְךָ
וּלְךָ נָאֶה לְהוֹדוֹת:

Thank You.

For
We are not alone,
We are not abandoned in the world.
We are persons,
And so there must exist within the universe
An acknowledgement of persons,
A personal presence
We acknowledge as Adonay.

We can feel secure here
Protected

Each one of our imperfect lives
Reveals an irreplaceable piece of a holy world.

Our lives, complex, are Your caress
Our souls, beclouded, are Your intimates
Miracles surround us
Every minute of an ordinary day,
At every corner of a troubled night
Are signs of You.

In You we find perfect motherlove and fathercaring
Which help us to accept
Our own parents' imperfections
And irreplaceable humanity.

Inscribe all the members of Your covenant
For a good life,
For all life

Its beauty, ugliness, tragedy, delight,
Is the truth of Your existence
And its goodness.
Thank You for it all.

For it all.

Shalom Rav (For Peace)

שָׁלוֹם רָב עַל יִשְׂרָאֵל עַמְּךָ תָּשִׂים לְעוֹלָם. כִּי אַתָּה
הוּא מֶלֶךְ אָדוֹן לְכָל־הַשָּׁלוֹם. וְטוֹב בְּעֵינֶיךָ לְבָרֵךְ
אֶת־עַמְּךָ יִשְׂרָאֵל בְּכָל־עֵת וּבְכָל־שָׁעָה בִּשְׁלוֹמֶךָ.
בְּסֵפֶר חַיִּים בְּרָכָה וְשָׁלוֹם וּפַרְנָסָה טוֹבָה נִזָּכֵר וְנִכָּתֵב
לְפָנֶיךָ אֲנַחְנוּ וְכָל־עַמְּךָ בֵּית יִשְׂרָאֵל לְחַיִּים טוֹבִים
וּלְשָׁלוֹם. בָּרוּךְ אַתָּה יְיָ עֹשֵׂה הַשָּׁלוֹם:

War is what we know,
Plan for, calculate,
Talk about so often
It seems as natural as breath.

Peace is what You know,
You created it with the world's first light
That it might keep at bay the chaos which preceded Your
    creation.
When You said to darkness: Let there be light!
You really said: Let there be Shalom.
When you said to the Sea: Let there be Israel!
You really said: Let there be messengers of Shalom.

Teach us how to resist the messengers of war
And place upon our breath
Shalom in abundance

That we may speak of it to every person
Every day.

You are praised
Who commands Your people Israel
Within a warring world
To speak
To act
To dare
For Shalom.

*   *   *

Alternative Reading (by Rabbi Nachman of Bratzlav)

May the will come from You,
   to annul wars and the shedding of blood from the universe,
And to extend a peace, great and wondrous, in the universe.
Nor again shall one people raise the sword against another
   and they shall learn war no more.

But let all the residents of earth recognize and know the
   innermost truth:
That we are not come into this world for quarrel and divi-
   sion,
Nor for hate and jealousy, contrariness and bloodshed;
But we are come into this world
You to recognize and know,
Who is blessed forever.

And let Your glory fill all our wits and minds, knowledge
   and hearts;
And may I be a chariot for the presence of Your divinity.
May I not again depart from the Sanctity as much as a
   hairsbreadth.
May I not again think one extraneous thought.

But may I ever cling to You and to Your sacred Torah,
   until I be worthy to introduce others into the knowledge
   of the truth of Your divinity
To announce to the human race Your power,
   and the honor of the glory of Your kingdom.

Elohai Ntzor (Concluding Meditation)

אֱלֹהַי נְצוֹר לְשׁוֹנִי מֵרָע וּשְׂפָתַי מִדַּבֵּר מִרְמָה
וְלִמְקַלְלַי נַפְשִׁי תִדּוֹם וְנַפְשִׁי כֶּעָפָר לַכֹּל תִּהְיֶה: פְּתַח
לִבִּי בְּתוֹרָתֶךָ וּבְמִצְוֹתֶיךָ תִּרְדּוֹף נַפְשִׁי. וְכָל
הַחוֹשְׁבִים עָלַי רָעָה מְהֵרָה הָפֵר עֲצָתָם וְקַלְקֵל
מַחֲשַׁבְתָּם: עֲשֵׂה לְמַעַן שְׁמֶךָ. עֲשֵׂה לְמַעַן יְמִינֶךָ. עֲשֵׂה
לְמַעַן קְדֻשָׁתֶךָ. עֲשֵׂה לְמַעַן תּוֹרָתֶךָ: לְמַעַן יֵחָלְצוּן
יְדִידֶיךָ הוֹשִׁיעָה יְמִינְךָ וַעֲנֵנִי: יִהְיוּ לְרָצוֹן אִמְרֵי פִי
וְהֶגְיוֹן לִבִּי לְפָנֶיךָ יְיָ צוּרִי וְגוֹאֲלִי: עֹשֶׂה שָׁלוֹם
בִּמְרוֹמָיו הוּא יַעֲשֶׂה שָׁלוֹם עָלֵינוּ וְעַל כָּל יִשְׂרָאֵל
וְאִמְרוּ אָמֵן:

My God,
Guard my tongue from passion unrestrained,
My lips from lying words.
Give me the strength of stillness
Before those who slander me,
And like dust, unchanged beneath incessant feet,
May my soul not suffer injury
From those who seek my ill.
Rather, merely thwart their plans
And turn their plots to naught.
For Your sake—
For Your power, Your holiness, Your Torah—

And for mine,
That those you love may escape unharmed.
Answer me,
Help me to come out all right.
May all the words of my mouth
And the thoughts within my heart
Be desirable to You,
Rock of mine, Restorer of my freedom.
The One who makes peace in the heavens high above
Shall surely do the work of peace with us,
All Israel and all the human family,
Therefore say with me: it will be so.

Yih'yu l'ratzon imrey fee, v'hegyon libee l'faneh-cha.
Adonay tzuree v'go'alee. Oseh shalom bimromav hu ya'aseh
shalom aleynu v'al kol Yisrael, v'imru amen.

Kaddish Shalem (Praise After Concluding the Amiḍah)

יִתְגַּדַּל וְיִתְקַדַּשׁ שְׁמֵהּ רַבָּא. בְּעָלְמָא דִּי בְרָא
כִרְעוּתֵהּ. וְיַמְלִיךְ מַלְכוּתֵהּ בְּחַיֵּיכוֹן וּבְיוֹמֵיכוֹן וּבְחַיֵּי
דְכָל בֵּית יִשְׂרָאֵל. בַּעֲגָלָא וּבִזְמַן קָרִיב וְאִמְרוּ. אָמֵן:

יְהֵא שְׁמֵהּ רַבָּא מְבָרַךְ לְעָלַם וּלְעָלְמֵי עָלְמַיָּא:

יִתְבָּרַךְ וְיִשְׁתַּבַּח וְיִתְפָּאַר וְיִתְרֹמַם וְיִתְנַשֵּׂא וְיִתְהַדָּר
וְיִתְעַלֶּה וְיִתְהַלָּל שְׁמֵהּ דְּקֻדְשָׁא. בְּרִיךְ הוּא. לְעֵלָּא
לְעֵלָּא מִן כָּל בִּרְכָתָא וְשִׁירָתָא תֻּשְׁבְּחָתָא וְנֶחֱמָתָא
דַּאֲמִירָן בְּעָלְמָא וְאִמְרוּ. אָמֵן:

תִּתְקַבֵּל צְלוֹתְהוֹן וּבָעוּתְהוֹן דְּכָל יִשְׂרָאֵל קֳדָם
אֲבוּהוֹן דִּי בִשְׁמַיָּא וְאִמְרוּ. אָמֵן:

יְהֵא שְׁלָמָא רַבָּא מִן שְׁמַיָּא וְחַיִּים עָלֵינוּ וְעַל כָּל
יִשְׂרָאֵל וְאִמְרוּ. אָמֵן:

עוֹשֶׂה שָׁלוֹם בִּמְרוֹמָיו הוּא יַעֲשֶׂה שָׁלוֹם עָלֵינוּ וְעַל
כָּל יִשְׂרָאֵל וְאִמְרוּ. אָמֵן:

May God's great name be praised and sanctified in the world! May Your Rule be established in our lifetime and the lifetime of the House of Israel. God's great name is blessed and praised far beyond all blessings and praises we could ever say in the world. May the praises and prayers of all Israel be accepted in heaven before You. May there be a great peace from heaven and life for us and all Israel. May the One who makes peace in the high places, make peace for us and all Israel! Amen.

ALEYNU

We have shared many words together. That we could speak them, and hear them spoken, means that there is a place in the world for them, that our songs of praise and prayers of hope have not gone empty from our mouths, but remain still in the air, waiting for other words to join them. Too often they are not joined, but lost in hopeless words, rhetoric propounded but not meant, accents without acts. If the hopes that we have shared tonight are not to have been shared in vain, we must not leave our words here in our seats, neatly folded in our books. Our words must leave with us, go streaming out the doors of this New Year with us, accompany us as we walk on the road, when we sit in our houses, when we lie down and when we rise up. They must emblazon the doorposts of our house, and seal themselves into our hands and before our eyes, that the world might remember the words it has so long forgotten, and form from them a new song which all might sing in celebration of the world we all desire. Before that hope, before the God who is the substance of that hope, let us bow the head and bend the knee in the holy spaces of our yearning, Whom we praise.

עָלֵינוּ לְשַׁבֵּחַ לַאֲדוֹן הַכֹּל לָתֵת גְּדֻלָּה לְיוֹצֵר בְּרֵאשִׁית
שֶׁלֹּא עָשָׂנוּ כְּגוֹיֵי הָאֲרָצוֹת וְלֹא שָׂמָנוּ כְּמִשְׁפְּחוֹת
הָאֲדָמָה שֶׁלֹּא שָׂם חֶלְקֵנוּ כָּהֶם וְגוֹרָלֵנוּ כְּכָל הֲמוֹנָם:
וַאֲנַחְנוּ כֹּרְעִים וּמִשְׁתַּחֲוִים וּמוֹדִים
לִפְנֵי מֶלֶךְ מַלְכֵי הַמְּלָכִים הַקָּדוֹשׁ בָּרוּךְ הוּא.
שֶׁהוּא נוֹטֶה שָׁמַיִם וְיוֹסֵד אָרֶץ וּמוֹשַׁב יְקָרוֹ בַּשָּׁמַיִם
מִמַּעַל וּשְׁכִינַת עֻזּוֹ בְּגָבְהֵי מְרוֹמִים: הוּא אֱלֹהֵינוּ אֵין
עוֹד. אֱמֶת מַלְכֵּנוּ אֶפֶס זוּלָתוֹ כַּכָּתוּב בְּתוֹרָתוֹ וְיָדַעְתָּ
הַיּוֹם וַהֲשֵׁבֹתָ אֶל לְבָבֶךָ כִּי יְיָ הוּא הָאֱלֹהִים בַּשָּׁמַיִם
מִמַּעַל וְעַל הָאָרֶץ מִתָּחַת. אֵין עוֹד:

A-ley-nu l'-sha-be-ach la-a-don hakol la-tet g'-du-lah l'-yo-tzer b'-re-sheet, she-lo a-sa-nu k'-go-yey ha-a-ra-tzot v'-lo sa-ma-nu k'-mish-p'chot ha-a-da-mah. She-lo sam chel-ke-nu ka-hem v'-go-ra-le-nu k'-chol ha-mo-nam.
Va-a-nach-nu ko-r'-im u-mish-ta-cha-vim u-mo-dim lif-ney me-lech mal-chey hamlachim ha-ka-dosh ba-ruch hu.
She-hu no-teh sha-ma-yim v'-yo-sed a-retz. U-mo-shav y'ka-roh ba-sha-ma-yim mi-ma-al, u-shchi-nat u-zo b'gav-hey m'romim. Hu e-lo-hey-nu, ein od.
Emet malkeynu efes zulato, ka-katuv b'Torato v'yadata hayom va-hashey-vo-ta el l'va-vecha, kee Adonay hu ha-Elohim ba-sha-ma-yim mi-ma-al v'al ha-aretz mi-tachat, ein od.

May the time not be distant, O God, when Your name shall be worshipped in all the earth, when despair shall disappear and error be no more. We pray that the day be not far off when all humanity shall find their way to calling on Your name, when corruption and evil shall give way to integrity and goodness, when the many kinds of humans dwelling on the earth shall recognize not alone their difference but their unity, that each people may in its unique manner work for the coming of God's united realm. Hear O Israel is only for the present; the day will come when all the earth will hear that Adonay is God, Adonay is One.

וְנֶאֱמַר וְהָיָה יְיָ לְמֶלֶךְ עַל כָּל הָאָרֶץ בַּיּוֹם הַהוּא יִהְיֶה
יְיָ אֶחָד וּשְׁמוֹ אֶחָד:

V'ne-e-mar: V'-ha-yah A-do-nai l'me-lech al kol ha-a-retz,
ba-yom ha-hu ba-yom ha-hu yih-yeh A-do-nai e-chad
u-sh'-mo e-chad

Mourner's Kaddish

יִתְגַּדַּל וְיִתְקַדַּשׁ שְׁמֵהּ רַבָּא. בְּעָלְמָא דִי בְרָא
כִרְעוּתֵהּ. וְיַמְלִיךְ מַלְכוּתֵהּ בְּחַיֵּיכוֹן וּבְיוֹמֵיכוֹן וּבְחַיֵּי
דְכָל בֵּית יִשְׂרָאֵל. בַּעֲגָלָא וּבִזְמַן קָרִיב וְאִמְרוּ. אָמֵן:

Yit-ga-dal v'yit-ka'dash sh'mey ra-bah.
B'al-ma dee v'rah chi-ru-tey.
V'yam-leech mal-chu-tey, b'cha-yey-chon
U-v'yo-mey-chon uv-cha-yey d'chol beyt yis-ra-el,
ba-a-ga-lah u-viz-man ka-reev. V'im-ru a-men.

יְהֵא שְׁמֵהּ רַבָּא מְבָרַךְ לְעָלַם וּלְעָלְמֵי עָלְמַיָּא:

Y'hey sh'may ra-bah m'va-rach l'alam u-l'al-mey
Al-ma-ya.

יִתְבָּרַךְ וְיִשְׁתַּבַּח וְיִתְפָּאַר וְיִתְרֹמַם וְיִתְנַשֵּׂא וְיִתְהַדָּר
וְיִתְעַלֶּה וְיִתְהַלָּל שְׁמֵהּ דְּקוּדְשָׁא. בְּרִיךְ הוּא. לְעֵלָּא
לְעֵלָּא מִן כָּל בִּרְכָתָא וְשִׁירָתָא תֻּשְׁבְּחָתָא וְנֶחֱמָתָא
דַּאֲמִירָן בְּעָלְמָא וְאִמְרוּ. אָמֵן:

Yit-ba-rach v'yish-ta-bach v'yit-pa-ar v'-yit-ro-mam
V'yit-na-sey v'yit-ha-dar v'yit-a-leh
V'yit-ha-lal sh-mey d-ku-d'shah. B'reech hu.
L'ey-lah l-ey-lah min kol bir-cha-tah
V'shir-a-tah tush-b'cha-tah v'ne-che-ma-tah
Da-a-mi-ran b'al-mah. V'im-ru: A-men.

יְהֵא שְׁלָמָא רַבָּא מִן שְׁמַיָּא וְחַיִּים עָלֵינוּ וְעַל כָּל
יִשְׂרָאֵל וְאִמְרוּ. אָמֵן:

Y'hey sh'la-mah ra-bah min sh'ma-yah
V'cha-yim a-ley-nu v'al kol Yis-ra-el.
V'im-ru: A-men.

עוֹשֶׂה שָׁלוֹם בִּמְרוֹמָיו הוּא יַעֲשֶׂה שָׁלוֹם עָלֵינוּ וְעַל
כָּל יִשְׂרָאֵל וְאִמְרוּ. אָמֵן:

O-seh sha-lom bim-ro-mav hu ya-a-seh
Sha-lom a-ley-nu v'al kol Yis-ra-el.
V'im-ru: A-men.

May God's great name be praised and sanctified in the
world! May Your Rule be established in our lifetime and
the lifetime of the House of Israel. God's great name is
blessed and praised far beyond all blessings and praises we
could ever say in the world.

May there be a great peace from heaven and life for us and
all Israel. May the One who makes peace in the high
places, make peace for us and all Israel! Amen.

Hopes for the New Year

Now all things are possible:
For the New Year and we have found each other
Arm in arm beneath the nurturing night,
Welcoming the day on which the world itself began,
The day which reunites our people in their ancient task:
Messengers of light before the darkness,
Messengers of peace before the world.

*   *   *

May we find the world in our lifetime,
And may our future be realized in the life to come.
May our hearts meditate in understanding,
Our mouths speak wisdom,
Our tongues sing songs of jubilation.
May our eyes look straight before us,
Our eyes afire with the light of Torah,
Our faces shining with the glow of heaven.
May our lips utter knowledge,
And our inward parts rejoice,
May our footsteps hasten toward the words
Of the Ancient of Days.

Adon Olam

*Adon olam asher malach, b'terem kol
y'tseer nivra,
l'ayt na-asa b'cheftso kol, azay
melech shmo nikra*

אֲדוֹן עוֹלָם אֲשֶׁר מָלַךְ
בְּטֶרֶם כָּל יְצִיר נִבְרָא:
לְעֵת נַעֲשָׂה בְחֶפְצוֹ כֹּל
אֲזַי מֶלֶךְ שְׁמוֹ נִקְרָא:

*V'acharey kichlot ha-kol
L'vado yimloch nora
V'hu haya, v'hu hoveh,
V'hu yihyeh b'tifara.*

וְאַחֲרֵי כִּכְלוֹת הַכֹּל
לְבַדּוֹ יִמְלוֹךְ נוֹרָא:
וְהוּא הָיָה וְהוּא הֹוֶה
וְהוּא יִהְיֶה בְּתִפְאָרָה:

*V'hu echad v'ayn sheynee, l'hamsheel
lo l'hachbeera:
B'lee raysheet b'lee tachleet, v'lo
ha-oz v'ha-misra.*

וְהוּא אֶחָד וְאֵין שֵׁנִי
לְהַמְשִׁיל לוֹ לְהַחְבִּירָה:
בְּלִי רֵאשִׁית בְּלִי תַכְלִית
וְלוֹ הָעֹז וְהַמִּשְׂרָה:

*V'hu aylee v'chai goalee, v'tsur
chevlee b'ayt tsara:
V'hu nee-see umanos lee, m'nat kosee
b'yom ekra.*

וְהוּא אֵלִי וְחַי גּוֹאֲלִי
וְצוּר חֶבְלִי בְּעֵת צָרָה:
וְהוּא נִסִּי וּמָנוֹס לִי
מְנָת כּוֹסִי בְּיוֹם אֶקְרָא:

B'yado afkeed ruchee, b'ayt eeshan
v'a-ee-ra:
v'im ruchee g'veeyatee, Adonay lee
v'lo ee-ra.

בְּיָדוֹ אַפְקִיד רוּחִי
בְּעֵת אִישַׁן וְאָעִירָה:
וְעִם רוּחִי גְּוִיָּתִי
יְיָ לִי וְלֹא אִירָא:

The Author of eternity reigned before any creature was
  brought forth.
When all was made, as S/He desired, God was hailed as
  Sovereign.
When all is ended S/He alone will reign in awesome
  majesty.
S/He was, is, and will be glorious for eternity.
God is One, and has no second-in-command, with whom
  to share dominion.
Beginningless and endless, God alone has strength to rule.
My God, my life's redeemer, my rock in distress,
My banner and my refuge, my cup, my portion whenever I
  call.
In God's hand I entrust the breath through which I live,
  when I sleep and when I rise,
Along with my breath God has my body; Adonay is with
  me, I have no fear.

MORNING SERVICE
FOR ROSH HASHANAH

רַבּוֹת מַחֲשָׁבוֹת בְּלֶב־אִישׁ, וַעֲצַת יְהוָֹה הִיא תָקוּם.

Rabot machshavot b'lev eesh
va-atzat Adonay hee takum.

There are many plans within the human heart;
Only those which carry forth the divine plan
Will be sustained. — Prov. 19:21

אַשְׁרֵינוּ, מַה טוֹב חֶלְקֵנוּ וּמַה נָּעִים גוֹרָלֵנוּ וּמַה יָפָה
יְרֻשָּׁתֵנוּ.

Ashreynu, ma tov chelkeynu
Uma na-im goraleynu
Uma yafa y'rushateynu.

How fortunate are we, how
good our portion, how pleasant
our lot, and how beautiful our
inheritance.

INTRODUCTORY READINGS

An Argument for Judgment Morning

When last we came together it was dark, but healing sleep has
brought us back together in the light, our souls prepared to
sense the daysmells of the year now born, to seek their Source

through words and melodies, thoughts and hopes, and the reassuring presence of this portion of our people close at hand.

This is the day on which, tradition has it, judgment is determined for those neither wholly righteous nor wholly wicked. To affirm that tradition is to affirm the significance of our actions in the world, to take responsibility for what we have and have not done, for what we want to do, and for what our weakness will not let us do. To judge ourselves as the Judge of all the world might judge us—how terrifying! Yet how exhilarating! To believe that behind all the changes in the world, some permanent goals can still be sought; that behind all the conflicting falsehoods, lie some values we can identify as truth.

Beneath the sunlight we have come to search for the brightness of that truth—about ourselves, about our people, about the land in which we live, about the work that we must do to burn off the haze which hides these truths from daily view. We are good people, and our failings often blind us to our goodness; yet we are not so good as we would have ourselves believe, and we must seek the road between both exaggerations of our worth.

Our people has been oppressed, and oppression still dogs our heels in whatever land we live; but we must not let our own tragedies blot out the suffering which other people, other peoples, must endure as well. As individuals we too can act like oppressors, and we must learn how to secure our own survival while still ensuring that we shall survive as a compassionate and moral race. The land in which we live burdens us with injustice it is not yet prepared to cure, with callousness to the suffering which persists behind the barriers we have built to keep it from our eyes, and with cruelty toward the earth and sky we live between. Yet there is goodness too within this land, and if we blind ourselves to the beauties which grow within its people and its earth, we shall find no foundation upon which to build a new society, no healthy seed from which, with our help and nurture, a just and peaceful land might grow.

It is not easy to judge ourselves, to judge our people, to judge our world. We may be too harsh, we may be too lenient. But the New Year, in all its morning brightness, reminds us it is time to begin.

*   *   *

To Conceive the World

Hayom harat olam: On Rosh Hashanah is the world conceived. But there is more: on Rosh Hashanah we help conceive the world. If we pray with enough intensity, if we involve ourselves sufficiently with the words and deeds and lives of our people and our God, our ecstasy can be so powerful that from it a new world can flow.

Jewishness means not only concentration on the details of life—the words and gestures of prayer, the exact requirements of mitzvot, even the calamities and urgent needs of our people—it is as well the love affair of our people's encounter with God. Life is not only responsibility, this day reminds us, but also love and exultation; the Shofar calls us to a realm where we may embrace what is holy and uplifting and cosmically incredible, and feel embraced by it so lustily that our souls near leap for joy beyond our bodies.

We are not alone, we Jews; we are part of a grand design in which we pulsate every minute of our lives as partners of God, as parts of an all-embracing human race, as parts of the Creation whose winds and water are our sisters, whose stars and grasses are our brothers.

To conceive the world today releases us to run upon the hills tomorrow, to let our mouths drop open in these days of awe to the awesomeness of life itself—the brilliance of a clear day's sky, the quiet of grey rain on green leaves, the miracle of a baby brought triumphantly from the womb, the magic of the person in whose company we feel like the most important person in the world, the triumph of being alone with ourselves, plumbing the

full depths of our intellect or our feeling. Where is God in the world, we ask? God is where we encounter all the ways in which our bodies and our minds connect with nature, with humanity, and with our people; to know we are not alone, to know we lie in passionate embrace with the world at every conscious moment: then it is that we are ready to conceive the world—today, now as we sit here, now as our lips begin to pour forth words and melodies that are the Jew's old love song on the morning that the world begins its life.

*   *   *

The Senses of New Year

Into all our senses comes this Day, this New Year Day, when we would carefully tune that instrument which is our body, that all our limbs might raise our souls before the throne of God and say, "Behold this person You created!"

When we hear the Shofar, will we hear as well the voices to which we have not listened—of our conscience, of good friends, wise teachers, our parents and our children? Will we hear our own voices, echoing these prayers and promises last year?

In the morning light, let us look with understanding and with love into the faces of our neighbors to find their hopes and longings there, helping those we care about to realize the good ones and desist from those that can bring only harm. Let us look this morning at ourselves as well, that in the days ahead we may tear down the battlements we have constructed to obscure our best selves from view. As we see the Torah open up before us, that self could stand with Abraham and Sarah, ready to face as they did the stiffest tests which life presents, still convinced that God is good, that justice undergirds the world.

In a world which seems too seldom just, we need the taste of honey to remind ourselves what sweetness is, resolving to bring more sweetness into our own lives and the lives of those about us. Have we been harsh of late? Rosh Hashanah reminds us to

treat gently those we care for, replacing the memory of an annoying habit with a recollection of the habits that we love, which themselves bring sweetness into our often sour world.

Beyond the windows of our praying place there lies another sweetness: the trees and grass, the autumn leaves and flowers of the Creation we are charged to guard. But mingled with them are the odors of offending cars, polluting factories, and nuclear arms in a profusion that could wipe the leaves and flowers from the earth. We need to pledge ourselves to greater vigilance for the earth and sky, to preserve the scents of the Creation formed this day.

These words upon our page, we hope, will touch our hearts. For words to touch us, we need to touch others, and at this season to recall those whose plight has failed to touch us, those times when we have turned away unfeeling from an entreating voice, a needy hand. We need to translate the prayers in the book to new resolves in mind and deeper feelings in the heart, or prayer is but ink on page, and not a pathway to the throne of God.

As we embark upon that path, let us concentrate all our senses on the mystery of this Day, this Year, that has begun. Let us be conscious of each other's presence as we pray, letting our neighbors' devotions lift our prayers on their intensity, that together we might raise our words and melodies up to heaven. The Throneroom waits for our arrival. The New Year calls us to ascend.

BIRCHOT HASHACHAR (Morning Blessings)

Elohai Nshama (For the Return of the Soul)

> *To awake from sleep each morning*
> *Recalls Your mystifying promise*
> *That death is not the end,*
> *But when this world awakens to the messianic dawn*
> *Souls and bodies will somehow join together once again*
> *In one grand reunion of the human race.*

When I awoke this morning
It was as though that mystery was rehearsed
For as I gradually emerged from sleep
My soul became aware of my body once again
In a small but wondrous reunion of my own humanity.

אֱלֹהַי, נְשָׁמָה שֶׁנָּתַתָּ בִּי טְהוֹרָה הִיא. אַתָּה בְרָאתָהּ
אַתָּה יְצַרְתָּהּ אַתָּה נְפַחְתָּהּ בִּי וְאַתָּה מְשַׁמְּרָהּ בְּקִרְבִּי.
וְאַתָּה עָתִיד לִטְּלָהּ מִמֶּנִּי וּלְהַחֲזִירָהּ בִּי לֶעָתִיד לָבֹא:
כָּל זְמַן שֶׁהַנְּשָׁמָה בְקִרְבִּי מוֹדֶה אֲנִי לְפָנֶיךָ יְיָ אֱלֹהַי
וֵאלֹהֵי אֲבוֹתַי (וֵאלֹהֵי אִמּוֹתַי) רִבּוֹן כָּל הַמַּעֲשִׂים
אֲדוֹן כָּל הַנְּשָׁמוֹת: בָּרוּךְ אַתָּה יְיָ הַמַּחֲזִיר נְשָׁמוֹת
לִפְגָרִים מֵתִים:

My God,
The soul You gave me is pure.
You created it
You sculpted it
You breathed it inside of me
You protect it.
At some future time
You will draw it forth from me
And give it back in the World to Come.
But all the time it remains in me
I shall give You thanks
My God
God of those who lived before me,
Author of all works,
Protector of all souls.

You who restore the soul to the body of us all,
You are praised.

Praises for Our Life

בָּרוּךְ אַתָּה יְיָ אֱלֹהֵינוּ מֶלֶךְ הָעוֹלָם אֲשֶׁר נָתַן לַשֶּׂכְוִי
בִינָה לְהַבְחִין בֵּין יוֹם וּבֵין לָיְלָה:

בָּרוּךְ אַתָּה יְיָ אֱלֹהֵינוּ מֶלֶךְ הָעוֹלָם שֶׁעֲשַׂנִי בְּצַלְמוֹ:

בָּרוּךְ אַתָּה יְיָ אֱלֹהֵינוּ מֶלֶךְ הָעוֹלָם שֶׁעֲשַׂנִי בֶּן (בַּת)
חוֹרִין:

בָּרוּךְ אַתָּה יְיָ אֱלֹהֵינוּ מֶלֶךְ הָעוֹלָם שֶׁעֲשַׂנִי יִשְׂרָאֵל:

בָּרוּךְ אַתָּה יְיָ אֱלֹהֵינוּ מֶלֶךְ הָעוֹלָם פּוֹקֵחַ עִוְרִים:

בָּרוּךְ אַתָּה יְיָ אֱלֹהֵינוּ מֶלֶךְ הָעוֹלָם מַלְבִּישׁ עֲרֻמִּים:

בָּרוּךְ אַתָּה יְיָ אֱלֹהֵינוּ מֶלֶךְ הָעוֹלָם מַתִּיר אֲסוּרִים:

בָּרוּךְ אַתָּה יְיָ אֱלֹהֵינוּ מֶלֶךְ הָעוֹלָם זוֹקֵף כְּפוּפִים:

בָּרוּךְ אַתָּה יְיָ אֱלֹהֵינוּ מֶלֶךְ הָעוֹלָם רוֹקַע הָאָרֶץ עַל
הַמָּיִם:

בָּרוּךְ אַתָּה יְיָ אֱלֹהֵינוּ מֶלֶךְ הָעוֹלָם שֶׁעָשָׂה לִי כָּל־
צָרְכִּי:

בָּרוּךְ אַתָּה יְיָ אֱלֹהֵינוּ מֶלֶךְ הָעוֹלָם הַמֵּכִין מִצְעֲדֵי
גָבֶר:

בָּרוּךְ אַתָּה יְיָ אֱלֹהֵינוּ מֶלֶךְ הָעוֹלָם אוֹזֵר יִשְׂרָאֵל
בִּגְבוּרָה:

בָּרוּךְ אַתָּה יְיָ אֱלֹהֵינוּ מֶלֶךְ הָעוֹלָם עוֹטֵר יִשְׂרָאֵל
בְּתִפְאָרָה:

בָּרוּךְ אַתָּה יְיָ אֱלֹהֵינוּ מֶלֶךְ הָעוֹלָם הַנּוֹתֵן לַיָּעֵף כֹּחַ:

Morning stirs us to praise You:
For the ability to distinguish day from night
For shaping us in Your image
For creating us to be free
For giving us the life of Jewish people
For opening our eyes
For clothing our bodies
For helping us break free when we are bound
For helping us rise when we are fallen
For placing us in an ordered universe

For enabling us to meet our needs
For guiding us in proper paths
For giving our people strength to endure
For crowning Israel with glory
For giving courage to those whom the world has tired out
For giving us the hope of a new day.

(To be read on Shabbat)

Today, on Rosh Hashanah, the world was conceived.
Today, on Shabbat, the world was completed.

Today, every day, the world begins again—
We see it new, more fully,
We encounter an old branch of a tree we knew for years
    as though its leaves and bark had never brushed our face
    before.

Today, Shabbat, the world is perfect, not for us to change—
    tradition asks us not to break the branch that bruised our
    walk,
    but let its leaves glisten
    in the same sun that warms us.

Rosh Hashanah reminds us
That everything is to grow, to change, to rise and flower and
    wax as full and fat and gorgeous as it can become;

Shabbat reminds us
That everything that is has value just as it is,
With no change,
Leaf without flower, seed without stalk,
Each of us
With all our imperfections.

Today the world began,
Charged to become everything that lies within the power of
    its creation.
Today the world is complete,
Charged to embrace even the weakness of a life
Brushed by God.

PSUKEY D'ZIMRA (Verses of Song)

Baruch She-amar

בָּרוּךְ שֶׁאָמַר וְהָיָה הָעוֹלָם. בָּרוּךְ הוּא. בָּרוּךְ עוֹשֶׂה
בְרֵאשִׁית. בָּרוּךְ אוֹמֵר וְעוֹשֶׂה. בָּרוּךְ גּוֹזֵר וּמְקַיֵּם.
בָּרוּךְ מְרַחֵם עַל הָאָרֶץ. בָּרוּךְ מְרַחֵם עַל הַבְּרִיּוֹת.
בָּרוּךְ מְשַׁלֵּם שָׂכָר טוֹב לִירֵאָיו. בָּרוּךְ חַי לָעַד וְקַיָּם
לָנֶצַח. בָּרוּךְ פּוֹדֶה וּמַצִּיל. בָּרוּךְ שְׁמוֹ. בָּרוּךְ אַתָּה יְיָ
אֱלֹהֵינוּ מֶלֶךְ הָעוֹלָם. הָאֵל הָאָב הָרַחֲמָן הַמְהֻלָּל בְּפִי
עַמּוֹ מְשֻׁבָּח וּמְפֹאָר בִּלְשׁוֹן חֲסִידָיו וַעֲבָדָיו. וּבְשִׁירֵי
דָוִד עַבְדֶּךָ. נְהַלֶּלְךָ יְיָ אֱלֹהֵינוּ. בִּשְׁבָחוֹת וּבִזְמִירוֹת
נְגַדֶּלְךָ וּנְשַׁבֵּחֲךָ וּנְפָאֶרְךָ וְנַזְכִּיר שִׁמְךָ וְנַמְלִיכְךָ מַלְכֵּנוּ
אֱלֹהֵינוּ יָחִיד חֵי הָעוֹלָמִים. מֶלֶךְ מְשֻׁבָּח וּמְפֹאָר עֲדֵי
עַד שְׁמוֹ הַגָּדוֹל. בָּרוּךְ אַתָּה יְיָ מֶלֶךְ מְהֻלָּל
בַּתִּשְׁבָּחוֹת:

Ba-ruch she-a-mar v'ha-yah ha-o-lam
Ba-ruch hu

Ba-ruch o-mer v'o-seh
Ba-ruch go-zer um-ka-yeim
Ba-ruch m'ra-cheim al ha-a-retz
Ba-ruch m'ra-cheim al ha bri-ot

Ba-ruch o-seh v'rei-sheet
M'sha-leim sa-char tov lirei-av
Chai v'ka-yam la-ne-tzach
Ba-ruch sh'mo

Blessed are You who spoke and the world came into being.
Blessed are You.
Blessed are You who speaks and acts,
Blessed are You who decrees and fulfills.
Blessed are You who is merciful to the land.

Blessed are You who is merciful to all creatures,
Who rewards those who fear You,
Who lives and exists forever.
Blessed is Your Name.

                        *   *   *   *

You are praised
Who spoke
And the universe came into being.

You are praised
Creating the world this very morning
Speaking in the speech we hear
Acting in the acts we see
Ordering nature
Upholding her orders
Embracing the earth and her children
With *rachamim,*
Rewarding with surprises
Those who look upon the world with awe.

You are praised
Alive this moment
Enduring forever
Securing a ransom for each of us in bondage
Bringing rescue for each of us in danger.

You are praised
Adonay our Elohim,
God, Monarch
In every time and place!
Av ha-rachaman,
Motherly father,
Unchanging, trusted source of love.

Hallels fill the mouth of Your people!
Praise and glory flow
From the tongue of Your servants,
Whose deeds of love
Add devotion to the law.

We too would sing hallel!
Help us reach Your realm
Through the songs of David,
Sovereign of Israel who served the Sovereign of the world.
With his words
Let us exalt and praise
The Sovereign of praise,
Source of life eternal.
You are praised,
Monarch, crowned with hallels full of glory!

Psalm 19

לַמְנַצֵּחַ, מִזְמוֹר לְדָוִד. הַשָּׁמַיִם מְסַפְּרִים כְּבוֹד־אֵל,
וּמַעֲשֵׂה יָדָיו מַגִּיד הָרָקִיעַ. יוֹם לְיוֹם יַבִּיעַ אֹמֶר,
וְלַיְלָה לְּלַיְלָה יְחַוֶּה־דָּעַת. אֵין־אֹמֶר וְאֵין דְּבָרִים, בְּלִי
נִשְׁמָע קוֹלָם. בְּכָל־הָאָרֶץ יָצָא קַוָּם, וּבִקְצֵה תֵבֵל
מִלֵּיהֶם; לַשֶּׁמֶשׁ שָׂם־אֹהֶל בָּהֶם. וְהוּא כְּחָתָן יֹצֵא
מֵחֻפָּתוֹ, יָשִׂישׂ כְּגִבּוֹר לָרוּץ אֹרַח. מִקְצֵה הַשָּׁמַיִם
מוֹצָאוֹ, וּתְקוּפָתוֹ עַל־קְצוֹתָם, וְאֵין נִסְתָּר מֵחַמָּתוֹ.
תּוֹרַת יְיָ תְּמִימָה, מְשִׁיבַת נָפֶשׁ; עֵדוּת יְיָ נֶאֱמָנָה,
מַחְכִּימַת פֶּתִי. פִּקּוּדֵי יְיָ יְשָׁרִים, מְשַׂמְּחֵי־לֵב; מִצְוַת יְיָ
בָּרָה, מְאִירַת עֵינָיִם. יִרְאַת יְיָ טְהוֹרָה, עוֹמֶדֶת לָעַד;
מִשְׁפְּטֵי־יְיָ אֱמֶת, צָדְקוּ יַחְדָּו. הַנֶּחֱמָדִים מִזָּהָב וּמִפַּז
רָב, וּמְתוּקִים מִדְּבַשׁ וְנֹפֶת צוּפִים. גַּם־עַבְדְּךָ נִזְהָר
בָּהֶם, בְּשָׁמְרָם עֵקֶב רָב. שְׁגִיאוֹת מִי־יָבִין; מִנִּסְתָּרוֹת
נַקֵּנִי. גַּם מִזֵּדִים חֲשֹׁךְ עַבְדֶּךָ, אַל־יִמְשְׁלוּ־בִי; אָז
אֵיתָם, וְנִקֵּיתִי מִפֶּשַׁע רָב. יִהְיוּ לְרָצוֹן אִמְרֵי־פִי וְהֶגְיוֹן
לִבִּי לְפָנֶיךָ, יְיָ, צוּרִי וְגֹאֲלִי.

(Psalm 19: An Interpretation)

Dawn clouds goldening
First rays of daily Glory
Billow into silent tales of God.

Departing,
Old day's dark
Brushes memory
Into new day's gentle light
In silent
Voiceless
Awe.

Glow widens into brilliance:
The sun bursts from his tent
A bridegroom exultant
From his first night's love
To stride his course from heaven to heaven
And earth to sea,
Dispelling shadows,
Melting darkness.

The world is sunlight,
Restoring the soul
Rejoicing the heart
Bringing light to the eyes
More welcomed than gold.

A Torah from heaven.

I have no light to give the morning.
My Torah,
My special human gift,
Is words.

As I bring my words forth from silence
Welcome them.
You who redeems the sun
From darkness.

Psalm 136

כִּי לְעוֹלָם חַסְדּוֹ:   הוֹדוּ לַייָ כִּי טוֹב
כִּי לְעוֹלָם חַסְדּוֹ:   הוֹדוּ לֵאלֹהֵי הָאֱלֹהִים

Hodu ladonay ki tov, ki l'olam chasdo!
Hodu leylohey ha-elohim, ki l'olam chasdo!

Give thanks to Adonay, for goodness is there,
Give thanks to the God above all gods,
For the eternal love shown to our people!

כִּי לְעוֹלָם חַסְדּוֹ:   הוֹדוּ לַאֲדֹנֵי הָאֲדֹנִים
כִּי לְעוֹלָם חַסְדּוֹ:   לְעֹשֵׂה נִפְלָאוֹת גְּדֹלוֹת לְבַדּוֹ

Hodu ladoney ha-adonim, ki l'olam chasdo!
L'osey nifla-ot g'dolot l'vado, ki l'olam chasdo!

Give thanks to the Power above all powers,
To the One who makes great wonders all alone,
And the eternal love shown to our people!

כִּי לְעוֹלָם חַסְדּוֹ:   לְעֹשֵׂה הַשָּׁמַיִם בִּתְבוּנָה
כִּי לְעוֹלָם חַסְדּוֹ:   לְרֹקַע הָאָרֶץ עַל הַמָּיִם

L'osey hashamay-im bit'vuna, ki l'olam chasdo!
L'roka' ha-aretz al ha-may-im, ki l'olam chasdo!

To the One who makes the heavens through discernment
Spreading out the earth above the waters,
And the eternal love shown to our people!

Psalm 92

מִזְמוֹר שִׁיר לְיוֹם הַשַּׁבָּת. טוֹב לְהֹדוֹת לַייָ, וּלְזַמֵּר
לְשִׁמְךָ עֶלְיוֹן. לְהַגִּיד בַּבֹּקֶר חַסְדֶּךָ, וֶאֱמוּנָתְךָ בַּלֵּילוֹת.
עֲלֵי־עָשׂוֹר וַעֲלֵי־נָבֶל, עֲלֵי הִגָּיוֹן בְּכִנּוֹר. כִּי שִׂמַּחְתַּנִי

יְיָ בְּפָעֳלֶךָ; בְּמַעֲשֵׂי יָדֶיךָ אֲרַנֵּן. מַה־גָּדְלוּ מַעֲשֶׂיךָ יְיָ,
מְאֹד עָמְקוּ מַחְשְׁבֹתֶיךָ. אִישׁ בַּעַר לֹא יֵדָע, וּכְסִיל
לֹא־יָבִין אֶת־זֹאת. בִּפְרֹחַ רְשָׁעִים כְּמוֹ עֵשֶׂב, וַיָּצִיצוּ
כָּל־פֹּעֲלֵי אָוֶן, לְהִשָּׁמְדָם עֲדֵי־עַד. וְאַתָּה מָרוֹם לְעֹלָם,
יְיָ. כִּי הִנֵּה אֹיְבֶיךָ, יְיָ, כִּי־הִנֵּה אֹיְבֶיךָ יֹאבֵדוּ, יִתְפָּרְדוּ
כָּל־פֹּעֲלֵי אָוֶן. וַתָּרֶם כִּרְאֵים קַרְנִי; בַּלֹּתִי בְּשֶׁמֶן רַעֲנָן.
וַתַּבֵּט עֵינִי בְּשׁוּרָי, בַּקָּמִים עָלַי מְרֵעִים תִּשְׁמַעְנָה
אָזְנָי. צַדִּיק כַּתָּמָר יִפְרָח, כְּאֶרֶז בַּלְּבָנוֹן יִשְׂגֶּה.
שְׁתוּלִים בְּבֵית יְיָ, בְּחַצְרוֹת אֱלֹהֵינוּ יַפְרִיחוּ. עוֹד
יְנוּבוּן בְּשֵׂיבָה, דְּשֵׁנִים וְרַעֲנַנִּים יִהְיוּ. לְהַגִּיד כִּי־יָשָׁר
יְיָ; צוּרִי, וְלֹא־עַוְלָתָה בּוֹ.

A Song by the Sabbath Day.

It is good to thank God.
To sing praises to Your name, Highest One.

To tell Your kindness in the morning
And Your good faith at night,
On the lute, the lyre and the ringing harp.

For Your work has made me joyous, Adonay,
I acclaim Your handiwork.

How great are Your works, Adonay,
And how very deep Your thoughts.

An insensitive person does not know this
And a fool does not understand.

But even when wicked people sprout up like weeds
And all kinds of trouble-makers blossom,
Ultimately they will be destroyed forever.

But You rule on high forever, God.
For Your enemies, Adonay,
Your enemies will perish,
And all the trouble-makers will be disunited.

You have raised my head like the wild ox,
Sure of my strength.
I am anointed with fresh oil.

My eyes looked on those who were spying on me.
My ears heard those who were plotting against me.

The just will blossom like the date palm.
They will stand tall like the cedar of Lebanon.
Rooted in Your chosen House,
They will blossom in the courts of our God.

Even in old age they will bear fruit.
Still they will be fresh and growing,
To bear witness that Adonay is fair and dependable
And there is no injustice in God's ways.

Tzadik katamar yifrach
K'erez ba-l'vanon yisgeh
Sh'tulim b'veyt Adonay
B'chatzrot Eloheynu yafrichu
Od y'nuvun b'seyvah
D'sheynim v'ra-ananim yih-yu
L'hagid ki yashar Adonay
Tzuri v'lo avlatah bo.

I Chronicles 16

הוֹדוּ לַיְיָ, קִרְאוּ בִשְׁמוֹ, הוֹדִיעוּ בָעַמִּים עֲלִילֹתָיו.
שִׁירוּ לוֹ, זַמְּרוּ לוֹ, שִׂיחוּ בְּכָל נִפְלְאוֹתָיו. הִתְהַלְלוּ
בְּשֵׁם קָדְשׁוֹ; יִשְׂמַח לֵב מְבַקְשֵׁי יְיָ. דִּרְשׁוּ יְיָ וְעֻזּוֹ,
בַּקְּשׁוּ פָנָיו תָּמִיד. זִכְרוּ נִפְלְאֹתָיו אֲשֶׁר עָשָׂה, מֹפְתָיו
וּמִשְׁפְּטֵי־פִיהוּ. זֶרַע יִשְׂרָאֵל עַבְדּוֹ, בְּנֵי יַעֲקֹב בְּחִירָיו.
הוּא יְיָ אֱלֹהֵינוּ, בְּכָל הָאָרֶץ מִשְׁפָּטָיו. זִכְרוּ לְעוֹלָם
בְּרִיתוֹ, דָּבָר צִוָּה לְאֶלֶף דּוֹר. אֲשֶׁר כָּרַת אֶת אַבְרָהָם,
וּשְׁבוּעָתוֹ לְיִצְחָק. וַיַּעֲמִידֶהָ לְיַעֲקֹב לְחֹק, לְיִשְׂרָאֵל
בְּרִית עוֹלָם. לֵאמֹר, לְךָ אֶתֵּן אֶרֶץ כְּנָעַן, חֶבֶל

נַחֲלַתְכֶם. בִּהְיוֹתְכֶם מְתֵי מִסְפָּר, כִּמְעַט וְגָרִים בָּהּ.
וַיִּתְהַלְּכוּ מִגּוֹי אֶל גּוֹי, וּמִמַּמְלָכָה אֶל עַם אַחֵר. לֹא
הִנִּיחַ לְאִישׁ לְעָשְׁקָם, וַיּוֹכַח עֲלֵיהֶם מְלָכִים. אַל תִּגְּעוּ
בִמְשִׁיחָי, וּבִנְבִיאַי אַל תָּרֵעוּ. שִׁירוּ לַיָי כָּל הָאָרֶץ,
בַּשְּׂרוּ מִיּוֹם אֶל יוֹם יְשׁוּעָתוֹ. סַפְּרוּ בַגּוֹיִם אֶת כְּבוֹדוֹ,
בְּכָל הָעַמִּים נִפְלְאֹתָיו. כִּי גָדוֹל יְיָ וּמְהֻלָּל מְאֹד,
וְנוֹרָא הוּא עַל כָּל אֱלֹהִים. כִּי כָּל אֱלֹהֵי הָעַמִּים
אֱלִילִים, וַיְיָ שָׁמַיִם עָשָׂה. הוֹד וְהָדָר לְפָנָיו, עֹז וְחֶדְוָה
בִּמְקֹמוֹ. הָבוּ לַיָי מִשְׁפְּחוֹת עַמִּים, הָבוּ לַיָי כָּבוֹד וָעֹז.
הָבוּ לַיָי כְּבוֹד שְׁמוֹ, שְׂאוּ מִנְחָה וּבֹאוּ לְפָנָיו, הִשְׁתַּחֲווּ
לַיָי בְּהַדְרַת קֹדֶשׁ. חִילוּ מִלְּפָנָיו כָּל הָאָרֶץ, אַף תִּכּוֹן
תֵּבֵל בַּל תִּמּוֹט. יִשְׂמְחוּ הַשָּׁמַיִם וְתָגֵל הָאָרֶץ, וְיֹאמְרוּ
בַגּוֹיִם יְיָ מָלָךְ. יִרְעַם הַיָּם וּמְלוֹאוֹ, יַעֲלֹץ הַשָּׂדֶה וְכָל
אֲשֶׁר בּוֹ. אָז יְרַנְּנוּ עֲצֵי הַיָּעַר, מִלִּפְנֵי יְיָ, כִּי בָא
לִשְׁפּוֹט אֶת הָאָרֶץ. הוֹדוּ לַיָי כִּי טוֹב, כִּי לְעוֹלָם
חַסְדּוֹ. וְאִמְרוּ, הוֹשִׁיעֵנוּ אֱלֹהֵי יִשְׁעֵנוּ, וְקַבְּצֵנוּ
וְהַצִּילֵנוּ מִן הַגּוֹיִם, לְהֹדוֹת לְשֵׁם קָדְשֶׁךָ, לְהִשְׁתַּבֵּחַ
בִּתְהִלָּתֶךָ. בָּרוּךְ יְיָ אֱלֹהֵי יִשְׂרָאֵל מִן הָעוֹלָם וְעַד
הָעֹלָם; וַיֹּאמְרוּ כָל הָעָם אָמֵן וְהַלֵּל לַיָי.

I Chronicles 16 (An Interpretive Version)

Thank the Lord, call upon His Name,
Spread the word of His great deeds among the peoples!

Sing to God's Shechina, strum the strings before Her,
Spread the tales of all Her wondrous acts!

May we find praise in the holiness of His Name,
May our heart rejoice as we seek the Lord.

Search out God's intimate Presence, trust in Her
  strength,
Seek an audience with Her every day.

Bring to mind the wondrous acts which He has done,
The miracles and the judgments that have streamed from
  His mouth.

The seed of Israel is Her faithful servant,
The children of Jacob are those She has chosen.

Adonay and Shechina, Lord and Presence,
Are separate names for an indivisible God.
In the One God sometimes we encounter Him,
In the One God sometimes we are addressed by Her.

Adonay is our God, transcending gender,
The world is God's court, transcending place.

Remember that the covenant with us is forever,
Commanded through our mothers and fathers for a thousand generations.

It was made first with Abraham and Sarah,
In blessings secured by Rebecca and Isaac,
Through the children of Israel and Leah and Rachel.

When God gave the earth of Canaan to their seed
They were few in number, strangers dwelling on their own
  land.
In their wanderings, God let no one harm them,
Deborah and Samuel, Huldah and Amos carried out the
  protecting will of God.

The holy breath was placed in women's mouths and
  men's,
God and the Shechina were One, and the holy people
  was one.

When Israel was exiled, the Shechina went with them,
When the ten tribes of the North were lost among their
  captors
God mourned Her separation from the Holy One.

Israel remains a scattered people,
With some in her own land, the rest dispersed around
    the world.

God remains a scattered God,
With some divinity in His own land, the rest dispersed
around Her world.

When Israel shall have embraced her unity again,
God and the Shechina will be One as well.

When each child of Israel and Leah does a mitzvah,
When each child of Israel and Rachel finds a mate among
    their people,
The Shechina takes another step out of exile,
God rejoices as Her Presence comes closer.

When anyone in Israel offers words of praise
When the Shma closes our eyes to separations and we
    affirm God's unity
The separations between He and She diminish,
The time approaches when they will address us all as
    One.

Sing, therefore, to Adonay, O earth where our seed is
    scattered!
Let our shouts of praise cause earth to quiver, quickening
    our seed,
That Israel, united, might blossom forth in victory over
    our dispersion
And the heavens and the earth, the fields and all within
    them
The trees in every forest
The seas and all their host,
Will sing before the Lord, for She is come to judge the
    earth,
Will shout to the Shechina, for His loving covenant
    endures forever!

Save us, God victorious over separations,
Gather us together that as women and men together we
   may be delivered,
Praised be the God of Israel in this world and eternity,
And let the people cry, Amen! Hallel to Adonay!

Psalm 146

הַלְלוּיָהּ; הַלְלִי נַפְשִׁי אֶת יְיָ. אֲהַלְלָה יְיָ בְּחַיָּי, אֲזַמְּרָה
לֵאלֹהַי בְּעוֹדִי. אַל תִּבְטְחוּ בִנְדִיבִים, בְּבֶן אָדָם שֶׁאֵין
לוֹ תְשׁוּעָה. תֵּצֵא רוּחוֹ יָשֻׁב לְאַדְמָתוֹ, בַּיּוֹם הַהוּא
אָבְדוּ עֶשְׁתֹּנֹתָיו. אַשְׁרֵי שֶׁאֵל יַעֲקֹב בְּעֶזְרוֹ, שִׂבְרוֹ עַל
יְיָ אֱלֹהָיו. עֹשֶׂה שָׁמַיִם וָאָרֶץ, אֶת הַיָּם, וְאֶת כָּל אֲשֶׁר
בָּם; הַשֹּׁמֵר אֱמֶת לְעוֹלָם. עֹשֶׂה מִשְׁפָּט לַעֲשׁוּקִים, נֹתֵן
לֶחֶם לָרְעֵבִים; יְיָ מַתִּיר אֲסוּרִים. יְיָ פֹּקֵחַ עִוְרִים, יְיָ
זֹקֵף כְּפוּפִים, יְיָ אֹהֵב צַדִּיקִים. יְיָ שֹׁמֵר אֶת גֵּרִים;
יָתוֹם וְאַלְמָנָה יְעוֹדֵד, וְדֶרֶךְ רְשָׁעִים יְעַוֵּת. יִמְלֹךְ יְיָ
לְעוֹלָם, אֱלֹהַיִךְ צִיּוֹן לְדֹר וָדֹר; הַלְלוּיָהּ.

Halleluya!
Sing hallel to Ya!
Praise Adonay, O my being!
Let me sing hallels all of my life,
As long as I am, let me sing to my God!
Put no trust in officials,
No human rulers will help you prevail,
When breath has left them
They return to their dust,
At which very moment their plans are for naught.

Seeking help from Jacob's God brings joy,
Finding hope in Adonay brings happiness.
Adonay is creating heaven and earth,

The sea and life in it,
Protecting truth till the end of time,
Working at justice for people oppressed,
Seeking bread for the hungry,
Untying those who are bound up,
Opening the eyes of those who will not see,
Raising those fallen to the ground,
Showing love for the tzadik, the just one, through deeds.

Adonay is protecting the stranger, the convert,
The orphan, the widow,
But if you are cruel, God is twisting your path.
One power will rule, O Zion, forever,
Your God will prevail through all generations,
Halleluya!

Psalm 148

הַלְלוּיָהּ; הַלְלוּ אֶת יְיָ מִן הַשָּׁמַיִם, הַלְלוּהוּ בַּמְּרוֹמִים.
הַלְלוּהוּ כָל מַלְאָכָיו, הַלְלוּהוּ כָּל צְבָאָיו. הַלְלוּהוּ
שֶׁמֶשׁ וְיָרֵחַ, הַלְלוּהוּ כָּל כּוֹכְבֵי אוֹר. הַלְלוּהוּ שְׁמֵי
הַשָּׁמַיִם, וְהַמַּיִם אֲשֶׁר מֵעַל הַשָּׁמָיִם. יְהַלְלוּ אֶת שֵׁם יְיָ,
כִּי הוּא צִוָּה וְנִבְרָאוּ. וַיַּעֲמִידֵם לָעַד לְעוֹלָם, חָק־נָתַן
וְלֹא יַעֲבוֹר. הַלְלוּ אֶת יְיָ מִן הָאָרֶץ, תַּנִּינִים וְכָל
תְּהֹמוֹת. אֵשׁ וּבָרָד, שֶׁלֶג וְקִיטוֹר, רוּחַ סְעָרָה עֹשָׂה
דְבָרוֹ. הֶהָרִים וְכָל גְּבָעוֹת, עֵץ פְּרִי וְכָל אֲרָזִים. הַחַיָּה
וְכָל בְּהֵמָה, רֶמֶשׂ וְצִפּוֹר כָּנָף, מַלְכֵי אֶרֶץ וְכָל לְאֻמִּים,
שָׂרִים וְכָל שֹׁפְטֵי אָרֶץ. בַּחוּרִים וְגַם בְּתוּלוֹת, זְקֵנִים
עִם נְעָרִים. יְהַלְלוּ אֶת שֵׁם יְיָ, כִּי נִשְׂגָּב שְׁמוֹ לְבַדּוֹ;
הוֹדוֹ עַל אֶרֶץ וְשָׁמָיִם. וַיָּרֶם קֶרֶן לְעַמּוֹ, תְּהִלָּה לְכָל
חֲסִידָיו, לִבְנֵי יִשְׂרָאֵל עַם קְרֹבוֹ; הַלְלוּיָהּ.

Halleluya!
Sing hallel to Adonay from heaven,
Sing hallel in the heights,
Sing hallel where the angels are,
Sing hallel all the hosts,
Sing hallel sun and moon
And all you glittering stars!
Sing hallel highest heavens,
Sing hallel sea,
And all beneath the sky,
Sing hallel to the source of love,
For at its command, all things became.
Adonay raised them up forever in their place,
And gave them a law they cannot disobey.

So sing hallel from out of the earth,
Great creatures of the sea and all the depths,
Fire and hail, snow and cloud,
Wild winds of the storm—all obeying God's word!
Mountains and hills, fruit trees and cedars,
Rampaging beasts and pasturing cows,
Creatures that crawl and birds soaring free,
Monarchs on earth, nations and rulers, all human judges,
Young men and women, old men and youths,
Sing hallel, shout praise:
Adonay!
Power to which none other can reach,
Splendor surpassing earth and sky,
Noble stature You brought to Your people,
Praise to Your followers,
Closeness to Israel,
Your kin here on earth.
To Ya sing hallel!
Halleluya!

Psalm 150

הַלְלוּיָהּ; הַלְלוּ אֵל בְּקָדְשׁוֹ, הַלְלוּהוּ בִּרְקִיעַ עֻזּוֹ.
הַלְלוּהוּ בִגְבוּרֹתָיו, הַלְלוּהוּ כְּרֹב גֻּדְלוֹ. הַלְלוּהוּ

בְּתֵקַע שׁוֹפָר, הַלְלוּהוּ בְּנֵבֶל וְכִנּוֹר. הַלְלוּהוּ בְתֹף
וּמָחוֹל, הַלְלוּהוּ בְּמִנִּים וְעֻגָב. הַלְלוּהוּ בְצִלְצְלֵי שָׁמַע,
הַלְלוּהוּ בְּצִלְצְלֵי תְרוּעָה. כֹּל הַנְּשָׁמָה תְּהַלֵּל יָהּ;
הַלְלוּיָהּ. כֹּל הַנְּשָׁמָה תְּהַלֵּל יָהּ; הַלְלוּיָהּ.

Halleluya!
Sing hallel to God in holy array,
Sing hallel to You in Your heavenly fort,
Sing hallel to You for the proofs of Your power,
Sing hallel to You for Your far-reaching might,
Sing hallel to You with a blast on the shofar,
Sing hallel to You with a plucking of lutes,
Sing hallel to You with a drum and a dance,
*Sing hallel to You with a strumming of strings,
Sing hallel to You with a crashing of cymbals,
All things alive, sing hallel to Ya! Halleluya!
All things alive, sing hallel to Ya! Halleluya!

*Halleluhu, Halleluhu
B'tziltz'ley Shama
Halleluhu, Halleluhu
B'tziltz'ley T'ruah
Kol han'shama t'hallel Ya
Halleluya, Halleluya!

Halleluya (5x)
Hallelu El b'kodsho
Halleluhu (2x) birki'a uzo
Halleluhu (6x) bigvurotav
Halleluhu (2x) k'rov gudlo
Halleluhu (6x) b'teka shofar
Halleluhu (2x) b'nevel v'chinor
Halleluhu (6x) b'tof umachol
Halleluhu (2x) b'minim v'ugav
Halleluhu (6x) b'tzilitz'ley shama
Halleluhu (2x) b'tzilitz'ley truah
Kol han'shama (2x) t'hallel Ya (2x)
Kol han'shama t'hallel Ya, Halleluya (2x)

Nishmat

נִשְׁמַת כָּל חַי תְּבָרֵךְ אֶת שִׁמְךָ, יְיָ אֱלֹהֵינוּ, וְרוּחַ כָּל
בָּשָׂר תְּפָאֵר וּתְרוֹמֵם זִכְרְךָ, מַלְכֵּנוּ, תָּמִיד. מִן הָעוֹלָם
וְעַד הָעוֹלָם אַתָּה אֵל, וּמִבַּלְעָדֶיךָ אֵין לָנוּ מֶלֶךְ גּוֹאֵל
וּמוֹשִׁיעַ, פּוֹדֶה וּמַצִּיל וּמְפַרְנֵס, וּמְרַחֵם בְּכָל עֵת צָרָה
וְצוּקָה; אֵין לָנוּ מֶלֶךְ אֶלָּא אָתָּה. אֱלֹהֵי הָרִאשׁוֹנִים
וְהָאַחֲרוֹנִים, אֱלוֹהַּ כָּל בְּרִיּוֹת, אֲדוֹן כָּל תּוֹלָדוֹת,
הַמְהֻלָּל בְּרֹב הַתִּשְׁבָּחוֹת, הַמְנַהֵג עוֹלָמוֹ בְּחֶסֶד
וּבְרִיּוֹתָיו בְּרַחֲמִים. וַיְיָ לֹא יָנוּם וְלֹא יִישָׁן, הַמְעוֹרֵר
יְשֵׁנִים, וְהַמֵּקִיץ נִרְדָּמִים, וְהַמֵּשִׂיחַ אִלְּמִים, וְהַמַּתִּיר
אֲסוּרִים, וְהַסּוֹמֵךְ נוֹפְלִים, וְהַזּוֹקֵף כְּפוּפִים. לְךָ לְבַדְּךָ
אֲנַחְנוּ מוֹדִים. אִלּוּ פִינוּ מָלֵא שִׁירָה כַּיָּם, וּלְשׁוֹנֵנוּ
רִנָּה כַּהֲמוֹן גַּלָּיו, וְשִׂפְתוֹתֵינוּ שֶׁבַח כְּמֶרְחֲבֵי רָקִיעַ,
וְעֵינֵינוּ מְאִירוֹת כַּשֶּׁמֶשׁ וְכַיָּרֵחַ, וְיָדֵינוּ פְרוּשׂוֹת
כְּנִשְׁרֵי שָׁמָיִם, וְרַגְלֵינוּ קַלּוֹת כָּאַיָּלוֹת, אֵין אֲנַחְנוּ
מַסְפִּיקִים לְהוֹדוֹת לְךָ, יְיָ אֱלֹהֵינוּ וֵאלֹהֵי אֲבוֹתֵינוּ
(וְאִמּוֹתֵינוּ), וּלְבָרֵךְ אֶת שִׁמְךָ עַל אַחַת מֵאָלֶף,
אֶלֶף אַלְפֵי אֲלָפִים וְרִבֵּי רְבָבוֹת פְּעָמִים הַטּוֹבוֹת
שֶׁעָשִׂיתָ עִם אֲבוֹתֵינוּ (וְאִמּוֹתֵינוּ) וְעִמָּנוּ. מִמִּצְרַיִם
גְּאַלְתָּנוּ, יְיָ אֱלֹהֵינוּ, וּמִבֵּית עֲבָדִים פְּדִיתָנוּ; בְּרָעָב
זַנְתָּנוּ. וּבְשָׂבָע כִּלְכַּלְתָּנוּ; מֵחֶרֶב הִצַּלְתָּנוּ. וּמִדֶּבֶר
מִלַּטְתָּנוּ, וּמֵחֳלָיִם רָעִים וְנֶאֱמָנִים דִּלִּיתָנוּ. עַד הֵנָּה
עֲזָרוּנוּ רַחֲמֶיךָ. וְלֹא עֲזָבוּנוּ חֲסָדֶיךָ; וְאַל תִּטְּשֵׁנוּ יְיָ
אֱלֹהֵינוּ, לָנֶצַח. עַל כֵּן, אֵבָרִים שֶׁפִּלַּגְתָּ בָּנוּ, וְרוּחַ
וּנְשָׁמָה שֶׁנָּפַחְתָּ בְּאַפֵּינוּ, וְלָשׁוֹן אֲשֶׁר שַׂמְתָּ
בְּפִינוּ, הֵן הֵם יוֹדוּ וִיבָרְכוּ, וִישַׁבְּחוּ וִיפָאֲרוּ, וִירוֹמְמוּ
וְיַעֲרִיצוּ, וְיַקְדִּישׁוּ וְיַמְלִיכוּ אֶת שִׁמְךָ, מַלְכֵּנוּ. כִּי כָל

פֶּה לְךָ יוֹדֶה, וְכָל לָשׁוֹן לְךָ תִשָּׁבַע, וְכָל בֶּרֶךְ לְךָ
תִכְרַע, וְכָל קוֹמָה לְפָנֶיךָ תִשְׁתַּחֲוֶה, וְכָל לְבָבוֹת
יִירָאוּךָ, וְכָל קֶרֶב וּכְלָיוֹת יְזַמְּרוּ לִשְׁמֶךָ, כַּדָּבָר
שֶׁכָּתוּב: כָּל עַצְמוֹתַי תֹּאמַרְנָה, יְיָ מִי כָמוֹךָ, מַצִּיל עָנִי
מֵחָזָק מִמֶּנּוּ, וְעָנִי וְאֶבְיוֹן מִגֹּזְלוֹ. מִי יִדְמֶה לָּךְ, וּמִי
יִשְׁוֶה לָּךְ, וּמִי יַעֲרָךְ־לָךְ, הָאֵל הַגָּדוֹל, הַגִּבּוֹר וְהַנּוֹרָא,
אֵל עֶלְיוֹן, קֹנֵה שָׁמַיִם וָאָרֶץ. נְהַלֶּלְךָ וּנְשַׁבֵּחֲךָ
וּנְפָאֶרְךָ, וּנְבָרֵךְ אֶת שֵׁם קָדְשֶׁךָ, כָּאָמוּר: לְדָוִד, בָּרְכִי
נַפְשִׁי אֶת יְיָ, וְכָל קְרָבַי אֶת שֵׁם קָדְשׁוֹ.

Let the soul of everything alive
Sing praises to Your name!
Let the breath of every creature glorify and praise
The signs of divinity in time,
The traces of holy rule in every place!
In the face of the evils of these years,
The pain and suffering of human life,
Let us feel the touch of forces
    freeing us from bondage,
    winning victories over enemies
    within us and without.

Adonay does not sleep.
Those who lead sleepy lives
God stirs awake,
Those who live without words
God stirs to speak.

If our mouths filled with song like the sea,
If our tongue could roar like the surf,
If our lips billowed praise like a bright day's sky—
Our eyes the sun, or by night the moon—
If our arms could spread like the pinions of eagles
And our legs make us fly over fields like gazelles—
Still would our lips lack words

And our bodies the space
To acknowledge the brilliance even of a handful of world
Pervaded by Adonay,
Or speak a blessing even for the tiniest goodness You have
    done,
God for our fathers, our mothers, and for us.

Yet these shall sing what praise they can:
The limbs with which You have constructed us shall be our
    strings,
The tongue You have placed in us shall be the bow,
The soul You have breathed in us shall resonate the
    melody.
Soon with my mouth
Every mouth shall give thanks,
Every tongue shall swear its truth,
Every knee shall bow down,
Every backbone fall prostrate,
Every heart shall fill with awe,
Every inner organ sing its praise,
And the psalm verse shall come true:
"All my bones shall say, 'Incomparable is Adonay!'"

David first plucked out the chords:
"O my soul, sing praises to Adonay;
To the one
Whose Name is holy
Shout with all my inmost being!"

Alternative Nishmat

Song-filled sea
Rejoicing waves
Sky shouting blue
Yellowbright sun
Exultant eagles
Deer flashing in the green
We can be them all.

The song is ours:
Rejoicing
Shouting
Yellowbright
Exultant
Flashing in the green
In praise of miracles.

Who can't believe in miracles
This morning?

Who can't find one leaf
Deserving infinite praise?

Praise God, my soul!
O inmost depths of me,
Praise Your holy space!

Hamelech

הַמֶּלֶךְ

יוֹשֵׁב עַל כִּסֵּא רָם וְנִשָּׂא׃

שׁוֹכֵן עַד מָרוֹם וְקָדוֹשׁ שְׁמוֹ. וְכָתוּב. רַנְּנוּ צַדִּיקִים בַּיָי
לַיְשָׁרִים נָאוָה תְהִלָּה׃ בְּפִי יְשָׁרִים תִּתְרוֹמָם. וּבְדִבְרֵי
צַדִּיקִים תִּתְבָּרַךְ. וּבִלְשׁוֹן חֲסִידִים תִּתְקַדָּשׁ. וּבְקֶרֶב
קְדוֹשִׁים תִּתְהַלָּל׃

Praised be the Sovereign, who sits upon the high and lofty
Throne!
The Shechina is our intimate forever, yet with a Name
exalted and holy.
Sing to Adonay, those who do justly, for praise becomes
the upright.
From the mouth of the upright comes God's praise,
Blessing is in the words of doers of justice,

Exaltation springs from the tongue of those who do more
than is required.
From the innermost parts of holy people does God's holiness shine forth.

יִשְׁתַּבַּח שִׁמְךָ לָעַד מַלְכֵּנוּ. הָאֵל הַמֶּלֶךְ הַגָּדוֹל
וְהַקָּדוֹשׁ בַּשָּׁמַיִם וּבָאָרֶץ. כִּי לְךָ נָאֶה יְיָ אֱלֹהֵינוּ
וֵאלֹהֵי אֲבוֹתֵינוּ (וֵאלֹהֵי אִמּוֹתֵינוּ) שִׁיר וּשְׁבָחָה הַלֵּל
וְזִמְרָה עֹז וּמֶמְשָׁלָה נֶצַח גְּדֻלָּה וּגְבוּרָה תְּהִלָּה
וְתִפְאֶרֶת קְדֻשָּׁה וּמַלְכוּת. בְּרָכוֹת וְהוֹדָאוֹת מֵעַתָּה
וְעַד עוֹלָם. בָּרוּךְ אַתָּה יְיָ אֵל מֶלֶךְ גָּדוֹל בַּתִּשְׁבָּחוֹת.
אֵל הַהוֹדָאוֹת אֲדוֹן הַנִּפְלָאוֹת. הַבּוֹחֵר בְּשִׁירֵי זִמְרָה.
מֶלֶךְ אֵל חֵי הָעוֹלָמִים:

You are praised, Adonay
Source of power in the universe
Sovereign extolled in thanks and praises,
God of awesome wonders
Guarantor of life eternal,
Who has chosen the verses of these our songs.

Reader's Kaddish

יִתְגַּדַּל וְיִתְקַדַּשׁ שְׁמֵהּ רַבָּא בְּעָלְמָא דִּי בְרָא כִרְעוּתֵהּ,
וְיַמְלִיךְ מַלְכוּתֵהּ בְּחַיֵּיכוֹן וּבְיוֹמֵיכוֹן וּבְחַיֵּי דְכָל בֵּית
יִשְׂרָאֵל, בַּעֲגָלָא וּבִזְמַן קָרִיב, וְאִמְרוּ אָמֵן:

יְהֵא שְׁמֵהּ רַבָּא מְבָרַךְ לְעָלַם וּלְעָלְמֵי עָלְמַיָּא.

יִתְבָּרַךְ וְיִשְׁתַּבַּח, וְיִתְפָּאַר וְיִתְרוֹמַם, וְיִתְנַשֵּׂא
וְיִתְהַדָּר, וְיִתְעַלֶּה וְיִתְהַלַּל שְׁמֵהּ דְּקֻדְשָׁא, בְּרִיךְ הוּא,
לְעֵלָּא לְעֵלָּא מִן כָּל בִּרְכָתָא וְשִׁירָתָא, תֻּשְׁבְּחָתָא
וְנֶחֱמָתָא, דַּאֲמִירָן בְּעָלְמָא, וְאִמְרוּ אָמֵן.

May God's great Name be magnified and sanctified in the world created according to the holy will, and may God's rule be known in your lifetime, in your own days, and in the life of the house of Israel, speedily, in a time close at hand.

May the Name of the Blessed Holy One be praised and extolled far beyond all praises and blessings we can ever say in the world. Amen.

In Praise of Praise

It will soon be time to praise God.

— Praise? For what, when the world is cruel!
— Praise? For what, when so many are suffering!
— The good in the world is done by good people—why should we praise God for good?
— It's hard to praise anyone; it makes us seem less.
— It seems like currying favor; how can we only praise virtues and not also criticize faults?

God is not anyone—God is our lover; and to praise our lover makes us seem more, for we praise the one who has chosen us to love.

God is our lover—and to praise our lover is to offer a gift, choosing words that will please, because we wish to add joy to one who has given so much joy to us. There will be prayers in which we can cry out for change—but now is the time to praise.

God is our lover—if we have not known that love, by offering praise we reach out to that which longs to reach to us. In saying "Baruch!", we take the first step, we ease the way for the Majesty of the universe to embrace us, and in the pause between our words we can listen for our love.

THE SHMA AND ITS BLESSINGS

בָּרְכוּ אֶת יְיָ הַמְבֹרָךְ:

Barchu et Adonay hamvorach:

Bend the knee in praise to God
Before whom all shall bow!

בָּרוּךְ יְיָ הַמְבֹרָךְ לְעוֹלָם וָעֶד:

Baruch Adonay hamvorach l'olam va-ed:

The knee is bent.
Praised be God before whom all shall bow
Throughout all time and space!

Yotzer (In Praise of the Creator)

בָּרוּךְ אַתָּה יְיָ אֱלֹהֵינוּ מֶלֶךְ הָעוֹלָם. יוֹצֵר אוֹר וּבוֹרֵא
חֹשֶׁךְ. עֹשֶׂה שָׁלוֹם וּבוֹרֵא אֶת הַכֹּל:
הַמֵּאִיר לָאָרֶץ וְלַדָּרִים עָלֶיהָ בְּרַחֲמִים. וּבְטוּבוֹ מְחַדֵּשׁ
בְּכָל יוֹם תָּמִיד מַעֲשֵׂה־בְרֵאשִׁית: מָה רַבּוּ מַעֲשֶׂיךָ יְיָ.
כֻּלָּם בְּחָכְמָה עָשִׂיתָ. מָלְאָה הָאָרֶץ קִנְיָנֶךָ: תִּתְבָּרַךְ יְיָ
אֱלֹהֵינוּ עַל־שֶׁבַח מַעֲשֵׂה יָדֶיךָ. וְעַל־מְאוֹרֵי־אוֹר
שֶׁעָשִׂיתָ יְפָאֲרוּךָ סֶּלָה: בָּרוּךְ אַתָּה יְיָ יוֹצֵר הַמְּאוֹרוֹת:

You create light and darkness,
The possibility of peace within a warring world,
All forms and creatures,
Who acknowledge their only common bond
In You.

You open daily the gates of the east,
Cleave the windows of the sky,

Bring forth the sun from its place,
The moon from its abode.

The sky, the sun, the moon, are far from us.
Yet their Creator created us,
And so their world is ours,
Their light is ours,
Though we must often gather up their light
From the dark places where it has fallen.

Bring forth their light,
That ours may shine anew.
You who have created light
Are praised.

Alternative Yotzer

You are praised
Who rolls out the rough, raw clay of the universe
Into delicate vessels of light
And from nothing at all
Creates the darkness which lets them shine.

You fashion harmony from all that You have made
And from nothing at all
Create the chaos that lets harmony be heard.

Your vessels pour light upon the universe
Flooding the cracks in our darkness
With the beams of Your compassion.
If we could walk upon that lighted path
We could perceive in a world that has turned old
A shimmering new Creation right before our eyes
Made just this moment
Just for us.

How much of life reveals Your presence!
How much Torah unfolds from each new flower,
From each new wave that breaks upon our sands!

You are praised
Who forms,
From the clay that cloaks our lives,
The delicate vessels which are our light.

Ahava Raba (In Praise of the Torah Giver)

אַהֲבָה רַבָּה אֲהַבְתָּנוּ יְיָ אֱלֹהֵינוּ חֶמְלָה גְדוֹלָה וִיתֵרָה
חָמַלְתָּ עָלֵינוּ: אָבִינוּ מַלְכֵּנוּ בַּעֲבוּר אֲבוֹתֵינוּ
(וְאִמּוֹתֵינוּ) שֶׁבָּטְחוּ בְךָ וַתְּלַמְּדֵם חֻקֵּי חַיִּים כֵּן תְּחָנֵּנוּ
וּתְלַמְּדֵנוּ: אָבִינוּ הָאָב הָרַחֲמָן הַמְרַחֵם. רַחֵם עָלֵינוּ
וְתֵן בְּלִבֵּנוּ לְהָבִין וּלְהַשְׂכִּיל לִשְׁמֹעַ לִלְמֹד וּלְלַמֵּד
לִשְׁמֹר וְלַעֲשׂוֹת וּלְקַיֵּם אֶת כָּל דִּבְרֵי תַלְמוּד תּוֹרָתֶךָ
בְּאַהֲבָה: וְהָאֵר עֵינֵינוּ בְּתוֹרָתֶךָ וְדַבֵּק לִבֵּנוּ בְּמִצְוֹתֶיךָ
וְיַחֵד לְבָבֵנוּ לְאַהֲבָה וּלְיִרְאָה אֶת שְׁמֶךָ וְלֹא נֵבוֹשׁ
לְעוֹלָם וָעֶד: כִּי בְשֵׁם קָדְשְׁךָ הַגָּדוֹל וְהַנּוֹרָא בָּטָחְנוּ
נָגִילָה וְנִשְׂמְחָה בִּישׁוּעָתֶךָ: וַהֲבִיאֵנוּ לְשָׁלוֹם מֵאַרְבַּע
כַּנְפוֹת הָאָרֶץ וְתוֹלִיכֵנוּ קוֹמְמִיּוּת לְאַרְצֵנוּ: כִּי אֵל
פּוֹעֵל יְשׁוּעוֹת אַתָּה וּבָנוּ בָחַרְתָּ מִכָּל־עַם וְלָשׁוֹן
וְקֵרַבְתָּנוּ לְשִׁמְךָ הַגָּדוֹל סֶלָה בֶּאֱמֶת לְהוֹדוֹת לְךָ
וּלְיַחֶדְךָ בְּאַהֲבָה: בָּרוּךְ אַתָּה יְיָ הַבּוֹחֵר בְּעַמּוֹ יִשְׂרָאֵל
בְּאַהֲבָה:

With acts of great love
You embrace us, Adonay our God.
With great acts of mercy
You encompass us.
You, Monarch, are our Sovereign, our father and our
    mother;
For the sake of our fathers and mothers who are no more,
Who trusted You,
Whom You taught laws for life—

Accept us,
Be our teacher too.

Our mother,
Our fathermother filled with compassion,
Sustain us with compassion
And permit our knowing hearts
To discern that we may understand,
Then listen that we may learn and teach,
Then observe that we may do and sustain
All the words of Your Torah we shall study
In love.

Give light for our eyes through Your Torah,
Bring close our knowing hearts to Your mitzvot,
And make the many truths our heart knows
One,
Through love and awe of Your Name,
And we shall never be confounded
In time and the world.
For in Your great and awesome Name,
Filled with kedusha,
We have trusted too,
And rejoiced and exulted
In the victories You have brought us.

Bring us then within shalom
From the four corners of the earth
And escort us, heads upright, to that part of earth
You call ours.
For You are God
Bringing victory,
Choosing a different task for us
From that which You have chosen for each other people
And every other tongue:
You have brought us close to Your great Name
Through truth,
That we may speak thankfully to You,
Proving Your Oneness
Through our love.

You are praised, Adonay,
Choosing Israel Your people
Through Your love.

*V'ha-eyr eyneynu b'Torah-techa v'dabeyk libeynu b'mitzvo-
techa*
V'yached l'vaveynu l'ahavah ul'yirah et sh'mecha.
V'lo ney-vosh v'lo nikaleym v'lo nikashel l'olam va-ed.

Give light for our eyes through Your Torah . . .

Alternative Ahava Raba

You were God
And we were Israel,
God alone
And lonely people,
Long ago.

You loved us a great love
And You taught us
How to respond to You

Through Mitzvot
Recollections
Celebrations
Torah

They are the light of our eyes
The uniqueness of our being.

In the joy of them
You have drawn us close to You.

In the truth of them
We have discovered You, the only One.

We are together still.

You respond to every people
In Your chosen way.
With Your love
You have chosen to respond to us.

With our love
We offer You our praise.

Preparation for the Shma

Let eyelids close, let disharmony disappear. . . .

Shma: Listen, hearken, let the words' familiar sounds dapple the darkness. . . .

Yisrael: Israel is each of us, Jacob wrestling with God, our people wrestling with our doubts and our destiny. . . .

Adonay: Your Name, Your innermost Name, the Name You love best, the compassionate Name we heard Moses call You face to face, the Name that means: I am. . . .

Eloheynu: O God whose rule is just, God who promised Israel eternity like the stars, God with us, *Gottenyu, oy, Gottenyu*. . . .

Adonay: Wherever we are is You; wherever the world is, is You. . . .

Echad: You alone, You are life. Disharmony and harmony, shaded light and dappled dark, wicked acts, compassionate people, justice and cruelty, all find their hidden purpose in Your innermost Name. Let disharmony (*soon , and in our own day!*) disappear.

The Shma: First Paragraph (Shma and V'ahavta)

שְׁמַע יִשְׂרָאֵל יְהֹוָה אֱלֹהֵינוּ יְהֹוָה אֶחָד:

Shma Yisrael Adonay Eloheynu Adonay Echad:

Listen, Israel! Adonay is God for us, Adonay alone is One.

בָּרוּךְ שֵׁם כְּבוֹד מַלְכוּתוֹ לְעוֹלָם וָעֶד:

Baruch sheym kvod malchuto l'olam vaed:

That Name is praised whose glorious Rule will outlast the world and time.

וְאָהַבְתָּ אֵת יְהוָֹה אֱלֹהֶיךָ בְּכָל־לְבָבְךָ וּבְכָל־נַפְשְׁךָ
וּבְכָל־מְאֹדֶךָ: וְהָיוּ הַדְּבָרִים הָאֵלֶּה אֲשֶׁר אָנֹכִי מְצַוְּךָ
הַיּוֹם עַל־לְבָבֶךָ: וְשִׁנַּנְתָּם לְבָנֶיךָ וְדִבַּרְתָּ בָּם בְּשִׁבְתְּךָ
בְּבֵיתֶךָ וּבְלֶכְתְּךָ בַדֶּרֶךְ וּבְשָׁכְבְּךָ וּבְקוּמֶךָ: וּקְשַׁרְתָּם
לְאוֹת עַל־יָדֶךָ וְהָיוּ לְטֹטָפֹת בֵּין עֵינֶיךָ: וּכְתַבְתָּם עַל־
מְזֻזוֹת בֵּיתֶךָ וּבִשְׁעָרֶיךָ:

V-a-hav-ta et A-do-nay E-lo-he-cha
b-chol l'-va-v'cha uv-chol nafsh'cha
uv-chol m'o-de-cha.
V'-ha-yu ha-d'-va-rim ha-e-leh
a-sher a-no-chi m'-tza-v'-cha
ha-yom al l'-va-ve-cha.

V'-shi-nan-tam l'-va-ne-cha
v'-di-bar-ta bam b'-shiv-t'cha
b'-vey-te-cha, uv-lech-t'cha
va-de-rech, uv-shoch-b'cha uvkumecha.
Uk-shar-tam l'-ot al ya-de-cha,
v'-ha-yu l'-to-ta-fot beyn ey-ne-cha.
uch-tav-tam al m'zu-zot bey-te-cha
Uvish'a-re-cha.

Thus you shall show your love for Adonay your God:
With every inclination of your knowing heart,
With all the strength through which you live,
With every benefit you have received.
For these words in which I am giving you mitzvot today
Shall enter into your knowing heart,
That you may help your children sink their teeth in them,
And speak through them
While sitting in your house,
While walking on the road,
At the time for lying down,

At the time for rising up.
You shall bind them in a sign upon your arm.
They shall become frontlets between your eyes
You shall inscribe them in mezuzot for your house,
Upon your gates.   .

The Shma: Second Paragraph (V'haya im Shamoa)

וְהָיָה אִם־שָׁמֹעַ תִּשְׁמְעוּ אֶל־מִצְוֹתַי אֲשֶׁר אָנֹכִי מְצַוֶּה
אֶתְכֶם הַיּוֹם לְאַהֲבָה אֶת־יְהוָֹה אֱלֹהֵיכֶם וּלְעָבְדוֹ
בְּכָל־לְבַבְכֶם וּבְכָל־נַפְשְׁכֶם: וְנָתַתִּי מְטַר־אַרְצְכֶם
בְּעִתּוֹ יוֹרֶה וּמַלְקוֹשׁ וְאָסַפְתָּ דְגָנֶךָ וְתִירֹשְׁךָ וְיִצְהָרֶךָ:
וְנָתַתִּי עֵשֶׂב בְּשָׂדְךָ לִבְהֶמְתֶּךָ וְאָכַלְתָּ וְשָׂבָעְתָּ: הִשָּׁמְרוּ
לָכֶם פֶּן־יִפְתֶּה לְבַבְכֶם וְסַרְתֶּם וַעֲבַדְתֶּם אֱלֹהִים
אֲחֵרִים וְהִשְׁתַּחֲוִיתֶם לָהֶם: וְחָרָה אַף־יְהוָֹה בָּכֶם
וְעָצַר אֶת־הַשָּׁמַיִם וְלֹא־יִהְיֶה מָטָר וְהָאֲדָמָה לֹא תִתֵּן
אֶת־יְבוּלָהּ וַאֲבַדְתֶּם מְהֵרָה מֵעַל הָאָרֶץ הַטֹּבָה אֲשֶׁר
יְהוָֹה נֹתֵן לָכֶם: וְשַׂמְתֶּם אֶת־דְּבָרַי אֵלֶּה עַל־לְבַבְכֶם
וְעַל־נַפְשְׁכֶם וּקְשַׁרְתֶּם אֹתָם לְאוֹת עַל־יֶדְכֶם וְהָיוּ
לְטוֹטָפֹת בֵּין עֵינֵיכֶם: וְלִמַּדְתֶּם אֹתָם אֶת־בְּנֵיכֶם
לְדַבֵּר בָּם בְּשִׁבְתְּךָ בְּבֵיתֶךָ וּבְלֶכְתְּךָ בַדֶּרֶךְ וּבְשָׁכְבְּךָ
וּבְקוּמֶךָ: וּכְתַבְתָּם עַל־מְזוּזוֹת בֵּיתֶךָ וּבִשְׁעָרֶיךָ: לְמַעַן
יִרְבּוּ יְמֵיכֶם וִימֵי בְנֵיכֶם עַל הָאֲדָמָה אֲשֶׁר נִשְׁבַּע יְהוָֹה
לַאֲבֹתֵיכֶם לָתֵת לָהֶם כִּימֵי הַשָּׁמַיִם עַל־הָאָרֶץ:

And if you listen intently to My mitzvot,
Which I am making your mitzvot this very day,
Showing your love for Adonay your God
And giving service
With every inclination of your knowing heart
And all the strength with which you live—

Then I shall give your land rain in its proper time,
Autumn rain and spring rain,
That you may harvest your grain,
Your wine and your oil.
I shall give grass to the field for your cows
That you may eat your fill.

But beware!
If you turn your knowing heart away
To serve gods that are alien,
Bowing down to different kinds of powers,
Then the breath of Adonay will flare against you
To shut up the heavens so there will be no rain,
So the ground will not give her produce,
And you will perish at once from the good earth
Which Adonay is giving you.
Therefore
Place these words upon your knowing heart
Teach them to your children throughout the day
Bind them to your heart and to your doorpost.
That your days upon the land that is God's gift
Will be as many as the days of heaven
Above the earth.

The Shma: Third Paragraph (Vayomer)

וַיֹּאמֶר יְהֹוָה אֶל־מֹשֶׁה לֵּאמֹר: דַּבֵּר אֶל־בְּנֵי יִשְׂרָאֵל
וְאָמַרְתָּ אֲלֵהֶם וְעָשׂוּ לָהֶם צִיצִת עַל־כַּנְפֵי בִגְדֵיהֶם
לְדֹרֹתָם וְנָתְנוּ עַל־צִיצִת הַכָּנָף פְּתִיל תְּכֵלֶת: וְהָיָה
לָכֶם לְצִיצִת וּרְאִיתֶם אֹתוֹ וּזְכַרְתֶּם אֶת־כָּל־מִצְוֹת
יְהֹוָה וַעֲשִׂיתֶם אֹתָם וְלֹא תָתוּרוּ אַחֲרֵי לְבַבְכֶם וְאַחֲרֵי
עֵינֵיכֶם אֲשֶׁר־אַתֶּם זֹנִים אַחֲרֵיהֶם: לְמַעַן תִּזְכְּרוּ
וַעֲשִׂיתֶם אֶת־כָּל־מִצְוֹתָי וִהְיִיתֶם קְדֹשִׁים לֵאלֹהֵיכֶם:
אֲנִי יְהֹוָה אֱלֹהֵיכֶם אֲשֶׁר הוֹצֵאתִי אֶתְכֶם מֵאֶרֶץ
מִצְרַיִם לִהְיוֹת לָכֶם לֵאלֹהִים אֲנִי יְהֹוָה אֱלֹהֵיכֶם:

God spoke to Moses saying: Speak to the people of Israel
and tell them to make fringes on the corners of their garments throughout their generations and to put a cord of
blue on the fringe of each corner. The fringe will be a
symbol of your commitment: When you see it, you will be
reminded of all God's commandments and you will fulfill
them, and you will not simply follow your own impulses
and desires which might lead you to be false to Me. In this
way you will remember and do all My commandments and
you will be wholly dedicated for your God. I am Adonay
your God who brought you out of the land of Egypt in
order to be your God. I am Adonay your God.

Alternative Vayomer

God spoke to Moses saying: Speak to the people of Israel
and tell them to make fringes on their garments throughout their generations and to put a cord of blue on the fringe
of each corner.

> Once we hid ourselves beneath the pallid sameness of
> everyone about us; now we need no longer turn aside
> from the mezuzah 'round the neck, the kipah on the
> head, which proclaim to others what we are, that
> what we are is lovely, that we wish our outside and
> our inside to be one.

The fringe will be a symbol of your commitment: when you
see it, you will be reminded of all God's commandments
and you will fulfill them, and you will not simply follow
your own impulses and desires which might lead you to be
false to Me.

> Each of us is not the only person who has walked the
> earth; others have been here before us, wearing these
> same symbols, uncovering the profundities of our
> common past. Once we fled their footsteps; now more
> of us may search the path they took to find the mean-
> ing of our ancient ground.

In this way you will remember and do all My command-
ments and you will be wholly dedicated for your God. I am
Adonay your God who brought you out of the land of
Egypt in order to be your God. I am Adonay your God.

> All Jews have their own Egypt; we must each free our-
> selves in our own way from the bonds that keep us
> from our true integrity. When that bond is burst,
> when we have ousted the illegitimate masters from
> our minds, then one day we each can come to God,
> each on our own ground, within our own flame, but
> each to the same ultimate reality whose power rules
> the sea, the earth, and each person's freely loving
> soul.

מִי־כָמֹכָה בָּאֵלִם יְיָ מִי כָּמֹכָה נֶאְדָּר בַּקֹּדֶשׁ נוֹרָא
תְהִלֹּת עֹשֵׂה־פֶלֶא:

Mi chamocha ba'eylim Adonay
Mi kamocha ne'dar ba-kodesh
Nora t-hilot o-sey feleh.

Who is like You Adonay, glorious in holiness and praise,
working wonders!

שִׁירָה חֲדָשָׁה שִׁבְּחוּ גְאוּלִים לְשִׁמְךָ עַל שְׂפַת הַיָּם.
יַחַד כֻּלָּם הוֹדוּ וְהִמְלִיכוּ וְאָמְרוּ.

Shira chadasha shib'chu g'ulim
L'shim-cha al-sfat ha-yam.
Yachad kulam hodu
V'himlichu v'am-ru:

A new song the redeemed sang to Your Name on the shore
of the sea. Together they acknowledged Your divine rule.

יְיָ יִמְלֹךְ לְעֹלָם וָעֶד:

Adonay yimloch l'olam va-ed.

Adonay will reign forever and ever!

צוּר יִשְׂרָאֵל קוּמָה בְּעֶזְרַת יִשְׂרָאֵל. וּפְדֵה כִנְאֻמֶךְ
יְהוּדָה וְיִשְׂרָאֵל. גֹּאֲלֵנוּ יְיָ צְבָאוֹת שְׁמוֹ קְדוֹשׁ יִשְׂרָאֵל:
בָּרוּךְ אַתָּה יְיָ גָּאַל יִשְׂרָאֵל:

Tzur Yisrael kuma b'ezrat Yisrael. Uf'dey chin'umecha Yehuda
v'Yisrael. Goaleynu Adonay tz'va-ot shmo k'dosh Yisrael.
Baruch attah Adonay ga-al Yisrael.

O Rock of Israel, come to Israel's help.
Fulfill Your promise of redemption for Judah and Israel.
Our Redeemer is Adonay of hosts, the Holy One of Israel.

Praised You are, O God, who will fulfill the time of
redemption for Israel and all humanity.

AMIDAH (THE GREAT PRAYER)

(The full traditional silent Amidah in Hebrew and English is
found on pages 156—171)

אֲדֹנָי שְׂפָתַי תִּפְתָּח וּפִי יַגִּיד תְּהִלָּתֶךְ:

Avot

בָּרוּךְ אַתָּה, יְיָ אֱלֹהֵינוּ וֵאלֹהֵי אֲבוֹתֵינוּ (וֵאלֹהֵי
אִמוֹתֵינוּ), אֱלֹהֵי אַבְרָהָם, אֱלֹהֵי יִצְחָק, וֵאלֹהֵי יַעֲקֹב,
(אֱלֹהֵי שָׂרָה, אֱלֹהֵי רִבְקָה, אֱלֹהֵי רָחֵל, וֵאלֹהֵי לֵאָה,)
הָאֵל הַגָּדוֹל הַגִּבּוֹר וְהַנּוֹרָא, אֵל עֶלְיוֹן, גּוֹמֵל חֲסָדִים
טוֹבִים, וְקֹנֵה הַכֹּל, וְזוֹכֵר חַסְדֵי אָבוֹת (וְאִמָּהוֹת),

וּמֵבִיא גוֹאֵל* לִבְנֵי בְנֵיהֶם לְמַעַן שְׁמוֹ בְּאַהֲבָה.
זָכְרֵנוּ לְחַיִּים, מֶלֶךְ חָפֵץ בַּחַיִּים, וְכָתְבֵנוּ בְּסֵפֶר
הַחַיִּים, לְמַעַנְךָ אֱלֹהִים חַיִּים: מֶלֶךְ עוֹזֵר וּמוֹשִׁיעַ
וּמָגֵן. בָּרוּךְ אַתָּה יְיָ, מָגֵן אַבְרָהָם (וְשָׂרָה).

In the Reform tradition, גְּאוּלָה*

Praised be the God of our fathers,
The God of Abraham, of Isaac, and of Jacob.
Praised be the God of our mothers,
Of Sarah, of Rebecca, of Leah, and of Rachel.
Praised be the source of strength and courage,
The source of kindness and good deeds.
Praised be the source of gentleness and love,
Of softness and kind words.
Praised be the man who transcends strength
Through gentleness,
Praised be the woman who perfects gentleness
Through strength.
Praised be the person who acts according to the best that is
    within,
Praised be the person who reaches out to touch the best in
    others.
Praised be the gentle faithfulness of Abraham
And the valiant strength of Sarah.
Praised be the God Who created with divinity
A woman and a man.

Gevurot

אַתָּה גִבּוֹר לְעוֹלָם אֲדֹנָי מְחַיֵּה מֵתִים* אַתָּה רַב
לְהוֹשִׁיעַ. מְכַלְכֵּל חַיִּים בְּחֶסֶד מְחַיֵּה מֵתִים* בְּרַחֲמִים
רַבִּים. סוֹמֵךְ נוֹפְלִים וְרוֹפֵא חוֹלִים וּמַתִּיר אֲסוּרִים
וּמְקַיֵּם אֱמוּנָתוֹ לִישֵׁנֵי עָפָר. מִי כָמוֹךָ בַּעַל גְּבוּרוֹת
וּמִי דּוֹמֶה לָּךְ. מֶלֶךְ מֵמִית וּמְחַיֶּה וּמַצְמִיחַ יְשׁוּעָה: מִי
כָמוֹךָ אַב הָרַחֲמִים זוֹכֵר יְצוּרָיו לְחַיִּים בְּרַחֲמִים:
וְנֶאֱמָן אַתָּה לְהַחֲיוֹת מֵתִים*. בָּרוּךְ אַתָּה יְיָ מְחַיֵּה
הַמֵּתִים*:

In the Reform tradition, הַכֹּל*

Adonay is forever mighty,
Restoring life to those marked out for death,
Liberating peoples once destined for defeat.

Adonay is forever mighty,
Banishing despair through the loving acts of human
    beings,
Reviving barren hopes within the womb of weary
    dreamers,
Cutting loose the fetters of the victims
Fallen underneath the sickness of our days,
Remembering those passed over by the dust of time.

May You extend Your mighty hand to us,
Restoring us,
Banishing our despair,
That from the dust of our uncaring age
We might bring to bud those loving acts that make us
Human.

(*When Musaf is to be offered, the service continues with Uv'chen
on page 96)*

UNETANEH TOKEF

Introductory Readings

We shall affirm the mighty holiness of this day, a day of awe and dread, for upon it is God's rule exalted, and the holy throne established in covenantal love.

When we really begin a new year it is decided,
And when we actually repent it is determined:

Who shall be truly alive,
And who shall merely exist;

Who shall be tormented by the fire of ambition,
And whose hopes shall be quenched by the waters of failure;

Who shall be pierced by the sharp sword of envy,
And who shall be torn by the wild beast of resentment;

Who shall hunger for companionship,
And who shall thirst for approval;

Who shall be shattered by storms of change,
And who shall be plagued by the pressures of conformity;

Who shall be strangled by insecurity,
And who shall be beaten into submission;

Who shall be content with their lot,
And who shall go wandering in search of satisfaction;

Who shall be serene,
And who shall be distraught.

But *Tshuvah, Tefillah* and *Tzedakah,*
Repentance, Prayer and Just Action,
Have the power to change
The character of our lives.

Therefore let us repent, pray, and do right,
So that this may be a genuinely new year of life.

                        *   *   *

On this Judgment Day, old legend relates,
Rabbi Amnon of Mainz, dying of the tortures of the eleventh
    century,
Saw God enthroned with the angelic host
Determining in the books of life and death
The verdict of everyone on earth.
His vision, Unetaneh Tokef, remains for us,
A reminder that the world is more awesome
Than our finite gallery of profane sights and ordinary thoughts,
It is a vaster realm of mystery and power
Which makes a claim upon our lives
And relates each one of us to spheres beyond our sight.

Unetaneh Tokef accounts with grim detail
The fires, floods, great storms, cruel swords
Whereby we each shall one day meet our death,
Yet also how our own repentance, prayer, and acts of human
    caring
Can mitigate the harshness of existence
And elevate survival to the plain of being human.

That there are powers far beyond ourselves reminds us
That because so much of life is not within our power,
Because nature and humanity can wreak such awful cruelty,
Just so must we struggle against all the cruelty we know,
And never cease within our prayers to demand
That the God who watched the tortures of Amnon of Mainz
And all the slaughters in the ages since his own
Bring quickly to an end the world's capacity for harm
And stir powerfully in the breasts of every creature
The repentance, prayer, and acts of human caring
That can make the vision of a God who metes out justice
A reality once more.

וּנְתַנֶּה תֹּקֶף קְדֻשַּׁת הַיּוֹם. כִּי הוּא נוֹרָא וְאָיוֹם. וּבוֹ
תִּנָּשֵׂא מַלְכוּתֶךָ. וְיִכּוֹן בְּחֶסֶד כִּסְאֶךָ. וְתֵשֵׁב עָלָיו
בֶּאֱמֶת. אֱמֶת כִּי אַתָּה הוּא דַיָּן וּמוֹכִיחַ וְיוֹדֵעַ וָעֵד.
וְכוֹתֵב וְחוֹתֵם וְסוֹפֵר וּמוֹנֶה. וְתִזְכֹּר כָּל־הַנִּשְׁכָּחוֹת.
וְתִפְתַּח אֶת־סֵפֶר הַזִּכְרוֹנוֹת. וּמֵאֵלָיו יִקָּרֵא. וְחוֹתָם
יַד כָּל־אָדָם בּוֹ.

Let us declare the holy power of this day, for it is awesome and mighty. Your sovereignty is exalted upon it, and
You faithfully take Your place upon Your throne established in love borne of the covenant between You and
ourselves. You are the true judge and witness, You write
and seal and inscribe and take account. You remember all
that we have forgotten, opening the Book of Remembrance from which everything is read and in which is
recorded the seal of every human being.

וּבְשׁוֹפָר גָּדוֹל יִתָּקַע. וְקוֹל דְּמָמָה דַקָּה יִשָּׁמַע.
וּמַלְאָכִים יֵחָפֵזוּן. וְחִיל וּרְעָדָה יֹאחֵזוּן. וְיֹאמְרוּ הִנֵּה
יוֹם הַדִּין. לִפְקֹד עַל צְבָא מָרוֹם בַּדִּין. כִּי לֹא יִזְכּוּ
בְעֵינֶיךָ בַּדִּין. וְכָל־בָּאֵי עוֹלָם יַעַבְרוּן לְפָנֶיךָ כִּבְנֵי
מָרוֹן: כְּבַקָּרַת רוֹעֶה עֶדְרוֹ. מַעֲבִיר צֹאנוֹ תַּחַת שִׁבְטוֹ.
כֵּן תַּעֲבִיר וְתִסְפֹּר וְתִמְנֶה. וְתִפְקֹד נֶפֶשׁ כָּל־חָי.
וְתַחְתֹּךְ קִצְבָה לְכָל־בְּרִיָּה. וְתִכְתּוֹב אֶת־גְּזַר דִּינָם:

The great Shofar is sounded, and a still small voice is
heard. The angels in heaven are dismayed and are seized
with fear and trembling, as they proclaim: "Behold the
Day of Judgment!" The hosts of heaven are to be
arraigned in judgment, for in Your eyes even they are not
free from guilt. All who live in the world pass today before
You, one by one, like a flock of sheep. As a shepherd

gathers the sheep and causes them to pass beneath the staff, so You pass and record, count and visit, every living soul, appointing the measure of every creature's life and decreeing its destiny.

Refrain:
B'rosh hashanah yikateyvun uvyom tzom kippur yehchateymun.
(On Rosh Hashanah it is written and on Yom Kippur it is decided)

בְּרֹאשׁ הַשָּׁנָה יִכָּתֵבוּן. וּבְיוֹם צוֹם כִּפּוּר יֵחָתֵמוּן. כַּמָּה
יַעַבְרוּן. וְכַמָּה יִבָּרֵאוּן. מִי יִחְיֶה. וּמִי יָמוּת. מִי בְקִצּוֹ.
וּמִי לֹא בְקִצּוֹ. מִי בָאֵשׁ. וּמִי בַמַּיִם. מִי בַחֶרֶב. וּמִי
בָחַיָּה. מִי בָרָעָב. וּמִי בַצָּמָא. מִי בָרַעַשׁ. וּמִי בַמַּגֵּפָה.
מִי בַחֲנִיקָה וּמִי בַסְּקִילָה. מִי יָנוּחַ. וּמִי יָנוּעַ. מִי יִשָּׁקֵט.
וּמִי יִטָּרֵף. מִי יִשָּׁלֵו. וּמִי יִתְיַסָּר. מִי יֵעָנִי. וּמִי יֵעָשֵׁר.
מִי יִשָּׁפֵל. וּמִי יָרוּם:

וּתְשׁוּבָה וּתְפִלָּה וּצְדָקָה
מַעֲבִירִין אֶת־רֹעַ הַגְּזֵרָה:

On Rosh Hashanah it is written and on Yom Kippur it is decided how many shall pass on and how many be created, who shall live and who shall die, who when their time comes and who before or after their time, who by fire and who by water, who by the sword and who by wild beasts, who by famine and who by drought, who by earthquake and who by epidemic, who by strangling and who by stoning; who shall have rest and who can never be still, who shall be serene and who torn apart, who shall be at ease and who afflicted, who shall be impoverished and who enriched, who shall be brought low and who raised high. But tshuvah, prayer, and charitable acts avert the severity of the decree.

Kedusha

נְקַדֵּשׁ אֶת־שִׁמְךָ בָּעוֹלָם כְּשֵׁם שֶׁמַּקְדִּישִׁים אוֹתוֹ
בִּשְׁמֵי מָרוֹם. כַּכָּתוּב עַל־יַד נְבִיאֶךָ וְקָרָא זֶה אֶל זֶה
וְאָמַר.

And so, along with the angels far above, we declare the
holiness of Your presence in the world just as it is declared
in the highest heavens, as it is written in Isaiah: "And each
called to the other saying:

קָדוֹשׁ קָדוֹשׁ קָדוֹשׁ יְיָ צְבָאוֹת. מְלֹא כָל־הָאָרֶץ
כְּבוֹדוֹ:

*Kadosh Kadosh Kadosh Adonay Tzvaot, mlo chol ha-aretz
kvodo:*

"Holy! Holy! Holy! is the Commander of the Hosts,
The fullness of all the earth is God's Glory."

אָז בְּקוֹל רַעַשׁ גָּדוֹל אַדִּיר וְחָזָק מַשְׁמִיעִים קוֹל
מִתְנַשְּׂאִים לְעֻמַּת שְׂרָפִים לְעֻמָּתָם בָּרוּךְ יֹאמֵרוּ.

Then with a great and powerful rushing voice they raise
themselves opposite the Seraphim and cry, "Praised be!"

בָּרוּךְ כְּבוֹד־יְיָ מִמְּקוֹמוֹ:

Baruch kvod Adonay mimkomo:

Praised be the Glory of Adonay from God's Place, the
World.

מִמְּקוֹמְךָ מַלְכֵּנוּ תוֹפִיעַ וְתִמְלוֹךְ עָלֵינוּ כִּי מְחַכִּים
אֲנַחְנוּ לָךְ: מָתַי תִּמְלוֹךְ בְּצִיּוֹן. בְּקָרוֹב בְּיָמֵינוּ לְעוֹלָם
וָעֶד תִּשְׁכּוֹן: תִּתְגַּדַּל וְתִתְקַדַּשׁ בְּתוֹךְ יְרוּשָׁלַיִם עִירְךָ

לְדוֹר וָדוֹר וּלְנֵצַח נְצָחִים: וְעֵינֵינוּ תִרְאֶינָה מַלְכוּתֶךָ
כַּדָּבָר הָאָמוּר בְּשִׁירֵי עֻזֶּךָ עַל־יְדֵי דָוִד מְשִׁיחַ צִדְקֶךָ:

From Your Place, O Majesty, appear and rule over us, for
we are awaiting you! When will You rule in Zion? May
Your presence be felt soon, in our own days, and forever!
Your holiness shall be felt in the midst of Jerusalem, Your
city, forever and ever to all eternity, and our eyes shall
behold the reality of Your rule as it is said in the songs
written of Your power by David, Your righteous
Anointed:

יִמְלֹךְ יְיָ לְעוֹלָם. אֱלֹהַיִךְ צִיּוֹן לְדֹר וָדֹר. הַלְלוּיָהּ:

Yimloch Adonay l'olam, Elohayich tziyon, ldor vador halleluya!

Adonay will reign forever, your God will reign, O Zion, to
all generations. Praise God!

לְדוֹר וָדוֹר נַגִּיד גָּדְלֶךָ. וּלְנֵצַח נְצָחִים קְדֻשָּׁתְךָ נַקְדִּישׁ.
וְשִׁבְחֲךָ אֱלֹהֵינוּ מִפִּינוּ לֹא יָמוּשׁ לְעוֹלָם וָעֶד. כִּי אֵל
מֶלֶךְ גָּדוֹל וְקָדוֹשׁ אָתָּה:

We shall tell our children of Your greatness, and they will
tell our grandchildren. In every generation till eternity we
shall proclaim Your holiness. Our lips shall never abandon
Your praise, for Your Majesty is great and holy.

U'vchen (Awe)

וּבְכֵן תֵּן פַּחְדְּךָ, יְיָ אֱלֹהֵינוּ, עַל כָּל מַעֲשֶׂיךָ, וְאֵימָתְךָ
עַל כָּל מַה שֶּׁבָּרֵאתָ, וְיִירָאוּךָ כָּל הַמַּעֲשִׂים וְיִשְׁתַּחֲווּ
לְפָנֶיךָ כָּל הַבְּרוּאִים, וְיֵעָשׂוּ כֻלָּם אֲגֻדָּה אַחַת לַעֲשׂוֹת
רְצוֹנְךָ בְּלֵבָב שָׁלֵם, כְּמוֹ שֶׁיָּדַעְנוּ, יְיָ אֱלֹהֵינוּ,

שֶׁהַשִּׁלְטוֹן לְפָנֶיךָ, עֹז בְּיָדְךָ וּגְבוּרָה בִּימִינֶךָ, וְשִׁמְךָ
נוֹרָא עַל כָּל מַה שֶׁבָּרָאתָ.

וּבְכֵן תֵּן כָּבוֹד, יְיָ, לְעַמֶּךָ, תְּהִלָּה לִירֵאֶיךָ וְתִקְוָה
לְדוֹרְשֶׁיךָ, וּפִתְחוֹן פֶּה לַמְיַחֲלִים לָךְ, שִׂמְחָה לְאַרְצֶךָ
וְשָׂשׂוֹן לְעִירֶךָ, וּצְמִיחַת קֶרֶן לְדָוִד עַבְדֶּךָ, וַעֲרִיכַת נֵר
לְבֶן־יִשַׁי מְשִׁיחֶךָ, בִּמְהֵרָה בְיָמֵינוּ.

וּבְכֵן צַדִּיקִים יִרְאוּ וְיִשְׂמָחוּ, וִישָׁרִים יַעֲלֹזוּ, וַחֲסִידִים
בְּרִנָּה יָגִילוּ, וְעוֹלָתָה תִּקְפָּץ־פִּיהָ, וְכָל הָרִשְׁעָה כֻּלָּה
כְּעָשָׁן תִּכְלֶה, כִּי תַעֲבִיר מֶמְשֶׁלֶת זָדוֹן מִן הָאָרֶץ.

וְתִמְלוֹךְ אַתָּה יְיָ לְבַדֶּךָ עַל כָּל מַעֲשֶׂיךָ בְּהַר צִיּוֹן
מִשְׁכַּן כְּבוֹדֶךָ וּבִירוּשָׁלַיִם עִיר קָדְשֶׁךָ. כַּכָּתוּב בְּדִבְרֵי
קָדְשֶׁךָ. יִמְלֹךְ יְיָ לְעוֹלָם אֱלֹהַיִךְ צִיּוֹן לְדֹר וָדֹר
הַלְלוּיָהּ:

קָדוֹשׁ אַתָּה וְנוֹרָא שְׁמֶךָ וְאֵין אֱלוֹהַּ מִבַּלְעָדֶיךָ
כַּכָּתוּב. וַיִּגְבַּהּ יְיָ צְבָאוֹת בַּמִּשְׁפָּט וְהָאֵל הַקָּדוֹשׁ
נִקְדַּשׁ בִּצְדָקָה. בָּרוּךְ אַתָּה יְיָ הַמֶּלֶךְ הַקָּדוֹשׁ:

Let us know awe again
Adonay our God
Help us in our regulated life
In our days oppressed by mere annoyances
To encounter greatness
Wonder and majesty
The surprise of good people
The worth of each of us.

Let us know hope again,
Adonay our God.
Help us in our placid life

In our days oppressed by too much self-concern
To do without that others might know having
To dare an act that will better someone's life
To find the love to share another's pain,
The strength to fight for causes beyond our own content-
  ment,
The courage to face down cynicism before an honest
  human being.

Let us know You again,
Adonay our God
Help us in our unconnected life
In our days oppressed by pains which have no purpose
To shed our fears
Of finding a reality beyond what we can see and touch
That one day we might find the nerve
To perceive within the seas and sky and earth and human
  race

You.

Ya'aleh V'yavo (For the Ascent of Our Thoughts)

אֱלֹהֵינוּ וֵאלֹהֵי אֲבוֹתֵינוּ (וֵאלֹהֵי אִמּוֹתֵינוּ) יַעֲלֶה וְיָבֹא
וְיַגִּיעַ וְיֵרָאֶה וְיֵרָצֶה וְיִשָּׁמַע וְיִפָּקֵד וְיִזָּכֵר זִכְרוֹנֵנוּ
וּפִקְדוֹנֵנוּ וְזִכְרוֹן אֲבוֹתֵינוּ (וְאִמּוֹתֵינוּ) וְזִכְרוֹן מָשִׁיחַ
בֶּן־דָּוִד עַבְדֶּךָ וְזִכְרוֹן יְרוּשָׁלַיִם עִיר קָדְשֶׁךָ וְזִכְרוֹן כָּל
עַמְּךָ בֵּית יִשְׂרָאֵל לְפָנֶיךָ. לִפְלֵיטָה וּלְטוֹבָה לְחֵן
וּלְחֶסֶד וּלְרַחֲמִים לְחַיִּים וּלְשָׁלוֹם בְּיוֹם הַזִּכָּרוֹן הַזֶּה.
זָכְרֵנוּ יְיָ אֱלֹהֵינוּ בּוֹ לְטוֹבָה. וּפָקְדֵנוּ בּוֹ לִבְרָכָה.
וְהוֹשִׁיעֵנוּ בּוֹ לְחַיִּים: וּבִדְבַר יְשׁוּעָה וְרַחֲמִים חוּס
וְחָנֵּנוּ וְרַחֵם עָלֵינוּ וְהוֹשִׁיעֵנוּ כִּי אֵלֶיךָ עֵינֵינוּ. כִּי אֵל
מֶלֶךְ חַנּוּן וְרַחוּם אָתָּה:

M'loch (Sanctifying Rosh Hashanah)

אֱלֹהֵינוּ וֵאלֹהֵי אֲבוֹתֵינוּ (וֵאלֹהֵי אִמוֹתֵינוּ). מְלוֹךְ עַל
כָּל הָעוֹלָם כֻּלּוֹ בִּכְבוֹדֶךָ וְהִנָּשֵׂא עַל כָּל הָאָרֶץ בִּיקָרֶךָ
וְהוֹפַע בַּהֲדַר גְּאוֹן עֻזֶּךָ עַל כָּל יוֹשְׁבֵי תֵבֵל אַרְצֶךָ.
וְיֵדַע כָּל פָּעוּל כִּי אַתָּה פְעַלְתּוֹ וְיָבִין כָּל יָצוּר כִּי אַתָּה
יְצַרְתּוֹ וְיֹאמַר כֹּל אֲשֶׁר נְשָׁמָה בְאַפּוֹ יְיָ אֱלֹהֵי יִשְׂרָאֵל
מֶלֶךְ וּמַלְכוּתוֹ בַּכֹּל מָשָׁלָה: אֱלֹהֵינוּ וֵאלֹהֵי אֲבוֹתֵינוּ
(וֵאלֹהֵי אִמוֹתֵינוּ) [רְצֵה בִמְנוּחָתֵנוּ] קַדְּשֵׁנוּ בְּמִצְוֹתֶיךָ
וְתֵן חֶלְקֵנוּ בְּתוֹרָתֶךָ שַׂבְּעֵנוּ מִטּוּבֶךָ וְשַׂמְּחֵנוּ
בִּישׁוּעָתֶךָ: [וְהַנְחִילֵנוּ יְיָ אֱלֹהֵינוּ בְּאַהֲבָה וּבְרָצוֹן
שַׁבַּת קָדְשֶׁךָ וְיָנוּחוּ בוֹ יִשְׂרָאֵל מְקַדְּשֵׁי שְׁמֶךָ] וְטַהֵר
לִבֵּנוּ לְעָבְדְּךָ בֶּאֱמֶת. כִּי אַתָּה אֱלֹהִים אֱמֶת וּדְבָרְךָ
אֱמֶת וְקַיָּם לָעַד. בָּרוּךְ אַתָּה יְיָ מֶלֶךְ עַל כָּל הָאָרֶץ
מְקַדֵּשׁ [הַשַּׁבָּת וְ]יִשְׂרָאֵל וְיוֹם הַזִּכָּרוֹן:

Our God and God of our ancestors:
May the thought of us
Our fathers and mothers long before us
The Messiah you have promised from the
    seed of David
Jerusalem, your holy city
Israel, Your covenanted people

May the thought of all these
Ascend and come before You

And reach You
And be pleasing to You

For liberation
For good
For graciousness
For covenantal love
For mother love

For life
For peace.

On this Day of Remembering
Remember us for our good
Keep us in mind for blessing
Save us for long life
Victory over our smallness
And peace.

Adonay our God,
Let this holy time
Lift us to Your presence
In life
In peace
In leaping joy.
You have promised us it will.
Find rest in our rest,
Holiness in our performance of mitzvot.
Help us find our being in Your Torah,
Feed us from Your store of good,
Bring us joy in Your victory over evil.
Wash clean our hearts
That we may serve You and Your creatures
Honestly.
Dower us with love and acceptance
Joyous delight
(Shabbat and) holy festivals,
That we who represent Your holiness
May know joy.

Through (Shabbat and) this Day of Remembrance
May we
Your people Israel
Find You.

Rtzey

רְצֵה יְיָ אֱלֹהֵינוּ בְּעַמְּךָ יִשְׂרָאֵל וּבִתְפִלָּתָם. וְהָשֵׁב אֶת
הָעֲבוֹדָה לִדְבִיר בֵּיתֶךָ וְאִשֵּׁי יִשְׂרָאֵל וּתְפִלָּתָם
בְּאַהֲבָה תְקַבֵּל בְּרָצוֹן. וּתְהִי לְרָצוֹן תָּמִיד עֲבוֹדַת
יִשְׂרָאֵל עַמֶּךָ. וְתֶחֱזֶינָה עֵינֵינוּ בְּשׁוּבְךָ לְצִיּוֹן בְּרַחֲמִים.
בָּרוּךְ אַתָּה יְיָ הַמַּחֲזִיר שְׁכִינָתוֹ לְצִיּוֹן:

An Interpretation

Not with bullocks have we come
Before the great altar
With our golden grains and oils
But here into this simple room
We've brought the offering of our dreams
Our laughter and our shouting
Our loneliness and terror
And kneaded them into the words we send into the air
Upon the breath that was Your offering
At our birth.

We hope You like them.

We hope You will bring them inside
To the most intimate part of Your house
We hope You will warm them
On the embers of the offerings Israel brought You long ago
We hope You will keep them
As part of the daily offering Israel gives back to You
With each new morning's breath.

May our gifts help build the altar
On which the offerings You like best
May be heaped up once again
Without the suffering of bullocks
With the overflowing altar as a guarantee
That not one person will go hungry

Ever again.
Our eyes will soon see You again
Enthroned in Zion on compassion's throne.

How much more we'd like to say
Than this morning's modest praise.
Hurray! is what we'd like to say
Hurray! for all the joy we have
Hurray! (the hardest offering)
For all the joy we've lost

Would You accept Hurray! upon Your altar?

Adonay, You are praise itself.
Your presence moves closer with each new morning's
    breath
Toward Zion.
Toward us.

Modim (Thanks to God)

מוֹדִים אֲנַחְנוּ לָךְ שָׁאַתָּה הוּא יְיָ אֱלֹהֵינוּ וֵאלֹהֵי
אֲבוֹתֵינוּ (וֵאלֹהֵי אִמּוֹתֵינוּ) לְעוֹלָם וָעֶד. צוּר חַיֵּינוּ
מָגֵן יִשְׁעֵנוּ אַתָּה הוּא לְדוֹר וָדוֹר. נוֹדֶה לְּךָ וּנְסַפֵּר
תְּהִלָּתֶךָ עַל חַיֵּינוּ הַמְּסוּרִים בְּיָדֶךָ וְעַל נִשְׁמוֹתֵינוּ
הַפְּקוּדוֹת לָךְ וְעַל נִסֶּיךָ שֶׁבְּכָל־יוֹם עִמָּנוּ וְעַל
נִפְלְאוֹתֶיךָ וְטוֹבוֹתֶיךָ שֶׁבְּכָל־עֵת עֶרֶב וָבֹקֶר וְצָהֳרָיִם.
הַטּוֹב כִּי לֹא כָלוּ רַחֲמֶיךָ וְהַמְרַחֵם כִּי לֹא
תַמּוּ חֲסָדֶיךָ מֵעוֹלָם קִוִּינוּ לָךְ:

וְעַל כֻּלָּם יִתְבָּרַךְ וְיִתְרוֹמַם שִׁמְךָ מַלְכֵּנוּ תָּמִיד לְעוֹלָם
וָעֶד:

וּכְתֹב לְחַיִּים טוֹבִים כָּל־בְּנֵי בְרִיתֶךָ:

וְכֹל הַחַיִּים יוֹדְוּךָ סֶּלָה וִיהַלְלוּ אֶת שִׁמְךָ בֶּאֱמֶת הָאֵל
יְשׁוּעָתֵנוּ וְעֶזְרָתֵנוּ סֶלָה. בָּרוּךְ אַתָּה יְיָ הַטּוֹב שִׁמְךָ
וּלְךָ נָאֶה לְהוֹדוֹת:

Adonay our God, we thank You and praise You for guard-
ing our lives and nourishing our souls. We thank You for
the wondrous workings of the world around us, which we
witness every day. You are a gracious Sovereign, whose
motherlove and compassion are without measure. May all
who worship in Your name be inscribed in the Book of Life
for a year of blessing, sustenance, and peace. Praised are
You, whose name is Good, to whom it is fitting to give
abundant praise.

Sim Shalom (Peace)

שִׁים שָׁלוֹם טוֹבָה וּבְרָכָה חֵן וָחֶסֶד וְרַחֲמִים עָלֵינוּ וְעַל
כָּל־יִשְׂרָאֵל עַמֶּךָ. בָּרְכֵנוּ אָבִינוּ כֻּלָּנוּ כְּאֶחָד בְּאוֹר
פָּנֶיךָ. כִּי בְאוֹר פָּנֶיךָ נָתַתָּ לָּנוּ יְיָ אֱלֹהֵינוּ תּוֹרַת חַיִּים
וְאַהֲבַת חֶסֶד וּצְדָקָה וּבְרָכָה וְרַחֲמִים וְחַיִּים וְשָׁלוֹם.
וְטוֹב בְּעֵינֶיךָ לְבָרֵךְ אֶת־עַמְּךָ יִשְׂרָאֵל בְּכָל־עֵת וּבְכָל־
שָׁעָה בִּשְׁלוֹמֶךָ.
בְּסֵפֶר חַיִּים בְּרָכָה וְשָׁלוֹם וּפַרְנָסָה טוֹבָה נִזָּכֵר וְנִכָּתֵב
לְפָנֶיךָ אֲנַחְנוּ וְכָל עַמְּךָ בֵּית יִשְׂרָאֵל לְחַיִּים טוֹבִים
וּלְשָׁלוֹם. בָּרוּךְ אַתָּה יְיָ עֹשֶׂה הַשָּׁלוֹם:

Let all these be possible:
Peace
Goodness
Lives that are a blessing
Gracious acts
The love of sharing

The love of creating
Light unbound
Torah alive
Sustenance for all
Abounding life.

They're there.
Help us find them here.

Private Meditation

The day has come
To take an accounting of my life.

Have I dreamed of late
Of the person I want to be,
Of the changes I would make
In my daily habits,
In the way I am with others,
In the friendship I show companions,
Woman friends, man friends, my partner,
In the regard I show my father and mother,
Who brought me out of childhood?

I have remained enchained too often to less than what I am.
But the day has come to take an accounting of my life.

Have I renewed of late
My vision of the world I want to live in,
Of the changes I would make
In the way my friends are with each other
The way we find out whom we love
The way we grow to educated people
The way in which the many kinds of needy people
Grope their way to justice?

I, who am my own kind of needy person, have been afraid of
visions.
But the day has come to take an accounting of my life.

Have I faced up of late
To the needs I really have—
Not for comforts which shelter my unsureness,
Not for honors which paper over my (really tawdry) self,
Not for handsome beauty in which my weakness masquerades,
Not for unattractiveness in which my strengths hide out—

I need to be loved.
Do I deserve to be?
I need to love another.
Can I commit my love?
Perhaps its object will be less than my visions
(And then I would be less)
Perhaps I am not brave enough
To find new vision
Through a real and breathing person.

I need to come in touch with my own power,
Not with titles,
Not possessions, money, high praise,
But with the power that is mine
As a child of the Power that is the universe
To be a comfort, a source of honor,
Handsome and beautiful from the moment I awoke this morn-
    ing
So strong
That I can risk the love of someone else
So sure
That I can risk to change the world
And know that even if it all comes crashing down
I shall survive it all—
Saddened a bit, shaken perhaps,
Not unvisited by tears
But my dreams shall not crash down
My visions not go glimmering.
So long as I have breath
I know I have the strength
To transform what I can be
To what I am.

The day has come
To take an accounting of my life.

(Silent, individual prayer may be encouraged here)

יִהְיוּ לְרָצוֹן אִמְרֵי פִי וְהֶגְיוֹן לִבִּי לְפָנֶיךָ יְיָ צוּרִי
וְגוֹאֲלִי: עֹשֶׂה שָׁלוֹם בִּמְרוֹמָיו הוּא יַעֲשֶׂה שָׁלוֹם
עָלֵינוּ וְעַל כָּל יִשְׂרָאֵל וְאִמְרוּ אָמֵן:

Yih'yu l'ratzon imrey fee, v'hegyon libee l'faneh-cha,
Adonay tzuree v'go'alee. Oseh shalom bimromav hu ya-aseh
shalom aleynu v'al kol Yisrael, v'imru Amen.

May all the words of my mouth
And the thoughts within my heart
Be desirable to You,
Rock of mine, Restorer of my freedom.
The One who makes peace in the heavens high above
Shall surely do the work of peace with us,
With all Israel, and all the human family,
Therefore say with me: it will be so.

Avinu Malkeynu: Our Forgiving Parent, Our Sovereign

אָבִינוּ מַלְכֵּנוּ חָטָאנוּ לְפָנֶיךָ:
Avinu Malkeynu, we have done wrong before You.

אָבִינוּ מַלְכֵּנוּ אֵין לָנוּ מֶלֶךְ אֶלָּא אָתָּה:
Avinu Malkeynu, we have no Sovereign except You.

אָבִינוּ מַלְכֵּנוּ חַדֵּשׁ עָלֵינוּ שָׁנָה טוֹבָה:
Avinu Malkeynu, let this be a good year for us.

אָבִינוּ מַלְכֵּנוּ הָפֵר עֲצַת אוֹיְבֵינוּ:
Avinu Malkeynu, destroy the power of every oppressor and
   adversary.

אָבִינוּ מַלְכֵּנוּ כַּלֵּה דֶּבֶר וְחֶרֶב וְרָעָב וּשְׁבִי וּמַשְׁחִית מִבְּנֵי בְרִיתֶךָ:

Avinu Malkeynu, remove from all Your children disease, war, famine, exile and destruction.

אָבִינוּ מַלְכֵּנוּ סְלַח וּמְחַל לְכָל־עֲוֹנוֹתֵינוּ:

Avinu Malkeynu, forgive and pardon all our wrong-doing.

אָבִינוּ מַלְכֵּנוּ הַחֲזִירֵנוּ בִּתְשׁוּבָה שְׁלֵמָה לְפָנֶיךָ:

Avinu Malkeynu, may we return to You in earnest repentance.

אָבִינוּ מַלְכֵּנוּ שְׁלַח רְפוּאָה שְׁלֵמָה לְחוֹלֵי עַמֶּךָ:

Avinu Malkeynu, send healing to all who are sick.

אָבִינוּ מַלְכֵּנוּ כָּתְבֵנוּ בְּסֵפֶר חַיִּים טוֹבִים:

Avinu Malkeynu, inscribe us in Your book for a life of good ness.

אָבִינוּ מַלְכֵּנוּ כָּתְבֵנוּ בְּסֵפֶר פַּרְנָסָה וְכַלְכָּלָה:

Avinu Malkeynu, inscribe us in the book of sustenance.

אָבִינוּ מַלְכֵּנוּ כָּתְבֵנוּ בְּסֵפֶר זְכָיּוֹת:

Avinu Malkeynu, inscribe us in the book of meritorious acts.

אָבִינוּ מַלְכֵּנוּ כָּתְבֵנוּ בְּסֵפֶר סְלִיחָה וּמְחִילָה:

Avinu Malkeynu, inscribe us in the book of forgiveness and reconciliation.

אָבִינוּ מַלְכֵּנוּ חֲמוֹל עָלֵינוּ וְעַל עוֹלָלֵינוּ וְטַפֵּנוּ:

Avinu Malkeynu. show mercy to us and to our children.

אָבִינוּ מַלְכֵּנוּ פְּתַח שַׁעֲרֵי שָׁמַיִם לִתְפִלָּתֵנוּ:

Avinu Malkeynu, open the gates of heaven to our prayer.

אָבִינוּ מַלְכֵּנוּ עֲשֵׂה לְמַעַן בָּאֵי בָאֵשׁ וּבַמַּיִם עַל־קִדּוּשׁ שְׁמֶךָ:

Avinu Malkeynu, do it for the sake of those who went through fire and water to honor Your name.

אָבִינוּ מַלְכֵּנוּ חָנֵּנוּ וַעֲנֵנוּ כִּי אֵין בָּנוּ מַעֲשִׂים עֲשֵׂה
עִמָּנוּ צְדָקָה וָחֶסֶד וְהוֹשִׁיעֵנוּ:

Avinu Malkeynu, be gracious and respond to us, for we have
too few good deeds; act toward us with justice tempered by
love, and bring us salvation.

Avinu Malkeynu chawneynu va'a-neinu ki ein banu ma'asim
Asey imanu tz'dakah va'chesed v'hoshi-eynu

Kaddish Shalem (Praise After Concluding the Amidah)

יִתְגַּדַּל וְיִתְקַדַּשׁ שְׁמֵהּ רַבָּא. בְּעָלְמָא דִּי בְרָא
כִרְעוּתֵהּ. וְיַמְלִיךְ מַלְכוּתֵהּ בְּחַיֵּיכוֹן וּבְיוֹמֵיכוֹן וּבְחַיֵּי
דְכָל בֵּית יִשְׂרָאֵל. בַּעֲגָלָא וּבִזְמַן קָרִיב וְאִמְרוּ. אָמֵן:

יְהֵא שְׁמֵהּ רַבָּא מְבָרַךְ לְעָלַם וּלְעָלְמֵי עָלְמַיָּא:

יִתְבָּרַךְ וְיִשְׁתַּבַּח וְיִתְפָּאַר וְיִתְרֹמַם וְיִתְנַשֵּׂא וְיִתְהַדָּר
וְיִתְעַלֶּה וְיִתְהַלָּל שְׁמֵהּ דְּקֻדְשָׁא. בְּרִיךְ הוּא. לְעֵלָּא
לְעֵלָּא מִן כָּל בִּרְכָתָא וְשִׁירָתָא תֻּשְׁבְּחָתָא וְנֶחֱמָתָא
דַּאֲמִירָן בְּעָלְמָא וְאִמְרוּ. אָמֵן:

תִּתְקַבֵּל צְלוֹתְהוֹן וּבָעוּתְהוֹן דְּכָל יִשְׂרָאֵל קֳדָם
אֲבוּהוֹן דִּי בִשְׁמַיָּא וְאִמְרוּ. אָמֵן:

יְהֵא שְׁלָמָא רַבָּא מִן שְׁמַיָּא וְחַיִּים עָלֵינוּ וְעַל כָּל
יִשְׂרָאֵל וְאִמְרוּ. אָמֵן:

עוֹשֶׂה שָׁלוֹם בִּמְרוֹמָיו הוּא יַעֲשֶׂה שָׁלוֹם עָלֵינוּ וְעַל
כָּל יִשְׂרָאֵל וְאִמְרוּ. אָמֵן:

May God's great name be praised and sanctified in the
world! May Your Rule be established in our lifetime and
the lifetime of the House of Israel. God's great name is
blessed and praised far beyond all blessings and praises we
can ever say in the world. May the praises and prayers of
all Israel be accepted in heaven before You. May there be a
great peace from heaven and life for us and all Israel. May
the One who makes peace in the high places, make peace
for us, for all Israel, and for all humanity. Amen.

TORAH SERVICE

אֵין כָּמוֹךָ בָאֱלֹהִים, אֲדֹנָי, וְאֵין כְּמַעֲשֶׂיךָ. מַלְכוּתְךָ
מַלְכוּת כָּל עֹלָמִים, וּמֶמְשַׁלְתְּךָ בְּכָל דֹּר וָדֹר. יְיָ מֶלֶךְ,
יְיָ מָלָךְ, יְיָ יִמְלֹךְ לְעוֹלָם וָעֶד. יְיָ עֹז לְעַמּוֹ יִתֵּן, יְיָ יְבָרֵךְ
אֶת עַמּוֹ בַשָּׁלוֹם.

אַב הָרַחֲמִים, הֵיטִיבָה בִרְצוֹנְךָ אֶת צִיּוֹן, תִּבְנֶה
חוֹמוֹת יְרוּשָׁלָיִם. כִּי בְךָ לְבַד בָּטָחְנוּ, מֶלֶךְ אֵל רָם
וְנִשָּׂא, אֲדוֹן עוֹלָמִים:

*Ayn kamocha va-elohim, Adonay, v'ayn k'ma-aseh-cha. Mal-
chut'cha malchut kol olamim, u-memshalt'cha b'chol dor
va'dor. Adonay melech, Adonay malach, Adonay yimloch
l'olam va-ed. Adonay oz l'amo yiteyn, Adonay y'varech et
amo va-shalom. Av ha-rachamim, hey-tiva vir'tzon'cha et
Tziyon: tivneh chomot Y'rushalayim. Ki v'cha l'vad batachnu,
melech El ram v'nissa, adon olamim.*

None is like You among the powers of the world,
No deeds compare to Yours.

>Your realm, O Majesty, is everlasting,
>Your rule extends to every generation.

Adonay is our Ruler, Adonay has been ruling,
Adonay will rule forever and ever.

Adonay gives strength to our people through Torah,
Through Torah Adonay has blessed us with peace.

Womb-gentle Father, do good in Zion:
Rebuild the walls in Jerusalem!

For You alone do we trust,
Sovereign God, high and exalted,
Power eternal.

(The ark is opened)

וַיְהִי בִּנְסֹעַ הָאָרֹן וַיֹּאמֶר מֹשֶׁה: קוּמָה יְיָ, וְיָפֻצוּ
אֹיְבֶיךָ, וְיָנֻסוּ מְשַׂנְאֶיךָ מִפָּנֶיךָ. כִּי מִצִּיּוֹן תֵּצֵא תוֹרָה,
וּדְבַר יְיָ מִירוּשָׁלָיִם. בָּרוּךְ שֶׁנָּתַן תּוֹרָה לְעַמּוֹ יִשְׂרָאֵל
בִּקְדֻשָּׁתוֹ.

When the ark began to move, Moses proclaimed: Arise,
Adonay, let Your enemies scatter, fleeing before You! For
one day from Zion Torah will go forth, and the word of
God from Jerusalem. Praised be the One who has shared
holiness with Israel in giving us the Torah.

*(The Thirteen Qualities of God are recited three times.
The passage is omitted on Shabbat)*

יְיָ יְיָ אֵל רַחוּם וְחַנּוּן אֶרֶךְ אַפַּיִם וְרַב חֶסֶד וֶאֱמֶת: נֹצֵר
חֶסֶד לָאֲלָפִים נֹשֵׂא עָוֹן וָפֶשַׁע וְחַטָּאָה וְנַקֵּה.

*Adonay, Adonay, El rachum v'chanun erech apayim v'rav
chesed ve-emet: notzer chesed la-alafim, nosey avon va-fesha
v'chata-ah v'nakey.*

Adonay, Adonay, God filled with mother love, slow to
anger, great in covenantal love and truth:
Keeping love for the thousands within the covenant, for-

giving perverse actions, rebelliousness, and the missing of the mark, and acquitting.

The Reader receives the Torah and the ark is closed

שְׁמַע יִשְׂרָאֵל יְיָ אֱלֹהֵינוּ יְיָ אֶחָד:

Shma Yisrael Adonay Eloheynu Adonay Echad:

Hear, O Israel, Adonay is our God, Adonay is One.

אֶחָד אֱלֹהֵינוּ גָּדוֹל אֲדוֹנֵינוּ קָדוֹשׁ וְנוֹרָא שְׁמוֹ:

Echad Eloheynu, Gadol Adoneynu, Kadosh v'Nora Shmo:

Our God is One, Adonay is One, with a holy and awesome name.

גַּדְּלוּ לַייָ אִתִּי. וּנְרוֹמְמָה שְׁמוֹ יַחְדָּו:

Gad'lu l'Adonay iti un'rom'ma shmo yachdav:

Magnify Adonay with me, and let us exalt the Name together.

Torah Procession

L'cha Adonay ha-g'dula v'ha-gvura v'hatiferet v'ha-netzach v'ha-hod, ki chol ba-shamayim uva-aretz l'cha Adonay ha-mamlacha v'hamitnasey l'chol l'rosh. Rom'mu Adonay Eloheynu v'hishtachavu la-hadom raglav kadosh hu. Rom'mu Adonay Eloheynu v'hishtachavu l'har kod'sho ki kadosh Adonay Eloheynu.

לְךָ יְיָ הַגְּדֻלָּה וְהַגְּבוּרָה וְהַתִּפְאֶרֶת וְהַנֵּצַח וְהַהוֹד. כִּי־כֹל בַּשָּׁמַיִם וּבָאָרֶץ לְךָ יְיָ הַמַּמְלָכָה וְהַמִּתְנַשֵּׂא לְכֹל לְרֹאשׁ. רוֹמְמוּ יְיָ אֱלֹהֵינוּ וְהִשְׁתַּחֲווּ לַהֲדֹם רַגְלָיו קָדוֹשׁ הוּא: רוֹמְמוּ יְיָ אֱלֹהֵינוּ וְהִשְׁתַּחֲווּ לְהַר קָדְשׁוֹ כִּי קָדוֹשׁ יְיָ אֱלֹהֵינוּ:

To You, Adonay, belong the greatness, the power, the glory, the everlasting victory, and the majesty, for to You

belongs everything in heaven and on earth, sovereignty
and the exaltation as head above all. Exalt Adonay our
God, and worship at the footstool of God, the holy One!
Exalt Adonay our God and worship at the holy mountain,
for Adonay our God is holy.

*(The Torah is placed on the reading desk. The Reader unrolls
it and, if individuals will be called to the Torah, says:)*

וְיַעֲזוֹר וְיָגֵן וְיוֹשִׁיעַ לְכָל הַחוֹסִים בּוֹ, וְנֹאמַר אָמֵן.
הַכֹּל הָבוּ גֹדֶל לֵאלֹהֵינוּ, וּתְנוּ כָבוֹד לַתּוֹרָה. (כֹּהֵן,
קְרָב;) יַעֲמֹד (תַּעֲמוֹד) . . . בָּרוּךְ שֶׁנָּתַן תּוֹרָה לְעַמּוֹ
יִשְׂרָאֵל בִּקְדֻשָׁתוֹ.

May God help, shield, and rescue all who trust in You,
Amen. Let everyone ascribe greatness to our God and
honor to the Torah. (*If appropriate,* Kohen, draw near.) I
call . . . Let us praise the One who in holiness has given the
Torah to the people Israel.

(All respond:)

וְאַתֶּם הַדְּבֵקִים בַּיְיָ אֱלֹהֵיכֶם, חַיִּים כֻּלְּכֶם הַיּוֹם.

*V-atem ha-d'vekim b'Adonay Eloheychem, chayim kul-chem
ha-yom.*

And you who have cleaved to Adonay your God are alive,
all of you, this day.

Blessings for the Reading of the Torah

Bar'chu et Adonay ham'vorach: בָּרְכוּ אֶת יְיָ הַמְבֹרָךְ:

בָּרוּךְ יְיָ הַמְבֹרָךְ לְעוֹלָם וָעֶד:
Baruch Adonay ham'vorach l'olam va-ed.

בָּרוּךְ אַתָּה יְיָ אֱלֹהֵינוּ מֶלֶךְ הָעוֹלָם אֲשֶׁר בָּחַר־בָּנוּ
מִכָּל הָעַמִּים וְנָתַן לָנוּ אֶת תּוֹרָתוֹ. בָּרוּךְ אַתָּה יְיָ נוֹתֵן
הַתּוֹרָה:

Baruch atta Adonay Eloheynu melech ha-olam,
asher bachar banu mikol ha-amim, v'natan lanu
et Torato. Baruch atta Adonay, noteyn ha-Torah.

(The Torah is read)

בָּרוּךְ אַתָּה יְיָ אֱלֹהֵינוּ מֶלֶךְ הָעוֹלָם אֲשֶׁר נָתַן לָנוּ
תּוֹרַת אֱמֶת וְחַיֵּי עוֹלָם נָטַע בְּתוֹכֵנוּ. בָּרוּךְ אַתָּה יְיָ
נוֹתֵן הַתּוֹרָה:

Baruch atta Adonay Eloheynu melech
ha-olam, asher natan lanu Torat emet,
v'chayey olam nata' b'tocheynu.
Baruch atta Adonay, noteyn ha-Torah.

You are praised forever, Adonay, ruler of the universe,
who has chosen us from among all peoples and given us
Your Torah. You gave us a Torah of truth and implanted
eternal life within us. You are praised, Adonay, who is giving us the Torah.

TORAH READINGS

TORAH READING FOR THE FIRST DAY (Genesis 21:1–21)

וַיהֹוָה פָּקַד אֶת־שָׂרָה כַּאֲשֶׁר אָמָר
וַיַּעַשׂ יהוה לְשָׂרָה כַּאֲשֶׁר דִּבֵּר: וַתַּהַר וַתֵּלֶד שָׂרָה לְאַבְרָהָם
בֵּן לִזְקֻנָיו לַמּוֹעֵד אֲשֶׁר־דִּבֶּר אֹתוֹ אֱלֹהִים: וַיִּקְרָא אַבְרָהָם
אֶת־שֶׁם־בְּנוֹ הַנּוֹלַד־לוֹ אֲשֶׁר־יָלְדָה־לוֹ שָׂרָה יִצְחָק: וַיָּמָל
אַבְרָהָם אֶת־יִצְחָק בְּנוֹ בֶּן־שְׁמֹנַת יָמִים כַּאֲשֶׁר צִוָּה אֹתוֹ
אֱלֹהִים: וְאַבְרָהָם בֶּן־מְאַת שָׁנָה בְּהִוָּלֶד לוֹ אֵת יִצְחָק בְּנוֹ:
וַתֹּאמֶר שָׂרָה צְחֹק עָשָׂה לִי אֱלֹהִים כָּל־הַשֹּׁמֵעַ יִצְחַק־לִי:

TORAH READING FOR THE FIRST DAY (Genesis 21:1–21)

Adonay took note of Sarah as promised, doing for Sarah
as had been said. Sarah became pregnant and bore to
Avraham a son in his old age, at the exact season which
God had told him. Avraham called the name of the boy
who had been born to him, whom Sarah bore him, Yitzchak ("the one who laughs"). Then Avraham circumcized
Yitzchak his son when he was eight days old, as God had
commanded him. Now Avraham was a hundred years old
when Yitzchak his son was born to him. And Sarah said:
God has made laughter (tzchok) for me; all who hear will
laugh at (or "laugh with") me. She said: "Who could have

וַתֹּאמֶר מִי מִלֵּל לְאַבְרָהָם הֵינִיקָה בָנִים שָׂרָה כִּי־יָלַדְתִּי בֵן
לִזְקֻנָיו: וַיִּגְדַּל הַיֶּלֶד וַיִּגָּמַל וַיַּעַשׂ אַבְרָהָם מִשְׁתֶּה גָדוֹל בְּיוֹם
הִגָּמֵל אֶת־יִצְחָק: וַתֵּרֶא שָׂרָה אֶת־בֶּן־הָגָר הַמִּצְרִית אֲשֶׁר־
יָלְדָה לְאַבְרָהָם מְצַחֵק: וַתֹּאמֶר לְאַבְרָהָם גָּרֵשׁ הָאָמָה הַזֹּאת
וְאֶת־בְּנָהּ כִּי לֹא יִירַשׁ בֶּן־הָאָמָה הַזֹּאת עִם־בְּנִי עִם־יִצְחָק:
וַיֵּרַע הַדָּבָר מְאֹד בְּעֵינֵי אַבְרָהָם עַל אוֹדֹת בְּנוֹ: וַיֹּאמֶר אֱלֹהִים
אֶל־אַבְרָהָם אַל־יֵרַע בְּעֵינֶיךָ עַל־הַנַּעַר וְעַל־אֲמָתֶךָ כֹּל אֲשֶׁר
תֹּאמַר אֵלֶיךָ שָׂרָה שְׁמַע בְּקֹלָהּ כִּי בְיִצְחָק יִקָּרֵא לְךָ זָרַע: וְגַם
אֶת־בֶּן־הָאָמָה לְגוֹי אֲשִׂימֶנּוּ כִּי זַרְעֲךָ הוּא: וַיַּשְׁכֵּם אַבְרָהָם ׀
בַּבֹּקֶר וַיִּקַּח־לֶחֶם וְחֵמַת מַיִם וַיִּתֵּן אֶל־הָגָר שָׂם עַל־שִׁכְמָהּ
וְאֶת־הַיֶּלֶד וַיְשַׁלְּחֶהָ וַתֵּלֶךְ וַתֵּתַע בְּמִדְבַּר בְּאֵר שָׁבַע: וַיִּכְלוּ
הַמַּיִם מִן־הַחֵמֶת וַתַּשְׁלֵךְ אֶת־הַיֶּלֶד תַּחַת אַחַד הַשִּׂיחִם: וַתֵּלֶךְ
וַתֵּשֶׁב לָהּ מִנֶּגֶד הַרְחֵק כִּמְטַחֲוֵי קֶשֶׁת כִּי אָמְרָה אַל־אֶרְאֶה
בְּמוֹת הַיָּלֶד וַתֵּשֶׁב מִנֶּגֶד וַתִּשָּׂא אֶת־קֹלָהּ וַתֵּבְךְּ: וַיִּשְׁמַע
אֱלֹהִים אֶת־קוֹל הַנַּעַר וַיִּקְרָא מַלְאַךְ אֱלֹהִים ׀ אֶל־הָגָר מִן־
הַשָּׁמַיִם וַיֹּאמֶר לָהּ מַה־לָּךְ הָגָר אַל־תִּירְאִי כִּי־שָׁמַע אֱלֹהִים
אֶל־קוֹל הַנַּעַר בַּאֲשֶׁר הוּא־שָׁם: קוּמִי שְׂאִי אֶת־הַנַּעַר וְהַחֲזִיקִי
אֶת־יָדֵךְ בּוֹ כִּי־לְגוֹי גָּדוֹל אֲשִׂימֶנּוּ: וַיִּפְקַח אֱלֹהִים אֶת־עֵינֶיהָ
וַתֵּרֶא בְּאֵר מָיִם וַתֵּלֶךְ וַתְּמַלֵּא אֶת־הַחֵמֶת מַיִם וַתַּשְׁקְ אֶת־
הַנָּעַר: וַיְהִי אֱלֹהִים אֶת־הַנַּעַר וַיִּגְדָּל וַיֵּשֶׁב בַּמִּדְבָּר וַיְהִי רֹבֶה
קַשָּׁת: וַיֵּשֶׁב

said to Avraham that Sarah would suckle children? For in his old age I have given birth to a son!" And the boy grew and was weaned, and Avraham made a great feast on the day Yitzchak was weaned.

But Sarah saw the son of Hagar the Egyptian—whom she had borne to Avraham—laughing mockingly (*m'tzachek*). And she said to Avraham: "Get rid of this servant and her son! The son of this servant shall not share in the inheritance along with my son, along with Yitzchak." The matter was very wrong in Avraham's eyes (or, "the matter distressed Avraham greatly") for it concerned his son. But God said to Avraham, "Let it not be wrong in your eyes (or, "Do not be distressed") concerning the lad and your servant; whatever Sarah says to you, hearken to her voice, for it is through Yitzchak that seed shall be named for you. As for the servant's son, I will make him into a nation too, for he is your seed."

And Avraham arose early in the morning, took bread and a skin of water and gave them to Hagar, putting them on her shoulder, and as he sent her away with the boy, she went wandering in the wilderness of Beer Sheva. When the water had been drained from the skin, she cast the child away under one of the bushes, and went off to sit down at a distance of a bowshot away, for she said, "I cannot watch the boy dying." And so she sat at a distance, lifted up her voice and wept.

Then God hearkened to the voice of the lad where he was, and a messenger of God called out to Hagar from heaven and said to her: "What is your plight, Hagar? Do not fear! For God has hearkened to the voice of the lad where he is. Arise, lift up the boy, and take him (or, "strengthen him") with your hand, for I shall make him a great nation." And God opened her eyes and she saw a well of water. She went to fill the skin with water, giving the lad some to drink.

And God was with the boy as he grew up, and he lived in the wilderness and became a bowman. He dwelt in the

בְּמִדְבַּר פָּארָן וַתִּקַח־לוֹ אִמּוֹ אִשָּׁה מֵאֶרֶץ מִצְרָיִם:

TORAH READING FOR THE SECOND DAY (Genesis 22:1—19)

וַיְהִי אַחַר הַדְּבָרִים הָאֵלֶּה וְהָאֱלֹהִים נִסָּה אֶת־אַבְרָהָם וַיֹּאמֶר
אֵלָיו אַבְרָהָם וַיֹּאמֶר הִנֵּנִי: וַיֹּאמֶר קַח־נָא אֶת־בִּנְךָ אֶת־
יְחִידְךָ אֲשֶׁר־אָהַבְתָּ אֶת־יִצְחָק וְלֶךְ־לְךָ אֶל־אֶרֶץ הַמֹּרִיָּה
וְהַעֲלֵהוּ שָׁם לְעֹלָה עַל אַחַד הֶהָרִים אֲשֶׁר אֹמַר אֵלֶיךָ: וַיַּשְׁכֵּם
אַבְרָהָם בַּבֹּקֶר וַיַּחֲבֹשׁ אֶת־חֲמֹרוֹ וַיִּקַּח אֶת־שְׁנֵי נְעָרָיו אִתּוֹ
וְאֵת יִצְחָק בְּנוֹ וַיְבַקַּע עֲצֵי עֹלָה וַיָּקָם וַיֵּלֶךְ אֶל־הַמָּקוֹם אֲשֶׁר־
אָמַר־לוֹ הָאֱלֹהִים: בַּיּוֹם הַשְּׁלִישִׁי וַיִּשָּׂא אַבְרָהָם אֶת־עֵינָיו
וַיַּרְא אֶת־הַמָּקוֹם מֵרָחֹק: וַיֹּאמֶר אַבְרָהָם אֶל־נְעָרָיו שְׁבוּ־לָכֶם
פֹּה עִם־הַחֲמוֹר וַאֲנִי וְהַנַּעַר נֵלְכָה עַד־כֹּה וְנִשְׁתַּחֲוֶה וְנָשׁוּבָה
אֲלֵיכֶם: וַיִּקַּח אַבְרָהָם אֶת־עֲצֵי הָעֹלָה וַיָּשֶׂם עַל־יִצְחָק בְּנוֹ
וַיִּקַּח בְּיָדוֹ אֶת־הָאֵשׁ וְאֶת־הַמַּאֲכֶלֶת וַיֵּלְכוּ שְׁנֵיהֶם יַחְדָּו:
וַיֹּאמֶר יִצְחָק אֶל־אַבְרָהָם אָבִיו וַיֹּאמֶר אָבִי וַיֹּאמֶר הִנֶּנִּי בְנִי
וַיֹּאמֶר הִנֵּה הָאֵשׁ וְהָעֵצִים וְאַיֵּה הַשֶּׂה לְעֹלָה: וַיֹּאמֶר אַבְרָהָם
אֱלֹהִים יִרְאֶה־לּוֹ הַשֶּׂה לְעֹלָה בְּנִי וַיֵּלְכוּ שְׁנֵיהֶם יַחְדָּו: וַיָּבֹאוּ
אֶל־הַמָּקוֹם אֲשֶׁר אָמַר־לוֹ הָאֱלֹהִים וַיִּבֶן שָׁם אַבְרָהָם אֶת־
הַמִּזְבֵּחַ וַיַּעֲרֹךְ אֶת־הָעֵצִים וַיַּעֲקֹד אֶת־יִצְחָק בְּנוֹ וַיָּשֶׂם אֹתוֹ
עַל־הַמִּזְבֵּחַ מִמַּעַל לָעֵצִים: וַיִּשְׁלַח אַבְרָהָם אֶת־יָדוֹ וַיִּקַּח
אֶת־הַמַּאֲכֶלֶת לִשְׁחֹט אֶת־בְּנוֹ: וַיִּקְרָא אֵלָיו מַלְאַךְ יהוה
מִן־הַשָּׁמַיִם וַיֹּאמֶר אַבְרָהָם। אַבְרָהָם וַיֹּאמֶר הִנֵּנִי:

wilderness of Paran and his mother acquired a wife for him from the land of Egypt.

TORAH READING FOR THE SECOND DAY (Genesis 22:1—19)

After these things God put Avraham to a test to prove him, saying to him, "Avraham!" He replied, "Here I am." Then God said, "Please take your son, your only one, whom you love, Yitzchak, and get yourself into the land of Moriah, and offer him up as a burnt offering there (or, "bring him up there for a going-up") on one of the mountains of which I will tell you."

So Avraham arose early in the morning, saddled his own donkey, and took two servants (or, "two of his servants") with him, and Yitzchak his son as well. He split wood for the burnt-offering and he rose up to go to the place which God had told him. On the third day Avraham lifted up his eyes and saw the place from afar. Then Avraham said to his servants, "Stay here with the donkey while I and the lad go over there; after we have bowed down in worship we shall return to you."

Then Avraham took the wood for the burnt-offering, putting it on Yitzchak his son and he took the fire and the knife in his hand, and the two of them walked together. Yitzchak said to Avraham his father: "My father." And he said, "Here I am, my son." And he said, "Here is the fire and the wood, but where is the sheep for the burnt-offering?" And Avraham said, "God will see to the sheep for the burnt-offering, my son," and the two of them walked together.

When they came to the place of which God had told him, Avraham built the altar there and arranged the wood and bound Yitzchak his son, placing him upon the altar on top of the wood. But just as Avraham was stretching out his hand for the knife to slay his son, there called to him a messenger of God from heaven, who said: "Avraham! Avraham!" And he said, "Here I am!"

וַיֹּאמֶר אַל־

תִּשְׁלַח יָדְךָ אֶל־הַנַּעַר וְאַל־תַּעַשׂ לוֹ מְאוּמָה כִּי עַתָּה יָדַעְתִּי
כִּי־יְרֵא אֱלֹהִים אַתָּה וְלֹא חָשַׂכְתָּ אֶת־בִּנְךָ אֶת־יְחִידְךָ מִמֶּנִּי:
וַיִּשָּׂא אַבְרָהָם אֶת־עֵינָיו וַיַּרְא וְהִנֵּה־אַיִל אַחַר נֶאֱחַז בַּסְּבַךְ
בְּקַרְנָיו וַיֵּלֶךְ אַבְרָהָם וַיִּקַּח אֶת־הָאַיִל וַיַּעֲלֵהוּ לְעֹלָה תַּחַת
בְּנוֹ: וַיִּקְרָא אַבְרָהָם שֵׁם־הַמָּקוֹם הַהוּא יְהוָה יִרְאֶה אֲשֶׁר
יֵאָמֵר הַיּוֹם בְּהַר יְהוָה יֵרָאֶה: וַיִּקְרָא מַלְאַךְ יְהוָה אֶל־אַבְרָהָם
שֵׁנִית מִן־הַשָּׁמָיִם: וַיֹּאמֶר בִּי נִשְׁבַּעְתִּי נְאֻם־יְהוָה כִּי יַעַן אֲשֶׁר
עָשִׂיתָ אֶת־הַדָּבָר הַזֶּה וְלֹא חָשַׂכְתָּ אֶת־בִּנְךָ אֶת־יְחִידֶךָ: כִּי־
בָרֵךְ אֲבָרֶכְךָ וְהַרְבָּה אַרְבֶּה אֶת־זַרְעֲךָ כְּכוֹכְבֵי הַשָּׁמַיִם וְכַחוֹל
אֲשֶׁר עַל־שְׂפַת הַיָּם וְיִרַשׁ זַרְעֲךָ אֵת שַׁעַר אֹיְבָיו: וְהִתְבָּרְכוּ
בְזַרְעֲךָ כֹּל גּוֹיֵי הָאָרֶץ עֵקֶב אֲשֶׁר שָׁמַעְתָּ בְּקֹלִי: וַיָּשָׁב אַבְרָהָם
אֶל־נְעָרָיו וַיָּקֻמוּ וַיֵּלְכוּ יַחְדָּו אֶל־בְּאֵר שָׁבַע וַיֵּשֶׁב אַבְרָהָם
בִּבְאֵר שָׁבַע:

And he said, "Do not stretch out your hand against the lad; don't do anything to him! For now I know (or, "have proven") that you are in awe of God (or, "that you fear God," or, "that you believe in God"), for you have not withheld your son, your only one, from me." And Avraham lifted up his eyes and saw a ram behind him, caught in the thicket by its horns, and Avraham went to take the ram and offered it up as a burnt-offering in place of his son. And Avraham called the name of that place "Adonay-yireh," which is why it is said even today, "On the mount of Adonay (things) can be seen."

Then the messenger of Adonay called to Avraham from heaven a second time and said, "'By my own self I swear,' said Adonay, 'because you performed this act and did not withhold your son, your only one, I shall bestow blessing upon you and multiply your seed greatly, like the stars of heaven and the sand on the shore of the sea, and your seed shall inherit the gate of their enemies. All the nations of the earth shall bless themselves by your seed (or, "using the example of your seed"), because you have hearkened to My voice."

And Avraham returned to his servants and they arose to walk together to Beer Sheva. And Avraham dwelt in Beer Sheva.

Reader's Kaddish

יִתְגַּדַּל וְיִתְקַדַּשׁ שְׁמֵהּ רַבָּא. בְּעָלְמָא דִּי בְרָא
כִרְעוּתֵהּ. וְיַמְלִיךְ מַלְכוּתֵהּ בְּחַיֵּיכוֹן וּבְיוֹמֵיכוֹן וּבְחַיֵּי
דְכָל בֵּית יִשְׂרָאֵל. בַּעֲגָלָא וּבִזְמַן קָרִיב וְאִמְרוּ. אָמֵן:

יְהֵא שְׁמֵהּ רַבָּא מְבָרַךְ לְעָלַם וּלְעָלְמֵי עָלְמַיָּא:

יִתְבָּרַךְ וְיִשְׁתַּבַּח וְיִתְפָּאַר וְיִתְרוֹמַם וְיִתְנַשֵּׂא וְיִתְהַדָּר
וְיִתְעַלֶּה וְיִתְהַלָּל שְׁמֵהּ דְּקֻדְשָׁא. בְּרִיךְ הוּא. לְעֵלָּא
לְעֵלָּא מִן כָּל בִּרְכָתָא וְשִׁירָתָא תֻּשְׁבְּחָתָא וְנֶחֱמָתָא
דַּאֲמִירָן בְּעָלְמָא וְאִמְרוּ. אָמֵן:

May God's great name be magnified and sanctified in the world created according to the holy will, and may God's rule be known in your lifetime, in your own days, and in the life of the house of Israel, speedily, in a time close at hand.

May the name of the blessed Holy One be praised and extolled far beyond all praises and blessings we can ever say in the world. Amen.

(When the Torah is raised, all rise and proclaim:)

וְזֹאת הַתּוֹרָה אֲשֶׁר שָׂם מֹשֶׁה לִפְנֵי בְּנֵי יִשְׂרָאֵל, עַל פִּי
יְיָ בְּיַד מֹשֶׁה.

V'zot ha-Torah asher sam Moshe lifney b'ney Yisrael al pi Adonay, b'yad Moshe.

This is the Torah which Moses placed before the children of Israel at the command of Adonay, through Moses.

(If there is a second scroll, it is now placed on the reading table.)

MAFTIR READING FROM THE SECOND SCROLL
(Numbers 29:1-6)

וּבַחֹ֨דֶשׁ הַשְּׁבִיעִ֜י בְּאֶחָ֣ד לַחֹ֗דֶשׁ מִקְרָא־קֹ֨דֶשׁ֙ יִהְיֶ֣ה לָכֶ֔ם כָּל־
מְלֶ֥אכֶת עֲבֹדָ֖ה לֹ֣א תַעֲשׂ֑וּ י֥וֹם תְּרוּעָ֖ה יִהְיֶ֥ה לָכֶֽם: וַעֲשִׂיתֶ֨ם
עֹלָ֜ה לְרֵ֤יחַ נִיחֹ֨חַ֙ לַֽיהוָ֔ה פַּ֧ר בֶּן־בָּקָ֛ר אֶחָ֖ד אַ֣יִל אֶחָ֑ד כְּבָשִׂ֧ים
בְּנֵי־שָׁנָ֛ה שִׁבְעָ֖ה תְּמִימִֽם: וּמִנְחָתָ֗ם סֹ֤לֶת בְּלוּלָ֣ה בַשֶּׁ֔מֶן שְׁלֹשָׁ֣ה
עֶשְׂרֹנִ֞ים לַפָּ֗ר שְׁנֵ֤י עֶשְׂרֹנִים֙ לָאָ֔יִל: וְעִשָּׂר֣וֹן אֶחָ֔ד לַכֶּ֖בֶשׂ הָאֶחָ֑ד
לְשִׁבְעַ֖ת הַכְּבָשִֽׂים: וּשְׂעִיר־עִזִּ֥ים אֶחָ֖ד חַטָּ֑את לְכַפֵּ֖ר עֲלֵיכֶֽם:
מִלְּבַד֩ עֹלַ֨ת הַחֹ֜דֶשׁ וּמִנְחָתָ֗הּ וְעֹלַ֤ת הַתָּמִיד֙ וּמִנְחָתָ֔הּ וְנִסְכֵּיהֶ֖ם
כְּמִשְׁפָּטָ֑ם לְרֵ֣יחַ נִיחֹ֔חַ אִשֶּׁ֖ה לַֽיהוָֽה:

In the seventh month, on the first day of the month, there
shall be a holy convocation for you; you shall not do any
weekday work. It will be for you a day when *t'ruah* is
sounded on the shofar. You shall present a burnt offering
with a pleasing aroma to Adonay: one bullock of the herd,
one ram, and seven yearling lambs, all unblemished. The
meal offering accompanying them—choice flour mixed
with oil—shall be: three-tenths of a measure for the bullock, two-tenths for the ram, and one-tenth for each of the
seven lambs. And there shall be one goat for a sin offering,
to make expiation in your behalf—in addition to the burnt
offering of the new moon with its meal offering and the
regular daily burnt offering with its meal offering, each
with its libation as prescribed, offerings by fire with a
pleasing aroma to Adonay.

(V'zot ha-Torah *is chanted again when the second scroll is
raised.*)

READING OF THE HAFTARAH

Blessing Preceding the Haftarah

בָּרוּךְ אַתָּה יְיָ אֱלֹהֵינוּ מֶלֶךְ הָעוֹלָם אֲשֶׁר בָּחַר
בִּנְבִיאִים טוֹבִים וְרָצָה בְדִבְרֵיהֶם הַנֶּאֱמָרִים בֶּאֱמֶת
בָּרוּךְ אַתָּה יְיָ הַבּוֹחֵר בַּתּוֹרָה וּבְמשֶׁה עַבְדּוֹ וּבְיִשְׂרָאֵל
עַמּוֹ וּבִנְבִיאֵי הָאֱמֶת וָצֶדֶק.

HAFTARAH FOR THE FIRST DAY (I Samuel 1:1—2:10)

וַיְהִי אִישׁ אֶחָד מִן־הָרָמָתַיִם צוֹפִים מֵהַר אֶפְרָיִם וּשְׁמוֹ אֶלְקָנָה
בֶּן־יְרֹחָם בֶּן־אֱלִיהוּא בֶּן־תֹּחוּ בֶן־צוּף אֶפְרָתִי: וְלוֹ שְׁתֵּי נָשִׁים
שֵׁם אַחַת חַנָּה וְשֵׁם הַשֵּׁנִית פְּנִנָּה וַיְהִי לִפְנִנָּה יְלָדִים וּלְחַנָּה
אֵין יְלָדִים: וְעָלָה הָאִישׁ הַהוּא מֵעִירוֹ מִיָּמִים ׀ יָמִימָה
לְהִשְׁתַּחֲוֹת וְלִזְבֹּחַ לַיהוָה צְבָאוֹת בְּשִׁלֹה וְשָׁם שְׁנֵי בְנֵי־עֵלִי
חָפְנִי וּפִנְחָס כֹּהֲנִים לַיהוָה: וַיְהִי הַיּוֹם וַיִּזְבַּח אֶלְקָנָה וְנָתַן
לִפְנִנָּה אִשְׁתּוֹ וּלְכָל־בָּנֶיהָ וּבְנוֹתֶיהָ מָנוֹת: וּלְחַנָּה יִתֵּן מָנָה
אַחַת אַפָּיִם כִּי אֶת־חַנָּה אָהֵב וַיהוָה סָגַר רַחְמָהּ: וְכִעֲסַתָּה
צָרָתָהּ גַּם־כַּעַס בַּעֲבוּר הַרְּעִמָהּ כִּי־סָגַר יְהוָה בְּעַד רַחְמָהּ:
וְכֵן יַעֲשֶׂה שָׁנָה בְשָׁנָה מִדֵּי עֲלֹתָהּ בְּבֵית יְהוָה כֵּן תַּכְעִסֶנָּה
וַתִּבְכֶּה וְלֹא תֹאכַל:

READING OF THE HAFTARAH

Blessing Preceding the Haftarah

You are praised, Adonay our God, Sovereign of the world, who has chosen good prophets, finding favor in their words which faithfully reflect Your truth. You are praised, Adonay, who has chosen Moses your servant, Israel Your people, and prophets who have spoken truth and justice.

HAFTARAH FOR THE FIRST DAY (I Samuel 1:1–2:10)

There was a man from Ramatayim-Zophim, from the hills of Ephraim, whose name was Elkanah, Yerocham's son, who was Elihu's son, who was Tochu's son, who was the son of Zuph of Ephrat. He had two wives, one named Chana (whose name means "graceful one"), and the other Penina (whose name means "pearl"). Penina had children, but Chana had no children. Now this man used to go up regularly to worship and make his offerings to Adonay of Hosts at Shilo where the two sons of Eli, Chofni and Pinchas, were kohanim with God. On a particular day after Elkanah had made his offerings, he gave portions to his wife Penina and all her sons and daughters, and to Chana he gave a special portion to cheer her up (translation by Rashi, the medieval Jewish commentator), for he loved Chana and God had closed her womb. Her rival used to provoke her to great anger to make her fretful because God had closed up her womb. This would happen every year. Whenever she went up to the house of God the other woman would get her angry, and she would cry so hard she could not eat.

וַיֹּאמֶר לָהּ אֶלְקָנָה אִישָׁהּ חַנָּה לָמֶה
תִבְכִּי וְלָמֶה לֹא תֹאכְלִי וְלָמֶה יֵרַע לְבָבֵךְ הֲלוֹא אָנֹכִי טוֹב
לָךְ מֵעֲשָׂרָה בָּנִים: וַתָּקָם חַנָּה אַחֲרֵי אָכְלָה בְשִׁלֹה וְאַחֲרֵי
שָׁתֹה וְעֵלִי הַכֹּהֵן יֹשֵׁב עַל־הַכִּסֵּא עַל־מְזוּזַת הֵיכַל יְהוָֹה: וְהִיא
מָרַת נָפֶשׁ וַתִּתְפַּלֵּל עַל־יְהוָֹה וּבָכֹה תִבְכֶּה: וַתִּדֹּר נֶדֶר וַתֹּאמַר
יְהוָֹה צְבָאוֹת אִס־רָאֹה תִרְאֶה ׀ בָּעֳנִי אֲמָתֶךָ וּזְכַרְתַּנִי וְלֹא־
תִשְׁכַּח אֶת־אֲמָתֶךָ וְנָתַתָּה לַאֲמָתְךָ זֶרַע אֲנָשִׁים וּנְתַתִּיו
לַיהוָֹה כָּל־יְמֵי חַיָּיו וּמוֹרָה לֹא־יַעֲלֶה עַל־רֹאשׁוֹ: וְהָיָה כִּי
הִרְבְּתָה לְהִתְפַּלֵּל לִפְנֵי יְהוָֹה וְעֵלִי שֹׁמֵר אֶת־פִּיהָ: וְחַנָּה הִיא
מְדַבֶּרֶת עַל־לִבָּהּ רַק שְׂפָתֶיהָ נָּעוֹת וְקוֹלָהּ לֹא יִשָּׁמֵעַ וַיַּחְשְׁבֶהָ
עֵלִי לְשִׁכֹּרָה: וַיֹּאמֶר אֵלֶיהָ עֵלִי עַד־מָתַי תִּשְׁתַּכָּרִין הָסִירִי
אֶת־יֵינֵךְ מֵעָלָיִךְ: וַתַּעַן חַנָּה וַתֹּאמֶר לֹא אֲדֹנִי אִשָּׁה קְשַׁת־
רוּחַ אָנֹכִי וְיַיִן וְשֵׁכָר לֹא שָׁתִיתִי וָאֶשְׁפֹּךְ אֶת־נַפְשִׁי לִפְנֵי יְהוָֹה:
אַל־תִּתֵּן אֶת־אֲמָתְךָ לִפְנֵי בַּת־בְּלִיָּעַל כִּי־מֵרֹב שִׂיחִי וְכַעְסִי
דִּבַּרְתִּי עַד־הֵנָּה: וַיַּעַן עֵלִי וַיֹּאמֶר לְכִי לְשָׁלוֹם וֵאלֹהֵי יִשְׂרָאֵל
יִתֵּן אֶת־שֵׁלָתֵךְ אֲשֶׁר שָׁאַלְתְּ מֵעִמּוֹ: וַתֹּאמֶר תִּמְצָא שִׁפְחָתְךָ
חֵן בְּעֵינֶיךָ וַתֵּלֶךְ הָאִשָּׁה לְדַרְכָּהּ וַתֹּאכַל וּפָנֶיהָ לֹא־הָיוּ־לָהּ
עוֹד: וַיַּשְׁכִּמוּ בַבֹּקֶר וַיִּשְׁתַּחֲווּ לִפְנֵי יְהוָֹה וַיָּשֻׁבוּ וַיָּבֹאוּ אֶל־
בֵּיתָם הָרָמָתָה וַיֵּדַע אֶלְקָנָה אֶת־חַנָּה אִשְׁתּוֹ וַיִּזְכְּרֶהָ יְהוָֹה:
וַיְהִי לִתְקֻפוֹת הַיָּמִים וַתַּהַר חַנָּה וַתֵּלֶד בֵּן וַתִּקְרָא אֶת־שְׁמוֹ
שְׁמוּאֵל כִּי מֵיהוָֹה שְׁאִלְתִּיו: וַיַּעַל הָאִישׁ אֶלְקָנָה וְכָל־בֵּיתוֹ
לִזְבֹּחַ לַיהוָֹה אֶת־זֶבַח הַיָּמִים וְאֶת־נִדְרוֹ:

And Elkanah said to his wife Chana, "Why are you crying so hard you cannot eat? Why is your heart distressed? Am I not better to you than ten children?"

But after the eating and drinking at Shilo, Chana arose while Eli was still sitting in his chair at the doorpost of the temple of God. Out of her bitter spirit she prayed before God, weeping all the while. Then she vowed a vow: "Adonay of Hosts, if You will cast Your glance upon the affliction of Your servant, if You will take notice of me and not forget Your servant and grant me a male child, then I will grant him to God all the days of his life, and a razor will never go upon his head."

Because she was praying before God a long time, Eli began to observe her mouth, and since Chana was uttering what was (weighing) on her heart, only her lips were moving, but her voice was not to be heard, and Eli thought she was intoxicated. And so Eli said to her: "How long will you stay intoxicated? Get rid of your wine!" But Chana replied, "No, sir, I am a woman who has been having a hard time. I have drunk neither wine nor liquor. I am pouring out my soul before God. Do not consider your servant a worthless woman, for it is out of anguish and lament that I have been speaking thus far." And Eli replied, "Go in peace, for the God of Israel will grant your request which you have petitioned." And saying, "May your servant find favor (*cheyn*) in your eyes," the woman went on her way, and her face was anguished (Rashi) no more.

They arose early in the morning and after worshipping before God they went back home to Ramah, where Elkanah knew Chana intimately, and Adonay took note of her. When the days of the year had finished their circuit Chana became pregnant and bore a son, whose name she called Shmuel, for "I have petitioned Adonay for him (*sh'iltiv*)."

Then Elkanah the husband and all his household went up to make the year's offering to God and to fulfill his vow.

וְחַנָּה לֹא עָלָתָה כִּי־
אָמְרָה לְאִישָׁהּ עַד יִגָּמֵל הַנַּעַר וַהֲבִאֹתִיו וְנִרְאָה אֶת־פְּנֵי יְהוָה
וְיָשַׁב שָׁם עַד־עוֹלָם: וַיֹּאמֶר לָהּ אֶלְקָנָה אִישָׁהּ עֲשִׂי הַטּוֹב
בְּעֵינַיִךְ שְׁבִי עַד־גָּמְלֵךְ אֹתוֹ אַךְ יָקֵם יְהוָה אֶת־דְּבָרוֹ וַתֵּשֶׁב
הָאִשָּׁה וַתֵּינֶק אֶת־בְּנָהּ עַד־גָּמְלָהּ אֹתוֹ: וַתַּעֲלֵהוּ עִמָּהּ כַּאֲשֶׁר
גְמָלַתּוּ בְּפָרִים שְׁלֹשָׁה וְאֵיפָה אַחַת קֶמַח וְנֵבֶל יַיִן וַתְּבִאֵהוּ
בֵית־יְהוָה שִׁלוֹ וְהַנַּעַר נָעַר: וַיִּשְׁחֲטוּ אֶת־הַפָּר וַיָּבִאוּ אֶת־
הַנַּעַר אֶל־עֵלִי: וַתֹּאמֶר בִּי אֲדֹנִי חֵי נַפְשְׁךָ אֲדֹנִי אֲנִי הָאִשָּׁה
הַנִּצֶּבֶת עִמְּכָה בָּזֶה לְהִתְפַּלֵּל אֶל־יְהוָה: אֶל־הַנַּעַר הַזֶּה
הִתְפַּלָּלְתִּי וַיִּתֵּן יְהוָה לִי אֶת־שְׁאֵלָתִי אֲשֶׁר שָׁאַלְתִּי מֵעִמּוֹ:
וְגַם אָנֹכִי הִשְׁאִלְתִּיהוּ לַיהוָה כָּל־הַיָּמִים אֲשֶׁר הָיָה הוּא שָׁאוּל
לַיהוָה וַיִּשְׁתַּחוּ שָׁם לַיהוָה: וַתִּתְפַּלֵּל חַנָּה
וַתֹּאמַר עָלַץ לִבִּי בַּיהוָה רָמָה קַרְנִי בַּיהוָה רָחַב פִּי עַל־אוֹיְבַי
כִּי שָׂמַחְתִּי בִּישׁוּעָתֶךָ: אֵין־קָדוֹשׁ כַּיהוָה כִּי־אֵין בִּלְתֶּךָ וְאֵין
צוּר כֵּאלֹהֵינוּ: אַל־תַּרְבּוּ תְדַבְּרוּ גְּבֹהָה גְבֹהָה יֵצֵא עָתָק
מִפִּיכֶם כִּי אֵל דֵּעוֹת יְהוָה וְלֹא נִתְכְּנוּ עֲלִלוֹת: קֶשֶׁת גִּבֹּרִים
חַתִּים וְנִכְשָׁלִים אָזְרוּ חָיִל: שְׂבֵעִים בַּלֶּחֶם נִשְׂכָּרוּ וּרְעֵבִים חָדֵלּוּ
עַד־עֲקָרָה יָלְדָה שִׁבְעָה וְרַבַּת בָּנִים אֻמְלָלָה: יְהוָה מֵמִית
וּמְחַיֶּה מוֹרִיד שְׁאוֹל וַיָּעַל:

But Chana did not go up, for she said to her husband,
"When the lad is weaned I shall bring him to appear before
Adonay, for then he must stay there forever." Elkanah
said to his wife, "Do what is good in your eyes; stay until
you have weaned him, but let Adonay fulfill the divine
plan." And the wife remained and nursed her son until she
had weaned him. After the weaning she brought him up
with her, along with three bullocks, an ephah of flour and a
flask of wine, and she brought him into the House of
Adonay at Shilo, while the boy was very young. When the
bullock had been slain and the boy was brought to Eli, she
said, "O sir, by your life, sir, I am the woman who was
standing with you in this place to pray to Adonay. I was
praying for this lad, and Adonay granted me my petition
which I had petitioned. And now I grant him (*hishiltiv*) to
Adonay all the days that he lives; he is a grant to Adonay."
And she bowed low in worship there to Adonay.

And Chana prayed:
Because of God, my heart exults,
Because of God my self-respect has been restored,
My mouth can open wide before my adversaries
For in the victory You have given me I have found great
    joy.
There is none holy as God, there is none beside You,
There is no Rock as sure as our God.
Do not speak with pride and haughtiness,
Let no arrogance stalk from your mouth,
For God is the power over knowledge,
By the divine are actions measured.
The bows of mighty men are beaten into pieces,
While those who stumble are girded with strength.
Those once sated, hire themselves out for bread,
While those who were ravenous have ceased to want.
The barren woman has borne seven,
While the one with many children is desolate.
Adonay brings both death and life,
Escorting us to the grave and raising us from it.

יהוה מוריש וּמַעֲשִׁיר מַשְׁפִּיל
אַף־מְרוֹמֵם: מֵקִים מֵעָפָר דָּל מֵאַשְׁפֹּת יָרִים אֶבְיוֹן לְהוֹשִׁיב
עִם־נְדִיבִים וְכִסֵּא כָבוֹד יַנְחִלֵם כִּי לַיהוָה מְצֻקֵי אֶרֶץ וַיָּשֶׁת
עֲלֵיהֶם תֵּבֵל: רַגְלֵי חֲסִידָו יִשְׁמֹר וּרְשָׁעִים בַּחֹשֶׁךְ יִדָּמּוּ כִּי־לֹא
בְכֹחַ יִגְבַּר־אִישׁ: יְהוָה יֵחַתּוּ מְרִיבָו עָלָו בַּשָּׁמַיִם יַרְעֵם יְהוָה
יָדִין אַפְסֵי־אָרֶץ וְיִתֶּן־עֹז לְמַלְכּוֹ וְיָרֵם קֶרֶן מְשִׁיחוֹ:

HAFTARAH FOR THE SECOND DAY
(Jeremiah 31:1–20)

כֹּה אָמַר יְהוָה מָצָא חֵן בַּמִּדְבָּר עַם
שְׂרִידֵי חֶרֶב הָלוֹךְ לְהַרְגִּיעוֹ יִשְׂרָאֵל: מֵרָחוֹק יְהוָה נִרְאָה לִי
וְאַהֲבַת עוֹלָם אֲהַבְתִּיךְ עַל־כֵּן מְשַׁכְתִּיךְ חָסֶד: עוֹד אֶבְנֵךְ
וְנִבְנֵית בְּתוּלַת יִשְׂרָאֵל עוֹד תַּעְדִּי תֻפַּיִךְ וְיָצָאת בִּמְחוֹל
מְשַׂחֲקִים: עוֹד תִּטְּעִי כְרָמִים בְּהָרֵי שֹׁמְרוֹן נָטְעוּ נֹטְעִים
וְחִלֵּלוּ: כִּי יֶשׁ־יוֹם קָרְאוּ נֹצְרִים בְּהַר אֶפְרָיִם קוּמוּ וְנַעֲלֶה צִיּוֹן
אֶל־יְהוָה אֱלֹהֵינוּ:   כִּי־כֹה ׀ אָמַר יְהוָה רָנּוּ
לְיַעֲקֹב שִׂמְחָה וְצַהֲלוּ בְּרֹאשׁ הַגּוֹיִם הַשְׁמִיעוּ הַלְלוּ וְאִמְרוּ
הוֹשַׁע יְהוָה אֶת־עַמְּךָ אֵת שְׁאֵרִית יִשְׂרָאֵל: הִנְנִי

Adonay brings both poverty and riches,
Casting us into humiliation and exalting us on the heights,
Helping poor people stand up out of the dust,
Raising up the needy from the trash heap,
To take their place with princes
And inherit the seat of honor.
For the pillars of the earth belong to God,
Who has set the world upon them.
God guards the steps of those who keep the covenant,
But the wicked shall be silenced into darkness,
For no one shall prevail through strength.
Those who strive against God shall be beaten into pieces,
Adonay will thunder against them in heaven.
God's judgment will prevail to the ends of the earth,
Granting strength only to a ruler divinely selected,
Raising up the person divinely anointed
To receive the honor of all the world.

(Blessings completing the reading of the Haftarah are found on page 134)

HAFTARAH FOR THE SECOND DAY
(Jeremiah 31:1–20)

So speaks Adonay: The people who has survived the sword has found grace (*chen*) in the wilderness on Israel's way to seek repose. From that far time Adonay appeared: "An eternal love (*ahavat olam*) I loved you, and so I have drawn you to Me in a covenant of love. I shall build you up again and you shall be rebuilt, O damsel Israel! Again you shall dress up with timbrel drums (*tof*) and go forth to join the playful dance! Again you shall plant vineyards on Samaria's hillsides, and having planted, the planters shall eat of their fruit. For there will be a day when those who stand guard on the hills of Ephraim shall call out: "Arise! Let us go up to Zion, to Adonay our God!"

So speaks Adonay: "Sing joyously for Jacob, shout from the heights of the nations, proclaim in exultation: 'Save Your people, Adonay, the remnant of Israel!' Here I am,

מֵבִיא אוֹתָם

מֵאֶרֶץ צָפוֹן וְקִבַּצְתִּים מִיַּרְכְּתֵי־אָרֶץ בָּם עִוֵּר וּפִסֵּחַ הָרָה

וְיֹלֶדֶת יַחְדָּו קָהָל גָּדוֹל יָשׁוּבוּ הֵנָּה: בִּבְכִי יָבֹאוּ וּבְתַחֲנוּנִים

אוֹבִילֵם אוֹלִיכֵם אֶל־נַחֲלֵי מַיִם בְּדֶרֶךְ יָשָׁר לֹא יִכָּשְׁלוּ בָּהּ כִּי־

הָיִיתִי לְיִשְׂרָאֵל לְאָב וְאֶפְרַיִם בְּכֹרִי הוּא: שִׁמְעוּ

דְבַר־יְהוָֹה גּוֹיִם וְהַגִּידוּ בָאִיִּים מִמֶּרְחָק וְאִמְרוּ מְזָרֵה יִשְׂרָאֵל

יְקַבְּצֶנּוּ וּשְׁמָרוֹ כְּרֹעֶה עֶדְרוֹ: כִּי־פָדָה יְהוָֹה אֶת־יַעֲקֹב וּגְאָלוֹ

מִיַּד חָזָק מִמֶּנּוּ: וּבָאוּ וְרִנְּנוּ בִמְרוֹם־צִיּוֹן וְנָהֲרוּ אֶל־טוּב יְהוָֹה

עַל־דָּגָן וְעַל־תִּירֹשׁ וְעַל־יִצְהָר וְעַל־בְּנֵי־צֹאן וּבָקָר וְהָיְתָה

נַפְשָׁם כְּגַן רָוֶה וְלֹא־יוֹסִיפוּ לְדַאֲבָה עוֹד: אָז תִּשְׂמַח בְּתוּלָה

בְּמָחוֹל וּבַחֻרִים וּזְקֵנִים יַחְדָּו וְהָפַכְתִּי אֶבְלָם לְשָׂשׂוֹן וְנִחַמְתִּים

וְשִׂמַּחְתִּים מִיגוֹנָם: וְרִוֵּיתִי נֶפֶשׁ הַכֹּהֲנִים דָּשֶׁן וְעַמִּי אֶת־טוּבִי

יִשְׂבָּעוּ נְאֻם־יְהוָֹה: כֹּה ׀ אָמַר יְהוָֹה קוֹל בְּרָמָה

נִשְׁמָע נְהִי בְּכִי תַמְרוּרִים רָחֵל מְבַכָּה עַל־בָּנֶיהָ מֵאֲנָה לְהִנָּחֵם

עַל־בָּנֶיהָ כִּי אֵינֶנּוּ:   כֹּה ׀ אָמַר יְהוָֹה מִנְעִי קוֹלֵךְ

מִבֶּכִי וְעֵינַיִךְ מִדִּמְעָה כִּי יֵשׁ שָׂכָר לִפְעֻלָּתֵךְ נְאֻם־יְהוָֹה וְשָׁבוּ

מֵאֶרֶץ אוֹיֵב: וְיֵשׁ־תִּקְוָה לְאַחֲרִיתֵךְ נְאֻם־יְהוָֹה וְשָׁבוּ בָנִים

לִגְבוּלָם: שָׁמוֹעַ שָׁמַעְתִּי אֶפְרַיִם מִתְנוֹדֵד יִסַּרְתַּנִי וָאִוָּסֵר כְּעֵגֶל

לֹא לֻמָּד הֲשִׁבֵנִי וְאָשׁוּבָה כִּי אַתָּה יְהוָֹה אֱלֹהָי: כִּי־אַחֲרֵי שׁוּבִי

נִחַמְתִּי וְאַחֲרֵי הִוָּדְעִי סָפַקְתִּי עַל־יָרֵךְ בֹּשְׁתִּי וְגַם־נִכְלַמְתִּי כִּי

נָשָׂאתִי חֶרְפַּת נְעוּרָי: הֲבֵן יַקִּיר לִי אֶפְרַיִם אִם יֶלֶד שַׁעֲשׁוּעִים

כִּי־מִדֵּי דַבְּרִי בּוֹ זָכֹר אֶזְכְּרֶנּוּ עוֹד עַל־כֵּן הָמוּ מֵעַי לוֹ רַחֵם

אֲרַחֲמֶנּוּ נְאֻם־יְהוָֹה:

bringing them from the north, gathering them from the corners of the earth, the blind and the lame among them, pregnant women together with women giving birth—what a great congregation is returning here!

"They come weeping and I lead them with compassion; I lead them to streams of water on a straight road that they might not stumble, for I have been become a parent to Israel, to My first-born Ephraim.

"Hear the word of Adonay, O nations, tell the tale to the islands far away! The One who scatters Israel is gathering them up, protecting them like a shepherd his flock (*ro'eh edro,* echoed in Untaneh Tokef). For Adonay has ransomed Jacob, and redeemed them from hands stronger than their own. They shall come singing to the heights of Zion, streaming brightly to God's goodness with grain and wine and oil, and the newborn of the flocks and herds; their life will become a garden well-watered, and they will feel weak no longer.

"Then shall damsels dance for joy, and young men and old along with them; I shall turn their mourning into rejoicing, and I shall bring comfort and celebration out of their pain. I shall satisfy priestly appetites with abundance, and my people shall be sated with My goodness," says Adonay.

So says Adonay: "A voice is heard in Ramah: wailing, bitter weeping! Rachel weeps for her children, refusing to be comforted, for they are no more." So says Adonay: "Take away the weeping from your voice, the tears from your eyes; for there will be a reward for your labor," says Adonay; "they will return from the land of the enemy. There will be hope for your future, says Adonay, and your children will return to their own borders. I have listened carefully to the wandering Ephraim as he bewailed his plight: 'You have chastised me, and I have felt chastised, like a calf untrained; bring me back, and I shall come back (or, let me do *tshuvah,* and I will do it), for you, Adonay, are my God. For after I returned (or, did *tshuvah*), I

repented, and after I was enlightened, I struck my thigh; I am ashamed, I am abashed, for I bear the disgrace of my youth.'

"Is not Ephraim my beloved child, the youngster of my delights? Whenever I speak of him it is as though he were still present before Me, and so My inmost being yearns for him; I will treat him with great compassion," says Adonay.

Blessings Completing the Reading of the Haftarah

בָּרוּךְ אַתָּה, יְיָ אֱלֹהֵינוּ, מֶלֶךְ הָעוֹלָם, צוּר כָּל הָעוֹלָמִים, צַדִּיק בְּכָל הַדּוֹרוֹת, הָאֵל הַנֶּאֱמָן, הָאוֹמֵר וְעוֹשֶׂה, הַמְדַבֵּר וּמְקַיֵּם, שֶׁכָּל דְּבָרָיו אֱמֶת וָצֶדֶק.

נֶאֱמָן אַתָּה הוּא, יְיָ אֱלֹהֵינוּ, וְנֶאֱמָנִים דְּבָרֶיךָ, וְדָבָר אֶחָד מִדְּבָרֶיךָ אָחוֹר לֹא יָשׁוּב רֵיקָם, כִּי אֵל מֶלֶךְ נֶאֱמָן וְרַחֲמָן אָתָּה. בָּרוּךְ אַתָּה יְיָ הָאֵל הַנֶּאֱמָן בְּכָל דְּבָרָיו.

You are praised, Adonay our God, sovereign of the world, eternal Rock, righteous ruler in all generations, faithful God, whose every word is true and just. Not one of your words shall return unfulfilled, for Your rule is trustworthy and compassionate. You are praised, God of faithful words.

רַחֵם עַל צִיּוֹן, כִּי הִיא בֵּית חַיֵּינוּ, וְלַעֲלוּבַת נֶפֶשׁ תּוֹשִׁיעַ בִּמְהֵרָה בְיָמֵינוּ. בָּרוּךְ אַתָּה יְיָ מְשַׂמֵּחַ צִיּוֹן בְּבָנֶיהָ.

Show compassion on Zion, for it is our eternal house, and rescue soon, in our days, those who are brought low. You are praised, Adonay, who brings Zion joy through her children.

שַׂמְּחֵנוּ, יְיָ אֱלֹהֵינוּ, בְּאֵלִיָּהוּ הַנָּבִיא עַבְדֶּךָ, וּבְמַלְכוּת
בֵּית דָּוִד מְשִׁיחֶךָ, בִּמְהֵרָה יָבֹא, וְיָגֵל לִבֵּנוּ; עַל כִּסְאוֹ
לֹא יֵשֵׁב זָר, וְלֹא יִנְחֲלוּ עוֹד אֲחֵרִים אֶת כְּבוֹדוֹ, כִּי
בְשֵׁם קָדְשְׁךָ נִשְׁבַּעְתָּ לּוֹ, שֶׁלֹּא יִכְבֶּה נֵרוֹ לְעוֹלָם וָעֶד.
בָּרוּךְ אַתָּה יְיָ מָגֵן דָּוִד.

Bring us joy, Adonay our God, with the coming of Your
servant, Elijah the prophet, and the reign of the house of
David, Your anointed. Let no stranger sit upon his throne,
nor any others inherit his glory, for You have sworn by
Your holy name that his light would never be extinguished
anywhere. You are praised, Adonay, shield of David.

עַל הַתּוֹרָה וְעַל הָעֲבוֹדָה וְעַל הַנְּבִיאִים [וְעַל יוֹם
הַשַּׁבָּת הַזֶּה] וְעַל יוֹם הַזִּכָּרוֹן הַזֶּה, שֶׁנָּתַתָּ לָּנוּ, יְיָ
אֱלֹהֵינוּ, [לִקְדֻשָּׁה וְלִמְנוּחָה], לְכָבוֹד וּלְתִפְאָרֶת.

עַל הַכֹּל, יְיָ אֱלֹהֵינוּ, אֲנַחְנוּ מוֹדִים לָךְ, וּמְבָרְכִים
אוֹתָךְ; יִתְבָּרַךְ שִׁמְךָ בְּפִי כָל חַי תָּמִיד, לְעוֹלָם וָעֶד.
וּדְבָרְךָ אֱמֶת וְקַיָּם לָעַד. בָּרוּךְ אַתָּה יְיָ מֶלֶךְ עַל כָּל
הָאָרֶץ, מְקַדֵּשׁ [הַשַּׁבָּת וְ]יִשְׂרָאֵל וְיוֹם הַזִּכָּרוֹן.

For the Torah, for serving You in prayer, for the prophets
(for this Shabbat) and for this Day of Remembrance which
You have granted us, Adonay our God, (for holiness and
rest), for glory, and for honor; indeed, for everything,
Adonay our God, we thank You and praise You. Your
name shall be praised forever in the mouths of all who live,
for Your word is true and upheld eternally. You are
praised, Adonay, Ruler over all the earth, who reveals
Your holiness through (Shabbat), Israel, and the Day of
Remembrance.

SHOFAR SERVICE

Introductions

The time has come to sound the horn, its solemn, soulful cry carrying us back to the time when sound and soul were first created; its yearning notes lifting us into the time to come, when a new and just Creation will dawn for all humanity.

Our Shofar sounds three themes: awakening us to the *Sovereignty of God* toward which we and all present rulers must direct their paths; to the *Memories* of the covenant of survival which God sealed with all humanity through Noah, and the covenant of promise sealed with us through Abraham; and finally the Shofar awakens us to itself, to the *Shofar Calls* of a future which we must dedicate ourselves to help ensure. For one day God alone will sound the Great Shofar for the freedom of humanity, when all the exiles will be gathered from the uttermost parts of the earth and led exultantly to a city which every soul shall know to be the city of God.

*   *   *

The ram found in Moriah's thicket lives for us today, in the ancient horn we sound as an announcement that the year has dawned and as an alarm to our sleepy souls that the Judgment Day has come. In this ram's horn we shall sound is present the ram which was the proof of Isaac's salvation, and so its sound connects our fate to his, and to all the individuals whose sacrifice informs our lives. Its call can awaken us to all the demands and proofs and trials to which God may call us in sounds we cannot predict until time shall purse her lips once more, and we must be prepared.

(All rise)

בָּרוּךְ אַתָּה יְיָ אֱלֹהֵינוּ, מֶלֶךְ הָעוֹלָם, אֲשֶׁר קִדְּשָׁנוּ בְּמִצְוֹתָיו, וְצִוָּנוּ לִשְׁמֹעַ קוֹל שׁוֹפָר.

בָּרוּךְ אַתָּה, יְיָ אֱלֹהֵינוּ, מֶלֶךְ הָעוֹלָם, שֶׁהֶחֱיָנוּ וְקִיְּמָנוּ
וְהִגִּיעָנוּ לַזְּמַן הַזֶּה.

Baruch atta Adonay Eloheynu melech ha-olam
asher kidd'sha-nu b'mitz-vo-tav v'tzee-vanu
lishmo-a kol shofar.

Baruch atta Adonay Eloheynu melech ha-olam
shehehiyanu v'kiymanu v'higianu lazman
ha-zeh.

You are praised, Adonay our God, Majesty of the universe, who made us holy through Your mitzvot and commanded us to listen to the sound of the shofar.

You are praised, Adonay our God, Majesty of the universe, who has kept us alive and sustained us and allowed
us to reach this wondrous time.

May it be Your will, our God, and God of our fathers and
mothers, that the notes of the shofar which we are sounding reach all the way up to Your glorious throne and intercede for us, so that You forgive us all our wrongs.
Praised are you, source of compassion.

תְּקִיעָה	שְׁבָרִים תְּרוּעָה	תְּקִיעָה
תְּקִיעָה	שְׁבָרִים תְּרוּעָה	תְּקִיעָה
תְּקִיעָה	שְׁבָרִים תְּרוּעָה	תְּקִיעָה

*(If there is to be a Musaf service, continue with Returning the
Scroll to the Ark, page 148)*

(All are seated)

MALCHUYOT: *Evocations of God's Sovereignty*

Today marks the birthday of the world. Today we affirm our
faith that the world makes sense, that there is design and purpose, order and beauty within it. And we affirm that we, who
are made in God's image, are called upon to continue the work

of creation, to finish the task of bringing order out of chaos,
light where there is darkness, understanding where there is
ignorance, and hope where there is despair.

*   *   *

Our prayer room is not this room,
A simple hall wherein we yearly gather for the Days of Awe.
Our prayer room is the most resplendent hall of all the universe,
With ceilings reaching higher than the highest heavens,
Blazing in the light of candelabra from the sun.
Our prayer room, illumined by the heavens,
Is the throne room of the Sovereign of earth and heaven,
The Monarch more powerful by far than any power we can
    know.
Creator of the whole illustrious expanse
And of every speck of dust that makes it up,
Creator of each one of us.
With each word of prayer we speak
We step before that cosmic throne,
Yet find there a very quiet, warmly shining Presence.

The Sovereign of all the universe
Is in the holy shimmer of a fragrant blossom,
The Sovereign of all the universe
Is in the holy words of care from a friend we love
The Sovereign of all the universe
Is in the holy words of this our ancient people
The Sovereign of all the universe
Stands before our words, before our standing bodies,
Before our ears which listen to the ancient horn.

*   *   *

Aleynu

We are called to praise the Source of all,
To hail the grandeur of the Sculptor of Creation,
Who did not make us like nations in other lands
Nor were we put on earth like other families of Adam's
    seed.

We were not given a portion like theirs,
Nor a destiny like others who throng the earth.
Our calling is to bow the head and bend the knee in
    worship
To pour forth thanks and praise
Only before the Sovereign greater than the most sovereign
    of all the sovereigns on earth,
The Holy One, whose very Soul is praise.

For You spread out the heavens and founded the earth,
establishing a dwelling for Your glory in the heavens high
above, and the presence of Your Shechina, Your might, in
the highest realms of space. You are our God, none other.
You, O majesty, are Truth, none beside You, as You have
written in Your Torah: "Today you shall know intimately,
placing it upon your heart, that Adonay is God, in the
heavens above and on earth below, none other."

Therefore do we hope in You, Adonay our God, confident
that soon we shall see the glory of Your might revealed,
ridding the world of all idolatries, cutting down all false
gods from their pedestals, reconstructing the world into a
realm where You can rule, Almighty One. Then everyone
of flesh and blood will be able to speak Your name, for
You will have turned toward You all the wicked of the
earth. All who live on this planet will recognize that they
too can know You intimately, that every knee can bend to
You, every tongue pledge faithfulness to You. Turning
toward You, Adonay our God, all will bow down and fall
prostrate, granting honor at last to Your glorious name,
and all will accept the yoke that joins them to Your sovereignty, that You may rule over them speedily to the end of
time. For Sovereignty is Yours, and in glory will You reign
forever, as it is written in Your Torah: Adonay will reign
forever and ever.

Biblical Proclamations of God's Sovereignty

From Psalm 24

שְׂאוּ שְׁעָרִים רָאשֵׁיכֶם, וְהִנָּשְׂאוּ פִּתְחֵי עוֹלָם, וְיָבוֹא
מֶלֶךְ הַכָּבוֹד. מִי זֶה מֶלֶךְ הַכָּבוֹד, יְיָ עִזּוּז וְגִבּוֹר, יְיָ
גִּבּוֹר מִלְחָמָה. שְׂאוּ שְׁעָרִים רָאשֵׁיכֶם, וּשְׂאוּ פִּתְחֵי
עוֹלָם, וְיָבֹא מֶלֶךְ הַכָּבוֹד. מִי הוּא זֶה מֶלֶךְ הַכָּבוֹד, יְיָ
צְבָאוֹת הוּא מֶלֶךְ הַכָּבוֹד, סֶלָה.

Lift your heads, Temple gates;
Raise yourselves, you doors to the timeless house!
Let the glorious Sovereign enter in!
Who is this glorious Sovereign?
Adonay, strong and mighty,
Adonay, our defender!
Lift your heads, Temple gates,
Raise yourselves, doors to the timeless house!
Let the glorious Sovereign enter in!
Who is this glorious Sovereign?
The Commander of the hosts of heaven and earth,
This is the glorious Sovereign!

*　　*　　*

So act that none beholds wrongdoing in Jacob, that none
sees wickedness among the children of Rachel and Leah;
by acting justly, you will show that Adonay is Your God,
whose rule is proclaimed by the Tru'ah of the Shofar.

That a monarch rules in Yeshurun is proclaimed
when the heads of the people gather together, when
all the tribes of Israel meet in common purpose.

Sovereignty belongs to You who rules among the nations,
robed in grandeur, girded with might, emblem of a world
secured immovably on its foundations.

Thus says Adonay, ruler of Israel and her Redeemer,
Commander of the Hosts: I am the first First One, I
am the Final One, there is no God beside Me.

The victorious ones shall ascend Mount Zion to judge the
hills of Esau, to weigh the acts of all who have ruled over
Your people, and so God's rule shall be declared.

And Adonay shall become Sovereign over all the
earth; on that day Adonay will be one and the divine
Name one!

Hear, O Israel, Adonay is our God, Adonay is One!

(All rise)

Our God
And God of those who have gone before us,
Help us to perceive Your sovereignty
In the royal splendor that pervades the universe,
In the holy power that creates of all creatures
A single household.
Let this holy time lift us to Your presence
In life,
In peace,
In leaping joy.

You are praised, Ruler over all the earth,
Whose holiness we encounter through (Shabbat), Israel,
    and the Day of Remembrance.

תְּקִיעָה	שְׁבָרִים תְּרוּעָה	תְּקִיעָה
תְּקִיעָה	שְׁבָרִים	תְּקִיעָה
תְּקִיעָה	תְּרוּעָה	תְּקִיעָה

הַיּוֹם הֲרַת עוֹלָם, הַיּוֹם יַעֲמִיד בַּמִּשְׁפָּט כָּל יְצוּרֵי
עוֹלָמִים, אִם כְּבָנִים אִם כַּעֲבָדִים. אִם כְּבָנִים, רַחֲמֵנוּ
כְּרַחֵם אָב עַל בָּנִים; וְאִם כַּעֲבָדִים עֵינֵינוּ לְךָ תְלוּיוֹת,
עַד שֶׁתְּחָנֵּנוּ וְתוֹצִיא כָאוֹר מִשְׁפָּטֵנוּ, אָיוֹם קָדוֹשׁ.

אֲרֶשֶׁת שְׂפָתֵינוּ יֶעֱרַב לְפָנֶיךָ, אֵל רָם וְנִשָׂא, מֵבִין
וּמַאֲזִין, מַבִּיט וּמַקְשִׁיב לְקוֹל תְּקִיעָתֵנוּ; וּתְקַבֵּל
בְּרַחֲמִים וּבְרָצוֹן סֵדֶר מַלְכִיּוֹתֵינוּ.

Today is the world conceived, today all humanity is
judged. May the words on our lips be pleasing, O exalted
God, who hearkens to the T'kiyah we sound today. O
accept with favor the order of our Malchuyot, the praise of
Your sovereignty.

(All are seated)

ZICHRONOT: Remembrances

You remember the creation of the universe,
You recollect every creature You formed from of old.
Before You is revealed
Everything that humans cannot see,
Everything that has been buried since the world began.
There is no forgetting before Your throne of Glory,
You remember every single act.

> When we become convinced that we do not matter,
> That our lives are only wrinkles in the tapestry of the
>   world,

You remember the creation of the universe,
You recollect every creature You formed from of old.

> When governments commit atrocious crimes,
> When they seem to have escaped unpunished from
>   their savagery,

There is no forgetting before Your throne of Glory,
You remember every single act.

> When the promise of Your creation seems obscured,
> When the thread of goodness merely leads us deeper
>   into the forest,

Before You is revealed
Everything that humans cannot see,
Everything that has been buried since the world began.

*   *   *

This is a day that has been since Your creative work began,
a Remembrance of the first day. It is a statute for Israel, a
law for the God of Jacob, of Rachel and of Leah. On this
day nations are judged: this one for the sword, this one for
peace; this one for famine, this one for plenty. On this day
human beings are judged; who is not taken note of on this
day? For the presence of each creature is called before You,
the record of every person's thoughts and deeds come
before You. Happy is the one who is conscious of You at
all times, who is aware of the courage You implanted in us
as Your gift. Those who seek You will not stumble, those
who trust in You will never be confounded.

Biblical Recollections of God's Remembrance

As you remembered Noah and with the wind dispersed the
    waters of the flood,
So too remember us upon the flood of cruelty that threat-
    ens this frail ark in which we live and pray.

As in Egypt You heard our screaming,
And remembered there Your pact with Abraham, Isaac,
    and Jacob,
Sarah, Rebecca, Rachel and Leah,
So too remember us
Enslaved to lives and lifestyles that we cannot change,
Oppressed by fears and Pharaohs that turn living waters
    into blood.

As after each pogrom and exile and oppression
When Israel turned to Torah once again
And you remembered our ancient covenant,
So too remember us

Dispersed in friendly lands and hostile,
Fighting for the survival of the Jewish people
While trying to be true to the ideals that have made our
    people Jews.

As You instructed Jeremiah:
Whisper in the ear of Jerusalem
How I remember our youthful passion,
So too remember now
To whisper in her ear again
The words and acts through which she may embrace her
    enemies in peace.

(All rise)

Our God
And God of all those who have gone before us,
Remember us for good,
For a peaceful victory over evil,
For the everlasting covenant of love You promised Abra-
    ham on Mount Moriah.
As Abraham there suppressed a father's natural mercy to
    do Your will,
So may Your mercy suppress Your anger at our failure to
    redo our world,
And fulfill for us the promise engraved in Your Torah
And in ours:

I will remember for their sake
The covenant of the first ones who sought Me,
When I brought them out of Egypt in their search for God,
In My search for a people.

Praised are You who has remembered the covenant,
With whom is no forgetting before the throne of Glory.

תְּקִיעָה	שְׁבָרִים תְּרוּעָה	תְּקִיעָה
תְּקִיעָה	שְׁבָרִים	תְּקִיעָה
תְּקִיעָה	תְּרוּעָה	תְּקִיעָה

הַיּוֹם הֲרַת עוֹלָם, הַיּוֹם יַעֲמִיד בַּמִּשְׁפָּט כָּל יְצוּרֵי
עוֹלָמִים, אִם כְּבָנִים אִם כַּעֲבָדִים. אִם כְּבָנִים, רַחֲמֵנוּ
כְּרַחֵם אָב עַל בָּנִים; וְאִם כַּעֲבָדִים עֵינֵינוּ לְךָ תְלוּיוֹת,
עַד שֶׁתְּחָנֵּנוּ וְתוֹצִיא כָאוֹר מִשְׁפָּטֵנוּ, אָיוֹם קָדוֹשׁ.

אֲרֶשֶׁת שְׂפָתֵינוּ יֶעֱרַב לְפָנֶיךָ, אֵל רָם וְנִשָּׂא, מֵבִין
וּמַאֲזִין, מַבִּיט וּמַקְשִׁיב לְקוֹל תְּקִיעָתֵנוּ; וּתְקַבֵּל
בְּרַחֲמִים וּבְרָצוֹן סֵדֶר זִכְרוֹנוֹתֵינוּ.

Today is the world conceived, today all humanity is
judged. May the words on our lips be pleasing, O exalted
God, who hearkens to the T'kiyah we sound today. O
accept with favor the order of our Zichronot, the praise of
Your Remembrance of the covenant.

(All are seated)

SHOFAROT: The Shofar Sounds

In the world of matter, sound travels great distances from place
to place, connecting two places far away from the other. In the
realm of spirit sound can also transcend space and rise to that
Place in which all lesser places merge. On Rosh Hashanah, the
first of the Ten Days of Returning, we begin our returning from
all the bad places whither our missteps have carried us, returning to that true Place which is our proper home. But it is possible to rise to that place only through the sacred sounds which
rise from lips moving in prayer and from pushing sounds out of
the Shofar up to heaven. As we stand in the place where we have
gone astray and lift the words and Shofar sounds toward
heaven, God hears our voice, and leads us out beyond our
present place up and up onto that realm which transcends place
and space to the Place of the World, to God, where everyone is
returned to the perfection of our creation.

*   *   *

There are sounds which first we heard as children which have
engraved themselves, like ancient riverbeds long dry, into our
inner ear. Years later, when we've grown, those early sounds
will open up those ancient streams, and the place and moment
of that early music will flow again across our memory, and we
are at once transported there, splashing in the cooling spray like
the children we still are, with all the joy and playfulness and awe
we thought had dried up in our long-sought maturity. Buried
even deeper in us than our childhood is the childhood of our
people, when we were wandering and playing at the foot of
Sinai, full of wonder and confusion, as the cloud appeared, and
holy fire, and thundervoices out of heaven and the sounds of a
Shofar. Each year when the Shofar sounds for us again, the
cloud appears above the riverbed of memory, and we know that
if sufficient wonder and confusion fill our minds, the holy fire
will burn once more, and voices from our modest Shofar will
thunder out of heaven once again. If only we can listen, the
moment and the place will flow again, and we can splash with
the child our people was at the beginning, in the stream.

*   *   *

Biblical Hearkenings to the Sounds of the Shofar

On the third day as morning dawned, there were thundervoices and lightning and a dense cloud upon the mountain
Sinai and a loud Shofarblast, and all the people in the
camp trembled.

> The sound of the Shofar grew louder and louder,
> Moses spoke, and God answered him in a thunder-
> voice.

As the commandments were spoken, all the people witnessed the thundervoices and the lightning, the Shofarblasts and the mountain smoking, and when the people
saw it, they fell back and stood at a distance.

> When the Temple stood, the priests proclaimed:
> Adonay has ascended with T'ruah! It is Adonay in
> the sound of Shofarblast!

Sound T'kiyah on the Shofar at each new moon, and every
full moon which is Festival! It is a statute for Israel, a law
from the God of Jacob.

All dwellers of earth, all inhabitants of the world:
when a banner is raised upon the mountains, look up!
When T'kiyah is sounded on the Shofar, listen!

On that day T'kiyah shall be sounded on the great Shofar,
and all the tribes lost beyond the Euphrates shall come
forth, and all those cast away into Egypt shall worship
once more on Jerusalem's holy mountain. Adonay shall
appear, the divine presence will go forth as lightning,
sounding T'kiyah on the Shofar and protecting Israel until
the end of time.

(All rise)

Our God and God of those who have gone before us,
Let there be heard from this Shofar we sound today
The promise of the great Shofar announcing our freedom.
Raise up a banner to gather our exiles,
Bring home from the four corners of the earth
All those scattered among strangers,
And help us all find that place which You have promised.
For You attend to the meaning of the Shofarblasts,
Sovereign of all the universe, You remember the promise
   of T'ruah.
You are praised, composer of the T'ruah in which we met
   at Sinai,
Who pays heed to that T'ruah Your people offers You
   today.

תְּקִיעָה	שְׁבָרִים תְּרוּעָה	תְּקִיעָה
תְּקִיעָה	שְׁבָרִים	תְּקִיעָה
תְּקִיעָה גְדוֹלָה	תְּרוּעָה	תְּקִיעָה

הַיּוֹם הֲרַת עוֹלָם, הַיּוֹם יַעֲמִיד בַּמִּשְׁפָּט כָּל יְצוּרֵי
עוֹלָמִים, אִם כְּבָנִים אִם כַּעֲבָדִים. אִם כְּבָנִים, רַחֲמֵנוּ

כְּרַחֵם אָב עַל בָּנִים; וְאִם כַּעֲבָדִים עֵינֵינוּ לְךָ תְלוּיוֹת,
עַד שֶׁתְּחָנֵּנוּ וְתוֹצִיא כָאוֹר מִשְׁפָּטֵנוּ, אָיוֹם קָדוֹשׁ.

אֲרֶשֶׁת שְׂפָתֵינוּ יֶעֱרַב לְפָנֶיךָ, אֵל רָם וְנִשָּׂא, מֵבִין
וּמַאֲזִין, מַבִּיט וּמַקְשִׁיב לְקוֹל תְּקִיעָתֵנוּ; וּתְקַבֵּל
בְּרַחֲמִים וּבְרָצוֹן סֵדֶר שׁוֹפְרוֹתֵינוּ.

Today is the world conceived, today all humanity is
judged. May the words on our lips be pleasing, O exalted
God, who hearkens to the T'kiyah we sound today. O
accept with favor the order of our Shofarot, the praise of
your ancient sounds and the hope for those You will sound
at the dawn of the age to come.

(Remain standing)

Returning the Scroll to the Ark

This is the covenant that I shall make with the house of
Israel after those days, Adonay proclaims:
I shall put my Torah in their inward parts, and on their
heart shall I write it, and I shall be their God and they shall
be My people. No more will you need to teach your neighbor to know God, for you shall all know Me, from the
smallest of you to the greatest of you, says Adonay.

יְהַלְלוּ אֶת שֵׁם יְיָ כִּי נִשְׂגָּב שְׁמוֹ לְבַדּוֹ:

O praise the Name of God, the most exalted name of all!

הוֹדוֹ עַל אֶרֶץ וְשָׁמָיִם וַיָּרֶם קֶרֶן לְעַמּוֹ תְּהִלָּה לְכָל
חֲסִידָיו לִבְנֵי יִשְׂרָאֵל עַם קְרֹבוֹ הַלְלוּיָהּ:

Hodo al eretz v'shamayim
Vayarem keren l'amo:
T'hilah l'chol chaseedav
livney Yisrael am kerovo
Halleluya.

God's glory is in the earth and heavens, and the people of
God is raised on high. The pious are become a praise, and

the children of Israel are become intimates of Adonay.
Halleluyah!

While the Torah is being placed in the ark:

וּבְנֻחֹה יֹאמַר: שׁוּבָה, יְיָ, רִבְבוֹת אַלְפֵי יִשְׂרָאֵל. קוּמָה
יְיָ לִמְנוּחָתֶךָ, אַתָּה וַאֲרוֹן עֻזֶּךָ. כֹּהֲנֶיךָ יִלְבְּשׁוּ צֶדֶק,
וַחֲסִידֶיךָ יְרַגֵּנוּ. בַּעֲבוּר דָּוִד עַבְדֶּךָ, אַל תָּשֵׁב פְּנֵי
מְשִׁיחֶךָ. כִּי לֶקַח טוֹב נָתַתִּי לָכֶם, תּוֹרָתִי אַל תַּעֲזֹבוּ.

And when the ark rested, Moses proclaimed: Return,
Adonay, to all the myriads of Israel! Rise up toward Your
resting place, You and the ark, the symbol of Your power.
Let the kohanim be clothed in righteousness, let Your
pious ones sing for joy! For Your servant David's sake, do
not turn away Your anointed one, the messiah. For I have
given you good teaching, indeed, My own Torah; do not
forsake it.

עֵץ חַיִּים הִיא לַמַּחֲזִיקִים בָּהּ וְתוֹמְכֶיהָ מְאֻשָּׁר: דְּרָכֶיהָ
דַרְכֵי־נֹעַם וְכָל־נְתִיבוֹתֶיהָ שָׁלוֹם: הֲשִׁיבֵנוּ יְיָ אֵלֶיךָ
וְנָשׁוּבָה: חַדֵּשׁ יָמֵינוּ כְּקֶדֶם:

Eytz chayim hee lamachazeekim ba
V'tomcheyha m'ushar;
D'racheyha darchey noam
V'chol n'teevoteyha shalom
Hasheeveynu Adonay eylecha v'nashuva,
Chadesh yameynu k'kedem.

It is a tree which ensures eternal life for those who take
hold of it, how fortunate are its supporters! Its ways are
pleasant ways, its paths comprise Shalom. Bring us back to
You, Adonay, that we might return, renew our life as in the
days when You and we began.

(Ark is closed)

(The Musaf Service will be found beginning on page 173)

ALEYNU

עָלֵינוּ לְשַׁבֵּחַ לַאֲדוֹן הַכֹּל לָתֵת גְּדֻלָּה לְיוֹצֵר בְּרֵאשִׁית
שֶׁלֹּא עָשָׂנוּ כְּגוֹיֵי הָאֲרָצוֹת וְלֹא שָׂמָנוּ כְּמִשְׁפְּחוֹת
הָאֲדָמָה שֶׁלֹּא שָׂם חֶלְקֵנוּ כָּהֶם וְגוֹרָלֵנוּ כְּכָל הֲמוֹנָם:
וַאֲנַחְנוּ כֹּרְעִים וּמִשְׁתַּחֲוִים וּמוֹדִים
לִפְנֵי מֶלֶךְ מַלְכֵי הַמְּלָכִים הַקָּדוֹשׁ בָּרוּךְ הוּא.
שֶׁהוּא נוֹטֶה שָׁמַיִם וְיוֹסֵד אֶרֶץ וּמוֹשַׁב יְקָרוֹ בַּשָּׁמַיִם
מִמַּעַל וּשְׁכִינַת עֻזּוֹ בְּגָבְהֵי מְרוֹמִים: הוּא אֱלֹהֵינוּ אֵין
עוֹד. אֱמֶת מַלְכֵּנוּ אֶפֶס זוּלָתוֹ כַּכָּתוּב בְּתוֹרָתוֹ וְיָדַעְתָּ
הַיּוֹם וַהֲשֵׁבֹתָ אֶל לְבָבֶךָ כִּי יְיָ הוּא הָאֱלֹהִים בַּשָּׁמַיִם
מִמַּעַל וְעַל הָאָרֶץ מִתָּחַת. אֵין עוֹד:

A-ley-nu l'sha-be-ach la-a-don hakol, la-tet g'dulah l'yo-tzer
b're-sheet, she-lo a-sa-nu k'go-yey ha-a-ra-tzot v'lo sa-ma-nu
k'mish-p'chot ha-a-da-mah. She-lo sam chel-ke-nu ka-hem,
v'go-ra-lenu k'chol ha-mo-nam. Va-anachnu ko-r'im u-mish-ta-cha-vim
u-mo-dim, lif-ney me-lech mal-chey ham'lachim ha-ka-dosh
baruch hu.
She-hu no-teh sha-ma-yim v'yo-sed a-retz. U-mo-shav y'ka-ro
ba-sha-ma-yim mi-ma-al, u-shchi-nat u-zo b'gav-hey m'ro-mim.
Hu Eloheynu, ein od. Emet malkeynu efes zulato, ka-katuv
b'Torato:
V'ya-da-ta ha-yom va-ha-shey-vo-ta el l'va-ve-cha, ki
Adonay hu
ha-Elohim ba-sha-ma-yim mi-ma-al v'al ha-aretz mi-tachat,
ein od.

May the time not be distant, O God,
When Your enduring rule shall be established
   in the midst of the earth;
When justice shall prevail in the land,
Evil destroyed,

And the strong shall no more oppress the weak;
May sin be taken away from every person,
And, heirs to a royal covenant,
May all people exercise the just power that is their birth-
   right
As human beings.
In youth may we gain wisdom,
Overflowing like a river with understanding;
Our soul profound enough to cover the earth,
Loved, each of us,
For the peace we bring to others.
May our deeds exceed our speech,
And may we never lift up our hand
But to conquer fear and doubt and grave despair.
Rise up like the sun, O God, over all humanity,
Cause light to go forth over all the lands between the seas,
And light up the universe with the joy of wholeness, of
   freedom and of peace.

וְנֶאֱמַר וְהָיָה יְיָ לְמֶלֶךְ עַל כָּל הָאָרֶץ בַּיּוֹם הַהוּא יִהְיֶה
יְיָ אֶחָד וּשְׁמוֹ אֶחָד:

V'ne-e-mar: v'ha-yah A-do-nay l'-me-lech al kol ha-a-retz,
Ba-yom ha-hu ba-yom ha-hu yih-yeh A-do-nay e-chad
u-sh'-mo e-chad.

Mourner's Kaddish

יִתְגַּדַּל וְיִתְקַדַּשׁ שְׁמֵהּ רַבָּא. בְּעָלְמָא דִּי בְרָא
כִרְעוּתֵהּ. וְיַמְלִיךְ מַלְכוּתֵהּ בְּחַיֵּיכוֹן וּבְיוֹמֵיכוֹן וּבְחַיֵּי
דְכָל בֵּית יִשְׂרָאֵל. בַּעֲגָלָא וּבִזְמַן קָרִיב וְאִמְרוּ. אָמֵן:

Yit-ga-dal v'yit-ka-dash sh'mey ra-bah, b'al-mah di v'rah
chi-ru-tey, v'yam-leech mal-chu-tey, b'cha-yey-chon uv'yo-
mey-chon uv-cha-yey d'chol bet Yis-ra-el, ba-a-ga-lah
u-viz-man ka-reev. V'im-ru A-men.

יְהֵא שְׁמֵהּ רַבָּא מְבָרַךְ לְעָלַם וּלְעָלְמֵי עָלְמַיָּא:

Y'hey sh'mey ra-bah m'va-rach l'a-lam ul'al-mey al-ma-ya.

יִתְבָּרַךְ וְיִשְׁתַּבַּח וְיִתְפָּאַר וְיִתְרֹמַם וְיִתְנַשֵּׂא וְיִתְהַדָּר
וְיִתְעַלֶּה וְיִתְהַלַּל שְׁמֵהּ דְּקוּדְשָׁא. בְּרִיךְ הוּא. לְעֵלָּא
לְעֵלָּא מִן כָּל בִּרְכָתָא וְשִׁירָתָא תֻּשְׁבְּחָתָא וְנֶחֱמָתָא
דַּאֲמִירָן בְּעָלְמָא וְאִמְרוּ. אָמֵן:

*Yit-ba-rach v'yish-ta-bach v'yit-pa-ar v'yit-ro-mam v'yit-na-
sey v'yit-ha-dar v'yit-a-leh v'yit-ha-lal sh'mey d'kudshah,
b'reech hu. L'ey-la l'ey-la min kol bir-cha-tah v'shir-a-tah,
tush-b'cha-tah v'ne-che-ma-tah da-a-mi-ran b'al-mah.
V'im-ru A-men.*

יְהֵא שְׁלָמָא רַבָּא מִן שְׁמַיָּא וְחַיִּים עָלֵינוּ וְעַל כָּל
יִשְׂרָאֵל וְאִמְרוּ. אָמֵן:

*Y'hey sh'la-mah ra-bah min sh'ma-ya v'cha-yim a-ley-nu v'al
kol Yis-ra-el. V'im-ru A-men.*

עוֹשֶׂה שָׁלוֹם בִּמְרוֹמָיו הוּא יַעֲשֶׂה שָׁלוֹם עָלֵינוּ וְעַל
כָּל יִשְׂרָאֵל וְאִמְרוּ. אָמֵן:

*O-seh sha-lom bim-ro-mav hu ya-a-seh sha-lom a-ley-nu
v'al kol Yis-ra-el. V'im-ru A-men.*

May God's great name be praised and sanctified in the
world! May Your Rule be established in our lifetime and
the lifetime of the House of Israel. God's great name is
blessed and praised far beyond all blessings and praises we
can ever say in the world.

May there be a great peace from heaven and life for us and
all Israel. May the One who makes peace in the high
places, make peace for us and all Israel! Amen.

Upon Departing Toward a New Beginning

We came together here to search for truth,
To face a judgment on ourselves, our people,
On the world which helps us grow and helps us stray.
In the time before we gather once again,
Let us not relent in searching how we might become
The people God created us to be.
Though we shall be separated from each other,
Let us be conscious of each other's presence,

For in the compassionate presence
Of those whose prayers we've shared today
We can grow closer to the compassionate presence
Of the God who wants to judge us worthy
Of a good, sweet year,
A year of health and fulfillment,
A year of peace.

*   *   *

Where is God in the world, we ask?
God is where we encounter
All the ways we may connect with nature,
With humanity, with our people,
To know we are not alone,
But lie in passionate embrace with the world
At every conscious moment.
Now we can begin to conceive the world:
Now, as we prepare to leave each other,
Now, as our lips conclude the melodies
Of the Jew's old love song
On this morning that the world begins
Its life.

A good and sweet, fulfilling New Year to us all!

*   *   *

Now, with senses newly quickened by the time we have
    spent together,
Let us walk out into the New Year with the lessons we have
    learned:
Having listened to the Shofar, let us listen also to the good
    voices in our lives,
Having looked into the Torah, let us look to find our best
    selves,
Having tasted honey, let us bring the taste of sweetness to
    the lives of those we love,
Having smelled the fragrant Year outside our praying
    place, let us work to preserve the fragrance from the
    destructive forces in the world,
Having touched the ancient thoughts and yearnings of our
    people, let us resolve to let the needs of others touch us,
    moving us to action in the days ahead.

L'shana Tovah tikateyvu: May we all be inscribed for a good and fruitful, healthy, peaceful year.

Ayn k'Eyloheynu

אֵין כֵּאלֹהֵינוּ. אֵין כַּאדוֹנֵינוּ. אֵין כְּמַלְכֵּנוּ. אֵין
כְּמוֹשִׁיעֵנוּ: מִי כֵאלֹהֵינוּ. מִי כַאדוֹנֵינוּ. מִי כְמַלְכֵּנוּ. מִי
כְמוֹשִׁיעֵנוּ: נוֹדֶה לֵאלֹהֵינוּ. נוֹדֶה לַאדוֹנֵינוּ. נוֹדֶה
לְמַלְכֵּנוּ. נוֹדֶה לְמוֹשִׁיעֵנוּ: בָּרוּךְ אֱלֹהֵינוּ. בָּרוּךְ
אֲדוֹנֵינוּ. בָּרוּךְ מַלְכֵּנוּ. בָּרוּךְ מוֹשִׁיעֵנוּ: אַתָּה הוּא
אֱלֹהֵינוּ. אַתָּה הוּא אֲדוֹנֵינוּ. אַתָּה הוּא מַלְכֵּנוּ. אַתָּה
הוּא מוֹשִׁיעֵנוּ. אַתָּה הוּא שֶׁהִקְטִירוּ אֲבוֹתֵנוּ לְפָנֶיךָ
אֵת קְטֹרֶת הַסַּמִּים:

Ayn k Eyloheynu, ayn kAdoneynu,
Ayn k'mal-keynu, ayn k'moshee-aynu.

Mi chEyloheynu, mi chAdoneynu,
Mi ch'malkeynu, mi ch'moshee-aynu.

Nodeh lEyloheynu, nodeh lAdoneynu,
Nodeh l'malkeynu, nodeh l'moshee-aynu.

Baruch Eloheynu, baruch Adoneynu,
Baruch malkeynu, baruch moshee-aynu.

Atah hu Eloheynu, atah hu Adoneynu,
Atah hu malkeynu, atah hu moshee-aynu.

Atah hu she-hikteeru avoteynu l'faneh-cha
et ktoret ha-samim.

There is none like our God, none like Adonay, none like our Ruler,
none like the One who brings us victory.
Who is like our God. . . .
We thank our God. . . .
Praised be our God. . . .
You are our God. . . .
You are the One to whose presence our fathers and mothers used to
offer up sweet incense.

V'ye-etayu: All the World Shall Come to Serve You

וְיֶאֱתָיוּ כֹל לְעָבְדֶךָ וִיבָרְכוּ שֵׁם כְּבוֹדֶךָ, וְיַגִּידוּ בָאִיִּים
צִדְקֶךָ, וְיִדְרְשׁוּךָ עַמִּים לֹא־יְדָעוּךָ. וִיהַלְלוּךָ כָּל־אַפְסֵי

אֶרֶץ, וְיֹאמְרוּ תָמִיד יִגְדַּל יְיָ. וְיִזְבְּחוּ לְךָ אֶת־זִבְחֵיהֶם,
וְיִזְנְחוּ אֶת עֲצַבֵּיהֶם, וְיַחְפְּרוּ עִם פְּסִילֵיהֶם. וְיַטּוּ שְׁכֶם־
אֶחָד לְעָבְדֶךָ, וְיִירָאוּךָ עִם שֶׁמֶשׁ מְבַקְשֵׁי פָנֶיךָ, וְיַכִּירוּ
כֹּחַ מַלְכוּתֶךָ, וִילַמְּדוּ תוֹעִים בִּינָה, וִימַלְּלוּ אֶת
גְּבוּרָתֶךָ, וְיִנַשְׂאוּךָ מִתְנַשֵּׂא לְכֹל לְרֹאשׁ. וִיסַלְּדוּ
בְחִילָה פָנֶיךָ, וִיעַטְּרוּךָ נֵזֶר תִּפְאָרָה, וְיִפְצְחוּ הָרִים
רִנָּה, וְיִצְהֲלוּ אִיִּים בְּמָלְכֶךָ, וִיקַבְּלוּ עֹל מַלְכוּתְךָ
עֲלֵיהֶם, וִירוֹמְמוּךָ בִּקְהַל עָם, וְיִשְׁמְעוּ רְחוֹקִים
וְיָבֹאוּ, וְיִתְּנוּ־לְךָ כֶּתֶר מְלוּכָה.

All the world shall come to serve You,
    And bless Your glorious name,
And Your righteousness triumphant
    The islands shall proclaim.

And the peoples shall go seeking
    Who knew You not before.
And the ends of earth shall praise You,
    And tell Your greatness o'er.

They shall build for You their altars,
    Their idols overthrown,
And their graven gods shall shame them,
    As they turn to You alone.
They shall worship You at sunrise,
    And feel Your sovereign might,
And impart their understanding
    To those astray in night.

When Your rule is universal
    The hills shall shout with song,
And the islands laugh exultant
    That they to God belong.
And through all Your congregations
    So loud Your praise shall be
That the utmost peoples, hearing,
    Shall hail Your sovereignty.

TRADITIONAL SILENT AMIDAH

אֲדֹנָי שְׂפָתַי תִּפְתָּח וּפִי יַגִּיד תְּהִלָּתֶךָ:

Avot

בָּרוּךְ אַתָּה, יְיָ אֱלֹהֵינוּ וֵאלֹהֵי אֲבוֹתֵינוּ (וְאִמּוֹתֵינוּ), אֱלֹהֵי אַבְרָהָם, אֱלֹהֵי יִצְחָק, וֵאלֹהֵי יַעֲקֹב, (אֱלֹהֵי שָׂרָה, אֱלֹהֵי רִבְקָה, אֱלֹהֵי רָחֵל, וֵאלֹהֵי לֵאָה,) הָאֵל הַגָּדוֹל הַגִּבּוֹר וְהַנּוֹרָא, אֵל עֶלְיוֹן, גּוֹמֵל חֲסָדִים טוֹבִים, וְקֹנֶה הַכֹּל, וְזוֹכֵר חַסְדֵי אָבוֹת (וְאִמָּהוֹת), וּמֵבִיא גוֹאֵל* לִבְנֵי בְנֵיהֶם לְמַעַן שְׁמוֹ בְּאַהֲבָה. זָכְרֵנוּ לְחַיִּים, מֶלֶךְ חָפֵץ בַּחַיִּים, וְכָתְבֵנוּ בְּסֵפֶר הַחַיִּים, לְמַעַנְךָ אֱלֹהִים חַיִּים: מֶלֶךְ עוֹזֵר וּמוֹשִׁיעַ וּמָגֵן. בָּרוּךְ אַתָּה יְיָ, מָגֵן אַבְרָהָם (וְשָׂרָה).

In the Reform tradition, גְּאוּלָה*

Gevurot

אַתָּה גִבּוֹר לְעוֹלָם אֲדֹנָי מְחַיֶּה מֵתִים* אַתָּה רַב לְהוֹשִׁיעַ. מְכַלְכֵּל חַיִּים בְּחֶסֶד מְחַיֶּה מֵתִים* בְּרַחֲמִים רַבִּים. סוֹמֵךְ נוֹפְלִים וְרוֹפֵא חוֹלִים וּמַתִּיר אֲסוּרִים וּמְקַיֵּם אֱמוּנָתוֹ לִישֵׁנֵי עָפָר. מִי כָמוֹךָ בַּעַל גְּבוּרוֹת וּמִי דוֹמֶה לָּךְ. מֶלֶךְ מֵמִית וּמְחַיֶּה וּמַצְמִיחַ יְשׁוּעָה. מִי כָמוֹךָ אַב הָרַחֲמִים זוֹכֵר יְצוּרָיו לְחַיִּים בְּרַחֲמִים: וְנֶאֱמָן אַתָּה לְהַחֲיוֹת מֵתִים* בָּרוּךְ אַתָּה יְיָ מְחַיֶּה הַמֵּתִים*:

In the Reform tradition, הַכֹּל*

TRADITIONAL SILENT AMIDAH

Adonay, open up my lips, that my mouth may sing Your praises.

Avot

You are praised, Adonay our God, God of our fathers (and mothers), of Abraham, of Isaac, of Jacob (of Sarah, of Rebecca, of Rachel, of Leah)—great, powerful, and awesome God, higher than all other powers, who loves us even when we are unworthy. Creator who nurtures all, You remember the worthy acts of our ancient fathers (and mothers), and You will return their love by bringing a redeemer* to their children's children for the sake of Your promise, as evidence of your love. Remember us with life, O Monarch who so treasures life! Inscribe us in the Book of Life for Your own sake, O God whose being is life. O Majesty who helps, saves and protects, You are praised, Adonay, source of strength for Abraham (and Sarah).

*In the Reform tradition, *redemption*

Gevurot

You are eternally powerful, Adonay, You have the power to give life to the dead*, You have the power to save us. You lovingly supply the needs of all living things. Out of Your compassion You grant the dead* eternal life. You support the weak, heal the sick, and free the enslaved; You keep Your word to those who sleep in the dust. Who is like You, source of all power? Who resembles You, Majesty, who gives both death and life and makes redemption flower?

Who is like You, motherly Father, who loves Your creatures with a compassion human parents long to give? We trust in Your promise one day to revive those we have lost to death. You are praised, Adonay, who gives the dead* eternal life.

*In the Reform tradition, *to all*

Kedushat Ha-Shem (The Holiness of God)

Atta Kadosh

אַתָּה קָדוֹשׁ וְשִׁמְךָ קָדוֹשׁ, וּקְדוֹשִׁים בְּכָל יוֹם יְהַלְלוּךָ
סֶּלָה.

Uv'chen

וּבְכֵן תֵּן פַּחְדְּךָ יְיָ אֱלֹהֵינוּ עַל כָּל מַעֲשֶׂיךָ וְאֵימָתְךָ עַל־
כָּל־מַה שֶׁבָּרָאתָ. וְיִירָאוּךָ כָּל הַמַּעֲשִׂים וְיִשְׁתַּחֲווּ
לְפָנֶיךָ כָּל הַבְּרוּאִים. וְיֵעָשׂוּ כֻלָּם אֲגֻדָּה אַחַת לַעֲשׂוֹת
רְצוֹנְךָ בְּלֵבָב שָׁלֵם. כְּמוֹ שֶׁיָּדַעְנוּ יְיָ אֱלֹהֵינוּ שֶׁהַשִּׁלְטוֹן
לְפָנֶיךָ עֹז בְּיָדְךָ וּגְבוּרָה בִּימִינֶךָ וְשִׁמְךָ נוֹרָא עַל כָּל
מַה שֶׁבָּרָאתָ:

וּבְכֵן תֵּן כָּבוֹד יְיָ לְעַמֶּךָ תְּהִלָּה לִירֵאֶיךָ וְתִקְוָה
לְדוֹרְשֶׁיךָ וּפִתְחוֹן פֶּה לַמְיַחֲלִים לָךְ. שִׂמְחָה לְאַרְצֶךָ
וְשָׂשׂוֹן לְעִירֶךָ וּצְמִיחַת קֶרֶן לְדָוִד עַבְדֶּךָ וַעֲרִיכַת נֵר
לְבֶן יִשַׁי מְשִׁיחֶךָ בִּמְהֵרָה בְיָמֵינוּ:

וּבְכֵן צַדִּיקִים יִרְאוּ וְיִשְׂמָחוּ וִישָׁרִים יַעֲלֹזוּ
וַחֲסִידִים בְּרִנָּה יָגִילוּ. וְעוֹלָתָה תִּקְפָּץ־פִּיהָ וְכָל
הָרִשְׁעָה כֻּלָּהּ כְּעָשָׁן תִּכְלֶה כִּי תַעֲבִיר מֶמְשֶׁלֶת זָדוֹן
מִן הָאָרֶץ:

וְתִמְלוֹךְ אַתָּה יְיָ לְבַדֶּךָ עַל כָּל מַעֲשֶׂיךָ בְּהַר צִיּוֹן
מִשְׁכַּן כְּבוֹדֶךָ וּבִירוּשָׁלַיִם עִיר קָדְשֶׁךָ. כַּכָּתוּב בְּדִבְרֵי
קָדְשֶׁךָ. יִמְלֹךְ יְיָ לְעוֹלָם אֱלֹהַיִךְ צִיּוֹן לְדֹר וָדֹר
הַלְלוּיָהּ:

קָדוֹשׁ אַתָּה וְנוֹרָא שְׁמֶךָ וְאֵין אֱלוֹהַּ מִבַּלְעָדֶיךָ

Kedushat Ha - Shem (The Holiness of God)

Atta Kadosh

You are holy, the meaning of Your name is holiness. We who strive to be holy yearn to praise You every day.

Uv'chen

Because of this, Adonay our God, make all Your creatures awestruck by Your greatness, help all that You have created to be conscious that You are the Judge of all they do. Help everything alive to align their desires to Your own, let all creation worship You, that everyone might sense their bond with each other and act to do Your will with harmonious hearts. Help us know, Adonay our God, that all sovereignty is Yours, You possess all strength, You grip all power. May all that You have created stand in awe of You.

Because of this, Adonay, share Your glory with Your people, Your praise with those who believe in You, Your hope with those who are searching for You. Give those who wait with You a chance to reveal Your presence to the world. Give joy to Your chosen land, exultation to Your special city. From David's family let there blossom a shoot as radiant as he; let the ideal world dawn for everyone, soon and in our own time.

When those who do justly see all this, they will rejoice; people of integrity will celebrate; those who serve God out of love will sing for joy. Injustice will shut its mouth at last, and cruelty will be blown away like smoke, for You will have swept away the arrogance of rulers from the earth.

You God, You alone, will reign over all that You have made, on Mount Zion the place of Your holy Temple, in Jerusalem Your holy city, as it says in the Bible, "Adonay shall reign forever, Your God, O Zion, throughout all generations."

You are holy, the Name which speaks Your being fills us with awe. There is no God but You. As it is written in Your

כַּכָּתוּב. וַיִּגְבַּה יְיָ צְבָאוֹת בַּמִּשְׁפָּט וְהָאֵל הַקָּדוֹשׁ
נִקְדַּשׁ בִּצְדָקָה. בָּרוּךְ אַתָּה יְיָ הַמֶּלֶךְ הַקָּדוֹשׁ:

Kedushat Ha-Yom (The Holiness of this Day)

Atta V'chartanu

אַתָּה בְחַרְתָּנוּ מִכָּל הָעַמִּים, אָהַבְתָּ אוֹתָנוּ וְרָצִיתָ בָּנוּ,
וְרוֹמַמְתָּנוּ מִכָּל הַלְּשׁוֹנוֹת, וְקִדַּשְׁתָּנוּ בְּמִצְוֹתֶיךָ,
וְקֵרַבְתָּנוּ מַלְכֵּנוּ לַעֲבוֹדָתֶךָ, וְשִׁמְךָ הַגָּדוֹל וְהַקָּדוֹשׁ
עָלֵינוּ קָרָאתָ.

Va-titen Lanu (Rosh Hashanah)

וַתִּתֶּן לָנוּ יְיָ אֱלֹהֵינוּ, בְּאַהֲבָה אֶת יוֹם [הַשַּׁבָּת הַזֶּה
וְאֶת יוֹם] הַזִּכָּרוֹן הַזֶּה, יוֹם [זִכְרוֹן] תְּרוּעָה [בְּאַהֲבָה]
מִקְרָא קֹדֶשׁ, זֵכֶר לִיצִיאַת מִצְרָיִם.

Va-titen Lanu (Yom Kippur)

וַתִּתֶּן לָנוּ יְיָ אֱלֹהֵינוּ, בְּאַהֲבָה אֶת יוֹם [הַשַּׁבָּת הַזֶּה
לִקְדֻשָּׁה וְלִמְנוּחָה, וְאֶת יוֹם] הַכִּפּוּרִים הַזֶּה לִמְחִילָה
וְלִסְלִיחָה וּלְכַפָּרָה, וְלִמְחָל־בּוֹ אֶת כָּל עֲוֹנוֹתֵינוּ,
[בְּאַהֲבָה] מִקְרָא קֹדֶשׁ, זֵכֶר לִיצִיאַת מִצְרָיִם.

Ya'aleh V'yavo

אֱלֹהֵינוּ וֵאלֹהֵי אֲבוֹתֵינוּ (וֵאלֹהֵי אִמּוֹתֵינוּ) יַעֲלֶה וְיָבֹא
וְיַגִּיעַ וְיֵרָאֶה וְיֵרָצֶה וְיִשָּׁמַע וְיִפָּקֵד וְיִזָּכֵר זִכְרוֹנֵנוּ
וּפִקְדוֹנֵנוּ וְזִכְרוֹן אֲבוֹתֵינוּ (וְאִמּוֹתֵינוּ) וְזִכְרוֹן מָשִׁיחַ

Bible, "Through justice the Commander of the hosts is exalted; through tzedakah, holiness flows from the holy God." You are praised, Adonay, Your majesty is holy.

Kedushat Ha-Yom (The Holiness of this Day)

Atta V'chartanu

You chose us from among all other nations to exemplify Your presence in the world. You showered us with love, You desired us, You exalted us that we might preserve the holy tongue, You imbued us with holiness through Your mitzvot, You drew us close to Your majesty through the prayers You chose, and You made us, with all our imperfections, the representatives of Your great and holy Name.

Va-titen Lanu (Rosh Hashanah)

As a gift of love, Adonay our God, You presented us (this day of Shabbat holiness and soul-rest, as well as) this Day of Remembrance, the day of (recollection of) sounding T'ruah on the Shofar (in love). It is a holy day on which we are called together; it is a remembrance of the Exodus from Egypt, when we first became Your people.

Va-titen Lanu (Yom Kippur)

As a gift of love, Adonay our God, You presented us (this day of Shabbat holiness and soul-rest, as well as) this Yom Kippur as a day of forgiveness, of the second chance, a day in which all our failures can be pardoned. It is a holy day on which we are called together; it is a remembrance of the Exodus from Egypt, when we first became Your people.

Ya'aleh V'ya-vo

Our God and God of those who came before us:

May the presence
    of us who come before You here
    of our ancient grandmothers and grandfathers

בֶּן דָּוִד עַבְדֶּךָ וְזִכְרוֹן יְרוּשָׁלַיִם עִיר קָדְשֶׁךָ וְזִכְרוֹן כָּל
עַמְּךָ בֵּית יִשְׂרָאֵל לְפָנֶיךָ. לִפְלֵיטָה וּלְטוֹבָה לְחֵן
וּלְחֶסֶד וּלְרַחֲמִים לְחַיִּים וּלְשָׁלוֹם בְּיוֹם הַזִּכָּרוֹן הַזֶּה.*
זָכְרֵנוּ יְיָ אֱלֹהֵינוּ בּוֹ לְטוֹבָה. וּפָקְדֵנוּ בוֹ לִבְרָכָה.
וְהוֹשִׁיעֵנוּ בוֹ לְחַיִּים: וּבִדְבַר יְשׁוּעָה וְרַחֲמִים חוּס
וְחָנֵּנוּ וְרַחֵם עָלֵינוּ וְהוֹשִׁיעֵנוּ כִּי אֵלֶיךָ עֵינֵינוּ. כִּי אֵל
מֶלֶךְ חַנּוּן וְרַחוּם אָתָּה:

(on Yom Kippur: *בְּיוֹם הַכִּפּוּרִים הַזֶּה)

M'loch al Kol Ha-olam (Sanctifying Rosh Hashanah)

אֱלֹהֵינוּ וֵאלֹהֵי אֲבוֹתֵינוּ (וֵאלֹהֵי אִמּוֹתֵינוּ) מְלוֹךְ עַל
כָּל הָעוֹלָם כֻּלּוֹ בִּכְבוֹדֶךָ וְהִנָּשֵׂא עַל כָּל הָאָרֶץ בִּיקָרֶךָ
וְהוֹפַע בַּהֲדַר גְּאוֹן עֻזֶּךָ עַל כָּל יוֹשְׁבֵי תֵבֵל אַרְצֶךָ.
וְיֵדַע כָּל פָּעוּל כִּי אַתָּה פְעַלְתּוֹ וְיָבִין כָּל יָצוּר כִּי אַתָּה
יְצַרְתּוֹ וְיֹאמַר כֹּל אֲשֶׁר נְשָׁמָה בְאַפּוֹ יְיָ אֱלֹהֵי יִשְׂרָאֵל

of our promised Messiah from Your servant David's
family
    of Jerusalem, the city filled with Your holiness
    of all Your people, the House of Israel

Ascend
    and come before You
    and come near to You
    and be noticed by You
    and be pleasing to You
    and be heeded by You
and be kept in mind by You
and be remembered by You

    for deliverance, for good, for grace, for kindness, for
    mercy, for life, for peace on this (Day of Remem-
    brance) (Yom Kippur).

Adonay our God:
    Remember us today for good
    Keep us in mind today for blessing
    Save us today for long life
    With a promise of victory over our weakness
    And compassion for our strength
    Hold us close
    Be gracious to us
    Save us
    Because our eyes are turned toward You,
    Because Your nature is grace and compassion,
    Because You are our Majesty.

M'loch al Kol Ha-olam (Sanctifying Rosh Hashanah)

Our God and God of our mothers and fathers, extend
Your rule in glory over the entire universe, that You may
be exalted in honor over the earth, appearing in the full
splendor of Your exalted power over all who dwell upon
the globe, Your planet. May every one of Your creatures
know that You created it, every form of life perceive that
You formed it, so that every being with breath in its nos-

מֶלֶךְ וּמַלְכוּתוֹ בַּכֹּל מָשָׁלָה: אֱלֹהֵינוּ וֵאלֹהֵי אֲבוֹתֵינוּ
(וֵאלֹהֵי אִמּוֹתֵינוּ) [רְצֵה בִמְנוּחָתֵנוּ] קַדְּשֵׁנוּ בְּמִצְוֹתֶיךָ
וְתֵן חֶלְקֵנוּ בְּתוֹרָתֶךָ שַׂבְּעֵנוּ מִטּוּבֶךָ וְשַׂמְּחֵנוּ
בִּישׁוּעָתֶךָ: [וְהַנְחִילֵנוּ יְיָ אֱלֹהֵינוּ בְּאַהֲבָה וּבְרָצוֹן
שַׁבַּת קָדְשֶׁךָ וְיָנוּחוּ בוֹ יִשְׂרָאֵל מְקַדְּשֵׁי שְׁמֶךָ] וְטַהֵר
לִבֵּנוּ לְעָבְדְּךָ בֶּאֱמֶת. כִּי אַתָּה אֱלֹהִים אֱמֶת וּדְבָרְךָ
אֱמֶת וְקַיָּם לָעַד. בָּרוּךְ אַתָּה יְיָ מֶלֶךְ עַל כָּל הָאָרֶץ
מְקַדֵּשׁ [הַשַּׁבָּת וְ]יִשְׂרָאֵל וְיוֹם הַזִּכָּרוֹן:

M'chal la-Avonoteynu (Sanctifying Yom Kippur)

אֱלֹהֵינוּ וֵאלֹהֵי אֲבוֹתֵינוּ (וֵאלֹהֵי אִמּוֹתֵינוּ) מְחַל
לַעֲוֹנוֹתֵינוּ בְּיוֹם [הַשַּׁבָּת הַזֶּה וּבְיוֹם] הַכִּפֻּרִים הַזֶּה.
מְחֵה וְהַעֲבֵר פְּשָׁעֵינוּ וְחַטֹּאתֵינוּ מִנֶּגֶד עֵינֶיךָ, כָּאָמוּר:
אָנֹכִי אָנֹכִי הוּא מוֹחֶה פְּשָׁעֶיךָ לְמַעֲנִי, וְחַטֹּאתֶיךָ לֹא
אֶזְכֹּר. וְנֶאֱמַר: מָחִיתִי כָעָב פְּשָׁעֶיךָ, וְכֶעָנָן חַטֹּאתֶיךָ;
שׁוּבָה אֵלַי כִּי גְאַלְתִּיךָ. וְנֶאֱמַר: כִּי בַיּוֹם הַזֶּה יְכַפֵּר
עֲלֵיכֶם לְטַהֵר אֶתְכֶם, מִכֹּל חַטֹּאתֵיכֶם לִפְנֵי יְיָ
תִּטְהָרוּ. אֱלֹהֵינוּ וֵאלֹהֵי אֲבוֹתֵינוּ (וֵאלֹהֵי אִמּוֹתֵינוּ),
[רְצֵה בִמְנוּחָתֵנוּ] קַדְּשֵׁנוּ בְּמִצְוֹתֶיךָ וְתֵן חֶלְקֵנוּ
בְּתוֹרָתֶךָ, שַׂבְּעֵנוּ מִטּוּבֶךָ וְשַׂמְּחֵנוּ בִּישׁוּעָתֶךָ.
[וְהַנְחִילֵנוּ, יְיָ אֱלֹהֵינוּ, בְּאַהֲבָה וּבְרָצוֹן שַׁבַּת קָדְשֶׁךָ,
וְיָנוּחוּ בוֹ יִשְׂרָאֵל מְקַדְּשֵׁי שְׁמֶךָ.] וְטַהֵר לִבֵּנוּ לְעָבְדְּךָ
בֶּאֱמֶת, כִּי אַתָּה סָלְחָן לְיִשְׂרָאֵל וּמָחֳלָן לְשִׁבְטֵי יְשֻׁרוּן
בְּכָל דּוֹר וָדוֹר, וּמִבַּלְעָדֶיךָ אֵין לָנוּ מֶלֶךְ מוֹחֵל וְסוֹלֵחַ

trils may proclaim: "Adonay, God of Israel, rules a realm encompassing all people!"

Our God and God of those who gave us life: (Be pleased with our soul-rest.) Imbue us with holiness through Your mitzvot and grant us our share in the understanding of Your Torah. Satiate us with Your goodness, fill us with the joy of victory over our selfish instincts, our cruel temptations. (Dower us, God, with the holiness of Your Shabbat; let the Jewish people, whose actions strive to manifest Your holiness, find soul-rest on this day.) Wash clean our hearts that we may serve You with true intentions, for You are the God of truth, and Your word is true, sustained forever. You are praised, Adonay, Sovereign over all the earth, who fills with holiness (Shabbat,) the Jewish people, and the Day of Remembrance.

M'chal la-Avonoteynu (Sanctifying Yom Kippur)

Our God and God of our mothers and fathers, pardon our failures on (this Shabbat and on) this Yom Kippur. Erase our malicious deeds, our human shortcomings; sweep them from Your sight. As it says in the Bible, "I myself will erase your malicious deeds for the sake of My mercy; I will not recall your shortcomings." As it says, "I have dissolved Your malicious deeds like a mist, your shortcomings like a cloud. Turn back to Me, do tshuvah, for I have redeemed you." And it says, "On this day God will give you a new start by purifying you. From all your shortcomings you will be clean in the sight of Adonay."

Our God and God of those who gave us life: (Be pleased with our soul-rest). Imbue us with holiness through Your mitzvot and grant us our share in the understanding of Your Torah. Satiate us with Your goodness, fill us with the joy of victory over our selfish instincts, our cruel temptations. (Dower us, God, with the holiness of your Shabbat; let the Jewish people, whose actions strive to manifest Your holiness, find soul-rest on this day.) Wash clean our hearts that we may serve You with true intentions. You are the forgiver of Israel, who grants pardon to the tribes You

אֶלָּא אָתָּה. בָּרוּךְ אַתָּה יְיָ מֶלֶךְ מוֹחֵל וְסוֹלֵחַ
לַעֲוֹנוֹתֵינוּ וְלַעֲוֹנוֹת עַמּוֹ בֵּית יִשְׂרָאֵל, וּמַעֲבִיר
אַשְׁמוֹתֵינוּ בְּכָל שָׁנָה וְשָׁנָה, מֶלֶךְ עַל כָּל הָאָרֶץ
מְקַדֵּשׁ [הַשַּׁבָּת וְ]יִשְׂרָאֵל וְיוֹם הַכִּפֻּרִים.

Avodah (Serving God)

R'tzey (Traditional version)

רְצֵה יְיָ אֱלֹהֵינוּ בְּעַמְּךָ יִשְׂרָאֵל וּבִתְפִלָּתָם. וְהָשֵׁב אֶת
הָעֲבוֹדָה לִדְבִיר בֵּיתֶךָ וְאִשֵּׁי יִשְׂרָאֵל וּתְפִלָּתָם
בְּאַהֲבָה תְקַבֵּל בְּרָצוֹן. וּתְהִי לְרָצוֹן תָּמִיד עֲבוֹדַת
יִשְׂרָאֵל עַמֶּךָ. וְתֶחֱזֶינָה עֵינֵינוּ בְּשׁוּבְךָ לְצִיּוֹן בְּרַחֲמִים.
בָּרוּךְ אַתָּה יְיָ הַמַּחֲזִיר שְׁכִינָתוֹ לְצִיּוֹן:

R'tzey (Reform version)

רְצֵה יְיָ אֱלֹהֵינוּ בְּעַמְּךָ יִשְׂרָאֵל, וּתְפִלָּתָם בְּאַהֲבָה
תְקַבֵּל, וּתְהִי לְרָצוֹן תָּמִיד עֲבוֹדַת יִשְׂרָאֵל עַמֶּךָ. אֵל
קָרוֹב לְכָל-קֹרְאָיו, פְּנֵה אֶל עֲבָדֶיךָ וְחָנֵּנוּ; שְׁפוֹךְ
רוּחֲךָ עָלֵינוּ, וְתֶחֱזֶינָה עֵינֵינוּ בְּשׁוּבְךָ לְצִיּוֹן בְּרַחֲמִים.
בָּרוּךְ אַתָּה יְיָ הַמַּחֲזִיר שְׁכִינָתוֹ לְצִיּוֹן:

Hoda-ah (Thanksgiving)

Modim

מוֹדִים אֲנַחְנוּ לָךְ שָׁאַתָּה הוּא יְיָ אֱלֹהֵינוּ וֵאלֹהֵי
אֲבוֹתֵינוּ (וֵאלֹהֵי אִמּוֹתֵינוּ) לְעוֹלָם וָעֶד. צוּר חַיֵּינוּ
מָגֵן יִשְׁעֵנוּ אַתָּה הוּא לְדוֹר וָדוֹר. נוֹדֶה לְּךָ וּנְסַפֵּר
תְּהִלָּתֶךָ עַל חַיֵּינוּ הַמְּסוּרִים בְּיָדֶךָ וְעַל נִשְׁמוֹתֵינוּ
הַפְּקוּדוֹת לָךְ וְעַל נִסֶּיךָ שֶׁבְּכָל-יוֹם עִמָּנוּ וְעַל
נִפְלְאוֹתֶיךָ וְטוֹבוֹתֶיךָ שֶׁבְּכָל-עֵת עֶרֶב וָבֹקֶר וְצָהֳרָיִם.
הַטּוֹב כִּי לֹא כָלוּ רַחֲמֶיךָ וְהַמְרַחֵם כִּי לֹא תַמּוּ חֲסָדֶיךָ

called Yeshurun, the upright. No other power beside You can forgive and excuse us. You are praised, Adonay, Monarch who forgives and excuses our wrongs and the wrongs of Your entire people Israel, who takes away our guilt each year; Ruler of all the earth, who fills with holiness (Shabbat,) the Jewish people, and Yom Kippur.

Avodah (Serving God)

R'tzey (Traditional version)

May You be pleased with Your people Israel, Adonay our God, and with their prayer. Restore to Your holy temple in Jerusalem the service You most desire, accepting Israel's holy offerings and holy words with love. May the intensity of Your people's worship please You always. May we see Your merciful return to Zion with our own eyes. You are praised, Adonay, whose nurturing presence You will again return to Zion.

R'tzey (Reform version)

May You be pleased with Your people Israel, Adonay our God, may You lovingly accept our prayer. May the intensity of Your people's prayers please You always. Turn Your gracious countenance to Your servants, pour out Your spirit upon us, that we might see Your merciful return to Zion with our own eyes. You are praised, Adonay, whose nuturing presence You will again return to Zion.

Hoda-ah (Thanksgiving)

Modim

Thank You.
    You are the Source of our life, and the life of those
    who carried us into this world.
You are our Rock, our shield, our defender.
In every generation we will thank You and retell Your praise
    for our lives which You shape with Your hand
    for our souls which You hold in trust
    for Your miracles which accompany us each day
    for Your wonders and Your favors which fill all
our moments

מֵעוֹלָם קִוִּינוּ לָךְ: וְעַל כֻּלָּם יִתְבָּרַךְ וְיִתְרוֹמַם שִׁמְךָ
מַלְכֵּנוּ תָּמִיד לְעוֹלָם וָעֶד: וּכְתֹב לְחַיִּים טוֹבִים כָּל־בְּנֵי
בְרִיתֶךָ: וְכֹל הַחַיִּים יוֹדוּךָ סֶּלָה וִיהַלְלוּ אֶת שִׁמְךָ
בֶּאֱמֶת הָאֵל יְשׁוּעָתֵנוּ וְעֶזְרָתֵנוּ סֶלָה. בָּרוּךְ אַתָּה יְיָ
הַטּוֹב שִׁמְךָ וּלְךָ נָאֶה לְהוֹדוֹת:

Birkat Shalom (Peace)

Shalom Rav (Evening Services)

שָׁלוֹם רָב עַל יִשְׂרָאֵל עַמְּךָ תָּשִׂים לְעוֹלָם. כִּי אַתָּה
הוּא מֶלֶךְ אָדוֹן לְכָל־הַשָּׁלוֹם. וְטוֹב בְּעֵינֶיךָ לְבָרֵךְ
אֶת־עַמְּךָ יִשְׂרָאֵל בְּכָל־עֵת וּבְכָל־שָׁעָה בִּשְׁלוֹמֶךָ.
בְּסֵפֶר חַיִּים בְּרָכָה וְשָׁלוֹם וּפַרְנָסָה טוֹבָה נִזָּכֵר וְנִכָּתֵב
לְפָנֶיךָ אֲנַחְנוּ וְכָל עַמְּךָ בֵּית יִשְׂרָאֵל לְחַיִּים טוֹבִים
וּלְשָׁלוֹם. בָּרוּךְ אַתָּה יְיָ עֹשֶׂה הַשָּׁלוֹם:

Sim Shalom (Morning, Yom Kippur Afternoon, and Ne'ilah Services)

שִׂים שָׁלוֹם טוֹבָה וּבְרָכָה חֵן וָחֶסֶד וְרַחֲמִים עָלֵינוּ וְעַל
כָּל־יִשְׂרָאֵל עַמֶּךָ. בָּרְכֵנוּ אָבִינוּ כֻּלָּנוּ כְּאֶחָד בְּאוֹר
פָּנֶיךָ. כִּי בְאוֹר פָּנֶיךָ נָתַתָּ לָּנוּ יְיָ אֱלֹהֵינוּ תּוֹרַת חַיִּים
וְאַהֲבַת חֶסֶד וּצְדָקָה וּבְרָכָה וְרַחֲמִים וְחַיִּים וְשָׁלוֹם.
וְטוֹב בְּעֵינֶיךָ לְבָרֵךְ אֶת־עַמְּךָ יִשְׂרָאֵל בְּכָל־עֵת וּבְכָל־
שָׁעָה בִּשְׁלוֹמֶךָ. בְּסֵפֶר חַיִּים בְּרָכָה וְשָׁלוֹם וּפַרְנָסָה

every evening, every morning, on dark days, and when the sun is high.

For You are the good God, whose nurture never dries up, the Compassionate One, whose acts of love are endless.

In Your eternity lies our hope.

For all these things, O Majesty, may Your Name be blessed and raised in high esteem by all who live, and inscribe for a good life the people of Your covenant, who pour forth thanks to You in ecstasy, along with everything alive, giving honest praise to Your Name, O God, who leads us forth from our adversaries in triumph, sela! You are praised, Adonay, whose name is Good, whose praise is comely on our lips.

Birkat Shalom (Peace)

Shalom Rav (Evening Services)

Spread peace, abundant and everlasting, over Your people Israel, for You are the source, the Majesty, of peace, wherever it is found. May it be good in Your eyes to bless Your people Israel at every season, at every moment, with that peace which is Your nature. May we and all the House of Israel be inscribed perpetually in the Book of life and blessing, peace and sustenance, for a worthwhile life and for peace. You are praised, Adonay, author of peace.

Sim Shalom (Morning, Yom Kippur Afternoon, and Ne'ilah Services)

Spread peace, goodness and blessing, grace, love, and compassion over us and over all Israel Your people. Bless us, Fathermother, all of us as one, in the radiance of Your countenance, for in the light of Your presence, Adonay our God, you gave us a Torah of life, love born of our covenant, justice, blessing, compassion, life, and peace. May it be good in Your eyes to bless Your people Israel at every season, at every moment, with that peace which is Your nature.

טוֹבָה נִזָּכֵר וְנִכָּתֵב לְפָנֶיךָ אֲנַחְנוּ וְכָל עַמְּךָ בֵּית
יִשְׂרָאֵל לְחַיִּים טוֹבִים וּלְשָׁלוֹם. בָּרוּךְ אַתָּה יְיָ עֹשֵׂה
הַשָּׁלוֹם:

*(Confessions for Yom Kippur will be found on pages
230–237)*

Personal Prayer

Elohai Ntzor

אֱלֹהַי נְצוֹר לְשׁוֹנִי מֵרָע וּשְׂפָתַי מִדַּבֵּר מִרְמָה
וְלִמְקַלְלַי נַפְשִׁי תִדּוֹם וְנַפְשִׁי כֶּעָפָר לַכֹּל תִּהְיֶה: פְּתַח
לִבִּי בְּתוֹרָתֶךָ וּבְמִצְוֹתֶיךָ תִּרְדּוֹף נַפְשִׁי. וְכָל
הַחוֹשְׁבִים עָלַי רָעָה מְהֵרָה הָפֵר עֲצָתָם וְקַלְקֵל
מַחֲשַׁבְתָּם: עֲשֵׂה לְמַעַן שְׁמֶךָ. עֲשֵׂה לְמַעַן יְמִינֶךָ. עֲשֵׂה
לְמַעַן קְדֻשָּׁתֶךָ עֲשֵׂה לְמַעַן תוֹרָתֶךָ: לְמַעַן יֵחָלְצוּן
יְדִידֶיךָ הוֹשִׁיעָה יְמִינְךָ וַעֲנֵנִי: יִהְיוּ לְרָצוֹן אִמְרֵי פִי
וְהֶגְיוֹן לִבִּי לְפָנֶיךָ יְיָ צוּרִי וְגוֹאֲלִי: עֹשֶׂה שָׁלוֹם
בִּמְרוֹמָיו הוּא יַעֲשֶׂה שָׁלוֹם עָלֵינוּ וְעַל כָּל יִשְׂרָאֵל
וְאִמְרוּ אָמֵן:

May we and all the House of Israel be inscribed perpetually in the Book of life and blessing, peace and sustenance,
for a worthwhile life and for peace. You are praised,
Adonay, author of peace.

(Confessions for Yom Kippur will be found on pages
230–237)

Personal Prayer

Elohai Ntzor

Adonay, keep my tongue from cruelty and my lips from
deceit. To those who defame me, let my soul keep silent;
teach my soul humility that I may learn even from those
who hate me. Open my heart to Your Torah and let my
soul search out Your mitzvot. As for all who think to harm
me, frustrate their plans and their purposes for the sake of
Your honor, to show You have the power to protect, for
the sake of Your holiness and Your Torah. Preserve those
who try to live by Your teachings. Save me with Your
power, Adonay, and answer me. May the words in my
mouth and the thoughts in My heart be equally acceptable
to You, Adonay my rescuer, my faithful Rock. O heavenly
peacemaker, make peace felt now among us, among all
Israel, among all Your creatures, that we all might say:
Amen.

MUSAF SERVICE

MUSAF SERVICE

Preparation

Bleat of lambs
Sweetness of new wheat
Oils pressed from ancient olives
Gifts we would have brought had we but lived
In offering distance of the sacred house.

Their sound and fragrance lingers on our page.

The centuries have changed them.
Musaf offerings for the special days
Have been pressed like yellowed roses lovingly preserved
In books
Torah proclamations of what we were supposed to offer
Have themselves become the offerings,
Grain and oils flow only from our lips.

Were the house still standing
Would we bring live lambs to slaughter?
Would we share our surplus as much with priests as
    with the poor?

We were driven from the house too soon to find the answer;
History has robbed us of the choice.

How can we know what mystery the ancients found
    within these rites
Unless our lips keep bringing forth their gifts?
How can we know whether lambs are what God wants
Unless we carry on the memory of what God wanted
Into that time which will proclaim God's ultimate plan,
And the destiny of lambs and priests,
The poor and the prosperous,
Will be explained at last?

Let then our offering be
Not only words pressed out of books
But voices
Voices filled with longing that the explanations might
        come soon
Longing that the centuries of suffering of lambs might
        be redeemed

Longing
That our words might give to all who can do naught but bleat
A voice

Longing
That to all the destitute
The innocents profaned
The suffering creatures with no choice but to be offered up
Time might grant at long, long last
A sacred house
A lasting home.

May the words we offer now
Once more release the fragrance
Of the yellow rose.

Reader's Kaddish

יִתְגַּדַּל וְיִתְקַדַּשׁ שְׁמֵהּ רַבָּא בְּעָלְמָא דִי בְרָא כִרְעוּתֵהּ;
וְיַמְלִיךְ מַלְכוּתֵהּ בְּחַיֵּיכוֹן וּבְיוֹמֵיכוֹן,וּבְחַיֵּי דְכָל בֵּית
יִשְׂרָאֵל, בַּעֲגָלָא וּבִזְמַן קָרִיב, וְאִמְרוּ אָמֵן:

יְהֵא שְׁמֵהּ רַבָּא מְבָרַךְ לְעָלַם וּלְעָלְמֵי עָלְמַיָּא.

יִתְבָּרַךְ וְיִשְׁתַּבַּח, וְיִתְפָּאַר וְיִתְרוֹמַם, וְיִתְנַשֵּׂא
וְיִתְהַדָּר, וְיִתְעַלֶּה וְיִתְהַלַּל שְׁמֵהּ דְּקֻדְשָׁא, בְּרִיךְ הוּא,
לְעֵלָּא לְעֵלָּא מִן כָּל בִּרְכָתָא וְשִׁירָתָא, תֻּשְׁבְּחָתָא
וְנֶחֱמָתָא, דַּאֲמִירָן בְּעָלְמָא, וְאִמְרוּ אָמֵן.

May God's great name be magnified and sanctified in the world created by the holy will, and may God's rule be known in your lifetime, in your own days, and in the life of the house of Israel, speedily, in a time close at hand.

May the name of the blessed Holy One be praised and extolled far beyond all praises and blessings we can ever say in the world. Amen.

MUSAF AMIDAH

אֲדֹנָי שְׂפָתַי תִּפְתָּח וּפִי יַגִּיד תְּהִלָּתֶךָ:

Avot

בָּרוּךְ אַתָּה, יְיָ אֱלֹהֵינוּ וֵאלֹהֵי אֲבוֹתֵינוּ (וֵאלֹהֵי
אִמּוֹתֵינוּ), אֱלֹהֵי אַבְרָהָם, אֱלֹהֵי יִצְחָק, וֵאלֹהֵי יַעֲקֹב,
(אֱלֹהֵי שָׂרָה, אֱלֹהֵי רִבְקָה, אֱלֹהֵי רָחֵל, וֵאלֹהֵי לֵאָה),
הָאֵל הַגָּדוֹל הַגִּבּוֹר וְהַנּוֹרָא, אֵל עֶלְיוֹן, גּוֹמֵל חֲסָדִים
טוֹבִים, וְקֹנֵה הַכֹּל, וְזוֹכֵר חַסְדֵי אָבוֹת (וְאִמָּהוֹת),
וּמֵבִיא גוֹאֵל* לִבְנֵי בְנֵיהֶם לְמַעַן שְׁמוֹ בְּאַהֲבָה.

(When the Reader offers the Amidah aloud, insert the following:)

(מִסּוֹד חֲכָמִים וּנְבוֹנִים, וּמִלֶּמֶד דַּעַת מְבִינִים,
אֶפְתְּחָה פִּי בִּתְפִלָּה וּבְתַחֲנוּנִים, לְחַלּוֹת וּלְחַנֵּן
פְּנֵי מֶלֶךְ מַלְכֵי הַמְּלָכִים וַאֲדוֹנֵי הָאֲדוֹנִים.)

זָכְרֵנוּ לְחַיִּים, מֶלֶךְ חָפֵץ בַּחַיִּים, וְכָתְבֵנוּ בְּסֵפֶר
הַחַיִּים, לְמַעַנְךָ אֱלֹהִים חַיִּים: מֶלֶךְ עוֹזֵר וּמוֹשִׁיעַ
וּמָגֵן. בָּרוּךְ אַתָּה יְיָ, מָגֵן אַבְרָהָם (וְשָׂרָה).

In the Reform tradition, גְּאוּלָה*

Gevurot

אַתָּה גִבּוֹר לְעוֹלָם אֲדֹנָי מְחַיֵּה מֵתִים* אַתָּה רַב
לְהוֹשִׁיעַ. מְכַלְכֵּל חַיִּים בְּחֶסֶד מְחַיֵּה מֵתִים* בְּרַחֲמִים
רַבִּים. סוֹמֵךְ נוֹפְלִים וְרוֹפֵא חוֹלִים וּמַתִּיר אֲסוּרִים
וּמְקַיֵּם אֱמוּנָתוֹ לִישֵׁנֵי עָפָר. מִי כָמוֹךָ בַּעַל גְּבוּרוֹת
וּמִי דּוֹמֶה לָךְ. מֶלֶךְ מֵמִית וּמְחַיֶּה וּמַצְמִיחַ יְשׁוּעָה: מִי
כָמוֹךָ אַב הָרַחֲמִים זוֹכֵר יְצוּרָיו לְחַיִּים בְּרַחֲמִים:

In the Reform tradition, הַכֹּל*

MUSAF AMIDAH

Adonay, open up my lips, that my mouth may sing Your praise.

Avot

You are praised, Adonay our God, God of our fathers (and mothers), of Abraham, of Isaac, of Jacob (of Sarah, of Rebecca, of Rachel, of Leah) — great, powerful, and awesome God, higher than all other powers, who loves us even when we are unworthy. Creator who nurtures all, You remember the worthy acts of our ancient fathers (and mothers), and You will return their love by bringing a redeemer* to their children's children for the sake of Your promise, as evidence of Your love.

(When the Reader offers the Amidah aloud, insert the following:)

> (With words borrowed from the profundity of the sages and the learning of the wise, let me open my mouth in prayerful entreaty as I come into the presence of the Ruler supreme above all earthly rulers, whose power is our hope.)

Remember us with life, O Monarch who so treasures life! Inscribe us in the Book of Life for Your own sake, O God whose being is life. O Majesty who helps, saves and protects, You are praised, Adonay, source of Abraham's strength(, of Sarah's nurture).

*In the Reform tradition, *redemption*

Gevurot

You are eternally powerful, Adonay, You have the power to give life to the dead,* You have the power to save us. You lovingly supply the needs of all living things. Out of Your compassion You grant the dead* eternal life. You support the weak, heal the sick, and free the enslaved; You keep Your word to those who sleep in the dust. Who is like You, source of all power? Who resembles You, Majesty, who gives both death and life and makes redemption flower?

*In the Reform tradition, *to all*

וְנֶאֱמָן אַתָּה לְהַחֲיוֹת מֵתִים*: בָּרוּךְ אַתָּה יְיָ מְחַיֵּה הַמֵּתִים*:

*In the Reform tradition, הַכֹּל

(When the Reader offers the Amidah aloud, continue with Unetaneh Tokef, below)

אַתָּה קָדוֹשׁ וְשִׁמְךָ קָדוֹשׁ וּקְדוֹשִׁים בְּכָל יוֹם יְהַלְלוּךָ סֶּלָה:

(Silent Amidah continues with U'v'chen, p. 184)

Unetaneh Tokef

וּנְתַנֶּה תְּקֶף קְדֻשַּׁת הַיּוֹם, כִּי הוּא נוֹרָא וְאָיוֹם; וּבוֹ תִנָּשֵׂא מַלְכוּתֶךָ, וְיִכּוֹן בְּחֶסֶד כִּסְאֶךָ, וְתֵשֵׁב עָלָיו בֶּאֱמֶת. אֱמֶת כִּי אַתָּה הוּא דַיָּן וּמוֹכִיחַ, וְיוֹדֵעַ וָעֵד, וְכוֹתֵב וְחוֹתֵם, וְסוֹפֵר וּמוֹנֶה, וְתִזְכּוֹר כָּל הַנִּשְׁכָּחוֹת: וְתִפְתַּח אֶת סֵפֶר הַזִּכְרוֹנוֹת, וּמֵאֵלָיו יִקָּרֵא, וְחוֹתַם יַד כָּל אָדָם בּוֹ.

וּבְשׁוֹפָר גָּדוֹל יִתָּקַע, וְקוֹל דְּמָמָה דַקָּה יִשָּׁמַע; וּמַלְאָכִים יֵחָפֵזוּן, וְחִיל וּרְעָדָה יֹאחֵזוּן, וְיֹאמְרוּ הִנֵּה יוֹם הַדִּין, לִפְקוֹד עַל צְבָא מָרוֹם בַּדִּין, כִּי לֹא יִזְכּוּ בְעֵינֶיךָ בַּדִּין. וְכָל בָּאֵי עוֹלָם יַעַבְרוּן לְפָנֶיךָ כִּבְנֵי מָרוֹן, כְּבַקָּרַת רוֹעֶה עֶדְרוֹ, מַעֲבִיר צֹאנוֹ תַּחַת שִׁבְטוֹ, כֵּן תַּעֲבִיר וְתִסְפּוֹר וְתִמְנֶה, וְתִפְקוֹד נֶפֶשׁ כָּל חַי, וְתַחְתּוֹךְ קִצְבָה לְכָל בְּרִיָּה, וְתִכְתּוֹב אֶת גְּזַר דִּינָם.

Who is like You, motherly Father, who loves Your creatures
with a compassion human parents long to give? We trust in
Your promise one day to revive those we have lost to death.
You are praised, Adonay, who gives the dead* eternal life.

*In the Reform tradition, *to all*

*(When the Reader offers the Amidah aloud, continue with
Unetaneh Tokef, below)*

Atta Kadosh

You are holy, the meaning of Your name is holiness. We who
strive to be holy yearn to praise You every day.

(Silent Amidah continues with U'v'chen, p. 185)

Unetaneh Tokef

Let us declare the holy power of this day, for it is awesome and
mighty. Your sovereignty is exalted upon it, and You faithfully
take Your place upon Your throne established in love borne of
the covenant between You and ourselves. You are the true
judge and witness, You write and seal and inscribe and take
account. You remember all that we have forgotten, opening the
Book of Remembrance from which everything is read and in
which is the seal of every human being.

The great Shofar is sounded, and a still small voice is heard. The
angels in heaven are dismayed and are seized with fear and
trembling, as they proclaim: "Behold the Day of Judgment!"
The hosts of heaven are to be arraigned in judgment, for in
Your eyes even they are not free from guilt. All who live in the
world pass today before You, one by one, like a flock of
sheep. As a shepherd gathers the sheep and causes them to pass
beneath the staff, so You pass and record, count and visit, every
living soul, appointing the measure of every creature's life and
decreeing its destiny.

בְּרֹאשׁ הַשָּׁנָה יִכָּתֵבוּן, וּבְיוֹם צוֹם כִּפּוּר יֵחָתֵמוּן, כַּמָּה יַעַבְרוּן, וְכַמָּה יִבָּרֵאוּן; מִי יִחְיֶה, וּמִי יָמוּת; מִי בְקִצּוֹ, וּמִי לֹא בְקִצּוֹ; מִי בָאֵשׁ, וּמִי בַמַּיִם; מִי בַחֶרֶב, וּמִי בַחַיָּה; מִי בָרָעָב, וּמִי בַצָּמָא; מִי בָרַעַשׁ, וּמִי בַמַּגֵּפָה; מִי בַחֲנִיקָה, וּמִי בַסְּקִילָה; מִי יָנוּחַ, וּמִי יָנוּעַ; מִי יִשָּׁקֵט, וּמִי יִטָּרֵף; מִי יִשָּׁלֵו וּמִי יִתְיַסָּר; מִי יֵעָנִי, וּמִי יֵעָשֵׁר; מִי יִשָּׁפֵל, וּמִי יָרוּם.

וּתְשׁוּבָה וּתְפִלָּה וּצְדָקָה
מַעֲבִירִין אֶת רֹעַ הַגְּזֵרָה.

כִּי כְּשִׁמְךָ כֵּן תְּהִלָּתֶךָ, קָשֶׁה לִכְעוֹס וְנוֹחַ לִרְצוֹת; כִּי לֹא תַחְפּוֹץ בְּמוֹת הַמֵּת, כִּי אִם בְּשׁוּבוֹ מִדַּרְכּוֹ וְחָיָה. וְעַד יוֹם מוֹתוֹ תְּחַכֶּה לוֹ, אִם יָשׁוּב מִיַּד תְּקַבְּלוֹ. אֱמֶת כִּי אַתָּה הוּא יוֹצְרָם, וְאַתָּה יוֹדֵעַ יִצְרָם, כִּי הֵם בָּשָׂר וָדָם.

אָדָם יְסוֹדוֹ מֵעָפָר וְסוֹפוֹ לֶעָפָר; בְּנַפְשׁוֹ יָבִיא לַחְמוֹ; מָשׁוּל כְּחֶרֶס הַנִּשְׁבָּר, כְּחָצִיר יָבֵשׁ, וּכְצִיץ נוֹבֵל, כְּצֵל עוֹבֵר, וּכְעָנָן כָּלָה, וּכְרוּחַ נוֹשָׁבֶת, וּכְאָבָק פּוֹרֵחַ, וְכַחֲלוֹם יָעוּף.
וְאַתָּה הוּא מֶלֶךְ אֵל חַי וְקַיָּם.

Kedusha

אֵין קִצְבָה לִשְׁנוֹתֶךָ, וְאֵין קֵץ לְאֹרֶךְ יָמֶיךָ; וְאֵין לְשַׁעֵר מַרְכְּבוֹת כְּבוֹדֶךָ, וְאֵין לְפָרֵשׁ עֲלוּם שְׁמֶךָ; שִׁמְךָ נָאֶה לְךָ וְאַתָּה נָאֶה לִשְׁמֶךָ, וּשְׁמֵנוּ קָרָאתָ בִּשְׁמֶךָ.
עֲשֵׂה לְמַעַן שְׁמֶךָ, וְקַדֵּשׁ אֶת שִׁמְךָ עַל מַקְדִּישֵׁי שְׁמֶךָ, בַּעֲבוּר כְּבוֹד שִׁמְךָ הַנַּעֲרָץ וְהַנִּקְדָּשׁ, כְּסוֹד שִׂיחַ שַׂרְפֵי

Refrain:
B'rosh hashanah yikateyvun uvyom tzom kippur yeychateymun.

(On Rosh Hashanah it is written and on Yom Kippur it is decided)

On Rosh Hashanah it is written and on Yom Kippur it is decided how many shall pass on and how many be created, who shall live and who shall die, who when their time comes and who before or after their time, who by fire and who by water, who by the sword and who by wild beasts, who by famine and who by drought, who by earthquake and who by epidemic, who by strangling and who by stoning, who shall have rest and who can never be still, who shall be serene and who torn apart, who shall be at ease and who afflicted, who shall be impoverished and who enriched, who shall be brought low and who raised high. But tshuvah, prayer, and charitable acts avert the severity of the decree.

Your praise is like Your nature: slow to anger and easy to placate. You do not want people to die, but to turn from their evil ways and live. Till our dying day You wait for us, and if we do tshuvah, You accept us back at once. True it is that You are our Creator and You know the drives that dominate flesh and blood.

We humans come from dust and end in dust. We expend our lives bringing forth bread. We are like a fragment of broken pottery, like dry grass; like a faded flower, a passing shadow; like a melting cloud, a blowing breeze; like flying dust, a dream dissolving.

But You are the Sovereign who lives forever!

Kedusha

O Being of endless years, of Glory unattainable! Your secrets are beyond discovery, the true meaning of Your Name is known to You alone, and yet You have included Your Name El in ours, in Israel. Act now for Your Name's sake, for the sake of Your glorious Being, filled with holiness and praise! Reveal the holy presence of Your Name before Your faithful ones, dwellers

קֹדֶשׁ, הַמַּקְדִּישִׁים שִׁמְךָ בַּקֹּדֶשׁ, דֲּרֵי מַעְלָה עִם דֲּרֵי
מַטָּה—

כַּכָּתוּב עַל יַד נְבִיאֶךָ: וְקָרָא זֶה אֶל זֶה וְאָמַר:

קָדוֹשׁ, קָדוֹשׁ, קָדוֹשׁ יְיָ צְבָאוֹת;
מְלֹא כָל הָאָרֶץ כְּבוֹדוֹ.
כְּבוֹדוֹ מָלֵא עוֹלָם, מְשָׁרְתָיו שׁוֹאֲלִים זֶה לָזֶה אַיֵּה
מְקוֹם כְּבוֹדוֹ, לְעֻמָּתָם בָּרוּךְ יֹאמֵרוּ—

בָּרוּךְ כְּבוֹד יְיָ מִמְּקוֹמוֹ.

מִמְּקוֹמוֹ הוּא יִפֶן בְּרַחֲמִים, וְיָחֹן עִם הַמְיַחֲדִים שְׁמוֹ
עֶרֶב וָבֹקֶר, בְּכָל יוֹם תָּמִיד, פַּעֲמַיִם בְּאַהֲבָה שְׁמַע
אוֹמְרִים:
שְׁמַע יִשְׂרָאֵל, יְיָ אֱלֹהֵינוּ, יְיָ אֶחָד.

הוּא אֱלֹהֵינוּ, הוּא אָבִינוּ, הוּא מַלְכֵּנוּ, הוּא מוֹשִׁיעֵנוּ,
וְהוּא יַשְׁמִיעֵנוּ בְּרַחֲמָיו שֵׁנִית לְעֵינֵי כָּל חָי; לִהְיוֹת
לָכֶם לֵאלֹהִים—

אֲנִי יְיָ אֱלֹהֵיכֶם.

אַדִּיר אַדִּירֵנוּ, יְיָ אֲדֹנֵינוּ, מָה אַדִּיר שִׁמְךָ בְּכָל הָאָרֶץ.
וְהָיָה יְיָ לְמֶלֶךְ עַל כָּל הָאָרֶץ, בַּיּוֹם הַהוּא יִהְיֶה יְיָ
אֶחָד וּשְׁמוֹ אֶחָד.

וּבְדִבְרֵי קָדְשְׁךָ כָּתוּב לֵאמֹר:

יִמְלֹךְ יְיָ לְעוֹלָם, אֱלֹהַיִךְ צִיּוֹן לְדֹר וָדֹר; הַלְלוּיָהּ.

there on high and dwellers here below, who in the mysterious tongue of Seraphim aflame with holiness, now declare the sanctity of Your Name:

As it is written in Isaiah: "And each called to the other, saying":

Kadosh Kadosh Kadosh Adonay Tzvaot, mlo chol ha-aretz kvodo:

Holy! Holy! Holy! is the Commander of the Hosts, the fullness of all the earth is God's glory.

Your Glory fills the world! Those who watch over it ask each other: Where is the place of God's glory?" And they all reply, "Baruch—"

Baruch kvod Adonay mimkomo:

Praised be the Glory of Adonay from God's Place, the World.

From that place, may You turn in compassion and grace to the people who declare Your Oneness evening and morning every day, as in love they proclaim, "Sh'ma—"

Sh'ma Yisrael Adonay Eloheynu Adonay Echad:

Hear, Israel, Adonay is our God, Adonay is One.

You are our God, our Nurturer, our Sovereign, our Deliverer. In Your mercy may You once again cause every living being to hear Your words:

Ani Adonay Eloheychem:
I, Adonay, am Your God.

Excellency, our Excellency, Adonay, Source of everything we are, how excellent is Your Name in all the earth! Adonay will reign as sovereign throughout all the earth, and on that day You will be the only One, Your Name the only One!

In the holy words of Psalms it is written:

Yimloch Adonay l'olam, Elohayich tziyon, l'dor vador, halleluya!

Adonay will reign forever, Your God will reign, O Zion to all generations. Praise God!

לְדוֹר וָדוֹר נַגִּיד גָּדְלֶךָ, וּלְנֵצַח נְצָחִים קְדֻשָּׁתְךָ נַקְדִּישׁ,
וְשִׁבְחֲךָ אֱלֹהֵינוּ מִפִּינוּ לֹא יָמוּשׁ לְעוֹלָם וָעֶד, כִּי אֵל
מֶלֶךְ גָּדוֹל וְקָדוֹשׁ אָתָּה.

Uv'chen

וּבְכֵן תֵּן פַּחְדְּךָ יְיָ אֱלֹהֵינוּ עַל כָּל מַעֲשֶׂיךָ וְאֵימָתְךָ עַל־
כָּל מַה שֶּׁבָּרָאתָ. וְיִירָאוּךָ כָּל הַמַּעֲשִׂים וְיִשְׁתַּחֲווּ
לְפָנֶיךָ כָּל הַבְּרוּאִים. וְיֵעָשׂוּ כֻלָּם אֲגֻדָּה אַחַת לַעֲשׂוֹת
רְצוֹנְךָ בְּלֵבָב שָׁלֵם. כְּמוֹ שֶׁיָּדַעְנוּ יְיָ אֱלֹהֵינוּ שֶׁהַשָּׁלְטוֹן
לְפָנֶיךָ, עֹז בְּיָדְךָ וּגְבוּרָה בִּימִינֶךָ, וְשִׁמְךָ נוֹרָא עַל כָּל
מַה שֶּׁבָּרָאתָ:

וּבְכֵן תֵּן כָּבוֹד יְיָ לְעַמֶּךָ תְּהִלָּה לִירֵאֶיךָ וְתִקְוָה
לְדוֹרְשֶׁיךָ וּפִתְחוֹן פֶּה לַמְיַחֲלִים לָךְ. שִׂמְחָה לְאַרְצֶךָ
וְשָׂשׂוֹן לְעִירֶךָ וּצְמִיחַת קֶרֶן לְדָוִד עַבְדֶּךָ וַעֲרִיכַת נֵר
לְבֶן יִשַׁי מְשִׁיחֶךָ בִּמְהֵרָה בְיָמֵינוּ.

וּבְכֵן צַדִּיקִים יִרְאוּ וְיִשְׂמָחוּ וִישָׁרִים יַעֲלֹזוּ וַחֲסִידִים
בְּרִנָּה יָגִילוּ. וְעוֹלָתָה תִּקְפָּץ־פִּיהָ וְכָל הָרִשְׁעָה כֻּלָּהּ
כְּעָשָׁן תִּכְלֶה כִּי תַעֲבִיר מֶמְשֶׁלֶת זָדוֹן מִן הָאָרֶץ:

(When Reader offers the Amidah aloud, insert the following:)

V'ye-etayu

(וְיֶאֱתָיוּ כֹל לְעָבְדֶּךָ, וִיבָרְכוּ שֵׁם כְּבוֹדֶךָ, וְיַגִּידוּ בָאִיִּים
צִדְקֶךָ. וְיִדְרְשׁוּךָ עַמִּים לֹא יְדָעוּךָ, וִיהַלְלוּךָ כָּל־אַפְסֵי
אָרֶץ, וְיֹאמְרוּ תָמִיד: יִגְדַּל יְיָ. וְיִזְבְּחוּ לְךָ אֶת־זִבְחֵיהֶם,

We shall tell our children of Your greatness and they will tell our grandchildren. In every generation till eternity we shall proclaim Your holiness. Our lips shall never abandon Your praise, for Your Majesty is great and holy.

Uv'chen

Because of this, Adonay our God, make all Your creatures awestruck by Your greatness, help all that You have created to be conscious that You are the Judge of all they do. Help everything alive to align their desires to Your own, let all creation worship You, that everyone might sense their bond with each other and act to do Your will with harmonious hearts. Help us know, Adonay our God, that all sovereignty is Yours, You possess all strength, You grip all power. May all that You have created stand in awe of You.

Because of this, Adonay, share Your glory with Your people, Your praise with those who believe in You, Your hope with those who are searching for You. Give those who wait with You a chance to reveal Your presence to the world. Give joy to Your chosen land, exultation to Your special city. From David's family let there blossom a shoot as radiant as he; let the ideal world dawn for everyone, soon and in our own time.

When those who do justly see all this, they will rejoice; people of integrity will celebrate; those who serve God out of love will sing for joy. Injustice will shut its mouth at last, and cruelty will be blown away like smoke, for You will have swept away the arrogance of rulers from the earth.

(When Reader offers the Amidah aloud, insert the following:)

V'ye-etayu

(All people will come together to worship You.
They will praise Your glorious Name,
Broadcasting Your justice everywhere.
Nations who never knew You will seek You out;
Far-flung peoples will praise You
Saying, "From now on, greatness belongs to God."
Burying their idols, they will present their offerings to You.
Everyone will lend a hand together

וְיִזְנְחוּ אֶת עֲצַבֵּיהֶם, וְיַחְפְּרוּ עִם פְּסִלֵיהֶם, וְיַטּוּ שְׁכֶם
אֶחָד לְעָבְדֶּךָ. וְיִירָאוּךָ עִם שֶׁמֶשׁ מְבַקְשֵׁי פָנֶיךָ, וְיַכִּירוּ
כֹּחַ מַלְכוּתֶךָ, וִילַמְּדוּ תוֹעִים בִּינָה. וִימַלְּלוּ אֶת
גְּבוּרָתֶךָ, וִינַשְּׂאוּךָ מִתְנַשֵּׂא לְכֹל לְרֹאשׁ. וִיסַלְּדוּ
בְחִילָה פָנֶיךָ, וִיעַטְּרוּךָ נֵזֶר תִּפְאָרָה. וְיִפְצְחוּ הָרִים
רִנָּה, וְיִצְהֲלוּ אִיִּים בְּמָלְכֶךָ, וִיקַבְּלוּ עֹל מַלְכוּתְךָ
עֲלֵיהֶם, וִירוֹמְמוּךָ בִּקְהַל עָם, וְיִשְׁמְעוּ רְחוֹקִים
וְיָבְוֹאוּ, וְיִתְּנוּ־לְךָ כֶּתֶר מְלוּכָה.)

V'timloch

וְתִמְלוֹךְ, אַתָּה יְיָ לְבַדֶּךָ, עַל כָּל מַעֲשֶׂיךָ, בְּהַר צִיּוֹן
מִשְׁכַּן כְּבוֹדֶךָ, וּבִירוּשָׁלַיִם עִיר קָדְשֶׁךָ, כַּכָּתוּב בְּדִבְרֵי
קָדְשֶׁךָ: יִמְלֹךְ יְיָ לְעוֹלָם, אֱלֹהַיִךְ צִיּוֹן לְדֹר וָדֹר;
הַלְלוּיָהּ.
קָדוֹשׁ אַתָּה וְנוֹרָא שְׁמֶךָ, וְאֵין אֱלוֹהַּ מִבַּלְעָדֶיךָ,
כַּכָּתוּב: וַיִּגְבַּהּ יְיָ צְבָאוֹת בַּמִּשְׁפָּט, וְהָאֵל הַקָּדוֹשׁ
נִקְדַּשׁ בִּצְדָקָה. בָּרוּךְ אַתָּה, יְיָ, הַמֶּלֶךְ הַקָּדוֹשׁ.

Atta V'chartanu

אַתָּה בְחַרְתָּנוּ מִכָּל הָעַמִּים, אָהַבְתָּ אוֹתָנוּ וְרָצִיתָ בָּנוּ,
וְרוֹמַמְתָּנוּ מִכָּל הַלְּשׁוֹנוֹת, וְקִדַּשְׁתָּנוּ בְּמִצְוֹתֶיךָ,
וְקֵרַבְתָּנוּ מַלְכֵּנוּ לַעֲבוֹדָתֶךָ, וְשִׁמְךָ הַגָּדוֹל וְהַקָּדוֹשׁ
עָלֵינוּ קָרָאתָ.

To do Your work in this world.
Those who had always been looking for You
Will greet the morning sun in their rush to honor You,
Realizing at last the power of Your Rule,
And they will teach all those who stray to understand.
As they talk about Your mighty powers,
People will come to declare You supreme,
You who have always been supreme;
And leaping in joy before You,
They will present You with a diadem of beauty.
Mountains will burst into song,
Continents will rejoice in Your reign,
Acclaiming You in cheering throngs
As they willingly accept Your Rule.
People in far-off lands will hear the news,
And they, too, will come
To crown you Sovereign.)

V'timloch

You God, You alone, will reign over all that You have made, on Mount Zion the place of Your holy Temple, in Jerusalem Your holy city, as it says in the Bible, "Adonay shall reign forever, Your God, O Zion, throughout all generations."

You are holy, the Name which speaks Your being fills us with awe. There is no God but You. As it is written in Your Bible, "Through justice the Commander of the hosts is exalted; through tzedakah, holiness flows from the holy God." You are praised, Adonay, Your majesty is holy.

Atta V'chartanu

You chose us from among all other nations to exemplify Your presence in the world. You showered us with love, You desired us, You exalted us that we might preserve the holy tongue, You imbued us with holiness through Your mitzvot, You drew us close to Your majesty through the prayers You chose, and You made us, with all our imperfections, the representatives of Your great and holy Name.

Va-titen lanu (Rosh Hashanah)

וַתִּתֶּן לָנוּ יְיָ אֱלֹהֵינוּ, בְּאַהֲבָה אֶת יוֹם [הַשַּׁבָּת הַזֶּה
וְאֶת יוֹם] הַזִּכָּרוֹן הַזֶּה, יוֹם [זִכְרוֹן] תְּרוּעָה [בְּאַהֲבָה]
מִקְרָא קֹדֶשׁ, זֵכֶר לִיצִיאַת מִצְרָיִם.

Va-titen lanu (Yom Kippur)

וַתִּתֶּן לָנוּ יְיָ אֱלֹהֵינוּ, בְּאַהֲבָה אֶת יוֹם [הַשַּׁבָּת הַזֶּה
לִקְדֻשָּׁה וְלִמְנוּחָה, וְאֶת יוֹם] הַכִּפּוּרִים הַזֶּה לִמְחִילָה
וְלִסְלִיחָה וּלְכַפָּרָה, וְלִמְחָל־בּוֹ אֶת כָּל עֲוֹנוֹתֵינוּ,
[בְּאַהֲבָה] מִקְרָא קֹדֶשׁ, זֵכֶר לִיצִיאַת מִצְרָיִם.

Umip'ney Chata-eynu

וּמִפְּנֵי חֲטָאֵינוּ גָּלִינוּ מֵאַרְצֵנוּ וְנִתְרַחַקְנוּ מֵעַל
אַדְמָתֵנוּ, וְאֵין אֲנַחְנוּ יְכוֹלִים לַעֲשׂוֹת חוֹבוֹתֵינוּ בְּבֵית
בְּחִירָתֶךָ, בַּבַּיִת הַגָּדוֹל וְהַקָּדוֹשׁ שֶׁנִּקְרָא שִׁמְךָ עָלָיו,
מִפְּנֵי הַיָּד שֶׁנִּשְׁתַּלְּחָה בְּמִקְדָּשֶׁךָ. יְהִי רָצוֹן מִלְּפָנֶיךָ, יְיָ
אֱלֹהֵינוּ וֵאלֹהֵי אֲבוֹתֵינוּ (וֵאלֹהֵי אִמּוֹתֵינוּ), מֶלֶךְ
רַחֲמָן, שֶׁתָּשׁוּב וּתְרַחֵם עָלֵינוּ וְעַל מִקְדָּשְׁךָ בְּרַחֲמֶיךָ
הָרַבִּים, וְתִבְנֵהוּ מְהֵרָה וּתְגַדֵּל כְּבוֹדוֹ. אָבִינוּ מַלְכֵּנוּ,
גַּלֵּה כְּבוֹד מַלְכוּתְךָ עָלֵינוּ מְהֵרָה, וְהוֹפַע וְהִנָּשֵׂא
עָלֵינוּ לְעֵינֵי כָּל חָי, וְקָרֵב פְּזוּרֵינוּ מִבֵּין הַגּוֹיִם,
וּנְפוּצוֹתֵינוּ כַּנֵּס מִיַּרְכְּתֵי אָרֶץ: וַהֲבִיאֵנוּ לְצִיּוֹן עִירְךָ
בְּרִנָּה, וְלִירוּשָׁלַיִם בֵּית מִקְדָּשְׁךָ בְּשִׂמְחַת עוֹלָם, וְשָׁם
נַעֲשֶׂה לְפָנֶיךָ אֶת קָרְבְּנוֹת חוֹבוֹתֵינוּ, תְּמִידִים כְּסִדְרָם
וּמוּסָפִים כְּהִלְכָתָם. *וְאֶת מוּסְפֵי [יוֹם הַשַּׁבָּת הַזֶּה
וְ]יוֹם הַזִּכָּרוֹן הַזֶּה* נַעֲשֶׂה וְנַקְרִיב לְפָנֶיךָ בְּאַהֲבָה
בְּמִצְוַת רְצוֹנֶךָ, כְּמוֹ שֶׁכָּתַבְתָּ עָלֵינוּ בְּתוֹרָתֶךָ, עַל יְדֵי
מֹשֶׁה עַבְדֶּךָ, מִפִּי כְבוֹדֶךָ, כָּאָמוּר:

* . . .**On Yom Kippur say,*

[וְאֶת מוּסַף יוֹם הַשַּׁבָּת הַזֶּה] וְאֶת מוּסַף יוֹם הַכִּפּוּרִים הַזֶּה

Va-titen lanu (Rosh Hashanah)

As a gift of love, Adonay our God, You presented us (this day of Shabbat holiness and soul-rest, as well as) this Day of Remembrance, the day of (recollection of) sounding T'ruah on the Shofar (in love). It is a holy day on which we are called together; it is a remembrance of the Exodus from Egypt, when we first became Your people.

Va-titen lanu (Yom Kippur)

As a gift of love, Adonay our God, You presented us (this day of Shabbat holiness and soul-rest, as well as) this Yom Kippur as a day of forgiveness, of the second chance, a day in which all our failures can be pardoned. It is a holy day on which we are called together; it is a remembrance of the Exodus from Egypt, when we first became Your people.

Umip'ney Chata-eynu

Because of our wrongdoing against You and each other, we were exiled from our land, sent far away from the ground of our humanity. We have not been able to perform our duties in your chosen Temple, that great and holy house called by Your own Name, because of the power sent against Your holy place. May it be your will, Adonay our God, God of those who knew that place — compassionate Sovereign — that in Your great mercy You may return to us and have mercy on us and on Your sacred site; rebuild it soon and let it reflect Your Glory even more than before.

Avinu Malkeynu, reveal Your majestic Glory to us soon; shine forth high above us in the sight of every living creature. Draw our scattered brothers and sisters close together from among the nations, gather up our dispersed people from the ends of the earth. Bring us to Zion Your city amid shouts of joy, to Jerusalem Your holy house in never-ending gladness. There in Your presence we will lovingly prepare whatever daily and additional Musaf offerings You desire (for this Sabbath day and) * for this Day of Remembering.* As you inscribed in glorious words to us in Your Torah, through Moses Your servant:

. . . On Yom Kippur say: *for this Day of Atonement*

(On Shabbat)

[וּבְיוֹם הַשַּׁבָּת שְׁנֵי כְבָשִׂים בְּנֵי שָׁנָה תְּמִימִם,
וּשְׁנֵי עֶשְׂרֹנִים סֹלֶת מִנְחָה בְּלוּלָה בַשֶּׁמֶן, וְנִסְכּוֹ.
עֹלַת שַׁבַּת בְּשַׁבַּתּוֹ, עַל עֹלַת הַתָּמִיד וְנִסְכָּהּ.]

(On Rosh Hashanah)

וּבַחֹדֶשׁ הַשְּׁבִיעִי, בְּאֶחָד לַחֹדֶשׁ, מִקְרָא קֹדֶשׁ
יִהְיֶה לָכֶם, כָּל מְלֶאכֶת עֲבֹדָה לֹא תַעֲשׂוּ, יוֹם
תְּרוּעָה יִהְיֶה לָכֶם. וַעֲשִׂיתֶם עֹלָה לְרֵיחַ נִיחֹחַ לַייָ
פַּר בֶּן־בָּקָר אֶחָד, אַיִל אֶחָד, כְּבָשִׂים בְּנֵי שָׁנָה
שִׁבְעָה, תְּמִימִם.
וּמִנְחָתָם וְנִסְכֵּיהֶם כִּמְדֻבָּר: שְׁלֹשָׁה עֶשְׂרֹנִים
לַפָּר, וּשְׁנֵי עֶשְׂרֹנִים לָאַיִל, וְעִשָּׂרוֹן לַכֶּבֶשׂ, וְיַיִן
כְּנִסְכּוֹ, וּשְׁנֵי שְׂעִירִים לְכַפֵּר, וּשְׁנֵי תְמִידִים
כְּהִלְכָתָם. מִלְּבַד עֹלַת הַחֹדֶשׁ וּמִנְחָתָהּ, וְעֹלַת
הַתָּמִיד וּמִנְחָתָהּ, וְנִסְכֵּיהֶם כְּמִשְׁפָּטָם, לְרֵיחַ
נִיחֹחַ אִשֶּׁה לַייָ.

(On Yom Kippur)

וּבֶעָשׂוֹר לַחֹדֶשׁ הַשְּׁבִיעִי הַזֶּה מִקְרָא קֹדֶשׁ יִהְיֶה
לָכֶם, וְעִנִּיתֶם אֶת־נַפְשֹׁתֵיכֶם; כָּל מְלָאכָה לֹא
תַעֲשׂוּ. וְהִקְרַבְתֶּם עֹלָה לַייָ, רֵיחַ נִיחֹחַ, פַּר בֶּן־
בָּקָר אֶחָד, אַיִל אֶחָד, כְּבָשִׂים בְּנֵי שָׁנָה שִׁבְעָה,
תְּמִימִם יִהְיוּ לָכֶם.
וּמִנְחָתָם וְנִסְכֵּיהֶם כִּמְדֻבָּר: שְׁלֹשָׁה עֶשְׂרֹנִים
לַפָּר וּשְׁנֵי עֶשְׂרֹנִים לָאַיִל, וְעִשָּׂרוֹן לַכֶּבֶשׂ, וְיַיִן
כְּנִסְכּוֹ, וּשְׁנֵי שְׂעִירִים לְכַפֵּר, וּשְׁנֵי תְמִידִים
כְּהִלְכָתָם.

(On Shabbat)

(On Shabbat, two unblemished yearling male lambs and two-tenths of an ephah of fine flour mixed with oil as a meal-offering, and the appropriate libation. This is the burnt-offering for each Shabbat in addition to the daily burnt-offering with its libation.)

(On Rosh Hashanah)

In the seventh month, on the first day of the month, there shall be a holy convocation for you; you shall not do any weekday work. It will be for you a day on which *t'ruah* is sounded on the shofar. You shall present a burnt offering with a pleasing aroma to Adonay: one bullock of the herd, one ram, and seven yearling lambs, all unblemished. The meal and liquid offerings to accompany them are worded as follows: three-tenths of a measure for the bullock, two-tenths for the ram, one-tenth for each lamb, and wine according to the required libation, as well as two goats offered in a sin-offering, to make expiation on your behalf, in addition to the two regular daily offerings and the new moon offerings with their prescribed libations, offerings by fire with a pleasing aroma to Adonay.

(On Yom Kippur)

In the seventh month, on the tenth day of the seventh month, there shall be a holy convocation for you; you shall not do any weekday work. You shall present a burnt-offering with a pleasing aroma to Adonay: one bullock of the herd, one ram, and seven yearling lambs, all unblemished. The meal and liquid offerings to accompany them are worded as follows: three-tenths of a measure for the bullock, two tenths for the ram, one-tenth for each lamb, and wine according to the required libation, as well as two goats offered in a sin-offering, to make expiation on your behalf, in addition to the two regular daily offerings.

(On Shabbat)

[יִשְׂמְחוּ בְמַלְכוּתְךָ שׁוֹמְרֵי שַׁבָּת וְקוֹרְאֵי עֹנֶג, עַם
מְקַדְּשֵׁי שְׁבִיעִי, כֻּלָּם יִשְׂבְּעוּ וְיִתְעַנְּגוּ מִטּוּבֶךָ;
וְהַשְּׁבִיעִי רָצִיתָ בּוֹ וְקִדַּשְׁתּוֹ, חֶמְדַּת יָמִים אוֹתוֹ
קָרָאתָ, זֵכֶר לְמַעֲשֵׂה בְרֵאשִׁית.]

(On Yom Kippur, the private Amidah continues with M'chal la-
Avonoteynu on p. 220)

Aleynu*

עָלֵינוּ לְשַׁבֵּחַ לַאֲדוֹן הַכֹּל, לָתֵת גְּדֻלָּה לְיוֹצֵר
בְּרֵאשִׁית, שֶׁלֹּא עָשָׂנוּ כְּגוֹיֵי הָאֲרָצוֹת, וְלֹא שָׂמָנוּ
כְּמִשְׁפְּחוֹת הָאֲדָמָה; שֶׁלֹּא שָׂם חֶלְקֵנוּ כָּהֶם,
וְגֹרָלֵנוּ כְּכָל הֲמוֹנָם. וַאֲנַחְנוּ כּוֹרְעִים וּמִשְׁתַּחֲוִים
וּמוֹדִים לִפְנֵי מֶלֶךְ מַלְכֵי הַמְּלָכִים, הַקָּדוֹשׁ בָּרוּךְ
הוּא, שֶׁהוּא נוֹטֶה שָׁמַיִם וְיֹסֵד אָרֶץ, וּמוֹשַׁב
יְקָרוֹ בַּשָּׁמַיִם מִמַּעַל, וּשְׁכִינַת עֻזּוֹ בְּגָבְהֵי
מְרוֹמִים. הוּא אֱלֹהֵינוּ, אֵין עוֹד; אֱמֶת מַלְכֵּנוּ,
אֶפֶס זוּלָתוֹ, כַּכָּתוּב בְּתוֹרָתוֹ: וְיָדַעְתָּ הַיּוֹם
וַהֲשֵׁבֹתָ אֶל לְבָבֶךָ, כִּי יְיָ הוּא הָאֱלֹהִים
בַּשָּׁמַיִם מִמַּעַל וְעַל הָאָרֶץ מִתָּחַת, אֵין עוֹד.

*On Rosh Hashanah, this marks the beginning of Malchuyot.

(When the Reader offers the Amidah aloud:)

Ochilah la-El

אוֹחִילָה לָאֵל, אֲחַלֶּה פָנָיו, אֶשְׁאֲלָה מִמֶּנּוּ מַעֲנֵה
לָשׁוֹן. אֲשֶׁר בִּקְהַל עָם אָשִׁירָה עֻזּוֹ, אַבִּיעָה

(On Shabbat)

(Those who observe Shabbat and call it a delight shall rejoice in Your realm; the people whose members set apart the seventh day shall fully enjoy Your goodness. You were pleased with the seventh day and set it apart; you called it the most desirable of days, a memento of Creation.)

(On Yom Kippur, the private Amidah continues with M'chal la-Avonoteynu on p. 221)

Aleynu*

We are called to praise the Source of all,
To hail the grandeur of the Sculptor of Creation,
Who did not make us like nations in other lands
Nor were we put on earth like other families of Adam's seed.
We were not given a portion like theirs,
Nor a destiny like others who throng the earth.
Our calling is to bow the head and bend the knee in worship
To pour forth thanks and praise
Only before the Sovereign greater than the most sovereign of all
    the sovereigns on earth,
The Holy One, whose very Soul is praise.

For You spread out the heavens and founded the earth, establishing a dwelling for Your glory in the heavens high above, and the presence of Your Shechina, Your might, in the highest realms of space. You are our God, none other. You, O Majesty, are Truth, none beside You, as You have written in Your Torah: "Today you shall know intimately, placing it upon your heart, that Adonay is God, in the heavens above and on earth below, none other."

*On Rosh Hashanah, this marks the beginning of Malchuyot.

(When the Reader offers the Amidah aloud:)

Ochilah la-El

I look to God, I seek You out,
I ask of You the gift of words,

רְנָנוֹת בְּעַד מִפְעָלָיו. לְאָדָם מַעַרְכֵי לֵב, וּמֵיְיָ
מַעֲנֵה לָשׁוֹן. יְיָ שְׂפָתַי תִּפְתָּח, וּפִי יַגִּיד תְּהִלָּתֶךָ.
יִהְיוּ לְרָצוֹן אִמְרֵי פִי וְהֶגְיוֹן לִבִּי לְפָנֶיךָ, יְיָ, צוּרִי
וְגוֹאֲלִי.

*(On Rosh Hashanah, continue with Malchuyot below. On Yom
Kippur, when the Reader offers the Amidah aloud, continue with
the Avodah service on p. 395, Eyleh Ezkerah on p. 404, and Sh'ma
Koleynu on p. 210.)*

(On Rosh Hashanah, continue with Malchuyot below. On Yom Kippur, when the Reader offers the Amidah aloud, continue with the Avodah service on p. 395, Eyleh Ezkerah on p. 404, and Sh'ma Koleynu on p. 210.)

Malchuyot (Continued)

עַל כֵּן נְקַוֶּה לְּךָ, יְיָ אֱלֹהֵינוּ, לִרְאוֹת מְהֵרָה
בְּתִפְאֶרֶת עֻזֶּךָ, לְהַעֲבִיר גִּלּוּלִים מִן הָאָרֶץ,
וְהָאֱלִילִים כָּרוֹת יִכָּרֵתוּן; לְתַקֵּן עוֹלָם בְּמַלְכוּת
שַׁדַּי, וְכָל בְּנֵי בָשָׂר יִקְרְאוּ בִשְׁמֶךָ, לְהַפְנוֹת אֵלֶיךָ
כָּל רִשְׁעֵי אָרֶץ. יַכִּירוּ וְיֵדְעוּ כָּל יוֹשְׁבֵי תֵבֵל, כִּי
לְךָ תִכְרַע כָּל בֶּרֶךְ, תִּשָּׁבַע כָּל לָשׁוֹן. לְפָנֶיךָ, יְיָ
אֱלֹהֵינוּ, יִכְרְעוּ וְיִפֹּלוּ, וְלִכְבוֹד שִׁמְךָ יְקָר יִתֵּנוּ,
וִיקַבְּלוּ כֻלָּם אֶת עֹל מַלְכוּתֶךָ, וְתִמְלוֹךְ עֲלֵיהֶם
מְהֵרָה לְעוֹלָם וָעֶד. כִּי הַמַּלְכוּת שֶׁלְּךָ הִיא,
וּלְעוֹלְמֵי עַד תִּמְלוֹךְ בְּכָבוֹד, כַּכָּתוּב בְּתוֹרָתֶךָ: יְיָ
יִמְלֹךְ לְעֹלָם וָעֶד.

Biblical Proclamations of God's Sovereignty

וְנֶאֱמַר: לֹא הִבִּיט אָוֶן בְּיַעֲקֹב, וְלֹא רָאָה עָמָל
בְּיִשְׂרָאֵל; יְיָ אֱלֹהָיו עִמּוֹ וּתְרוּעַת מֶלֶךְ בּוֹ.
וְנֶאֱמַר: וַיְהִי בִישֻׁרוּן מֶלֶךְ, בְּהִתְאַסֵּף רָאשֵׁי עָם,

That I may sing Your glory before the people,
And praise Your acts before humanity.
We may arrange the thoughts in our hearts,
But only You can give them words.
Adonay, open up my lips that my mouth may sing Your praise.
May the words in my mouth and the thoughts in my heart
Be equally acceptable to You, Adonay,
My rescuer, my faithful Rock.

*(On Rosh Hashanah, continue with Malchuyot below. On Yom
Kippur, when the Reader offers the Amidah aloud, continue with
the Avodah service on p. 395, Eyleh Ezkerah on p. 404, and Sh'ma
Koleynu on p. 211.)*

Malchuyot (Continued)

Therefore do we hope in You, Adonay our God, confident that
soon we shall see the glory of Your might revealed, ridding the
world of all its idolatries, cutting down all false gods from their
pedestals, reconstructing the world into a realm where You can
rule, Almighty One. Then everyone of flesh and blood will be
able to speak Your Name, for You will have turned toward You
all the wicked of the earth. All who live on this planet will recognize that they too can know You intimately, that every knee can
bend to You, every tongue pledge faithfulness to You. Turning
toward You, Adonay our God, all will bow down and fall prostrate, granting honor at last to Your glorious name, and all will
accept the yoke that joins them to Your sovereignty, that You
may rule over them speedily to the end of time. For Sovereignty
is Yours, and in glory will You reign forever, as it is written in
Your Torah: Adonay will reign forever and ever.

Biblical Proclamations of God's Sovereignty (Selection)

So act that none beholds wrongdoing in Jacob, that none sees
wickedness among the children of Rachel and Leah; by acting
justly, you will show that Adonay is Your God, whose rule is
proclaimed by the T'ruah of the Shofar.

יַחַד שִׁבְטֵי יִשְׂרָאֵל. וּבְדִבְרֵי קָדְשְׁךָ כָּתוּב לֵאמֹר:
כִּי לַיָי הַמְּלוּכָה וּמוֹשֵׁל בַּגּוֹיִם. וְנֶאֱמַר: יְיָ מָלָךְ
גֵּאוּת לָבֵשׁ, לָבֵשׁ יְיָ, עֹז הִתְאַזָּר, אַף תִּכּוֹן תֵּבֵל
בַּל תִּמּוֹט. וְנֶאֱמַר: שְׂאוּ שְׁעָרִים רָאשֵׁיכֶם,
וְהִנָּשְׂאוּ פִּתְחֵי עוֹלָם, וְיָבוֹא מֶלֶךְ הַכָּבוֹד. מִי זֶה
מֶלֶךְ הַכָּבוֹד, יְיָ עִזּוּז וְגִבּוֹר, יְיָ גִּבּוֹר מִלְחָמָה.
שְׂאוּ שְׁעָרִים רָאשֵׁיכֶם, וּשְׂאוּ פִּתְחֵי עוֹלָם, וְיָבֹא
מֶלֶךְ הַכָּבוֹד. מִי הוּא זֶה מֶלֶךְ הַכָּבוֹד, יְיָ צְבָאוֹת
הוּא מֶלֶךְ הַכָּבוֹד, סֶלָה. וְעַל יְדֵי עֲבָדֶיךָ הַנְּבִיאִים
כָּתוּב לֵאמֹר: כֹּה אָמַר יְיָ, מֶלֶךְ יִשְׂרָאֵל וְגֹאֲלוֹ, יְיָ
צְבָאוֹת, אֲנִי רִאשׁוֹן וַאֲנִי אַחֲרוֹן, וּמִבַּלְעָדַי אֵין
אֱלֹהִים. וְנֶאֱמַר: וְעָלוּ מוֹשִׁיעִים בְּהַר צִיּוֹן לִשְׁפֹּט
אֶת הַר עֵשָׂו, וְהָיְתָה לַיָי הַמְּלוּכָה. וְנֶאֱמַר: וְהָיָה
יְיָ לְמֶלֶךְ עַל כָּל הָאָרֶץ; בַּיּוֹם הַהוּא
יִהְיֶה יְיָ אֶחָד וּשְׁמוֹ אֶחָד. וּבְתוֹרָתְךָ כָּתוּב לֵאמֹר:
שְׁמַע יִשְׂרָאֵל, יְיָ אֱלֹהֵינוּ, יְיָ אֶחָד.

M'loch al Kol Ha-Olam (Conclusion of Malchuyot)

אֱלֹהֵינוּ וֵאלֹהֵי אֲבוֹתֵינוּ (וְאֱלֹהֵי אִמּוֹתֵינוּ), מְלוֹךְ
עַל כָּל הָעוֹלָם כֻּלּוֹ בִּכְבוֹדֶךָ, וְהִנָּשֵׂא עַל כָּל
הָאָרֶץ בִּיקָרֶךָ, וְהוֹפַע בַּהֲדַר גְּאוֹן עֻזֶּךָ, עַל כָּל

That a monarch rules in Yeshurun is proclaimed when the heads of the people gather together, when all the tribes of Israel meet in common purpose.

Sovereignty belongs to You who rules among the nations, robed in grandeur, girded with might, emblem of a world secured immovably on its foundations.

Lift your heads, Temple gates;
Raise yourselves, you doors to the timeless house!
Let the glorious Sovereign enter in!
Who is this glorious Sovereign?
Adonay, strong and mighty,
Adonay, our defender!
Lift your heads, Temple gates,
Raise yourselves, doors to the timeless house!
Let the glorious Sovereign enter in!
Who is this glorious Sovereign?
The Commander of the hosts of heaven and earth,
This is the glorious Sovereign!

Thus says Adonay, ruler of Israel and her Redeemer, Commander of the Hosts: I am the first First One, I am the Final One, there is no God beside Me.

The victorious ones shall ascend Mount Zion to judge the hills of Esau, to weigh the acts of all who have ruled over Your people, and so God's rule shall be declared.

And Adonay shall become Sovereign over all the earth; on that day Adonay will be one and the divine Name one!

Hear, O Israel, Adonay is our God, Adonay is One!

M'loch al Kol Ha-Olam (Conclusion of Malchuyot)

Our God and God of our fathers (and mothers), extend Your rule in glory over the entire universe, that You may be exalted in honor over the earth, appearing in the full splendor of Your exalted power over all who dwell upon the globe, Your planet. May every one of Your creatures know that You created it,

יוֹשְׁבֵי תֵבֵל אַרְצֶךָ, וְיֵדַע כָּל פָּעוּל כִּי אַתָּה
פְעַלְתּוֹ, וְיָבִין כָּל יָצוּר כִּי אַתָּה יְצַרְתּוֹ, וְיֹאמַר
כֹּל אֲשֶׁר נְשָׁמָה בְּאַפּוֹ, יְיָ אֱלֹהֵי יִשְׂרָאֵל מֶלֶךְ,
וּמַלְכוּתוֹ בַּכֹּל מָשָׁלָה.

אֱלֹהֵינוּ וֵאלֹהֵי אֲבוֹתֵינוּ (וֵאלֹהֵי אִמּוֹתֵינוּ), [רְצֵה
בִמְנוּחָתֵנוּ] קַדְּשֵׁנוּ בְּמִצְוֹתֶיךָ וְתֵן חֶלְקֵנוּ
בְּתוֹרָתֶךָ, שַׂבְּעֵנוּ מִטּוּבֶךָ וְשַׂמְּחֵנוּ בִּישׁוּעָתֶךָ.
[וְהַנְחִילֵנוּ, יְיָ אֱלֹהֵינוּ, בְּאַהֲבָה וּבְרָצוֹן שַׁבַּת
קָדְשֶׁךָ, וְיָנְוּחוּ בוֹ יִשְׂרָאֵל מְקַדְּשֵׁי שְׁמֶךָ]. וְטַהֵר
לִבֵּנוּ לְעָבְדְּךָ בֶּאֱמֶת, כִּי אַתָּה אֱלֹהִים אֱמֶת,
וּדְבָרְךָ אֱמֶת וְקַיָּם לָעַד. בָּרוּךְ אַתָּה, יְיָ, מֶלֶךְ
עַל כָּל הָאָרֶץ, מְקַדֵּשׁ [הַשַּׁבָּת וְ]יִשְׂרָאֵל וְיוֹם
הַזִּכָּרוֹן.

The following is said when the Reader offers the Amidah aloud:

תקיעה שברים תרועה תקיעה
תקיעה שברים תקיעה
תקיעה תרועה תקיעה

הַיּוֹם הֲרַת עוֹלָם, הַיּוֹם יַעֲמִיד בַּמִּשְׁפָּט כָּל יְצוּרֵי
עוֹלָמִים, אִם כְּבָנִים אִם כַּעֲבָדִים. אִם כְּבָנִים
רַחֲמֵנוּ כְּרַחֵם אָב עַל בָּנִים; וְאִם כַּעֲבָדִים עֵינֵינוּ
לְךָ תְלוּיוֹת, עַד שֶׁתְּחָנֵּנוּ וְתוֹצִיא כָאוֹר מִשְׁפָּטֵנוּ,
אָיוֹם קָדוֹשׁ.

(On Shabbat omit:)

אֲרֶשֶׁת שְׂפָתֵינוּ יֶעֱרַב לְפָנֶיךָ, אֵל רָם וְנִשָּׂא, מֵבִין
וּמַאֲזִין, מַבִּיט וּמַקְשִׁיב לְקוֹל תְּקִיעָתֵנוּ, וּתְקַבֵּל
בְּרַחֲמִים וּבְרָצוֹן סֵדֶר מַלְכִיּוֹתֵינוּ.

every form of life perceive that You formed it, so that every being with breath in its nostrils may proclaim: "Adonay, God of Israel, rules a realm encompassing all people!"

Our God and God of those who gave us life: (Be pleased with our soul-rest.) Imbue us with holiness through Your mitzvot and grant us our share in the understanding of Your Torah. Satiate us with Your goodness, fill us with the joy of victory over our selfish instincts, our cruel temptations. (Dower us, God, with the holiness of Your Shabbat; let the Jewish people, whose actions strive to manifest Your holiness, find soul-rest on this day.) Wash clean our hearts that we may serve You with true intentions, for You are the God of truth, and Your word is true, sustained forever. You are praised, Adonay, Sovereign over all the earth, who fills with holiness (Shabbat,) the Jewish people, and the Day of Remembrance.

The following is said when the Reader offers the Amidah aloud:

TKIYAH   SHVARIM-TRUAH   TKIYAH
TKIYAH   SHVARIM   TKIYAH
TKIYAH   TRUAH   TKIYAH

This is the day the world was conceived. On this day all living creatures — as Your children or as Your servants — stand up for judgment. If as children, have mercy on us as a parent has mercy on children. If as servants, our eyes yearn for You to be gracious to us. O awesome, holy God, return us a verdict as clear as light!

(On Shabbat omit:)

May the request of our lips please You, high and transcendant God, who hearkens to the Tkiyah we are sounding. O accept with favor the order of our Malchuyot, the praise of Your Sovereignty.

Zichronot

אַתָּה זוֹכֵר מַעֲשֵׂה עוֹלָם, וּפוֹקֵד כָּל יְצוּרֵי קֶדֶם. לְפָנֶיךָ נִגְלוּ כָּל תַּעֲלוּמוֹת, וַהֲמוֹן נִסְתָּרוֹת שֶׁמִּבְּרֵאשִׁית. אֵין שִׁכְחָה לִפְנֵי כִסֵּא כְבוֹדֶךָ, וְאֵין נִסְתָּר מִנֶּגֶד עֵינֶיךָ. אַתָּה זוֹכֵר אֶת כָּל הַמִּפְעָל, וְגַם כָּל הַיְצוּר לֹא נִכְחָד מִמֶּךָּ. הַכֹּל גָּלוּי וְיָדוּעַ לְפָנֶיךָ, יְיָ אֱלֹהֵינוּ, צוֹפֶה וּמַבִּיט עַד סוֹף כָּל הַדּוֹרוֹת. כִּי תָבִיא חֹק זִכָּרוֹן, לְהִפָּקֵד כָּל רוּחַ וָנֶפֶשׁ, לְהִזָּכֵר מַעֲשִׂים רַבִּים וַהֲמוֹן בְּרִיּוֹת לְאֵין תַּכְלִית, מֵרֵאשִׁית כָּזֹאת הוֹדַעְתָּ, וּמִלְּפָנִים אוֹתָהּ גִּלִּיתָ.

זֶה הַיּוֹם תְּחִלַּת מַעֲשֶׂיךָ, זִכָּרוֹן לְיוֹם רִאשׁוֹן; כִּי חֹק לְיִשְׂרָאֵל הוּא, מִשְׁפָּט לֵאלֹהֵי יַעֲקֹב. וְעַל הַמְּדִינוֹת בּוֹ יֵאָמֵר: אֵיזוֹ לַחֶרֶב, וְאֵיזוֹ לַשָּׁלוֹם, אֵיזוֹ לָרָעָב, וְאֵיזוֹ לְשֹׂבַע. וּבְרִיּוֹת בּוֹ יִפָּקֵדוּ, לְהַזְכִּירָם לַחַיִּים וְלַמָּוֶת. מִי לֹא נִפְקָד כְּהַיּוֹם הַזֶּה; כִּי זֵכֶר כָּל הַיְצוּר לְפָנֶיךָ בָּא, מַעֲשֵׂה אִישׁ וּפְקֻדָּתוֹ, וַעֲלִילוֹת מִצְעֲדֵי גֶבֶר, מַחְשְׁבוֹת אָדָם וְתַחְבּוּלוֹתָיו, וְיִצְרֵי מַעַלְלֵי אִישׁ.

אַשְׁרֵי אִישׁ שֶׁלֹּא יִשְׁכָּחֶךָ, וּבֶן־אָדָם יִתְאַמֶּץ־בָּךְ. כִּי דוֹרְשֶׁיךָ לְעוֹלָם לֹא יִכָּשֵׁלוּ, וְלֹא יִכָּלְמוּ לָנֶצַח כָּל הַחוֹסִים בָּךְ. כִּי זֵכֶר כָּל הַמַּעֲשִׂים לְפָנֶיךָ בָּא, וְאַתָּה דוֹרֵשׁ מַעֲשֵׂה כֻלָּם. וְגַם אֶת נֹחַ בְּאַהֲבָה זָכַרְתָּ, וַתִּפְקְדֵהוּ בִּדְבַר יְשׁוּעָה וְרַחֲמִים, בַּהֲבִיאֲךָ אֶת מֵי הַמַּבּוּל לְשַׁחֵת כָּל בָּשָׂר מִפְּנֵי רֹעַ מַעַלְלֵיהֶם.עַל כֵּן זִכְרוֹנוֹ בָּא לְפָנֶיךָ, יְיָ אֱלֹהֵינוּ, לְהַרְבּוֹת זַרְעוֹ כְּעַפְרוֹת תֵּבֵל, וְצֶאֱצָאָיו כְּחוֹל

Zichronot

You remember all that has ever been created; You recall every creature that was formed in earliest times. Before You all hidden things are revealed, all mysteries since the very beginning. For You on Your glorious throne, there is no such thing as forgetting; there is nothing hidden from Your sight. You are mindful of every act, and no creature is concealed from You. Everything is open and known to You, Adonay our God, for You look out and scan time till the end of all generations. From the very beginning You made this known, from earliest times You disclosed this: that you would bring about a fixed day of remembering, on which to be especially mindful of every living creature, on which to remember the many deeds of untold numbers of people. This day is the anniversary of the first day of creation; it is "a law for Israel, a judgment by the God of Jacob." On this day sentence is passed on states for the sword or for peace, for hunger or for plenty. And on this day sentence is passed on individuals for life or for death. Who is not remembered on a day such as this when before You come the past deeds of every person, our devious steps, our cruel designs, our innermost wiles?

Yet how fortunate are those who do not forget You, even as You do not forget them! How fortunate are those who take strength from You for the future, even while You are judging them! Those who seek You never stumble, those who take shelter in You are never disgraced, because when the memory of all their deeds comes before You, You search out each deed for an extenuating cause. So it was that you lovingly remembered Noah, granting him merciful aid when you brought the flood-waters to destroy all creatures because of their evil doings. So it was that the memory of Noah came before You, Adonay our God, and though You were destroying his contemporaries, You

הַיָּם, כַּכָּתוּב בְּתוֹרָתֶךָ: וַיִּזְכֹּר אֱלֹהִים אֶת נֹחַ, וְאֵת כָּל הַחַיָּה וְאֶת כָּל הַבְּהֵמָה אֲשֶׁר אִתּוֹ בַּתֵּבָה, וַיַּעֲבֵר אֱלֹהִים רוּחַ עַל הָאָרֶץ, וַיָּשֹׁכּוּ הַמָּיִם.

Biblical Recollections of God's Remembrance

וְנֶאֱמַר: וַיִּשְׁמַע אֱלֹהִים אֶת נַאֲקָתָם, וַיִּזְכֹּר אֱלֹהִים אֶת בְּרִיתוֹ אֶת אַבְרָהָם, אֶת יִצְחָק וְאֶת יַעֲקֹב. וְנֶאֱמַר: וְזָכַרְתִּי אֶת בְּרִיתִי יַעֲקוֹב, וְאַף אֶת בְּרִיתִי יִצְחָק, וְאַף אֶת בְּרִיתִי אַבְרָהָם אֶזְכֹּר, וְהָאָרֶץ אֶזְכֹּר. וּבְדִבְרֵי קָדְשְׁךָ כָּתוּב לֵאמֹר:זֵכֶר עָשָׂה לְנִפְלְאֹתָיו, חַנּוּן וְרַחוּם יְיָ. וְנֶאֱמַר: טֶרֶף נָתַן לִירֵאָיו, יִזְכֹּר לְעוֹלָם בְּרִיתוֹ. וְנֶאֱמַר: וַיִּזְכֹּר לָהֶם בְּרִיתוֹ, וַיִּנָּחֵם כְּרֹב חֲסָדָיו. וְעַל יְדֵי עֲבָדֶיךָ הַנְּבִיאִים כָּתוּב לֵאמֹר: הָלוֹךְ וְקָרָאתָ בְאָזְנֵי יְרוּשָׁלַיִם לֵאמֹר, כֹּה אָמַר יְיָ, זָכַרְתִּי לָךְ חֶסֶד נְעוּרַיִךְ, אַהֲבַת כְּלוּלֹתָיִךְ, לֶכְתֵּךְ אַחֲרַי בַּמִּדְבָּר, בְּאֶרֶץ לֹא זְרוּעָה. וְנֶאֱמַר: וְזָכַרְתִּי אֲנִי אֶת בְּרִיתִי אוֹתָךְ בִּימֵי נְעוּרָיִךְ וַהֲקִימוֹתִי לָךְ בְּרִית עוֹלָם. וְנֶאֱמַר: הֲבֵן יַקִּיר לִי אֶפְרַיִם, אִם יֶלֶד שַׁעֲשׁוּעִים, כִּי מִדֵּי דַבְּרִי בּוֹ זָכֹר אֶזְכְּרֶנּוּ עוֹד, עַל כֵּן הָמוּ מֵעַי לוֹ, רַחֵם אֲרַחֲמֶנּוּ נְאֻם יְיָ.

made his descendants increase like the dust of the earth, like the
sand at the seashore.

Biblical Recollections of God's Remembrance (An Interpretation)

As you remembered Noah and with the wind dispersed the
    waters of the flood,
So too remember us upon the flood of cruelty that threatens this
    frail ark in which we live and pray.

As in Egypt you heard our screaming,
And remembered there Your pact with Abraham, Isaac, and
    Jacob,
Sarah, Rebecca, Rachel and Leah,
So too remember us
Enslaved to lives and lifestyles that we cannot change,
Oppressed by fears and Pharaohs that turn living waters into
    blood.

As after each pogrom and exile and oppression
When Israel turned to Torah once again
And you remembered our ancient covenant,
So too remember us
Dispersed in friendly lands and hostile,
Fighting for the survival of the Jewish people
While trying to be true to the ideals that have made our people
    Jews.

As You instructed Jeremiah:
Whisper in the ear of Jerusalem
How I remember our youthful passion,
So too remember now
To whisper in her ear again
The words and acts through which she may embrace her
    enemies in peace.

Conclusion of Zichronot

אֱלֹהֵינוּ וֵאלֹהֵי אֲבוֹתֵינוּ (וֵאלֹהֵי אִמּוֹתֵינוּ), זָכְרֵנוּ
בְּזִכָּרוֹן טוֹב לְפָנֶיךָ, וּפָקְדֵנוּ בִּפְקֻדַּת יְשׁוּעָה
וְרַחֲמִים מִשְּׁמֵי שְׁמֵי קֶדֶם. וּזְכָר־לָנוּ, יְיָ אֱלֹהֵינוּ,
אֶת הַבְּרִית וְאֶת הַחֶסֶד, וְאֶת הַשְּׁבוּעָה אֲשֶׁר
נִשְׁבַּעְתָּ לְאַבְרָהָם אָבִינוּ בְּהַר הַמֹּרִיָּה. וְתֵרָאֶה
לְפָנֶיךָ עֲקֵדָה שֶׁעָקַד אַבְרָהָם אָבִינוּ אֶת יִצְחָק בְּנוֹ
עַל גַּבֵּי הַמִּזְבֵּחַ, וְכָבַשׁ רַחֲמָיו לַעֲשׂוֹת רְצוֹנְךָ
בְּלֵבָב שָׁלֵם. כֵּן יִכְבְּשׁוּ רַחֲמֶיךָ אֶת כַּעַסְךָ מֵעָלֵינוּ,
וּבְטוּבְךָ הַגָּדוֹל יָשׁוּב חֲרוֹן אַפְּךָ מֵעַמְּךָ וּמֵעִירְךָ
וּמִנַּחֲלָתֶךָ. וְקַיֶּם־לָנוּ, יְיָ אֱלֹהֵינוּ, אֶת הַדָּבָר
שֶׁהִבְטַחְתָּנוּ בְּתוֹרָתֶךָ, עַל יְדֵי מֹשֶׁה עַבְדֶּךָ,
מִפִּי כְבוֹדֶךָ, כָּאָמוּר: וְזָכַרְתִּי לָהֶם בְּרִית
רִאשׁוֹנִים, אֲשֶׁר הוֹצֵאתִי אֹתָם מֵאֶרֶץ מִצְרַיִם
לְעֵינֵי הַגּוֹיִם לִהְיוֹת לָהֶם לֵאלֹהִים, אֲנִי יְיָ. כִּי
זוֹכֵר כָּל הַנִּשְׁכָּחוֹת אַתָּה הוּא מֵעוֹלָם, וְאֵין
שִׁכְחָה לִפְנֵי כִסֵּא כְבוֹדֶךָ. וַעֲקֵדַת יִצְחָק לְזַרְעוֹ
הַיּוֹם בְּרַחֲמִים תִּזְכּוֹר. בָּרוּךְ אַתָּה, יְיָ, זוֹכֵר
הַבְּרִית.

The following is said when the Reader offers the Amidah aloud:

תקיעה שברים תרועה תקיעה
תקיעה שברים תקיעה
תקיעה תרועה תקיעה

הַיּוֹם הֲרַת עוֹלָם, הַיּוֹם יַעֲמִיד בַּמִּשְׁפָּט כָּל יְצוּרֵי
עוֹלָמִים, אִם כְּבָנִים אִם כַּעֲבָדִים. אִם כְּבָנִים,

Conclusion of Zichronot

Our God and God of our fathers (and mothers): Remember us with favor, think of us with the thoughts of help and mercy which You were thinking even before space and time began. Adonay our God, remember in our favor the covenant, the solemn promise of blessing, which You made to our father Abraham on Mount Moriah, in return for his willingness to offer You his son. Recall the sight of our father Abraham binding his son Isaac on the altar, holding back his mercy in order to do Your will wholeheartedly; recall Isaac offering himself to You, holding back his fear in order to serve You with devotion; and let Your mercy hold back Your anger from us. In your great goodness, let Your wrath turn back from Your people, from Your city, and from the land which You gave us as our heritage. Adonay our God, fulfill what You promised us in Your Torah through Your servant Moses: "When they are in exile I will remember in their favor the covenant which I made with their forebears, whom I liberated from the land of Egypt in the sight of the nations, so that I might be their God. I am Adonay." You who have always remembered all forgotten things; You, on Your glorious throne, for whom there is no such thing as forgetting: remember on this day with mercy the binding of Isaac on the altar. Praised are You, Adonay, who remembers the covenant.

The following is said when the Reader offers the Amidah aloud:

TKIYAH   SHVARIM-TRUAH   TKIYAH
TKIYAH   SHVARIM   TKIYAH
TKIYAH   TRUAH   TKIYAH

This is the day the world was conceived. On this day all living creatures — as Your children or as Your servants — stand up for judgment. If as children, have mercy on us as a parent has mercy on children. If as servants, our eyes

רַחֲמֵנוּ כְּרַחֵם אָב עַל בָּנִים; וְאִם כַּעֲבָדִים עֵינֵינוּ
לְךָ תְלוּיוֹת, עַד שֶׁתְּחָנֵּנוּ וְתוֹצִיא כָאוֹר מִשְׁפָּטֵנוּ,
אָיוֹם קָדוֹשׁ.

(on Shabbat omit:)

אֲרֶשֶׁת שְׂפָתֵינוּ יֶעֱרַב לְפָנֶיךָ, אֵל רָם וְנִשָּׂא, מֵבִין
וּמַאֲזִין, מַבִּיט וּמַקְשִׁיב לְקוֹל תְּקִיעָתֵנוּ; וּתְקַבֵּל
בְּרַחֲמִים וּבְרָצוֹן סֵדֶר זִכְרוֹנוֹתֵינוּ.

Shofarot

אַתָּה נִגְלֵיתָ בַּעֲנַן כְּבוֹדֶךָ, עַל עַם קָדְשֶׁךָ, לְדַבֵּר
עִמָּם. מִן הַשָּׁמַיִם הִשְׁמַעְתָּם קוֹלֶךָ, וְנִגְלֵיתָ
עֲלֵיהֶם בְּעַרְפַלֵּי טָהַר. גַּם כָּל הָעוֹלָם כֻּלּוֹ חָל
מִפָּנֶיךָ, וּבְרִיּוֹת בְּרֵאשִׁית חָרְדוּ מִמֶּךָּ, בְּהִגָּלוֹתְךָ
מַלְכֵּנוּ עַל הַר סִינַי לְלַמֵּד לְעַמְּךָ תּוֹרָה וּמִצְוֹת,
וַתַּשְׁמִיעֵם אֶת הוֹד קוֹלֶךָ, וְדִבְּרוֹת קָדְשְׁךָ
מִלַּהֲבוֹת אֵשׁ. בְּקֹלֹת וּבְרָקִים עֲלֵיהֶם נִגְלֵיתָ,
וּבְקוֹל שֹׁפָר עֲלֵיהֶם הוֹפָעְתָ, כַּכָּתוּב בְּתוֹרָתֶךָ:

Biblical Hearkenings to the Sounds of the Shofar

וַיְהִי בַיּוֹם הַשְּׁלִישִׁי בִּהְיֹת הַבֹּקֶר, וַיְהִי קֹלֹת
וּבְרָקִים, וְעָנָן כָּבֵד עַל הָהָר, וְקֹל שֹׁפָר
חָזָק מְאֹד, וַיֶּחֱרַד כָּל הָעָם אֲשֶׁר בַּמַּחֲנֶה. וְנֶאֱמַר:
וַיְהִי קוֹל הַשֹּׁפָר הוֹלֵךְ וְחָזֵק מְאֹד, מֹשֶׁה יְדַבֵּר
וְהָאֱלֹהִים יַעֲנֶנּוּ בְקוֹל. וְנֶאֱמַר: וְכָל הָעָם רֹאִים
אֶת הַקּוֹלֹת וְאֶת הַלַּפִּידִם, וְאֵת קוֹל הַשֹּׁפָר, וְאֶת
הָהָר עָשֵׁן; וַיַּרְא הָעָם וַיָּנֻעוּ וַיַּעַמְדוּ מֵרָחוֹק.
וּבְדִבְרֵי קָדְשְׁךָ כָּתוּב לֵאמֹר: עָלָה אֱלֹהִים
בִּתְרוּעָה, יְיָ בְּקוֹל שׁוֹפָר. וְנֶאֱמַר: בַּחֲצֹצְרוֹת
וְקוֹל שׁוֹפָר הָרִיעוּ לִפְנֵי הַמֶּלֶךְ יְיָ. וְנֶאֱמַר: תִּקְעוּ
בַחֹדֶשׁ שׁוֹפָר, בַּכֶּסֶה לְיוֹם חַגֵּנוּ. כִּי חֹק לְיִשְׂרָאֵל

yearn for You to be gracious to us. O awesome, holy God,
return us a verdict as clear as light!

(on Shabbat omit:)

May the request of our lips please You, high and transcendant God, who hearkens to the Tkiyah we are sounding. O
accept with favor the order of our Zichronot, the prayer
that You may ever remember in mercy Your covenant with
Your people Israel.

Shofarot

You revealed Yourself through a cloud of glory to speak with
Your holy people. You sent Your voice to them from the
heavens and signalled Your presence among them by deep dark
clouds. The whole world trembled at Your presence, all the
works of creation shook in awe of you, our Sovereign, when
You revealed Yourself on Mount Sinai to teach Your people the
Torah and its commandments. You caused them to hear Your
majestic voice, to see Your holy words in flashes of fire. With
thunder and lightening You revealed yourself to them, with the
sound of the shofar You appeared to them.

Biblical Hearkenings to the Sounds of the Shofar (Selection)

On the third day as morning dawned, there were thundervoices
and lightning and a dense cloud upon the mountain Sinai and a
loud Shofarblast, and all the people in the camp trembled.

The sound of the Shofar grew louder and louder, Moses
spoke, and God answered him in a thundervoice.

As the commandments were spoken, all the people witnessed
the thundervoices and the lightning, the Shofarblasts and the
mountain smoking, and when the people saw it, they fell back
and stood at a distance.

הוּא, מִשְׁפָּט לֵאלֹהֵי יַעֲקֹב. וְנֶאֱמַר: הַלְלוּיָהּ,
הַלְלוּ אֵל בְּקָדְשׁוֹ, הַלְלוּהוּ בִּרְקִיעַ עֻזּוֹ. הַלְלוּהוּ
בִגְבוּרֹתָיו, הַלְלוּהוּ כְּרֹב גֻּדְלוֹ. הַלְלוּהוּ בְּתֵקַע
שׁוֹפָר, הַלְלוּהוּ בְּנֵבֶל וְכִנּוֹר. הַלְלוּהוּ בְּתֹף
וּמָחוֹל, הַלְלוּהוּ בְּמִנִּים וְעֻגָב. הַלְלוּהוּ בְּצִלְצְלֵי
שָׁמַע, הַלְלוּהוּ בְּצִלְצְלֵי תְרוּעָה. כֹּל הַנְּשָׁמָה
תְּהַלֵּל יָהּ, הַלְלוּיָהּ. וְעַל יְדֵי עֲבָדֶיךָ הַנְּבִיאִים
כָּתוּב לֵאמֹר: כָּל יֹשְׁבֵי תֵבֵל וְשֹׁכְנֵי אָרֶץ,
כִּנְשֹׂא נֵס הָרִים תִּרְאוּ, וְכִתְקֹעַ שׁוֹפָר תִּשְׁמָעוּ.
וְנֶאֱמַר: וְהָיָה בַּיּוֹם הַהוּא יִתָּקַע בְּשׁוֹפָר גָּדוֹל,
וּבָאוּ הָאֹבְדִים בְּאֶרֶץ אַשּׁוּר וְהַנִּדָּחִים בְּאֶרֶץ
מִצְרָיִם, וְהִשְׁתַּחֲווּ לַיָי בְּהַר הַקֹּדֶשׁ בִּירוּשָׁלָיִם.
וְנֶאֱמַר: וַיָי עֲלֵיהֶם יֵרָאֶה, וְיָצָא כַבָּרָק חִצּוֹ;
וַאדֹנָי אֱלֹהִים בַּשּׁוֹפָר יִתְקַע, וְהָלַךְ בְּסַעֲרוֹת
תֵּימָן. יְיָ צְבָאוֹת יָגֵן עֲלֵיהֶם. כֵּן תָּגֵן עַל עַמְּךָ
יִשְׂרָאֵל בִּשְׁלוֹמֶךָ.

Conclusion of Shofarot

אֱלֹהֵינוּ וֵאלֹהֵי אֲבוֹתֵינוּ (וֵאלֹהֵי אִמּוֹתֵינוּ), תְּקַע
בְּשׁוֹפָר גָּדוֹל לְחֵרוּתֵנוּ, וְשָׂא נֵס לְקַבֵּץ גָּלֻיּוֹתֵינוּ,
וְקָרֵב פְּזוּרֵינוּ מִבֵּין הַגּוֹיִם, וּנְפוּצוֹתֵינוּ כַּנֵּס מִיַּרְכְּתֵי
אָרֶץ. וַהֲבִיאֵנוּ לְצִיּוֹן עִירְךָ בְּרִנָּה, וְלִירוּשָׁלַיִם בֵּית
מִקְדָּשְׁךָ בְּשִׂמְחַת עוֹלָם. וְשָׁם נַעֲשֶׂה לְפָנֶיךָ אֶת
קָרְבְּנוֹת חוֹבוֹתֵינוּ כִּמְצֻוֶּה עָלֵינוּ בְּתוֹרָתֶךָ, עַל יְדֵי
מֹשֶׁה עַבְדֶּךָ, מִפִּי כְבוֹדֶךָ כָּאָמוּר:

וּבְיוֹם שִׂמְחַתְכֶם, וּבְמוֹעֲדֵיכֶם וּבְרָאשֵׁי חָדְשֵׁיכֶם,
וּתְקַעְתֶּם בַּחֲצֹצְרֹת עַל עֹלֹתֵיכֶם וְעַל זִבְחֵי שַׁלְמֵיכֶם;
וְהָיוּ לָכֶם לְזִכָּרוֹן לִפְנֵי אֱלֹהֵיכֶם, אֲנִי יְיָ אֱלֹהֵיכֶם. כִּי

When the Temple stood, the priests proclaimed: Adonay has ascended with Truah! It is Adonay in the sound of Shofarblast!

Sound Tkiyah on the Shofar at each new moon, and every full moon which is Festival! It is a statute for Israel, a law from the God of Jacob.

All dwellers of earth, all inhabitants of the world: when a banner is raised upon the mountains, look up! When Tkiyah is sounded on the Shofar, listen!

On that day Tkiyah shall be sounded on the great Shofar, and all the tribes lost beyond the Euphrates shall come forth, and all those cast away into Egypt shall worship once more on Jerusalem's holy mountain. Adonay shall appear, the divine presence will go forth as lightning, sounding Tkiyah on the Shofar and protecting Israel until the end of time.

Conclusion of Shofarot

Our God and God of our fathers (and mothers): sound that great shofar of our liberation, raise that ensign to bring our exiled people together. Draw our scattered brothers and sisters together from among the nations, gather up our dispersed people from the ends of the earth. Bring us to Zion Your city amid shouts of joy, to Jerusalem the site of Your holy Temple in never-ending gladness. There we will prepare in Your honor the symbolic offerings required of us by Your Torah. We will offer them up to the sound of silver trumpets, as you had Moses command us; for it is written:

On your celebration days — your festivals and new moon days — you shall sound the silver trumpets over all the offerings you bring that they may convey your presence before Adonay your God. I am Adonay your God.

אַתָּה שׁוֹמֵעַ קוֹל שׁוֹפָר, וּמַאֲזִין תְּרוּעָה, וְאֵין דּוֹמֶה
לָךְ. בָּרוּךְ אַתָּה, יְיָ, שׁוֹמֵעַ קוֹל תְּרוּעַת עַמּוֹ יִשְׂרָאֵל
בְּרַחֲמִים.

The following is said when the Reader offers the Amidah aloud:

תקיעה שברים תרועה תקיעה

תקיעה שברים תקיעה

תקיעה תרועה   תקיעה גדולה

הַיּוֹם הֲרַת עוֹלָם, הַיּוֹם יַעֲמִיד בַּמִּשְׁפָּט כָּל יְצוּרֵי
עוֹלָמִים, אִם כְּבָנִים אִם כַּעֲבָדִים. אִם כְּבָנִים, רַחֲמֵנוּ
כְּרַחֵם אָב עַל בָּנִים; וְאִם כַּעֲבָדִים עֵינֵינוּ לְךָ תְלוּיוֹת,
עַד שֶׁתְּחָנֵּנוּ וְתוֹצִיא כָאוֹר מִשְׁפָּטֵנוּ, אָיוֹם קָדוֹשׁ.

(on Shabbat omit:)

אֲרֶשֶׁת שְׂפָתֵינוּ יֶעֱרַב לְפָנֶיךָ, אֵל רָם וְנִשָּׂא, מֵבִין
וּמַאֲזִין, מַבִּיט וּמַקְשִׁיב לְקוֹל תְּקִיעָתֵנוּ; וּתְקַבֵּל
בְּרַחֲמִים וּבְרָצוֹן סֵדֶר שׁוֹפְרוֹתֵינוּ.

Musaf for Rosh Hashanah continues with Rtzey on p. 222

(When Reader offers Yom Kippur Amidah aloud, continue here:)

Sh'ma Koleynu

שְׁמַע קוֹלֵנוּ, יְיָ אֱלֹהֵינוּ, חוּס וְרַחֵם עָלֵינוּ, וְקַבֵּל
בְּרַחֲמִים וּבְרָצוֹן אֶת תְּפִלָּתֵנוּ.

הֲשִׁיבֵנוּ יְיָ אֵלֶיךָ וְנָשׁוּבָה, חַדֵּשׁ יָמֵינוּ כְּקֶדֶם.

אֲמָרֵינוּ הַאֲזִינָה יְיָ, בִּינָה הֲגִיגֵנוּ. יִהְיוּ לְרָצוֹן אִמְרֵי
פִינוּ וְהֶגְיוֹן לִבֵּנוּ לְפָנֶיךָ, יְיָ צוּרֵנוּ וְגוֹאֲלֵנוּ.

For You understand the shofar's sounds, you give ear to its wordless prayer — there is no one like You! Praised are you, Adonay, who listens with mercy to the sound of Your people's shofar.

The following is said when the Reader offers the Amidah aloud:

TKIYAH   SHVARIM-TRUAH   TKIYAH
TKIYAH   SHVARIM   TKIYAH
TKIYAH   TRUAH   TKIYAH GDOLAH

This is the day the world was conceived. On this day all living creatures — as Your children or as Your servants — stand up for judgment. If as children, have mercy on us as a parent has mercy on children. If as servants, our eyes yearn for You to be gracious to us. O awesome, holy God, return us a verdict as clear as light!

(on Shabbat omit:)

May the request of our lips please You, high and transcendant God, who hearkens to the Tkiyah we are sounding. O accept with favor the order of our Shofarot, the praise of Your ancient sounds and the hope for those You will sound at the dawn of the age to come.

Musaf for Rosh Hashanah continues with Rtzey on p. 223

(When Reader offers Yom Kippur Amidah aloud, continue here:)

Sh'ma Koleynu

Hear our voice, Adonay our God, and take pity on us. Have mercy on us and accept our prayers with love and good will.

Turn us back to You, Adonay, that we may return to You in tshuvah. Renew our days with You as they once were.

Give ear to our words, Adonay, understand our thoughts in the way we intend them. May the words of our mouth and the thoughts in our heart be equally acceptable in Your presence, Adonay our Rock and Redeemer.

אַל תַּשְׁלִיכֵנוּ מִלְּפָנֶיךָ, וְרוּחַ קָדְשְׁךָ אַל תִּקַּח מִמֶּנּוּ.

אַל תַּשְׁלִיכֵנוּ לְעֵת זִקְנָה, כִּכְלוֹת כֹּחֵנוּ אַל תַּעַזְבֵנוּ.

אַל תַּעַזְבֵנוּ, יְיָ אֱלֹהֵינוּ, אַל תִּרְחַק מִמֶּנּוּ. עֲשֵׂה עִמָּנוּ אוֹת לְטוֹבָה, וְיִרְאוּ שׂוֹנְאֵינוּ וְיֵבְשׁוּ, כִּי אַתָּה יְיָ עֲזַרְתָּנוּ וְנִחַמְתָּנוּ. כִּי לְךָ יְיָ הוֹחָלְנוּ, אַתָּה תַעֲנֶה, אֲדֹנָי אֱלֹהֵינוּ.

אֱלֹהֵינוּ וֵאלֹהֵי אֲבוֹתֵינוּ (וְאלֹהֵי אִמּוֹתֵינוּ), אַל תַּעַזְבֵנוּ וְאַל תִּטְּשֵׁנוּ, וְאַל תַּכְלִימֵנוּ וְאַל תָּפֵר בְּרִיתְךָ אִתָּנוּ. קָרְבֵנוּ לְתוֹרָתֶךָ, לַמְּדֵנוּ מִצְוֹתֶיךָ, הוֹרֵנוּ דְרָכֶיךָ, הַט לִבֵּנוּ לְיִרְאָה אֶת שְׁמֶךָ, וּמוֹל אֶת לְבָבֵנוּ לְאַהֲבָתֶךָ, וְנָשׁוּב אֵלֶיךָ בֶּאֱמֶת וּבְלֵב שָׁלֵם. וּלְמַעַן שִׁמְךָ הַגָּדוֹל תִּמְחַל וְתִסְלַח לַעֲוֹנֵנוּ, כַּכָּתוּב בְּדִבְרֵי קָדְשֶׁךָ: לְמַעַן שִׁמְךָ יְיָ, וְסָלַחְתָּ לַעֲוֹנִי כִּי רַב הוּא.

Ki Anu Amecha

אֱלֹהֵינוּ וֵאלֹהֵי אֲבוֹתֵינוּ (וְאלֹהֵי אִמּוֹתֵינוּ), סְלַח לָנוּ, מְחַל לָנוּ, כַּפֶּר-לָנוּ.

כִּי אָנוּ עַמֶּךָ, וְאַתָּה אֱלֹהֵינוּ; אָנוּ בָנֶיךָ, וְאַתָּה אָבִינוּ. אָנוּ עֲבָדֶיךָ וְאַתָּה אֲדוֹנֵינוּ; אָנוּ קְהָלֶךָ, וְאַתָּה חֶלְקֵנוּ. אָנוּ נַחֲלָתֶךָ, וְאַתָּה גוֹרָלֵנוּ; אָנוּ צֹאנֶךָ, וְאַתָּה רוֹעֵנוּ. אָנוּ כַרְמֶךָ, וְאַתָּה נוֹטְרֵנוּ; אָנוּ פְעֻלָּתֶךָ, וְאַתָּה יוֹצְרֵנוּ. אָנוּ רַעְיָתֶךָ, וְאַתָּה דוֹדֵנוּ; אָנוּ סְגֻלָּתֶךָ, וְאַתָּה קְרוֹבֵנוּ.

Cast us not away from Your sight, remove not the breath
of Your holiness that gives us insight into Your will.

Cast us not away in our old age, abandon us not when our
strength fails us.

Abandon us not, Adonay our God, do not estrange Yourself from us! Show us a sign of Your favor, that those who
seek our misfortune will stand in awe and be ashamed, seeing that You, Adonay, have aided and comforted us.

We have watched and waited for You, Adonay our God, please
answer us now.

Adonay our God and God of our fathers (and mothers): do not
abandon us in shame as a people who used to have a covenant
with You. Instead, draw us closer to Your Torah, teach us Your
mitzvot, show us Your ways, give our minds the inclination to
know Your awe-filled Name. Cut away from our hearts the
foreskin of indifference that keeps us from loving You, that we
may return to You in earnest with a full heart.

For the sake of Your great Name, forgive and pardon us our
sins, as it is written in Your Torah: "For the sake of Your
Name, Adonay, forgive my sin though it be great."

Ki Anu Amecha

Our God and God of our fathers (and mothers): forgive us,
wipe the slate clean, grant us atonement:

For we are Your people, and You our God.
We are Your children, and You the One who gave us life.
We are Your servants, and You the One who acquires us.
We are Your congregation, and You our only One.
We are Your heritage, and You our Destiny.
We are Your flock, and You our Shepherd.
We are Your vineyard, and You our Protector.
We are Your creatures, and You our Creator.
We are Your companion, and You our beloved.
We are Your treasure, and You the intimate who redeems us.

אָנוּ עַמֶּךָ, וְאַתָּה מַלְכֵּנוּ; אָנוּ מַאֲמִירֶיךָ, וְאַתָּה
מַאֲמִירֵנוּ.

CONFESSIONS

Preparation

אֱלֹהֵינוּ וֵאלֹהֵי אֲבוֹתֵינוּ (וֵאלֹהֵי אִמּוֹתֵינוּ), תָּבֹא
לְפָנֶיךָ תְּפִלָּתֵנוּ, וְאַל תִּתְעַלַּם מִתְּחִנָּתֵנוּ; שֶׁאֵין
אֲנַחְנוּ עַזֵּי פָנִים וּקְשֵׁי עֹרֶף לוֹמַר לְפָנֶיךָ, יְיָ אֱלֹהֵינוּ
וֵאלֹהֵי אֲבוֹתֵינוּ (וֵאלֹהֵי אִמּוֹתֵינוּ), צַדִּיקִים אֲנַחְנוּ
וְלֹא חָטָאנוּ; אֲבָל אֲנַחְנוּ חָטָאנוּ.

Ashamnu

אָשַׁמְנוּ, בָּגַדְנוּ, גָּזַלְנוּ, דִּבַּרְנוּ דְֹפִי; הֶעֱוִינוּ, וְהִרְשַׁעְנוּ,
זַדְנוּ, חָמַסְנוּ, טָפַלְנוּ שֶׁקֶר; יָעַצְנוּ רָע, כִּזַּבְנוּ, לַצְנוּ,
מָרַדְנוּ, נִאַצְנוּ, סָרַרְנוּ, עָוִינוּ, פָּשַׁעְנוּ, צָרַרְנוּ, קִשִּׁינוּ
עֹרֶף; רָשַׁעְנוּ, שִׁחַתְנוּ, תִּעַבְנוּ, תָּעִינוּ, תִּעְתָּעְנוּ.

We are Your people, and You our Sovereign.
We have chosen You, and You have chosen us.

*Ki anu amecha v'atta Eloheynu, anu vanecha v'atta avinu.
Anu avadecha v'atta Adoneynu, anu k'halecha v'atta chelkeynu.
Anu nachalatecha v'atta goraleynu, anu tzonecha v'atta
ro-eynu.
Anu charmecha v'atta notreynu, anu f'ulatecha v'atta yotzreynu.
Anu ra'yatecha v'atta dodeynu, anu s'gulatecha v'atta k'roveynu.
Anu amecha v'atta malkeynu, anu ma'amirecha v'atta
ma'amireynu.*

CONFESSIONS

Preparation

Our God and God of our fathers (and mothers): Let our prayer enter Your presence; O do not turn aside from our entreaty! For we are not so obstinate and stubborn as to say before You, "We are righteous, we have done no wrong." For indeed, we have done wrong. We have sinned.

Ashamnu
Ashamnu, bagadnu, gazalnu, dibarnu dofi, he-evinu, v'hirshanu, zadnu, chamasnu, tafalnu sheker, ya-atznu ra, kizavnu, latznu, maradnu, ni-atznu, sararnu, avinu, pashanu, tzararnu, kishinu oref, rashanu, shichatnu, ti-avnu, ta-inu, ti'ta'nu.

We have been negligent; we have betrayed;
We have robbed; we have slandered;
We have been perverse; we have been wicked;
We have sinned wilfully; we have done violence;
We have been deceitful; we have given evil advice;
We have lied; we have mocked;
We have rebelled; we have been iniquitous;
We have trespassed; we have oppressed;
We have been obstinate; we have acted wickedly;
We have been corrupt; we have committed abominations;
We have gone astray; we have led others astray.

סַרְנוּ מִמִּצְוֹתֶיךָ וּמִמִּשְׁפָּטֶיךָ הַטּוֹבִים, וְלֹא שָׁוָה לָנוּ. וְאַתָּה צַדִּיק עַל כָּל הַבָּא עָלֵינוּ, כִּי אֱמֶת עָשִׂיתָ וַאֲנַחְנוּ הִרְשָׁעְנוּ. מַה נֹּאמַר לְפָנֶיךָ יוֹשֵׁב מָרוֹם, וּמַה נְּסַפֵּר לְפָנֶיךָ שׁוֹכֵן שְׁחָקִים הֲלֹא כָּל הַנִּסְתָּרוֹת וְהַנִּגְלוֹת אַתָּה יוֹדֵעַ.

אַתָּה יוֹדֵעַ רָזֵי עוֹלָם, וְתַעֲלוּמוֹת סִתְרֵי כָל חָי. אַתָּה חוֹפֵשׂ כָּל חַדְרֵי בָטֶן, וּבוֹחֵן כְּלָיוֹת וָלֵב. אֵין דָּבָר נֶעְלָם מִמֶּךָּ, וְאֵין נִסְתָּר מִנֶּגֶד עֵינֶיךָ. וּבְכֵן יְהִי רָצוֹן מִלְּפָנֶיךָ, יְיָ אֱלֹהֵינוּ וֵאלֹהֵי אֲבוֹתֵינוּ (וֵאלֹהֵי אִמּוֹתֵינוּ), שֶׁתִּסְלַח לָנוּ עַל כָּל חַטֹּאתֵינוּ, וְתִמְחַל לָנוּ עַל כָּל עֲוֹנוֹתֵינוּ, וּתְכַפֶּר־לָנוּ עַל כָּל פְּשָׁעֵינוּ.

Al Cheyt

עַל חֵטְא שֶׁחָטָאנוּ לְפָנֶיךָ בְּאֹנֶס וּבְרָצוֹן,
וְעַל חֵטְא שֶׁחָטָאנוּ לְפָנֶיךָ בְּאִמּוּץ הַלֵּב.
עַל חֵטְא שֶׁחָטָאנוּ לְפָנֶיךָ בִּבְלִי דָעַת,
וְעַל חֵטְא שֶׁחָטָאנוּ לְפָנֶיךָ בְּבִטּוּי שְׂפָתָיִם.
עַל חֵטְא שֶׁחָטָאנוּ לְפָנֶיךָ בְּגִלּוּי עֲרָיוֹת,
וְעַל חֵטְא שֶׁחָטָאנוּ לְפָנֶיךָ בַּגָּלוּי וּבַסָּתֶר.
עַל חֵטְא שֶׁחָטָאנוּ לְפָנֶיךָ בְּדַעַת וּבְמִרְמָה,
וְעַל חֵטְא שֶׁחָטָאנוּ לְפָנֶיךָ בְּדִבּוּר פֶּה.
עַל חֵטְא שֶׁחָטָאנוּ לְפָנֶיךָ בְּהוֹנָאַת רֵעַ,
וְעַל חֵטְא שֶׁחָטָאנוּ לְפָנֶיךָ בְּהִרְהוּר הַלֵּב.

We have turned aside from Your mitzvot,
From Your laws which point us toward the good,
And no good has come to us from our misdeeds.
Yet You do justly with everyone who comes before You,
For You have acted out of truth, while we have too often acted
    falsely.
What shall we say before You who dwells in the heights,
What stories can we tell to You who dwells in heaven?
Do You not already know all that we reveal and all that we have
    tried to hide?

Indeed, you know the mysteries of the universe,
And the best kept secrets of every living thing.
You search out the innermost rooms of our life,
With care You examine all our feelings, all our thoughts.
Not one thing is hidden from You, nothing escapes Your gaze.
God who preserves the memory of all our ancestors,
If You would only wipe away the memory of all our wrongs
And grant atonement for all our sins.

Al Cheyt

For the wrong we did before You under coercion or of our own
free will:
And for the wrong we did before You by hardening our hearts.

For the wrong we did before You unintentionally;
And for the wrong we did before You through idle talk and
meaningless resolutions.

For the wrong we did before You by using sex exploitatively;
And for the wrong we did before You in public and in private.

For the wrong we did before You knowingly and deceptively;
And for the wrong we did before You by offensive language.

For the wrong we did before You by oppressing another person:
And for the wrong we did before You by malicious thoughts.

עַל חֵטְא שֶׁחָטָאנוּ לְפָנֶיךָ בִּוְעִידַת זְנוּת,

וְעַל חֵטְא שֶׁחָטָאנוּ לְפָנֶיךָ בְּוִדּוּי פֶּה.

עַל חֵטְא שֶׁחָטָאנוּ לְפָנֶיךָ בְּזִלְזוּל הוֹרִים וּמוֹרִים,

וְעַל חֵטְא שֶׁחָטָאנוּ לְפָנֶיךָ בְּזָדוֹן וּבִשְׁגָגָה.

עַל חֵטְא שֶׁחָטָאנוּ לְפָנֶיךָ בְּחֹזֶק יָד,

וְעַל חֵטְא שֶׁחָטָאנוּ לְפָנֶיךָ בְּחִלּוּל הַשֵּׁם.

עַל חֵטְא שֶׁחָטָאנוּ לְפָנֶיךָ בְּטֻמְאַת שְׂפָתָיִם,

וְעַל חֵטְא שֶׁחָטָאנוּ לְפָנֶיךָ בְּטִפְשׁוּת פֶּה,

עַל חֵטְא שֶׁחָטָאנוּ לְפָנֶיךָ בְּיֵצֶר הָרָע,

וְעַל חֵטְא שֶׁחָטָאנוּ לְפָנֶיךָ בְּיוֹדְעִים וּבְלֹא יוֹדְעִים.

וְעַל כֻּלָּם, אֱלוֹהַּ סְלִיחוֹת, סְלַח לָנוּ, מְחַל לָנוּ, כַּפֶּר־לָנוּ.

עַל חֵטְא שֶׁחָטָאנוּ לְפָנֶיךָ בְּכַחַשׁ וּבְכָזָב,

וְעַל חֵטְא שֶׁחָטָאנוּ לְפָנֶיךָ בְּכַפַּת שֹׁחַד.

עַל חֵטְא שֶׁחָטָאנוּ לְפָנֶיךָ בְּלָצוֹן,

וְעַל חֵטְא שֶׁחָטָאנוּ לְפָנֶיךָ בְּלָשׁוֹן הָרָע.

עַל חֵטְא שֶׁחָטָאנוּ לְפָנֶיךָ בְּמַשָּׂא וּבְמַתָּן,

וְעַל חֵטְא שֶׁחָטָאנוּ לְפָנֶיךָ בְּמַאֲכָל וּבְמִשְׁתֶּה.

עַל חֵטְא שֶׁחָטָאנוּ לְפָנֶיךָ בְּנֶשֶׁךְ וּבְמַרְבִּית,

וְעַל חֵטְא שֶׁחָטָאנוּ לְפָנֶיךָ בִּנְטִיַּת גָּרוֹן.

עַל חֵטְא שֶׁחָטָאנוּ לְפָנֶיךָ בְּשִׂיחַ שִׂפְתוֹתֵינוּ,

וְעַל חֵטְא שֶׁחָטָאנוּ לְפָנֶיךָ בְּשִׁקּוּר עָיִן.

For the wrong we did before You by promiscuity;
And for the wrong we did before You by confessing insincerely.

For the wrong we did before You by contempt for parents and teachers;
And for the wrong we did before You intentionally or by accident.

For the wrong we did before You by violence;
And for the wrong we did before You by failing to be true to our heritage, thus defaming Your Name in the world.

For the wrong we did before You by ugly language;
And for the wrong we did before You by foolish talk.

For the wrong we did before You by the unbridled passions of our *yetzer ha-ra*;
And for the wrong we did before You knowingly and unknowingly.

V'al kulam, Eloah slichot, s'lach lanu, m'chal lanu, kapper lanu.

For all our wrongs, God of forgiveness, forgive us, wipe the slate clean, grant us atonement.

For the wrong we did before You by lying and deceiving;
And for the wrong we did before You by accepting bribes.

For the wrong we did before You by scoffing and mocking;
And for the wrong we did before You by speaking ill of other people.
For the wrong we did before You in our work;
And for the wrong we did before You in the foods we eat and the amount we drink.

For the wrong we did before You by refusing to be generous;
And for the wrong we did before you by being proud and haughty.

For the wrong we did before You by the content of our conversation;
And for the wrong we did before You by immodest or demeaning glances.

עַל חֵטְא שֶׁחָטָאנוּ לְפָנֶיךָ בְּעֵינַיִם רָמוֹת,

וְעַל חֵטְא שֶׁחָטָאנוּ לְפָנֶיךָ בְּעַזּוּת מֶצַח.

וְעַל כֻּלָּם אֱלוֹהַּ סְלִיחוֹת, סְלַח לָנוּ, מְחַל לָנוּ, כַּפֶּר־
לָנוּ.

עַל חֵטְא שֶׁחָטָאנוּ לְפָנֶיךָ בִּפְרִיקַת עֹל,
וְעַל חֵטְא שֶׁחָטָאנוּ לְפָנֶיךָ בִּפְלִילוּת.
עַל חֵטְא שֶׁחָטָאנוּ לְפָנֶיךָ בִּצְדִיַּת רֵעַ,
וְעַל חֵטְא שֶׁחָטָאנוּ לְפָנֶיךָ בְּצָרוּת עָיִן.
עַל חֵטְא שֶׁחָטָאנוּ לְפָנֶיךָ בְּקַלּוּת רֹאשׁ,
וְעַל חֵטְא שֶׁחָטָאנוּ לְפָנֶיךָ בְּקַשְׁיוּת עֹרֶף.
עַל חֵטְא שֶׁחָטָאנוּ לְפָנֶיךָ בְּרִיצַת רַגְלַיִם לְהָרַע,
וְעַל חֵטְא שֶׁחָטָאנוּ לְפָנֶיךָ בִּרְכִילוּת.
עַל חֵטְא שֶׁחָטָאנוּ לְפָנֶיךָ בִּשְׁבוּעַת שָׁוְא,
וְעַל חֵטְא שֶׁחָטָאנוּ לְפָנֶיךָ בְּשִׂנְאַת חִנָּם.
עַל חֵטְא שֶׁחָטָאנוּ לְפָנֶיךָ בִּתְשׂוּמֶת־יָד,
וְעַל חֵטְא שֶׁחָטָאנוּ לְפָנֶיךָ בְּתִמְהוֹן לֵבָב.

וְעַל כֻּלָּם, אֱלוֹהַּ סְלִיחוֹת, סְלַח לָנוּ, מְחַל לָנוּ, כַּפֶּר־
לָנוּ.

*(Yom Kippur Amidah, when offered privately and aloud by the
Reader, continues here:)*

M'chal la-Avonoteynu (Sanctifying Yom Kippur)

אֱלֹהֵינוּ וֵאלֹהֵי אֲבוֹתֵינוּ (וֵאלֹהֵי אִמּוֹתֵינוּ), מְחַל
לַעֲוֹנוֹתֵינוּ בְּיוֹם [הַשַּׁבָּת הַזֶּה וּבְיוֹם] הַכִּפֻּרִים הַזֶּה.
מְחֵה וְהַעֲבֵר פְּשָׁעֵינוּ וְחַטֹּאתֵינוּ מִנֶּגֶד עֵינֶיךָ,
כָּאָמוּר: אָנֹכִי אָנֹכִי הוּא מֹחֶה פְּשָׁעֶיךָ לְמַעֲנִי,

For the wrong we did before You by scornful glances;
And for the wrong we did before You by a defiant manner.

V'al kulam, Eloah s'lichot, s'lach lanu, m'chal lanu, kapper lanu.

For all our wrongs, God of forgiveness, forgive us, wipe the slate clean, grant us atonement.

For the wrong we did before You in rejecting Your authority;
And for the wrong we did before You in making harsh judgments on other people.

For the wrong we did before You by plotting against others;
And for the wrong we did before You by tormenting others.

For the wrong we did before You by dismissing serious matters with a joke;
And for the wrong we did before You by being obstinate.

For the wrong we did before You by running to do evil;
And for the wrong we did before You by gossiping.

For the wrong we did before You by swearing falsely;
And for the wrong we did before You by hating others without cause.

For the wrong we did before You by betraying a trust;
And for the wrong we did before You out of confusion, unaware of the significance of our actions.

V'al kulam, Eloah s'lichot, s'lach lanu, m'chal lanu, kapper lanu.

For all our wrongs, O God of forgiveness, forgive us, wipe the slate clean, grant us atonement.

(Yom Kippur Amidah, when offered privately and aloud by the Reader, continues here:)

M'chal la-Avonoteynu (Sanctifying Yom Kippur)

Our God and God of our mothers and fathers, pardon our failures on (this Shabbat and on) this Yom Kippur. Erase our malicious deeds, our human shortcomings; sweep them from Your sight. As it says in the Bible, "I myself will erase your malicious deeds for the sake of My mercy; I will not recall your shortcomings." As it says, "I have dissolved Your malicious

וְחַטֹּאתֶיךָ לֹא אֶזְכֹּר. וְנֶאֱמַר: מָחִיתִי כָעָב פְּשָׁעֶיךָ,
וְכֶעָנָן חַטֹּאתֶיךָ; שׁוּבָה אֵלַי כִּי גְאַלְתִּיךָ. וְנֶאֱמַר: כִּי
בַיּוֹם הַזֶּה יְכַפֵּר עֲלֵיכֶם לְטַהֵר אֶתְכֶם, מִכֹּל
חַטֹּאתֵיכֶם לִפְנֵי יְיָ תִּטְהָרוּ. אֱלֹהֵינוּ וֵאלֹהֵי אֲבוֹתֵינוּ
(וֵאלֹהֵי אִמּוֹתֵינוּ), [רְצֵה בִמְנוּחָתֵנוּ] קַדְּשֵׁנוּ בְּמִצְוֹתֶיךָ
וְתֵן חֶלְקֵנוּ בְּתוֹרָתֶךָ, שַׂבְּעֵנוּ מִטּוּבֶךָ, וְשַׂמְּחֵנוּ
בִּישׁוּעָתֶךָ. [וְהַנְחִילֵנוּ, יְיָ אֱלֹהֵינוּ, בְּאַהֲבָה וּבְרָצוֹן
שַׁבַּת קָדְשֶׁךָ, וְיָנְוּחוּ בָוֹ יִשְׂרָאֵל מְקַדְּשֵׁי שְׁמֶךָ). וְטַהֵר
לִבֵּנוּ לְעָבְדְּךָ בֶּאֱמֶת, כִּי אַתָּה סָלְחָן לְיִשְׂרָאֵל וּמָחֳלָן
לְשִׁבְטֵי יְשֻׁרוּן בְּכָל דּוֹר וָדוֹר, וּמִבַּלְעָדֶיךָ אֵין לָנוּ
מֶלֶךְ מוֹחֵל וְסוֹלֵחַ אֶלָּא אָתָּה. בָּרוּךְ אַתָּה, יְיָ, מֶלֶךְ
מוֹחֵל וְסוֹלֵחַ לַעֲוֹנוֹתֵינוּ וְלַעֲוֹנוֹת עַמּוֹ בֵּית יִשְׂרָאֵל,
וּמַעֲבִיר אַשְׁמוֹתֵינוּ בְּכָל שָׁנָה וְשָׁנָה, מֶלֶךְ עַל כָּל
הָאָרֶץ מְקַדֵּשׁ [הַשַּׁבָּת וְ]יִשְׂרָאֵל וְיוֹם הַכִּפֻּרִים.

(Rosh Hashanah and Yom Kippur Amidah continues here:)

Rtzey

רְצֵה, יְיָ אֱלֹהֵינוּ, בְּעַמְּךָ יִשְׂרָאֵל וּבִתְפִלָּתָם; וְהָשֵׁב
אֶת הָעֲבוֹדָה לִדְבִיר בֵּיתֶךָ, וְאִשֵּׁי יִשְׂרָאֵל וּתְפִלָּתָם
בְּאַהֲבָה תְקַבֵּל בְּרָצוֹן, וּתְהִי לְרָצוֹן תָּמִיד עֲבוֹדַת
יִשְׂרָאֵל עַמֶּךָ.

וְתֶחֱזֶינָה עֵינֵינוּ בְּשׁוּבְךָ לְצִיּוֹן בְּרַחֲמִים. בָּרוּךְ אַתָּה,
יְיָ, הַמַּחֲזִיר שְׁכִינָתוֹ לְצִיּוֹן.

Modim

מוֹדִים אֲנַחְנוּ לָךְ, שָׁאַתָּה הוּא יְיָ אֱלֹהֵינוּ וֵאלֹהֵי
אֲבוֹתֵינוּ (וֵאלֹהֵי אִמּוֹתֵינוּ) לְעוֹלָם וָעֶד. צוּר חַיֵּינוּ,
מָגֵן יִשְׁעֵנוּ אַתָּה הוּא. לְדוֹר וָדוֹר נוֹדֶה לְךָ, וּנְסַפֵּר

deeds like a mist, your shortcomings like a cloud. Turn back to
Me, do tshuvah, for I have redeemed you." And it says, "On
this day God will give you a new start by purifying you. From
all your shortcomings you will be clean in the sight of Adonay."

Our God and God of those who gave us life: (Be pleased with
our soul-rest). Imbue us with holiness through Your mitzvot
and grant us our share in the understanding of Your Torah.
Satiate us with Your goodness, fill us with the joy of victory
over our selfish instincts, our cruel temptations. (Dower us,
God, with the holiness of Your Shabbat; let the Jewish people,
whose actions strive to manifest Your holiness, find soul-rest on
this day.) Wash clean our hearts that we may serve You with
true intentions. You are the forgiver of Israel, who grants pardon to the tribes You called Yeshurun, the upright. No other
power beside You can forgive and excuse us. You are praised,
Adonay, Monarch who forgives and excuses our wrongs and
the wrongs of Your entire people Israel, who takes away our
guilt each year; Ruler of all the earth, who fills with holiness
(Shabbat,) the Jewish people, and Yom Kippur.

(Rosh Hashanah and Yom Kippur Amidah continues here:)

Rtzey

May You be pleased with Your people Israel, Adonay our God,
and with their prayer. Restore to Your holy temple in Jerusalem
the service You most desire, accepting Israel's holy offerings
and holy words with love. May the intensity of Your people's
worship please You always. May we see Your merciful return to
Zion with our own eyes. You are praised, Adonay, whose nurturing presence You will again return to Zion.

Modim

Thank You.
You are the Source of our life, and the life of those who carried
   us into this world.
You are our Rock, our shield, our defender.
In every generation we will thank you and retell Your praise

תְּהִלָּתֶךָ, עַל חַיֵּינוּ הַמְּסוּרִים בְּיָדֶךָ, וְעַל נִשְׁמוֹתֵינוּ הַפְּקוּדוֹת לָךְ, וְעַל נִסֶּיךָ שֶׁבְּכָל יוֹם עִמָּנוּ, וְעַל נִפְלְאוֹתֶיךָ וְטוֹבוֹתֶיךָ שֶׁבְּכָל עֵת, עֶרֶב וָבֹקֶר וְצָהֳרָיִם. הַטוֹב כִּי לֹא כָלוּ רַחֲמֶיךָ, וְהַמְרַחֵם כִּי לֹא תַמּוּ חֲסָדֶיךָ, מֵעוֹלָם קִוִּינוּ לָךְ.

(When the Reader offers the Amidah aloud, all respond with the following Modim:)

(מוֹדִים אֲנַחְנוּ לָךְ שָׁאַתָּה הוּא יְיָ אֱלֹהֵינוּ וֵאלֹהֵי אֲבוֹתֵינוּ (וְאלֹהֵי אִמּוֹתֵינוּ) אֱלֹהֵי כָל־בָּשָׂר יוֹצְרֵנוּ יוֹצֵר בְּרֵאשִׁית. בְּרָכוֹת וְהוֹדָאוֹת לְשִׁמְךָ הַגָּדוֹל וְהַקָּדוֹשׁ עַל שֶׁהֶחֱיִיתָנוּ וְקִיַּמְתָּנוּ. כֵּן תְּחַיֵּנוּ וּתְקַיְּמֵנוּ וְתֶאֱסוֹף גָּלֻיּוֹתֵינוּ לְחַצְרוֹת קָדְשֶׁךָ לִשְׁמֹר חֻקֶּיךָ וְלַעֲשׂוֹת רְצוֹנֶךָ וּלְעָבְדְּךָ בְּלֵבָב שָׁלֵם עַל שֶׁאֲנַחְנוּ מוֹדִים לָךְ. בָּרוּךְ אֵל הַהוֹדָאוֹת:)

וְעַל כֻּלָּם יִתְבָּרַךְ וְיִתְרוֹמַם שִׁמְךָ, מַלְכֵּנוּ, תָּמִיד לְעוֹלָם וָעֶד.

וּכְתוֹב לְחַיִּים טוֹבִים כָּל בְּנֵי בְרִיתֶךָ.

וְכֹל הַחַיִּים יוֹדוּךָ סֶּלָה, וִיהַלְלוּ אֶת שִׁמְךָ בֶּאֱמֶת, הָאֵל, יְשׁוּעָתֵנוּ וְעֶזְרָתֵנוּ סֶלָה. בָּרוּךְ אַתָּה, יְיָ, הַטוֹב שִׁמְךָ, וּלְךָ נָאֶה לְהוֹדוֹת.

(When the Reader offers the Rosh Hashanah or Yom Kippur Amidah aloud, continue with Birkat Kohanim on p. 226)

Sim Shalom

שִׂים שָׁלוֹם, טוֹבָה וּבְרָכָה, חֵן וָחֶסֶד וְרַחֲמִים, עָלֵינוּ וְעַל כָּל יִשְׂרָאֵל עַמֶּךָ. בָּרְכֵנוּ אָבִינוּ, כֻּלָּנוּ כְּאֶחָד,

for our lives which You shape with Your hand
for our souls which You hold in trust
for Your miracles which accompany us each day
for Your wonders and Your favors which fill all our
    moments every evening, every morning, on dark days,
    and when the sun is high.

For You are the good God, whose nurture never dries up, the
    Compassionate One, whose acts of love are endless.
In Your eternity lies our hope.

*(When the Reader offers the Amidah aloud, all respond with the
following Modim:)*

(We are grateful to You, Adonay, our God and God of our
fathers (and mothers). You are the God of all flesh, our
Creator, Creator of the beginnings of all life. We shall pour
forth thanks and blessings to Your great and holy Name,
for You have given our people life and sustained us
through the generations. May You continue to grant life to
us all and sustain us. Gather up our scattered people and
bring us into Your holy courts, where we may keep all of
Your commands and do Your will, serving You with hearts
that have found peace, for we are grateful to You. You are
praised, God, to whom unbounded thanks are due.)

For all these things, O Majesty, may Your Name be blessed and
raised in high esteem by all who live, and inscribe for a good life
the people of Your covenant, who pour forth thanks to You in
ecstasy, along with everything alive, giving honest praise to
Your name, O God, who leads us forth from our adversaries in
triumph, sela! You are praised, Adonay, whose name is Good,
whose praise is comely on our lips.

*(When the Reader offers the Rosh Hashanah or Yom Kippur
Amidah aloud, continue with Birkat Kohanim on p. 227)*
Sim Shalom

Spread peace, goodness and blessing, grace, love, and compassion over us and over all Israel Your people. Bless us Father-

בְּאוֹר פָּנֶיךָ; כִּי בְאוֹר פָּנֶיךָ נָתַתָּ לָנוּ, יְיָ אֱלֹהֵינוּ,
תּוֹרַת חַיִּים וְאַהֲבַת חֶסֶד, וּצְדָקָה וּבְרָכָה וְרַחֲמִים,
וְחַיִּים וְשָׁלוֹם. וְטוֹב בְּעֵינֶיךָ לְבָרֵךְ אֶת עַמְּךָ יִשְׂרָאֵל
בְּכָל עֵת וּבְכָל שָׁעָה בִּשְׁלוֹמֶךָ.

בְּסֵפֶר חַיִּים, בְּרָכָה וְשָׁלוֹם וּפַרְנָסָה טוֹבָה, נִזָּכֵר
וְנִכָּתֵב לְפָנֶיךָ, אֲנַחְנוּ וְכָל עַמְּךָ בֵּית יִשְׂרָאֵל, לְחַיִּים
טוֹבִים וּלְשָׁלוֹם. בָּרוּךְ אַתָּה, יְיָ, עוֹשֵׂה הַשָּׁלוֹם.

*(Private Rosh Hashanah Amidah continues with Elohai Nizor on
p. 238; private Yom Kippur Amidah continues with Confessions on
p. 230)*

*(When the Reader offers the Rosh Hashanah or Yom Kippur
Amidah aloud, continue here:)*

Birkat Kohanim

אֱלֹהֵינוּ וֵאלֹהֵי אֲבוֹתֵינוּ (וֵאלֹהֵי אִמּוֹתֵינוּ), בָּרְכֵנוּ
בַבְּרָכָה הַמְשֻׁלֶּשֶׁת בַּתּוֹרָה הַכְּתוּבָה עַל יְדֵי מֹשֶׁה
עַבְדֶּךָ. הָאֲמוּרָה מִפִּי אַהֲרֹן וּבָנָיו כֹּהֲנִים. עַם קְדוֹשֶׁךָ
כָּאָמוּר:

Congregation	*Reader*
כֵּן יְהִי רָצוֹן:	יְבָרֶכְךָ יְיָ וְיִשְׁמְרֶךָ:
כֵּן יְהִי רָצוֹן:	יָאֵר יְיָ פָּנָיו אֵלֶיךָ וִיחֻנֶּךָ:
כֵּן יְהִי רָצוֹן:	יִשָּׂא יְיָ פָּנָיו אֵלֶיךָ וְיָשֵׂם לְךָ שָׁלוֹם:

Sim Shalom

שִׂים שָׁלוֹם, טוֹבָה וּבְרָכָה, חֵן וָחֶסֶד וְרַחֲמִים, עָלֵינוּ
וְעַל כָּל יִשְׂרָאֵל עַמֶּךָ. בָּרְכֵנוּ אָבִינוּ, כֻּלָּנוּ כְּאֶחָד,
בְּאוֹר פָּנֶיךָ. כִּי בְאוֹר פָּנֶיךָ נָתַתָּ לָנוּ, יְיָ אֱלֹהֵינוּ,

mother, all of us as one, in the radiance of Your countenance, for in the light of Your presence, Adonay our God, You gave us a Torah of life, love born of our covenant, justice, blessing, compassion, life, and peace. May it be good in Your eyes to bless Your people Israel at every season, at every moment, with that peace which is Your nature.

May we and all the House of Israel be inscribed perpetually in the Book of life and blessing, peace and sustenance, for a worthwhile life and for peace. You are praised, Adonay, author of peace.

(Private Rosh Hashanah Amidah continues with Elohai Nizor on p. 239; private Yom Kippur Amidah continues with Confessions on p. 231)

(When the Reader offers the Rosh Hashanah or Yom Kippur Amidah aloud, continue here:)

Birkat Kohanim

Our God and God of our fathers (and mothers), favor us with the threefold blessing written in Your Torah through Your servant Moses and spoken by Aaron and his descendants, the holy company of Kohanim, through the ages:

Reader	*Congregation*
May God bless you and protect you.	May it be God's will.
May the light of God's countenance favor you with enlightenment and grace.	May it be God's will.
May God's countenance be raised up to You that you may find peace.	May it be God's will.

Sim Shalom

Spread peace, goodness and blessing, grace, love, and compassion over us and over all Israel Your people. Bless us Father-mother, all of us as one, in the radiance of Your countenance, for in the light of Your presence, Adonay our God, You gave us

תּוֹרַת חַיִּים וְאַהֲבַת חֶסֶד, וּצְדָקָה וּבְרָכָה, וְרַחֲמִים, וְחַיִּים וְשָׁלוֹם. וְטוֹב בְּעֵינֶיךָ לְבָרֵךְ אֶת עַמְּךָ יִשְׂרָאֵל בְּכָל עֵת וּבְכָל שָׁעָה בִּשְׁלוֹמֶךָ.

בְּסֵפֶר חַיִּים, בְּרָכָה וְשָׁלוֹם וּפַרְנָסָה טוֹבָה, נִזָּכֵר וְנִכָּתֵב לְפָנֶיךָ, אֲנַחְנוּ וְכָל עַמְּךָ בֵּית יִשְׂרָאֵל, לְחַיִּים טוֹבִים וּלְשָׁלוֹם.

וְנֶאֱמַר: כִּי בִי יִרְבּוּ יָמֶיךָ, וְיוֹסִיפוּ לְךָ שְׁנוֹת חַיִּים. לְחַיִּים טוֹבִים תִּכְתְּבֵנוּ, אֱלֹהִים חַיִּים. כָּתְבֵנוּ בְּסֵפֶר הַחַיִּים, כַּכָּתוּב: וְאַתֶּם הַדְּבֵקִים בַּיְיָ אֱלֹהֵיכֶם, חַיִּים כֻּלְּכֶם הַיּוֹם.

הַיּוֹם תְּאַמְּצֵנוּ	אָמֵן.
הַיּוֹם תְּבָרְכֵנוּ	אָמֵן.
הַיּוֹם תְּגַדְּלֵנוּ	אָמֵן.
הַיּוֹם תִּדְרְשֵׁנוּ לְטוֹבָה	אָמֵן.
הַיּוֹם תִּכְתְּבֵנוּ לְחַיִּים טוֹבִים	אָמֵן.
הַיּוֹם תְּקַבֵּל בְּרַחֲמִים וּבְרָצוֹן אֶת תְּפִלָּתֵנוּ	אָמֵן.
הַיּוֹם תִּשְׁמַע שַׁוְעָתֵנוּ	אָמֵן.
הַיּוֹם תִּתְמְכֵנוּ בִּימִין צִדְקֶךָ	אָמֵן.

כְּהַיּוֹם הַזֶּה תְּבִיאֵנוּ שָׂשִׂים וּשְׂמֵחִים בְּבִנְיַן שָׁלֵם, כַּכָּתוּב עַל יַד נְבִיאֶךָ: וַהֲבִיאוֹתִים אֶל הַר קָדְשִׁי, וְשִׂמַּחְתִּים בְּבֵית תְּפִלָּתִי, עוֹלֹתֵיהֶם וְזִבְחֵיהֶם לְרָצוֹן עַל מִזְבְּחִי, כִּי בֵיתִי בֵּית תְּפִלָּה יִקָּרֵא לְכָל הָעַמִּים. וְנֶאֱמַר: וַיְצַוֵּנוּ יְיָ לַעֲשׂוֹת אֶת כָּל הַחֻקִּים הָאֵלֶּה, לְיִרְאָה אֶת יְיָ אֱלֹהֵינוּ, לְטוֹב לָנוּ כָּל הַיָּמִים, לְחַיּוֹתֵנוּ כְּהַיּוֹם הַזֶּה. וְנֶאֱמַר: וּצְדָקָה תִּהְיֶה לָּנוּ, כִּי נִשְׁמֹר לַעֲשׂוֹת אֶת כָּל הַמִּצְוָה הַזֹּאת לִפְנֵי יְיָ אֱלֹהֵינוּ, כַּאֲשֶׁר צִוָּנוּ. וּצְדָקָה וּבְרָכָה וְרַחֲמִים וְחַיִּים

a Torah of life, love born of our covenant, justice, blessing, compassion, life, and peace. May it be good in Your eyes to bless Your people Israel at every season, at every moment, with that peace which is Your nature.

May we and all the House of Israel be inscribed perpetually in the Book of life and blessing, peace and sustenance, for a worthwhile life and for peace.

For it is said, "Through Me shall your days be multiplied, and years of life be added to you." May we be inscribed for a good life, O God of life. Inscribe us in the Book of Life, as it is written, "And you who cling to Adonay Your God are all alive today."

Today, please strengthen us.   Amen.
Today, please bless us.   Amen.
Today, please exalt us.   Amen.
Today, please seek our good.   Amen.
Today, please inscribe us for a good life.   Amen.
Today, please accept our prayers with favor and
      compassion.   Amen.
Today, please hear our cries.   Amen.
Today, please support us with Your vindicating
      power.   Amen.

On a day like today please bring us exultantly to Jerusalem restored, as it is written by Your prophet: "I shall bring them into My holy mountain, and I shall give them joy in My house of prayer, permitting them to place the offerings I desire upon My altar, for My house shall be called a house of prayer for all peoples." Then we and all Israel shall have justice, blessing,

וְשָׁלוֹם יִהְיֶה לָנוּ וּלְכָל יִשְׂרָאֵל עַד הָעוֹלָם. בָּרוּךְ
אַתָּה יְיָ, עוֹשֶׂה הַשָּׁלוֹם.

*(The Rosh Hashanah and Yom Kippur Amidahs offered by the
Reader conclude with Kaddish Shalem on p. 238)*

(The private Yom Kippur Amidah continues here:)

CONFESSIONS
Preparation

אֱלֹהֵינוּ וֵאלֹהֵי אֲבוֹתֵינוּ (וֵאלֹהֵי אִמּוֹתֵינוּ), תָּבֹא
לְפָנֶיךָ תְּפִלָּתֵנוּ, וְאַל תִּתְעַלַּם מִתְּחִנָּתֵנוּ; שֶׁאֵין
אֲנַחְנוּ עַזֵּי פָנִים וּקְשֵׁי עֹרֶף לוֹמַר לְפָנֶיךָ, יְיָ אֱלֹהֵינוּ
וֵאלֹהֵי אֲבוֹתֵינוּ (וֵאלֹהֵי אִמּוֹתֵינוּ), צַדִּיקִים אֲנַחְנוּ
וְלֹא חָטָאנוּ; אֲבָל אֲנַחְנוּ חָטָאנוּ.

Ashamnu

אָשַׁמְנוּ, בָּגַדְנוּ, גָּזַלְנוּ דִבַּרְנוּ דֹפִי; הֶעֱוִינוּ, וְהִרְשַׁעְנוּ,
זַדְנוּ, חָמַסְנוּ, טָפַלְנוּ שֶׁקֶר; יָעַצְנוּ רָע, כִּזַּבְנוּ, לַצְנוּ,
מָרַדְנוּ, נִאַצְנוּ, סָרַרְנוּ, עָוִינוּ, פָּשַׁעְנוּ, צָרַרְנוּ, קִשִּׁינוּ
עֹרֶף; רָשַׁעְנוּ, שִׁחַתְנוּ, תִּעַבְנוּ, תָּעִינוּ, תִּעְתָּעְנוּ.

סַרְנוּ מִמִּצְוֹתֶיךָ וּמִמִּשְׁפָּטֶיךָ הַטּוֹבִים, וְלֹא שָׁוָה לָנוּ.
וְאַתָּה צַדִּיק עַל כָּל הַבָּא עָלֵינוּ כִּי אֱמֶת עָשִׂיתָ

compassion, life and peace forever more. You are praised, Adonay, author of peace.

(The Rosh Hashanah and Yom Kippur Amidahs offered by the Reader conclude with Kaddish Shalem on p. 239)

(The private Yom Kippur Amidah continues here:)

CONFESSIONS

Preparation

Our God and God of our fathers (and mothers): Let our prayer enter Your presence; O do not turn aside from our entreaty! For we are not so obstinate and stubborn as to say before You, "We are righteous, we have done no wrong." For indeed, we have done wrong. We have sinned.

Ashamnu

Ashamnu, bagadnu, gazalnu, dibarnu dofi, he-evinu, v'hirshanu, zadnu, chamasnu, tafalnu sheker, ya-atznu ra, kizavnu, latznu, maradnu, ni-atznu, sararnu, avinu, pashanu, tzararnu, kishinu oref, rashanu, shichatnu, ti-avnu, ta-inu, ti'ta'nu.

We have been negligent; we have betrayed;
We have robbed; we have slandered;
We have been perverse; we have been wicked;
We have sinned willfully; we have done violence;
We have been deceitful; we have given evil advice;
We have lied; we have mocked;
We have rebelled; we have been iniquitous;
We have trespassed; we have oppressed;
We have been obstinate; we have acted wickedly;
We have been corrupt; we have committed abominations;
We have gone astray; we have led others astray.

We have turned aside from Your mitzvot,
From Your laws which point us toward the good,
And no good has come to us from our misdeeds.

וַאֲנַֽחְנוּ הִרְשַֽׁעְנוּ. מַה נֹּאמַר לְפָנֶֽיךָ יוֹשֵׁב מָרוֹם, וּמַה
נְּסַפֵּר לְפָנֶֽיךָ שׁוֹכֵן שְׁחָקִים, הֲלֹא כָּל הַנִּסְתָּרוֹת
וְהַנִּגְלוֹת אַתָּה יוֹדֵֽעַ.

אַתָּה יוֹדֵֽעַ רָזֵי עוֹלָם, וְתַעֲלוּמוֹת סִתְרֵי כָל חָי. אַתָּה
חוֹפֵשׂ כָּל חַדְרֵי בָֽטֶן, וּבוֹחֵן כְּלָיוֹת וָלֵב. אֵין דָּבָר
נֶעְלָם מִמֶּֽךָּ. וְאֵין נִסְתָּר מִנֶּֽגֶד עֵינֶֽיךָ. וּבְכֵן יְהִי רָצוֹן
מִלְּפָנֶֽיךָ, יְיָ אֱלֹהֵֽינוּ וֵאלֹהֵי אֲבוֹתֵֽינוּ (וֵאלֹהֵי
אִמּוֹתֵֽינוּ), שֶׁתִּסְלַח לָֽנוּ עַל כָּל חַטֹּאתֵֽינוּ, וְתִמְחַל לָֽנוּ
עַל כָּל עֲוֹנוֹתֵֽינוּ, וּתְכַפֶּר־לָֽנוּ עַל כָּל פְּשָׁעֵֽינוּ.

Al Cheyt

עַל חֵטְא שֶׁחָטָֽאנוּ לְפָנֶֽיךָ בְּאֹֽנֶס וּבְרָצוֹן,
וְעַל חֵטְא שֶׁחָטָֽאנוּ לְפָנֶֽיךָ בְּאִמּוּץ הַלֵּב.
עַל חֵטְא שֶׁחָטָֽאנוּ לְפָנֶֽיךָ בִּבְלִי דָֽעַת,
וְעַל חֵטְא שֶׁחָטָֽאנוּ לְפָנֶֽיךָ בְּבִטּוּי שְׂפָתָֽיִם.
עַל חֵטְא שֶׁחָטָֽאנוּ לְפָנֶֽיךָ בְּגִלּוּי עֲרָיוֹת,
וְעַל חֵטְא שֶׁחָטָֽאנוּ לְפָנֶֽיךָ בַּגָּלוּי וּבַסָּֽתֶר.
עַל חֵטְא שֶׁחָטָֽאנוּ לְפָנֶֽיךָ בְּדַֽעַת וּבְמִרְמָה,
וְעַל חֵטְא שֶׁחָטָֽאנוּ לְפָנֶֽיךָ בְּדִבּוּר פֶּה.
עַל חֵטְא שֶׁחָטָֽאנוּ לְפָנֶֽיךָ בְּהוֹנָֽאַת רֵֽעַ,
וְעַל חֵטְא שֶׁחָטָֽאנוּ לְפָנֶֽיךָ בְּהַרְהוֹר הַלֵּב.
עַל חֵטְא שֶׁחָטָֽאנוּ לְפָנֶֽיךָ בִּוְעִידַת זְנוּת,
וְעַל חֵטְא שֶׁחָטָֽאנוּ לְפָנֶֽיךָ בְּוִדּוּי פֶּה.

Yet You do justly with everyone who comes before You,
For You have acted out of truth, while we have too often acted
    falsely.
What shall we say before You who dwells in the heights,
What stories can we tell to You who dwells in heaven?
Do You not already know all that we reveal and all that we have
  tried to hide?

Indeed, You know the mysteries of the universe,
And the best kept secrets of every living thing.
You search out the innermost rooms of our life,
With care You examine all our feelings, all our thoughts.
Not one thing is hidden from You, nothing escapes Your gaze.
God who preserves the memory of all our ancestors,
If You would only wipe away the memory of all our wrongs
And grant atonement for all our sins.

Al Cheyt

For the wrong we did before You under coercion or of our own
free will;
And for the wrong we did before You by hardening our hearts.

For the wrong we did before You unintentionally;
And for the wrong we did before You through idle talk and
meaningless resolutions.

For the wrong we did before You by using sex exploitatively;
And for the wrong we did before You in public and in private.

For the wrong we did before You knowingly and deceptively;
And for the wrong we did before You by offensive language.

For the wrong we did before You by oppressing another person;
And for the wrong we did before You by malicious thoughts.

For the wrong we did before You by promiscuity;
And for the wrong we did before You by confessing insincerely.

עַל חֵטְא שֶׁחָטָאנוּ לְפָנֶיךָ בְּזִלְזוּל הוֹרִים וּמוֹרִים,

וְעַל חֵטְא שֶׁחָטָאנוּ לְפָנֶיךָ בְּזָדוֹן וּבִשְׁגָגָה.

עַל חֵטְא שֶׁחָטָאנוּ לְפָנֶיךָ בְּחֹזֶק יָד,

וְעַל חֵטְא שֶׁחָטָאנוּ לְפָנֶיךָ בְּחִלּוּל הַשֵּׁם.

עַל חֵטְא שֶׁחָטָאנוּ לְפָנֶיךָ בְּטֻמְאַת שְׂפָתָיִם,

וְעַל חֵטְא שֶׁחָטָאנוּ לְפָנֶיךָ בְּטִפְשׁוּת פֶּה.

עַל חֵטְא שֶׁחָטָאנוּ לְפָנֶיךָ בְּיֵצֶר הָרָע,

וְעַל חֵטְא שֶׁחָטָאנוּ לְפָנֶיךָ בְּיוֹדְעִים וּבְלֹא יוֹדְעִים.

וְעַל כֻּלָּם, אֱלוֹהַּ סְלִיחוֹת, סְלַח לָנוּ, מְחַל לָנוּ, כַּפֶּר־
לָנוּ.

עַל חֵטְא שֶׁחָטָאנוּ לְפָנֶיךָ בְּכַחַשׁ וּבְכָזָב,

וְעַל חֵטְא שֶׁחָטָאנוּ לְפָנֶיךָ בְּכַפַּת שֹׁחַד.

עַל חֵטְא שֶׁחָטָאנוּ לְפָנֶיךָ בְּלָצוֹן,

וְעַל חֵטְא שֶׁחָטָאנוּ לְפָנֶיךָ בְּלָשׁוֹן הָרָע.

עַל חֵטְא שֶׁחָטָאנוּ לְפָנֶיךָ בְּמַשָּׂא וּבְמַתָּן,

וְעַל חֵטְא שֶׁחָטָאנוּ לְפָנֶיךָ בְּמַאֲכָל וּבְמִשְׁתֶּה.

עַל חֵטְא שֶׁחָטָאנוּ לְפָנֶיךָ בְּנֶשֶׁךְ וּבְמַרְבִּית,

וְעַל חֵטְא שֶׁחָטָאנוּ לְפָנֶיךָ בִּנְטִיַּת גָּרוֹן.

עַל חֵטְא שֶׁחָטָאנוּ לְפָנֶיךָ בְּשִׂיחַ שִׂפְתוֹתֵינוּ,

וְעַל חֵטְא שֶׁחָטָאנוּ לְפָנֶיךָ בְּשִׁקּוּר עָיִן.

עַל חֵטְא שֶׁחָטָאנוּ לְפָנֶיךָ בְּעֵינַיִם רָמוֹת,

וְעַל חֵטְא שֶׁחָטָאנוּ לְפָנֶיךָ בְּעַזּוּת מֵצַח.

For the wrong we did before You by contempt for parents and teachers;
And for the wrong we did before You intentionally or by accident.

For the wrong we did before You by violence;
And for the wrong we did before You by failing to be true to our heritage, thus defaming Your Name in the world.

For the wrong we did before You by ugly language;
And for the wrong we did before You by foolish talk.

For the wrong we did before You by the unbridled passions of our *yetzer ha-ra*;
And for the wrong we did before You knowingly and unknowingly.

V'al kulam, Eloah slichot, s'lach lanu, m'chal lanu, kapper lanu.

For all our wrongs, God of forgiveness, forgive us, wipe the slate clean, grant us atonement.

For the wrong we did before You by lying and deceiving;
And for the wrong we did before You by accepting bribes.

For the wrong we did before You by scoffing and mocking;
And for the wrong we did before You by speaking ill of other people.

For the wrong we did before You in our work;
And for the wrong we did before You in the foods we eat and the amount we drink.

For the wrong we did before You by refusing to be generous;
And for the wrong we did before you by being proud and haughty.

For the wrong we did before You by the content of our conversation;
And for the wrong we did before You by immodest or demeaning glances.

For the wrong we did before You by scornful glances;
And for the wrong we did before You by a defiant manner.

וְעַל כֻּלָּם, אֱלוֹהַּ סְלִיחוֹת, סְלַח לָנוּ, מְחַל לָנוּ, כַּפֶּר־לָנוּ.

עַל חֵטְא שֶׁחָטָאנוּ לְפָנֶיךָ בִּפְרִיקַת עֹל,

וְעַל חֵטְא שֶׁחָטָאנוּ לְפָנֶיךָ בִּפְלִילוּת.

עַל חֵטְא שֶׁחָטָאנוּ לְפָנֶיךָ בִּצְדִיַּת רֵעַ,

וְעַל חֵטְא שֶׁחָטָאנוּ לְפָנֶיךָ בְּצָרוּת עָיִן.

עַל חֵטְא שֶׁחָטָאנוּ לְפָנֶיךָ בְּקַלּוּת רֹאשׁ,

וְעַל חֵטְא שֶׁחָטָאנוּ לְפָנֶיךָ בְּקַשְׁיוּת עֹרֶף.

עַל חֵטְא שֶׁחָטָאנוּ לְפָנֶיךָ בְּרִיצַת רַגְלַיִם לְהָרַע,

וְעַל חֵטְא שֶׁחָטָאנוּ לְפָנֶיךָ בִּרְכִילוּת.

עַל חֵטְא שֶׁחָטָאנוּ לְפָנֶיךָ בִּשְׁבוּעַת שָׁוְא,

וְעַל חֵטְא שֶׁחָטָאנוּ לְפָנֶיךָ בְּשִׂנְאַת חִנָּם.

עַל חֵטְא שֶׁחָטָאנוּ לְפָנֶיךָ בִּתְשֽׂוּמֶת־יָד,

וְעַל חֵטְא שֶׁחָטָאנוּ לְפָנֶיךָ בְּתִמְהוֹן לֵבָב.

וְעַל כֻּלָּם, אֱלוֹהַּ סְלִיחוֹת, סְלַח לָנוּ, מְחַל לָנוּ, כַּפֶּר־לָנוּ.

Elohai Ad She-lo Notzarti

אֱלֹהַי, עַד שֶׁלֹּא נוֹצַרְתִּי אֵינִי כְדַאי, וְעַכְשָׁו שֶׁנּוֹצַרְתִּי כְּאִלּוּ לֹא נוֹצַרְתִּי; עָפָר אֲנִי בְּחַיַּי, קַל וָחֹֽמֶר בְּמִיתָתִי; הֲרֵי אֲנִי לְפָנֶיךָ כִּכְלִי מָלֵא בוּשָׁה וּכְלִמָּה. יְהִי רָצוֹן מִלְּפָנֶיךָ, יְיָ אֱלֹהַי וֵאלֹהֵי אֲבוֹתַי (וֵאלֹהֵי אִמּוֹתַי), שֶׁלֹּא אֶחֱטָא עוֹד; וּמַה שֶּׁחָטָֽאתִי לְפָנֶיךָ מָרֵק בְּרַחֲמֶיךָ הָרַבִּים, אֲבָל לֹא עַל יְדֵי יִסּוּרִים וָחֳלָיִם רָעִים.

V'al kulam, Eloah s'lichot, s'lach lanu, m'chal lanu, kapper lanu.

For all our wrongs, God of forgiveness, forgive us, wipe the slate clean, grant us atonement.

For the wrong we did before You in rejecting Your authority; And for the wrong we did before You in making harsh judgments on other people.

For the wrong we did before You by plotting against others; And for the wrong we did before You by tormenting others.

For the wrong we did before You by dismissing serious matters with a joke; And for the wrong we did before You by being obstinate.

For the wrong we did before You by running to do evil; And for the wrong we did before You by gossiping.

For the wrong we did before You by swearing falsely; And for the wrong we did before You by hating others without cause.

For the wrong we did before You by betraying a trust; And for the wrong we did before You out of confusion, unaware of the significance of our actions.

V'al kulam, Eloah s'lichot, s'lach lanu, m'chal lanu, kapper lanu.

For all our wrongs, O God of forgiveness, forgive us, wipe the slate clean, grant us atonement.

Elohai Ad She-lo Notzarti

My God, before I was formed, my worth was no more than promise; yet now that I am here, I have failed to fulfill the promise. Living, I am animated dust; dead, inanimate clay. I was meant to be a crystal cup filled with deeds of love, but I am earthenware and filled with shame. May it be Your will, Adonay my God and God of my fathers (and mothers), that I sin no more. As for the wrongs I did You, purge them out of mercy toward me, but not through terrible tests or suffering.

(Private Rosh Hashanah and Yom Kippur Amidahs conclude here:)

Elohai Ntzor

אֱלֹהַי, נְצֹר לְשׁוֹנִי מֵרָע, וּשְׂפָתַי מִדַּבֵּר מִרְמָה; וְלִמְקַלְלַי נַפְשִׁי תִדּוֹם, וְנַפְשִׁי כֶּעָפָר לַכֹּל תִּהְיֶה. פְּתַח לִבִּי בְּתוֹרָתֶךָ, וּבְמִצְוֹתֶיךָ תִּרְדּוֹף נַפְשִׁי; וְכָל הַחוֹשְׁבִים עָלַי רָעָה, מְהֵרָה הָפֵר עֲצָתָם וְקַלְקֵל מַחֲשַׁבְתָּם. עֲשֵׂה לְמַעַן שְׁמֶךָ, עֲשֵׂה לְמַעַן יְמִינֶךָ, עֲשֵׂה לְמַעַן קְדֻשָּׁתֶךָ, עֲשֵׂה לְמַעַן תּוֹרָתֶךָ. לְמַעַן יֵחָלְצוּן יְדִידֶיךָ, הוֹשִׁיעָה יְמִינְךָ וַעֲנֵנִי. יִהְיוּ לְרָצוֹן אִמְרֵי פִי וְהֶגְיוֹן לִבִּי לְפָנֶיךָ, יְיָ, צוּרִי וְגוֹאֲלִי. עֹשֶׂה שָׁלוֹם בִּמְרוֹמָיו, הוּא יַעֲשֶׂה שָׁלוֹם עָלֵינוּ וְעַל כָּל יִשְׂרָאֵל, וְאִמְרוּ אָמֵן.

יְהִי רָצוֹן מִלְּפָנֶיךָ, יְיָ אֱלֹהֵינוּ וֵאלֹהֵי אֲבוֹתֵינוּ (וֵאלֹהֵי אִמּוֹתֵינוּ) שֶׁיִּבָּנֶה בֵּית הַמִּקְדָּשׁ בִּמְהֵרָה בְיָמֵינוּ, וְתֵן חֶלְקֵנוּ בְּתוֹרָתֶךָ. וְשָׁם נַעֲבָדְךָ בְּיִרְאָה, כִּימֵי עוֹלָם וּכְשָׁנִים קַדְמוֹנִיּוֹת. וְעָרְבָה לַיָי מִנְחַת יְהוּדָה וִירוּשָׁלָיִם, כִּימֵי עוֹלָם וּכְשָׁנִים קַדְמוֹנִיּוֹת.

(When the Reader offers the Rosh Hashanah or Yom Kippur Amidah aloud, continue here:)

Kaddish Shalem

יִתְגַּדַּל וְיִתְקַדַּשׁ שְׁמֵהּ רַבָּא בְּעָלְמָא דִּי בְרָא כִרְעוּתֵהּ: וְיַמְלִיךְ מַלְכוּתֵהּ בְּחַיֵּיכוֹן וּבְיוֹמֵיכוֹן, וּבְחַיֵּי דְכָל בֵּית יִשְׂרָאֵל, בַּעֲגָלָא וּבִזְמַן קָרִיב, וְאִמְרוּ אָמֵן.

יְהֵא שְׁמֵהּ רַבָּא מְבָרַךְ לְעָלַם וּלְעָלְמֵי עָלְמַיָּא.

יִתְבָּרַךְ וְיִשְׁתַּבַּח, וְיִתְפָּאַר וְיִתְרוֹמַם, וְיִתְנַשֵּׂא וְיִתְהַדָּר, וְיִתְעַלֶּה וְיִתְהַלָּל שְׁמֵהּ דְּקֻדְשָׁא, בְּרִיךְ הוּא,

(Private Rosh Hashanah and Yom Kippur Amidahs conclude here:)

Elohai Ntzor

Adonay, keep my tongue from cruelty and my lips from deceit. To those who defame me, let my soul keep silent; teach my soul humility that I may learn even from those who hate me. Open my heart to Your Torah and let my soul search out Your mitzvot. As for all who think to harm me, frustrate their plans and their purposes for the sake of Your honor, to show You have the power to protect, for the sake of Your holiness and Your Torah. Preserve those who try to live by Your teachings. Save me with Your power, Adonay, and answer me. May the words in my mouth and the thoughts in My heart be equally acceptable to You, Adonay my rescuer, my faithful Rock. O heavenly peacemaker, make peace felt now among us, among all Israel, among all Your creatures, that we all might say: Amen.

Adonay our God and God of our fathers (and mothers), let the holy house be built soon, even in our own days, in the manner You desire, that the promise of Your Torah may be fulfilled. O let us serve You there filled with awe, as in the early days when the world and we were young! May You find sweetness in the gifts of Judah and Jerusalem, as in the early days, when the world and we were young.

(When the Reader offers the Rosh Hashanah or Yom Kippur Amidah aloud, continue here:)

Kaddish Shalem

Let the greatness and holiness of God's great Name be proclaimed in the world God was pleased to create. May the Messianic age come in your lifetime and in your days and within the life of the whole House of Israel, speedily and soon. Amen!

Let God's great name be blessed forever and ever!

Let the Name of the Holy Blessed One be praised, exalted,

לְעֵלָּא לְעֵלָּא מִן כָּל בִּרְכָתָא וְשִׁירָתָא, תֻּשְׁבְּחָתָא
וְנֶחֱמָתָא, דַּאֲמִירָן בְּעָלְמָא, וְאִמְרוּ אָמֵן.

תִּתְקַבַּל צְלוֹתְהוֹן וּבָעוּתְהוֹן דְּכָל בֵּית יִשְׂרָאֵל קֳדָם
אֲבוּהוֹן דִּי בִשְׁמַיָּא, וְאִמְרוּ אָמֵן.

יְהֵא שְׁלָמָא רַבָּא מִן שְׁמַיָּא, וְחַיִּים, עָלֵינוּ וְעַל כָּל
יִשְׂרָאֵל, וְאִמְרוּ אָמֵן.

עֹשֶׂה שָׁלוֹם בִּמְרוֹמָיו, הוּא יַעֲשֶׂה שָׁלוֹם עָלֵינוּ וְעַל
כָּל יִשְׂרָאֵל, וְאִמְרוּ אָמֵן.

*(Musaf for Yom Kippur concludes here. Rosh Hashanah Musaf
concludes with Ayn Keyloheynu, p. 154; Aleynu, p. 150;
Mourner's Kaddish, p. 151; Adon Olam is found on p. 46).*

honored, and adored far beyond all blessing and song, praise and comfort that can ever be uttered. Amen!

May the prayers and entreaties of the whole House of Israel be accepted by God in heaven. Amen!

May Heaven send an abundance of peace and life to us and to all Israel. Amen!

May the One who harmonizes opposing forces in the universe make harmony and peace possible for us and for all Israel. Amen!

(Musaf for Yom Kippur concludes here. Rosh Hashanah Musaf concludes with Ayn Keyloheynu, p. 154; Aleynu, p. 150; Mourner's Kaddish, p. 151; Adon Olam is found on p. 46).

YOM KIPPUR

EVENING SERVICE FOR YOM KIPPUR

Meditation

The night descends once more on the delusive sunlight of our careless lives, closing the door against our fantasies and leaving us to face ourselves. How longed-for! Alone, our privacy at last secured, alone with our own lives, our own yearnings, our own desires and dreams. Yet how frightening! Alone, without the mirror of others to convince us of our worth, without the excuse of others to blame for what disturbs us. In charge of our own mistakes, desires, weaknesses, and longings—*our own*, whatever their origin, but ours to bear, confront, and overcome—alone.

This is a Day then of Alonement, but of Atonement too, as, grappling with the consequences of our weakness, we would seek the strength to act upon our better natures, to value our own worth enough to trust our feelings, and accept the worth of others not as threat or competition, but as insights into a different kind of worth from ours. What I am is good, we would like to say to ourselves—and believe it.

But what I am is also right, we want to say; I have power to determine my own course. For us to atone is no longer to accept a myriad of separate moral systems—my parents', my children's, my friends', my professor's, my employer's, my own. Atonement is to know that there is but one moral system, which is God's—and that each of us has equal insight into the divine will. A small child must be guided, but an adult must come to see that God is revealed equally to those who seek to do the right, who are concerned with others and not themselves alone, and so I need not always accept the words of others which conflict with what I feel is right; nor need I turn aside from others' words in fear lest in accepting them I surrender something of myself.

To admit our errors, to confess our faults, we need not abase ourselves, nor wallow in unworthiness. The source behind our

faults is often our failure to admit our worth, to rely on our inner sense of what is right, lest others laugh at us, mistreat us, or profess a higher standard than we can ever reach. Could we on this Day of At-one-ment feel at one, at home, with ourselves, the cruelties we do which spring from fear, unsureness, guilt, or doubt might disappear. Sometimes we strut and preen too much, yet that too stems from a need to find our worth outside ourselves, through fame or recognition, and if others will not give it, then we must tout ourselves. We shall say many things about ourselves this Atonement Day, confessing error, thoughtlessness, misdeed, and wrong. But before we do, before we honestly confront our failings, we must first confront our virtue, and know that whatever wrongs we have committed, we could not recognize our wrongs were not our basic natures fundamentally, irrevocably right. What we must seek first of all this day is the conviction of our inner worth, that no matter what we do we are the child of God, a valued and irreplaceable jewel in the crown that is God's universe.

We shall speak many words this awesome Day. We shall confess to sins we know not, vow an openness we are not secure enough to give, pray ourselves into a virtue we are sure to mar as soon as prayerbooks are closed and intensive introspection ended. The earnestness of our vows, and the humanness of our weakness are all a piece of that tapestry which is our unique and very special life, whose beauty we shall strive to deepen through this Day in the all-embracing darkness of ourselves, our people, and our God.

Silent Reflection

Permission

בִּישִׁיבָה שֶׁל מַעְלָה וּבִישִׁיבָה שֶׁל מַטָּה.
עַל דַּעַת הַמָּקוֹם וְעַל דַּעַת הַקָּהָל.
אָנוּ מַתִּירִין לְהִתְפַּלֵּל עִם הָעֲבַרְיָנִים.

Permission

By the authority of the heavenly court,
And by the authority of the earthly court,
With the permission of God the Ever-Present,
And with the permission of this congregation,
We who have ourselves transgressed
Declare it lawful to pray with others
Who have wronged either God or human beings:
The keeper of Shabbat who, by her silence,
Allowed crime to flourish among her associates
Consents to pray with the supporter of the oppressed
Who disdained to put on t'filin.
The one who gave tzedakah but cheated on exams
Consents to pray with the one who worked hard for Israel
But exploited his friend.
Joined in the recognition of our own failings,
We pledge to pray both for ourselves and for
The others around us who have fallen short.

Candle Lighting

בָּרוּךְ אַתָּה יְיָ אֱלֹהֵינוּ מֶלֶךְ הָעוֹלָם אֲשֶׁר קִדְּשָׁנוּ
בְּמִצְוֹתָיו וְצִוָּנוּ לְהַדְלִיק נֵר שֶׁל [שַׁבָּת וְשֶׁל] יוֹם
הַכִּפֻּרִים:

Baruch atta Adonay Eloheynu melech ha-olam, asher kid-shanu b'mitzvotav, vitzivanu l'hadlik ner shel (Shabbat v'shel) Yom Hakipurim.

Praised be Adonay our God, Majesty of the universe, who makes us holy in the mitzvah of lighting candles, whose light can burn the darkness out of our souls, and warm the self within us to which we seek return.

Preparations for Kol Nidrey

We need courage to make vows in the heat of convictions born of this weighty day, to make promises that shall bind us even when the days that follow Yom Kippur have

cooled our passions down. How shall we feel a month from now, or when spring has come around? What new terrors, what great madness now unseen will roll down in torrents on our lives in months ahead, before which must pale the solemn hopes of this earnest day? We cannot know what will befall our vows when we have separated from each other, when the year begins to color in the changes that it has in store—and so on this Atonement eve we would make our promises, and yet promise in the same breath that if time invalidates their meaning, we shall change our promise, and feel no guilt.

To vow in the face of change—yet to change the face of vows when time's new knowledge has changed the meaning of the vow: that is the double courage we would seek tonight, this night of Kol Nidrey, when all vows, all bonds, all devotions, promises, obligations, penalties, and oaths are there before us to be undertaken: but which time and we must unvow or vow differently as truth reveals itself anew. May it all, whatever it shall be, come to us for good.

*   *   *

Prayer of ancient origins, in mystic chant,
    Protecting us since ancient times from impulsive oaths,
    Pouring forth, tradition has supposed, from the anguished
    lips of secret Jews.

Long ago, in one forbidding land after another
Our mothers masqueraded in a faith forced on them by tyrants,
Our fathers prayed from their cellars that God would annul
    their alien vows,
And help them find the hard way back to their ancestral truth.

Kol Nidrey reminds us who do not have to hide
How many fearful cellars we inhabit
That close us off from full acceptance of the Jewish faith,
That muffle our acceptance of our parents' pledge at Sinai,

Forced on them by no one,
Freely made in the sunlight of the day.
Now at nightfall
May we hear within the mystic chant
The hidden origins of our birth into the Jewish people,
And may we be protected from every impulse to betray our heri-
   tage,
To masquerade as someone who we never were
And cannot be.

Prayer of ancient anguish,
Let it form our lips into the anguish of the Jew
We have not dared to be,
Let its painful strains seize hold of our inconstant hearts
Till tears of grief pour forth
For all the alien vows we've sworn,
For all the hard ancestral truths we've casually denied
For all we've turned our backs to since our faith began.

What lies within the cellars of our souls tonight?

O hidden origins!
O mystic chant!
O Kol Nidrey!

*   *   *

All the vows on our lips,
The burdens in our hearts,
The pent-up regrets
About which we brooded and spoke
Through prayers without end
On last Atonement Day
Did not change our way of life,
Did not bring deliverance
In the year that has gone.
From mountain peaks of fervor
We fell to common ways
At the close of the fast.

Will You hear our regret?
Will You open our prison,
Release us from shackles of habit?
Will You answer our prayers,
Forgive our wrongs,
Though we sin again and again?
In moments of weakness
We do not remember
Promises of Atonement Day.
Look past forgetfulness,
Take only from our hearts;
Forgive us, pardon us.

*   *   *

In the darkness of time still unknown, holding close the
teaching of a people who has known that time is holy, we
rise for Kol Nidrey, to share its truths together in
the atoning closeness of this night:

Kol Nidrey

כָּל נִדְרֵי. וֶאֱסָרֵי. וַחֲרָמֵי. וְקוֹנָמֵי. וְכִנּוּיֵי. וְקִנּוּסֵי.
וּשְׁבוּעוֹת. דִּנְדַרְנָא. וּדְאִשְׁתַּבַּעְנָא. וּדְאַחֲרִימְנָא.
וְדְאָסַרְנָא עַל נַפְשָׁתָנָא. מִיּוֹם כִּפֻּרִים זֶה עַד יוֹם
כִּפֻּרִים הַבָּא עָלֵינוּ לְטוֹבָה. כֻּלְהוֹן אִחֲרַטְנָא בְהוֹן.
כֻּלְהוֹן יְהוֹן שָׁרָן. שְׁבִיקִין. שְׁבִיתִין. בְּטֵלִין וּמְבֻטָּלִין.
לָא שְׁרִירִין וְלָא קַיָּמִין: נִדְרָנָא לָא נִדְרֵי. וֶאֱסָרָנָא לָא
אֱסָרֵי. וּשְׁבוּעָתָנָא לָא שְׁבוּעוֹת:

Kol nidrey ve'esarey va'charamey v'konamey v'chinuyey v'kinu-
* sey ush'vuot*
Dindarna ud'ishtaba-na ud'achareemna v'di-asarna al naf-
* shatana*
Mee-yom kippurim zeh ad yom kippurim ha-ba, aleynu l'tova
Kul-hon icharatna v'hon, kul-hon y'hon sharan,
Sh'veekeen, sh'veeteen, b'tayleen um'vutaleen
La sh'reereen v'la kayameen.
Nidrana la nidrey, ve'esarana la esarey, ush'vuatana la sh'vuot.

(All vows, bonds, devotions, promises, obligations, penalties and oaths, wherewith we have vowed, sworn, devoted, and bound ourselves, from this Day of Atonement to the next Day of Atonement—may it come to us for good—all these we repent us of them. They shall be absolved, released, annulled, made void and of no effect; they shall not be binding nor shall they have any power. Our vows shall not be vows; our bonds shall not be bonds; and our oaths shall not be oaths.)

וְנִסְלַח לְכָל־עֲדַת בְּנֵי יִשְׂרָאֵל וְלַגֵּר הַגָּר בְּתוֹכָם
כִּי לְכָל הָעָם בִּשְׁגָגָה:
סְלַח־נָא לַעֲוֹן הָעָם הַזֶּה כְּגֹדֶל חַסְדֶּךָ
וְכַאֲשֶׁר נָשָׂאתָה לָעָם הַזֶּה מִמִּצְרַיִם וְעַד הֵנָּה: וְשָׁם
נֶאֱמַר:
וַיֹּאמֶר יְיָ סָלַחְתִּי כִּדְבָרֶךָ:

Forgive the wrongdoings of this people, and all who dwell in their midst, according to the greatness of Your covenantal love. For in all of us Your people is there unwitting transgression.

Adonay has said, "I have forgiven as you have asked."

בָּרוּךְ אַתָּה יְיָ אֱלֹהֵינוּ מֶלֶךְ הָעוֹלָם
שֶׁהֶחֱיָנוּ וְקִיְּמָנוּ וְהִגִּיעָנוּ לַזְּמַן הַזֶּה:

*Baruch atta Adonay Eloheynu melech
ha-olam she-hechiyanu v'kiyyimanu
v'higiyanu lazman hazeh.*

You are praised, Adonay our God, through whose rule the world coheres, through whom we live and are sustained, and to whose time for atonement we have come once more.

Psalm 92 (On Shabbat)

A Song for Shabbat.
It is good to thank God,

To sing praises to Your name, Highest One.

To tell Your kindness in the morning
And Your good faith at night,
On the lute, the lyre, and the ringing harp.

For You have made me happy, Adonay, in Your work.
I acclaim Your handiwork.

How great are Your works, O God,
And how very deep Your thoughts.

An insensitive person does not know this
And a fool does not understand.

But even when wicked people sprout up like weeds
And all kinds of trouble-makers blossom,
Ultimately they will be destroyed forever.

But You rule on high forever, Adonay.
For Your enemies, Adonay,
Your enemies will perish,
And all the trouble-makers will be disunited.

You have raised my head like the wild ox
In prideful power.
I am anointed with fresh oil.

My eyes looked on those who were spying on me.
My ears heard those who were plotting against me.

The just will blossom like the date palm.
They will stand tall like the cedar of Lebanon.
Rooted in the House of Adonay.
They will blossom in the courts of our God.

Even in old age they will bear fruit,
Still they will be fresh and growing,
To bear witness that Adonay is fair and dependable
And there is no injustice in God's ways.

צַדִּיק כַּתָּמָר יִפְרָח, כְּאֶרֶז בַּלְבָנוֹן יִשְׂגֶּה. שְׁתוּלִים
בְּבֵית יְיָ, בְּחַצְרוֹת אֱלֹהֵינוּ יַפְרִיחוּ. עוֹד יְנוּבוּן
בְּשֵׂיבָה, דְּשֵׁנִים וְרַעֲנַנִּים יִהְיוּ. לְהַגִּיד כִּי־יָשָׁר
יְיָ; צוּרִי, וְלֹא־עַוְלָתָה בּוֹ.

Tzadik katamar yifrach
K'erez bal'vanon yisgeh
Sh'tulim b'veyt Adonay
B'chatzrot Eloheynu yafrichu
Od y'nuvun b'seyvah
D'sheynim v'ra-ananim yihyu
L'hagid ki yashar Adonay
Tzuri v'lo avlatah bo.

Meditation Before Barchu

Praise Me, says God, and I will know that you love Me.
Curse Me, I will know that you love Me.
   Praise Me or curse Me, I will know that you love Me.
Sing out My graces, says God.
Raise your fist against Me and revile, says God.
   Sing My graces or revile, reviling is also praise, says
God.
But if you sit fenced off in your apathy,
   Entrenched in "I couldn't care less," says God,
If you look at the stars and yawn, says God,
   If you see suffering and don't cry out,
If you don't praise and don't revile,
   Then I created you in vain, says God.

THE SHMA AND ITS BLESSINGS

בָּרְכוּ אֶת יְיָ הַמְבֹרָךְ:

Barchu et Adonay hamvorach:

Proclaim how blessed is Adonay,
Source of blessing for all the world!

בָּרוּךְ יְיָ הַמְבֹרָךְ לְעוֹלָם וָעֶד:

Baruch Adonay hamvorach l'olam vaed:

Blessed is Adonay,
Source of blessing for all the world forever and ever!

Maariv Aravim (In Praise of the Evening-Bringer)

בָּרוּךְ אַתָּה יְיָ אֱלֹהֵינוּ מֶלֶךְ הָעוֹלָם אֲשֶׁר בִּדְבָרוֹ
מַעֲרִיב עֲרָבִים בְּחָכְמָה פּוֹתֵחַ שְׁעָרִים וּבִתְבוּנָה
מְשַׁנֶּה עִתִּים וּמַחֲלִיף אֶת־הַזְּמַנִּים וּמְסַדֵּר אֶת־
הַכּוֹכָבִים בְּמִשְׁמְרוֹתֵיהֶם בָּרָקִיעַ כִּרְצוֹנוֹ. בּוֹרֵא יוֹם
וָלַיְלָה גּוֹלֵל אוֹר מִפְּנֵי חֹשֶׁךְ וְחֹשֶׁךְ מִפְּנֵי אוֹר וּמַעֲבִיר
יוֹם וּמֵבִיא לָיְלָה וּמַבְדִּיל בֵּין יוֹם וּבֵין לָיְלָה יְיָ צְבָאוֹת
שְׁמוֹ. אֵל חַי וְקַיָּם תָּמִיד יִמְלוֹךְ עָלֵינוּ לְעוֹלָם וָעֶד.
בָּרוּךְ אַתָּה יְיָ הַמַּעֲרִיב עֲרָבִים:

You are praised, Adonay
Author of time and space
Who brings on evening with a word,
Opens heaven's gates with wisdom,
Adjusts the ages with sensitive judgment,
Varies the seasons,
And orders the orbits of a sky full of stars.

You create each day and each night afresh,
Roll light in front of darkness
And darkness in front of light
So gently
That no moment is quite like the one before
Or after.

Second by second
You make day pass into night
And You alone know the boundary point
Dividing one from the other.
Unifier of all beings is Your name.

Timeless God,
Rule forever.

You Who bring the evening in
Are praised.

Alternative Maariv Aravim

There was darkness once before the world began
Not like tonight—
A great black quilt all stitched with stars
To snuggle sleeping earth against the void—
Once the void was all there was
Dark sky, dark water
Only the breath of God rippling the waves ...

Until that breath formed words:
"Let there be light."
And darkness fled into the shadows of the light
Plotting its return once brightness dimmed.

God dispersed the light throughout the void
Sewing stars in picture patterns on the fabric of the night
Cutting out round moons and crescent shapes
To relieve the power of the black expanse
Embroidering gold strands of day into the darkness
Threading purple darkness into day.

We are the void!
Dark sins, dark cruelties
Only the breath of God rippling our lips
Until that breath forms words:
"Return to Me."

But our darkness does not flee

It knows how hard returning is
From snuggling darkness
Into blinding light.
So God disperses light throughout our being
Merely touching us with radiance:
"Just confess this single wrong."
Brushing us gently with a glowing promise:
"I shall forgive this sin."
To relieve the power of God's blazing glory
Glimpses of our golden soul peek out from this day's
    prayers
Glints of purple from our royal lineage wink in all Your
    words.

And gradually
As night grows into day and day again is night
Your gentle pardon will turn around the guilt that tar-
nishes our soul
And Your breath will fill our mouths:
"From all your wrongs will you be clean!"
And we like cleansing night
All stitched with stars
Will snuggle once again against the void . . .

You whose light delivers us from darkness
You are praised.

Ahavat Olam (In Praise of the Torah-Giver)

אַהֲבַת עוֹלָם בֵּית יִשְׂרָאֵל עַמְּךָ אָהָבְתָּ תּוֹרָה וּמִצְוֹת
חֻקִּים וּמִשְׁפָּטִים אוֹתָנוּ לִמַּדְתָּ. עַל כֵּן יְיָ אֱלֹהֵינוּ
בְּשָׁכְבֵּנוּ וּבְקוּמֵנוּ נָשִׂיחַ בְּחֻקֶּיךָ. וְנִשְׂמַח בְּדִבְרֵי
תוֹרָתֶךָ וּבְמִצְוֹתֶיךָ לְעוֹלָם וָעֶד. כִּי הֵם חַיֵּינוּ וְאֹרֶךְ
יָמֵינוּ וּבָהֶם נֶהְגֶּה יוֹמָם וָלָיְלָה. וְאַהֲבָתְךָ אַל תָּסִיר
מִמֶּנוּ לְעוֹלָמִים. בָּרוּךְ אַתָּה יְיָ אוֹהֵב עַמּוֹ יִשְׂרָאֵל:

An eternal love You have loved the house of Israel Your people. You have taught us Torah and mitzvot, statutes that have ruled our lives since ancient days, judgments that form our sentences today. Lying down and rising up, Adonay our God, we shall strive to make Your laws the substance of our speech, to exult forever in each word of Torah we can learn, in each commanded deed we can fulfill. By meditating on them we shall find the purpose of our days; by acting on them we shall learn how to lengthen our life. In darkness and in light, may these words of Your love ever be upon our lips. Whatever our merit in our own eyes, may we never be deprived of Your love. Help us reciprocate Your love, Adonay, through our praise.

Alternative Ahavat Olam

You were God
And we were Israel,
Your shy, untutored lover
Long ago.

You loved us a great love
And you taught us
How to respond to You

Through Torah
Mitzvot
Statutes
Judgments

We go to sleep with them
And with them we awake.

We shall enjoy them forever.

They give us life
They prolong our days
We form our words around them
At nighttime,
In daytime.

Now,
Long after long ago,
Do not withdraw Your love from us.

Lover of Israel,
You are praised.

The Shma: First Paragraph (Shma and V'ahavta)

שְׁמַע יִשְׂרָאֵל יְהֹוָה אֱלֹהֵינוּ יְהֹוָה אֶחָד:

Shma Yisrael Adonay Eloheynu Adonay Echad:

Listen, Israel! Adonay is our God, Adonay alone is One.

בָּרוּךְ שֵׁם כְּבוֹד מַלְכוּתוֹ לְעוֹלָם וָעֶד:

Baruch sheym kvod malchuto l'olam vaed:

The Name is praised whose glorious Sovereignty will outlast the world and time.

וְאָהַבְתָּ אֵת יְהֹוָה אֱלֹהֶיךָ בְּכָל־לְבָבְךָ וּבְכָל־נַפְשְׁךָ
וּבְכָל־מְאֹדֶךָ: וְהָיוּ הַדְּבָרִים הָאֵלֶּה אֲשֶׁר אָנֹכִי מְצַוְּךָ
הַיּוֹם עַל־לְבָבֶךָ: וְשִׁנַּנְתָּם לְבָנֶיךָ וְדִבַּרְתָּ בָּם בְּשִׁבְתְּךָ
בְּבֵיתֶךָ וּבְלֶכְתְּךָ בַדֶּרֶךְ וּבְשָׁכְבְּךָ וּבְקוּמֶךָ: וּקְשַׁרְתָּם
לְאוֹת עַל־יָדֶךָ וְהָיוּ לְטֹטָפֹת בֵּין עֵינֶיךָ: וּכְתַבְתָּם עַל־
מְזֻזוֹת בֵּיתֶךָ וּבִשְׁעָרֶיךָ:

Thus you shall show your love for Adonay your God:
With every inclination of your knowing heart,
With all the strength through which you live,
With every benefit you have received.
For these words in which I am giving you mitzvot today
Shall stand over against your knowing heart,
That you may help your children sink their teeth in them,

And speak through them
While sitting in your house,
While walking on the road,
At the time for lying down,
At the time for rising up.
You shall bind them in a sign upon your arm.
They shall become frontlets between your eyes.
You shall inscribe them in mezuzot for your house,
Upon your gates.

The Shma: Second Paragraph (V'haya im Shamo'a)

וְהָיָה אִם־שָׁמֹעַ תִּשְׁמְעוּ אֶל־מִצְוֹתַי אֲשֶׁר אָנֹכִי מְצַוֶּה
אֶתְכֶם הַיּוֹם לְאַהֲבָה אֶת־יְהֹוָה אֱלֹהֵיכֶם וּלְעָבְדוֹ
בְּכָל־לְבַבְכֶם וּבְכָל־נַפְשְׁכֶם: וְנָתַתִּי מְטַר־אַרְצְכֶם
בְּעִתּוֹ יוֹרֶה וּמַלְקוֹשׁ וְאָסַפְתָּ דְגָנֶךָ וְתִירֹשְׁךָ וְיִצְהָרֶךָ:
וְנָתַתִּי עֵשֶׂב בְּשָׂדְךָ לִבְהֶמְתֶּךָ וְאָכַלְתָּ וְשָׂבָעְתָּ: הִשָּׁמְרוּ
לָכֶם פֶּן־יִפְתֶּה לְבַבְכֶם וְסַרְתֶּם וַעֲבַדְתֶּם אֱלֹהִים
אֲחֵרִים וְהִשְׁתַּחֲוִיתֶם לָהֶם: וְחָרָה אַף־יְהֹוָה בָּכֶם
וְעָצַר אֶת־הַשָּׁמַיִם וְלֹא־יִהְיֶה מָטָר וְהָאֲדָמָה לֹא תִתֵּן
אֶת־יְבוּלָהּ וַאֲבַדְתֶּם מְהֵרָה מֵעַל הָאָרֶץ הַטֹּבָה אֲשֶׁר
יְהֹוָה נֹתֵן לָכֶם: וְשַׂמְתֶּם אֶת־דְּבָרַי אֵלֶּה עַל־לְבַבְכֶם
וְעַל־נַפְשְׁכֶם וּקְשַׁרְתֶּם אֹתָם לְאוֹת עַל־יֶדְכֶם וְהָיוּ
לְטוֹטָפֹת בֵּין עֵינֵיכֶם: וְלִמַּדְתֶּם אֹתָם אֶת־בְּנֵיכֶם
לְדַבֵּר בָּם בְּשִׁבְתְּךָ בְּבֵיתֶךָ וּבְלֶכְתְּךָ בַדֶּרֶךְ וּבְשָׁכְבְּךָ
וּבְקוּמֶךָ: וּכְתַבְתָּם עַל־מְזוּזוֹת בֵּיתֶךָ וּבִשְׁעָרֶיךָ: לְמַעַן
יִרְבּוּ יְמֵיכֶם וִימֵי בְנֵיכֶם עַל הָאֲדָמָה אֲשֶׁר נִשְׁבַּע יְהֹוָה
לַאֲבֹתֵיכֶם לָתֵת לָהֶם כִּימֵי הַשָּׁמַיִם עַל־הָאָרֶץ:

If we can hear the words from Sinai
Then love will flow from us
And we shall serve all that is holy
With all our intellect and all our passion
And all our life.

If we can serve all that is holy
We shall be doing all that humans can
To help the rains to flow
The grasses to be green
The grains to grow up golden like the sun
And the rivers to be filled with life once more.
All the children of God shall eat
And there will be enough.

But if we turn from Sinai's words
And serve only what is common and profane
Making gods of our own comfort or our power
Then the holiness of life will contract for us
Our world will grow inhospitable
To rains from heaven
And the produce of the earth will not be ours.
Or worse
It will be ours unjustly
And our acts shall isolate us
From the flowing waves of green and gold.

Let us therefore
Lace these words
Into our passion and our intellect
And bind them, all of us,
As a sign upon our hands and our eyes,
Writing them on mezuzot for our doors and gates,
Teaching them to our children,
Listening to our children teaching us.
That our generation may be as numerous
As the stars of heaven and the dust of earth,
As faithful as the living waters
That unite them all.

The Shma: Third Paragraph (Vayomer)

וַיֹּאמֶר יְהוָֹה אֶל־מֹשֶׁה לֵּאמֹר: דַּבֵּר אֶל־בְּנֵי יִשְׂרָאֵל
וְאָמַרְתָּ אֲלֵהֶם וְעָשׂוּ לָהֶם צִיצִת עַל־כַּנְפֵי בִגְדֵיהֶם
לְדֹרֹתָם וְנָתְנוּ עַל־צִיצִת הַכָּנָף פְּתִיל תְּכֵלֶת: וְהָיָה
לָכֶם לְצִיצִת וּרְאִיתֶם אֹתוֹ וּזְכַרְתֶּם אֶת־כָּל־מִצְוֹת
יְהוָֹה וַעֲשִׂיתֶם אֹתָם וְלֹא תָתוּרוּ אַחֲרֵי לְבַבְכֶם וְאַחֲרֵי
עֵינֵיכֶם אֲשֶׁר־אַתֶּם זֹנִים אַחֲרֵיהֶם: לְמַעַן תִּזְכְּרוּ
וַעֲשִׂיתֶם אֶת־כָּל־מִצְוֹתָי וִהְיִיתֶם קְדֹשִׁים לֵאלֹהֵיכֶם:
אֲנִי יְהוָֹה אֱלֹהֵיכֶם אֲשֶׁר הוֹצֵאתִי אֶתְכֶם מֵאֶרֶץ
מִצְרַיִם לִהְיוֹת לָכֶם לֵאלֹהִים אֲנִי יְהוָֹה אֱלֹהֵיכֶם:

God said to Moses:
Let Israel throughout her generations make tzitzit
Fringes, with a thread of blue,
On the corners of her garments
To look at and remember all the mitzvot of God
And do them.

Otherwise
All of you will follow only what your eyes see
And your hearts desire,
Forgetting that everything you see
And whatever you desire
Are signs of My presence in the world.

But looking at the knotted fringes
You will remember as a knot around the finger
That everything you see
And whatever you desire
Can be seen and done
As one of my mitzvot.

Thus will you share the holiness of God
Who saw you as slaves in Egypt
And desired you
To become a people of God.

I am Adonay your God.

Emet Ve-emunah: The Redemption

אֱמֶת וֶאֱמוּנָה כָּל זֹאת, וְקַיָּם עָלֵינוּ כִּי הוּא יְיָ אֱלֹהֵינוּ
וְאֵין זוּלָתוֹ, וַאֲנַחְנוּ יִשְׂרָאֵל עַמּוֹ. הַפּוֹדֵנוּ מִיַּד מְלָכִים,
מַלְכֵּנוּ הַגּוֹאֲלֵנוּ מִכַּף כָּל הֶעָרִיצִים; הָאֵל הַנִּפְרָע לָנוּ
מִצָּרֵינוּ, וְהַמְשַׁלֵּם גְּמוּל לְכָל אֹיְבֵי נַפְשֵׁנוּ; הָעֹשֶׂה
גְדֹלוֹת עַד אֵין חֵקֶר, וְנִפְלָאוֹת עַד אֵין מִסְפָּר; הַשָּׂם
נַפְשֵׁנוּ בַּחַיִּים, וְלֹא נָתַן לַמּוֹט רַגְלֵנוּ; הַמַּדְרִיכֵנוּ עַל
בָּמוֹת אֹיְבֵינוּ, וַיָּרֶם קַרְנֵנוּ עַל כָּל שׂוֹנְאֵינוּ; הָעֹשֶׂה לָנוּ
נִסִּים וּנְקָמָה בְּפַרְעֹה, אוֹתוֹת וּמוֹפְתִים בְּאַדְמַת בְּנֵי
חָם; הַמַּכֶּה בְעֶבְרָתוֹ כָּל בְּכוֹרֵי מִצְרָיִם, וַיּוֹצֵא אֶת
עַמּוֹ יִשְׂרָאֵל מִתּוֹכָם לְחֵרוּת עוֹלָם. הַמַּעֲבִיר בָּנָיו בֵּין
גִּזְרֵי יַם סוּף; אֶת רוֹדְפֵיהֶם וְאֶת שׂוֹנְאֵיהֶם בִּתְהֹמוֹת
טִבַּע. וְרָאוּ בָנָיו גְּבוּרָתוֹ; שִׁבְּחוּ וְהוֹדוּ לִשְׁמוֹ,
וּמַלְכוּתוֹ בְּרָצוֹן קִבְּלוּ עֲלֵיהֶם. מֹשֶׁה וּבְנֵי יִשְׂרָאֵל לְךָ
עָנוּ שִׁירָה בְּשִׂמְחָה רַבָּה, וְאָמְרוּ כֻלָּם:

(A Contemporary Interpretation)

Our faith is true.

Everything we have said this evening can be sustained:
Adonay alone is God
And we Israel have proven by our life,
Our survival as a vibrant people through all our tragedies,
That we remain a people loved
Protected
By God.
You have rescued us from vicious rulers
And have ruled us in their stead,
Ultimately repaying our oppressors with deserved destruc-
tion,

Though often the wait was long until they met their due.

You continue to do great things for us,
Wonders more than we can count.
You have done so since You let us go from Egypt,
Punishing the cruel Egyptians that we might find eternal
   liberty.
But innocent Egyptians suffered also in the taking of the
   first-born,
The price of living among those who torture innocents
They thought were not their own.

In recalling our people's redemption from Egyptian
   bondage
We look to the coming of a more perfect redemption
When all the world will understand
That innocents are the responsibility of everyone,
And the most vicious rulers will be turned
Without delay
Into providers of harmony and freedom.
On that day all people will sing in joy
The redemption song of Israel at the Red Sea shore,
Praising the God supreme above all rulers,
Swift protector of all You rule.

מִי כָמֹכָה בָּאֵלִם יְיָ מִי כָּמֹכָה נֶאְדָּר בַּקֹּדֶשׁ נוֹרָא
תְהִלֹּת עֹשֵׂה פֶלֶא:

Mi chamocha ba-eylim Adonay:
Mi kamochah ne'dar ba-kodesh
Nora t'hilot osey fe-leh.

Who is like You, Eternal One, among
   the gods others worship?
Who is like You, majestic in holiness,
   awesome in splendor, doing wonders?

מַלְכוּתְךָ רָאוּ בָנֶיךָ בּוֹקֵעַ יָם לִפְנֵי מֹשֶׁה זֶה אֵלִי עָנוּ
וְאָמְרוּ:

Malchut'cha ra'u va-necha
Bokea yam lifney Mosheh
Zeh eli, anu v'am'ru:

יְיָ יִמְלֹךְ לְעֹלָם וָעֶד:

Adonay Yimloch l'olam va-ed.

In their escape from the sea, Your children saw Your sovereign
might displayed. "This is my God!" they cried. "The Eternal will
reign forever and ever!"

וְנֶאֱמַר כִּי פָדָה יְיָ אֶת יַעֲקֹב וּגְאָלוֹ מִיַּד חָזָק מִמֶּנּוּ.
בָּרוּךְ אַתָּה יְיָ גָּאַל יִשְׂרָאֵל:

V'ne-emar ki fadah Adonay et Ya-akov
U'g'alo miyad chazak memenu.
Baruch atah Adonay, ga-al Yisrael.

Now let all come to say: The Eternal has redeemed Jacob and
rescued Israel from a power stronger than our own.
You are praised, Eternal One, who redeemed Israel.

Hashkivenu (Night Prayer)

הַשְׁכִּיבֵנוּ יְיָ אֱלֹהֵינוּ לְשָׁלוֹם וְהַעֲמִידֵנוּ מַלְכֵּנוּ לְחַיִּים.
וּפְרוֹשׂ עָלֵינוּ סֻכַּת שְׁלוֹמֶךָ וְתַקְּנֵנוּ בְּעֵצָה טוֹבָה
מִלְּפָנֶיךָ וְהוֹשִׁיעֵנוּ לְמַעַן שְׁמֶךָ. וְהָגֵן בַּעֲדֵנוּ וְהָסֵר
מֵעָלֵינוּ אוֹיֵב דֶּבֶר וְחֶרֶב וְרָעָב וְיָגוֹן וְהָסֵר שָׂטָן
מִלְּפָנֵינוּ וּמֵאַחֲרֵינוּ וּבְצֵל כְּנָפֶיךָ תַּסְתִּירֵנוּ. כִּי אֵל
שׁוֹמְרֵנוּ וּמַצִּילֵנוּ אָתָּה כִּי אֵל מֶלֶךְ חַנּוּן וְרַחוּם אָתָּה.
וּשְׁמוֹר צֵאתֵנוּ וּבוֹאֵנוּ לְחַיִּים וּלְשָׁלוֹם מֵעַתָּה וְעַד
עוֹלָם. וּפְרוֹשׂ עָלֵינוּ סֻכַּת שְׁלוֹמֶךָ. בָּרוּךְ אַתָּה יְיָ
הַפּוֹרֵשׂ סֻכַּת שָׁלוֹם עָלֵינוּ וְעַל כָּל־עַמּוֹ יִשְׂרָאֵל וְעַל
יְרוּשָׁלָיִם:

Give us a place to rest, Adonay our God,
And peace.
Help us, O Majesty, to stand up to life.

Spread over us Your peace-filled sukkah
That through Your good counsel
We might be repaired.

Liberate us from the place we are
That we might effect Your name.

Shield us from enmity
From slaughter
From hunger of the body and the soul
From unexpected sorrow
From those who would accuse us of being merely human.

Bring us into shelter
In the soft, long evening shadows
Of Your truth,
For with You is protection and safekeeping
And in Your presence is royal acceptance and gentle love.

Watch over us as we go forth.
Prepare for us as we return
A peaceful welcome
Life
A future
And now.

Spread over us Your peace-filled sukkah
And over all we love
Over our Jerusalem
And Yours.

Go with us.

Uf'ros aleynu sukat shlomecha.

(Spread over us Your peace-filled sukkah.)

(On Shabbat)

וְשָׁמְרוּ בְנֵי־יִשְׂרָאֵל אֶת־הַשַּׁבָּת. לַעֲשׂוֹת אֶת־הַשַּׁבָּת
לְדֹרֹתָם בְּרִית עוֹלָם בֵּינִי וּבֵין בְּנֵי יִשְׂרָאֵל אוֹת הִיא
לְעֹלָם. כִּי־שֵׁשֶׁת יָמִים עָשָׂה יְיָ אֶת־הַשָּׁמַיִם וְאֶת־
הָאָרֶץ וּבַיּוֹם הַשְּׁבִיעִי שָׁבַת וַיִּנָּפַשׁ:

V'shamru v'ney Yisrael et ha-shabbat
La-asot et ha-shabbat l'dorotam brit olam
Beynee uveyn b'ney Yisrael
ot hee l'olam.
Kee shey-shet yamim asah Adonay
et ha-shamayim v'et ha-aretz
uva-yom hash'vee-ee shavat vayinafash.

For the children of Israel shall keep Shabbat,
Doing what is fitting
Through all their generations
To make Shabbat an eternal covenant
Between Me and the children of Israel
A sign throughout all time and space.
For Adonay did the work of heaven and earth
Six days,
And on the seventh day God ceased work,
Rested,
And breathed a new soul into the world.

Ki va-yom ha-zeh

כִּי־בַיּוֹם הַזֶּה יְכַפֵּר עֲלֵיכֶם לְטַהֵר אֶתְכֶם מִכֹּל
חַטֹּאתֵיכֶם לִפְנֵי יְיָ תִּטְהָרוּ:

On this day atonement will be made for you to purify you
   from all your wrongs.
In the presence of Adonay shall you be pure.

Reader's Kaddish

Reader

יִתְגַּדַּל וְיִתְקַדַּשׁ שְׁמֵהּ רַבָּא. בְּעָלְמָא דִי בְרָא
כִרְעוּתֵהּ. וְיַמְלִיךְ מַלְכוּתֵהּ בְּחַיֵּיכוֹן וּבְיוֹמֵיכוֹן וּבְחַיֵּי
דְכָל בֵּית יִשְׂרָאֵל. בַּעֲגָלָא וּבִזְמַן קָרִיב וְאִמְרוּ. אָמֵן:

Congregation and Reader

יְהֵא שְׁמֵהּ רַבָּא מְבָרַךְ לְעָלַם וּלְעָלְמֵי עָלְמַיָּא:

Reader

יִתְבָּרַךְ וְיִשְׁתַּבַּח וְיִתְפָּאַר וְיִתְרוֹמַם וְיִתְנַשֵּׂא וְיִתְהַדָּר
וְיִתְעַלֶּה וְיִתְהַלָּל שְׁמֵהּ דְּקוּדְשָׁא. בְּרִיךְ הוּא. לְעֵלָּא
לְעֵלָּא מִן כָּל בִּרְכָתָא וְשִׁירָתָא תֻּשְׁבְּחָתָא וְנֶחֱמָתָא
דַּאֲמִירָן בְּעָלְמָא וְאִמְרוּ אָמֵן:

May God's great Name be magnified and sanctified in the world created according to the holy will, and may God's rule be known in your lifetime, in your own days, and in the life of the house of Israel, speedily, in a time close at hand.

May the Name of the blessed Holy One be praised and extolled far beyond all praises and blessings we can ever say in the world. Amen.

OPTIONAL READINGS

On Doing Wrong

(a) If we say, "I will sin and repent, then I will sin again and repent again," we are not in a position to repent. Likewise, if we say, "I will sin, and the Day of Atonement will atone for me," the Day of Atonement will not atone for us.

For transgressions between a person and God, the Day
of Atonement atones; but for transgressions between one
person and another, the Day of Atonement does not atone
unless the wrongdoer has first become reconciled with the
person wronged.

*   *   *

(b) If I am guilty of a sin and confess it but do not change
my ways, what am I like? It is as though I held a defiling
object in my hand at the same time as I was immersing
myself in purifying waters. All the waters in the world
would not cleanse me! I would remain unclean so long as I
held on to my defilement.

*   *   *

(c) Do not suppose that repentance is required only for
transgressions involving some outward act such as sexual
immorality, robbery or theft; but, just as we must repent of
these, so we must search out our evil thoughts and repent
of anger, enmity, jealousy, mockery and the pursuit of
wealth and honor, as well as gluttony and the like; from all
these we must turn in repentance. Indeed, these sins are
harder to deal with than those which involve action, for as
long as we are steeped in them, we find it difficult to turn
away from them. That is why Scripture says, "Let the
wicked forsake their ways, and those bent on evil their
thoughts."

*   *   *

(d) Let not we who are repenting imagine that we are far
below the rung of the righteous on account of the iniquities
and sins we have committed. On the contrary, we are
beloved and precious to the Creator as though we had
never sinned at all. Indeed, our reward is especially great,
for, though we have tasted wrongdoing, we have broken
away from it and overcome our inclination. Accordingly
the Sages said: "In a place where the repentant stand, the

completely righteous may not stand." That is to say, they stand on a higher rung than those who have never sinned, because they have had to make a greater effort to subdue their impulses.

*   *   *

(e) The Blessed Holy One says to the people Israel: "My children, I have created the evil inclination, and I have created the Torah as a remedy for it; if you occupy yourselves with the Torah, you will not be delivered into its power."

*   *   *

(f) Everyone has been given free will. If we wish to turn to the good way and be righteous, we have the power to do so; and if we wish to turn to the evil way and be wicked, we are free to do that. Everyone is capable of being righteous like Moses or wicked like Jeroboam, learned or ignorant, merciful or cruel, mean or generous. Nobody forces us, or decides for us, or pulls us in one direction or the other; but we ourselves, each by our own volition, chooses the path we wish.

On Doing Tshuvah for Wrong

Maimonides tells us: If a person has either willfully or unintentionally transgressed any of the Torah's commands, whether positive or negative, and the person wishes to return from wrongdoing, he or she must confess to God. How does one confess? By saying the words of the great confession, the Al Cheyt: "Adonay, I have done You unintentional wrongs; I have done You willful wrongs; I have even rebelled against You. I have done this and this particular act. Now I feel ashamed and full of regret for my acts, and I will never repeat this thing which I have done." This is the essence of confession.

*   *   *

Maimonides says, "Tshuvah is when a wrongdoer leaves off doing a wrong act, puts it out of the mind, and resolves never to repeat it." We might say, "Tshuvah is when a wrongdoer leaves off the wrong act, and asks why the act was done. If it is part of a recurrent pattern, the person should try to understand the pattern as best he or she can, and then begin, alone or with the help of others, to change the pattern into a more desirable one. It is only if one says, 'That's the way I am,' without attempting any self-understanding or change, that a person rules out the possibility of tshuvah."

*   *   *

The act of tshuvah and the day of Yom Kippur achieve atonement only for wrongs between human beings and God, as outlined in the Torah. But for wrongs between one person and another—if one has wounded, cursed, or robbed another human being—we can never achieve atonement, Maimonides reminds us, until we make good our neighbor's loss, and have won the wronged person over once more. Even if we return the money or property owed, we must still ask for forgiveness. On the other hand, the wronged person must not be cruel and refuse to grant forgiveness. One should be slow to anger and quick to be pacified. When someone who has offended you comes asking forgiveness, forgive the person with a sincere and willing heart. (We might add: forgive the person even if you know the act was part of a pattern and may recur, particularly if the person is trying hard to change.) Even if the other person has wronged and troubled you a great deal, do not seek revenge or bear a grudge. That is the way of the seed of Israel.

*   *   *

As it is with human beings and God or with each other, is it the same with peoples and nations? How many blacks

have we wronged, how many poor people, how many
oppressed Jews in other lands have we ignored, how many
disabled people have we stared at, or turned away from?
How callous we have been to starving people all over the
globe, to the fragility of our earth and air! What unconcern
we've shown to the danger of nuclear weapons, which
could destroy the earth and the air, rich and poor, Jew and
Gentile, in a single horrifying moment! Yom Kippur
comes to turn us away from complacency to a realization
that too many things are endangered in the world, and that
if we are in earnest this Kol Nidrey night, we shall vow to
work at rescuing this poor, precious world so long as time,
and we, remain.

*   *   *

We who have not been sufficiently concerned for our
people in Israel, vow to deepen our concern.

We who have been content merely to go to rallies or sign
petitions, vow to act so as to affect deeply our brothers and
sisters.

We who once cheered for victory, vow to try to understand
that wars mean death and sorrow, lifelong pain, and
tragedy.

We who have been concerned, who have acted effectively,
who have understood the tragedy of war, vow to work for
the time when war shall cease forever between Jew and
Arab.

We who have loved our bleeding people, vow to search for
the capacity to love all people, that we may help turn our
enemy into our friend, a child of God, like each of us.

AMIDAH (THE GREAT PRAYER)

(The traditional silent Amidah, in Hebrew and English, is found on pages 156–171.)

Alternative Prayers for the Amidah

This is my prayer to You, O my God:
Let me not swerve from my life's path,
Let not my spirit wither and shrivel
In its thirst for You
And lose the dew
With which You sprinkled it
When I was young.

Let my heart be open
To every broken thing,
To orphaned life,
To every stumbler
Wandering unknown
And groping in the shadow.

Bless my eyes, purify me to see
Human beauty rise in the world,
And my people's grandeur
In its land redeemed,
Scattering its scent
Over all the earth.

Deepen and broaden my senses
To absorb a fresh
Green, flowering world,
To take from it the secret
Of blossoming in silence.

Grant me strength to yield fine fruits,
Quintessence of my life,
Steeped in my very being,
Without expectation of reward.

And when my time comes—
Let me slip into the night
Demanding nothing, God, of any person
Or of You.

*   *   *

I pray to You, O God.
From all my heart.

With fervor and zeal,
For the uncertainty of those who wait;
For the helplessness of the dying;
For the sadness of the misunderstood,
For those who request in vain;

For all those abused, scorned and disdained;
For the silly, the wicked, the miserable;
For those who hurry in pain
To the nearest physician;
For those who return from work
With trembling and anguished hearts to their homes;

For those who are roughly treated and pushed aside,
For those who are hissed on the stage;
For all who are clumsy, ugly, tiresome and dull,
For the weak, the beaten, the oppressed,
For those who cannot find rest
During long sleepless nights;

For those who are afraid of death,
For those who wait in hospitals;
For those who have missed the train;

For all the inhabitants of our earth
And all their pains and troubles,
Their worries, sufferings, disappointments,
All their griefs, afflictions, sorrows,
Longings, failures, defeats;

For everything which is not joy,
Comfort, happiness, bliss—
Let these shine forever upon them
With tender love and brightness,

     I pray to You with fervor, God,
     I pray from the depths of my heart.

*   *   *

Praised are You
For Your wisdom that is hidden
For Your dreams that You have cherished from eternity
That we might one day become people
In the fullness of the light.

Praised are You
For what no eye has seen
No ear has heard
But has arisen in our hearts
Since You first spoke Your word to us.

Your dream has become our conscience
May it never again be silent in us
May it never again be
As though we had not heard it.

Praised are You
For making people responsible
For making all people liable
For the future of each other.

Praised are You
Who have called:
"Where are you?"
"Where is your brother, your sister?"
Did you give one person to the other
For their children to kill each other?

Praised are You
For people who hear Your word
And do it—

They are like trees
Planted by living water.

Praised are You
For all those who support each other
Who give comfort and light
Who in their secret way make life easier to bear.

Praised are You
In those who walk on Your path
Who know and honor You
Doing justice
Who honor the stranger in their midst
Who do not reap the corners of their fields
Or keep the laborer's wage until the morning.

Praised are You
For people who believe in peace and love
Despite the power of the facts
For those who endure in this world
Unrewarded
And do not hate the light.

Praised are You for nameless people
Who suffer daily under others' cruelties
Who dare to oppose the cruelties they see
Because they hope in the day You are preparing
When cruelties will end.

Praised are You for all who are foolish
Who do not insist on what is theirs
Who do not want power
Who only hunger for Your rule to be made manifest
Praised are You.

*   *   *

It is easier sometimes
To say "I'm sorry" to a friend,
A parent, a child,
Than to accept "I'm sorry"
From them.

If they've hurt me
Can "I'm sorry" erase the pain?
If they've trifled with me
Is "I'm sorry" enough
To restore my well-being?
If I accept "I'm sorry" too easily
Will I appear over-eager for their approval?
It's often easier to ask forgiveness
Than to forgive.

Yet
What do *I* mean when *I* say "I'm sorry?"
Is it merely a way to smoothe an awkward moment,
To relieve my own anxieties with a formal phrase?
Perhaps I say my own "I'm sorry"s too easily
And so suspect that others do the same.
If I become more committed to my own "I'm sorry"s
I might more readily believe
That others are committed to theirs.

But sometimes I withhold forgiveness
As a means of punishment,
Exercising power over a friend,
Taking revenge by nursing my hurt inside.
But by withholding "I forgive you,"
I really withhold myself from the very people
Whose caring could alleviate my pain.

For how can other people really hurt me
Or shoot holes in my well-being?
I may not be prepared for their remarks,
I may suddenly feel that my friend is not so good a friend,
But let me ask myself:
What leads *me* to cause another's hurt?
Do I mean to?

Not too often.
Usually I speak a hurtful word out of my own uncertainty,
When I feel threatened or belittled.
I really intend not to wound another

But to shore up my own defenses.
It's fair to assume that others utter hurts the same way.
Perhaps if I listened to the person behind the remark,
Asked why my friend needed to belittle me just then
I might be able to ease my friend's pain
At the same time as I protect my own well-being.

To forgive readily
Not only helps another
It helps me feel whole as well.

*   *   *

I am not a bad person
Why then have I come here to talk about my faults?
I am not as good as I would like to be.
I am not as good as God desires me to be.

How do I know what God desires of me?

Jews from long ago tell me what God desires of me.
Jews—and everyone else—who live today tell me what I
    should desire.

Jews who live today tell me I need someone who loves me.

Jews from long ago say I don't.
They say I need to know God loves me.

God loves me?
I'm not convinced some days my parents love me.
It's hard enough to accept their love—
Their gifts of words or things—
They crowd my need to feel like an adult.

So how can I feel God's love?

Jews from long ago say:
        How would you like your mother to be?
        How would you like your father to be?
        Your parents have the potential to be that way,
        But God is that way now.

The kind of parent-love you want
You want because it's there for you,
It's there in God.
Open your arms to it, accept it, embrace it.
And you will more easily embrace your parents.
Not for what you want them to be
But for what they are.

How do you need the one you love to be?
The kind of lover you need
Is there for you in God,
Lover of Israel from ancient days.
And so you can accept your lover's shortcomings
Because God will compensate for them
Until, with years of growing,
You feel confident enough in yourselves, each other,
To emulate the One
Who taught Israel how to love.

Jews who live today tell me I need to be successful.
Jews from long ago tell me I need to be honest and gentle
And know some Torah.

What do I gain from that?

Jews from long ago say:

It's right.
But it also gives you something back.
When you're honest, you encourage others to be
honest too.
When you're gentle, you often melt the harshness in
the one you're talking to.
When you study Torah, it stimulates your thoughts,
your feelings.
Torah gives you love.

Jews who live today tell me I need to compete effectively
with other people.
Jews from long ago say I need to be concerned for other
people's pain.

Why should I?
Who's concerned for my pain?

Jews from long ago say:

> When you start thinking about other people's pain,
> You think less and less about your own.
> When you see others as sufferers and not competitors
> Their successes will not be threats to you
> But signs of a victory over weakness you can celebrate
>   with them.
> When others in pain feel your concern, they will start
>   looking at you differently
> And soon you'll feel their caring,
> As your pain lessens and others' caring grows
> Suddenly you will know
> That God cares too.

I am loved.
I deserve to be loved.
I can be as good as God desires me to be.
I am as good as God desires me to be.
If only I could believe it.
If only I could act the way Jews from long ago say I am.

I know the path to believing it
Begins tonight.

                    *   *   *

May the words in my mouth
And the thoughts in My heart
Be acceptable equally before You,
Adonay my rescuer,
My faithful Rock.
O heavenly peacemaker,
Let me know Your peace,
Make peace felt among all Your people Israel
And all Your creatures wherever they may dwell,
That all of us might one day say together:
Amen.
Amen.

Piyyut: *Ya'aleh*

יַעֲלֶה	תַּחֲנוּנֵנוּ	מֵעֶרֶב.
וְיָבֹא	שַׁוְעָתֵנוּ	מִבֹּקֶר.
וְיֵרָאֶה	רִנּוּנֵנוּ	עַד עָרֶב:
יַעֲלֶה	קוֹלֵנוּ	מֵעֶרֶב.
וְיָבֹא	צִדְקָתֵנוּ	מִבֹּקֶר.
וְיֵרָאֶה	פִּדְיוֹנֵנוּ	עַד עָרֶב:
יַעֲלֶה	עִנּוּיֵנוּ	מֵעֶרֶב.
וְיָבֹא	סְלִיחָתֵנוּ	מִבֹּקֶר.
וְיֵרָאֶה	נַאֲקָתֵנוּ	עַד עָרֶב:
יַעֲלֶה	מְנוּסֵנוּ	מֵעֶרֶב.
וְיָבֹא	לְמַעֲנוּ	מִבֹּקֶר.
וְיֵרָאֶה	כִּפּוּרֵנוּ	עַד עָרֶב:

May our petitions rise out of the night,
Our cries enter out of the dawn,
And let our joyous song appear out of the dusk.

May our voices rise out of the night,
Our vindication enter out of the dawn,
And let our redemption appear out of the dusk.

May our affliction rise out of the night,
Our pardon enter out of the dawn,
And let our cries appear out of the dusk.

O may our refuge rise out of the night,
And enter for Your sake out of the dawn,
And let our atonement appear out of the dusk.

Piyyut: *Ki Anu Amecha*

אָנוּ בָנֶיךָ וְאַתָּה אָבִינוּ:	כִּי אָנוּ עַמֶּךָ וְאַתָּה אֱלֹהֵינוּ.
אָנוּ קְהָלֶךָ וְאַתָּה חֶלְקֵנוּ:	אָנוּ עֲבָדֶיךָ וְאַתָּה אֲדוֹנֵנוּ.
אָנוּ צֹאנֶךָ וְאַתָּה רוֹעֵנוּ:	אָנוּ נַחֲלָתֶךָ וְאַתָּה גוֹרָלֵנוּ.

אָנוּ כַרְמֶךָ וְאַתָּה נוֹטְרֵנוּ.   אָנוּ פְעֻלָּתֶךָ וְאַתָּה יוֹצְרֵנוּ:

אָנוּ רַעְיָתֶךָ וְאַתָּה דוֹדֵנוּ.   אָנוּ סְגֻלָּתֶךָ וְאַתָּה קְרוֹבֵנוּ.

אָנוּ עַמֶּךָ וְאַתָּה מַלְכֵּנוּ.   אָנוּ מַאֲמִירֶךָ וְאַתָּה מַאֲמִירֵנוּ:

Ki anu amecha v'atta Eloheynu, anu vanecha v'atta avinu.
Anu avadecha v'atta Adoneynu, anu k'halecha v'atta chelkeynu.
Anu nachalatecha v'atta goraleynu, anu tzonecha v'atta ro-eynu.
Anu charmecha v'atta notreynu, anu f'ulatecha v'atta yotzreynu.
Anu ra'yatecha v'atta dodeynu, anu s'gulatecha v'atta k'roveynu.
Anu amecha v'atta malkeynu, anu ma'amirecha v'atta ma'amireynu.

For we are Your people, and You our God.
We are Your children, and You the One who gave us life.
We are Your servants, and You the One who acquires us.
We are Your congregation, and You our only One.
We are Your heritage, and You our Destiny.
We are Your flock, and You our Shepherd.
We are Your vineyard, and You our Protector.
We are Your creatures, and You our Creator.
We are Your companion, and You our Beloved.
We are Your treasure, and You the intimate who redeems us.
We are Your people, and You our Sovereign.
We have chosen You, and You have chosen us.

CONFESSION

Preparations

אֱלֹהֵינוּ וֵאלֹהֵי אֲבוֹתֵינוּ (וֵאלֹהֵי אִמּוֹתֵינוּ), תָּבֹא
לְפָנֶיךָ תְּפִלָּתֵנוּ, וְאַל תִּתְעַלַּם מִתְּחִנָּתֵנוּ; שֶׁאֵין
אֲנַחְנוּ עַזֵּי פָנִים וּקְשֵׁי עֹרֶף לוֹמַר לְפָנֶיךָ, יְיָ אֱלֹהֵינוּ
וֵאלֹהֵי אֲבוֹתֵינוּ (וֵאלֹהֵי אִמּוֹתֵינוּ), צַדִּיקִים אֲנַחְנוּ
וְלֹא חָטָאנוּ; אֲבָל אֲנַחְנוּ חָטָאנוּ.

God of those who sought You out in ages past
Let our prayer also come before You
And do not turn aside from our entreaty.
For we are not so obstinate and stubborn
As to say before You:
We are righteous, we have done no wrong.
For indeed, we have done wrong,
And we join now in confession before You.

*   *   *

This is a time to open wide our vision of ourselves, to
stretch our souls that they might conceive a life of the
broadest possibility, the most profound concern, the most
intense conviction. Let us bare our feelings to the world
that we might enlarge our hopes to fill the world as we join,
together and in silence, to confess our weakness in the past.

*   *   *

Now we join together for confession of our wrongs, asking
God to pardon us for sins we may not even be aware we've
done, sins which in the company we keep may even be con-
sidered virtues. To join in this confession is to join our
values to the word of God's commands, to forsake—even
for just the day of Yom Kippur—that world of looser
values we inhabit all the year. To join in this confession is
to say: words matter, words can hurt; reputations matter,
gossip hurts; too much small talk wastes time we could
spend exploring Torah with each other, exploring other
insights, sharing feelings. To join in this confession says:
our actions matter—not only do they touch the lives of
other people, but the smallest thing we do is witnessed by
the eyes of God. Before that God, let us join as one community to acknowledge what we've done.

(Private confession may be encouraged here)

Ashamnu: An Alphabet of Wrongdoing

Of these things we have been guilty: we have Acted out of malice; we have Back-bitten; we have been Contemptuous of others; we have Double-crossed; we have given Evil advice; we have Falsified the truth; we have Gloated over our achievements; we have Hated wrong-doers; we have been Insolent; we have Jeered convictions not our own; we have Knifed friends in the back; we have Lost our self-control; we have Manipulated; we have Nullified the humanity of others; we have Oppressed our brothers and sisters; we have told Petty lies; we have Quietly acquiesced in wrong; we have Refused to back down from positions we could see were incorrect; we have Sneered at serious matters; we have Trifled with other humans; we have Usurped others' positions; we have practiced Violence; we have committed X-number of sins of which we have not been aware; we have said Yes when we should have cried out no; we have lacked the Zeal to struggle for our convictions through unrewarding months and years.

אָשַׁמְנוּ. בָּגַדְנוּ. גָּזַלְנוּ. דִּבַּרְנוּ דֹפִי. הֶעֱוִינוּ. וְהִרְשַׁעְנוּ. זַדְנוּ. חָמַסְנוּ. טָפַלְנוּ שֶׁקֶר. יָעַצְנוּ רָע. כִּזַּבְנוּ. לַצְנוּ. מָרַדְנוּ. נִאַצְנוּ. סָרַרְנוּ. עָוִינוּ. פָּשַׁעְנוּ. צָרַרְנוּ. קִשִּׁינוּ עֹרֶף. רָשַׁעְנוּ. שִׁחַתְנוּ. תִּעַבְנוּ. תָּעִינוּ. תִּעְתָּעְנוּ:

Ashamnu, bagadnu, gazalnu, dibarnu dofi, he-evinu, v'hirsha-nu, zadnu, chamasnu, tafalnu sheker, ya-atznu ra, kizavnu, latznu, maradnu, ni-atznu, sararnu, avinu, pashanu, tzararnu, kishinu oref, rashanu, shichatnu, ti-avnu, ta-inu, ti'ta'nu.

סַרְנוּ מִמִּצְוֹתֶיךָ וּמִמִּשְׁפָּטֶיךָ הַטּוֹבִים, וְלֹא שָׁוָה לָנוּ. וְאַתָּה צַדִּיק עַל כָּל הַבָּא עָלֵינוּ, כִּי אֱמֶת עָשִׂיתָ וַאֲנַחְנוּ הִרְשָׁעְנוּ. מַה נֹּאמַר לְפָנֶיךָ יוֹשֵׁב מָרוֹם, וּמַה נְּסַפֵּר לְפָנֶיךָ שׁוֹכֵן שְׁחָקִים הֲלֹא כָּל הַנִּסְתָּרוֹת וְהַנִּגְלוֹת אַתָּה יוֹדֵעַ.

We have turned aside from Your mitzvot
From Your laws which point us toward the good,
And no good has come to us from our misdeeds.
Yet You do justly with everyone who comes before You,
For You have acted out of truth, while we have too often acted
  falsely.
What shall we say before You who dwells in the heights,
What stories can we tell to You who dwells in heaven?
Do You not already know all that we reveal and all that we have
  tried to hide?

אַתָּה יוֹדֵעַ רָזֵי עוֹלָם, וְתַעֲלוּמוֹת סִתְרֵי כָל חָי. אַתָּה
חוֹפֵשׂ כָּל חַדְרֵי בָטֶן, וּבוֹחֵן כְּלָיוֹת וָלֵב. אֵין דָּבָר
נֶעְלָם מִמֶּךָ, וְאֵין נִסְתָּר מִנֶּגֶד עֵינֶיךָ. וּבְכֵן יְהִי רָצוֹן
מִלְּפָנֶיךָ, יְיָ אֱלֹהֵינוּ וֵאלֹהֵי אֲבוֹתֵינוּ (וֵאלֹהֵי
אִמּוֹתֵינוּ), שֶׁתִּסְלַח לָנוּ עַל כָּל חַטֹּאתֵינוּ, וְתִמְחַל לָנוּ
עַל כָּל עֲוֹנוֹתֵינוּ, וּתְכַפֶּר־לָנוּ עַל כָּל פְּשָׁעֵינוּ.

Indeed, You know the mysteries of the universe,
And the best kept secrets of every living thing.
You search out the innermost rooms of our life,
With care You examine all our feelings, all our thoughts.
Not one thing is hidden from You, nothing escapes Your gaze.
God who preserves the memory of all our ancestors,
If you would only wipe away the memory of all our wrongs
And grant atonement for all our sins.

Al Chet: The Great Confession

עַל חֵטְא שֶׁחָטָאנוּ לְפָנֶיךָ בְּאֹנֶס וּבְרָצוֹן.
וְעַל חֵטְא שֶׁחָטָאנוּ לְפָנֶיךָ בְּאִמּוּץ הַלֵּב:
עַל חֵטְא שֶׁחָטָאנוּ לְפָנֶיךָ בִּבְלִי דָעַת.

For the wrong we did before You under coercion or of our own free will;
And for the wrong we did before You by hardening our hearts.

For the wrong we did before You unintentionally;
And for the wrong we did before You through idle talk and meaningless resolutions.

For the wrong we did before You by using sex exploitatively;
And for the wrong we did before You in public and in private.

For the wrong we did before You knowingly and deceptively;
And for the wrong we did before You by offensive language.

For the wrong we did before You by oppressing another person;
And for the wrong we did before You by malicious thoughts.

For the wrong we did before You by promiscuity;
And for the wrong we did before You by confessing insincerely.

For the wrong we did before You by contempt for parents and teachers;
And for the wrong we did before You by violence.

For the wrong we did before You by failing to be true to our heritage, thus defaming Your Name in the world;
And for the wrong we did before You by unbridled passion.

וְעַל כֻּלָּם, אֱלוֹהַ סְלִיחוֹת, סְלַח לָנוּ, מְחַל לָנוּ, כַּפֶּר־לָנוּ.

V'al kulam, Eloah slichot, s'lach lanu, m'chal lanu, kapper lanu.

For all our wrongs, God of forgiveness, forgive us, wipe the slate clean, grant us atonement.

עַל חֵטְא שֶׁחָטָאנוּ לְפָנֶיךָ בְּכַחַשׁ וּבְכָזָב.
וְעַל חֵטְא שֶׁחָטָאנוּ לְפָנֶיךָ בְּכַפַּת שֹׁחַד:
עַל חֵטְא שֶׁחָטָאנוּ לְפָנֶיךָ בְּלָצוֹן.

For the wrong we did before You by lying and deceiving,
And for the wrong we did before You by accepting bribes.

For the wrong we did before You by scoffing and mocking,
And for the wrong we did before You by speaking ill of
other people.

For the wrong we did before You in our work,
And for the wrong we did before You in the foods we eat
and the amount we drink.

For the wrong we did before You by refusing to be
generous,
And for the wrong we did before You by being proud and
haughty.

For the wrong we did before You in rejecting Your authority,
And for the wrong we did before You in making harsh
judgments on other people.

וְעַל כֻּלָּם, אֱלוֹהַ סְלִיחוֹת, סְלַח לָנוּ, מְחַל לָנוּ, כַּפֶּר־
לָנוּ.

V'al kulam, Eloah s'lichot, s'lach lanu, m'chal lanu, kapper lanu.

For all our wrongs, O God of forgiveness, forgive us,
wipe the slate clean, grant us atonement.

עַל חֵטְא שֶׁחָטָאנוּ לְפָנֶיךָ בִּצְדִיַּת רֵעַ.
וְעַל חֵטְא שֶׁחָטָאנוּ לְפָנֶיךָ בְּצָרוּת עָיִן:
עַל חֵטְא שֶׁחָטָאנוּ לְפָנֶיךָ בְּקַלּוּת רֹאשׁ.

For the wrong we did before You by plotting against others,
And for the wrong we did before You by tormenting others.

For the wrong we did before You by dismissing serious matters with a joke,
And for the wrong we did before You by being obstinate.

For the wrong we did before You by running to do evil,
And for the wrong we did before You by gossiping.

For the wrong we did before You by swearing falsely,
And for the wrong we did before You by hating others without cause.

For the wrong we did before You by betraying a trust,
And for the wrong we did before You out of confusion, unaware of the significance of our actions.

וְעַל כֻּלָם, אֱלוֹהַ סְלִיחוֹת, סְלַח לָנוּ, מְחַל לָנוּ, כַּפֶּר־
לָנוּ.

V'al kulam, Eloah s'lichot, s'lach lanu, m'chal lanu, kapper lanu.

For all our wrongs, O God of forgiveness, forgive us, wipe the slate clean, grant us atonement.

Avinu Malkeynu: Our Forgiving Parent, Our Sovereign

אָבִינוּ מַלְכֵּנוּ חָטָאנוּ לְפָנֶיךָ:

Avinu Malkeynu, we have done wrong before You.

אָבִינוּ מַלְכֵּנוּ אֵין לָנוּ מֶלֶךְ אֶלָא אַתָּה:

Avinu Malkeynu, we have no Sovereign except You.

אָבִינוּ מַלְכֵּנוּ חַדֵּשׁ עָלֵינוּ שָׁנָה טוֹבָה:

Avinu Malkeynu, let this be a good year for us.

אָבִינוּ מַלְכֵּנוּ הָפֵר עֲצַת אוֹיְבֵינוּ:

Avinu Malkeynu, destroy the power of every oppressor and adversary.
:

אָבִינוּ מַלְכֵּנוּ כַּלֵּה כָּל צַר וּמַשְׂטִין מֵעָלֵינוּ:

Avinu Malkeynu, destroy the power of every oppressor
and adversary.

אָבִינוּ מַלְכֵּנוּ כַּלֵּה דֶּבֶר וְחֶרֶב וְרָעָב וּשְׁבִי וּמַשְׁחִית
מִבְּנֵי בְרִיתֶךָ:

Avinu Malkeynu, remove from all Your children disease,
war, famine, exile and destruction.

אָבִינוּ מַלְכֵּנוּ סְלַח וּמְחַל לְכָל־עֲוֹנוֹתֵינוּ:

Avinu Malkeynu, forgive and pardon all our wrongdoing.

אָבִינוּ מַלְכֵּנוּ הַחֲזִירֵנוּ בִּתְשׁוּבָה שְׁלֵמָה לְפָנֶיךָ:

Avinu Malkeynu, may we return to You in earnest repentance.

אָבִינוּ מַלְכֵּנוּ שְׁלַח רְפוּאָה שְׁלֵמָה לְחוֹלֵי עַמֶּךָ:

Avinu Malkeynu, send healing to all who are sick.

אָבִינוּ מַלְכֵּנוּ כָּתְבֵנוּ בְּסֵפֶר חַיִּים טוֹבִים:

Avinu Malkeynu, inscribe us in Your book for a life of
goodness.

אָבִינוּ מַלְכֵּנוּ כָּתְבֵנוּ בְּסֵפֶר גְּאֻלָּה וִישׁוּעָה:

Avinu Malkeynu, inscribe us in the book of redemption
and freedom.

אָבִינוּ מַלְכֵּנוּ כָּתְבֵנוּ בְּסֵפֶר פַּרְנָסָה וְכַלְכָּלָה:

Avinu Malkeynu, inscribe us in the book of sustenance.

אָבִינוּ מַלְכֵּנוּ כָּתְבֵנוּ בְּסֵפֶר זְכֻיּוֹת:

Avinu Malkeynu, inscribe us in the book of meritorious
acts.

אָבִינוּ מַלְכֵּנוּ כָּתְבֵנוּ בְּסֵפֶר סְלִיחָה וּמְחִילָה:

Avinu Malkeynu, inscribe us in the book of forgiveness
and reconciliation.

אָבִינוּ מַלְכֵּנוּ שְׁמַע קוֹלֵנוּ, חוּס וְרַחֵם עָלֵינוּ:

Avinu Malkeynu, listen to our voice, spare us, show us
Your compassion.

אָבִינוּ מַלְכֵּנוּ קַבֵּל בְּרַחֲמִים וּבְרָצוֹן אֶת תְּפִלָּתֵנוּ:

Avinu Malkeynu, accept our prayer with compassion and
favor.

אָבִינוּ מַלְכֵּנוּ פְּתַח שַׁעֲרֵי שָׁמַיִם לִתְפִלָּתֵנוּ:

Avinu Malkeynu, open the gates of heaven to our prayer.

אָבִינוּ מַלְכֵּנוּ נָא אַל תְּשִׁיבֵנוּ רֵיקָם מִלְּפָנֶיךָ:

Avinu Malkeynu, do not turn us away empty from Your
presence.

אָבִינוּ מַלְכֵּנוּ תְּהֵא הַשָּׁעָה הַזֹּאת שְׁעַת רַחֲמִים וְעֵת
רָצוֹן מִלְּפָנֶיךָ:

Avinu Malkeynu, let this hour be an hour of compassion
and a time of acceptance in Your presence.

אָבִינוּ מַלְכֵּנוּ חֲמוֹל עָלֵינוּ וְעַל עוֹלָלֵינוּ וְטַפֵּנוּ:

Avinu Malkeynu, show mercy to us and to our children.

אָבִינוּ מַלְכֵּנוּ חָנֵּנוּ וַעֲנֵנוּ כִּי אֵין בָּנוּ מַעֲשִׂים עֲשֵׂה
עִמָּנוּ צְדָקָה וָחֶסֶד וְהוֹשִׁיעֵנוּ:

Avinu Malkeynu, be gracious and respond to us, for we
have too few good deeds; act toward us with justice tempered by love, and bring us salvation.

Avinu Malkeynu
Chawneynu va'a-neinu
Ki ein banu ma'a'sim
Asey imanu
Tz'dakah va'chesed
V'hoshi-eynu.

ALEYNU

עָלֵינוּ לְשַׁבֵּחַ לַאֲדוֹן הַכֹּל לָתֵת גְּדֻלָּה לְיוֹצֵר בְּרֵאשִׁית
שֶׁלֹּא עָשָׂנוּ כְּגוֹיֵי הָאֲרָצוֹת וְלֹא שָׂמָנוּ כְּמִשְׁפְּחוֹת
הָאֲדָמָה שֶׁלֹּא שָׂם חֶלְקֵנוּ כָּהֶם וְגוֹרָלֵנוּ כְּכָל הֲמוֹנָם:

וַאֲנַחְנוּ כֹּרְעִים וּמִשְׁתַּחֲוִים וּמוֹדִים
לִפְנֵי מֶלֶךְ מַלְכֵי הַמְּלָכִים הַקָּדוֹשׁ בָּרוּךְ הוּא.

שֶׁהוּא נוֹטֶה שָׁמַיִם וְיוֹסֵד אָרֶץ וּמוֹשַׁב יְקָרוֹ בַּשָּׁמַיִם
מִמַּעַל וּשְׁכִינַת עֻזּוֹ בְּגָבְהֵי מְרוֹמִים: הוּא אֱלֹהֵינוּ אֵין
עוֹד:

*A-ley-nu l'sha-be-ach la-a-don hakol, la-tet g'du-lah l'yo-
tzer b're-sheet, she-lo a-sa-nu k'-go-yey ha-a-ra-tzot, v'lo
sa-ma-nu k'mish-p'chot ha-a-da-mah; she-lo sam chel-ke-
nu ka-hem, v'go-ra-le-nu k'-chol ha-mo-nam.
Va-a-nachnu ko-r'im u-mish-ta-cha-vim u-mo-dim lif-ney
me-lech mal-chey ha-m'la-chim, ha-ka-dosh ba-ruch hu.
She-hu no-teh sha-ma-yim v'yo-sed a-retz, u-mo-shav
y'ka-roh ba-sha-ma-yim mi-ma-al, u-shchi-nat u-zo b'gav
hey m'ro-mim. Hu E-lo-hey-nu, ein od.*

We place our hope in You, Adonay our God, confident
that soon we shall see the glory of Your might revealed,
ridding the world of all its idolatries, cutting down all false
gods from their pedestals, reconstructing the world into a
realm where You can rule. Then everyone of flesh and
blood will be able to speak Your Name, for You will have
turned toward You all the wicked of the earth. All who live
on this planet will recognize that they too can
know You intimately, that every knee can bend to You,
every tongue pledge faithfulness to You. Turning toward
You, Adonay our God, all will grant honor at last to Your
glorious Name, and all will accept the yoke that joins them
to Your sovereignty, that You may rule over them speedily
to the end of time. For Sovereignty is Yours, and in glory
will You reign forever, as it is written in Your Torah:
Adonay will reign forever and ever.

וְנֶאֱמַר וְהָיָה יְיָ לְמֶלֶךְ עַל כָּל הָאָרֶץ בַּיּוֹם הַהוּא יִהְיֶה
יְיָ אֶחָד וּשְׁמוֹ אֶחָד:

V'ne-e-mar: v'ha-yah A-do-nay l'me-lech al kol ha-a-retz;
ba-yom ha-hu yih-yeh A-do-nay e-chad u-sh'mo e-chad.

Mourner's Kaddish

יִתְגַּדַּל וְיִתְקַדַּשׁ שְׁמֵהּ רַבָּא. בְּעָלְמָא דִי בְרָא
כִרְעוּתֵהּ. וְיַמְלִיךְ מַלְכוּתֵהּ בְּחַיֵּיכוֹן וּבְיוֹמֵיכוֹן וּבְחַיֵּי
דְכָל בֵּית יִשְׂרָאֵל. בַּעֲגָלָא וּבִזְמַן קָרִיב וְאִמְרוּ. אָמֵן:

Yit-ga-dal v'yit-ka-dash shmay raba. B'al-ma di v'ra chir-u-
tay. V'yam-leech mal-chu-tay b'cha-yay-chon uv-yo-may-
chon uv-cha-yay d'chol bait Yis-ra-el ba-a-ga-lah u-viz-man
ka-reev. V'im-ru a-men.

יְהֵא שְׁמֵהּ רַבָּא מְבָרַךְ לְעָלַם וּלְעָלְמֵי עָלְמַיָּא:

Y'hay shamay raba m'va-rach l'a-lam ul-al-may al-ma-ya.

יִתְבָּרַךְ וְיִשְׁתַּבַּח וְיִתְפָּאַר וְיִתְרוֹמַם וְיִתְנַשֵּׂא וְיִתְהַדָּר
וְיִתְעַלֶּה וְיִתְהַלָּל שְׁמֵהּ דְקֻדְשָׁא. בְּרִיךְ הוּא. לְעֵלָּא
לְעֵלָּא מִן כָּל בִּרְכָתָא וְשִׁירָתָא תֻּשְׁבְּחָתָא וְנֶחֱמָתָא
דַּאֲמִירָן בְּעָלְמָא וְאִמְרוּ. אָמֵן:

Yit-ba-rach v'yish-ta-bach v'yit-pa-ar v'-yit-ro-mam v'yit-
na-say v'yit-ha-dar v'yit-a-leh v'yit-ha-lal sh-mey d-ku-
d'shah. B'reech hu. L'ay-lah l-ey-lah min kol bir-cha-tah
v'shir-a-tah tush-b'cha-tah v'ne-che-ma-tah da-a-mi-ran
b'al-mah. V'im-ru: A-men.

יְהֵא שְׁלָמָא רַבָּא מִן שְׁמַיָּא וְחַיִּים עָלֵינוּ וְעַל כָּל
יִשְׂרָאֵל וְאִמְרוּ. אָמֵן:

Y'hay shlama raba meen shmaya v'cha-yeem aleynu v'al kol
Yisrael. V'im-ru a-men.

עוֹשֶׂה שָׁלוֹם בִּמְרוֹמָיו הוּא יַעֲשֶׂה שָׁלוֹם עָלֵינוּ וְעַל
כָּל יִשְׂרָאֵל וְאִמְרוּ. אָמֵן:

*O-seh shalom bim'ro-mav hu ya-a-seh shalom aleynu v'al kol
Yisrael. V'im-ru a-men.*

May God's great name be praised and sanctified in the
world! May Your Rule be established in our lifetime and
the lifetime of the House of Israel. God's great name is
blessed and praised far beyond all blessings and praises we
can ever say in the world.

May there be a great peace from heaven and life for us and
all Israel. May the One who makes peace in the high
places make peace for us and all Israel! Amen.

SONGS

1) Esa Eynai

Esa eynai el he-harim	אֶשָּׂא עֵינַי אֶל הֶהָרִים
Mey-ayin yavo ezri;	מֵאַיִן יָבוֹא עֶזְרִי
Ezri meyim Adonay	עֶזְרִי מֵעִם יְיָ
Oseh shamayim va-aretz.	עוֹשֶׂה שָׁמַיִם וָאָרֶץ:

(I lift up my eyes to the mountains,
From whence shall come my help?
My help is with Adonay,
Maker of heaven and earth.)

2) Adon Olam

Adon olam asher malach, b'terem kol	אֲדוֹן עוֹלָם אֲשֶׁר מָלַךְ
y'tseer nivra.	בְּטֶרֶם כָּל יְצִיר נִבְרָא:
l'ayt na-asa b'cheftso kol, azay	לְעֵת נַעֲשָׂה בְחֶפְצוֹ כֹּל
melech shmo nikra.	אֲזַי מֶלֶךְ שְׁמוֹ נִקְרָא:

V'acharay kichlot ha-kol
L'vado yimloch nora
V'hu haya, v'hu hoveh,
V'hu yihyeh b'tifara.

V'hu echad v'ayn sheynee, l'hamsheel lo l'hachbeera:
B'lee raysheet b'lee tachleet, v'lo ha-oz v'ha-misra.

V'hu aylee v'chai go-a-lee, v'tsur chevlee b'ayt tsara:
Vhu nee-see umanos lee, m'nat kosee b'yom ekra.

B'yado afkeed ruchee, b'ayt eeshan v'a-ee-ra:
v'im ruchee g'vee-ya-tee, Adonay lee v'lo ee-ra.

וְאַחֲרֵי כִּכְלוֹת הַכֹּל
לְבַדּוֹ יִמְלוֹךְ נוֹרָא:
וְהוּא הָיָה וְהוּא הֹוֶה
וְהוּא יִהְיֶה בְּתִפְאָרָה:
וְהוּא אֶחָד וְאֵין שֵׁנִי
לְהַמְשִׁיל לוֹ לְהַחְבִּירָה:
בְּלִי רֵאשִׁית בְּלִי תַכְלִית
וְלוֹ הָעֹז וְהַמִּשְׂרָה:
וְהוּא אֵלִי וְחַי גּוֹאֲלִי
וְצוּר חֶבְלִי בְּעֵת צָרָה:
וְהוּא נִסִּי וּמָנוֹס לִי
מְנָת כּוֹסִי בְּיוֹם אֶקְרָא:
בְּיָדוֹ אַפְקִיד רוּחִי
בְּעֵת אִישַׁן וְאָעִירָה:
וְעִם רוּחִי גְּוִיָּתִי
יְיָ לִי וְלֹא אִירָא:

The Author of eternity reigned before any creature was brought forth.
When all was made, as S/He desired, God was hailed as Sovereign.
When all is ended, S/He alone will reign in awesome majesty.
S/He was, is, and will be glorious for eternity.
God is One, and has no second-in-command, with whom to share dominion,
Beginningless and endless, God alone has strength to rule.
My God, my life's redeemer, my rock in distress,
My banner and my refuge, my cup, my portion whenever I call.
In God's hand I entrust the breath through which I live, when I sleep and when I rise,
Along with my breath God has my body; Adonay is with me, I have no fear.

MORNING SERVICE
FOR
YOM KIPPUR

MORNING SERVICE FOR YOM KIPPUR

PREPARATIONS FOR PRAYER

Psalm 130

A reaching-up song.

From far down deep
I call You,
God.
Adonay
    hear my voice—
Let Your ears be tuned
    to the voice of my pleading.
O God,
If You should keep count of wrongs,
Who would be left standing?
But pardon is with You,
That we might revere You.
I am waiting, Adonay,
My soul is waiting—
It is Your word I await.
My soul watches for Adonay more than
    those who watch for the dawn,
    more than those who watch for the dawn . . .
Let Israel await our Sovereign,
For with the Eternal is love,
With God is great freedom:
Yes,
God will free Israel
From all our wrongdoing.

*   *   *

Levi Yitzchak of Berditchev stood by the reader's table prepared to sound the shofar. The congregation waited patiently for him to begin. After a long interval, the shammes hesitatingly approached Levi Yitzchak and asked the cause for the delay.

The rabbi whispered to the shammes:
"A stranger is seated near the door of the synagogue who never learned to pray. But he has just said to God:
"Ruler of the universe, You understand the true meaning of prayers and You know those that are most acceptable. Since I know only the letters of the alphabet, I shall repeat them and You can compose from them the prayers I should recite on this sacred day."
"The Almighty is now preoccupied with composing prayers from the letters. Therefore, we must wait."

*   *   *

Ruler of the World,

Open your lips within me,
for I cannot speak—

Send words to me
From Your holy place,
From heaven,
So that I may create the mode of Your praise,
And find Your will,
And bring You peace.

May Your compassion
And Your boundless love make You open
To give me these words,
The words of prayer,
And to accept them from me.

May my words, Your words,
Be sweet and whole
As the words of David the King,
Singer of Psalms before You.

You who give joy to the broken in spirit,
Help me to rejoice—
For alone I am very low.
I stand here tired;
In thirst and hunger I stand,

Empty and dry.
Turn my sorrow to joy, O God,
As I raise my soul toward You.

Hineni

הִנְנִי הֶעָנִי מִמַּעַשׂ, נִרְעָשׁ וְנִפְחָד מִפַּחַד יוֹשֵׁב תְּהִלּוֹת
יִשְׂרָאֵל, בָּאתִי לַעֲמֹד וּלְהִתְחַנֵּן לְפָנֶיךָ עַל עַמְּךָ
יִשְׂרָאֵל אֲשֶׁר שְׁלָחוּנִי, אַף עַל פִּי שֶׁאֵינִי כְדַאי וְהָגוּן
לְכָךְ. לָכֵן אֲבַקֵּשׁ מִמְּךָ, אֱלֹהֵי אַבְרָהָם, אֱלֹהֵי יִצְחָק,
וֵאלֹהֵי יַעֲקֹב, יְיָ יְיָ, אֵל רַחוּם וְחַנּוּן, אֱלֹהֵי יִשְׂרָאֵל,
שַׁדַּי אָיוֹם וְנוֹרָא, הֱיֵה נָא מַצְלִיחַ דַּרְכִּי אֲשֶׁר אֲנִי
הוֹלֵךְ, לַעֲמֹד וּלְבַקֵּשׁ רַחֲמִים עָלַי וְעַל שׁוֹלְחָי. נָא אַל
תַּפְשִׁיעֵם בְּחַטֹּאתַי, וְאַל תְּחַיְּבֵם בַּעֲוֹנוֹתַי, כִּי חוֹטֵא
וּפוֹשֵׁעַ אָנִי. וְאַל יִכָּלְמוּ בִּפְשָׁעַי, וְאַל יֵבוֹשׁוּ הֵם בִּי
וְאַל אֵבוֹשׁ אֲנִי בָּהֶם. קַבֵּל תְּפִלָּתִי כִּתְפִלַּת זָקֵן וְרָגִיל,
וּפִרְקוֹ נָאֶה, וּזְקָנוֹ מְגֻדָּל, וְקוֹלוֹ נָעִים, וּמְעֹרָב בְּדַעַת
עִם הַבְּרִיּוֹת. וְתִגְעַר בַּשָּׂטָן לְבַל יַשְׂטִינֵנִי, וִיהִי נָא
דְלוּגֵנוּ עָלֶיךָ אַהֲבָה, וְעַל כָּל פְּשָׁעִים תְּכַסֶּה בְּאַהֲבָה.
וְכָל צָרוֹת וְרָעוֹת הָפָךְ־נָא לָנוּ וּלְכָל יִשְׂרָאֵל לְשָׂשׂוֹן
וּלְשִׂמְחָה, לְחַיִּים וּלְשָׁלוֹם. הָאֱמֶת וְהַשָּׁלוֹם אֱהָבוּ,
וְלֹא יְהִי שׁוּם מִכְשׁוֹל בִּתְפִלָּתִי.

Here have I come,
Poor in deeds but rich in awe,
To present Your people's case before You
Though I am hardly worthy of my task.

God of Abraham, of Isaac, of Jacob,
Of Sarah, Rebecca, Rachel and Leah,
Through Your presence I feel mercy and compassion,
Awe and wonder.
Help me fulfill my commission.

Let others not suffer for my failings
Nor be blamed for my transgressions,
For I have done wrong.
I have missed the mark
And overturned an order that once was good.
May others not suffer shame for my faults,
Nor I suffer shame for theirs.

Accept my prayers for my brothers and sisters
As though they poured forth from lips schooled in devo-
tion,
From a person of noble mien and flowing locks.

Let no stray thoughts distract me.

Turn our grief into joy and life and peace,
We must learn to work for truth and peace.

May I offer up my prayers without stumbling.

וִיהִי רָצוֹן מִלְפָנֶיךָ, יְיָ, אֱלֹהֵי אַבְרָהָם יִצְחָק
וְיַעֲקֹב, הָאֵל הַגָּדוֹל הַגִּבּוֹר וְהַנּוֹרָא, אֵל עֶלְיוֹן, אֶהְיֶה
אֲשֶׁר אֶהְיֶה, שֶׁכָּל הַמַּלְאָכִים שֶׁהֵם מַעֲלֵי תְפִלּוֹת
יָבִיאוּ תְפִלָּתִי לִפְנֵי כִסֵּא כְבוֹדֶךָ, וְיַצִּיגוּ אוֹתָהּ לְפָנֶיךָ,
בַּעֲבוּר כָּל הַצַּדִּיקִים וְהַחֲסִידִים, הַתְּמִימִים וְהַיְּשָׁרִים,
וּבַעֲבוּר כְּבוֹד שִׁמְךָ הַגָּדוֹל וְהַנּוֹרָא, כִּי אַתָּה שׁוֹמֵעַ
תְּפִלַּת עַמְּךָ יִשְׂרָאֵל בְּרַחֲמִים. בָּרוּךְ אַתָּה שׁוֹמֵעַ
תְּפִלָּה.

God of our first mothers and fathers,
You who told Moses, "I am Being itself,"
And Moses replied, O great and mighty, awesome God on
High!"
May it be Your will
That the angels who raise up prayers to heaven on their
wings
Bring in each one of our prayers before Your glorious
throne

And offer them before You
For the sake of all the just and upright people who have
  come before us
And for the sake of Your great and awesome Name.

How You love to hear Your people's prayers!

Thank You
For hearing ours.

BIRCHOT HA-SHACHAR (Praises for the Morning)

בָּרוּךְ אַתָּה, יְיָ אֱלֹהֵינוּ, מֶלֶךְ הָעוֹלָם, אֲשֶׁר קִדְּשָׁנוּ
בְּמִצְוֹתָיו וְצִוָּנוּ עַל נְטִילַת יָדָיִם.

You are praised, Adonay, Majesty of the universe, who has
shown us holiness as we pour water over our hands upon
arising, washing away the sleep of oblivion with the flowing stream of life.

בָּרוּךְ אַתָּה, יְיָ אֱלֹהֵינוּ, מֶלֶךְ הָעוֹלָם, אֲשֶׁר יָצַר אֶת
הָאָדָם בְּחָכְמָה, וּבָרָא בוֹ נְקָבִים נְקָבִים, חֲלוּלִים
חֲלוּלִים. גָּלוּי וְיָדוּעַ לִפְנֵי כִסֵּא כְבוֹדֶךָ, שֶׁאִם יִפָּתֵחַ
אֶחָד מֵהֶם אוֹ יִסָּתֵם אֶחָד מֵהֶם אִי אֶפְשַׁר לְהִתְקַיֵּם
וְלַעֲמוֹד לְפָנֶיךָ. בָּרוּךְ אַתָּה יְיָ, רוֹפֵא כָל בָּשָׂר
וּמַפְלִיא לַעֲשׂוֹת.

You are praised, Adonay, Majesty of the universe, who has
shown us holiness as we empty fluids from our bodies,
celebrating the wisdom with which you formed each gland
and duct and orifice within us. For if the wrong one opens
up or closes down before its time, it is known all the way
up to Your glorious throne how difficult it is to stand
upright before You. You are praised, Adonay, worker of
miracles in the healing of all flesh.

בָּרוּךְ אַתָּה, יְיָ אֱלֹהֵינוּ, מֶלֶךְ הָעוֹלָם, אֲשֶׁר קִדְּשָׁנוּ בְּמִצְוֹתָיו וְצִוָּנוּ לַעֲסוֹק בְּדִבְרֵי תוֹרָה.

You are praised, Adonay, Majesty of the universe, who has shown us holiness through the mitzvah that words of Torah must occupy us in all we do each day.

וְהַעֲרֶב־נָא, יְיָ אֱלֹהֵינוּ, אֶת דִּבְרֵי תוֹרָתְךָ בְּפִינוּ, וּבְפִי עַמְּךָ בֵּית יִשְׂרָאֵל, וְנִהְיֶה אֲנַחְנוּ וְצֶאֱצָאֵינוּ, וְצֶאֱצָאֵי עַמְּךָ בֵּית יִשְׂרָאֵל, כֻּלָּנוּ יוֹדְעֵי שְׁמֶךָ וְלוֹמְדֵי תוֹרָתֶךָ לִשְׁמָהּ. בָּרוּךְ אַתָּה יְיָ הַמְלַמֵּד תּוֹרָה לְעַמּוֹ יִשְׂרָאֵל.

Make the words of Torah sweet inside our mouths, Adonay our God, and in the mouths of Your people Israel, that together with our children and everyone's children within the house of Israel, we may become familiar with Your name and eager students of Your Torah. You are praised, Adonay, Torah teacher of Israel.

בָּרוּךְ אַתָּה, יְיָ אֱלֹהֵינוּ, מֶלֶךְ הָעוֹלָם, אֲשֶׁר בָּחַר בָּנוּ מִכָּל הָעַמִּים, וְנָתַן לָנוּ אֶת תּוֹרָתוֹ. בָּרוּךְ אַתָּה יְיָ, נוֹתֵן הַתּוֹרָה.

You are praised, Adonay, Majesty of the universe, who has chosen us from all peoples to accept Your Torah. For this gift, which has assured our destiny in the universe, we praise You in the words of the gift itself:

יְבָרֶכְךָ יְיָ וְיִשְׁמְרֶךָ. יָאֵר יְיָ פָּנָיו אֵלֶיךָ וִיחֻנֶּךָּ. יִשָּׂא יְיָ פָּנָיו אֵלֶיךָ וְיָשֵׂם לְךָ שָׁלוֹם.

May Adonay bless you and keep you.

May God shower fruitfulness and safekeeping upon us.

May Adonay cast over you the radiance of the divine face
in all its fullness and grace.

> May God suffuse us with the light of divine accept-
> ance and answer our prayers even when we are not
> deserving.

May Adonay raise up the face of the divine before your
face, and give you peace.

> May God's face behold ours in all our shame and
> glory, and let us find the harmony of the universe in
> our hearts and in our families, that we might help
> extend the harmony of peace to all the world.

(based on Numbers 6:24–25)

Says the Talmud: These are acts and words whose fruit we
can enjoy both in this world and store up in the cornucopia
of the world to come: honoring father and mother, deeds
of lovingkindness, regular attendance at the house of
study, hospitality to strangers, visiting the sick, giving support to new brides and bridegrooms, honoring the dead by
attending the funeral, sincerity in prayer, and making
peace with one another. Equivalent to them all is the study
of Torah which motivates us to perform the rest.

(Shabbat 127a)

Elohai N'shama

אֱלֹהַי. נְשָׁמָה שֶׁנָּתַתָּ בִּי טְהוֹרָה הִיא. אַתָּה בְרָאתָהּ
אַתָּה יְצַרְתָּהּ אַתָּה נְפַחְתָּהּ בִּי וְאַתָּה מְשַׁמְּרָהּ בְּקִרְבִּי.
וְאַתָּה עָתִיד לִטְּלָהּ מִמֶּנִּי וּלְהַחֲזִירָהּ בִּי לֶעָתִיד לָבֹא:
כָּל זְמַן שֶׁהַנְּשָׁמָה בְקִרְבִּי מוֹדֶה אֲנִי לְפָנֶיךָ יְיָ אֱלֹהַי
וֵאלֹהֵי אֲבוֹתַי (וֵאלֹהֵי אִמּוֹתַי) רִבּוֹן כָּל הַמַּעֲשִׂים
אֲדוֹן כָּל הַנְּשָׁמוֹת: בָּרוּךְ אַתָּה יְיָ הַמַּחֲזִיר נְשָׁמוֹת
לִפְגָרִים מֵתִים:

My God,
The soul You gave me is pure
You created it
You sculpted it
You breathed it inside of me
You protect it.

At some future time
You will draw it forth from me
And give it back in the World to Come.
But all the time it remains in me
I shall give You thanks
My God
God of those who lived before me,
Author of all works,
Protector of all souls.

You who restore the soul to the body of us all,
You are praised.

Praises for Our Life

בָּרוּךְ אַתָּה יְיָ אֱלֹהֵינוּ מֶלֶךְ הָעוֹלָם אֲשֶׁר נָתַן לַשֶּׂכְוִי
בִּינָה לְהַבְחִין בֵּין יוֹם וּבֵין לָיְלָה:
בָּרוּךְ אַתָּה יְיָ אֱלֹהֵינוּ מֶלֶךְ הָעוֹלָם שֶׁעָשַׂנִי בְּצַלְמוֹ:
בָּרוּךְ אַתָּה יְיָ אֱלֹהֵינוּ מֶלֶךְ הָעוֹלָם שֶׁעָשַׂנִי בֶּן (בַּת)
חוֹרִין:
בָּרוּךְ אַתָּה יְיָ אֱלֹהֵינוּ מֶלֶךְ הָעוֹלָם שֶׁעָשַׂנִי יִשְׂרָאֵל:
בָּרוּךְ אַתָּה יְיָ אֱלֹהֵינוּ מֶלֶךְ הָעוֹלָם פּוֹקֵחַ עִוְרִים:
בָּרוּךְ אַתָּה יְיָ אֱלֹהֵינוּ מֶלֶךְ הָעוֹלָם מַלְבִּישׁ עֲרֻמִּים:
בָּרוּךְ אַתָּה יְיָ אֱלֹהֵינוּ מֶלֶךְ הָעוֹלָם מַתִּיר אֲסוּרִים:
בָּרוּךְ אַתָּה יְיָ אֱלֹהֵינוּ מֶלֶךְ הָעוֹלָם זוֹקֵף כְּפוּפִים:
בָּרוּךְ אַתָּה יְיָ אֱלֹהֵינוּ מֶלֶךְ הָעוֹלָם רוֹקַע הָאָרֶץ עַל
הַמָּיִם:

בָּרוּךְ אַתָּה יְיָ אֱלֹהֵינוּ מֶלֶךְ הָעוֹלָם שֶׁעָשָׂה לִי כָּל־
צָרְכִּי:

בָּרוּךְ אַתָּה יְיָ אֱלֹהֵינוּ מֶלֶךְ הָעוֹלָם הַמֵּכִין מִצְעֲדֵי
גָבֶר:

בָּרוּךְ אַתָּה יְיָ אֱלֹהֵינוּ מֶלֶךְ הָעוֹלָם אוֹזֵר יִשְׂרָאֵל
בִּגְבוּרָה:

בָּרוּךְ אַתָּה יְיָ אֱלֹהֵינוּ מֶלֶךְ הָעוֹלָם עוֹטֵר יִשְׂרָאֵל
בְּתִפְאָרָה:

בָּרוּךְ אַתָּה יְיָ אֱלֹהֵינוּ מֶלֶךְ הָעוֹלָם הַנּוֹתֵן לַיָּעֵף כֹּחַ:

Morning stirs us to praise You:

For the ability to distinguish day from night
For shaping us in Your image
For creating us to be free
For giving us the life of Jewish people
For opening our eyes
For clothing our bodies
For helping us break free when we are bound
For helping us rise when we are fallen
For placing us in an ordered universe
For enabling us to meet our needs
For guiding us in proper paths
For giving our people strength to endure
For crowning Israel with glory
For giving courage to those whom the world has tired out
For giving us the hope of a new day.

PESUKEY D'ZIMRAH (Verses of Song)

Baruch She-amar (Introductory Blessing for Psalms)

בָּרוּךְ שֶׁאָמַר וְהָיָה הָעוֹלָם. בָּרוּךְ הוּא. בָּרוּךְ עוֹשֶׂה
בְרֵאשִׁית. בָּרוּךְ אוֹמֵר וְעוֹשֶׂה. בָּרוּךְ גּוֹזֵר וּמְקַיֵּם.
בָּרוּךְ מְרַחֵם עַל הָאָרֶץ. בָּרוּךְ מְרַחֵם עַל הַבְּרִיּוֹת.

בָּרוּךְ מְשַׁלֵּם שָׂכָר טוֹב לִירֵאָיו. בָּרוּךְ חַי לָעַד וְקַיָּם
לָנֶצַח. בָּרוּךְ פּוֹדֶה וּמַצִּיל. בָּרוּךְ שְׁמוֹ. בָּרוּךְ אַתָּה יְיָ
אֱלֹהֵינוּ מֶלֶךְ הָעוֹלָם. הָאֵל הָאָב הָרַחֲמָן הַמְהֻלָּל בְּפִי
עַמּוֹ מְשֻׁבָּח וּמְפֹאָר בִּלְשׁוֹן חֲסִידָיו וַעֲבָדָיו. וּבְשִׁירֵי
דָוִד עַבְדֶּךָ. נְהַלֶּלְךָ יְיָ אֱלֹהֵינוּ. בִּשְׁבָחוֹת וּבִזְמִירוֹת
נְגַדֶּלְךָ וּנְשַׁבֵּחֲךָ וּנְפָאֶרְךָ וְנַזְכִּיר שִׁמְךָ וְנַמְלִיכְךָ מַלְכֵּנוּ
אֱלֹהֵינוּ יָחִיד חֵי הָעוֹלָמִים. מֶלֶךְ מְשֻׁבָּח וּמְפֹאָר עֲדֵי
עַד שְׁמוֹ הַגָּדוֹל. בָּרוּךְ אַתָּה יְיָ מֶלֶךְ מְהֻלָּל
בַּתִּשְׁבָּחוֹת:

Ba-ruch she-a-mar v'ha-yah ha-o-lam
Ba-ruch hu
Ba-ruch o-mer v'o-seh
Ba-ruch go-zer um-ka-yeim
Ba-ruch m'ra-cheim al ha-a-retz
Ba-ruch m'ra-cheim al ha bri-ot
Ba-ruch o-seh v'rei-sheet
M'sha-leim sa-char tov lirei-av
Chai v'ka-yam la-ne-tzach
Ba-ruch sh'mo

Blessed are You who spoke and the world came into being.
Blessed are You.
Blessed are You who speaks and acts,
Blessed are You who decrees and fulfills.
Blessed are You who is merciful to the land.
Blessed are You who is merciful to all creatures,
Who rewards those who fear You,
Who lives and exists forever.
Blessed is Your Name.

An Offering of Psalms

רוֹמְמוּ יְיָ אֱלֹהֵינוּ, וְהִשְׁתַּחֲווּ לַהֲדֹם רַגְלָיו, קָדוֹשׁ
הוּא. רוֹמְמוּ יְיָ אֱלֹהֵינוּ, וְהִשְׁתַּחֲווּ לְהַר קָדְשׁוֹ, כִּי
קָדוֹשׁ יְיָ אֱלֹהֵינוּ. וְהוּא רַחוּם יְכַפֵּר עָוֹן וְלֹא יַשְׁחִית,
וְהִרְבָּה לְהָשִׁיב אַפּוֹ, וְלֹא יָעִיר כָּל־חֲמָתוֹ. אַתָּה, יְיָ,

לֹא תִכְלָא רַחֲמֶיךָ מִמֶּנִּי, חַסְדְּךָ וַאֲמִתְּךָ תָּמִיד יִצְּרוּנִי.
זְכֹר רַחֲמֶיךָ יְיָ, וַחֲסָדֶיךָ, כִּי מֵעוֹלָם הֵמָּה. תְּנוּ עֹז
לֵאלֹהִים, עַל יִשְׂרָאֵל גַּאֲוָתוֹ, וְעֻזּוֹ בַּשְּׁחָקִים. נוֹרָא
אֱלֹהִים מִמִּקְדָּשֶׁיךָ; אֵל יִשְׂרָאֵל, הוּא נֹתֵן עֹז
וְתַעֲצֻמוֹת לָעָם; בָּרוּךְ אֱלֹהִים. אֵל נְקָמוֹת, יְיָ, אֵל
נְקָמוֹת, הוֹפִיעַ. הִנָּשֵׂא, שֹׁפֵט הָאָרֶץ, הָשֵׁב גְּמוּל עַל
גֵּאִים. לַיְיָ הַיְשׁוּעָה, עַל עַמְּךָ בִרְכָתֶךָ סֶּלָה. יְיָ צְבָאוֹת
עִמָּנוּ, מִשְׂגָּב לָנוּ אֱלֹהֵי יַעֲקֹב סֶלָה. יְיָ צְבָאוֹת, אַשְׁרֵי
אָדָם בֹּטֵחַ בָּךְ. יְיָ הוֹשִׁיעָה; הַמֶּלֶךְ יַעֲנֵנוּ בְיוֹם קָרְאֵנוּ.
הוֹשִׁיעָה אֶת עַמֶּךָ, וּבָרֵךְ אֶת נַחֲלָתֶךָ, וּרְעֵם וְנַשְּׂאֵם
עַד הָעוֹלָם. נַפְשֵׁנוּ חִכְּתָה לַיְיָ, עֶזְרֵנוּ וּמָגִנֵּנוּ הוּא. כִּי
בוֹ יִשְׂמַח לִבֵּנוּ, כִּי בְשֵׁם קָדְשׁוֹ בָטָחְנוּ. יְהִי חַסְדְּךָ יְיָ
עָלֵינוּ, כַּאֲשֶׁר יִחַלְנוּ לָךְ. הַרְאֵנוּ יְיָ חַסְדֶּךָ, וְיֶשְׁעֲךָ
תִּתֶּן־לָנוּ. קוּמָה עֶזְרָתָה לָּנוּ, וּפְדֵנוּ לְמַעַן חַסְדֶּךָ. אָנֹכִי
יְיָ אֱלֹהֶיךָ הַמַּעַלְךָ מֵאֶרֶץ מִצְרָיִם, הַרְחֶב־פִּיךָ
וַאֲמַלְאֵהוּ. אַשְׁרֵי הָעָם שֶׁכָּכָה לּוֹ, אַשְׁרֵי הָעָם שֶׁיְיָ
אֱלֹהָיו. וַאֲנִי בְּחַסְדְּךָ בָטַחְתִּי, יָגֵל לִבִּי בִּישׁוּעָתֶךָ;
אָשִׁירָה לַיְיָ, כִּי גָמַל עָלָי.

(An Interpretation)

Exalt Adonay from the earth, footstool of the throne of
   God,
Exalt Adonay upon the holy mountain, for Adonay our
   God is holiness itself.

The God who bore us is filled with compassion,
Wiping out our sins with divine atonement,
Refusing to destroy those who have gone astray.
God will not be angry with us overlong
I know You will not withhold Your mercy from Me,
Child of Your womb that I am.

Remember the day You bore Me, Adonay,
Remember all the love that flowed from You
Into my tiny, kicking, wailing frame.
I am tiny still before Your power,
And on this day I wail once more
Before the self I might have been and can be still.
How awesome You are when I touch Your holiness!
How awesome I might be if my actions showed the holi-
  ness with which You formed me!
God of Israel,
Give Your people strength to fulfill Your purposes,
Praised be God!

God of avenging justice,
Avenge those who have suffered in innocence,
Show Yourself, O Judge of all the earth,
Bestow upon the arrogant what they deserve.
Such a victory is comely only to God;
Grant to Your people the blessing of fruitfulness and
  peace.
O Commander of the hosts,
Happy are those who trust in You!
Show us Your victory, Adonay,
Over our enemies and over ourselves.
O Majesty, answer us on this day when we call.

Psalm 34

לְדָוִד, בְּשַׁנּוֹתוֹ אֶת טַעְמוֹ לִפְנֵי אֲבִימֶלֶךְ, וַיְגָרְשֵׁהוּ
וַיֵּלַךְ. אֲבָרְכָה אֶת יְיָ בְּכָל עֵת; תָּמִיד תְּהִלָּתוֹ בְּפִי. בַּיְיָ
תִּתְהַלֵּל נַפְשִׁי; יִשְׁמְעוּ עֲנָוִים וְיִשְׂמָחוּ. גַּדְּלוּ לַיְיָ אִתִּי,
וּנְרוֹמְמָה שְׁמוֹ יַחְדָּו. דָּרַשְׁתִּי אֶת יְיָ וְעָנָנִי, וּמִכָּל
מְגוּרוֹתַי הִצִּילָנִי. הִבִּיטוּ אֵלָיו וְנָהָרוּ, וּפְנֵיהֶם אַל
יֶחְפָּרוּ. זֶה עָנִי קָרָא וַיְיָ שָׁמֵעַ, וּמִכָּל צָרוֹתָיו הוֹשִׁיעוֹ.
חֹנֶה מַלְאַךְ יְיָ סָבִיב לִירֵאָיו וַיְחַלְּצֵם. טַעֲמוּ וּרְאוּ כִּי־
טוֹב יְיָ; אַשְׁרֵי הַגֶּבֶר יֶחֱסֶה בּוֹ. יְראוּ אֶת יְיָ, קְדֹשָׁיו, כִּי

אֵין מַחְסוֹר לִירֵאָיו. כְּפִירִים רָשׁוּ וְרָעֵבוּ, וְדֹרְשֵׁי יְיָ
לֹא יַחְסְרוּ כָל טוֹב. לְכוּ בָנִים, שִׁמְעוּ לִי, יִרְאַת יְיָ
אֲלַמֶּדְכֶם. מִי הָאִישׁ הֶחָפֵץ חַיִּים, אֹהֵב יָמִים לִרְאוֹת
טוֹב. נְצֹר לְשׁוֹנְךָ מֵרָע, וּשְׂפָתֶיךָ מִדַּבֵּר מִרְמָה. סוּר
מֵרָע וַעֲשֵׂה טוֹב, בַּקֵּשׁ שָׁלוֹם וְרָדְפֵהוּ. עֵינֵי יְיָ אֶל
צַדִּיקִים, וְאָזְנָיו אֶל שַׁוְעָתָם. פְּנֵי יְיָ בְּעֹשֵׂי רָע,
לְהַכְרִית מֵאֶרֶץ זִכְרָם. צָעֲקוּ וַיְיָ שָׁמֵעַ, וּמִכָּל צָרוֹתָם
הִצִּילָם. קָרוֹב יְיָ לְנִשְׁבְּרֵי לֵב, וְאֶת־דַּכְּאֵי רוּחַ יוֹשִׁיעַ.
רַבּוֹת רָעוֹת צַדִּיק, וּמִכֻּלָּם יַצִּילֶנּוּ יְיָ. שֹׁמֵר כָּל
עַצְמוֹתָיו, אַחַת מֵהֵנָּה לֹא נִשְׁבָּרָה. תְּמוֹתֵת רָשָׁע רָעָה,
וְשֹׂנְאֵי צַדִּיק יֶאְשָׁמוּ. פּוֹדֶה יְיָ נֶפֶשׁ עֲבָדָיו, וְלֹא
יֶאְשְׁמוּ כָּל הַחוֹסִים בּוֹ.

Of David, pretending to taste madness before Abimelech,
  who spared his life and sent him away.

I shall sing of God's fruitfulness in every season,
God's praise is always in my mouth.
Let my hymn to Adonay be my life,
That it may bring joy to listeners
Who live with humility.
Declare the greatness of Adonay with me,
Let us raise high the divine name together!

I have sought God out, and I was answered,
From every single fear was I delivered!
When we look to God, our face turns bright with joy,
Not red with shame.
This poor man cried out, and Adonay was listening;
And he felt rescued from all his troubles.
Whoever holds God in awe, an angel encamps around her,
  setting her free.
So taste the world and see how good is Adonay,
How happy is everyone who truly trusts in God.

Hold God in awe if you would be a holy person,

For those who do, feel nothing lacking in their lives.
Those who seek, like animals, only to abate their appetite
Know only want and hunger,
But those who seek God feel the lack of nothing.

Come, my daughters and sons, listen to what I say,
For I can teach you the awe that is God's presence.
How can you be people who desire life,
Who love to see the good all your days?
Keep your tongue from speaking ill of others,
Your lips from uttering deceit.
Turn from wrongdoing, and do what is good,
Seek peace and harmony, actively pursue it!

For the eyes of God turn toward just men and women,
To their cries Adonay responds.
God's countenance is set against those who do ill,
Their presence is cut off from the earth.

To whose cry does God listen, who shall be rescued from
    troubles?
When our hearts are broken, Adonay is very close,
When our spirits feel shattered, God's rescue is near.
Good people may suffer many sorrows,
But God is working to save them,
Protecting all their limbs—
I believe not one of them will be broken.

Wicked people get destroyed in their own wickedness,
And those who hate good people will be condemned as
    guilty.
Adonay is at work rescuing those who try to be servants of
    the Almighty:
We never need feel guilt
When we trust in God.

Psalm 91

יֹשֵׁב בְּסֵתֶר עֶלְיוֹן, בְּצֵל שַׁדַּי יִתְלוֹנָן. אֹמַר לַיָי מַחְסִי
וּמְצוּדָתִי, אֱלֹהַי אֶבְטַח בּוֹ. כִּי הוּא יַצִּילְךָ מִפַּח יָקוּשׁ,

מִדֶּבֶר הַוּוֹת. בְּאֶבְרָתוֹ יֶסֶךְ לָךְ, וְתַחַת כְּנָפָיו תֶּחְסֶה;
צִנָּה וְסֹחֵרָה אֲמִתּוֹ. לֹא תִירָא מִפַּחַד לָיְלָה, מֵחֵץ
יָעוּף יוֹמָם. מִדֶּבֶר בָּאֹפֶל יַהֲלֹךְ, מִקֶּטֶב יָשׁוּד צָהֳרָיִם.
יִפֹּל מִצִּדְּךָ אֶלֶף, וּרְבָבָה מִימִינֶךָ; אֵלֶיךָ לֹא יִגָּשׁ. רַק
בְּעֵינֶיךָ תַבִּיט, וְשִׁלֻּמַת רְשָׁעִים תִּרְאֶה. כִּי אַתָּה, יְיָ,
מַחְסִי; עֶלְיוֹן שַׂמְתָּ מְעוֹנֶךָ. לֹא-תְאֻנֶּה אֵלֶיךָ רָעָה,
וְנֶגַע לֹא יִקְרַב בְּאָהֳלֶךָ. כִּי מַלְאָכָיו יְצַוֶּה לָּךְ, לִשְׁמָרְךָ
בְּכָל דְּרָכֶיךָ. עַל כַּפַּיִם יִשָּׂאוּנְךָ, פֶּן-תִּגֹּף בָּאֶבֶן רַגְלֶךָ.
עַל שַׁחַל וָפֶתֶן תִּדְרֹךְ, תִּרְמֹס כְּפִיר וְתַנִּין. כִּי בִי חָשַׁק
וַאֲפַלְּטֵהוּ; אֲשַׂגְּבֵהוּ כִּי יָדַע שְׁמִי. יִקְרָאֵנִי וְאֶעֱנֵהוּ,
עִמּוֹ אָנֹכִי בְצָרָה, אֲחַלְּצֵהוּ וַאֲכַבְּדֵהוּ. אֹרֶךְ יָמִים
אַשְׂבִּיעֵהוּ, וְאַרְאֵהוּ בִּישׁוּעָתִי. אֹרֶךְ יָמִים אַשְׂבִּיעֵהוּ,
וְאַרְאֵהוּ בִּישׁוּעָתִי.

O you who dwell in the shelter of the Most High
And seek shade in the presence of the Almighty,
I say of the Eternal, my refuge and stronghold,
My God in whom I trust,
That Adonay will save you from the hidden trap,
From the ruinous plague.

Like branches on a succah
God will cover you with outstretched pinions,
And beneath the wings of the divine
Will be your refuge.

The truth that is God's
Is surer than the thickest armor,
So do not be afraid of the terrors of the night
Of arrows shooting by in daytime
Of the plague that stalks in the darkness
Of the horror that ravages at noon.

Even if a thousand fall on your left, ten thousand on your
    right,
Nothing will touch you.
You need only look with your eyes,
And you will see the fate of those who do evil.

For You, Adonay, are my refuge,
And when you, my friend, make the Most High your
    shelter,
No misfortune will cause you to suffer,
No calamity will affect the tent of your inner self.

It is as though God had sent angels to guard all your paths,
To carry you upon their hands, lest you slip on a stone.
You can walk amid cubs and vipers,
You can trample fierce lions and snakes.

To you God says,
Because you are devoted to Me I will deliver you
I will protect you, for you know Me intimately.
Call upon Me and I will respond,
I am with you in trouble,
I will rescue you and bring you honor,
I will give you the satisfaction of a life that feels complete,
I will let you see the proof
That I have saved you.

Psalm 92

מִזְמוֹר שִׁיר לְיוֹם הַשַּׁבָּת. טוֹב לְהֹדוֹת לַיְיָ, וּלְזַמֵּר
לְשִׁמְךָ עֶלְיוֹן. לְהַגִּיד בַּבֹּקֶר חַסְדֶּךָ, וֶאֱמוּנָתְךָ בַּלֵּילוֹת.
עֲלֵי עָשׂוֹר וַעֲלֵי נָבֶל, עֲלֵי הִגָּיוֹן בְּכִנּוֹר. כִּי שִׂמַּחְתַּנִי יְיָ
בְּפָעֳלֶךָ, בְּמַעֲשֵׂי יָדֶיךָ אֲרַנֵּן. מַה גָּדְלוּ מַעֲשֶׂיךָ, יְיָ;
מְאֹד עָמְקוּ מַחְשְׁבֹתֶיךָ. אִישׁ בַּעַר לֹא יֵדָע, וּכְסִיל לֹא
יָבִין אֶת־זֹאת. בִּפְרֹחַ רְשָׁעִים כְּמוֹ עֵשֶׂב, וַיָּצִיצוּ כָּל
פֹּעֲלֵי אָוֶן, לְהִשָּׁמְדָם עֲדֵי עַד. וְאַתָּה מָרוֹם לְעֹלָם, יְיָ.
כִּי הִנֵּה אֹיְבֶיךָ, יְיָ, כִּי הִנֵּה אֹיְבֶיךָ יֹאבֵדוּ, יִתְפָּרְדוּ כָּל

פֹּעֲלֵי אָוֶן. וַתָּרֶם כִּרְאֵים קַרְנִי, בַּלֹּתִי בְּשֶׁמֶן רַעֲנָן.
וַתַּבֵּט עֵינִי בְּשׁוּרָי, בַּקָּמִים עָלַי מְרֵעִים תִּשְׁמַעְנָה
אָזְנָי. צַדִּיק כַּתָּמָר יִפְרָח, כְּאֶרֶז בַּלְּבָנוֹן יִשְׂגֶּה.
שְׁתוּלִים בְּבֵית יְיָ, בְּחַצְרוֹת אֱלֹהֵינוּ יַפְרִיחוּ. עוֹד
יְנוּבוּן בְּשֵׂיבָה, דְּשֵׁנִים וְרַעֲנַנִּים יִהְיוּ. לְהַגִּיד כִּי יָשָׁר
יְיָ; צוּרִי, וְלֹא עַוְלָתָה בּוֹ.

A Song by Shabbat.
It is good to thank God,
To sing praises to Your Name, Highest One.

To tell Your kindness in the morning
And Your good faith at night
On the lute, the lyre, and the ringing harp.

For You have made me happy, Adonay, in Your work.
I acclaim Your handiwork.

How great are Your works, Adonay,
And how very deep Your thoughts.

An insensitive person does not know this
And a fool does not understand.

But even when wicked people sprout up like weeds
And all kinds of trouble-makers blossom,
Ultimately they will be destroyed forever.

But You rule on high forever, God.
For Your enemies, Adonay,
Your enemies will perish,
And all the trouble-makers will be disunited.

You have raised my head like the wild ox
In prideful power.
I am anointed with fresh oil.

My eyes looked on those who were spying on me.
My ears heard those who were plotting against me.

The just will blossom like the date palm.
They will stand tall like the cedar of Lebanon.
Rooted in Your chosen House,
They will blossom in the courts of our God.

Even in old age they will bear fruit.
Still they will be fresh and growing,
To bear witness that Adonay is fair and dependable
And there is no injustice in God's ways.

Tzadik katamar yifrach
K'erez bal'vanon yisgeh
Sh'tulim b'veyt Adonay
B'chatzrot Eloheynu yafrichu
Od y'nuvun b'seyvah
D'sheynim v'ra-ananim yih-yu
L'hagid ki yashar Adonay
Tsuri v'lo avlatah bo.

Psalm 150

הַלְלוּיָהּ; הַלְלוּ אֵל בְּקָדְשׁוֹ, הַלְלוּהוּ בִּרְקִיעַ עֻזּוֹ.
הַלְלוּהוּ בִגְבוּרֹתָיו, הַלְלוּהוּ כְּרֹב גֻּדְלוֹ. הַלְלוּהוּ
בְּתֵקַע שׁוֹפָר, הַלְלוּהוּ בְּנֵבֶל וְכִנּוֹר. הַלְלוּהוּ בְּתֹף
וּמָחוֹל, הַלְלוּהוּ בְּמִנִּים וְעֻגָב. הַלְלוּהוּ בְּצִלְצְלֵי שָׁמַע,
הַלְלוּהוּ בְּצִלְצְלֵי תְרוּעָה. כֹּל הַנְּשָׁמָה תְּהַלֵּל יָהּ;
הַלְלוּיָהּ. כֹּל הַנְּשָׁמָה תְּהַלֵּל יָהּ; הַלְלוּיָהּ.

Halleluyah!
Praise God in holy space;
Praise God in the expanses of holy power;
Praise God for Your great deeds for us.
Praise God with shofar's blast,
Praise God with the lute and harp;
Praise God with drum and dance,
Praise God with strings and wind.
Praise God with tambourines,

Praise God with clashing cymbals.
Let every breathing soul praise God.
Halleluyah!

Halleluhu halleluhu b'tzil-tz'lay sha-mah
Halleluhu halleluhu b'tzil-tz'lay t'ru-ah
Kol ha-n'shah-mah t'hallel-ya
Halleluyah!

Nishmat

נִשְׁמַת כָּל חַי תְּבָרֵךְ אֶת שִׁמְךָ, יְיָ אֱלֹהֵינוּ, וְרוּחַ כָּל
בָּשָׂר תְּפָאֵר וּתְרוֹמֵם זִכְרְךָ, מַלְכֵּנוּ, תָּמִיד. מִן הָעוֹלָם
וְעַד הָעוֹלָם אַתָּה אֵל, וּמִבַּלְעָדֶיךָ אֵין לָנוּ מֶלֶךְ גּוֹאֵל
וּמוֹשִׁיעַ, פּוֹדֶה וּמַצִּיל וּמְפַרְנֵס, וּמְרַחֵם בְּכָל עֵת צָרָה
וְצוּקָה; אֵין לָנוּ מֶלֶךְ אֶלָּא אָתָּה. אֱלֹהֵי הָרִאשׁוֹנִים
וְהָאַחֲרוֹנִים, אֱלוֹהַּ כָּל בְּרִיּוֹת, אֲדוֹן כָּל תּוֹלָדוֹת,
הַמְהֻלָּל בְּרֹב הַתִּשְׁבָּחוֹת, הַמְנַהֵג עוֹלָמוֹ בְּחֶסֶד
וּבְרִיּוֹתָיו בְּרַחֲמִים. וַיְיָ לֹא יָנוּם וְלֹא יִישָׁן, הַמְעוֹרֵר
יְשֵׁנִים, וְהַמֵּקִיץ נִרְדָּמִים, וְהַמֵּשִׂיחַ אִלְּמִים, וְהַמַּתִּיר
אֲסוּרִים, וְהַסּוֹמֵךְ נוֹפְלִים, וְהַזּוֹקֵף כְּפוּפִים. לְךָ לְבַדְּךָ
אֲנַחְנוּ מוֹדִים. אִלּוּ פִינוּ מָלֵא שִׁירָה כַּיָּם, וּלְשׁוֹנֵנוּ
רִנָּה כַּהֲמוֹן גַּלָּיו, וְשִׂפְתוֹתֵינוּ שֶׁבַח כְּמֶרְחֲבֵי רָקִיעַ,
וְעֵינֵינוּ מְאִירוֹת כַּשֶּׁמֶשׁ וְכַיָּרֵחַ, וְיָדֵינוּ פְרוּשׂוֹת
כְּנִשְׁרֵי שָׁמָיִם, וְרַגְלֵינוּ קַלּוֹת כָּאַיָּלוֹת, אֵין אֲנַחְנוּ
מַסְפִּיקִים לְהוֹדוֹת לְךָ, יְיָ אֱלֹהֵינוּ וֵאלֹהֵי אֲבוֹתֵינוּ
(וְאִמּוֹתֵינוּ), וּלְבָרֵךְ אֶת שְׁמֶךָ עַל אַחַת מֵאָלֶף,
אֶלֶף אַלְפֵי אֲלָפִים וְרִבֵּי רְבָבוֹת פְּעָמִים. הַטּוֹבוֹת
שֶׁעָשִׂיתָ עִם אֲבוֹתֵינוּ (וְאִמּוֹתֵינוּ) וְעִמָּנוּ. מִמִּצְרַיִם
גְּאַלְתָּנוּ, יְיָ אֱלֹהֵינוּ, וּמִבֵּית עֲבָדִים פְּדִיתָנוּ; בְּרָעָב
זַנְתָּנוּ. וּבְשָׂבָע כִּלְכַּלְתָּנוּ; מֵחֶרֶב הִצַּלְתָּנוּ. וּמִדֶּבֶר

מִלַּטְתָּנוּ, וּמֵחֳלָיִם רָעִים וְנֶאֱמָנִים דִּלִּיתָנוּ. עַד הֵנָּה
עֲזָרוּנוּ רַחֲמֶיךָ. וְלֹא עֲזָבוּנוּ חֲסָדֶיךָ; וְאַל תִּטְּשֵׁנוּ יְיָ
אֱלֹהֵינוּ, לָנֶצַח. עַל כֵּן, אֵבָרִים שֶׁפִּלַּגְתָּ בָּנוּ, וְרוּחַ
וּנְשָׁמָה שֶׁנָּפַחְתָּ בְּאַפֵּינוּ, וְלָשׁוֹן אֲשֶׁר שַׂמְתָּ
בְּפִינוּ, הֵן הֵם יוֹדוּ וִיבָרְכוּ, וִישַׁבְּחוּ וִיפָאֲרוּ, וִירוֹמְמוּ
וְיַעֲרִיצוּ, וְיַקְדִּישׁוּ וְיַמְלִיכוּ אֶת שִׁמְךָ, מַלְכֵּנוּ. כִּי כָל
פֶּה לְךָ יוֹדֶה, וְכָל לָשׁוֹן לְךָ תִשָּׁבַע, וְכָל בֶּרֶךְ לְךָ
תִכְרַע, וְכָל קוֹמָה לְפָנֶיךָ תִשְׁתַּחֲוֶה, וְכָל לְבָבוֹת
יִירָאוּךָ, וְכָל קֶרֶב וּכְלָיוֹת יְזַמְּרוּ לִשְׁמֶךָ, כַּדָּבָר
שֶׁכָּתוּב: כָּל עַצְמוֹתַי תֹּאמַרְנָה, יְיָ מִי כָמוֹךָ, מַצִּיל עָנִי
מֵחָזָק מִמֶּנּוּ, וְעָנִי וְאֶבְיוֹן מִגֹּזְלוֹ. מִי יִדְמֶה לָּךְ, וּמִי
יִשְׁוֶה לָּךְ, וּמִי יַעֲרָךְ־לָךְ, הָאֵל הַגָּדוֹל, הַגִּבּוֹר וְהַנּוֹרָא,
אֵל עֶלְיוֹן, קֹנֵה שָׁמַיִם וָאָרֶץ. נְהַלֶּלְךָ וּנְשַׁבֵּחֲךָ
וּנְפָאֶרְךָ, וּנְבָרֵךְ אֶת שֵׁם קָדְשֶׁךָ, כָּאָמוּר: לְדָוִד, בָּרְכִי
נַפְשִׁי אֶת יְיָ, וְכָל קְרָבַי אֶת שֵׁם קָדְשׁוֹ.

Let the soul of everything alive
Sing praises to Your name!
Let the breath of every creature glorify and praise
The signs of divinity in time,
The trace of holy rule in every place!
In the face of the evils of these years,
The pain and suffering of human life,
Let us feel the touch of forces
    freeing us from bondage,
    winning victories over enemies
    within us and without.

Adonay does not sleep.
Those who lead sleepy lives
God stirs awake,
Those who live without words
God stirs to speak.

If our mouths filled with song like the sea,
If our tongue could roar like the surf,
If our lips billowed praise like a bright day's sky—
Our eyes the sun, or by night the moon—
If our arms could spread like the pinions of eagles
And our legs make us fly over fields like gazelles—
Still would our lips lack words
And our bodies the space
To acknowledge the brilliance even of a handful of world
Pervaded by Adonay,
Or speak a blessing even for the tiniest goodness You have
    done,
God for our fathers, our mothers, and for us.

Yet these shall sing what praise they can:
The limbs with which You have constructed us shall be our
    strings,
The tongue You have placed in us shall be the bow,
The soul You have breathed in us shall resonate the
    melody.
Soon with my mouth
Every mouth shall give thanks,
Every tongue shall swear its truth,
Every knee shall bow down,
Every backbone fall prostrate,
Every heart shall fill with awe,
Every inner organ sing its praise,
And the psalm verse shall come true:
"All my bones shall say, 'Incomparable is Adonay!'"

David first plucked out the chords:
"O my soul, sing praises to Adonay;
To the one
Whose name is holy
Shout with all my inmost being!"

Hamelech

הַמֶּלֶךְ

יוֹשֵׁב עַל כִּסֵּא רָם וְנִשָּׂא:

שׁוֹכֵן עַד מָרוֹם וְקָדוֹשׁ שְׁמוֹ. וְכָתוּב. רַנְּנוּ צַדִּיקִים בַּייָ
לַיְשָׁרִים נָאוָה תְהִלָּה: בְּפִי יְשָׁרִים תִּתְרוֹמָם. וּבְדִבְרֵי
צַדִּיקִים תִּתְבָּרַךְ. וּבִלְשׁוֹן חֲסִידִים תִּתְקַדָּשׁ. וּבְקֶרֶב
קְדוֹשִׁים תִּתְהַלָּל:

Praised be the Sovereign, who sits upon the high and lofty
   Throne!
The Shechina is our intimate forever, yet with a Name
   exalted and holy.
Sing to Adonay, those who do justly, for praise becomes
   the upright.
From the mouth of the upright comes God's praise,
Blessing is in the words of doers of justice,
Exaltation springs from the tongue of those who do more
   than is required.
From the innermost parts of holy people does God's holi-
   ness shine forth.

יִשְׁתַּבַּח שִׁמְךָ לָעַד מַלְכֵּנוּ. הָאֵל הַמֶּלֶךְ הַגָּדוֹל
וְהַקָּדוֹשׁ בַּשָּׁמַיִם וּבָאָרֶץ. כִּי לְךָ נָאֶה יְיָ אֱלֹהֵינוּ
וֵאלֹהֵי אֲבוֹתֵינוּ (וֵאלֹהֵי אִמּוֹתֵינוּ) שִׁיר וּשְׁבָחָה
הַלֵּל וְזִמְרָה עֹז וּמֶמְשָׁלָה נֶצַח גְּדֻלָּה וּגְבוּרָה תְּהִלָּה
וְתִפְאֶרֶת קְדֻשָּׁה וּמַלְכוּת בְּרָכוֹת וְהוֹדָאוֹת מֵעַתָּה
וְעַד עוֹלָם. בָּרוּךְ אַתָּה יְיָ אֵל מֶלֶךְ גָּדוֹל בַּתִּשְׁבָּחוֹת.
אֵל הַהוֹדָאוֹת אֲדוֹן הַנִּפְלָאוֹת. הַבּוֹחֵר בְּשִׁירֵי זִמְרָה.
מֶלֶךְ אֵל חֵי הָעוֹלָמִים:

You are praised, Adonay,
Source of power in the universe
Sovereign extolled in thanks and praises,
God of awesome wonders
Guarantor of life eternal,
Who has chosen the verses of these our songs.

Reader's Kaddish

יִתְגַּדֵּל וְיִתְקַדַּשׁ שְׁמֵהּ רַבָּא בְּעָלְמָא דִּי בְרָא כִרְעוּתֵהּ;
וְיַמְלִיךְ מַלְכוּתֵהּ בְּחַיֵּיכוֹן וּבְיוֹמֵיכוֹן, וּבְחַיֵּי דְכָל בֵּית
יִשְׂרָאֵל, בַּעֲגָלָא וּבִזְמַן קָרִיב, וְאִמְרוּ אָמֵן:

יְהֵא שְׁמֵהּ רַבָּא מְבָרַךְ לְעָלַם וּלְעָלְמֵי עָלְמַיָּא.

יִתְבָּרַךְ וְיִשְׁתַּבַּח, וְיִתְפָּאַר וְיִתְרוֹמַם, וְיִתְנַשֵּׂא
וְיִתְהַדָּר, וְיִתְעַלֶּה וְיִתְהַלָּל שְׁמֵהּ דְּקֻדְשָׁא, בְּרִיךְ הוּא,
לְעֵלָּא לְעֵלָּא מִן כָּל בִּרְכָתָא וְשִׁירָתָא, תֻּשְׁבְּחָתָא
וְנֶחֱמָתָא, דַּאֲמִירָן בְּעָלְמָא, וְאִמְרוּ אָמֵן.

May God's great name be magnified and sanctified in the world created according to the holy will, and may God's rule be known in your lifetime, in your own days, and in the life of the house of Israel, speedily, in a time close at hand.

May the name of the blessed Holy One be praised and extolled far beyond all praises and blessings we can ever say in the world. Amen.

THE SHMA AND ITS BLESSINGS

בָּרְכוּ אֶת יְיָ הַמְבֹרָךְ:

Bar'chu et Adonay ham'vorach:

Declare the power of God whose blessings shine through all the earth!

בָּרוּךְ יְיָ הַמְבֹרָךְ לְעוֹלָם וָעֶד:

Baruch Adonay ham'vorach l'olam va-ed:

How powerful is God whose blessings shall shine through all the earth forever and ever!

Yotzer: The Unity of the Creation

בָּרוּךְ אַתָּה יְיָ אֱלֹהֵינוּ מֶלֶךְ הָעוֹלָם. יוֹצֵר אוֹר וּבוֹרֵא
חְשֶׁךְ. עֹשֶׂה שָׁלוֹם וּבוֹרֵא אֶת הַכֹּל:

הַמֵּאִיר לָאָרֶץ וְלַדָּרִים עָלֶיהָ בְּרַחֲמִים. וּבְטוּבוֹ מְחַדֵּשׁ
בְּכָל יוֹם תָּמִיד מַעֲשֵׂה־בְרֵאשִׁית: מָה רַבּוּ מַעֲשֶׂיךָ יְיָ.
כֻּלָּם בְּחָכְמָה עָשִׂיתָ. מָלְאָה הָאָרֶץ קִנְיָנֶךָ: תִּתְבָּרַךְ יְיָ
אֱלֹהֵינוּ עַל־שֶׁבַח מַעֲשֵׂה יָדֶיךָ וְעַל מְאוֹרֵי־אוֹר
שֶׁעָשִׂיתָ יְפָאֲרוּךָ סֶּלָה: בָּרוּךְ אַתָּה יְיָ יוֹצֵר הַמְּאוֹרוֹת:

How powerful is God
Majesty of the universe
Sculptor of pure light
Inventor of secret darkness
Creator of one single harmony
Inventor of every single unrelated thing
Teeming in the morning light.

In the morning light
Your compassion warms every hidden soul
In the daily flowering of Your goodness
The bees bring promise of both pain and honey
Your breath blows golden leaves in heaps, burying their
    brilliance
Yet from that sheltered darkness new trees rise up toward
    the light.
Your breath conducts a hundred struggling organs in our
    body
Into the unified and graceful dance that is our day.

How many little beauties You have made—
Your collection fills the world!
Through Your wisdom each single unrelated thing

Fills a place in a single harmony
Wrapped in the wondrous ribbon of Your light.

How You are praised, Adonay,
Sculptor of secrets for each one of Your creatures
Teeming
With Your one light.

Alternative Yotzer

In some special way every person completes the universe.
If I do not play my part, I injure the pattern of all exist-
    ence.

The same stream of life that runs through my veins night
    and day
runs through the world and dances in rhythmic measures.

It is the same life that shoots in joy through the dust of the
    earth
in numberless blades of grass and
breaks into tumultuous waves of leaves and flowers.

It is the same life that is rocked
in the ocean-cradle of birth and death,
in ebb and flow.

I feel my limbs are made glorious
by the touch of this world of life.
And my pride is from the life-throb
of ages dancing in my blood this moment.

Ahavah Rabah: the Unity of Truth

אַהֲבָה רַבָּה אֲהַבְתָּנוּ יְיָ אֱלֹהֵינוּ חֶמְלָה גְדוֹלָה וִיתֵרָה
חָמַלְתָּ עָלֵינוּ: אָבִינוּ מַלְכֵּנוּ בַּעֲבוּר אֲבוֹתֵינוּ
(וְאִמוֹתֵינוּ) שֶׁבָּטְחוּ בְךָ וַתְּלַמְּדֵם חֻקֵי חַיִּים כֵּן תְּחָנֵּנוּ
וּתְלַמְּדֵנוּ: אָבִינוּ הָאָב הָרַחֲמָן הַמְרַחֵם. רַחֵם
עָלֵינוּ וְתֵן בְּלִבֵּנוּ לְהָבִין וּלְהַשְׂכִּיל לִשְׁמֹעַ לִלְמֹד

וּלְלַמֵּד לִשְׁמֹר וְלַעֲשׂוֹת וּלְקַיֵּם אֶת כָּל דִּבְרֵי תַלְמוּד
תּוֹרָתֶךָ בְּאַהֲבָה: וְהָאֵר עֵינֵינוּ בְּתוֹרָתֶךָ וְדַבֵּק לִבֵּנוּ
בְּמִצְוֹתֶיךָ וְיַחֵד לְבָבֵנוּ לְאַהֲבָה וּלְיִרְאָה אֶת שְׁמֶךָ וְלֹא
נֵבוֹשׁ לְעוֹלָם וָעֶד: כִּי בְשֵׁם קָדְשְׁךָ הַגָּדוֹל וְהַנּוֹרָא
בָּטָחְנוּ נָגִילָה וְנִשְׂמְחָה בִּישׁוּעָתֶךָ: וַהֲבִיאֵנוּ לְשָׁלוֹם
מֵאַרְבַּע כַּנְפוֹת הָאָרֶץ וְתוֹלִיכֵנוּ קוֹמְמִיּוּת לְאַרְצֵנוּ:
כִּי אֵל פּוֹעֵל יְשׁוּעוֹת אָתָּה וּבָנוּ בָחַרְתָּ מִכָּל־עַם
וְלָשׁוֹן וְקֵרַבְתָּנוּ לְשִׁמְךָ הַגָּדוֹל סֶלָה בֶּאֱמֶת לְהוֹדוֹת
לְךָ וּלְיַחֶדְךָ בְּאַהֲבָה: בָּרוּךְ אַתָּה יְיָ הַבּוֹחֵר בְּעַמּוֹ
יִשְׂרָאֵל בְּאַהֲבָה:

With acts of great love
You embrace us, Adonay our God.
With great acts of mercy
You encompass us.
You, Monarch, are our Sovereign, our father and our
   mother,
For the sake of our fathers and mothers who are no more,
Who trusted You,
Whom You taught laws for life—
Accept us,
Be our teacher too.

Our mother,
Our fathermother filled with compassion
Sustain us with compassion
And permit our knowing hearts
To discern that we may understand,
Then listen that we may learn and teach,
Then observe that we may do and sustain
All the words of Your Torah we shall study
In love.

Give light for our eyes through Your Torah,
Bring close our knowing hearts to Your mitzvot,
And make the many truths our heart knows

One,
Through love and awe of Your name,
And we shall never be confounded
In time and the world.
For in Your great and awesome name,
Filled with kedusha,
We have trusted too,
And rejoiced and exulted
In the victories You have brought us.

Alternative Ahava Rabah

God means:
What is behind our soul is beyond our spirit;
What is at the source of our selves
Is at the Goal of our ways.
God is the heart of all, eager to receive
And eager to give.

When God becomes our form of thinking
We begin to sense all people in one person,
The whole world in a grain of sand,
Eternity in a moment.
To worldly ethics
One human being is less than two human beings,
To the religious mind
If a person has caused a single soul to perish,
It is as though he had caused a whole world to perish,
And if one has saved a single soul,
It is as though she had saved a whole world.

If in the afterglow of a religious insight
I can see a way to gather up
My scattered life,
To unite what lies in strife;
A way that is good
For all people as it is for me—
I will know it is God's way.

The Shma: First Paragraph (Shma and V'ahavta)

שְׁמַע יִשְׂרָאֵל יְהֹוָה אֱלֹהֵינוּ יְהֹוָה אֶחָד:

Shma Yisrael Adonay Eloheynu Adonay Echad:

Listen, Israel! Adonay is our God, Adonay alone is One.

בָּרוּךְ שֵׁם כְּבוֹד מַלְכוּתוֹ לְעוֹלָם וָעֶד:

Baruch sheym kvod malchuto l'olam vaed:

The Name is praised whose glorious rule will outlast the world and time.

וְאָהַבְתָּ אֵת יְהֹוָה אֱלֹהֶיךָ בְּכָל־לְבָבְךָ וּבְכָל־נַפְשְׁךָ
וּבְכָל־מְאֹדֶךָ: וְהָיוּ הַדְּבָרִים הָאֵלֶּה אֲשֶׁר אָנֹכִי מְצַוְּךָ
הַיּוֹם עַל־לְבָבֶךָ: וְשִׁנַּנְתָּם לְבָנֶיךָ וְדִבַּרְתָּ בָּם בְּשִׁבְתְּךָ
בְּבֵיתֶךָ וּבְלֶכְתְּךָ בַדֶּרֶךְ וּבְשָׁכְבְּךָ וּבְקוּמֶךָ: וּקְשַׁרְתָּם
לְאוֹת עַל יָדֶךָ וְהָיוּ לְטֹטָפֹת בֵּין עֵינֶיךָ: וּכְתַבְתָּם עַל־
מְזֻזוֹת בֵּיתֶךָ וּבִשְׁעָרֶיךָ:

V'a-hav-ta et A-do-nay E-lo-hecha b'chol l'va-v'cha uv'chol naf-sh'cha uv'chol m'o-de-cha. V'ha-yu ha-d'va-rim ha-ey-leh a-sher a-no-chi m'tzav-cha ha-yom al l'va-ve-cha. V'shi-nan-tam l'va-ne-cha v'dibarta bam b'shiv-t'cha b'vey-te-cha, uv-lech-t'cha va-de-rech, uv'shoch-b'cha uvkumecha. Uk'shar-tam l'ot al ya-de-cha, v'ha-yu l'to-ta-fot beyn ey-ne-cha. Uch-tav-tam al m'zu-zot bey-te-cha u-vish-a-re-cha.

Thus you shall show your love for Adonay your God:
With every inclination of your knowing heart,
With all the strength through which you live,
With every benefit you have received.
For these words in which I am giving you mitzvot today
Shall enter into your knowing heart,
That you may help your children sink their teeth in them,

And speak through them
While sitting in your house,
While walking on the road,
At the time for lying down,
At the time for rising up.
You shall bind them in a sign upon your arm.
They shall become frontlets between your eyes.
You shall inscribe them in mezuzot for your house,
Upon your gates.

The Shma: Second Paragraph (V'haya im Shamoa)

וְהָיָה אִם־שָׁמֹעַ תִּשְׁמְעוּ אֶל־מִצְוֹתַי אֲשֶׁר אָנֹכִי מְצַוֶּה
אֶתְכֶם הַיּוֹם לְאַהֲבָה אֶת־יְהֹוָה אֱלֹהֵיכֶם וּלְעָבְדוֹ
בְּכָל־לְבַבְכֶם וּבְכָל־נַפְשְׁכֶם: וְנָתַתִּי מְטַר־אַרְצְכֶם
בְּעִתּוֹ יוֹרֶה וּמַלְקוֹשׁ וְאָסַפְתָּ דְגָנֶךָ וְתִירשְׁךָ וְיִצְהָרֶךָ:
וְנָתַתִּי עֵשֶׂב בְּשָׂדְךָ לִבְהֶמְתֶּךָ וְאָכַלְתָּ וְשָׂבָעְתָּ: הִשָּׁמְרוּ
לָכֶם פֶּן־יִפְתֶּה לְבַבְכֶם וְסַרְתֶּם וַעֲבַדְתֶּם אֱלֹהִים
אֲחֵרִים וְהִשְׁתַּחֲוִיתֶם לָהֶם: וְחָרָה אַף־יְהֹוָה בָּכֶם
וְעָצַר אֶת־הַשָּׁמַיִם וְלֹא־יִהְיֶה מָטָר וְהָאֲדָמָה לֹא תִתֵּן
אֶת־יְבוּלָהּ וַאֲבַדְתֶּם מְהֵרָה מֵעַל הָאָרֶץ הַטֹּבָה אֲשֶׁר
יְהֹוָה נֹתֵן לָכֶם: וְשַׂמְתֶּם אֶת־דְּבָרַי אֵלֶּה עַל־לְבַבְכֶם
וְעַל־נַפְשְׁכֶם וּקְשַׁרְתֶּם אֹתָם לְאוֹת עַל־יֶדְכֶם וְהָיוּ
לְטוֹטָפֹת בֵּין עֵינֵיכֶם: וְלִמַּדְתֶּם אֹתָם אֶת־בְּנֵיכֶם
לְדַבֵּר בָּם בְּשִׁבְתְּךָ בְּבֵיתֶךָ וּבְלֶכְתְּךָ בַדֶּרֶךְ וּבְשָׁכְבְּךָ
וּבְקוּמֶךָ: וּכְתַבְתָּם עַל־מְזוּזוֹת בֵּיתֶךָ וּבִשְׁעָרֶיךָ: לְמַעַן
יִרְבּוּ יְמֵיכֶם וִימֵי בְנֵיכֶם עַל הָאֲדָמָה אֲשֶׁר נִשְׁבַּע יְהֹוָה
לַאֲבֹתֵיכֶם לָתֵת לָהֶם כִּימֵי הַשָּׁמַיִם עַל־הָאָרֶץ:

If you will pay attention to My commandments which I
command you today, I will free you from worry about
physical sustenance so that you can devote your mind to

Torah and your body to right action. I will give rain in its
season for your harvest, and good pasture for your cattle.
But if you open to temptations and serve other sorts of
gods, then the anger of God will wax hot against you, closing the heavens and holding back the rain. Earth will not
yield its produce, and you shall fast disappear from the
good land which God has given you. Therefore place My
words upon your heart and soul, bind them to your arm,
that your days may increase upon the land.

The Shma: Third Paragraph (Vayomer)

וַיֹּאמֶר יְהֹוָה אֶל־מֹשֶׁה לֵּאמֹר: דַּבֵּר אֶל־בְּנֵי יִשְׂרָאֵל
וְאָמַרְתָּ אֲלֵהֶם וְעָשׂוּ לָהֶם צִיצִת עַל־כַּנְפֵי בִגְדֵיהֶם
לְדֹרֹתָם וְנָתְנוּ עַל־צִיצִת הַכָּנָף פְּתִיל תְּכֵלֶת: וְהָיָה
לָכֶם לְצִיצִת וּרְאִיתֶם אֹתוֹ וּזְכַרְתֶּם אֶת־כָּל־מִצְוֹת
יְהֹוָה וַעֲשִׂיתֶם אֹתָם וְלֹא תָתוּרוּ אַחֲרֵי לְבַבְכֶם וְאַחֲרֵי
עֵינֵיכֶם אֲשֶׁר־אַתֶּם זֹנִים אַחֲרֵיהֶם: לְמַעַן תִּזְכְּרוּ
וַעֲשִׂיתֶם אֶת־כָּל־מִצְוֹתָי וִהְיִיתֶם קְדֹשִׁים לֵאלֹהֵיכֶם:
אֲנִי יְהֹוָה אֱלֹהֵיכֶם אֲשֶׁר הוֹצֵאתִי אֶתְכֶם מֵאֶרֶץ
מִצְרַיִם לִהְיוֹת לָכֶם לֵאלֹהִים אֲנִי יְיָ אֱלֹהֵיכֶם:

God spoke to Moses saying: Speak to the people of Israel
and tell them to make fringes on the corners of their garments throughout their generations and to put a cord of
blue on the fringe of each corner. The fringe will be a symbol of your commitment: When you see it, you will be
reminded of all God's commandments and you will fulfill
them, and you will not simply follow your own
impulses and desires which might lead you to be false to
Me. In this way you will remember and do all My commandments and you will be wholly dedicated for your
God. I am Adonay your God who brought you out of the
land of Egypt in order to be your God. I am Adonay your
God.

Alternative Vayomer

Time is the border of eternity. Time is eternity formed
into tassels. The moments of our lives are like luxuriant
tassels. They are attached to the garment and are made of
the same cloth. It is through spiritual living that we realize
that the infinite can be confined in a measured line.

Life without integrity is like loosely hanging threads,
easily straying from the main cloth, while in acts of piety
we learn to understand that every instant is like a thread
raveling out of eternity to form a delicate tassel. We must
not cast off the threads but weave them into the design of
an eternal fabric.

The days of our lives are representatives of eternity
rather than fugitives, and we must live as if the fate of all of
time would totally depend upon a single moment.

Emet V'yatziv: Redemption

אֱמֶת וְיַצִּיב, וְנָכוֹן וְקַיָּם, וְיָשָׁר וְנֶאֱמָן, וְאָהוּב וְחָבִיב,
וְנֶחְמָד וְנָעִים, וְנוֹרָא וְאַדִּיר, וּמְתֻקָּן וּמְקֻבָּל, וְטוֹב
וְיָפֶה הַדָּבָר הַזֶּה עָלֵינוּ לְעוֹלָם וָעֶד. אֱמֶת, אֱלֹהֵי
עוֹלָם מַלְכֵּנוּ, צוּר יַעֲקֹב מָגֵן יִשְׁעֵנוּ. לְדֹר וָדֹר הוּא
קַיָּם, וּשְׁמוֹ קַיָּם, וְכִסְאוֹ נָכוֹן, וּמַלְכוּתוֹ וֶאֱמוּנָתוֹ לָעַד
קַיֶּמֶת. וּדְבָרָיו חָיִים וְקַיָּמִים, נֶאֱמָנִים וְנֶחֱמָדִים, לָעַד
וּלְעוֹלְמֵי עוֹלָמִים, עַל אֲבוֹתֵינוּ (וְעַל אִמּוֹתֵנוּ) וְעָלֵינוּ,
עַל בָּנֵינוּ וְעַל דּוֹרוֹתֵינוּ, וְעַל כָּל דּוֹרוֹת זֶרַע יִשְׂרָאֵל
עֲבָדֶיךָ.

עַל הָרִאשׁוֹנִים וְעַל הָאַחֲרוֹנִים דָּבָר טוֹב וְקַיָּם לְעוֹלָם
וָעֶד, אֱמֶת וֶאֱמוּנָה, חֹק וְלֹא יַעֲבֹר. אֱמֶת, שָׁאַתָּה
הוּא יְיָ אֱלֹהֵינוּ וֵאלֹהֵי אֲבוֹתֵינוּ (וֵאלֹהֵי אִמּוֹתֵינוּ),
מַלְכֵּנוּ מֶלֶךְ אֲבוֹתֵינוּ (וּמֶלֶךְ אִמּוֹתֵינוּ), גְּאָלֵנוּ גֹּאֵל
אֲבוֹתֵינוּ (וְגֹאֵל אִמּוֹתֵינוּ), יוֹצְרֵנוּ צוּר יְשׁוּעָתֵנוּ,
פּוֹדֵנוּ וּמַצִּילֵנוּ; מֵעוֹלָם שְׁמֶךָ, אֵין אֱלֹהִים זוּלָתֶךָ.

עֶזְרַת אֲבוֹתֵינוּ (וְעֶזְרַת אִמּוֹתֵינוּ) אַתָּה הוּא מֵעוֹלָם,
מָגֵן וּמוֹשִׁיעַ לִבְנֵיהֶם אַחֲרֵיהֶם בְּכָל דּוֹר וָדוֹר. בְּרוֹם
עוֹלָם מוֹשָׁבֶךָ, וּמִשְׁפָּטֶיךָ וְצִדְקָתְךָ עַד אַפְסֵי אָרֶץ.
אַשְׁרֵי אִישׁ שֶׁיִּשְׁמַע לְמִצְוֹתֶיךָ, וְתוֹרָתְךָ וּדְבָרְךָ יָשִׂים
עַל לִבּוֹ. אֱמֶת אַתָּה הוּא אָדוֹן לְעַמֶּךָ, וּמֶלֶךְ גִּבּוֹר
לָרִיב רִיבָם. אֱמֶת אַתָּה הוּא רִאשׁוֹן וְאַתָּה הוּא
אַחֲרוֹן, וּמִבַּלְעָדֶיךָ אֵין לָנוּ מֶלֶךְ גּוֹאֵל וּמוֹשִׁיעַ.
מִמִּצְרַיִם גְּאַלְתָּנוּ, יְיָ אֱלֹהֵינוּ, וּמִבֵּית עֲבָדִים פְּדִיתָנוּ.
כָּל בְּכוֹרֵיהֶם הָרָגְתָּ, וּבְכוֹרְךָ גָּאָלְתָּ, וְיַם סוּף בָּקַעְתָּ,
וְזֵדִים טִבַּעְתָּ, וִידִידִים הֶעֱבַרְתָּ; וַיְכַסּוּ מַיִם צָרֵיהֶם,
אֶחָד מֵהֶם לֹא נוֹתָר. עַל זֹאת שִׁבְּחוּ אֲהוּבִים וְרוֹמְמוּ
אֵל, וְנָתְנוּ יְדִידִים זְמִירוֹת שִׁירוֹת וְתִשְׁבָּחוֹת, בְּרָכוֹת
וְהוֹדָאוֹת לַמֶּלֶךְ, אֵל חַי וְקַיָּם. רָם וְנִשָּׂא, גָּדוֹל וְנוֹרָא,
מַשְׁפִּיל גֵּאִים וּמַגְבִּיהַּ שְׁפָלִים, מוֹצִיא אֲסִירִים וּפוֹדֶה
עֲנָוִים, וְעוֹזֵר דַּלִּים, וְעוֹנֶה לְעַמּוֹ בְּעֵת שַׁוְּעָם אֵלָיו.
תְּהִלּוֹת לְאֵל עֶלְיוֹן, בָּרוּךְ הוּא וּמְבֹרָךְ. מֹשֶׁה וּבְנֵי
יִשְׂרָאֵל לְךָ עָנוּ שִׁירָה בְּשִׂמְחָה רַבָּה, וְאָמְרוּ כֻלָּם:

True and certain and faithful and beloved
Precious and pleasing and awesome and grand
Correct and accepted and good and beautiful
Are all these words of the Shma which we have uttered.

Whatever truths we learn, however far we stray
These words of Your majesty will call to us,
For they proclaim the miracle of the vast universe,
The miracle of our small people's life.

Whatever homes we build, however far we stray
These words will carve out a place for Your throne,
They will teach us sounds with which we may pronounce
Your name.

Our mothers nursed us through these words,
Our children shall nurse theirs as well.
At the breast we learned of Your redemption.
Growing up we discovered Your saving power.

Happy are those who hear of Your mitzvot,
Who place Your words upon their heart.
Happy are those who rehearse the tale of Your deliverance
    in Egypt,
Who remember our liberation from the hovels of the
    slaves.

How cruelly did Pharaoh's hosts misuse us!
How cruelly did they meet their end!
Can we grieve that their first-born were drowned
While ours were saved?
How many first-born have we lost through the ages,
How many nursing babies have been drowned in our
    oppressors' bile?

Therefore Miriam the prophet led our mothers in praise of
    You at the Sea
Commanding timbrel and harp to exalt the Sovereign of
    the universe,
God of the true and certain, the awesome and grand,
Who defeats the arrogant and exalts the humble,
Ransoms the oppressed and supports the poor,
Responds to the people of God when they cry out—

Of course we should sing praise to God on high!
Our Ruler is bringing near the day when no one will be
    drowned,
No mothers will weep, no fathers struggle to be brave,
But all shall proclaim in the whole vast universe
The miracle of every people's life:
Adonay will reign forever and ever!

מִי כָמֹכָה בָּאֵלִם יְיָ מִי כָּמֹכָה נֶאְדָּר בַּקֹּדֶשׁ נוֹרָא
תְהִלֹּת עֹשֵׂה פֶלֶא:

Mi chamocha ba-eylim Adonay; mi kamocha ne-edar ba-kodesh; nora t'hilot o-sey fe-leh.

Who is like You, Adonay, among the gods that are worshiped? Who is like You, majestic in holiness, doing wonders?

שִׁירָה חֲדָשָׁה שִׁבְּחוּ גְאוּלִים לְשִׁמְךָ עַל שְׂפַת הַיָּם. יַחַד כֻּלָּם הוֹדוּ וְהִמְלִיכוּ וְאָמְרוּ.

Shira chadasha shib'chu g'ulim l'shim-cha al sfat ha-yam. Yachad kulam hodu v'him-lichu v'am-ru:

A new song the redeemed sang in praise to Your Name at the shore of the sea. Together they all gave thanks and declared You their Sovereign, saying:

יְיָ יִמְלֹךְ לְעֹלָם וָעֶד:

Adonay yimloch l'olam va-ed.

Adonay will rule forever and ever!

צוּר יִשְׂרָאֵל קוּמָה בְּעֶזְרַת יִשְׂרָאֵל. וּפְדֵה כִנְאֻמֶךָ יְהוּדָה וְיִשְׂרָאֵל. גֹּאֲלֵנוּ יְיָ צְבָאוֹת שְׁמוֹ קְדוֹשׁ יִשְׂרָאֵל: בָּרוּךְ אַתָּה יְיָ גָּאַל יִשְׂרָאֵל:

Tzur Yisrael, kuma b'ezrat Yisrael. Uf'dey chin'umecha Yehuda v'Yisrael. Go-aleynu Adonay Tz'va-ot sh'mo, k'dosh Yisrael. Baruch atta Adonay, ga-al Yisrael.

O Rock of Israel, rise up to help Israel, keeping Your promise to redeem Judah and Israel. Our Redeemer, Commander of the Hosts is Your name, O Holy One of Israel. You are praised, who has redeemed Israel.

AMIDAH (THE GREAT PRAYER)

AMIDAH (THE GREAT PRAYER)

*(The full traditional silent Amidah in Hebrew and English is
found on pages 156–171)*

אֲדֹנָי שְׂפָתַי תִּפְתָּח וּפִי יַגִּיד תְּהִלָּתֶךָ:

Avot: God of Our Ancestors

בָּרוּךְ אַתָּה, יְיָ אֱלֹהֵינוּ וֵאלֹהֵי אֲבוֹתֵינוּ (וְאלֹהֵי
אִמּוֹתֵינוּ), אֱלֹהֵי אַבְרָהָם, אֱלֹהֵי יִצְחָק, וֵאלֹהֵי יַעֲקֹב,
(אֱלֹהֵי שָׂרָה, אֱלֹהֵי רִבְקָה, אֱלֹהֵי רָחֵל, וֵאלֹהֵי לֵאָה,)
הָאֵל הַגָּדוֹל הַגִּבּוֹר וְהַנּוֹרָא, אֵל עֶלְיוֹן, גּוֹמֵל חֲסָדִים
טוֹבִים, וְקֹנֵה הַכֹּל, וְזוֹכֵר חַסְדֵי אָבוֹת (וְאִמָּהוֹת),
וּמֵבִיא גוֹאֵל* לִבְנֵי בְנֵיהֶם לְמַעַן שְׁמוֹ בְּאַהֲבָה.
זָכְרֵנוּ לְחַיִּים, מֶלֶךְ חָפֵץ בַּחַיִּים, וְכָתְבֵנוּ בְּסֵפֶר
הַחַיִּים, לְמַעַנְךָ אֱלֹהִים חַיִּים: מֶלֶךְ עוֹזֵר וּמוֹשִׁיעַ
וּמָגֵן. בָּרוּךְ אַתָּה יְיָ, מָגֵן אַבְרָהָם (וְשָׂרָה).

In the Reform tradition, גְּאוּלָה*

You are praised, Adonay, Source of life for all the world,
Our God, Source of light for a handful of ancients
Who shepherded a people toward Your promise.

You walked with Abraham and Isaac,
Showed Sarah how to laugh,
Entrusted Rebecca with our destiny,
Helped Jacob wrestle with his soul
And with the nation You created out of Leah and Rachel.

You are a noble God, mighty and awesome,
Enthroned on high
Engaged on earth
Showing us by Your example
How to support those burdened by their need.

With all the creatures You have formed since then
The ancients' faith moves You still,
For their sake Your love is at work
Forming a world in which redemption can arrive
For the children of the ancients
To fulfill Your promise.

With all our faults, with all our virtues,
We are the children of the ancients whom You love.
O Majesty,
Source of life for all the world,
May our lives move You too.
Inscribe us in the Book of Life
To fulfill Your promise, O God of Life.
Sovereign, helper, deliverer, protector,
You are praised, Adonay,
Shield of Abraham, Support of Sarah.

When You laugh with them,
Remember us.

Gevurot: God's Power

Will we rejoin the dead someday
Will they awake
Who sleep beneath the dust
As we who sleep throughout the night
Rise up when morning comes?

Will we rejoin the dead someday
Will those who sleep beneath the dust
Awake
And rise to greet us as we climb the mountain?

How much we have to tell them
How much we want to know from them!
How awesome it will be to meet our fathers there
To embrace our mothers once again
To speak with those who all our lives
Have just been silent names on stones

Long worn away,
To embrace as our own
Heroes and martyrs of peoples not our own
When the reunion on the mountain makes a human race now
   torn asunder
One.

אַתָּה גִבּוֹר לְעוֹלָם אֲדֹנָי מְחַיֵּה מֵתִים* אַתָּה רַב
לְהוֹשִׁיעַ. מְכַלְכֵּל חַיִּים בְּחֶסֶד מְחַיֵּה מֵתִים* בְּרַחֲמִים
רַבִּים. סוֹמֵךְ נוֹפְלִים וְרוֹפֵא חוֹלִים וּמַתִּיר אֲסוּרִים
וּמְקַיֵּם אֱמוּנָתוֹ לִישֵׁנֵי עָפָר. מִי כָמוֹךָ בַּעַל גְּבוּרוֹת
וּמִי דּוֹמֶה לָּךְ. מֶלֶךְ מֵמִית וּמְחַיֶּה וּמַצְמִיחַ יְשׁוּעָה. מִי
כָמוֹךָ אַב הָרַחֲמִים זוֹכֵר יְצוּרָיו לְחַיִּים בְּרַחֲמִים.
וְנֶאֱמָן אַתָּה לְהַחֲיוֹת מֵתִים. בָּרוּךְ אַתָּה יְיָ מְחַיֵּה
הַמֵּתִים*.

*הַכֹּל ,In the Reform tradition

You are mighty forever, Adonay!
You who brought Adam forth from the earth
Will one day bring all their children back from the earth
As naturally as You support the fallen,
Heal the sick,
Free the captives,
Just so do You keep faith
With those now sleeping in the dust.

Who is like You, Source of might,
Sovereign of the living and the dead
Who will bring forth blossoms of salvation out of the
   ground?

Who is like You, creator of the womb,
Whose life-giving love remembers every birth?

We trust in You to turn death into life.
You are praised, Adonay,
Who will reunite the living and the dead.

(When Musaf is to be offered, the service continues with
Kedushah on page 336)

UNETANEH TOKEF

Introductory Readings

We shall affirm the mighty holiness of this day, a day of awe and dread, for upon it is God's rule exalted, and the holy throne established in covenantal love.

> When we really begin a new year it is decided,
> And when we actually repent it is determined:

Who shall be truly alive,
And who shall merely exist;

> Who shall be tormented by the fire of ambition,
> And whose hopes shall be quenched by the waters of failure;

Who shall be pierced by the sharp sword of envy,
And who shall be torn by the wild beast of resentment;

> Who shall hunger for companionship,
> And who shall thirst for approval;

Who shall be shattered by storms of change,
And who shall be plagued by the pressures of conformity;

> Who shall be strangled by insecurity,
> And who shall be beaten into submission;

Who shall be content with their lot,
And who shall go wandering in search of satisfaction;

> Who shall be serene,
> And who shall be distraught.

But *Tshuvah, Tefillah* and *Tzedakah,*
Repentance, Prayer and Just Action,
Have the power to change
The character of our lives.

> Therefore let us repent, pray, and do right,
> So that this may be a genuinely new year of life.

*   *   *

On this Judgment Day, old legend relates,
Rabbi Amnon of Mainz, dying of the tortures of the
  eleventh century,
Saw God enthroned with the angelic host
Determining in the books of life and death
The verdict of everyone on earth.
His vision, Unetaneh Tokef, remains for us,
A reminder that the world is more awesome
Than our finite gallery of profane sights and ordinary
  thoughts,
It is a vaster realm of mystery and power
Which makes a claim upon our lives
And relates each one of us to spheres beyond our sight.

Unetaneh Tokef accounts with grim detail
The fires, floods, great storms, cruel swords
Whereby we each shall one day meet our death,
Yet also how our own repentance, prayer, and acts of
  human caring
Can mitigate the harshness of existence
And elevate survival to the plain of being human.

That there are powers far beyond ourselves reminds us
That because so much of life is not within our power,
Because nature and humanity can wreak such awful
  cruelty,
Just so must we struggle against all the cruelty we know,
And never cease within our prayers to demand
That the God who watched the tortures of Amnon of
  Mainz
And all the slaughters in the ages since his own
Bring quickly to an end the world's capacity for harm
And stir powerfully in the breasts of every creature
The repentance, prayer, and acts of human caring
That can make the vision of a God who metes out justice
A reality once more.

וּנְתַנֶּה תֹּקֶף קְדֻשַּׁת הַיּוֹם. כִּי הוּא נוֹרָא וְאָיוֹם. וּבוֹ
תִּנָּשֵׂא מַלְכוּתֶךָ. וְיִכּוֹן בְּחֶסֶד כִּסְאֶךָ. וְתֵשֵׁב עָלָיו

בֶּאֱמֶת. אֱמֶת כִּי אַתָּה הוּא דַיָּן וּמוֹכִיחַ וְיוֹדֵעַ וָעֵד.
וְכוֹתֵב וְחוֹתֵם וְסוֹפֵר וּמוֹנֶה. וְתִזְכֹּר כָּל־הַנִּשְׁכָּחוֹת.
וְתִפְתַּח אֶת־סֵפֶר הַזִּכְרוֹנוֹת. וּמֵאֵלָיו יִקָּרֵא. וְחוֹתָם
יַד כָּל־אָדָם בּוֹ.

Let us declare the holy power of this day, for it is awesome
and mighty. Your sovereignty is exalted upon it, and You
faithfully take Your place upon Your throne established in
love born of the covenant between You and ourselves. You
are the true judge and witness, You write and seal and
inscribe and take account. You remember all that we have
forgotten, opening the Book of Remembrance from which
everything is read and in which is recorded the seal of every
human being.

וּבְשׁוֹפָר גָּדוֹל יִתָּקַע. וְקוֹל דְּמָמָה דַקָּה יִשָּׁמַע.
וּמַלְאָכִים יֵחָפֵזוּן. וְחִיל וּרְעָדָה יֹאחֵזוּן. וְיֹאמְרוּ הִנֵּה
יוֹם הַדִּין. לִפְקֹד עַל צְבָא מָרוֹם בַּדִּין. כִּי לֹא יִזְכּוּ
בְעֵינֶיךָ בַּדִּין. וְכָל־בָּאֵי עוֹלָם יַעַבְרוּן לְפָנֶיךָ כִּבְנֵי
מָרוֹן: כְּבַקָּרַת רוֹעֶה עֶדְרוֹ. מַעֲבִיר צֹאנוֹ תַּחַת שִׁבְטוֹ.
כֵּן תַּעֲבִיר וְתִסְפֹּר וְתִמְנֶה. וְתִפְקֹד נֶפֶשׁ כָּל־חָי.
וְתַחְתֹּךְ קִצְבָה לְכָל־בְּרִיָּה. וְתִכְתּוֹב אֶת־גְּזַר דִּינָם:

The great Shofar is sounded, and a still small voice is
heard. The angels in heaven are dismayed and are seized
with fear and trembling, as they proclaim: "Behold the
Day of Judgment!" The hosts of heaven are to be
arraigned in judgment, for in Your eyes even they are not
free from guilt. All who live in the world pass today before
You, one by one, like a flock of sheep. As a shepherd
gathers the sheep and causes them to pass beneath the
staff, so You pass and record, count and visit, every living
soul, appointing the measure of every creature's life and
decreeing its destiny.

Refrain:
B'rosh hashanah yikateyvun uvyom tzom kippur yeychateymun
(On Rosh Hashanah it is written and on Yom Kippur it is
decided)

בְּרֹאשׁ הַשָּׁנָה יִכָּתֵבוּן. וּבְיוֹם צוֹם כִּפּוּר יֵחָתֵמוּן. כַּמָּה
יַעַבְרוּן. וְכַמָּה יִבָּרֵאוּן. מִי יִחְיֶה. וּמִי יָמוּת. מִי בְקִצּוֹ.
וּמִי לֹא בְקִצּוֹ. מִי בָאֵשׁ. וּמִי בַמַּיִם. מִי בַחֶרֶב. וּמִי
בַחַיָּה. מִי בָרָעָב. וּמִי בַצָּמָא. מִי בָרַעַשׁ. וּמִי בַמַּגֵּפָה.
מִי בַחֲנִיקָה וּמִי בַסְּקִילָה. מִי יָנוּחַ. וּמִי יָנוּעַ. מִי יִשָּׁקֵט.
וּמִי יִטָּרֵף. מִי יִשָּׁלֵו. וּמִי יִתְיַסָּר. מִי יֵעָנִי. וּמִי יֵעָשֵׁר.
מִי יִשָּׁפֵל. וּמִי יָרוּם:

וּתְשׁוּבָה וּתְפִלָּה וּצְדָקָה
מַעֲבִירִין אֶת־רֹעַ הַגְּזֵרָה:

On Rosh Hashanah is written and on Yom Kippur is
decided how many shall pass on and how many be created,
who shall live and who shall die, who when their time
comes and who before or after their time, who by fire and
who by water, who by the sword and who by wild beasts,
who by famine and who by drought, who by earthquake
and who by epidemic, who by strangling and who by stoning; who shall have rest and who can never be still, who
shall be serene and who torn apart, who shall be at ease
and who afflicted, who shall be impoverished and who
enriched, who shall be brought low and who raised high.
But tshuvah, prayer, and charitable acts avert the severity
of the decree.

Kedusha

נַעֲרִיצְךָ וְנַקְדִּישְׁךָ כְּסוֹד שִׂיחַ שַׂרְפֵי קֹדֶשׁ הַמַּקְדִּישִׁים
שִׁמְךָ בַּקֹּדֶשׁ, כַּכָּתוּב עַל־יַד נְבִיאֶךָ וְקָרָא זֶה אֶל זֶה
וְאָמַר.

In the secret sounds of Seraphim we sing of Your sanctity,
as it is written in Isaiah: "And each called to the other
saying:

קָדוֹשׁ קָדוֹשׁ קָדוֹשׁ יְיָ צְבָאוֹת. מְלֹא כָל־הָאָרֶץ
כְּבוֹדוֹ:

*Kadosh Kadosh Kadosh Adonay Tzvaot, mlo chol ha-aretz
kvodo:*

Holy! Holy! Holy! is the Commander of the Hosts,
The fullness of all the earth is God's Glory."

כְּבוֹדוֹ מָלֵא עוֹלָם, מְשָׁרְתָיו שׁוֹאֲלִים זֶה לָזֶה אַיֵּה
מְקוֹם כְּבוֹדוֹ, לְעֻמָּתָם בָּרוּךְ יֹאמֵרוּ—

Your glory fills the world! Those who watch over it ask
each other: "Where is the place of God's glory?" And they
all reply, "Baruch—"

בָּרוּךְ כְּבוֹד יְיָ מִמְּקוֹמוֹ.

Baruch kvod Adonay mimkomo:

Praised be the Glory of Adonay from God's Place, the
World.

מִמְּקוֹמוֹ הוּא יִפֶן בְּרַחֲמִים, וְיָחֹן עַם הַמְיַחֲדִים שְׁמוֹ
עֶרֶב וָבֹקֶר, בְּכָל יוֹם תָּמִיד , פַּעֲמַיִם בְּאַהֲבָה שְׁמַע
אוֹמְרִים:

From that place, may You turn in compassion and grace to
the people who declare Your Oneness evening and morning every day, as in love they proclaim, "Sh'ma—"

שְׁמַע יִשְׂרָאֵל, יְיָ אֱלֹהֵינוּ, יְיָ אֶחָד.

Sh'ma Yisrael Adonay Eloheynu Adonay Echad:

Hear, Israel, Adonay is our God, Adonay is One.

הוּא אֱלֹהֵינוּ, הוּא אָבִינוּ, הוּא מַלְכֵּנוּ, הוּא מוֹשִׁיעֵנוּ,
וְהוּא יַשְׁמִיעֵנוּ בְּרַחֲמָיו שֵׁנִית לְעֵינֵי כָּל חָי; לִהְיוֹת
לָכֶם לֵאלֹהִים—

You are our God, our Nurturer, our Sovereign, our
Deliverer. In Your mercy may You once again cause every
living being to hear Your words:

אֲנִי יְיָ אֱלֹהֵיכֶם.

Ani Adonay Eloheychem:

I, Adonay, am Your God.

אַדִּיר אַדִּירֵנוּ, יְיָ אֲדֹנֵינוּ, מָה אַדִּיר שִׁמְךָ בְּכָל הָאָרֶץ.
וְהָיָה יְיָ לְמֶלֶךְ עַל כָּל הָאָרֶץ, בַּיּוֹם הַהוּא יִהְיֶה יְיָ
אֶחָד וּשְׁמוֹ אֶחָד.

וּבְדִבְרֵי קָדְשְׁךָ כָּתוּב לֵאמֹר:

Excellency, our Excellency, Adonay, Source of everything we
are, how excellent is Your Name in all the earth! Adonay will
reign as sovereign throughout all the earth, and on that day You
will be the only One, Your Name the only One!

In the holy words of Psalms it is written:

יִמְלֹךְ יְיָ לְעוֹלָם. אֱלֹהַיִךְ צִיּוֹן לְדֹר וָדֹר. הַלְלוּיָהּ:

Yimloch Adonay l'olam, Elohayich tziyon, ldor vador halleluya!

Adonay will reign forever, your God will reign, O Zion, to
all generations. Praise God!

לְדוֹר וָדוֹר נַגִּיד גָּדְלֶךָ. וּלְנֵצַח נְצָחִים קְדֻשָּׁתְךָ נַקְדִּישׁ.
וְשִׁבְחֲךָ אֱלֹהֵינוּ מִפִּינוּ לֹא יָמוּשׁ לְעוֹלָם וָעֶד. כִּי אֵל
מֶלֶךְ גָּדוֹל וְקָדוֹשׁ אָתָּה:

We shall tell our children of Your greatness, and they will
tell our grandchildren. In every generation till eternity we
shall proclaim Your holiness. Our lips shall never abandon
Your praise, for Your majesty is great and holy.

On Fear and Awe: Reflections on the Uvchen

If we could only look at the world not with fears of other
people, but with awe of God! If we could only refrain from com-
paring ourselves with others, and realize instead that each of us
is an absolutely unique model of the image of God, each pos-
sessing a remarkable blend of knowledge, goodness, strength,

attractiveness—shared by no other human being! Then we
could appreciate others' strengths, not as competition but as
complements to our own . . . as a solitary bird, winging its way
across a majestic canyon, is not dwarfed by the expanse, but
harmonizes with the great quiet. Such a canyon, resplendent in
its myriad shapes and hues, is the human race we
live among; such a bird is each of us, whose unique and soaring
song can show those silent crags how wondrous is God's awe: it
fills the world.

Uvchen (Awe)

וּבְכֵן תֵּן פַּחְדְּךָ יְיָ אֱלֹהֵינוּ עַל כָּל מַעֲשֶׂיךָ וְאֵימָתְךָ עַל
כָּל מַה שֶׁבָּרָאתָ. וְיִירָאוּךָ כָּל הַמַּעֲשִׂים וְיִשְׁתַּחֲווּ
לְפָנֶיךָ כָּל הַבְּרוּאִים. וְיֵעָשׂוּ כֻלָּם אֲגֻדָּה אַחַת לַעֲשׂוֹת
רְצוֹנְךָ בְּלֵבָב שָׁלֵם. כְּמוֹ שֶׁיָּדַעְנוּ יְיָ אֱלֹהֵינוּ שֶׁהַשִּׁלְטוֹן
לְפָנֶיךָ עֹז בְּיָדְךָ וּגְבוּרָה בִּימִינֶךָ וְשִׁמְךָ נוֹרָא עַל כָּל
מַה שֶׁבָּרָאתָ:

May all Your creatures be filled with awe for You and may
all the peoples of the earth accept Your rule. May they
unite together in one harmonious assembly to act according to Your will.

וּבְכֵן תֵּן כָּבוֹד יְיָ לְעַמֶּךָ תְּהִלָּה לִירֵאֶיךָ וְתִקְוָה
לְדוֹרְשֶׁיךָ וּפִתְחוֹן פֶּה לַמְיַחֲלִים לָךְ. שִׂמְחָה לְאַרְצֶךָ
וְשָׂשׂוֹן לְעִירֶךָ וּצְמִיחַת קֶרֶן לְדָוִד עַבְדֶּךָ וַעֲרִיכַת נֵר
לְבֶן־יִשַׁי מְשִׁיחֶךָ בִּמְהֵרָה בְיָמֵינוּ:

Grant glory to Your people Israel, joy to its land, gladness
to Jerusalem. May those who stand in awe of You know
hope and confidence, fulfillment and salvation.

וּבְכֵן צַדִּיקִים יִרְאוּ וְיִשְׂמָחוּ וִישָׁרִים יַעֲלֹזוּ וַחֲסִידִים
בְּרִנָּה יָגִילוּ. וְעוֹלָתָה תִּקְפָּץ־פִּיהָ וְכָל־הָרִשְׁעָה כֻּלָּהּ
כְּעָשָׁן תִּכְלֶה כִּי תַעֲבִיר מֶמְשֶׁלֶת זָדוֹן מִן הָאָרֶץ:

Bring near the day, O God, when good people will have
reason to be glad, when suffering will be turned to song
and tyranny shall vanish like smoke.

Ya'aleh V'yavo: For the Ascent of Our Prayers

אֱלֹהֵינוּ וֵאלֹהֵי אֲבוֹתֵינוּ (וֵאלֹהֵי אִמּוֹתֵינוּ) יַעֲלֶה וְיָבֹא
וְיַגִּיעַ וְיֵרָאֶה וְיֵרָצֶה וְיִשָּׁמַע וְיִפָּקֵד וְיִזָּכֵר זִכְרוֹנֵנוּ
וּפִקְדוֹנֵנוּ וְזִכְרוֹן אֲבוֹתֵינוּ (וְזִכְרוֹן אִמּוֹתֵינוּ) וְזִכְרוֹן
מָשִׁיחַ בֶּן־דָּוִד עַבְדֶּךָ וְזִכְרוֹן יְרוּשָׁלַיִם עִיר קָדְשֶׁךָ
וְזִכְרוֹן כָּל עַמְּךָ בֵּית יִשְׂרָאֵל לְפָנֶיךָ. לִפְלֵיטָה וּלְטוֹבָה
לְחֵן וּלְחֶסֶד וּלְרַחֲמִים לְחַיִּים וּלְשָׁלוֹם בְּיוֹם הַכִּפֻּרִים
הַזֶּה. זָכְרֵנוּ יְיָ אֱלֹהֵינוּ בּוֹ לְטוֹבָה. וּפָקְדֵנוּ בוֹ לִבְרָכָה.
וְהוֹשִׁיעֵנוּ בוֹ לְחַיִּים: וּבִדְבַר יְשׁוּעָה וְרַחֲמִים חוּס
וְחָנֵּנוּ וְרַחֵם עָלֵינוּ וְהוֹשִׁיעֵנוּ כִּי אֵלֶיךָ עֵינֵינוּ. כִּי אֵל
מֶלֶךְ חַנּוּן וְרַחוּם אָתָּה:

Our God and God of our fathers and mothers, remember
them on this Yom Kippur and be gracious to us all. Look
with compassion upon the people standing in Your
presence praying for the days of Messiah and for Jerusalem Your holy city. Grant us life, well-being, lovingkindness and peace. Bless us, Adonay our God, with all that is
good. Remember Your promise of mercy and redemption.
Be merciful to us and save us, for we place our hope in
You, gracious and merciful God, our Sovereign.

*   *   *

Forgive us, Source of all forgiving mothers' love,
For all those mitzvot and deeds beyond mitzvot
Whose purposes we know we have transgressed,
And those we have transgressed unawares.
Today we shall again confess to those we know
But those that are unknown to us are known to You.

Perhaps not all those mitzvot our people have preserved
Have come from You,
Perhaps not all those mitzvot our people have preserved
Are compatible one with the other,
We may believe that some demands should be added
To the mitzvot our people have preserved.
We know our beliefs may be wrong,
And we pray You will forgive those erring judgments
Made with honest seeking, careful thought,
And the fearsome knowledge
That our judgments fall always short of the ideal.
Yet honor our seeking
You seeker after human hearts
And help us never to leave off our search
Within the Torah human beings have preserved
To find the Torah with which You alone
Created the world
And intended it should be governed.

Bring near that time
When Israel's Torah and Yours will be the same,
And forgive us the hope
That what we have found and lost and sought throughout
     the centuries
May become a part of Your Torah,
As losing You and finding You
Is part of ours.

*   *   *

My God,
Before I was formed I was as nothing.
As I consider all the selfish, thoughtless acts
I have performed
It is as though I were as nothing now,

So short have I fallen
Of the person I would like to be.
I am as dust
Even though I am alive.
Saying this in front of You
Fills me with shame.

May it be Your will
That I do no selfish act again.
May it be Your will
That I do no thoughtless act again.

Like all human beings,
I shall probably repeat those acts.
Yet I should like to believe
That I could overcome them.

As I have been strong enough
To confess my errors in front of You
So may You now help me
In my resolve for better deeds,
To feel forgiven,
To feel the special worth of my life.

Help me to feel that I can become
The person I was formed to be.

May the words of my mouth,
These difficult and painful words,
Be acceptable in front of You,
My Rock,
My Redeemer.

Silent Reflection

Shma Koleynu

שְׁמַע קוֹלֵנוּ יְיָ אֱלֹהֵינוּ חוּס וְרַחֵם עָלֵינוּ וְקַבֵּל
בְּרַחֲמִים וּבְרָצוֹן אֶת־תְּפִלָּתֵנוּ:
הֲשִׁיבֵנוּ יְיָ אֵלֶיךָ וְנָשׁוּבָה חַדֵּשׁ יָמֵינוּ כְּקֶדֶם:
אַל־תַּשְׁלִיכֵנוּ מִלְּפָנֶיךָ וְרוּחַ קָדְשְׁךָ אַל־תִּקַּח מִמֶּנּוּ:

אַל־תַּשְׁלִיכֵנוּ לְעֵת זִקְנָה כִּכְלוֹת כֹּחֵנוּ אַל־תַּעַזְבֵנוּ:
אַל־תַּעַזְבֵנוּ יְיָ אֱלֹהֵינוּ אַל־תִּרְחַק מִמֶּנּוּ:

Behind our very different lives
There is one voice today:
Spare us, show us compassion.
Accept as one lone impassioned prayer
All the divers thoughts that fill this room.
Bring us closer to Your presence
Make our days as fresh, as new, as in our youngest years.
Help us drink so deeply of our life
That we may never feel cast out from You,
Aware always of the holiness which seasons our days
Of the youthfulness which we possess
Whatever the number of our years,
And when our strength ebbs finally away
May You embrace us with Your own.

אֱלֹהֵינוּ וֵאלֹהֵי אֲבוֹתֵינוּ (וֵאלֹהֵי אִמּוֹתֵינוּ) סְלַח־לָנוּ.
מְחַל־לָנוּ. כַּפֶּר־לָנוּ:

Our God and God of our people—forgive us, pardon us,
grant us atonement.

Ki Anu Amecha

כִּי אָנוּ עַמֶּךָ וְאַתָּה אֱלֹהֵינוּ.   אָנוּ בָנֶיךָ וְאַתָּה אָבִינוּ:
אָנוּ עֲבָדֶיךָ וְאַתָּה אֲדוֹנֵנוּ.   אָנוּ קְהָלֶךָ וְאַתָּה חֶלְקֵנוּ:
אָנוּ נַחֲלָתֶךָ וְאַתָּה גוֹרָלֵנוּ.   אָנוּ צֹאנֶךָ וְאַתָּה רוֹעֵנוּ:
אָנוּ כַרְמֶךָ וְאַתָּה נוֹטְרֵנוּ.   אָנוּ פְעֻלָּתֶךָ וְאַתָּה יוֹצְרֵנוּ:
אָנוּ רַעְיָתֶךָ וְאַתָּה דוֹדֵנוּ.   אָנוּ סְגֻלָּתֶךָ וְאַתָּה קְרוֹבֵנוּ.
אָנוּ עַמֶּךָ וְאַתָּה מַלְכֵּנוּ.   אָנוּ מַאֲמִירֶיךָ וְאַתָּה מַאֲמִירֵנוּ:

Ki anu amecha v'attah Eloheynu,
anu vanecha v'atta avinu.

Anu avadecha v'atta Adoneynu,
anu k'halecha v'atta chelkeynu.

Anu nach-alatecha v'atta goraleynu,
Anu tzonecha v'atta ro-eynu.

Anu charmecha v'atta notreynu,
Anu f'ulatecha v'atta yotzreynu.

Anu ra'yatecha v'atta dodeynu,
Anu s'gulatecha v'atta k'roveynu.

Anu amecha v'atta malkeynu,
Anu ma-amirecha v'atta ma'amireynu.

For we are Your people, and You our God.
We are Your children, and You the One who gave us life.
We are Your servants, and You the One who acquires us.
We are Your congregation, and You our only One.
We are Your heritage, and You our Destiny.
We are Your flock, and You our Shepherd.
We are Your vineyard, and You our Protector.
We are Your creatures, and You our Creator.
We are Your companion, and You our Beloved.
We are Your treasure, and You the intimate who redeems us.
We are Your people, and You our Sovereign.
We have chosen You, and You have chosen us.

Rtzey: Acceptance of Our Prayer (Traditional Version)

רְצֵה יְיָ אֱלֹהֵינוּ בְּעַמְּךָ יִשְׂרָאֵל וּבִתְפִלָּתָם. וְהָשֵׁב אֶת
הָעֲבוֹדָה לִדְבִיר בֵּיתֶךָ וְאִשֵּׁי יִשְׂרָאֵל וּתְפִלָּתָם
בְּאַהֲבָה תְקַבֵּל בְּרָצוֹן. וּתְהִי לְרָצוֹן תָּמִיד עֲבוֹדַת
יִשְׂרָאֵל עַמֶּךָ. וְתֶחֱזֶינָה עֵינֵינוּ בְּשׁוּבְךָ לְצִיּוֹן בְּרַחֲמִים.
בָּרוּךְ אַתָּה יְיָ הַמַּחֲזִיר שְׁכִינָתוֹ לְצִיּוֹן:

Rtzey (Reform Version)

רְצֵה יְיָ אֱלֹהֵינוּ בְּעַמְּךָ יִשְׂרָאֵל, וּתְפִלָּתָם בְּאַהֲבָה
תְקַבֵּל, וּתְהִי לְרָצוֹן תָּמִיד עֲבוֹדַת יִשְׂרָאֵל עַמֶּךָ. אֵל
קָרוֹב לְכָל־קֹרְאָיו, פְּנֵה אֶל עֲבָדֶיךָ וְחָנֵּנוּ; שְׁפוֹךְ
רוּחֲךָ עָלֵינוּ, וְתֶחֱזֶינָה עֵינֵינוּ בְּשׁוּבְךָ לְצִיּוֹן בְּרַחֲמִים.
בָּרוּךְ אַתָּה יְיָ הַמַּחֲזִיר שְׁכִינָתוֹ לְצִיּוֹן:

Accept us, Your people, Adonay our God.
Help us fashion the service You desire.
Receive our prayers as though they ascended from the fire
  on the ancient altar,
Speed the descent of Your compassionate presence
To Zion,
To us.

Restorer of holy intimacy to Zion,
You are praised.

Modim: Thanks to God

מוֹדִים אֲנַחְנוּ לָךְ שָׁאַתָּה הוּא יְיָ אֱלֹהֵינוּ וֵאלֹהֵי
אֲבוֹתֵינוּ (וֵאלֹהֵי אִמּוֹתֵינוּ) לְעוֹלָם וָעֶד. צוּר חַיֵּינוּ
מָגֵן יִשְׁעֵנוּ אַתָּה הוּא לְדוֹר וָדוֹר. נוֹדֶה לְּךָ וּנְסַפֵּר
תְּהִלָּתֶךָ עַל חַיֵּינוּ הַמְּסוּרִים בְּיָדֶךָ וְעַל נִשְׁמוֹתֵינוּ
הַפְּקוּדוֹת לָךְ וְעַל נִסֶּיךָ שֶׁבְּכָל־יוֹם עִמָּנוּ וְעַל
נִפְלְאוֹתֶיךָ וְטוֹבוֹתֶיךָ שֶׁבְּכָל־עֵת עֶרֶב וָבֹקֶר וְצָהֳרָיִם.
הַטּוֹב כִּי לֹא כָלוּ רַחֲמֶיךָ וְהַמְרַחֵם כִּי לֹא
תַמּוּ חֲסָדֶיךָ מֵעוֹלָם קִוִּינוּ לָךְ:

וְעַל כֻּלָּם יִתְבָּרַךְ וְיִתְרוֹמַם שִׁמְךָ מַלְכֵּנוּ תָּמִיד לְעוֹלָם
וָעֶד:

וּכְתֹב לְחַיִּים טוֹבִים כָּל־בְּנֵי בְרִיתֶךָ:

וְכֹל הַחַיִּים יוֹדוּךָ סֶּלָה וִיהַלְלוּ אֶת שִׁמְךָ בֶּאֱמֶת הָאֵל
יְשׁוּעָתֵנוּ וְעֶזְרָתֵנוּ סֶלָה. בָּרוּךְ אַתָּה יְיָ הַטּוֹב שִׁמְךָ
וּלְךָ נָאֶה לְהוֹדוֹת:

Thank You.

For
We are not alone,
We are not abandoned in the world.
We are persons,

And so there must exist within the universe
An acknowledgement of persons,
A personal presence
We acknowledge as Adonay.

We can feel secure here
Protected
Each one of our imperfect lives
Reveals an irreplaceable piece of a holy world.

Our lives, complex, are Your caress
Our souls, beclouded, are Your intimates
Miracles surround us
Every minute of an ordinary day,
At every corner of a troubled night
Are signs of You.

In You we find perfect motherlove and fathercaring
Which help us to accept
Our own parents' imperfections
And irreplaceable humanity.

Inscribe all the members of Your covenant
For a good life,
For all life
Its beauty, ugliness, tragedy, delight,
Is the truth of Your existence
And its goodness.
Thank You for it all.

For it all.

Sim Shalom: Peace

שִׂים שָׁלוֹם טוֹבָה וּבְרָכָה חֵן וָחֶסֶד וְרַחֲמִים עָלֵינוּ וְעַל
כָּל־יִשְׂרָאֵל עַמֶּךָ. בָּרְכֵנוּ אָבִינוּ כֻּלָּנוּ כְּאֶחָד בְּאוֹר
פָּנֶיךָ. כִּי בְאוֹר פָּנֶיךָ נָתַתָּ לָּנוּ יְיָ אֱלֹהֵינוּ תּוֹרַת חַיִּים
וְאַהֲבַת חֶסֶד וּצְדָקָה וּבְרָכָה וְרַחֲמִים וְחַיִּים וְשָׁלוֹם.
וְטוֹב בְּעֵינֶיךָ לְבָרֵךְ אֶת־עַמְּךָ יִשְׂרָאֵל בְּכָל־עֵת וּבְכָל־
שָׁעָה בִּשְׁלוֹמֶךָ.

בְּסֵפֶר חַיִּים בְּרָכָה וְשָׁלוֹם וּפַרְנָסָה טוֹבָה נִזָּכֵר
וְנִכָּתֵב לְפָנֶיךָ אֲנַחְנוּ וְכָל עַמְּךָ בֵּית יִשְׂרָאֵל לְחַיִּים
טוֹבִים וּלְשָׁלוֹם. בָּרוּךְ אַתָּה יְיָ עֹשֶׂה הַשָּׁלוֹם:

We have chosen to be guided by a way which is divine, and
we have been chosen within the divine plan to help make
that way a reality. Through a world of evil actions, cruelty,
and death, we must seek a path of hopefulness and caring
that will open upon a world of just acts, compassion,
and peace. The psalms remind us that we must seek peace
and pursue it; we cannot be content merely to make peace
in our own household, but rather go forth to work for
peace wherever people struggle in its cause.

May we the House of Israel and all the peoples of the earth
be remembered in the book of life, blessing, sustenance,
and peace.

Praised are You, Adonay, source of peace.

יְבָרֶכְךָ יְיָ וְיִשְׁמְרֶךָ:

May Adonay bless you and keep you.

יָאֵר יְיָ פָּנָיו אֵלֶיךָ וִיחֻנֶּךָ:

May Adonay cast over you the
radiance of the divine face
in all its fullness and grace.

יִשָּׂא יְיָ פָּנָיו אֵלֶיךָ וְיָשֵׂם לְךָ שָׁלוֹם:

May Adonay raise up the face of
the divine before your face,
and establish peace for you,
your families, and all the world.

CONFESSION

Preparation

אֱלֹהֵינוּ וֵאלֹהֵי אֲבוֹתֵינוּ (וֵאלֹהֵי אִמוֹתֵינוּ), תָּבֹא
לְפָנֶיךָ תְּפִלָּתֵנוּ, וְאַל תִּתְעַלַּם מִתְּחִנָּתֵנוּ; שֶׁאֵין
אֲנַחְנוּ עַזֵּי פָנִים וּקְשֵׁי עֹרֶף לוֹמַר לְפָנֶיךָ, יְיָ אֱלֹהֵינוּ
וֵאלֹהֵי אֲבוֹתֵינוּ, צַדִּיקִים אֲנַחְנוּ וְלֹא חָטָאנוּ; אֲבָל
אֲנַחְנוּ חָטָאנוּ.

God of those who sought You out in ages past
Let our prayer also come before You
And do not turn aside from our entreaty.
For we are not so obstinate and stubborn
As to say before You:
We are righteous, we have done no wrong.
For indeed, we have done wrong,
And we join now in confession before You.

* * *

Ashamnu: An Alphabet of Wrongdoing

Of these things we have been guilty: we have Acted out of
malice; we have Back-bitten; we have been Contemptuous
of others; we have Double-crossed; we have given Evil
advice; we have Falsified the truth; we have Gloated over
our achievements; we have Hated wrong-doers; we have
been Insolent; we have Jeered convictions not our own; we
have Knifed friends in the back; we have Lost our self-
control; we have Manipulated; we have Nullified the
humanity of others; we have Oppressed our brothers and
sisters; we have told Petty lies; we have Quietly acquiesced
in wrong; we have Refused to back down from positions
we could see were incorrect; we have Sneered at serious
matters; we have Trifled with other humans; we have

Usurped others' positions; we have practiced Violence; we
have supported War by our lack of long-term commit-
ments; we have committed X-number of sins of which we
have not been aware; we have said Yes when we should
have cried out no; we have lacked the Zeal to struggle for
our convictions through unrewarding months and years.

אָשַׁמְנוּ. בָּגַדְנוּ. גָּזַלְנוּ. דִּבַּרְנוּ דְפִי. הֶעֱוִינוּ. וְהִרְשַׁעְנוּ.
זַדְנוּ. חָמַסְנוּ. טָפַלְנוּ שֶׁקֶר. יָעַצְנוּ רָע. כִּזַּבְנוּ. לַצְנוּ.
מָרַדְנוּ. נִאַצְנוּ. סָרַרְנוּ. עָוִינוּ. פָּשַׁעְנוּ. צָרַרְנוּ. קִשִּׁינוּ
עֹרֶף. רָשַׁעְנוּ. שִׁחַתְנוּ. תִּעַבְנוּ. תָּעִינוּ. תִּעְתָּעְנוּ:

Ashamnu, bagadnu, gazalnu, dibarnu dofi, he-evinu,
V'hirshanu, zadnu, chamasnu, tafalnu sheker, ya-atznu ra,
Kizavnu, latznu, maradnu, ni-atznu, sararnu, avinu, pashanu.
Tzararnu, kishinu oref, rashanu, shichatnu, ti-avnu, ta-inu,
Ti'ta'nu.

סַרְנוּ מִמִּצְוֹתֶיךָ וּמִמִּשְׁפָּטֶיךָ הַטּוֹבִים, וְלֹא שָׁוָה לָנוּ.
וְאַתָּה צַדִּיק עַל כָּל הַבָּא עָלֵינוּ, כִּי אֱמֶת עָשִׂיתָ
וַאֲנַחְנוּ הִרְשָׁעְנוּ. מַה נֹּאמַר לְפָנֶיךָ יוֹשֵׁב מָרוֹם, וּמַה
נְּסַפֵּר לְפָנֶיךָ שׁוֹכֵן שְׁחָקִים הֲלֹא כָּל הַנִּסְתָּרוֹת
וְהַנִּגְלוֹת אַתָּה יוֹדֵעַ.

We have turned aside from Your mitzvot
From Your laws which point us toward the good,
And no good has come to us from our misdeeds.
Yet You do justly with everyone who comes before You,
For You have acted out of truth, while we have too often acted
    falsely.
What shall we say before You who dwells in the heights,
What stories can we tell to You who dwells in heaven?
Do You not already know all that we reveal and all that we
    have tried to hide?

אַתָּה יוֹדֵעַ רָזֵי עוֹלָם, וְתַעֲלוּמוֹת סִתְרֵי כָל חָי. אַתָּה
חוֹפֵשׂ כָּל חַדְרֵי בָטֶן, וּבוֹחֵן כְּלָיוֹת וָלֵב. אֵין דָּבָר

נֶעְלָם מִמֶּךָ, וְאֵין נִסְתָּר מִנֶּגֶד עֵינֶיךָ. וּבְכֵן יְהִי רָצוֹן
מִלְּפָנֶיךָ, יְיָ אֱלֹהֵינוּ וֵאלֹהֵי אֲבוֹתֵינוּ (וֵאלֹהֵי
אִמּוֹתֵינוּ), שֶׁתִּסְלַח לָנוּ עַל כָּל חַטֹּאתֵינוּ, וְתִמְחַל לָנוּ
עַל כָּל עֲווֹנוֹתֵינוּ, וּתְכַפֶּר־לָנוּ עַל כָּל פְּשָׁעֵינוּ.

Indeed, You know the mysteries of the universe,
And the best kept secrets of every living thing.
You search out the innermost rooms of our life,
With care You examine all our feelings, all our thoughts.
Not one thing is hidden from You, nothing escapes Your gaze.
God who preserves the memory of all our ancestors,
If You would only wipe away the memory of all our wrongs
And grant atonement for all our sins.

Al Cheyt: The Great Confession

עַל חֵטְא שֶׁחָטָאנוּ לְפָנֶיךָ בְּאֹנֶס וּבְרָצוֹן.
וְעַל חֵטְא שֶׁחָטָאנוּ לְפָנֶיךָ בְּאִמּוּץ הַלֵּב:
עַל חֵטְא שֶׁחָטָאנוּ לְפָנֶיךָ בִּבְלִי דָעַת.

For the wrong we did before You under coercion or of our
own free will,
And for the wrong we did before You by hardening our
hearts.

For the wrong we did before You unintentionally;
And for the wrong we did before You through idle talk and
meaningless resolutions.

For the wrong we did before You by using sex exploitatively;
And for the wrong we did before You in public and in
private.

For the wrong we did before You knowingly and deceptively;
And for the wrong we did before You by offensive language.

For the wrong we did before You by oppressing another
person;
And for the wrong we did before You by malicious
thoughts.

For the wrong we did before You by promiscuity,
And for the wrong we did before You by confessing insincerely.

For the wrong we did before You by contempt for parents
and teachers;
And for the wrong we did before You by violence.

For the wrong we did before You by failing to be true to
our heritage, thus defaming Your Name in the world;
And for the wrong we did before You by unbridled
passion.

וְעַל כֻּלָּם, אֱלוֹהַּ סְלִיחוֹת, סְלַח לָנוּ, מְחַל לָנוּ, כַּפֶּר־
לָנוּ.

V'al kulam, Eloah slichot, s'lach lanu, m'chal lanu, kapper lanu.

For all our wrongs, God of forgiveness, forgive us, wipe
the slate clean, grant us atonement.

עַל חֵטְא שֶׁחָטָאנוּ לְפָנֶיךָ בְּכַחַשׁ וּבְכָזָב.
וְעַל חֵטְא שֶׁחָטָאנוּ לְפָנֶיךָ בְּכַפַּת שֹׁחַד:
עַל חֵטְא שֶׁחָטָאנוּ לְפָנֶיךָ בְּלָצוֹן.

For the wrong we did before You by lying and deceiving,
And for the wrong we did before You by accepting bribes.

For the wrong we did before You by scoffing and mocking,
And for the wrong we did before You by speaking ill of
other people.

For the wrong we did before You in our work,
And for the wrong we did before You in the foods we eat
and the amount we drink.

For the wrong we did before You by refusing to be
generous,
And for the wrong we did before you by being proud and
haughty.

For the wrong we did before You in rejecting Your
authority,
And for the wrong we did before You in making harsh
judgments on other people.

וְעַל כֻּלָּם, אֱלוֹהַ סְלִיחוֹת, סְלַח לָנוּ, מְחַל לָנוּ, כַּפֶּר־
לָנוּ.

V'al kulam, Eloah s'lichot, s'lach lanu, m'chal lanu, kapper lanu.

For all these wrongs, O God of forgiveness, forgive us,
wipe the slate clean, grant us atonement.

עַל חֵטְא שֶׁחָטָאנוּ לְפָנֶיךָ בִּצְדִיַּת רֶעַ.
וְעַל חֵטְא שֶׁחָטָאנוּ לְפָנֶיךָ בְּצָרוּת עָיִן:
עַל חֵטְא שֶׁחָטָאנוּ לְפָנֶיךָ בְּקַלּוּת רֹאשׁ.

For the wrong we did before You by plotting against
others,
And for the wrong we did before You by tormenting
others.

For the wrong we did before You by dismissing serious
matters with a joke,
And for the wrong we did before You by being obstinate.

For the wrong we did before You by running to do evil,
And for the wrong we did before You by gossiping.

For the wrong we did before You by swearing falsely,
And for the wrong we did before You by hating others
without cause.

For the wrong we did before You by betraying a trust,
And for the wrong we did before You out of confusion,
unaware of the significance of our actions.

וְעַל כֻּלָּם, אֱלוֹהַ סְלִיחוֹת, סְלַח לָנוּ, מְחַל לָנוּ, כַּפֶּר־
לָנוּ.

V'al kulam, Eloah s'lichot, s'lach lanu, m'chal lanu, kapper lanu.

For all these wrongs, O God of forgiveness, forgive us,
  wipe the slate clean, grant us atonement.

An Alternative Al Cheyt

For the wrong we did before You by listening to voices at
  odds with what we knew was right;
For the wrong we did before You by not listening to voices
  telling us unpleasant truths;
For the wrong we did before You by closing our ears to the
  poor and the hungry;
For the wrong we did before You by not working at rela-
  tionships;
For the wrong we did before You by making no time for
  those who needed us;
For the wrong we did before You by abusing our health;
For the wrong we did before You by giving in to illegiti-
  mate pressure;
For the wrong we did before You by unnecessary anger;
For the wrong we did before You by giving in to bullies;
For the wrong we did before You by talking of others' fail-
  ings behind their backs instead of face to face;

וְעַל כֻּלָּם, אֱלוֹהַ סְלִיחוֹת, סְלַח לָנוּ, מְחַל לָנוּ, כַּפֶּר־
לָנוּ.

V'al kulam Eloah s'lichot, s'lach lanu, m'chal lanu, kapper lanu.

For all these wrongs, O God of forgiveness, forgive us,
  wipe the slate clean, grant us atonement.

For the wrong we did before You by insensitivity to the
  plight of Jews in oppressive countries;
For the wrong we did before You by forgiving in Jews what
  we condemn in others;

For the wrong we did before You by forgiving in others
  what we condemn in Jews;

For the wrong we did before You by taking Israel for
  granted;

For the wrong we did before You by polluting our environ-
  ment;

For the wrong we did before You by cutting ourselves off
  from people of other races and cultures;

For the wrong we did before You by being afraid of others'
  disabilities;

For the wrong we did before You by ignoring our own
  weaknesses;

For the wrong we did before You by callous treatment of
  those with whom we live;

For the wrong we did before You by callous treatment of
  those with whom we work or study;

For the wrong we did before You by disrespect for those
  older or younger than ourselves;

For the wrong we did before You by ignoring the sensitivi-
  ties of children;

וְעַל כֻּלָּם, אֱלוֹהַּ סְלִיחוֹת, סְלַח לָנוּ, מְחַל לָנוּ, כַּפֶּר־
לָנוּ.

V'al kulam Eloah s'lichot, s'lach lanu, m'chal lanu, kapper lanu.

For all these wrongs, O God of forgiveness, forgive us,
  wipe the slate clean, grant us atonement.

For the wrong we did before You by ignoring the ever-
  present threat of war;

For the wrong we did before You by blinding our eyes to
  the danger of nuclear arms;

For the wrong we did before You by punishing others for
  lacks we see in ourselves;

For the wrong we did before You by bearing grudges;

For the wrong we did before You by indulging in excessive
  luxuries;

For the wrong we did before You by giving less tzedakah
  than we could afford;

For the wrong we did before You by manipulating others
for our own gain;

For the wrong we did before You by manipulating others'
feelings for our own well-being;

For the wrong we did before You by making those we love
feel guilty;

For the wrong we did before You by ignoring important
issues in our own community and country;

For the wrong we did before You by being ashamed to act
morally in public;

For the wrong we did before You by preventing others
from showing their own strengths;

וְעַל כֻּלָּם, אֱלוֹהַ סְלִיחוֹת, סְלַח לָנוּ, מְחַל לָנוּ, כַּפֶּר־
לָנוּ.

V'al kulam Eloah s'lichot, s'lach lanu, m'chal lanu, kapper lanu.

For all these wrongs, O God of forgiveness, forgive us,
wipe the slate clean, grant us atonement.

Avinu Malkeynu: Our Forgiving Parent, Our Sovereign

אָבִינוּ מַלְכֵּנוּ חָטָאנוּ לְפָנֶיךָ:

Avinu Malkeynu, we have done wrong before You.

אָבִינוּ מַלְכֵּנוּ אֵין לָנוּ מֶלֶךְ אֶלָּא אָתָּה:

Avinu Malkeynu, we have no Sovereign except You.

אָבִינוּ מַלְכֵּנוּ חַדֵּשׁ עָלֵינוּ שָׁנָה טוֹבָה:

Avinu Malkeynu, let this be a good year for us.

אָבִינוּ מַלְכֵּנוּ הָפֵר עֲצַת אוֹיְבֵינוּ:

Avinu Malkeynu, destroy the power of every oppressor
and adversary.

אָבִינוּ מַלְכֵּנוּ כַּלֵּה דֶּבֶר וְחֶרֶב וְרָעָב וּשְׁבִי וּמַשְׁחִית
מִבְּנֵי בְרִיתֶךָ:

Avinu Malkeynu, remove from all Your children disease,
war, famine, exile and destruction.

אָבִינוּ מַלְכֵּנוּ סְלַח וּמְחַל לְכָל־עֲוֹנוֹתֵינוּ:

Avinu Malkeynu, forgive and pardon all our wrongdoing.

אָבִינוּ מַלְכֵּנוּ הַחֲזִירֵנוּ בִּתְשׁוּבָה שְׁלֵמָה לְפָנֶיךָ:

Avinu Malkeynu, may we return to You in earnest repentance.

אָבִינוּ מַלְכֵּנוּ שְׁלַח רְפוּאָה שְׁלֵמָה לְחוֹלֵי עַמֶּךָ:

Avinu Malkeynu, send healing to all who are sick.

אָבִינוּ מַלְכֵּנוּ כָּתְבֵנוּ בְּסֵפֶר חַיִּים טוֹבִים:

Avinu Malkeynu, inscribe us in Your book for a life of
goodness.

אָבִינוּ מַלְכֵּנוּ כָּתְבֵנוּ בְּסֵפֶר פַּרְנָסָה וְכַלְכָּלָה:

Avinu Malkeynu, inscribe us in the book of sustenance.

אָבִינוּ מַלְכֵּנוּ כָּתְבֵנוּ בְּסֵפֶר זְכֻיּוֹת:

Avinu Malkeynu, inscribe us in the book of meritorious
acts.

אָבִינוּ מַלְכֵּנוּ כָּתְבֵנוּ בְּסֵפֶר סְלִיחָה וּמְחִילָה:

Avinu Malkeynu, inscribe us in the book of forgiveness
and reconciliation.

אָבִינוּ מַלְכֵּנוּ חֲמוֹל עָלֵינוּ וְעַל עוֹלָלֵינוּ וְטַפֵּנוּ:

Avinu Malkeynu, show mercy to us and to our children.

אָבִינוּ מַלְכֵּנוּ פְּתַח שַׁעֲרֵי שָׁמַיִם לִתְפִלָּתֵנוּ:

Avinu Malkeynu, open the gates of heaven to our prayer.

אָבִינוּ מַלְכֵּנוּ עֲשֵׂה לְמַעַן בָּאֵי בָאֵשׁ וּבַמַּיִם עַל־קִדּוּשׁ
שְׁמֶךָ:

Avinu Malkeynu, do it for the sake of those who went
through fire and water to honor Your name.

אָבִינוּ מַלְכֵּנוּ חָנֵּנוּ וַעֲנֵנוּ כִּי אֵין בָּנוּ מַעֲשִׂים עֲשֵׂה
עִמָּנוּ צְדָקָה וָחֶסֶד וְהוֹשִׁיעֵנוּ:

Avinu Malkeynu, be gracious and respond to us, for we
have too few good deeds; act toward us with justice tempered by love, and bring us salvation.

Avinu Malkeynu
chawneynu va'a-neinu
Ki ein banu ma'a'sim
Asey imanu
Tz'dakah va'chesed
V'hoshi-eynu.

Kaddish Shalem

יִתְגַּדַּל וְיִתְקַדַּשׁ שְׁמֵהּ רַבָּא. בְּעָלְמָא דִי בְרָא
כִרְעוּתֵהּ. וְיַמְלִיךְ מַלְכוּתֵהּ בְּחַיֵּיכוֹן וּבְיוֹמֵיכוֹן וּבְחַיֵּי
דְכָל בֵּית יִשְׂרָאֵל. בַּעֲגָלָא וּבִזְמַן קָרִיב וְאִמְרוּ. אָמֵן:

יְהֵא שְׁמֵהּ רַבָּא מְבָרַךְ לְעָלַם וּלְעָלְמֵי עָלְמַיָּא:

יִתְבָּרַךְ וְיִשְׁתַּבַּח וְיִתְפָּאַר וְיִתְרוֹמַם וְיִתְנַשֵּׂא וְיִתְהַדָּר
וְיִתְעַלֶּה וְיִתְהַלָּל שְׁמֵהּ דְּקֻדְשָׁא. בְּרִיךְ הוּא. לְעֵלָּא
לְעֵלָּא מִן כָּל בִּרְכָתָא וְשִׁירָתָא תֻּשְׁבְּחָתָא וְנֶחֱמָתָא
דַּאֲמִירָן בְּעָלְמָא וְאִמְרוּ. אָמֵן:

תִּתְקַבֵּל צְלוֹתְהוֹן וּבָעוּתְהוֹן דְּכָל יִשְׂרָאֵל קֳדָם
אֲבוּהוֹן דִּי בִשְׁמַיָּא וְאִמְרוּ. אָמֵן:
יְהֵא שְׁלָמָא רַבָּא מִן שְׁמַיָּא וְחַיִּים עָלֵינוּ וְעַל כָּל
יִשְׂרָאֵל וְאִמְרוּ. אָמֵן:
עוֹשֶׂה שָׁלוֹם בִּמְרוֹמָיו הוּא יַעֲשֶׂה שָׁלוֹם עָלֵינוּ וְעַל
כָּל יִשְׂרָאֵל וְאִמְרוּ. אָמֵן:

May God's great name be praised and sanctified in the
world! May Your Rule be established in our lifetime and
the lifetime of the House of Israel. God's great name is
blessed and praised far beyond all blessings and praises we
say in the world. May the praises and prayers of all Israel
be accepted in heaven before You. May there be a great
peace from heaven and life for us and all Israel. May the
One who makes peace in the high places, make peace for us
and all Israel! Amen.

TORAH SERVICE

אֵין כָּמוֹךְ בָאֱלֹהִים, אֲדֹנָי, וְאֵין כְּמַעֲשֶׂיךָ. מַלְכוּתְךָ
מַלְכוּת כָּל עֹלָמִים, וּמֶמְשַׁלְתְּךָ בְּכָל דֹּר נָדֹר. יְיָ מֶלֶךְ,
יְיָ מָלָךְ, יְיָ יִמְלֹךְ לְעוֹלָם וָעֶד. יְיָ עֹז לְעַמּוֹ יִתֵּן, יְיָ יְבָרֵךְ
אֶת עַמּוֹ בַשָּׁלוֹם. אַב הָרַחֲמִים, הֵיטִיבָה בִרְצוֹנְךָ אֶת
צִיּוֹן, תִּבְנֶה חוֹמוֹת יְרוּשָׁלָיִם. כִּי בְךָ לְבַד בָּטָחְנוּ, מֶלֶךְ
אֵל רָם וְנִשָּׂא, אֲדוֹן עוֹלָמִים:

Ayn kamocha va-elohim, Adonay, v'ayn k'ma-aseh-cha. Mal-
chut'cha malchut kol olamim, u-memshalt'cha b'chol dor va-
dor. Adonay melech, Adonay malach, Adonay yimloch l'olam
va-ed. Adonay oz l'amo yiteyn, Adonay y'varech et amo va'sha-
lom. Av ha-rachamim, hey-tiva vir'tzon'cha et Tziyon: tivneh
chomot Y'rushalayim. Ki v'cha l'vad batachnu, melech El ram
v'nissa, adon olamim.

None is like You among the powers of the world,
No deeds compare to Yours.

    Your realm, O Majesty, is everlasting,
    Your rule extends to every generation.

Adonay is our Ruler, Adonay has been ruling,
Adonay will rule forever and ever.

    Adonay gives strength to our people through Torah,
    Through Torah Adonay has blessed us with peace.

Womb-gentle Father, do good in Zion:
Rebuild the walls in Jerusalem!

    For You alone do we trust,
    Sovereign God, high and exalted,
    Power eternal.

(The ark is opened)

וַיְהִי בִּנְסֹעַ הָאָרֹן וַיֹּאמֶר מֹשֶׁה: קוּמָה יְיָ, וְיָפֻצוּ
אֹיְבֶיךָ, וְיָנֻסוּ מְשַׂנְאֶיךָ מִפָּנֶיךָ. כִּי מִצִּיּוֹן תֵּצֵא תוֹרָה,

וּדְבַר יְיָ מִירוּשָׁלָיִם. בָּרוּךְ שֶׁנָּתַן תּוֹרָה לְעַמּוֹ יִשְׂרָאֵל
בִּקְדֻשָׁתוֹ.

Whenever the ark started on its journey, Moses proclaimed: Arise, Adonay, let Your enemies scatter, fleeing
before You! For one day from Zion Torah will go forth,
and the word of God from Jerusalem. Praised be the One
who has shared holiness with Israel in giving us the Torah.

*(The Thirteen Qualities of God are recited three times. The pas-
sage is omitted on Shabbat.)*

יְיָ יְיָ אֵל רַחוּם וְחַנּוּן אֶרֶךְ אַפַּיִם וְרַב חֶסֶד וֶאֱמֶת: נֹצֵר
חֶסֶד לָאֲלָפִים נֹשֵׂא עָוֹן וָפֶשַׁע וְחַטָאָה וְנַקֵּה.

*Adonay, Adonay, El rachum v'chanun, erech apayim v'rav
chesed ve-emet: notzer chesed la-alafim, nosey avon va-fesha
v'chata-ah v'nakey.*

Adonay, Adonay, God filled with mother love, slow to
anger, great in covenantal love and truth:
Keeping love for the thousands within the covenant, forgiving perverse actions, rebelliousness, and the missing of
the mark; and acquitting.

(The reader receives the Torah and the ark is closed)

שְׁמַע יִשְׂרָאֵל יְיָ אֱלֹהֵינוּ יְיָ אֶחָד:

Shma Yisrael Adonay Eloheynu Adonay Echad:
Hear, O Israel, Adonay is our God, Adonay is One.

אֶחָד אֱלֹהֵינוּ גָּדוֹל אֲדוֹנֵינוּ קָדוֹשׁ וְנוֹרָא שְׁמוֹ:

Echad Eloheynu, gadol Adoneynu, kadosh v'nora shmo:
Our God is One, Adonay is One, with a holy and awesome
name.

גַּדְּלוּ לַייָ אִתִּי. וּנְרוֹמְמָה שְׁמוֹ יַחְדָּו:

Gad'lu l'Adonay iti un'rom'ma shmo yachdav:
Magnify Adonay with me, and let us exalt the Name
together.

Torah Procession

L'cha Adonay ha-g'dula
v'ha-gvura v'hatiferet
v'ha-netzach v'ha-hod,
ki chol ba'shamayim uva-aretz
l'cha Adonay ha'mamlacha
v'hamitnasey l'chol l'rosh.
Rom'mu Adonay Eloheynu
v'hishtachavu la'hadom raglav
kadosh hu. Rom'mu Adonay
Eloheynu v'hishtachavu l'har
kod'sho ki kadosh Adonay
Eloheynu.

לְךָ יְיָ הַגְּדֻלָּה וְהַגְּבוּרָה
וְהַתִּפְאֶרֶת וְהַנֵּצַח וְהַהוֹד.
כִּי־כֹל בַּשָּׁמַיִם וּבָאָרֶץ לְךָ יְיָ
הַמַּמְלָכָה וְהַמִּתְנַשֵּׂא לְכֹל
לְרֹאשׁ. רוֹמְמוּ יְיָ אֱלֹהֵינוּ
וְהִשְׁתַּחֲווּ לַהֲדֹם רַגְלָיו
קָדוֹשׁ הוּא: רוֹמְמוּ יְיָ
אֱלֹהֵינוּ וְהִשְׁתַּחֲווּ לְהַר
קָדְשׁוֹ כִּי קָדוֹשׁ יְיָ אֱלֹהֵינוּ:

To You, Adonay, belong the greatness, the power, the glory, the everlasting victory, and the majesty, for to You belongs everything in heaven and on earth, sovereignty and the exaltation as head above all. Exalt Adonay our God, and worship at the footstool of God, the holy One! Exalt Adonay our God and worship at the holy mountain, for Adonay our God is holy.

(The Torah is placed on the reading desk. The Reader unrolls it and, if individuals will be called to the Torah, says:)

וְיַעֲזוֹר וְיָגֵן וְיוֹשִׁיעַ לְכָל הַחוֹסִים בּוֹ, וְנֹאמַר אָמֵן.
הַכֹּל הָבוּ גֹדֶל לֵאלֹהֵינוּ, וּתְנוּ כָבוֹד לַתּוֹרָה. (כֹּהֵן,
קְרָב;) יַעֲמֹד (תַּעֲמוֹד) ... בָּרוּךְ שֶׁנָּתַן תּוֹרָה לְעַמּוֹ
יִשְׂרָאֵל בִּקְדֻשָּׁתוֹ.

May God help, shield, and rescue all who trust in You, Amen. Let everyone ascribe greatness to our God and honor to the Torah. (*If appropriate,* Kohen, draw near.) I call ... Let us praise the One who in holiness has given the Torah to the people Israel.

(All respond:)

וְאַתֶּם הַדְּבֵקִים בַּיָ אֱלֹהֵיכֶם, חַיִּים כֻּלְּכֶם הַיּוֹם.

V-atem ha-d'vekim b'Adonay Eloheychem, chayim kul-chem ha-yom.

And you who have cleaved to Adonay your God are alive, all of you, this day.

Blessings for the Reading of the Torah

בָּרְכוּ אֶת־יְיָ הַמְבֹרָךְ:

בָּרוּךְ יְיָ הַמְבֹרָךְ לְעוֹלָם וָעֶד:

בָּרוּךְ אַתָּה יְיָ אֱלֹהֵינוּ מֶלֶךְ הָעוֹלָם אֲשֶׁר בָּחַר־בָּנוּ מִכָּל־הָעַמִּים וְנָתַן־לָנוּ אֶת־תּוֹרָתוֹ. בָּרוּךְ אַתָּה יְיָ נוֹתֵן הַתּוֹרָה:

Bar'chu et Adonay ham'vorach:

Baruch Adonay ham'vorach l'olam va-ed. Baruch atta Adonay Eloheynu melech ha-olam, asher bachar banu mikol ha-amim, v'natan lanu et Torato. Baruch atta Adonay, noteyn ha-Torah.

(The Torah is read)

בָּרוּךְ אַתָּה יְיָ אֱלֹהֵינוּ מֶלֶךְ הָעוֹלָם אֲשֶׁר נָתַן־לָנוּ תּוֹרַת אֱמֶת וְחַיֵּי עוֹלָם נָטַע בְּתוֹכֵנוּ. בָּרוּךְ אַתָּה יְיָ נוֹתֵן הַתּוֹרָה:

Baruch atta Adonay Eloheynu melech ha-olam, asher natan lanu Torat emet, v'chayey olam nata' b'tocheynu. Baruch atta Adonay, noteyn ha-Torah.

You are praised forever, Adonay, ruler of the universe, who has chosen us from among all peoples and given us Your Torah. You gave us a Torah of truth and implanted eternal life within us. You are praised, Adonay, who is giving us the Torah.

TORAH READING
FOR YOM KIPPUR MORNING
(Leviticus 16)

וַיְדַבֵּר יהוה אֶל־מֹשֶׁה אַחֲרֵי מוֹת שְׁנֵי בְּנֵי אַהֲרֹן בְּקָרְבָתָם
לִפְנֵי־יהוה וַיָּמֻתוּ: וַיֹּאמֶר יהוה אֶל־מֹשֶׁה דַּבֵּר אֶל־אַהֲרֹן אָחִיךָ
וְאַל־יָבֹא בְכָל־עֵת אֶל־הַקֹּדֶשׁ מִבֵּית לַפָּרֹכֶת אֶל־פְּנֵי הַכַּפֹּרֶת
אֲשֶׁר עַל־הָאָרֹן וְלֹא יָמוּת כִּי בֶּעָנָן אֵרָאֶה עַל־הַכַּפֹּרֶת: בְּזֹאת
יָבֹא אַהֲרֹן אֶל־הַקֹּדֶשׁ בְּפַר בֶּן־בָּקָר לְחַטָּאת וְאַיִל לְעֹלָה:
כְּתֹנֶת־בַּד קֹדֶשׁ יִלְבָּשׁ וּמִכְנְסֵי־בַד יִהְיוּ עַל־בְּשָׂרוֹ וּבְאַבְנֵט
בַּד יַחְגֹּר וּבְמִצְנֶפֶת בַּד יִצְנֹף בִּגְדֵי־קֹדֶשׁ הֵם וְרָחַץ בַּמַּיִם אֶת־
בְּשָׂרוֹ וּלְבֵשָׁם: וּמֵאֵת עֲדַת בְּנֵי יִשְׂרָאֵל יִקַּח שְׁנֵי־שְׂעִירֵי עִזִּים
לְחַטָּאת וְאַיִל אֶחָד לְעֹלָה: וְהִקְרִיב אַהֲרֹן אֶת־פַּר הַחַטָּאת
אֲשֶׁר־לוֹ וְכִפֶּר בַּעֲדוֹ וּבְעַד בֵּיתוֹ: וְלָקַח אֶת־שְׁנֵי הַשְּׂעִירִם
וְהֶעֱמִיד אֹתָם לִפְנֵי יהוה פֶּתַח אֹהֶל מוֹעֵד: וְנָתַן אַהֲרֹן עַל־
שְׁנֵי הַשְּׂעִירִם גֹּרָלוֹת גּוֹרָל אֶחָד לַיהוה וְגוֹרָל אֶחָד לַעֲזָאזֵל:
וְהִקְרִיב אַהֲרֹן אֶת־הַשָּׂעִיר אֲשֶׁר עָלָה עָלָיו הַגּוֹרָל לַיהוה
וְעָשָׂהוּ חַטָּאת: וְהַשָּׂעִיר אֲשֶׁר עָלָה עָלָיו הַגּוֹרָל לַעֲזָאזֵל יָעֳמַד־
חַי לִפְנֵי יהוה לְכַפֵּר עָלָיו לְשַׁלַּח אֹתוֹ לַעֲזָאזֵל הַמִּדְבָּרָה:
וְהִקְרִיב אַהֲרֹן אֶת־פַּר הַחַטָּאת אֲשֶׁר־לוֹ וְכִפֶּר בַּעֲדוֹ וּבְעַד
בֵּיתוֹ וְשָׁחַט אֶת־פַּר הַחַטָּאת אֲשֶׁר־לוֹ: וְלָקַח מְלֹא־הַמַּחְתָּה
גַּחֲלֵי־אֵשׁ מֵעַל הַמִּזְבֵּחַ מִלִּפְנֵי יהוה וּמְלֹא חָפְנָיו קְטֹרֶת סַמִּים
דַּקָּה וְהֵבִיא מִבֵּית

TORAH READING

FOR YOM KIPPUR MORNING

(Leviticus 16)

This is what Adonay said to Moses after Aaron's two sons had died when they drew near to the presence of God:

Tell your brother Aaron that he should not enter the holy place inside the parochet (or curtain) before the kaporet (or ark-cover) at any time he chooses, lest he die; for I am able to be seen in the cloud over the kaporet. In this manner shall Aaron enter the holy place: with a young bullock for a sin-offering and a ram for a burnt-offering; in the linen tunic appropriate for holy use shall he dress, linen trousers shall be on his body, he shall put a linen sash around his waist, and wind a linen turban around his head; these are clothes set aside for holy use, and before he puts them on he shall wash with water.

From the congregation of Israelites Aaron shall take two male goats for a sin-offering and a ram for a burnt-offering. Let Aaron then bring near in offering the bullock for his own sin-offering to seek atonement for himself and for his household.

He shall then take the two goats and stand them up in the presence of Adonay at the entrance to the tent of meeting. Upon the two goats Aaron shall place lots, one lot for Adonay, one lot for Azazel. Aaron shall bring near in offering the goat upon which fell the lot for Adonay and make it the sin-offering, while the goat upon which fell the lot for Azazel shall be stood up live by its legs in the presence of Adonay that atonement may be sought through it, to be sent away to Azazel toward the wilderness. Next Aaron shall bring near in offering the other bullock for his own sin-offering and seek atonement for himself and (the kohanim of) his household, and he shall slaughter the bullock for his sin-offering.

Let him then take a pan full of fire-coals from off the altar, from the presence of Adonay, and two handfuls of spices finely ground for incense and bring them inside the

לַפָּרֹכֶת: וְנָתַן אֶת־הַקְּטֹרֶת עַל־הָאֵשׁ לִפְנֵי
יְהֹוָה וְכִסָּה וֹ עֲנַן הַקְּטֹרֶת אֶת־הַכַּפֹּרֶת אֲשֶׁר עַל־הָעֵדוּת וְלֹא
יָמוּת: וְלָקַח מִדַּם הַפָּר וְהִזָּה בְאֶצְבָּעוֹ עַל־פְּנֵי הַכַּפֹּרֶת קֵדְמָה
וְלִפְנֵי הַכַּפֹּרֶת יַזֶּה שֶׁבַע־פְּעָמִים מִן־הַדָּם בְּאֶצְבָּעוֹ: וְשָׁחַט
אֶת־שְׂעִיר הַחַטָּאת אֲשֶׁר לָעָם וְהֵבִיא אֶת־דָּמוֹ אֶל־מִבֵּית
לַפָּרֹכֶת וְעָשָׂה אֶת־דָּמוֹ כַּאֲשֶׁר עָשָׂה לְדַם הַפָּר וְהִזָּה אֹתוֹ עַל־
הַכַּפֹּרֶת וְלִפְנֵי הַכַּפֹּרֶת: וְכִפֶּר עַל־הַקֹּדֶשׁ מִטֻּמְאֹת בְּנֵי יִשְׂרָאֵל
וּמִפִּשְׁעֵיהֶם לְכָל־חַטֹּאתָם וְכֵן יַעֲשֶׂה לְאֹהֶל מוֹעֵד הַשֹּׁכֵן אִתָּם
בְּתוֹךְ טֻמְאֹתָם: וְכָל־אָדָם לֹא־יִהְיֶה וֹ בְּאֹהֶל מוֹעֵד בְּבֹאוֹ
לְכַפֵּר בַּקֹּדֶשׁ עַד־צֵאתוֹ וְכִפֶּר בַּעֲדוֹ וּבְעַד בֵּיתוֹ וּבְעַד כָּל־
קְהַל יִשְׂרָאֵל: וְיָצָא אֶל־הַמִּזְבֵּחַ אֲשֶׁר לִפְנֵי־יְהֹוָה וְכִפֶּר עָלָיו
וְלָקַח מִדַּם הַפָּר וּמִדַּם הַשָּׂעִיר וְנָתַן עַל־קַרְנוֹת הַמִּזְבֵּחַ סָבִיב:
וְהִזָּה עָלָיו מִן־הַדָּם בְּאֶצְבָּעוֹ שֶׁבַע פְּעָמִים וְטִהֲרוֹ וְקִדְּשׁוֹ
מִטֻּמְאֹת בְּנֵי יִשְׂרָאֵל: וְכִלָּה מִכַּפֵּר אֶת־הַקֹּדֶשׁ וְאֶת־אֹהֶל
מוֹעֵד וְאֶת־הַמִּזְבֵּחַ וְהִקְרִיב אֶת־הַשָּׂעִיר הֶחָי: וְסָמַךְ אַהֲרֹן
אֶת־שְׁתֵּי יָדָו עַל־רֹאשׁ הַשָּׂעִיר הַחַי וְהִתְוַדָּה עָלָיו אֶת־כָּל־
עֲוֺנֹת בְּנֵי יִשְׂרָאֵל וְאֶת־כָּל־פִּשְׁעֵיהֶם לְכָל־חַטֹּאתָם וְנָתַן אֹתָם
עַל־רֹאשׁ הַשָּׂעִיר וְשִׁלַּח בְּיַד־אִישׁ עִתִּי הַמִּדְבָּרָה: וְנָשָׂא
הַשָּׂעִיר עָלָיו אֶת־כָּל־עֲוֺנֹתָם אֶל־אֶרֶץ גְּזֵרָה וְשִׁלַּח אֶת־הַשָּׂעִיר
בַּמִּדְבָּר: וּבָא אַהֲרֹן אֶל־אֹהֶל מוֹעֵד

parochet. He should then put the incense on the fire in the presence of Adonay so that a cloud of incense covers the kaporet above the ark of witness (*i. e.,* the ark holding the tablets which bear witness to God's revelation of Torah to Israel), and he shall not die. Let him then take some of the bullock's blood and sprinkling it with his finger on the eastern face of the kaporet, let him sprinkle some of the blood in front of the kaporet seven times with his finger. He should then slaughter the goat for the people's sin-offering and bring its blood inside the parochet and do with its blood as he did with the bullock's blood, sprinkling it upon the kaporet and in front of the kaporet. Let him then seek atonement for the holy place from the impurities of the Israelites, and from their rebellious acts, whatever their wrongs may be, and let him do the same for the tent of meeting which abides with them in the midst of their impurities. There shall be no other person in the tent of meeting from the time that he goes in to seek atonement for the holy place until he comes out, that he may seek atonement for himself and his household and the entire congregation of Israel.

Let him then go forth to the altar which is in the presence of Adonay and seek atonement for it, taking some of the bullock's blood and the goat's blood and putting it all over the horns of the altar. He should sprinkle some of the blood upon it seven times with his finger to purify it and renew its holiness after the impurities of the Israelites. When he finishes seeking atonement for the holy place, the tent of meeting, and the altar, he shall bring near the live goat in offering. Aaron shall lay his two hands on the live goat's head and confess there all the crooked deeds of the Israelites and all their rebellious acts, whatever their wrongs may be, transferring them to the goat's head, and he shall send the animal away into the wilderness with a man standing ready for the task. And so the goat shall carry all the crooked acts away with him to an isolated place, and the goat shall be set free in the wilderness.

Then Aaron shall come into the tent of meeting and

וּפָשַׁט אֶת־בִּגְדֵי הַבָּד
אֲשֶׁר לָבַשׁ בְּבֹאוֹ אֶל־הַקֹּדֶשׁ וְהִנִּיחָם שָׁם: וְרָחַץ אֶת־בְּשָׂרוֹ
בַמַּיִם בְּמָקוֹם קָדוֹשׁ וְלָבַשׁ אֶת־בְּגָדָיו וְיָצָא וְעָשָׂה אֶת־עֹלָתוֹ
וְאֶת־עֹלַת הָעָם וְכִפֶּר בַּעֲדוֹ וּבְעַד הָעָם: וְאֵת חֵלֶב הַחַטָּאת
יַקְטִיר הַמִּזְבֵּחָה: וְהַמְשַׁלֵּחַ אֶת־הַשָּׂעִיר לַעֲזָאזֵל יְכַבֵּס בְּגָדָיו
וְרָחַץ אֶת־בְּשָׂרוֹ בַּמָּיִם וְאַחֲרֵי־כֵן יָבוֹא אֶל־הַמַּחֲנֶה: וְאֵת
פַּר הַחַטָּאת וְאֵת। שְׂעִיר הַחַטָּאת אֲשֶׁר הוּבָא אֶת־דָּמָם לְכַפֵּר
בַּקֹּדֶשׁ יוֹצִיא אֶל־מִחוּץ לַמַּחֲנֶה וְשָׂרְפוּ בָאֵשׁ אֶת־עֹרֹתָם וְאֶת־
בְּשָׂרָם וְאֶת־פִּרְשָׁם: וְהַשֹּׂרֵף אֹתָם יְכַבֵּס בְּגָדָיו וְרָחַץ אֶת־
בְּשָׂרוֹ בַּמָּיִם וְאַחֲרֵי־כֵן יָבוֹא אֶל־הַמַּחֲנֶה: וְהָיְתָה לָכֶם לְחֻקַּת
עוֹלָם בַּחֹדֶשׁ הַשְּׁבִיעִי בֶּעָשׂוֹר לַחֹדֶשׁ תְּעַנּוּ אֶת־נַפְשֹׁתֵיכֶם
וְכָל־מְלָאכָה לֹא תַעֲשׂוּ הָאֶזְרָח וְהַגֵּר הַגָּר בְּתוֹכְכֶם: כִּי־בַיּוֹם
הַזֶּה יְכַפֵּר עֲלֵיכֶם לְטַהֵר אֶתְכֶם מִכֹּל חַטֹּאתֵיכֶם לִפְנֵי יְהוָה
תִּטְהָרוּ: שַׁבַּת שַׁבָּתוֹן הִיא לָכֶם וְעִנִּיתֶם אֶת־נַפְשֹׁתֵיכֶם חֻקַּת
עוֹלָם: וְכִפֶּר הַכֹּהֵן אֲשֶׁר־יִמְשַׁח אֹתוֹ וַאֲשֶׁר יְמַלֵּא אֶת־יָדוֹ
לְכַהֵן תַּחַת אָבִיו וְלָבַשׁ אֶת־בִּגְדֵי הַבָּד בִּגְדֵי הַקֹּדֶשׁ: וְכִפֶּר
אֶת־מִקְדַּשׁ הַקֹּדֶשׁ וְאֶת־אֹהֶל מוֹעֵד וְאֶת־הַמִּזְבֵּחַ יְכַפֵּר וְעַל
הַכֹּהֲנִים וְעַל־כָּל־עַם הַקָּהָל יְכַפֵּר: וְהָיְתָה־זֹּאת לָכֶם לְחֻקַּת
עוֹלָם לְכַפֵּר עַל־בְּנֵי יִשְׂרָאֵל מִכָּל־חַטֹּאתָם אַחַת בַּשָּׁנָה וַיַּעַשׂ
כַּאֲשֶׁר צִוָּה יְהוָה אֶת־מֹשֶׁה:

take off the linen garments which he put on when he entered the holy place and leave them there. After he has washed his body with water in the holy area, he shall put on his regular vestments and go out to make his own burnt-offering and that of the people, that he may seek atonement for himself and for the people.

After Aaron shall turn the fat part of the sin-offering into smoke going up from the altar, the person who sent the goat away to Azazel shall scour his clothes and wash his body in water, following which he may enter the camp. The goat brought for the sin-offering whose blood was used to seek atonement for the holy place shall be brought outside the camp, and its skin, flesh, and dung shall be burnt in the fire. The one who burns it shall scour the clothes, wash in water, and may then come into the camp.

This shall be an eternal statute for you: in the seventh month, on the tenth of the month, you shall afflict yourselves. You shall do no work, neither the native nor the stranger who dwells among you. For on this day atonement shall be made for you to purify you from all your wrongs; in the presence of Adonay you shall be pure.

It shall be a complete Shabbat for you when you afflict yourselves, an eternal statute.

The kohen who is anointed and the one who is empowered to serve as kohen in place of his father shall put on linen garments set aside for holy use. He shall seek atonement for the holy sanctuary, the tent of meeting, and the altar, on behalf of the kohanim and on behalf of the people of the congregation. And this shall be an eternal statute for you, that atonement might be granted to the Israelites from all their wrongs once each year.

And all that Adonay commanded Moses was accomplished.

ALTERNATIVE TORAH READING (Deuteronomy 29:9–14; 30:11–20)

אַתֶּם נִצָּבִים הַיּוֹם כֻּלְּכֶם לִפְנֵי יהוה אֱלֹהֵיכֶם רָאשֵׁיכֶם שִׁבְטֵיכֶם
זִקְנֵיכֶם וְשֹׁטְרֵיכֶם כֹּל אִישׁ יִשְׂרָאֵל: טַפְּכֶם נְשֵׁיכֶם וְגֵרְךָ אֲשֶׁר
בְּקֶרֶב מַחֲנֶיךָ מֵחֹטֵב עֵצֶיךָ עַד שֹׁאֵב מֵימֶיךָ: לְעָבְרְךָ בִּבְרִית
יהוה אֱלֹהֶיךָ וּבְאָלָתוֹ אֲשֶׁר יהוה אֱלֹהֶיךָ כֹּרֵת עִמְּךָ הַיּוֹם:
לְמַעַן הָקִים־אֹתְךָ הַיּוֹם ו לוֹ לְעָם וְהוּא יִהְיֶה־לְּךָ לֵאלֹהִים כַּאֲשֶׁר
דִּבֶּר־לָךְ וְכַאֲשֶׁר נִשְׁבַּע לַאֲבֹתֶיךָ לְאַבְרָהָם לְיִצְחָק וּלְיַעֲקֹב:
וְלֹא אִתְּכֶם לְבַדְּכֶם אָנֹכִי כֹּרֵת אֶת־הַבְּרִית הַזֹּאת וְאֶת־הָאָלָה
הַזֹּאת: כִּי אֶת־אֲשֶׁר יֶשְׁנוֹ פֹּה עִמָּנוּ עֹמֵד הַיּוֹם לִפְנֵי יהוה אֱלֹהֵינוּ
וְאֵת אֲשֶׁר אֵינֶנּוּ פֹּה עִמָּנוּ הַיּוֹם:

כִּי הַמִּצְוָה הַזֹּאת אֲשֶׁר אָנֹכִי מְצַוְּךָ הַיּוֹם
לֹא־נִפְלֵאת הִוא מִמְּךָ וְלֹא־רְחֹקָה הִוא: לֹא בַשָּׁמַיִם הִוא
לֵאמֹר מִי יַעֲלֶה־לָּנוּ הַשָּׁמַיְמָה וְיִקָּחֶהָ לָּנוּ וְיַשְׁמִעֵנוּ אֹתָהּ
וְנַעֲשֶׂנָּה: וְלֹא־מֵעֵבֶר לַיָּם הִוא לֵאמֹר מִי יַעֲבָר־לָנוּ אֶל־עֵבֶר
הַיָּם וְיִקָּחֶהָ לָּנוּ וְיַשְׁמִעֵנוּ אֹתָהּ וְנַעֲשֶׂנָּה: כִּי־קָרוֹב אֵלֶיךָ הַדָּבָר
מְאֹד בְּפִיךָ וּבִלְבָבְךָ לַעֲשֹׂתוֹ:   רְאֵה נָתַתִּי לְפָנֶיךָ
הַיּוֹם אֶת־הַחַיִּים וְאֶת־הַטּוֹב וְאֶת־הַמָּוֶת וְאֶת־הָרָע: אֲשֶׁר
אָנֹכִי מְצַוְּךָ הַיּוֹם לְאַהֲבָה אֶת־יהוה אֱלֹהֶיךָ לָלֶכֶת בִּדְרָכָיו
וְלִשְׁמֹר מִצְוֹתָיו וְחֻקֹּתָיו וּמִשְׁפָּטָיו וְחָיִיתָ וְרָבִיתָ וּבֵרַכְךָ יהוה
אֱלֹהֶיךָ בָּאָרֶץ אֲשֶׁר־אַתָּה בָא־שָׁמָּה לְרִשְׁתָּהּ: וְאִם־יִפְנֶה
לְבָבְךָ וְלֹא תִשְׁמָע וְנִדַּחְתָּ וְהִשְׁתַּחֲוִיתָ לֵאלֹהִים אֲחֵרִים
וַעֲבַדְתָּם: הִגַּדְתִּי לָכֶם הַיּוֹם כִּי אָבֹד תֹּאבֵדוּן לֹא־תַאֲרִיכֻן
יָמִים עַל־הָאֲדָמָה אֲשֶׁר אַתָּה עֹבֵר אֶת־הַיַּרְדֵּן לָבוֹא שָׁמָּה
לְרִשְׁתָּהּ: הַעִדֹתִי בָכֶם הַיּוֹם אֶת־הַשָּׁמַיִם וְאֶת־הָאָרֶץ הַחַיִּים
וְהַמָּוֶת נָתַתִּי לְפָנֶיךָ הַבְּרָכָה וְהַקְּלָלָה וּבָחַרְתָּ בַּחַיִּים לְמַעַן
תִּחְיֶה אַתָּה וְזַרְעֶךָ: לְאַהֲבָה אֶת־יהוה אֱלֹהֶיךָ לִשְׁמֹעַ בְּקֹלוֹ
וּלְדָבְקָה־בוֹ כִּי הוּא חַיֶּיךָ וְאֹרֶךְ יָמֶיךָ לָשֶׁבֶת עַל־הָאֲדָמָה
אֲשֶׁר נִשְׁבַּע יהוה לַאֲבֹתֶיךָ לְאַבְרָהָם לְיִצְחָק וּלְיַעֲקֹב לָתֵת
לָהֶם:

ALTERNATIVE TORAH READING (Deuteronomy 29:9–14; 30:11–20)

You stand today—all of You—before Adonay your God: your leaders, your tribes, your elders, your officials, every man, woman, and child in Israel, the stranger in the midst of your camp, from the one who chops your wood to the one who draws your water, that you may enter into the sworn covenant of Adonay your God which Adonay your God is confirming with you this very day, for the purpose of establishing you as the people whose only God is Adonay, as you have been promised, and as God swore to your fathers, to Abraham, to Isaac, and to Jacob. But it is not only with you that I am making this sworn covenant, but with whoever is standing here with us today before Adonay your God, and with whoever is not here with us today.

For this mitzvah which I am commanding you today is not too wondrous for you to follow, nor too remote from you; it is not in heaven, that you should say, "Who will ascend to heaven to obtain it for us and explain it to us that we may do it?" Nor is it beyond the sea that you should say, "Who will cross over the sea to obtain it for us and explain it to us that we may do it?" For the word is very close to you, in your own mouth and heart, so you can do it.

See, I have set before you today life and good (or "order, prosperity") and death and evil (or "chaos," or "adversity"), in that I am commanding you today to love Adonay, to walk in the ways and keep the mitzvot, the statutes, and the judgments of your God, that you may live and increase as Adonay your God blesses you in the land into which you have come to inherit. But if your heart turns aside and you do not hearken, but let yourself be led astray to worship other gods and serve them, then I tell you today that you will surely perish, you shall not live long upon the land whither you have crossed the Jordan to

inherit. Today I call as witness against you heaven and earth: life and death have I set before you, blessing and curse, that you might choose life, and you and your seed might live, loving Adonay your God, hearkening to God's voice, and cleaving to the One who is your life and the length of your days, dwelling upon the land which Adonay your God promised to your fathers, to Abraham, Isaac, and Jacob, to give them.

Reader's Kaddish

יִתְגַּדַּל וְיִתְקַדַּשׁ שְׁמֵהּ רַבָּא. בְּעָלְמָא דִּי בְרָא
כִרְעוּתֵהּ. וְיַמְלִיךְ מַלְכוּתֵהּ בְּחַיֵּיכוֹן וּבְיוֹמֵיכוֹן וּבְחַיֵּי
דְכָל בֵּית יִשְׂרָאֵל. בַּעֲגָלָא וּבִזְמַן קָרִיב וְאִמְרוּ. אָמֵן:

יְהֵא שְׁמֵהּ רַבָּא מְבָרַךְ לְעָלַם וּלְעָלְמֵי עָלְמַיָּא:

יִתְבָּרַךְ וְיִשְׁתַּבַּח וְיִתְפָּאַר וְיִתְרֹמַם וְיִתְנַשֵּׂא וְיִתְהַדָּר
וְיִתְעַלֶּה וְיִתְהַלַּל שְׁמֵהּ דְּקֻדְשָׁא. בְּרִיךְ הוּא. לְעֵלָּא
לְעֵלָּא מִן כָּל בִּרְכָתָא וְשִׁירָתָא תֻּשְׁבְּחָתָא וְנֶחֱמָתָא
דַּאֲמִירָן בְּעָלְמָא וְאִמְרוּ. אָמֵן:

May God's great name be magnified and sanctified in the world created according to the holy will, and may God's rule be known in your lifetime, in your own days, and in the life of the house of Israel, speedily, in a time close at hand.

May the name of the blessed Holy One be praised and extolled far beyond all praises and blessings we can ever say in the world. Amen.

(When the Torah is raised, all rise and proclaim:)

וְזֹאת הַתּוֹרָה אֲשֶׁר שָׂם מֹשֶׁה לִפְנֵי בְּנֵי יִשְׂרָאֵל, עַל פִּי
יְיָ בְּיַד מֹשֶׁה.

V'zot ha-Torah asher sam Moshe lifney b'ney Yisrael al pi Adonay, b'yad Moshe.

This is the Torah which Moses placed before the children of Israel at the command of Adonay, through Moses.

(If there is a second scroll, it is now placed on the reading table.)

MAFTIR READING FROM THE SECOND SCROLL
(Numbers 29:7–11)

וּבֶעָשׂוֹר

לֶחֹדֶשׁ הַשְּׁבִיעִי הַזֶּה מִקְרָא־קֹדֶשׁ יִהְיֶה לָכֶם וְעִנִּיתֶם אֶת־
נַפְשֹׁתֵיכֶם כָּל־מְלָאכָה לֹא תַעֲשׂוּ: וְהִקְרַבְתֶּם עֹלָה לַיהוה רֵיחַ
נִיחֹחַ פַּר בֶּן־בָּקָר אֶחָד אַיִל אֶחָד כְּבָשִׂים בְּנֵי־שָׁנָה שִׁבְעָה תְּמִימִם
יִהְיוּ לָכֶם: וּמִנְחָתָם סֹלֶת בְּלוּלָה בַשֶּׁמֶן שְׁלֹשָׁה עֶשְׂרֹנִים לַפָּר
שְׁנֵי עֶשְׂרֹנִים לָאַיִל הָאֶחָד: עִשָּׂרוֹן עִשָּׂרוֹן לַכֶּבֶשׂ הָאֶחָד לְשִׁבְעַת
הַכְּבָשִׂים: שְׂעִיר־עִזִּים אֶחָד חַטָּאת מִלְּבַד חַטַּאת הַכִּפֻּרִים
וְעֹלַת הַתָּמִיד וּמִנְחָתָהּ וְנִסְכֵּיהֶם:

On the tenth day of the same seventh month there shall be a holy convocation for you in which you shall afflict yourselves; you shall not do any work. You shall bring near in offering for yourselves a burnt offering with a pleasing aroma to Adonay: one bullock of the herd, one ram and seven yearling lambs, all unblemished. The meal offering—choice flour mixed with oil—accompanying them shall be: three-tenths of a measure for the bullock, two-tenths for the ram, one-tenth for each of the seven lambs. And there shall be one goat for a sin-offering in addition to the sin-offering for atonement and the regular daily burnt-offering with its meal offering, each with its libation as prescribed.

(Vzot Ha-Torah *is chanted again when the second scroll is raised*)

READING OF THE HAFTARAH

בָּרוּךְ אַתָּה יְיָ אֱלֹהֵינוּ מֶלֶךְ הָעוֹלָם אֲשֶׁר בָּחַר
בִּנְבִיאִים טוֹבִים וְרָצָה בְדִבְרֵיהֶם הַנֶּאֱמָרִים בֶּאֱמֶת.
בָּרוּךְ אַתָּה יְיָ הַבּוֹחֵר בַּתּוֹרָה וּבְמֹשֶׁה עַבְדּוֹ וּבְיִשְׂרָאֵל
עַמּוֹ וּבִנְבִיאֵי הָאֱמֶת וָצֶדֶק.

HAFTARAH FOR YOM KIPPUR MORNING
(Isaiah 57:14–58:14)

וְאָמַר סֹלּוּ־סֹלּוּ פַּנּוּ־דָרֶךְ הָרִימוּ
מִכְשׁוֹל מִדֶּרֶךְ עַמִּי: כִּי כֹה אָמַר רָם וְנִשָּׂא שֹׁכֵן
עַד וְקָדוֹשׁ שְׁמוֹ מָרוֹם וְקָדוֹשׁ אֶשְׁכּוֹן וְאֶת־דַּכָּא וּשְׁפַל־רוּחַ
לְהַחֲיוֹת רוּחַ שְׁפָלִים וּלְהַחֲיוֹת לֵב נִדְכָּאִים: כִּי לֹא לְעוֹלָם
אָרִיב וְלֹא לָנֶצַח אֶקְצוֹף כִּי־רוּחַ מִלְּפָנַי יַעֲטוֹף וּנְשָׁמוֹת אֲנִי
עָשִׂיתִי: בַּעֲוֹן בִּצְעוֹ קָצַפְתִּי וְאַכֵּהוּ הַסְתֵּר וְאֶקְצֹף וַיֵּלֶךְ שׁוֹבָב
בְּדֶרֶךְ לִבּוֹ: דְּרָכָיו רָאִיתִי וְאֶרְפָּאֵהוּ וְאַנְחֵהוּ וַאֲשַׁלֵּם נִחֻמִים
לוֹ וְלַאֲבֵלָיו: בּוֹרֵא נִוב שְׂפָתָיִם שָׁלוֹם שָׁלוֹם לָרָחוֹק וְלַקָּרוֹב
אָמַר יְהוָה וּרְפָאתִיו: וְהָרְשָׁעִים כַּיָּם נִגְרָשׁ כִּי הַשְׁקֵט לֹא
יוּכָל וַיִּגְרְשׁוּ מֵימָיו רֶפֶשׁ וָטִיט: אֵין שָׁלוֹם אָמַר אֱלֹהַי
לָרְשָׁעִים: קְרָא בְגָרוֹן אַל־תַּחְשֹׂךְ כַּשּׁוֹפָר הָרֵם
קוֹלֶךָ וְהַגֵּד לְעַמִּי פִּשְׁעָם וּלְבֵית יַעֲקֹב חַטֹּאתָם:

READING OF THE HAFTARAH

You are praised, Adonay our God, Sovereign of the world, who has chosen good prophets, finding favor in their words which faithfully reflect Your truth. You are praised, Adonay, who has chosen Moses Your servant, Israel Your people, and prophets who have spoken truth and justice.

HAFTARAH FOR YOM KIPPUR MORNING
(Isaiah 57:14–58:14)

God said:
Build a road, clear a path,
Cast away all stumbling-blocks from my people's path,
For thus says the Most High and exalted, who dwells in
   eternity, whose name is Holy One:
I dwell in the heights, in holy space,
But equally with those of crushed and humble spirits,
   to breathe new life into the humble,
To renew the heart of those who are crushed.
Not forever will I dispute, not eternally will I be angry.
For breath unfolds from My presence, I make souls.
I smote them angrily for the sin of greed,
Angrily I slipped out of sight,
   and they all turned back to the path of their own desires.
Having observed their paths, now I will heal them,
I will guide them, offering a recompense of solace to them
   and their mourners.
I who create the fruit of the lips
Say, "Shalom, shalom!" to far and near,
I, Adonay, will heal them.
But the wicked will be like the tossing sea, finding no rest,
Its waters tossing up mud and slime;
Shalom is not, says my God, for the wicked.

So give a full-throated cry, hold nothing back,
Raise your voice to the pitch of a Shofar,
And tell my people of their rebelliousness,
Proclaim their wrongs to the house of Jacob.

וְאוֹתִי יוֹם יוֹם

יִדְרֹשׁוּן וְדַעַת דְּרָכַי יֶחְפָּצוּן כְּגוֹי אֲשֶׁר־צְדָקָה עָשָׂה וּמִשְׁפַּט
אֱלֹהָיו לֹא עָזָב יִשְׁאָלוּנִי מִשְׁפְּטֵי־צֶדֶק קִרְבַת אֱלֹהִים יֶחְפָּצוּן:
לָמָּה צַּמְנוּ וְלֹא רָאִיתָ עִנִּינוּ נַפְשֵׁנוּ וְלֹא תֵדָע הֵן בְּיוֹם צֹמְכֶם
תִּמְצְאוּ־חֵפֶץ וְכָל־עַצְּבֵיכֶם תִּנְגֹּשׂוּ: הֵן לְרִיב וּמַצָּה תָּצוּמוּ
וּלְהַכּוֹת בְּאֶגְרֹף רֶשַׁע לֹא־תָצוּמוּ כַיּוֹם לְהַשְׁמִיעַ בַּמָּרוֹם
קוֹלְכֶם: הֲכָזֶה יִהְיֶה צוֹם אֶבְחָרֵהוּ יוֹם עַנּוֹת אָדָם נַפְשׁוֹ הֲלָכֹף
כְּאַגְמֹן רֹאשׁוֹ וְשַׂק וָאֵפֶר יַצִּיעַ הֲלָזֶה תִּקְרָא־צוֹם וְיוֹם רָצוֹן
לַיהוָה: הֲלוֹא זֶה צוֹם אֶבְחָרֵהוּ פַּתֵּחַ חַרְצֻבּוֹת רֶשַׁע הַתֵּר
אֲגֻדּוֹת מוֹטָה וְשַׁלַּח רְצוּצִים חָפְשִׁים וְכָל־מוֹטָה תְּנַתֵּקוּ: הֲלוֹא
פָרֹס לָרָעֵב לַחְמֶךָ וַעֲנִיִּים מְרוּדִים תָּבִיא בָיִת כִּי־תִרְאֶה עָרֹם
וְכִסִּיתוֹ וּמִבְּשָׂרְךָ לֹא תִתְעַלָּם: אָז יִבָּקַע כַּשַּׁחַר אוֹרֶךָ וַאֲרֻכָתְךָ
מְהֵרָה תִצְמָח וְהָלַךְ לְפָנֶיךָ צִדְקֶךָ כְּבוֹד יְהוָה יַאַסְפֶךָ:

True, every day they ask Me questions—
How they would love the intimate knowledge of My paths!
They pretend to be a nation which has always acted justly,
Which has not forsaken the decisions of its God.
They ask Me for decisions that would declare them inno-
    cent,
How they would love to be near to God!
"For what purpose have we fasted, when You were not
    watching?
"Why should we have afflicted ourselves when You
    seemed not to know?"

Look here: on the day you fasted you were looking for
    business,
Grinding down the toilers who work under you!
Look here: you fast to dispute, to make trouble,
Pummeling everyone with wicked fists,
You're not fasting today
To raise your voice to heaven's height!

Is a fast like this the one I asked for?
A day for self affliction, to bend the head like a reed in a
    marsh,
To sprawl in sackcloth on the ashes?
Is this what you call a fast,
A day to seek the favor of God?

Is not this the fast I ask for:
To unlock the shackles of evil,
To loosen the thongs of the yoke,
To send forth crushed souls to freedom,
To tear every yoke in two!
To tear up your loaves for the hungry,
To bring the poor wanderer home,
When you see the naked, clothe them,
When you see your own flesh and blood, do not turn aside!
Then your light will burst forth like the morning,
And new flesh will soon cover your wounds;
Your reputation for justice will precede you
And the glory of God will follow close behind.

אָז

תִּקְרָא וַיהוה יַעֲנֶה תְּשַׁוַּע וְיֹאמַר הִנֵּנִי אִם־תָּסִיר מִתּוֹכְךָ
מוֹטָה שְׁלַח אֶצְבַּע וְדַבֶּר־אָוֶן: וְתָפֵק לָרָעֵב נַפְשֶׁךָ וְנֶפֶשׁ נַעֲנָה
תַּשְׂבִּיעַ וְזָרַח בַּחֹשֶׁךְ אוֹרֶךָ וַאֲפֵלָתְךָ כַּצָּהֳרָיִם: וְנָחֲךָ יהוה
תָּמִיד וְהִשְׂבִּיעַ בְּצַחְצָחוֹת נַפְשֶׁךָ וְעַצְמֹתֶיךָ יַחֲלִיץ וְהָיִיתָ כְּגַן
רָוֶה וּכְמוֹצָא מַיִם אֲשֶׁר לֹא־יְכַזְּבוּ מֵימָיו: וּבָנוּ מִמְּךָ חָרְבוֹת
עוֹלָם מוֹסְדֵי דוֹר־וָדוֹר תְּקוֹמֵם וְקֹרָא לְךָ גֹּדֵר פֶּרֶץ מְשׁוֹבֵב
נְתִיבוֹת לָשָׁבֶת: אִם־תָּשִׁיב מִשַּׁבָּת רַגְלֶךָ עֲשׂוֹת חֲפָצֶךָ בְּיוֹם
קָדְשִׁי וְקָרָאתָ לַשַּׁבָּת עֹנֶג לִקְדוֹשׁ יהוה מְכֻבָּד וְכִבַּדְתּוֹ
מֵעֲשׂוֹת דְּרָכֶיךָ מִמְּצוֹא חֶפְצְךָ וְדַבֵּר דָּבָר: אָז תִּתְעַנַּג עַל־
יהוה וְהִרְכַּבְתִּיךָ עַל־בָּמֳתֵי אָרֶץ וְהַאֲכַלְתִּיךָ נַחֲלַת יַעֲקֹב
אָבִיךָ כִּי פִּי יהוה דִּבֵּר:

Then when you call, Adonay will respond,
As soon as you cry out, God will say, "Here I am!"
If from your midst you remove
The oppressive yoke, the menacing hand, the abusive
  words,
If you reach out to the soul of the hungry,
If you ease the soul of the bruised,
Then your light will shine forth in the darkness,
And your shadows will change into noon;
Adonay will guide you forever,
Nourishing your soul like the sun,
Restoring your bones to vigor;
You will become a well-watered garden,
A spring of unfailing fresh water.
From your midst will step forth rebuilders of ruins,
They will restore the foundations of old,
You will be known as repairers of walls long breached,
People who reclaim old paths to dwell in once more.

If you restrain your feet from Shabbat violations,
From doing business on the day of My holiness,
If you call Shabbat a delight, God's holy time worthy of
  honor,
Honoring it by abandoning your customary ways,
From doing business and making idle talk,
Then you will become the delight of Adonay
And I shall lift you over the high places of the earth.
I shall nurture you out of the heritage of Jacob your father,
For the mouth of God has spoken.

Blessings Completing the Reading of the Haftarah

בָּרוּךְ אַתָּה, יְיָ אֱלֹהֵינוּ, מֶלֶךְ הָעוֹלָם, צוּר כָּל הָעוֹלָמִים, צַדִּיק בְּכָל הַדּוֹרוֹת, הָאֵל הַנֶּאֱמָן, הָאוֹמֵר וְעוֹשֶׂה, הַמְדַבֵּר וּמְקַיֵּם, שֶׁכָּל דְּבָרָיו אֱמֶת וָצֶדֶק.

נֶאֱמָן אַתָּה הוּא, יְיָ אֱלֹהֵינוּ, וְנֶאֱמָנִים דְּבָרֶיךָ, וְדָבָר אֶחָד מִדְּבָרֶיךָ אָחוֹר לֹא יָשׁוּב רֵיקָם, כִּי אֵל מֶלֶךְ נֶאֱמָן וְרַחֲמָן אָתָּה. בָּרוּךְ אַתָּה, יְיָ, הָאֵל הַנֶּאֱמָן בְּכָל דְּבָרָיו.

רַחֵם עַל צִיּוֹן, כִּי הִיא בֵּית חַיֵּינוּ, וְלַעֲלוּבַת נֶפֶשׁ תּוֹשִׁיעַ בִּמְהֵרָה בְיָמֵינוּ. בָּרוּךְ אַתָּה יְיָ מְשַׂמֵּחַ צִיּוֹן בְּבָנֶיהָ.

שַׂמְּחֵנוּ, יְיָ אֱלֹהֵינוּ, בְּאֵלִיָּהוּ הַנָּבִיא עַבְדֶּךָ, וּבְמַלְכוּת בֵּית דָּוִד מְשִׁיחֶךָ, בִּמְהֵרָה יָבֹא, וְיָגֵל לִבֵּנוּ; עַל כִּסְאוֹ לֹא יֵשֶׁב זָר, וְלֹא יִנְחֲלוּ עוֹד אֲחֵרִים אֶת כְּבוֹדוֹ, כִּי בְשֵׁם קָדְשְׁךָ נִשְׁבַּעְתָּ לּוֹ, שֶׁלֹּא יִכְבֶּה נֵרוֹ לְעוֹלָם וָעֶד. בָּרוּךְ אַתָּה יְיָ מָגֵן דָּוִד.

עַל הַתּוֹרָה וְעַל הָעֲבוֹדָה וְעַל הַנְּבִיאִים וְעַל יוֹם [הַשַּׁבָּת הַזֶּה וְעַל יוֹם] הַכִּפֻּרִים הַזֶּה, שֶׁנָּתַתָּ לָּנוּ, יְיָ אֱלֹהֵינוּ, [לִקְדֻשָּׁה וְלִמְנוּחָה] לִמְחִילָה וְלִסְלִיחָה וּלְכַפָּרָה, לְכָבוֹד וּלְתִפְאָרֶת.

עַל הַכֹּל, יְיָ אֱלֹהֵינוּ, אֲנַחְנוּ מוֹדִים לָךְ, וּמְבָרְכִים אוֹתָךְ; יִתְבָּרַךְ שִׁמְךָ בְּפִי כָּל חַי תָּמִיד, לְעוֹלָם וָעֶד. וּדְבָרְךָ אֱמֶת וְקַיָּם לָעַד. בָּרוּךְ אַתָּה, יְיָ מֶלֶךְ מוֹחֵל וְסוֹלֵחַ לַעֲבוֹנוֹתֵינוּ וְלַעֲוֹנוֹת עַמּוֹ בֵּית יִשְׂרָאֵל, וּמַעֲבִיר אַשְׁמוֹתֵינוּ בְּכָל שָׁנָה וְשָׁנָה. מֶלֶךְ עַל כָּל הָאָרֶץ, מְקַדֵּשׁ [הַשַּׁבָּת וְ]יִשְׂרָאֵל וְיוֹם הַכִּפֻּרִים.

Blessings Completing the Reading of the Haftarah

You are praised, Adonay our God, Sovereign of the world, eternal Rock, righteous ruler in all generations, faithful God, whose every word is true and just. Not one of your words shall return unfulfilled, for Your rule is trustworthy and compassionate. You are praised, God of faithful words.

Show compassion on Zion, for it is our eternal house, and rescue those who are brought low, soon, in our days. You are praised, Adonay, who brings Zion joy through her children.

Bring us joy, Adonay our God, with the coming of Your servant, Elijah the prophet, and the reign of the house of David Your anointed. Let no stranger sit upon his throne, nor any others inherit his glory, for You have sworn by Your holy name that his light would never be extinguished anywhere. You are praised, Adonay, shield of David.

For the Torah, for serving You in prayer, for the prophets, (for this Shabbat) and for this Day of Atonement which You have granted us, Adonay our God, (for holiness and rest,) for pardon and atonement, for glory, and for honor; indeed, for everything, Adonay our God, we thank You and praise You. Your name shall be praised forever in the mouths of all who live, for Your word is true and upheld eternally. You are praised, Adonay, who pardons our wrongdoing and the wrongdoing of Your people Israel, removing our guilt year after year, Ruler over all the earth, who reveals Your holiness through (Shabbat,) Israel, and the Day of Atonement.

YIZKOR SERVICE

יְיָ מָה־אָדָם וַתֵּדָעֵהוּ. בֶּן־אֱנוֹשׁ וַתְּחַשְּׁבֵהוּ: אָדָם
לַהֶבֶל דָּמָה. יָמָיו כְּצֵל עוֹבֵר: בַּבֹּקֶר יָצִיץ וְחָלָף.
לָעֶרֶב יְמוֹלֵל וְיָבֵשׁ: תָּשֵׁב אֱנוֹשׁ עַד־דַּכָּא. וַתֹּאמֶר
שׁוּבוּ בְנֵי אָדָם: לוּ חָכְמוּ יַשְׂכִּילוּ זֹאת יָבִינוּ
לְאַחֲרִיתָם: כִּי לֹא בְמוֹתוֹ יִקַּח הַכֹּל. לֹא־יֵרֵד אַחֲרָיו
כְּבוֹדוֹ: שְׁמָר־תָּם וּרְאֵה יָשָׁר. כִּי־אַחֲרִית לְאִישׁ
שָׁלוֹם: פָּדָה יְיָ נֶפֶשׁ עֲבָדָיו. וְלֹא יֶאְשְׁמוּ כָּל־הַחֹסִים
בּוֹ:

Adonay, what are we human beings that You should know
  about us,
We children of the flesh that You should take acount of us?
A person is like a vapor,
Our days as quickly passing as a shadow.
In the morning we flourish and grow tall,
In the evening we are cut down, dried up.
You turn us to contrition saying,
Do Tshuvah, children of the flesh!
Would that we were wise, and understood what will hap-
  pen to us in the end,
For when we die we take nothing away,
Our glory will not descend along with us.
Observe the innocent person, take notice of the upright,
For the end of such a person is peace.
Adonay can be trusted to redeem the soul of Godly people,
No one who trusts in God shall be confounded.

* * *

At the rising of the sun and at its going down
we remember them.

At the blowing of the wind and in the chill of winter
we remember them.

At the opening of the buds and in the rebirth of spring
we remember them.

    At the blueness of the skies and in the warmth of
    summer
    we remember them.

At the rustling of the leaves and in the beauty of autumn
we remember them.

    At the beginning of the year and when it ends
    we remember them.

As long as we live, they too will live:
for they are now a part of us,
as we remember them.

    When we are weary and in need of strength
    we remember them.

When we are lost and sick at heart
we remember them.

    When we have joy we crave to share
    we remember them.

When we have decisions that are difficult to make
we remember them.

    When we have achievements that are based on theirs
    we remember them.

As long as we live, they too will live;
for they are now a part of us,
as we remember them.

Selected Readings

Your joy is your sorrow unmasked.
The selfsame well from which your laughter rises was
    oftentimes filled with your tears.
And how else can it be?
The deeper that sorrow carves into your being, the more
    joy you can contain.

Is not the cup that holds your wine the very cup that was
  burned in the potter's oven?
And is not the lute that soothes your spirit, the very wood
  that was hollowed with knives?
When you are joyous, look deep into your heart and you
  shall find it is only that which has given you sorrow that
  is giving you joy.
When you are sorrowful look again in your heart, and you
  shall see that in truth you were weeping for that which
  has been your delight.
Some of you say, "Joy is greater than sorrow," and others
  say, "Nay, sorrow is the greater."
But I say to you, they are inseparable.
Together they come, and when one sits alone with you at
  your board, remember that the other is asleep upon your
  bed.
Verily you are suspended like scales between your sorrow
  and your joy.
Only when you are empty are you at standstill and
  balanced.
When the Treasure-keeper lifts you to weigh his gold or his
  silver, then must your joy or your sorrow rise or fall.

*   *   *

  Life is not fair. The wrong people get sick and the
wrong people get robbed and the wrong people get killed
in wars and in accidents. Some people see life's unfairness
and decide, "There is no God; the world is nothing but
chaos." Others see the same unfairness and ask themselves,
"Where do I get my sense of what is fair and unfair? Where
did I get my sense of outrage and indignation, my instinc-
tive response of sympathy? Don't I get these things from
God? Doesn't God plant in me a little bit of the divine
outrage at my injustice and oppression, just as God did for
the prophets of the Bible? Isn't my feeling of compassion
for the afflicted just a reflection of the compassion God
feels in seeing the suffering of God's creatures? Our

responding to life's unfairness with sympathy and righteous indignation, God's compassion and God's anger
working through us, may be the surest proof of all of God's
reality.

*   *   *

How often in a puzzling time
We turn around to mama
Asking, "What does all this mean?"

How often in a quiet hour
We turn around to the beloved of our life
Asking, "Do you remember when we both . . .?"

We feel the answer.
The knowing nod near moves the breeze
But there is no breeze.

The answer murmurs only in our mind
The smile lives somewhere in our eyes
No one else can see what has sown itself in us.

We are their earth.

Our words, our accents,
Half our songs, our tears,
All are flowers from their lives
Sweetening our blood
Perfuming our flesh.

Others say, "What a good person you are . . ."
We know the roots
However we two struggled when they stood beside us
From the struggle or beyond it rose
So much of us,
So much we need
To keep the conversation going.

"I'm my own person!" we always said.
But we weren't.
We never were.

Without them we are
Less.

And more
Because their shouting colors bloom
In us, if anywhere,
We must move the breeze along
To spread the fragrance
To listen past the breezes to the blow of breezes
Where the answers
(We)
Begin.

                    *   *   *

Strangers' eyes don't see
how in my small room I open a door
and begin my nightly stroll among the graves.
(How much earth—if you can call it earth—does it take to
    bury smoke?)
There are valleys and hills
and hidden twisted paths,
enough to last a whole night's journey.
In the dark I see shining towards me
faces of epitaphs
wailing their song.
Graves of the whole
vanished Jewish world
blossom in my one-man tent.
And I pray:
Be a father, a mother to me,
a sister, a brother,
my own children, body-kin,
real as pain,
from my own blood and skin,
be my own dead,
let me grasp and take in
these destroyed millions.

At dawn I shut the door
to my people's house of death.
I sit at the table and doze off,
humming a tune.
The enemy had no dominion over them.
Fathers, mothers, children from their cradles
ringed around death and overcame him.
All the children, astonished,
ran to meet the fear of death
without tears, like little Jewish bedtime stories.
And soon they flickered into flames
like small namesakes of God.

Who else, like me, has
his own nighttime
dead garden?
Who is destined for this, as I am?
Who has so much dead earth waiting for him, as for me?
And when I die
who will inherit my small house of death
and that shining gift, an eternal deathday light
forever flickering?

Private Memorials

In memory of a father:

יִזְכּוֹר אֱלֹהִים נִשְׁמַת אָבִי מוֹרִי ... שֶׁהָלַךְ לְעוֹלָמוֹ.
בַּעֲבוּר שֶׁאֲנִי נוֹדֵר (נוֹדֶרֶת) צְדָקָה בַּעֲדוֹ, בִּשְׂכַר זֶה,
תְּהֵא נַפְשׁוֹ צְרוּרָה בִּצְרוֹר הַחַיִּים עִם נִשְׁמוֹת
אַבְרָהָם יִצְחָק וְיַעֲקֹב, שָׂרָה רִבְקָה רָחֵל וְלֵאָה, וְעִם
שְׁאָר צַדִּיקִים וְצִדְקָנִיּוֹת שֶׁבְּגַן עֵדֶן. אָמֵן.

May God remember the soul of my father, my teacher
_____, who has gone to his eternal rest. In remembrance
of him, I shall perform acts of tzedakah and kindness. May

his soul be treasured in the cluster of immortals, along with
Abraham, Isaac, Jacob, Sarah, Rebecca, Rachel and Leah,
and all the righteous men and women who have merited a
share in the world to come. Amen.

In memory of a mother:

יִזְכּוֹר אֱלֹהִים נִשְׁמַת אִמִּי מוֹרָתִי ... שֶׁהָלְכָה
לְעוֹלָמָהּ. בַּעֲבוּר שֶׁאֲנִי נוֹדֵר (נוֹדֶרֶת) צְדָקָה בַּעֲדָהּ,
בִּשְׂכַר זֶה, תְּהֵא נַפְשָׁהּ צְרוּרָה בִּצְרוֹר הַחַיִּים עִם
נִשְׁמוֹת אַבְרָהָם יִצְחָק וְיַעֲקֹב, שָׂרָה רִבְקָה רָחֵל
וְלֵאָה, וְעִם שְׁאָר צַדִּיקִים וְצִדְקָנִיּוֹת שֶׁבְּגַן עֵדֶן. אָמֵן.

May God remember the soul of my mother, my teacher
_____, who has gone to her eternal rest. In remembrance
of her, I shall perform acts of tzedakah and kindness. May
her soul be treasured in the cluster of immortals, along
with Abraham, Isaac, Jacob, Sarah, Rebecca, Rachel, and
Leah, and all the righteous men and women who have
merited a share in the world to come. Amen.

In memory of a husband:

יִזְכּוֹר אֱלֹהִים נִשְׁמַת אִישִׁי הַיָּקָר ... שֶׁהָלַךְ
לְעוֹלָמוֹ. בַּעֲבוּר שֶׁאֲנִי נוֹדֶרֶת צְדָקָה בַּעֲדוֹ, בִּשְׂכַר זֶה,
תְּהֵא נַפְשׁוֹ צְרוּרָה בִּצְרוֹר הַחַיִּים עִם נִשְׁמוֹת
אַבְרָהָם יִצְחָק וְיַעֲקֹב, שָׂרָה רִבְקָה רָחֵל וְלֵאָה, וְעִם
שְׁאָר צַדִּיקִים וְצִדְקָנִיּוֹת שֶׁבְּגַן עֵדֶן. אָמֵן.

May God remember the soul of my beloved husband
_____, who has gone to his eternal rest. In remembrance
of him, I shall perform acts of tzedakah and kindness.
May his soul be treasured in the cluster of immortals,
along with Abraham, Isaac, Jacob, Sarah, Rebecca,
Rachel, and Leah, and all the righteous men and women
who have merited a share in the world to come. Amen.

In memory of a wife:

יִזְכּוֹר אֱלֹהִים נִשְׁמַת אִשְׁתִּי הַיְקָרָה ... שֶׁהָלְכָה
לְעוֹלָמָהּ. בַּעֲבוּר שֶׁאֲנִי נוֹדֵר צְדָקָה בַּעֲדָהּ, בִּשְׂכַר זֶה,
תְּהֵא נַפְשָׁהּ צְרוּרָה בִּצְרוֹר הַחַיִּים עִם נִשְׁמוֹת
אַבְרָהָם יִצְחָק וְיַעֲקֹב, שָׂרָה רִבְקָה רָחֵל וְלֵאָה, וְעִם
שְׁאָר צַדִּיקִים וְצִדְקָנִיּוֹת שֶׁבְּגַן עֵדֶן. אָמֵן.

May God remember the soul of my beloved wife _____,
who has gone to her eternal rest. In remembrance of her, I
shall perform acts of tzedakah and kindness. May her
soul be treasured in the cluster of immortals, along with
Sarah, Rebecca, Rachel, Leah, Abraham, Isaac, and
Jacob, and all the righteous men and women who have
merited a share in the world to come. Amen.

In memory of other relatives and friends:

יִזְכּוֹר אֱלֹהִים נִשְׁמוֹת קְרוֹבַי וִידִידַי שֶׁהָלְכוּ לְעוֹלָמָם.
בַּעֲבוּר שֶׁאֲנִי נוֹדֵר (נוֹדֶרֶת) צְדָקָה בְּעַד הַזְכָּרַת
נִשְׁמָתָם. בִּשְׂכַר זֶה תִּהְיֶינָה נַפְשׁוֹתֵיהֶם צְרוּרוֹת
בִּצְרוֹר הַחַיִּים עִם נִשְׁמוֹת אַבְרָהָם יִצְחָק וְיַעֲקֹב,
שָׂרָה רִבְקָה רָחֵל וְלֵאָה, וְעִם שְׁאָר צַדִּיקִים וְצִדְקָנִיּוֹת
שֶׁבְּגַן עֵדֶן. אָמֵן.

May God remember the soul of _____ and of all my
relatives and friends who have gone to their eternal rest. In
remembrance of them, I shall perform acts of tzedakah
and kindness. May their souls be treasured in the cluster of
immortals, along with Abraham, Isaac, Jacob, Sarah,
Rebecca, Rachel, and Leah, and all the righteous men and
women who have merited a share in the world to come.
Amen.

In memory of Jewish martyrs:

יִזְכּוֹר אֱלֹהִים נִשְׁמוֹת הַקְּדוֹשִׁים וְהַטְּהוֹרִים שֶׁנֶּהֶרְגוּ,
שֶׁנִּשְׁחֲטוּ וְשֶׁנִּשְׂרְפוּ וְשֶׁנִּטְבְּעוּ וְשֶׁנֶּחֶנְקוּ עַל קִדּוּשׁ
הַשֵּׁם. בַּעֲבוּר שֶׁאֲנִי נוֹדֵר (נוֹדֶרֶת) צְדָקָה בְּעַד הַזְכָּרַת
נִשְׁמוֹתֵיהֶם, בִּשְׂכַר זֶה, תִּהְיֶינָה נַפְשׁוֹתֵיהֶם צְרוּרוֹת
בִּצְרוֹר הַחַיִּים עִם נִשְׁמוֹת אַבְרָהָם יִצְחָק וְיַעֲקֹב,
שָׂרָה רִבְקָה רָחֵל וְלֵאָה, וְעִם שְׁאָר צַדִּיקִים וְצִדְקָנִיּוֹת
שֶׁבְּגַן עֵדֶן, וְנֹאמַר אָמֵן.

May God remember the souls of our martyrs, holy and
pure, who dedicated their deaths to God. In remembrance
of them I shall perform acts of tzedakah and kindness.
May their souls be treasured in the cluster of immortals,
along with Abraham, Isaac, Jacob, Sarah, Rebecca,
Rachel, and Leah, and all the righteous men and women
who have merited a share in the world to come. Amen.

El Maley Rachamim (for a man)

אֵל מָלֵא רַחֲמִים, שׁוֹכֵן בַּמְּרוֹמִים, הַמְצֵא מְנוּחָה
נְכוֹנָה תַּחַת כַּנְפֵי הַשְּׁכִינָה, בְּמַעֲלוֹת קְדוֹשִׁים
וּטְהוֹרִים כְּזֹהַר הָרָקִיעַ מַזְהִירִים, אֶת נִשְׁמַת ...
שֶׁהָלַךְ לְעוֹלָמוֹ. בַּעַל הָרַחֲמִים יַסְתִּירֵהוּ בְּסֵתֶר כְּנָפָיו
לְעוֹלָמִים, וְיִצְרוֹר בִּצְרוֹר הַחַיִּים אֶת נִשְׁמָתוֹ. יְיָ הוּא
נַחֲלָתוֹ; וְיָנוּחַ עַל מִשְׁכָּבוֹ בְּשָׁלוֹם, וְנֹאמַר אָמֵן.

O God in heaven, filled with compassion for those You
bring into this world, grant complete repose to the soul
of ..., who has entered his eternal home. Sheltered by
Your divine wings, may he join the company of the holy

and pure who shine as bright as heaven. Bring his soul into the bond of life that, with You as his portion, he may repose in peace. Amen.

El Maley Rachamim (for a woman)

אֵל מָלֵא רַחֲמִים, שׁוֹכֵן בַּמְּרוֹמִים, הַמְצֵא מְנוּחָה נְכוֹנָה תַּחַת כַּנְפֵי הַשְּׁכִינָה, בְּמַעֲלוֹת קְדוֹשִׁים וּטְהוֹרִים כְּזְהַר הָרָקִיעַ מַזְהִירִים, אֶת נִשְׁמַת ... שֶׁהָלְכָה לְעוֹלָמָהּ. בַּעַל הָרַחֲמִים יַסְתִּירֶהָ בְּסֵתֶר כְּנָפָיו לְעוֹלָמִים, וְיִצְרוֹר בִּצְרוֹר הַחַיִּים אֶת נִשְׁמָתָהּ. יְיָ הוּא נַחֲלָתָהּ; וְתָנוּחַ עַל מִשְׁכָּבָהּ בְּשָׁלוֹם, וְנֹאמַר אָמֵן.

O God in heaven, filled with compassion for those You bring into this world, grant complete repose to the soul of . . ., who has entered her eternal home. Sheltered by Your divine wings, may she join the company of the holy and pure who shine as bright as heaven. Bring her soul into the bond of life that, with You as her portion, she may repose in peace. Amen.

(Together)

It is hard to speak of oneness when our world is not complete, when those who once brought wholeness to our life have gone, and naught but memory can fill the emptiness their passing leaves behind. But memory can tell us only what we were, in company with those we loved; it cannot help us find what each of us, alone, must now become. Yet no person is really alone; those who live no more echo still within our thoughts and words, and what they did has become woven into what we are. We do best homage to our dead by living our lives fully even in the shadow of our loss. For each of our lives is worth the life of the whole

world; In each one is the breath of the Ultimate One. In affirming the One, we affirm the worth of each one whose life, now ended, brought us closer to the Source of Life, in whose union no person is alone and every life finds purpose.

Standing now before the Source of Life, the ultimate author of our purpose, let us join in hopefulness and praise, in blessing, and in trust:

El Maley Rachamim (for all our departed)

אֵל מָלֵא רַחֲמִים. שׁוֹכֵן בַּמְּרוֹמִים. הַמְצֵא מְנוּחָה
נְכוֹנָה תַּחַת כַּנְפֵי הַשְּׁכִינָה. בְּמַעֲלוֹת קְדוֹשִׁים
וּטְהוֹרִים כְּזֹהַר הָרָקִיעַ מַזְהִירִים, אֶת־נִשְׁמוֹת כָּל־
אֵלֶּה שֶׁהִזְכַּרְנוּ הַיּוֹם וְאֶת־נִשְׁמוֹת כָּל־אַחֵינוּ בְּנֵי
יִשְׂרָאֵל שֶׁמָּסְרוּ נַפְשָׁם עַל־קְדֻשַׁת הַשֵּׁם. בַּעַל
הָרַחֲמִים יַסְתִּירֵם בְּסֵתֶר כְּנָפָיו לְעוֹלָמִים. וְיִצְרוֹר
בִּצְרוֹר הַחַיִּים אֶת־נִשְׁמָתָם. יְיָ הוּא נַחֲלָתָם. וְיָנוּחוּ
עַל־מִשְׁכְּבוֹתָם בְּשָׁלוֹם. וְנֹאמַר אָמֵן:

O God in heaven, filled with compassion for those You bring into this world, grant complete repose to the souls of all those we are remembering today, and to all our people who have given their lives to sanctify Your name. Sheltered by Your divine wings, may they join the company of the holy and pure who shine as bright as heaven. Bring their souls into the bond of life that, with You as their portion, they may repose in peace. Amen.

Mourner's Kaddish

יִתְגַּדַּל וְיִתְקַדַּשׁ שְׁמֵהּ רַבָּא. בְּעָלְמָא דִי בְרָא

כִּרְעוּתֵהּ. וְיַמְלִיךְ מַלְכוּתֵהּ בְּחַיֵּיכוֹן וּבְיוֹמֵיכוֹן וּבְחַיֵּי
דְכָל בֵּית יִשְׂרָאֵל. בַּעֲגָלָא וּבִזְמַן קָרִיב וְאִמְרוּ. אָמֵן:

*Yit-ga-dal v'yit-ka-dash sh'mey ra-bah, b'al-mah di v'rah
chi-ru-tey,*
*V'yam-leech mal-chu-tey, b'cha-yey-chon uv'yo-mey-chon
uv-cha-yey*
*d'chol bet Yis-ra-el, ba-a-ga-lah u-viz-man ka-reev. V'im-ru
A-men.*

יְהֵא שְׁמֵהּ רַבָּא מְבָרַךְ לְעָלַם וּלְעָלְמֵי עָלְמַיָּא:

Y'hey sh'mey ra-bah m'vo-rach l'a-lam ul-al-mey al-ma-ya.

יִתְבָּרַךְ וְיִשְׁתַּבַּח וְיִתְפָּאַר וְיִתְרוֹמַם וְיִתְנַשֵּׂא וְיִתְהַדָּר
וְיִתְעַלֶּה וְיִתְהַלָּל שְׁמֵהּ דְּקֻדְשָׁא. בְּרִיךְ הוּא. לְעֵלָּא
לְעֵלָּא מִן כָּל בִּרְכָתָא וְשִׁירָתָא תֻּשְׁבְּחָתָא וְנֶחֱמָתָא
דַּאֲמִירָן בְּעָלְמָא וְאִמְרוּ. אָמֵן:

*Yit-ba-rach v'yish-ta-bach v'yit-pa-ar v'yit-ro-mam v'yit-
na-sey*
*v'yit-ha-dar v'yit-a-leh v'yit-ha-lal sh'mey d-kud'sha, b'reech
hu.*
*L'ey-la l'ey-la min kol bir-cha-tah v'shir-a-tah, tush-b'cha-tah
v'ne-che-ma-tah da-a-mi-ran b'al-mah. V'im-ru A-men.*

יְהֵא שְׁלָמָא רַבָּא מִן שְׁמַיָּא וְחַיִּים עָלֵינוּ וְעַל כָּל
יִשְׂרָאֵל וְאִמְרוּ. אָמֵן:

*Y'hey sh'la-mah ra-bah min sh'ma-ya v'cha-yim
a-ley-nu v'al kol Yis-ra-el. V'im-ru A-men.*

עוֹשֶׂה שָׁלוֹם בִּמְרוֹמָיו הוּא יַעֲשֶׂה שָׁלוֹם עָלֵינוּ וְעַל
כָּל יִשְׂרָאֵל וְאִמְרוּ. אָמֵן:

*O-seh sha-lom bim-ro-mav hu ya-a-seh sha-lom a-ley-nu
v'al kol Yis-ra-el. V'im-ru A-men.*

May God's great name be praised and sanctified in the world! May Your Rule be established in our lifetime and the lifetime of the House of Israel. God's great name is blessed and praised far beyond all blessings and praises we can ever say in the world.

May there be a great peace from heaven and life for us and all Israel. May the One who makes peace in the high places, make peace for us and all Israel. Amen.

(Remain standing)

Returning the Scroll to the Ark

This is the covenant that I shall make with the house of Israel after those days, Adonay proclaims:
I shall put my Torah in their inward parts, and on their heart shall I write it, and I shall be their God and they shall be My people. No more will you need to teach your neighbor to know God, for you shall all know Me, from the smallest of you to the greatest of you, says Adonay.

יְהַלְלוּ אֶת שֵׁם יְיָ כִּי נִשְׂגָּב שְׁמוֹ לְבַדּוֹ׃

O praise the Name of God, the most exalted name of all!

הוֹדוֹ עַל אֶרֶץ וְשָׁמָיִם וַיָּרֶם קֶרֶן לְעַמּוֹ תְּהִלָּה לְכָל
חֲסִידָיו לִבְנֵי יִשְׂרָאֵל עַם קְרֹבוֹ הַלְלוּיָהּ׃

Hodo al eretz v'shamayim
Vayarem keren l'amo:
T'hilah l'chol chaseedav
*   livney Yisrael am kerovo*
Halleluya.

God's glory is in the earth and heavens, and the people of God is raised on high. The pious are become a praise, and the children of Israel are become intimates of Adonay. Halleluyah!

While the Torah is being placed in the ark:

וּבְנֻחֹה יֹאמַר: שׁוּבָה, יְיָ, רִבְבוֹת אַלְפֵי יִשְׂרָאֵל. קוּמָה
יְיָ לִמְנוּחָתֶךָ, אַתָּה וַאֲרוֹן עֻזֶּךָ. כֹּהֲנֶיךָ יִלְבְּשׁוּ צֶדֶק,
וַחֲסִידֶיךָ יְרַנֵּנוּ. בַּעֲבוּר דָּוִד עַבְדֶּךָ, אַל תָּשֵׁב פְּנֵי
מְשִׁיחֶךָ. כִּי לֶקַח טוֹב נָתַתִּי לָכֶם, תּוֹרָתִי אַל תַּעֲזֹבוּ.

And when the ark rested, Moses proclaimed: Return,
Adonay, to all the myriads of Israel! Rise up toward Your
resting place, You and the ark, the symbol of Your power.
Let the kohanim be clothed in righteousness, let Your
pious ones sing for joy! For Your servant David's sake, do
not turn away Your anointed one, the messiah. For I have
given you good teaching, indeed, My own Torah; do not
forsake it.

עֵץ חַיִּים הִיא לַמַּחֲזִיקִים בָּהּ וְתֹמְכֶיהָ מְאֻשָּׁר: דְּרָכֶיהָ
דַרְכֵי־נֹעַם וְכָל־נְתִיבוֹתֶיהָ שָׁלוֹם: הֲשִׁיבֵנוּ יְהֹוָה אֵלֶיךָ
וְנָשׁוּבָה חַדֵּשׁ יָמֵינוּ כְּקֶדֶם:

Eytz chayim hee lamachazeekim ba
V'tomcheyha m'ushar;
D'racheyha darchey noam
V'chol n'teevoteyha shalom
Hasheeveynu Adonay eylecha v'nashuva,
Chadesh yameynu k'kedem.

It is a tree which ensures eternal life for those who take
hold of it, how fortunate are its supporters! Its ways are
pleasant ways, its paths comprise Shalom. Bring us back to
You, Adonay, that we might return, renew our life as in the
days when You and we began.

The Ark is closed

AFTERNOON SERVICE
FOR
YOM KIPPUR

AFTERNOON READINGS
FOR YOM KIPPUR

THE AVODAH SERVICE

Introduction

Sacrifice . . . the word almost makes us shudder. Ancient, faceless functionaries offering up something helpless to a God who does not need it and cannot want it; taking in vain the life of an innocent animal, ruining good grain that might feed human beings.

At best it embarrasses us: pagan peoples offered sacrifices; the sacrificial period in Jewish life seems to be an historical anomaly, properly replaced by prayer when the Temple was destroyed.

De we mourn the Temple? Yes, surely—for the human lives that were destroyed when it was sacked, for the glory of an independent Jewish life that went up in its flames. In the Musaf service we mourn whatever wrongs our people may have done to contribute to the destruction: injustice and callousness to the poor, the prophets said, would destroy the First Temple; baseless hatred, the rabbis said, doomed the Second.

Do we mourn the end of sacrifices? Do we pray for their restoration? We know many Jews do, and so we identify with their sorrow and their hope. Many of us, who may still hope for the Messiah or a messianic age, hope that God will create a form of worship for the new age that will require no innocent blood, that will offer up a bounteous harvest not only to the divine, but to a human race which shall know hunger never again.

And yet . . . memory of the sacrifices will not go away. If we remove their mention from our prayers, change the Torah readings so we do not have to confront them—still the prayerbook continues to describe the offerings presented every day,

every Shabbat and holiday, and now at this moment of Yom Kippur, when the tradition calls on us to read of the sacrifices offered up by the High Kohen, the High Priest, as his contribution to the rite of atonement sought by his people every year while the Temple stood. We cannot pretend that the sacrifices never happened, or that they were not the most compelling aspect of the Jew's encounter with God for a thousand years. Indeed, because the prayers which comprise our encounter grew up around the sacrifices, because the sacrifices gave their names and times to our prayers, we can only deepen our own relationship to God when we try to understand the sacrifices which underlie them.

To begin with, sacrifice is a Latin word, meaning "holy act." The Hebrew word is korban, from the root *krv,* meaning "near." Ancient Jews brought the animal or the grain near to God, believing that "the earth is God's and the fullness thereof," and therefore since all food comes from God, it is only proper to return the choicest foods to their source as an act that reflected its name, *korban,* drawing near. For when one placed hands on the offering one almost said, "Accept this as if it were I myself." When the physical animal or grain was placed on the fire of the altar, the fire changed its physical form into smoke, essentially invisible, a form in which it mingled with the invisible places where God dwells. As the presenters watched the smoke of the offering of their own hand disperse through the air and enter the presence of God, they might imagine that they themselves were entering that presence, feeling themselves lifted up along with their gift before the very throne of Glory.

The kohanim who offered korbanot offered prayers as well, in one of the chambers of the great Temple, in very much the form and the order in which we do today, though their prayer service was much shorter. At the same time, Jews would gather together in their town when the kohanim from their area went up to Jerusalem to offer korbanot. The local Jews would meet to read psalms and Torah verses and chant prayers themselves. Thus when the Temple was destroyed it was inevitable that prayers would replace *korbanot*—indeed, Rabbi Yochanan

ben Zakkai ruled that while *korbanot* were called Avodah (Service), prayers were also Avodah—*Avodah She-ba-lev*, the Service rendered from the heart. For prayers are words, quite invisible, easily able to mingle with the invisible places where God dwells. The words of our prayers are some of the very ones God used in creating the world, and so it is only proper to return the choicest words to their source as an act of gratitude and replenishment. As we listen to these offerings of our own hearts disperse through the air and enter the presence of God, it is as though we ourselves were entering that presence, and we can feel ourselves lifted up along with our gift before the very throne of Glory.

The Avodah service on Yom Kippur is a challenge to explore through words the dimensions of our people's ancient encounters with God. What was once a yearly experience of drama through detail is for us an outpouring of words in great detail, with the drama dependent on our own imaginations and our own ability to translate words into prayer. As a preface to the Avodah Service this afternoon, in fact, a very simple prayer may be appropriate:

> Help us, O God, to lift ourselves upon these very ordinary words that they may carry us back to our people's most extraordinary experience of You, that we who mingle with each other here today may draw near to You once more in awe and intimacy and great forgiveness.

A Preparation for the Avodah

When the great Rabbi Israel Baal Shem-Tov saw misfortune threatening the Jews, it was his custom to go into a certain part of the forest to meditate. There he would light a fire, say a special prayer, and the miracle would be accomplished and the misfortune averted.

Later, when his disciple, the celebrated Magid of Mezritch, had occasion, for the same reason, to intercede with heaven, he would go to the same place in the forest and say:

"Master of the Universe, listen!

I do not know how to light the fire, but I am
still able to say the prayer."

and again, the miracle would be accomplished.

Still later, Rabbi Moshe-Leib of Sasov, in order to save his
people once more, would go into the forest and say:

"I do not know how to light the fire, I do not
know the prayer, but I know the place and this
must be sufficient."

It was sufficient and the miracle was accomplished.

Then it fell to Rabbi Israel of Rizhyn to overcome misfortune. Sitting in his armchair, his head in his hands, he
spoke to God:

"I am unable to light the fire and I do not know the
prayer. I cannot even find the place in the forest. All I
can do is to tell the story, and this must be sufficient."

And it was sufficient.

Listen, God. We are going to tell the story.

AVODAH

Strong and Powerful are You. Whose might compares
to You? Upon the cold dark waters You created light,
revealing an earth in bud and blossom. In the sky You set
great lights, and from the seas You brought forth multi-
tudes of fish. You sent flights of birds across the heavens;
upon the clods of earth You brought forth animals—a
whole world filled with food and drink but none to sit
down at table. And so You kneaded from the clay a human
being in Your image, into whom You breathed Your pure
breath. Commanded not to eat from the Tree of Knowing
Good and Evil, Adam and Eve disobeyed, and from that
time forward humans have earned their bread by the sweat
of their brow and brought forth children in painful travail.

Their first children, Cain and Abel, strove together,
and Cain brought murder into the world. Violence

increased and You determined to flood the world, saving only Noah, and his children filled the earth once more. Yet some sought to build a tower into heaven that they might have a name in the world, and so You broke up their single language into many parts and scattered them and their words across the world.

But beloved Abraham used words to make You known in the world. You in turn promised him generations who would turn the pain of childbirth into the fruit of Your covenant, and You offered him a land from which the sweat of his brow would produce the proof of Your promise. From his loins upon that land grew Isaac, brought upon the altar for a burnt-offering, followed by Jacob, a lamb without a taint, father of the twelve tribes, each one unblemished for the service of God.

Your choice of Jacob's sons to minister to you was faithful Levi, out of whose tribe You chose the family of Aaron, the Kohanim, to serve in the Holy of Holies, to reside inside the Temple seven days, and carry out the service of atonement on Yom Kippur. No longer would the Creation You formed stand in danger of destruction, for upon that altar would You be reconciled with Israel, bearer of Your promise for the world.

Each year while the sacred Temple stood, the same procedure would be followed:

Seven days before Yom Kippur, the High Kohen was taken from his home to an apartment in the Temple, where he remained secluded for the week and practiced the service. He had to be physically and spiritually cleansed and had to devote his mind wholly to the task before him, for on Yom Kippur he was to wear the sacred garments and enter the Holy of Holies.

During the week of purification, an alternate kohen was made ready to take the High Kohen's place if anything happened to disqualify him. Sages would read the details of the service to the High Kohen in case he had forgotten

them or had never learned them. All week he was allowed
to eat and drink whatever he liked, but from sunset on the
day preceding Yom Kippur, he was required to eat lightly,
since much food induces sleep.

He stayed awake all the preceding night. If he was learned,
he would discuss Torah; if not, sages would discuss it in his
presence. If he began to fall asleep, his fellow kohanim
would snap their fingers and say to him, "Lord High
Kohen, you ought to stand up and drive sleep away by
walking on the pavement." Thus, his friends and colleagues would divert him until the time of the daily morning offering.

He would then be taken to the place of immersion, since no
one was ever permitted to officiate in the Temple before
immersion, even if he was ceremonially clean. During the
course of Yom Kippur, the High Kohen would immerse
himself five times.

All read

He consecrated his own atonement offering by making this
confession over it: "Adonay, I have done wrong against
you, I and my household. Adonay, forgive the wrongs and
failings of which I and my household have been guilty in
your sight, as it is written in the Torah set forth by your
servant Moses: 'On this day, God will give you a new start
by purifying you. From all your guilt in the sight of
Adonay you shall be clean.'"

When the kohanim and the people, who were standing in
the Temple court, heard God's glorious and revered Name
expressly pronounced by the High Kohen in holiness and
purity, they bowed down, prostrated themselves, and worshipped. They fell upon their faces and responded: *Baruch
shem k'vod malchuto l'olam va-ed*: "Praised be the true
Name whose glorious sovereignty extends beyond all time
and all worlds."

וְכַךְ הָיָה אוֹמֵר. אָנָּא הַשֵּׁם. חָטָאתִי. עָוִיתִי. פָּשַׁעְתִּי
לְפָנֶיךָ אֲנִי וּבֵיתִי וּבְנֵי אַהֲרֹן עַם קְדוֹשֶׁךָ. אָנָּא בַשֵּׁם.
כַּפֶּר־נָא. לַחֲטָאִים. וְלַעֲוֹנוֹת. וְלַפְּשָׁעִים. שֶׁחָטָאתִי
וְשֶׁעָוִיתִי. וְשֶׁפָּשַׁעְתִּי לְפָנֶיךָ אֲנִי וּבֵיתִי וּבְנֵי אַהֲרֹן עַם
קְדוֹשֶׁךָ. כַּכָּתוּב בְּתוֹרַת מֹשֶׁה עַבְדֶּךָ מִפִּי כְבוֹדֶךָ.
כִּי־בַיּוֹם הַזֶּה יְכַפֵּר עֲלֵיכֶם לְטַהֵר אֶתְכֶם מִכֹּל
חַטֹּאתֵיכֶם לִפְנֵי יְהֹוָה—

וְהַכֹּהֲנִים וְהָעָם הָעוֹמְדִים בָּעֲזָרָה, כְּשֶׁהָיוּ שׁוֹמְעִים
אֶת הַשֵּׁם הַנִּכְבָּד וְהַנּוֹרָא, מְפֹרָשׁ יוֹצֵא מִפִּי כֹהֵן גָּדוֹל
בִּקְדֻשָּׁה וּבְטָהֳרָה, הָיוּ כּוֹרְעִים וּמִשְׁתַּחֲוִים וּמוֹדִים
וְנוֹפְלִים עַל פְּנֵיהֶם, וְאוֹמְרִים: בָּרוּךְ שֵׁם כְּבוֹד
מַלְכוּתוֹ לְעוֹלָם וָעֶד.

He returned to his own offering, and this time he said the following confession over it: "Adonay, I have done wrong against you, I and my household and the family of Aaron, your priestly community. Adonay, forgive the wrongs and failings of which I and my household and the family of Aaron, Your priestly community, have been guilty in your sight, as it says in the Torah set forth by your servant Moses: 'On this day, God will give you a new start by purifying you. From all your guilt in the sight of Adonay you shall be clean.'"

All read

When the kohanim and the people, who were standing in the Temple court, heard God's glorious and revered name expressly pronounced by the High Kohen in holiness and purity, they bowed down and prostrated themselves and worshipped. They fell upon their faces and responded: *Baruch shem k'vod malchuto l'olam va-ed*: "Praised be the true name whose glorious sovereignty extends beyond all time and all worlds."

וְהַכֹּהֲנִים וְהָעָם הָעוֹמְדִים בָּעֲזָרָה, כְּשֶׁהָיוּ שׁוֹמְעִים
אֶת הַשֵּׁם הַנִּכְבָּד וְהַנּוֹרָא, מְפֹרָשׁ יוֹצֵא מִפִּי כֹהֵן גָּדוֹל
בִּקְדֻשָּׁה וּבְטָהֳרָה, הָיוּ כּוֹרְעִים וּמִשְׁתַּחֲוִים וּמוֹדִים
וְנוֹפְלִים עַל פְּנֵיהֶם, וְאוֹמְרִים: בָּרוּךְ שֵׁם כְּבוֹד
מַלְכוּתוֹ לְעוֹלָם וָעֶד.

He would prolong the intoning of the divine name, until
the worshippers had completed the response, whereupon
he would finish the verse by saying the word *tit'haru*—
"you shall be clean." And You, in Your goodness, would
awaken Your mercy and forgive the family of Aaron, Your
priestly community.

He would now enter the Holy of Holies. Only the High
Kohen was permitted to enter that room and only on this
day of the year when he went to ask God's pardon for the
entire community of Israel. Before he entered it, the High
Kohen was addressed by the eldest of the kohanim: "Consider that you are about to come before the Sovereign of all
Sovereigns, whose presence fills the universe. Know that if
you fail to concentrate on what you are about to do, or if
you harbor selfish thoughts, you will fall dead, and the
atonement of Israel will not be attained, for upon Israel
rests the burden of teaching people to be holy, and upon
you rests the burden of teaching Israel to be holy. Have
you searched your heart to make certain that you do not
come before the Sovereign while the enemy is still within
you?" The High Kohen replied that he had searched his
deeds and had turned his heart back toward God and had
urged his fellow kohanim to do likewise. The High Kohen
entered the Holy of Holies and presented the sacred
incense, whose sweet smell symbolized Israel's intention to
please God by the keeping of mitzvot. He then hurried out
to where the atonement offering for the community of
Israel stood, and made the following confession over it:
"Adonay, your people, the house of Israel, have done
wrong against you. Adonay, forgive the wrongs and fail-

ings of which your people, the house of Israel, have been
guilty in your sight, as it is written in the Torah set forth by
your servant Moses: 'On this day, God will give you a new
start by purifying you. From all your guilt, in the sight of
Adonay you shall be clean.'"

All read

When the kohanim and the people, who were standing in
the Temple court, heard God's glorious and revered name
expressly pronounced by the High Kohen in holiness and
purity, they bowed down, prostrated themselves and worshipped. They fell upon their faces and responded: *Baruch
shem k'vod malchuto l'olam va-ed*: "Praised be the true
name whose glorious sovereignty extends beyond all time
and all worlds."

וְהַכֹּהֲנִים וְהָעָם הָעוֹמְדִים בָּעֲזָרָה, כְּשֶׁהָיוּ שׁוֹמְעִים
אֶת הַשֵּׁם הַנִּכְבָּד וְהַנּוֹרָא, מְפֹרָשׁ יוֹצֵא מִפִּי כֹהֵן גָּדוֹל
בִּקְדֻשָׁה וּבְטָהֳרָה, הָיוּ כּוֹרְעִים וּמִשְׁתַּחֲוִים וּמוֹדִים
וְנוֹפְלִים עַל פְּנֵיהֶם, וְאוֹמְרִים: בָּרוּךְ שֵׁם כְּבוֹד
מַלְכוּתוֹ לְעוֹלָם וָעֶד.

He would prolong the intoning of the divine name, until
the worshippers had completed the response, whereupon
he would finish the verse by saying *tit'haru*—"you shall be
clean." And You in Your goodness would awaken Your
mercy and forgive Your people, the house of Israel.

Now, the High Kohen sent one goat away to the wilderness with the person standing in readiness, and offered up
the other goat and the bullock in the manner prescribed.
He read aloud the portions of the Torah concerning Yom
Kippur, then offered up the remaining offerings of the day,
burned the incense, and lighted the lamps. He bathed five
times, changed from linen garments to gold, and the
people escorted him home.

He was elated, his face shone like the sun, as the people escorted their faithful messenger home, joyous in the knowledge that scarlet had turned to white, that all their sins were washed away. The clouds distilled their dew; the watered fields yielded their produce; and the harvesters sang psalms of praise as they carried home their sheaves. The land rang with song from end to end, letting wayfarers know how good God is. The faithful messenger had indeed fulfilled his mission. How fortunate the people whose lot this is! How fortunate the people whose God is Adonay! Happy the eye that saw all this, happy the ear that heard all this!

EYLEH EZKARAH: The Ten Martyrs

Introduction

Since the destruction of the Temple in Jerusalem, prayer has taken the place of sacrifice, but that does not imply that sacrifice was abolished when the sacrificial rite went out of existence. Prayer is not a substitute for sacrifice. Prayer *is* sacrifice. What has changed is the substance of sacrifice: the self took the place of the thing. The spirit is the same.

"Accept the offerings of praise, Adonay," says the Psalmist (119:108). "Let my prayer be counted as incense before You, and the lifting of my hands as an evening sacrifice" (141:2). In moments of prayer we try to surrender our vanities, to burn our insolence, to abandon bias, cant, envy. We lay all our forces before God. The word is but an altar. We do not sacrifice. We are the sacrifice.

To the saints, prayer is a hazard, a venture of peril. Every person who prays is a Kohen at the greatest of all temples. The whole universe is the temple. With good prayer we may purify it, with improper prayer we may contaminate it. With good prayer we may "build worlds," with improper prayer we may "destroy worlds." According to Rabbi Ami (Taanit 8a), a person's prayer is answered only if one stakes one's very life on it. "It is a miracle that a person survives the hour of worship," the Baal Shem said.

The readiness to make the supreme sacrifice for the sake of God's name, for the sake of the truth that God is One, has long been the essence of our devotion in proclaiming the Shma, Hear, O Israel. When following the Bar Kochba rebellion, the Roman government prohibited the teaching of Torah, the great Rabbi Akiba continued to expound the words of God and to convey them to others. Thereupon he was arrested and eventually condemned to the hand of the executioner. The Talmud tells us:

"When the Romans brought Rabbi Akiba out to execution, it was time for reading the Shma; and though they were combing his flesh with iron combs, he continued to take upon himself the yoke of the Rule of heaven," he continued to read the words of the Shema: Hear, O Israel, Adonay is our God, Adonay is One. Thou shalt love Adonay thy God with all thy heart, with all thy soul, and with all thy might. His disciples said to him: "Our master, thus far! (Although suffering such agonies, you still say the Shma!)" And Rabbi Akiba answered them: "Throughout my life I have been troubled with this verse, 'And thou shalt love Adonay, thy God . . . with all thy soul,' which means: Even if I take thy life. For said I, 'When will it be in my power to fulfill it? Now that the opportunity is mine, shall I not fulfill it?'"

He prolonged the word *echad* ("one" in "Hear, O Israel") until his soul departed with the word *echad*. A heavenly voice issued forth and announced, "Happy art thou, Rabbi Akiba, that thy soul went out with the word *echad.*"

*   *   *

Rabbi Akiba was not alone. Ten of the greatest scholars of their age, a minyan of saints, were put to death by the Romans for daring to teach Torah when the Emperor Hadrian had forbidden it.

On this most holy day, to read of the heroism of these ten holy men reminds us that Torah is not an escape from the world, but a confrontation with it; to study Torah is to raise the banner of holiness before a society profaned. In

some generations, our learning shall win new followers for God; in others it may cause our blood to flow again across the banner before truth wins out. But because the ultimate triumph of Torah is sure, to read of the death of the Ten Martyrs is not only to weep for their suffering, but also to resolve to learn even more Torah in the year to come, thus helping to redeem the death of great teachers by proclaiming the eternal life of the word of God.

Let our prayer, the Eyleh Ezkarah, the Remembrance of the Ten Martyrs, be counted as incense before You, even as the ten sages, unable to bring their offerings in the ruined Temple, offered themselves, when no other choice remained.

EYLEH EZKARAH

These I will remember, and I will pour out my soul's grief for them. Evildoers have consumed us as the fire consumes a forgotten cake in the oven. There was no reprieve for the ten done to death by the Emperor of Rome. Learned in law from the mouths of the sages, the Emperor turned to the Bible and read, "Whoever kidnaps and sells a person, or if the person is even found in his possession, shall be put to death."

He commanded that his palace be filled with shoes, and in his insolence, summoned ten great sages, masters of Torah and teaching. "Judge this case," he told them. "Neither twist it nor lie, but tell me the clear truth: If a person is found to have kidnapped one of his brothers of the family of Israel and enslaved and sold him, what is the verdict?"

"That thief must die," they answered.

"Then what of your fathers who bartered their brother Joseph to a caravan of Ishmaelites in exchange for shoes? Accept the doom of Heaven, for since the days of your fathers there have been none like you. Had they been alive, I would have judged them in your presence, but instead you shall take upon yourselves the sin of your fathers."

"Give us three days to learn whether this sentence was

ordained in Heaven. If we are obligated to pay this price, we will bear the sentence of the Merciful One."

Shaking and trembling, all turned their eyes to Rabbi Ishmael, the high Kohen, charging him to pronounce the true name of God and ascend to discover whether God were the source of the sentence.

Rabbi Ishmael purified himself. In soaring hymns, he spoke the Name and rose to the Placeless World. There he asked a being in priestly garb and was answered, "Accept it upon yourselves, O righteous and beloved, for I have heard from behind the curtain that you would be ensnared in this manner." So he returned and told his comrades, and the evil Emperor commanded violent deaths for them.

First they took Rabbi Ishmael and Rabban Shimon ben Gamliel, and each sought to be the first to die, for neither wanted to witness the death of his friend. So they were commanded to draw lots and the lot fell on Rabban Shimon, and with a sword they hewed off his head. Rabbi Ishmael picked it up and cried bitterly, "O tongue, so quick to share its beautiful teachings, through no fault of yours do you now lick dust."

The wicked king's daughter heard his weeping and saw his beauty, and lust flamed in her heart. She asked for his life, but her father refused her. Instead, the skin was flayed from his face, but when they reached the place of the tefillin he cried bitterly to God and died.

The angels cried out in dismay, "Is this the Torah and is this its reward? The enemy derides Your great and awe-filled name and confutes and scorns the words of the Torah."

A voice from heaven answered, "Another sound and I will turn the world to water—my creation shall become chaos once more. This is my decree. Accept it, lovers of the timeless Torah."

Then Rabbi Akiva was led out to die, the great sage who had said, "The command 'You shall love your neighbor as yourself' is the unifying principle of all Torah." While they flayed his flesh with double-edged iron combs,

he prayed and gave no sign of pain. And when they asked him why he recited the Shma, he replied, "All my life I have tried to serve God with my whole heart and with all that I own, but only now have I been permitted to serve God with my life." He died whispering. "Adonay is one."

Rabbi Chaninah ben Tradyon, seized while illegally teaching the Torah, was wrapped in his own Torah scroll and set afire. A wet sponge was placed on his heart so that he would die slowly. Up, up, beyond the flames he turned his eyes, and his students asked, "What do you see?" He answered, "The parchment burns, the letters fly away." "Lean down to the fire and die," his students counseled. But he replied, "No one may hasten his own death." His executioner was filled with wonder and compassion. "Master," he asked, "if I take away the sponge from your heart, so that you will die more quickly, will I have a share in the next world of yours?" And Rabbi Chaninah answered, "Yes," because he knew that God rewards all acts of kindness. The executioner removed the sponge and cast himself into the flames. And a voice from heaven was heard declaring, "Rabbi Chaninah and his executioner have entered Paradise together."

One by one, ten great sages were murdered, their blood spilled in vengeance for an act committed two thousand years before, an act whose perpetrators had been forgiven by their victim. Yet the ten dedicated their deaths to the holiness of God.

They were our masters and teachers,

Ishmael the High Priest
Shimon ben Gamliel
Akiva
Chaninah ben Tradyon
Hutzpit the Interpreter
Elazar ben Shamua
Chaninah ben Chakmai
Yeshevav the Scribe
Judah ben Dama
Judah ben Bava

"The house of Jacob shall become a fire," You told us, "and the house of Joseph a flame, but the house of Rome shall be like straw, and it shall be consumed." Now the straw has quenched the fire.

This befell us and we pour out our hearts in the telling. From Your high place hear our prayer: "Adonay, Adonay, merciful and gracious God, look down from heaven and attend to us, look out from behind the curtain and for the sake of our martyred sages blot out our wrongdoings, O Sovereign God who rules from a merciful throne. O our Creator, we have done wrong! O our Creator, grant us pardon!

(If Musaf is offered aloud, continue on pp. 210–211 with Sh'ma Koleynu. If there is no Musaf, Ashamnu, p. 348, and Al Cheyt, p. 350 or p. 353, may be recited here.)

Reflections on the Martyrology

In reading of these Ten Martyrs, we of this generation cannot help but direct our thoughts to the six million of our people, who were slaughtered during World War II. We think of the way they were abandoned to their fate by powerful governments which, aware of the savage plans of the enemy, violated the moral imperative: "Neither shall you stand idly by the blood of your neighbor" (Leviticus 19:16). They were thus also guilty, for the silent spectator to a crime is as guilty as is the agent of the deed.

But the mood of this martyrology is not one of protest or even indignation. Composed soon after the first Crusade (1096 C.E.), this dirge is a reflection of the utter bewilderment of that generation in their inability to understand the meaning of the martyred death of countless innocents. Such unspeakable tragedies had to be explained without impugning the purity and the nobility of the character of the victims, and without accusing God of abandoning this hunted and tormented people. For this reason, they resorted to the midrashic tradition of the Ten Martyrs, which told of a previous instance of martyrs suf-

fering death, not for their own sins, but in expiation of the sins of previous generations.

This strange concept collides with the teaching that individuals are answerable only for their own conduct, a teaching formulated by Ezekiel in repudiation of the idea of collective and inherited guilt. Yet the Rabbis did not hesitate to avow that in times of widespread moral corruption, the righteous are "seized" for the guilt of their generation, and that where there are no righteous people in a particular generation, the children are "seized" for its guilt (Shab. 33b). This conception of the corporate moral solidarity and responsibility of the community is also reflected in an idea, found in the Apocrypha, that martyrs suffer because of the sinfulness of the entire people. Thus Eleazar, when tortured by his heathen persecutors, prays:

> Thou knowest O God, that though I might have saved myself, I die in fiery torment for the sake of Thee. Be merciful to Thy people and let my punishment be sufficient for their sake. Make my blood an expiation for them and take my life as a ransom for theirs (IV Macc. 6:27–28).

Eleazar gives voice here to the rabbinic conception that the death of the righteous is an expiation for the sins of all Israel (Jerusalem Talmud, Yoma 38b).

Experience had led our sages to the sad conclusion that sin is contagious in its punitive consequences, that it exacts its toll of innocent victims through the generations. History confirms that seeds of war, hatred, and suspicion, planted in one age, yield their fruits decades later. Moreover, when we fail to live by the ideals for which the martyrs have died, we increase the extent of our own guilt, for then we act as if they had died in vain. Israel Friedlaender, shortly before his own martyr's death while on a mission of mercy in Poland, wrote as follows:

> While our hearts are pained for the martyrs who have died, we must not let that for which they died languish and disappear.

TORAH SERVICE

The story of the Ten Teachers should encourage us not to weep at their martyrdom, but to redeem their suffering by learning more Torah in the year to come. For the Torah is the tree of life, the promise of immortality planted within our people and, insofar as we study it, within each one of us. The tree of life in the midst of the Garden was denied to Adam and Eve when they were expelled from Eden, but its fruit dwells in the midst of the soul of Israel, to be plucked anew with each new Torah teaching we acquire. On this fast day for the soul, words of Torah are the sweets God permitted us, the nourishment that we who seek forgiveness need the most.

וַיְהִי בִּנְסֹעַ הָאָרֹן וַיֹּאמֶר מֹשֶׁה: קוּמָה יְיָ, וְיָפֻצוּ אֹיְבֶיךָ, וְיָנֻסוּ מְשַׂנְאֶיךָ מִפָּנֶיךָ. כִּי מִצִּיּוֹן תֵּצֵא תוֹרָה, וּדְבַר יְיָ מִירוּשָׁלָיִם. בָּרוּךְ שֶׁנָּתַן תּוֹרָה לְעַמּוֹ יִשְׂרָאֵל בִּקְדֻשָׁתוֹ.

When the ark began to move, Moses proclaimed: Arise, Adonay, let Your enemies scatter, fleeing before You! For one day from Zion Torah will go forth, and the word of God from Jerusalem. Praised be the One who has shared holiness with Israel in giving us the Torah.

(The reader receives the Torah and the ark is closed)

שְׁמַע יִשְׂרָאֵל יְיָ אֱלֹהֵינוּ יְיָ אֶחָד:

Shma Yisrael Adonay Eloheynu Adonay Echad:

Hear, O Israel, Adonay is our God, Adonay is One.

אֶחָד אֱלֹהֵינוּ גָּדוֹל אֲדוֹנֵינוּ קָדוֹשׁ וְנוֹרָא שְׁמוֹ:

Echad Eloheynu, Gadol Adoneynu, Kadosh v'nora shmo:

Our God is One, Adonay is One, with a holy and awesome Name.

גַּדְּלוּ לַיְיָ אִתִּי. וּנְרוֹמְמָה שְׁמוֹ יַחְדָּו:

Gad'lu l'Adonay iti un'rom'ma shmo yachdav:

Magnify Adonay with me, and let us exalt the Name together.

Torah Procession

L'cha Adonay ha-g'dula
v'ha-gvura v'hatiferet
v'ha-netzach v'ha-hod,
ki chol ba-shamayim uva-aretz
l'cha Adonay ha-mamlacha
v'hamitnasey l'chol l'rosh.
Rom'mu Adonay Eloheynu
v'hishtachavu la-hadom raglav
kadosh hu. Rom'mu Adonay
Eloheynu v'hishtachavu l'har
kod'sho ki kadosh Adonay
Eloheynu.

לְךָ יְיָ הַגְּדֻלָּה וְהַגְּבוּרָה
וְהַתִּפְאֶרֶת וְהַנֵּצַח וְהַהוֹד.
כִּי־כֹל בַּשָּׁמַיִם וּבָאָרֶץ לְךָ יְיָ
הַמַּמְלָכָה וְהַמִּתְנַשֵּׂא לְכֹל
לְרֹאשׁ. רוֹמְמוּ יְיָ אֱלֹהֵינוּ
וְהִשְׁתַּחֲווּ לַהֲדֹם רַגְלָיו
קָדוֹשׁ הוּא: רוֹמְמוּ יְיָ
אֱלֹהֵינוּ וְהִשְׁתַּחֲווּ לְהַר
קָדְשׁוֹ כִּי קָדוֹשׁ יְיָ אֱלֹהֵינוּ:

To You, Adonay, belong the greatness, the power, the glory, the everlasting victory, and the majesty, for to You belongs everything in heaven and on earth, sovereignty and the exaltation as head above all. Exalt Adonay our God, and worship at the footstool of God, the holy One! Exalt Adonay our God and worship at the holy mountain, for Adonay our God is holy.

(The Torah is placed on the reading desk. The Reader unrolls it and, if individuals will be called to the Torah, says:)

הַכֹּל הָבוּ גֹדֶל לֵאלֹהֵינוּ, וּתְנוּ כָבוֹד לַתּוֹרָה. (כֹּהֵן,
קְרָב;) יַעֲמֹד (תַּעֲמֹד) ... בָּרוּךְ שֶׁנָּתַן תּוֹרָה לְעַמּוֹ
יִשְׂרָאֵל בִּקְדֻשָּׁתוֹ.

Let everyone ascribe greatness to our God and honor to the Torah. (*If appropriate,* Kohen, draw near.) I call . . ... Let us praise the One who in holiness has given the Torah to the people Israel.

(All respond:)

וְאַתֶּם הַדְּבֵקִים בַּיָי אֱלֹהֵיכֶם, חַיִּים כֻּלְכֶם הַיּוֹם.

V'atem ha-d'vekim b'Adonay Eloheychem, chayim kul-chem
ha-yom.

And you who have cleaved to Adonay your God are alive,
all of you, this day.

Blessings for the Reading of the Torah

בָּרְכוּ אֶת־יְיָ הַמְבֹרָךְ:
בָּרוּךְ יְיָ הַמְבֹרָךְ לְעוֹלָם וָעֶד:
בָּרוּךְ אַתָּה יְיָ אֱלֹהֵינוּ מֶלֶךְ הָעוֹלָם אֲשֶׁר בָּחַר־בָּנוּ
מִכָּל־הָעַמִּים וְנָתַן־לָנוּ אֶת־תּוֹרָתוֹ. בָּרוּךְ אַתָּה יְיָ
נוֹתֵן הַתּוֹרָה:

Bar'chu et Adonay ham'vorach:
Baruch Adonay ham'vorach l'olam va-ed.
Baruch atta Adonay Eloheynu melech ha-olam,
asher bachar banu mikol ha-amim, v'natan lanu
et Torato. Baruch atta Adonay, noteyn
ha-Torah.

(The Torah is read)

בָּרוּךְ אַתָּה יְיָ אֱלֹהֵינוּ מֶלֶךְ הָעוֹלָם אֲשֶׁר נָתַן־לָנוּ
תּוֹרַת אֱמֶת וְחַיֵּי עוֹלָם נָטַע בְּתוֹכֵנוּ. בָּרוּךְ אַתָּה יְיָ
נוֹתֵן הַתּוֹרָה:

Baruch atta Adonay Eloheynu melech
ha-olam, asher natan lanu Torat emet,
v'chayey olam nata' b'tocheynu.
Baruch atta Adonay, noteyn ha-Torah.

You are praised forever, Adonay, ruler of the universe,
who has chosen us from among all peoples and given us
Your Torah. You gave us a Torah of truth and implanted
eternal life within us. You are praised, Adonay, who is
giving us the Torah.

TORAH READING
FOR YOM KIPPUR AFTERNOON
(Leviticus 18)

וַיְדַבֵּר יהוה אֶל־מֹשֶׁה לֵּאמֹר׃ דַּבֵּר אֶל־בְּנֵי יִשְׂרָאֵל וְאָמַרְתָּ
אֲלֵהֶם אֲנִי יהוה אֱלֹהֵיכֶם׃ כְּמַעֲשֵׂה אֶרֶץ־מִצְרַיִם אֲשֶׁר יְשַׁבְתֶּם־
בָּהּ לֹא תַעֲשׂוּ וּכְמַעֲשֵׂה אֶרֶץ־כְּנַעַן אֲשֶׁר אֲנִי מֵבִיא אֶתְכֶם
שָׁמָּה לֹא תַעֲשׂוּ וּבְחֻקֹּתֵיהֶם לֹא תֵלֵכוּ׃ אֶת־מִשְׁפָּטַי תַּעֲשׂוּ
וְאֶת־חֻקֹּתַי תִּשְׁמְרוּ לָלֶכֶת בָּהֶם אֲנִי יהוה אֱלֹהֵיכֶם׃ וּשְׁמַרְתֶּם
אֶת־חֻקֹּתַי וְאֶת־מִשְׁפָּטַי אֲשֶׁר יַעֲשֶׂה אֹתָם הָאָדָם וָחַי בָּהֶם אֲנִי
יהוה׃   אִישׁ אִישׁ אֶל־כָּל־שְׁאֵר בְּשָׂרוֹ לֹא תִקְרְבוּ
לְגַלּוֹת עֶרְוָה אֲנִי יהוה׃   עֶרְוַת אָבִיךָ וְעֶרְוַת אִמְּךָ
לֹא תְגַלֵּה אִמְּךָ הִוא לֹא תְגַלֶּה עֶרְוָתָהּ׃   עֶרְוַת
אֵשֶׁת־אָבִיךָ לֹא תְגַלֵּה עֶרְוַת אָבִיךָ הִוא׃   עֶרְוַת
אֲחוֹתְךָ בַת־אָבִיךָ אוֹ בַת־אִמֶּךָ מוֹלֶדֶת בַּיִת אוֹ מוֹלֶדֶת חוּץ
לֹא תְגַלֶּה עֶרְוָתָן׃   עֶרְוַת בַּת־בִּנְךָ אוֹ בַת־
בִּתְּךָ לֹא תְגַלֶּה עֶרְוָתָן כִּי עֶרְוָתְךָ הֵנָּה׃   עֶרְוַת
בַּת־אֵשֶׁת אָבִיךָ מוֹלֶדֶת אָבִיךָ אֲחוֹתְךָ הִוא לֹא תְגַלֶּה
עֶרְוָתָהּ׃   עֶרְוַת אֲחוֹת־אָבִיךָ לֹא תְגַלֵּה שְׁאֵר
אָבִיךָ הִוא׃   עֶרְוַת אֲחוֹת־אִמְּךָ לֹא תְגַלֵּה כִּי־
שְׁאֵר אִמְּךָ הִוא׃   עֶרְוַת אֲחִי־אָבִיךָ לֹא תְגַלֵּה אֶל־
אִשְׁתּוֹ לֹא תִקְרָב דֹּדָתְךָ הִוא׃   עֶרְוַת כַּלָּתְךָ לֹא
תְגַלֵּה אֵשֶׁת בִּנְךָ הִוא לֹא תְגַלֶּה עֶרְוָתָהּ׃   עֶרְוַת
אֵשֶׁת־אָחִיךָ לֹא תְגַלֵּה עֶרְוַת אָחִיךָ הִוא׃   עֶרְוַת
אִשָּׁה וּבִתָּהּ לֹא תְגַלֵּה אֶת־בַּת־בְּנָהּ וְאֶת־בַּת־בִּתָּהּ לֹא
תִקַּח לְגַלּוֹת עֶרְוָתָהּ שַׁאֲרָה הֵנָּה זִמָּה הִוא׃ וְאִשָּׁה אֶל־
אֲחֹתָהּ לֹא תִקָּח לִצְרֹר לְגַלּוֹת עֶרְוָתָהּ עָלֶיהָ בְּחַיֶּיהָ׃ וְאֶל־
אִשָּׁה בְּנִדַּת טֻמְאָתָהּ לֹא תִקְרַב לְגַלּוֹת עֶרְוָתָהּ׃ וְאֶל־אֵשֶׁת
עֲמִיתְךָ לֹא־תִתֵּן שְׁכָבְתְּךָ לְזָרַע לְטָמְאָה־בָהּ׃

TORAH READING
FOR YOM KIPPUR AFTERNOON
(Leviticus 18)

Adonay said to Moses: Speak to the Israelites and tell them: I, Adonay, am your God. Do not act according to the practices of the land of Egypt where you live, nor of the land of Canaan where I have brought you; in their statutes you may not walk. Rather practice My precepts and observe My statutes; walk in them. I, Adonay, am your God. Keep My statutes and My judgments, through which, by observing, a person may live. I am Adonay.

No one may come near to a close relative to uncover that person's nakedness; I am Adonay.

The nakedness of these may not be uncovered: Your father and mother, for she is your mother; your father's wife, for it is your father's nakedness; your sister, or your father's daughter, or your mother's daughter, whether born at home or outside; the daughter of your son or daughter, for they are your nakedness; the daughter of your father's wife, begotten by your father, for she is your sister; your father's sister, for she is your father's close relative; your mother's sister, for she is your mother's close relative; the wife of your father's brother— you shall not come close to her, she is your aunt; your daughter-in-law, for she is your son's wife; your brother's wife, for that is the nakedness of your brother.

You shall not uncover the nakedness of a wife and her daughter; nor shall you marry the daughter of her son or daughter; they are her close relatives; it would be depravity.

You shall not marry a woman as a rival to her sister, uncovering her nakedness during the other's lifetime.

You shall not come near a woman during her monthly period of *tum'ah* (a time of endings and beginnings; usually, but imprecisely, translated "impurity") to uncover her nakedness.

You shall not have sexual relations with your neighbor's wife and become *tam'ei* ("impure") through her.

וּמִזַּרְעֲךָ לֹא־
תִתֵּן לְהַעֲבִיר לַמֹּלֶךְ וְלֹא תְחַלֵּל אֶת־שֵׁם אֱלֹהֶיךָ אֲנִי יְהוָה:
וְאֶת־זָכָר לֹא תִשְׁכַּב מִשְׁכְּבֵי אִשָּׁה תּוֹעֵבָה הִוא: וּבְכָל־בְּהֵמָה
לֹא־תִתֵּן שְׁכָבְתְּךָ לְטָמְאָה־בָהּ וְאִשָּׁה לֹא־תַעֲמֹד לִפְנֵי בְהֵמָה
לְרִבְעָהּ תֶּבֶל הוּא: אַל־תִּטַּמְּאוּ בְּכָל־אֵלֶּה כִּי בְכָל־אֵלֶּה
נִטְמְאוּ הַגּוֹיִם אֲשֶׁר־אֲנִי מְשַׁלֵּחַ מִפְּנֵיכֶם: וַתִּטְמָא הָאָרֶץ
וָאֶפְקֹד עֲ נָהּ עָלֶיהָ וַתָּקִא הָאָרֶץ אֶת־יֹשְׁבֶיהָ: וּשְׁמַרְתֶּם אַתֶּם
אֶת־חֻקֹּתַי וְאֶת־מִשְׁפָּטַי וְלֹא תַעֲשׂוּ מִכֹּל הַתּוֹעֵבֹת הָאֵלֶּה
הָאֶזְרָח וְהַגֵּר הַגָּר בְּתוֹכְכֶם: כִּי אֶת־כָּל־הַתּוֹעֵבֹת הָאֵל עָשׂוּ
אַנְשֵׁי־הָאָרֶץ אֲשֶׁר לִפְנֵיכֶם וַתִּטְמָא הָאָרֶץ: וְלֹא־תָקִיא הָאָרֶץ
אֶתְכֶם בְּטַמַּאֲכֶם אֹתָהּ כַּאֲשֶׁר קָאָה אֶת־הַגּוֹי אֲשֶׁר לִפְנֵיכֶם:
כִּי כָּל־אֲשֶׁר יַעֲשֶׂה מִכֹּל הַתּוֹעֵבֹת הָאֵלֶּה וְנִכְרְתוּ הַנְּפָשׁוֹת
הָעֹשֹׂת מִקֶּרֶב עַמָּם: וּשְׁמַרְתֶּם אֶת־מִשְׁמַרְתִּי לְבִלְתִּי עֲשׂוֹת
מֵחֻקּוֹת הַתּוֹעֵבֹת אֲשֶׁר נַעֲשׂוּ לִפְנֵיכֶם וְלֹא תִטַּמְּאוּ בָּהֶם אֲנִי
יְהוָה אֱלֹהֵיכֶם:

ALTERNATIVE TORAH READING
FOR YOM KIPPUR AFTERNOON
(Leviticus 19: 1–18, 32–37)

וַיְדַבֵּר יְהוָה אֶל־מֹשֶׁה לֵּאמֹר: דַּבֵּר אֶל־כָּל־עֲדַת בְּנֵי־יִשְׂרָאֵל
וְאָמַרְתָּ אֲלֵהֶם קְדֹשִׁים תִּהְיוּ כִּי קָדוֹשׁ אֲנִי יְהוָה אֱלֹהֵיכֶם:
אִישׁ אִמּוֹ וְאָבִיו תִּירָאוּ וְאֶת־שַׁבְּתֹתַי תִּשְׁמֹרוּ אֲנִי יְהוָה
אֱלֹהֵיכֶם: אַל־תִּפְנוּ אֶל־הָאֱלִילִם וֵאלֹהֵי מַסֵּכָה לֹא תַעֲשׂוּ
לָכֶם אֲנִי יְהוָה

You shall not let any of your offspring be offered up to Molech, thus profaning the name of your God. I am Adonay.

You shall not lie with a man as with a woman; it is an abhorrence (or, an emulation of the practices of pagan religion).

You shall not have sexual relations with an animal, thus becoming *tam'ei*; nor shall a woman come before an animal to lie with it; it is a perversion.

You shall not make yourselves *tam'ei* in any of these ways, for the Gentiles whom I am casting out before you have made themselves *tam'ei* in these ways. When the land became *tam'ei*, I visited its sin upon it, and the land spewed out its inhabitants. It is up to you to observe My statutes and My judgments, and not to engage in any of these abhorrent (or pagan) acts, neither the native nor the stranger who resides in your midst. For the people of the land who preceded you practiced all these abhorrent (or pagan) things, and the land became *tam'ei*. Let not the land spew you out because you have made it *tam'ei*, as it spewed out the nation which preceded you. For each and every person who practices any of these abhorrent (or pagan) acts shall be cut off from the midst of their people. Therefore observe My observances and do not practice any of these abhorrent (or pagan) statutes which were done before you, that you may not become *tam'ei* through them. I, Adonay, am your God.

ALTERNATIVE TORAH READING
FOR YOM KIPPUR AFTERNOON
(Leviticus 19: 1–18, 32–37)

Adonay spoke to Moses saying: Speak to the entire congregation of Israelites and say to them: You shall be *kadosh* (holy, separate) for I, Adonay your God, am *kadosh*: each person shall fear (or regard with awe, *yi'rah*) your mother and father and observe my sabbaths; I, Adonay, am your God. Do not turn to godlets (or idols), nor shall you make gods out of metal; I, Adonay, am your

אֱלֹהֵיכֶם: וְכִי תִזְבְּחוּ זֶבַח שְׁלָמִים לַיהוָה
לִרְצֹנְכֶם תִּזְבָּחֻהוּ: בְּיוֹם זִבְחֲכֶם יֵאָכֵל וּמִמָּחֳרָת וְהַנּוֹתָר עַד־
יוֹם הַשְּׁלִישִׁי בָּאֵשׁ יִשָּׂרֵף: וְאִם הֵאָכֹל יֵאָכֵל בַּיּוֹם הַשְּׁלִישִׁי
פִּגּוּל הוּא לֹא יֵרָצֶה: וְאֹכְלָיו עֲוֺנוֹ יִשָּׂא כִּי־אֶת־קֹדֶשׁ יְהוָה
חִלֵּל וְנִכְרְתָה הַנֶּפֶשׁ הַהִוא מֵעַמֶּיהָ: וּבְקֻצְרְכֶם אֶת־קְצִיר
אַרְצְכֶם לֹא תְכַלֶּה פְּאַת שָׂדְךָ לִקְצֹר וְלֶקֶט קְצִירְךָ לֹא תְלַקֵּט:
וְכַרְמְךָ לֹא תְעוֹלֵל וּפֶרֶט כַּרְמְךָ לֹא תְלַקֵּט לֶעָנִי וְלַגֵּר תַּעֲזֹב
אֹתָם אֲנִי יְהוָה אֱלֹהֵיכֶם: לֹא תִּגְנֹבוּ וְלֹא־תְכַחֲשׁוּ וְלֹא־תְשַׁקְּרוּ
אִישׁ בַּעֲמִיתוֹ: וְלֹא־תִשָּׁבְעוּ בִשְׁמִי לַשָּׁקֶר וְחִלַּלְתָּ אֶת־שֵׁם
אֱלֹהֶיךָ אֲנִי יְהוָה: לֹא־תַעֲשֹׁק אֶת־רֵעֲךָ וְלֹא תִגְזֹל לֹא־תָלִין
פְּעֻלַּת שָׂכִיר אִתְּךָ עַד־בֹּקֶר: לֹא־תְקַלֵּל חֵרֵשׁ וְלִפְנֵי עִוֵּר לֹא
תִתֵּן מִכְשֹׁל וְיָרֵאתָ מֵּאֱלֹהֶיךָ אֲנִי יְהוָה: לֹא־תַעֲשׂוּ עָוֶל בַּמִּשְׁפָּט
לֹא־תִשָּׂא פְנֵי־דָל וְלֹא תֶהְדַּר פְּנֵי גָדוֹל בְּצֶדֶק תִּשְׁפֹּט עֲמִיתֶךָ:
לֹא־תֵלֵךְ רָכִיל בְּעַמֶּיךָ לֹא תַעֲמֹד עַל־דַּם רֵעֶךָ אֲנִי יְהוָה:
לֹא־תִשְׂנָא אֶת־אָחִיךָ בִּלְבָבֶךָ הוֹכֵחַ תּוֹכִיחַ אֶת־עֲמִיתֶךָ וְלֹא־
תִשָּׂא עָלָיו חֵטְא: לֹא־תִקֹּם וְלֹא־תִטֹּר אֶת־בְּנֵי עַמֶּךָ וְאָהַבְתָּ
לְרֵעֲךָ כָּמוֹךָ אֲנִי יְהוָה:

God. When you offer a whole-offering (*sh'lamim*) to Adonay, you shall offer it in a manner that shall cause it to be accepted. It shall be eaten on the day you offer it and on the day after; but whatever remains by the third day shall be burnt up in the fire, for if it should be eaten at all on the third day it is vile (*pigul*); it shall not be accepted. Those who eat it shall bear their own sin, for each of them has made common that which is holy (*kodesh*) to Adonay, and so that person shall be cut off from the people.

When you reap the harvest of your land you shall not completely harvest the corner of your field, nor shall you gather in all of your harvest that there is to gather, nor shall you glean your vineyard, nor gather in the fallen fruit of your vineyard, but instead leave them for the poor and the stranger; I, Adonay, am your God. Do not steal, act deceitfully, or lie to your neighbor; do not take a false oath using My name, thus making common use of the name of your God; I am Adonay. Do not oppress your neighbor; do not rob, nor let the wages of someone you have hired remain with you till the next morning. Do not curse a deaf person nor put a stumbling-block before a blind person, but rather fear (or hold in awe) your God; I am Adonay. You shall do no wickedness in judgment through elevating the presence of a poor person or honoring the presence of a great one; with justice shall you judge your people. You shall not go about gossiping with your people, nor shall you stand idly by the blood of your neighbor; I am Adonay. You shall not hate your brother in your heart; rather, issue a rebuke to your neighbor and you will not bear sin on that person's account. You shall not take revenge nor bear a grudge against the members of your people, but you shall love your neighbor as yourself. I am Adonay.

מִפְּנֵי שֵׂיבָה תָּקוּם וְהָדַרְתָּ פְּנֵי זָקֵן

וְיָרֵאתָ מֵאֱלֹהֶיךָ אֲנִי יְהוָה: וְכִי־יָגוּר אִתְּךָ גֵּר
בְּאַרְצְכֶם לֹא תוֹנוּ אֹתוֹ: כְּאֶזְרָח מִכֶּם יִהְיֶה לָכֶם הַגֵּר וְהַגֵּר
אִתְּכֶם וְאָהַבְתָּ לוֹ כָּמוֹךָ כִּי־גֵרִים הֱיִיתֶם בְּאֶרֶץ מִצְרָיִם אֲנִי
יְהוָה אֱלֹהֵיכֶם: לֹא־תַעֲשׂוּ עָוֶל בַּמִּשְׁפָּט בַּמִּדָּה בַּמִּשְׁקָל
וּבַמְּשׂוּרָה: מֹאזְנֵי צֶדֶק אַבְנֵי־צֶדֶק אֵיפַת צֶדֶק וְהִין צֶדֶק יִהְיֶה
לָכֶם אֲנִי יְהוָה אֱלֹהֵיכֶם אֲשֶׁר־הוֹצֵאתִי אֶתְכֶם מֵאֶרֶץ מִצְרָיִם:
וּשְׁמַרְתֶּם אֶת־כָּל־חֻקֹּתַי וְאֶת־כָּל־מִשְׁפָּטַי וַעֲשִׂיתֶם אֹתָם
אֲנִי יְהוָה:

Rise up before age, and honor the presence of an old person, that you may stand in awe (or fear) of your God; I am Adonay.

If a stranger (in later ages, a convert) should dwell with you in your land, do not oppress such a person. Like a native among you should your stranger be who dwells with you, and you should love that person as yourself, for you were strangers in the land of Egypt; I, Adonay, am your God. You shall do no wickedness in judgment, through measures, weights, or quantity. You shall have just measures, just weights, a just *ephah* (dry measure), and a just *hin* (liquid measure); I am Adonay your God who brought you out of the land of Egypt, that you might observe all My statutes and all My judgments and do them; I am Adonay.

When the Torah is raised, all rise and proclaim:

וְזֹאת הַתּוֹרָה אֲשֶׁר שָׂם מֹשֶׁה לִפְנֵי בְּנֵי יִשְׂרָאֵל, עַל פִּי יְיָ בְּיַד מֹשֶׁה.

V'zot ha-Torah asher sam Moshe lifney b'ney Yisrael al pi Adonay, b'yad Moshe.

This is the Torah which Moses placed before the children of Israel at the command of Adonay, through Moses.

READING OF THE HAFTARAH

בָּרוּךְ אַתָּה יְיָ אֱלֹהֵינוּ מֶלֶךְ הָעוֹלָם אֲשֶׁר בָּחַר בִּנְבִיאִים טוֹבִים וְרָצָה בְדִבְרֵיהֶם הַנֶּאֱמָרִים בֶּאֱמֶת. בָּרוּךְ אַתָּה יְהֹוָה הַבּוֹחֵר בַּתּוֹרָה וּבְמֹשֶׁה עַבְדּוֹ וּבְיִשְׂרָאֵל עַמּוֹ וּבִנְבִיאֵי הָאֱמֶת וָצֶדֶק.

You are praised, Adonay our God, Sovereign of the world, who has chosen good prophets, finding favor in their words which faithfully reflect Your truth. You are praised, Adonay, who has chosen Moses your servant, Israel Your people, and prophets who have spoken truth and justice.

HAFTARAH FOR YOM KIPPUR AFTERNOON
The Book of Jonah

וַיְהִי דְּבַר־יהוה אֶל־יוֹנָה בֶן־אֲמִתַּי לֵאמֹר: קוּם לֵךְ אֶל־נִינְוֵה א
הָעִיר הַגְּדוֹלָה וּקְרָא עָלֶיהָ כִּי־עָלְתָה רָעָתָם לְפָנָי: וַיָּקָם יוֹנָה
לִבְרֹחַ תַּרְשִׁישָׁה מִלִּפְנֵי יהוה וַיֵּרֶד יָפוֹ וַיִּמְצָא אֳנִיָּה ׀ בָּאָה
תַרְשִׁישׁ וַיִּתֵּן שְׂכָרָהּ וַיֵּרֶד בָּהּ לָבוֹא עִמָּהֶם תַּרְשִׁישָׁה מִלִּפְנֵי
יהוה: וַיהוה הֵטִיל רוּחַ־גְּדוֹלָה אֶל־הַיָּם וַיְהִי סַעַר־גָּדוֹל בַּיָּם
וְהָאֳנִיָּה חִשְּׁבָה לְהִשָּׁבֵר: וַיִּירְאוּ הַמַּלָּחִים וַיִּזְעֲקוּ אִישׁ אֶל־
אֱלֹהָיו וַיָּטִלוּ אֶת־הַכֵּלִים אֲשֶׁר בָּאֳנִיָּה אֶל־הַיָּם לְהָקֵל
מֵעֲלֵיהֶם וְיוֹנָה יָרַד אֶל־יַרְכְּתֵי הַסְּפִינָה וַיִּשְׁכַּב וַיֵּרָדַם: וַיִּקְרַב
אֵלָיו רַב הַחֹבֵל וַיֹּאמֶר לוֹ מַה־לְּךָ נִרְדָּם קוּם קְרָא אֶל־אֱלֹהֶיךָ
אוּלַי יִתְעַשֵּׁת הָאֱלֹהִים לָנוּ וְלֹא נֹאבֵד: וַיֹּאמְרוּ אִישׁ אֶל־רֵעֵהוּ
לְכוּ וְנַפִּילָה גוֹרָלוֹת וְנֵדְעָה בְּשֶׁלְּמִי הָרָעָה הַזֹּאת לָנוּ וַיַּפִּלוּ
גּוֹרָלוֹת וַיִּפֹּל הַגּוֹרָל עַל־יוֹנָה: וַיֹּאמְרוּ אֵלָיו הַגִּידָה־נָּא לָנוּ
בַּאֲשֶׁר לְמִי־הָרָעָה הַזֹּאת לָנוּ מַה־מְּלַאכְתְּךָ וּמֵאַיִן תָּבוֹא מָה
אַרְצֶךָ וְאֵי־מִזֶּה עַם אָתָּה: וַיֹּאמֶר אֲלֵיהֶם עִבְרִי אָנֹכִי וְאֶת־
יהוה אֱלֹהֵי הַשָּׁמַיִם אֲנִי יָרֵא אֲשֶׁר־עָשָׂה אֶת־הַיָּם וְאֶת־
הַיַּבָּשָׁה: וַיִּירְאוּ הָאֲנָשִׁים יִרְאָה גְדוֹלָה וַיֹּאמְרוּ אֵלָיו מַה־זֹּאת
עָשִׂיתָ כִּי־יָדְעוּ הָאֲנָשִׁים כִּי־מִלִּפְנֵי יהוה הוּא בֹרֵחַ כִּי הִגִּיד
לָהֶם: וַיֹּאמְרוּ אֵלָיו מַה־נַּעֲשֶׂה לָּךְ וְיִשְׁתֹּק הַיָּם מֵעָלֵינוּ כִּי הַיָּם
הוֹלֵךְ וְסֹעֵר: וַיֹּאמֶר אֲלֵיהֶם שָׂאוּנִי וַהֲטִילֻנִי אֶל־הַיָּם וְיִשְׁתֹּק
הַיָּם מֵעֲלֵיכֶם כִּי יוֹדֵעַ אָנִי כִּי בְשֶׁלִּי הַסַּעַר הַגָּדוֹל הַזֶּה עֲלֵיכֶם:
וַיַּחְתְּרוּ הָאֲנָשִׁים לְהָשִׁיב

HAFTARAH FOR YOM KIPPUR AFTERNOON
(The Book of Jonah)

CHAPTER I

The word of Adonay came to Jonah, Amittai's son, saying: "Get up, go to Nineveh, the great city, and cry out to her that the evil of her inhabitants has come up before Me." But Jonah got up to flee to Tarshish, from before the face of Adonay, and he went down to Jaffa, found a ship going to Tarshish, paid the fare, and went down into the ship to go with its crew to Tarshish, away from the presence of Adonay.

But Adonay heaved a great wind into the sea, and such a great storm arose at sea that the ship thought she was about to break in pieces. The old salts grew terrified, and each one of them cried out to their own god, and they heaved all the baggage in the ship into the sea to reduce the weight.

Meanwhile Jonah had gone down into the thighs (or, the hold) of the vessel to lie down, and fell asleep. But the chief sailor approached him and said, "How can you be sleeping? Get up, cry out to your God, perhaps God will take notice of us and we will not be lost."

They said to each other, "Come, let us cast (or, "make fall") lots to find out on whose account this terrible thing has happened to us. So they cast lots, and the lot fell on Jonah. So they said to him: "Please tell us, since it is on your account that this terrible thing has happened to us, what is your work? Where do you come from? What is your land? From which people are you?" And he said to them, "I am a Hebrew, and I stand in awe of (or, "fear" or "worship") Adonay, the God of the heavens, who made the sea and the dry land." Then a great fear came upon the men and they said, "What is this you have done?" For the men now knew, since he had told them, that he was fleeing from the face of Adonay. They asked him, as the sea grew ever more stormy, "What shall we do with you so the sea may be calm for us?" He told them, "Pick me up and heave me into the sea and the sea will calm down for you. For I know that it is on my account that this great storm has come upon you." But instead the men dug their oars into the water, trying to row back

אֶל־הַיַּבָּשָׁה וְלֹא יָכֹלוּ כִּי הַיָּם הוֹלֵךְ
וְסֹעֵר עֲלֵיהֶם: וַיִּקְרְאוּ אֶל־יְהֹוָה וַיֹּאמְרוּ אָנָּה יְהֹוָה אַל־נָא
נֹאבְדָה בְּנֶפֶשׁ הָאִישׁ הַזֶּה וְאַל־תִּתֵּן עָלֵינוּ דָּם נָקִיא כִּי־אַתָּה
יְהֹוָה כַּאֲשֶׁר חָפַצְתָּ עָשִׂיתָ: וַיִּשְׂאוּ אֶת־יוֹנָה וַיְטִלֻהוּ אֶל־הַיָּם
וַיַּעֲמֹד הַיָּם מִזַּעְפּוֹ: וַיִּירְאוּ הָאֲנָשִׁים יִרְאָה גְדוֹלָה אֶת־יְהֹוָה
וַיִּזְבְּחוּ־זֶבַח לַיהֹוָה וַיִּדְּרוּ נְדָרִים: וַיְמַן יְהֹוָה דָּג גָּדוֹל לִבְלֹעַ אֶת־

ב

יוֹנָה וַיְהִי יוֹנָה בִּמְעֵי הַדָּג שְׁלֹשָׁה יָמִים וּשְׁלֹשָׁה לֵילוֹת: וַיִּתְפַּלֵּל
יוֹנָה אֶל־יְהֹוָה אֱלֹהָיו מִמְּעֵי הַדָּגָה: וַיֹּאמֶר קָרָאתִי מִצָּרָה לִי
אֶל־יְהֹוָה וַיַּעֲנֵנִי מִבֶּטֶן שְׁאוֹל שִׁוַּעְתִּי שָׁמַעְתָּ קוֹלִי: וַתַּשְׁלִיכֵנִי
מְצוּלָה בִּלְבַב יַמִּים וְנָהָר יְסֹבְבֵנִי כָּל־מִשְׁבָּרֶיךָ וְגַלֶּיךָ עָלַי
עָבָרוּ: וַאֲנִי אָמַרְתִּי נִגְרַשְׁתִּי מִנֶּגֶד עֵינֶיךָ אַךְ אוֹסִיף לְהַבִּיט אֶל־
הֵיכַל קָדְשֶׁךָ: אֲפָפוּנִי מַיִם עַד־נֶפֶשׁ תְּהוֹם יְסֹבְבֵנִי סוּף חָבוּשׁ
לְרֹאשִׁי: לְקִצְבֵי הָרִים יָרַדְתִּי הָאָרֶץ בְּרִחֶיהָ בַעֲדִי לְעוֹלָם
וַתַּעַל מִשַּׁחַת חַיַּי יְהֹוָה אֱלֹהָי: בְּהִתְעַטֵּף עָלַי נַפְשִׁי אֶת־יְהֹוָה
זָכָרְתִּי וַתָּבוֹא אֵלֶיךָ תְּפִלָּתִי אֶל־הֵיכַל קָדְשֶׁךָ: מְשַׁמְּרִים הַבְלֵי־
שָׁוְא חַסְדָּם יַעֲזֹבוּ: וַאֲנִי בְּקוֹל תּוֹדָה אֶזְבְּחָה־לָּךְ אֲשֶׁר נָדַרְתִּי
אֲשַׁלֵּמָה יְשׁוּעָתָה לַיהֹוָה: וַיֹּאמֶר יְהֹוָה לַדָּג וַיָּקֵא
אֶת־יוֹנָה אֶל־הַיַּבָּשָׁה:

to dry land, but they failed, for the sea was growing ever more stormy around them.

So they cried to Adonay, saying, "Please, Adonay, let us not lose our lives for this man, and at the same time let us not be guilty of shedding innocent blood, for it was You, Adonay, who desired this and made it happen this way." And as soon as they picked Jonah up and heaved him into the sea, the sea stopped raging. Then a great fear (or awe) of Adonay came upon the men and they offered an offering to Adonay and vowed vows.

CHAPTER II

Adonay appointed a great fish to swallow Jonah, and Jonah was in the belly of the fish three days and three nights. And Jonah prayed to Adonay his God from the bowels of the fish, saying:

I have cried out in my pain to Adonay and God has answered me,

From the belly of Sh'ol I have pleaded, and You heard my voice,

You had cast me into the depths—into the heart of the seas— the flood surrounded me,

All your rolling waves broke over me.

I said to myself: I am cast adrift from Your sight,

But I shall look again upon the temple of Your holiness.

Water surrounded me, I was gasping for breath,

The deeps closed in on me, my head was tangled in weeds,

I went down to the bottom of the mountains, the earth was drawing the bars against me forever,

But You brought up my life from the pit, Adonay my God.

When the breath of life was fading from within me,

I invoked the presence of Adonay, my prayer entered into Your presence, to the temple of Your holiness.

Those who heed the vaporous falsehood of idols forsake the love of Your covenant,

But I with thankful voice shall make an offering to You; what I have vowed I shall fulfill. Victory belongs to Adonay!

And Adonay spoke to the fish, who spewed Jonah forth onto the dry land.

ג   וַיְהִי דְבַר־יְהֹוָה אֶל־יוֹנָה

שֵׁנִית לֵאמֹר: קוּם לֵךְ אֶל־נִינְוֵה הָעִיר הַגְּדוֹלָה וּקְרָא אֵלֶיהָ

אֶת־הַקְּרִיאָה אֲשֶׁר אָנֹכִי דֹּבֵר אֵלֶיךָ: וַיָּקָם יוֹנָה וַיֵּלֶךְ אֶל־נִינְוֵה

כִּדְבַר יְהֹוָה וְנִינְוֵה הָיְתָה עִיר־גְּדוֹלָה לֵאלֹהִים מַהֲלַךְ שְׁלֹשֶׁת

ג   יָמִים: וַיָּחֶל יוֹנָה לָבוֹא בָעִיר מַהֲלַךְ יוֹם אֶחָד וַיִּקְרָא וַיֹּאמַר

עוֹד אַרְבָּעִים יוֹם וְנִינְוֵה נֶהְפָּכֶת: וַיַּאֲמִינוּ אַנְשֵׁי נִינְוֵה בֵּאלֹהִים

וַיִּקְרְאוּ־צוֹם וַיִּלְבְּשׁוּ שַׂקִּים מִגְּדוֹלָם וְעַד־קְטַנָּם: וַיִּגַּע הַדָּבָר

אֶל־מֶלֶךְ נִינְוֵה וַיָּקָם מִכִּסְאוֹ וַיַּעֲבֵר אַדַּרְתּוֹ מֵעָלָיו וַיְכַס שַׂק

וַיֵּשֶׁב עַל־הָאֵפֶר: וַיַּזְעֵק וַיֹּאמֶר בְּנִינְוֵה מִטַּעַם הַמֶּלֶךְ וּגְדֹלָיו

לֵאמֹר הָאָדָם וְהַבְּהֵמָה הַבָּקָר וְהַצֹּאן אַל־יִטְעֲמוּ מְאוּמָה אַל־

יִרְעוּ וּמַיִם אַל־יִשְׁתּוּ: וְיִתְכַּסּוּ שַׂקִּים הָאָדָם וְהַבְּהֵמָה וְיִקְרְאוּ

אֶל־אֱלֹהִים בְּחָזְקָה וְיָשֻׁבוּ אִישׁ מִדַּרְכּוֹ הָרָעָה וּמִן־הֶחָמָס אֲשֶׁר

בְּכַפֵּיהֶם: מִי־יוֹדֵעַ יָשׁוּב וְנִחַם הָאֱלֹהִים וְשָׁב מֵחֲרוֹן אַפּוֹ וְלֹא

נֹאבֵד: וַיַּרְא הָאֱלֹהִים אֶת־מַעֲשֵׂיהֶם כִּי־שָׁבוּ מִדַּרְכָּם הָרָעָה

וַיִּנָּחֶם הָאֱלֹהִים עַל־הָרָעָה אֲשֶׁר־דִּבֶּר לַעֲשׂוֹת־לָהֶם וְלֹא

ד   עָשָׂה: וַיֵּרַע אֶל־יוֹנָה רָעָה גְדוֹלָה וַיִּחַר לוֹ: וַיִּתְפַּלֵּל אֶל־יְהֹוָה

וַיֹּאמַר אָנָּה יְהֹוָה הֲלוֹא־זֶה דְבָרִי עַד־הֱיוֹתִי עַל־אַדְמָתִי עַל־כֵּן

קִדַּמְתִּי לִבְרֹחַ תַּרְשִׁישָׁה כִּי יָדַעְתִּי כִּי אַתָּה אֵל־חַנּוּן וְרַחוּם

אֶרֶךְ אַפַּיִם וְרַב־חֶסֶד וְנִחָם עַל־הָרָעָה: וְעַתָּה יְהֹוָה קַח־נָא

אֶת־נַפְשִׁי מִמֶּנִּי כִּי טוֹב מוֹתִי מֵחַיָּי: וַיֹּאמֶר יְהֹוָה הַהֵיטֵב חָרָה

לָךְ: וַיֵּצֵא יוֹנָה מִן־הָעִיר וַיֵּשֶׁב מִקֶּדֶם לָעִיר וַיַּעַשׂ לוֹ שָׁם סֻכָּה

וַיֵּשֶׁב תַּחְתֶּיהָ בַּצֵּל עַד אֲשֶׁר יִרְאֶה מַה־יִּהְיֶה בָּעִיר: וַיְמַן יְהֹוָה־

אֱלֹהִים קִיקָיוֹן וַיַּעַל ׀ מֵעַל

CHAPTER III

The word of Adonay came to Jonah a second time, saying:
"Get up, go to Nineveh, the great city, and cry out to her the cry
which I told you." And Jonah got up and went to Nineveh
according to the word of Adonay, for Nineveh was a great city
in God's sight, requiring three days to walk across it. As soon as
Jonah began entering the city on his first day's walk he cried
out: "Another forty days and Nineveh is overthrown!" The
people of Nineveh believed God and dispatched criers to
announce a fast. From the greatest to the smallest they dressed
in sackcloth. When the matter reached the king of Nineveh he
got up from his throne, removed his cloak, covered himself with
sackcloth and sat in ashes. He issued a proclamation in
Nineveh: "By decree of the king and his notables, as follows:
Neither human beings nor animals, neither cattle nor sheep
shall taste anything; they shall not graze and they shall not
drink water. Humans and animals shall cover themselves with
sackcloth, they shall cry out to God with all their might, and all
people must turn back (or, do *tshuvah*) from their evil way and
from the violence they have done. Who knows whether God will
turn back and relent, turning from the divine anger, so that we
shall not be lost?" And God saw by their actions that they had
turned back from their evil way, and God relented of the evil
which God had promised to wreak upon them, and did not do
it.

CHAPTER IV

But to Jonah this appeared to be a great evil, and he was
angry. He prayed to Adonay and said, "Please, Adonay, were
these not my words when I was on my own soil? This is why I
fled beforehand to Tarshish, for I know that You are *El Chanun
v'rachum,* a gracious and merciful God, long-suffering and
abundant in covenantal love, and relenting in matters of punishment. So now, Adonay, please take my life from me, for dying is
better for me than living."

And Adonay said, "Is anger better for you?"

Then Jonah went out of the city and sat on the east side,
where he made himself a *sukkah,* a little booth, and sat under it
in the shade to see what would happen to the city. And Adonay,
who is God, appointed a castor-bean plant to grow up over

לְיוֹנָה לִהְיוֹת צֵל עַל־רֹאשׁוֹ לְהַצִּיל

לוֹ מֵרָעָתוֹ וַיִּשְׂמַח יוֹנָה עַל־הַקִּיקָיוֹן שִׂמְחָה גְדוֹלָה: וַיְמַן

הָאֱלֹהִים תּוֹלַעַת בַּעֲלוֹת הַשַּׁחַר לַמָּחֳרָת וַתַּךְ אֶת־הַקִּיקָיוֹן

וַיִּיבָשׁ: וַיְהִי ׀ כִּזְרֹחַ הַשֶּׁמֶשׁ וַיְמַן אֱלֹהִים רוּחַ קָדִים חֲרִישִׁית

וַתַּךְ הַשֶּׁמֶשׁ עַל־רֹאשׁ יוֹנָה וַיִּתְעַלָּף וַיִּשְׁאַל אֶת־נַפְשׁוֹ לָמוּת

וַיֹּאמֶר טוֹב מוֹתִי מֵחַיָּי: וַיֹּאמֶר אֱלֹהִים אֶל־יוֹנָה הַהֵיטֵב חָרָה־

לְךָ עַל־הַקִּיקָיוֹן וַיֹּאמֶר הֵיטֵב חָרָה־לִי עַד־מָוֶת: וַיֹּאמֶר יְהוָֹה

אַתָּה חַסְתָּ עַל־הַקִּיקָיוֹן אֲשֶׁר לֹא־עָמַלְתָּ בּוֹ וְלֹא גִדַּלְתּוֹ

שֶׁבִּן־לַיְלָה הָיָה וּבִן־לַיְלָה אָבָד: וַאֲנִי לֹא אָחוּס עַל־נִינְוֵה

הָעִיר הַגְּדוֹלָה אֲשֶׁר יֶשׁ־בָּהּ הַרְבֵּה מִשְׁתֵּים־עֶשְׂרֵה רִבּוֹ

אָדָם אֲשֶׁר לֹא־יָדַע בֵּין־יְמִינוֹ לִשְׂמֹאלוֹ וּבְהֵמָה רַבָּה:

Blessings Completing the Reading of the Haftarah

בָּרוּךְ אַתָּה, יְהֹוָה אֱלֹהֵינוּ, מֶלֶךְ הָעוֹלָם, צוּר כָּל
הָעוֹלָמִים, צַדִּיק בְּכָל הַדּוֹרוֹת, הָאֵל הַנֶּאֱמָן, הָאוֹמֵר
וְעוֹשֶׂה, הַמְדַבֵּר וּמְקַיֵּם, שֶׁכָּל דְּבָרָיו אֱמֶת וָצֶדֶק.
נֶאֱמָן אַתָּה הוּא, יְהֹוָה אֱלֹהֵינוּ, וְנֶאֱמָנִים דְּבָרֶיךָ,
וְדָבָר אֶחָד מִדְּבָרֶיךָ אָחוֹר לֹא יָשׁוּב רֵיקָם, כִּי אֵל
מֶלֶךְ נֶאֱמָן וְרַחֲמָן אָתָּה. בָּרוּךְ אַתָּה, יְהֹוָה, הָאֵל
הַנֶּאֱמָן בְּכָל דְּבָרָיו.
רַחֵם עַל צִיּוֹן, כִּי הִיא בֵּית חַיֵּינוּ, וְלַעֲלוּבַת נֶפֶשׁ
תּוֹשִׁיעַ בִּמְהֵרָה בְיָמֵינוּ. בָּרוּךְ אַתָּה, יְהֹוָה, מְשַׂמֵּחַ
צִיּוֹן בְּבָנֶיהָ.
שַׂמְּחֵנוּ, יְהֹוָה אֱלֹהֵינוּ, בְּאֵלִיָּהוּ הַנָּבִיא עַבְדֶּךָ,
וּבְמַלְכוּת בֵּית דָּוִד מְשִׁיחֶךָ. בִּמְהֵרָה יָבֹא, וְיָגֵל לִבֵּנוּ;
עַל כִּסְאוֹ לֹא יֵשֶׁב זָר, וְלֹא יִנְחֲלוּ עוֹד אֲחֵרִים אֶת
כְּבוֹדוֹ, כִּי בְשֵׁם קָדְשְׁךָ נִשְׁבַּעְתָּ לּוֹ, שֶׁלֹּא יִכְבֶּה נֵרוֹ
לְעוֹלָם וָעֶד. בָּרוּךְ אַתָּה, יְהֹוָה, מָגֵן דָּוִד.

Jonah to shade his head and save him from the evil weather, and a great happiness came upon Jonah because of the bean plant. Then God appointed a worm in the warm early morning the next day, striking at the bean plant, which withered away. When the sun rose God appointed a sultry east wind, with the sun striking Jonah's head till he felt faint, and he longed to die, saying, "Dying is better for me than living." And God said to Jonah, "Is anger for the bean-plant better for you?" And he said, "Anger enough to die."

And Adonay said, "You had compassion for the bean-plant, which you did not work to raise; one night it was there, the next it was gone.

"And upon the great city Nineveh, with 120,000 human beings who don't know right from left, and much cattle besides, should I not have compassion?"

Blessings Completing the Reading of the Haftarah

You are praised, Adonay our God, Sovereign of the world, eternal Rock, righteous ruler in all generations, faithful God whose every word is true and just. Not one of your words shall return unfulfilled, for Your rule is trustworthy and compassionate. You are praised, God of faithful words.

Show compassion on Zion, for it is our eternal house, and rescue those who are brought low, soon, in our days. You are praised, Adonay, who brings Zion joy through her children.

Bring us joy, Adonay our God, with the coming of Your servant, Elijah the prophet, and the reign of the house of David Your anointed. Let no stranger sit upon his throne, nor any others inherit his glory, for You have sworn by Your holy name that his light would never be extinguished anywhere. You are praised, Adonay, shield of David.

Returning the Scroll to the Ark

יְהַלְלוּ אֶת שֵׁם יְהֹוָה, כִּי נִשְׂגָּב שְׁמוֹ לְבַדּוֹ:

O praise the Name of God; the most exalted name of all!

הוֹדוֹ עַל־אֶרֶץ וְשָׁמָיִם וַיָּרֶם קֶרֶן לְעַמּוֹ
תְּהִלָּה לְכָל־חֲסִידָיו לִבְנֵי יִשְׂרָאֵל עַם קְרֹבוֹ
הַלְלוּיָהּ:

Hodo al eretz v'shamayim
Vayarem keren l'amo:
T'hilah l'chol chaseedav
 livney Yisrael am kerovo
 Halleluya.

God's glory is in the earth and heavens, and the people of
God is raised on high. The pious are become a praise, and
the children of Israel are become intimates of Adonay.
Halleluyah!

While the Torah is being placed in the ark:

וּבְנֻחֹה יֹאמַר: שׁוּבָה, יְהֹוָה, רִבְבוֹת אַלְפֵי יִשְׂרָאֵל.
קוּמָה יְהֹוָה לִמְנוּחָתֶךָ, אַתָּה וַאֲרוֹן עֻזֶּךָ. כֹּהֲנֶיךָ
יִלְבְּשׁוּ צֶדֶק, וַחֲסִידֶיךָ יְרַנֵּנוּ. בַּעֲבוּר דָּוִד עַבְדֶּךָ, אַל
תָּשֵׁב פְּנֵי מְשִׁיחֶךָ. כִּי לֶקַח טוֹב נָתַתִּי לָכֶם, תּוֹרָתִי אַל
תַּעֲזֹבוּ.

And when the ark rested, Moses proclaimed: Return,
Adonay, to all the myriads of Israel! Rise up toward Your
resting place, You and the ark, the symbol of Your power.
Let the kohanim be clothed in righteousness, let Your
pious ones sing for joy! For Your servant David's sake, do
not turn away Your anointed one, the messiah. For I have
given you good teaching, indeed, My own Torah; do not
forsake it.

עֵץ חַיִּים הִיא לַמַּחֲזִיקִים בָּהּ וְתוֹמְכֶיהָ מְאֻשָּׁר: דְּרָכֶיהָ
דַרְכֵי־נֹעַם וְכָל־נְתִיבוֹתֶיהָ שָׁלוֹם: הֲשִׁיבֵנוּ יְיָ אֵלֶיךָ
וְנָשׁוּבָה חַדֵּשׁ יָמֵינוּ כְּקֶדֶם:

Eytz chayim hee lamachazeekim ba v'tomcheyha m'ushar; d'ra-cheyah darchey noam v'chol n'teevoteyha shalom. Hashee-veynu Adonay eylecha v'nashuva chadesh yameynu k'kedem.

It is a tree which ensures eternal life for those who take hold of it; how fortunate are its supporters! Its ways are pleasant ways, its paths comprise Shalom. Bring us back to You, Adonay, that we might return, renew our life as in the days when You and we began.

The ark is closed

Reader's Kaddish

יִתְגַּדַּל וְיִתְקַדַּשׁ שְׁמֵהּ רַבָּא. בְּעָלְמָא דִּי בְרָא
כִרְעוּתֵהּ. וְיַמְלִיךְ מַלְכוּתֵהּ בְּחַיֵּיכוֹן וּבְיוֹמֵיכוֹן וּבְחַיֵּי
דְכָל בֵּית יִשְׂרָאֵל בַּעֲגָלָא וּבִזְמַן קָרִיב וְאִמְרוּ. אָמֵן:
יְהֵא שְׁמֵהּ רַבָּא מְבָרַךְ לְעָלַם וּלְעָלְמֵי עָלְמַיָּא:
יִתְבָּרַךְ וְיִשְׁתַּבַּח וְיִתְפָּאַר וְיִתְרוֹמַם וְיִתְנַשֵּׂא וְיִתְהַדָּר
וְיִתְעַלֶּה וְיִתְהַלָּל שְׁמֵהּ דְּקֻדְשָׁא. בְּרִיךְ הוּא. לְעֵלָּא
לְעֵלָּא מִן כָּל בִּרְכָתָא וְשִׁירָתָא תֻּשְׁבְּחָתָא וְנֶחֱמָתָא
דַּאֲמִירָן בְּעָלְמָא וְאִמְרוּ. אָמֵן:

May God's great name be magnified and sanctified in the world created according to the holy will, and may God's rule be known in your lifetime, in your own days, and in the life of the house of Israel, speedily, in a time close at hand. May the name of the blessed Holy One be praised and extolled far beyond all praises and blessings we can ever say in the world. Amen.

(The traditional silent Amidah in Hebrew and English may be found on pages 156 through 171)

CONFESSION

Preparation

We have turned aside from Your mitzvot,
From Your laws which point us toward the good,
And no good has come to us from our misdeeds.
Yet You do justly with everyone who comes before You,
For You have acted out of truth, while we have too often acted falsely.
What more shall we say this afternoon before You who dwells in the heights?
Even with all we have confessed this day,
Do You not already know all that we reveal and all that we have tried to hide?

You who knows the mysteries of the universe
And the best kept secrets of every living thing,
You have been searching out the innermost rooms of our life today,
Examining all our feelings, all our thoughts!
Not one thing is hidden from You now, nothing escapes Your gaze.
O God who preserves the memory of our ancestors,
If You would only wipe away the memory of all our wrongs and grant atonement for all our sins!

Al Chet: The Great Confession

עַל חֵטְא שֶׁחָטָאנוּ לְפָנֶיךָ בְּאֹנֶס וּבְרָצוֹן.
וְעַל חֵטְא שֶׁחָטָאנוּ לְפָנֶיךָ בְּאִמּוּץ הַלֵּב:
עַל חֵטְא שֶׁחָטָאנוּ לְפָנֶיךָ בִּבְלִי דָעַת.

For the wrong we did before You under coercion or of our own free will;
And for the wrong we did before You by hardening our hearts.

For the wrong we did before You unintentionally;
And for the wrong we did before You through idle talk and meaningless resolutions.

For the wrong we did before You by using sex exploitatively;
And for the wrong we did before You in public and in private.

For the wrong we did before You knowingly and deceptively;
And for the wrong we did before You by offensive language.

For the wrong we did before You by oppressing another person;
And for the wrong we did before You by malicious thoughts.

For the wrong we did before You by promiscuity;
And for the wrong we did before You by confessing insincerely.

For the wrong we did before You by contempt for parents and teachers;
And for the wrong we did before You by violence.

For the wrong we did before You by failing to be true to our heritage, thus defaming Your Name in the world;
And for the wrong we did before You by ugly language.

וְעַל כֻּלָּם, אֱלוֹהַּ סְלִיחוֹת, סְלַח לָנוּ, מְחַל לָנוּ, כַּפֶּר־
לָנוּ.

V'al kulam, Eloah slichot, s'lach lanu, m'chal lanu, kapper lanu.

For all our wrongs, God of forgiveness, forgive us, wipe the slate clean, grant us atonement.

עַל חֵטְא שֶׁחָטָאנוּ לְפָנֶיךָ בְּכַחַשׁ וּבְכָזָב.
וְעַל חֵטְא שֶׁחָטָאנוּ לְפָנֶיךָ בְּכַפַּת שְׁחַד:
עַל חֵטְא שֶׁחָטָאנוּ לְפָנֶיךָ בְּלָצוֹן.

For the wrong we did before You by lying and deceiving;
And for the wrong we did before You by accepting bribes.

For the wrong we did before You by scoffing and mocking;
And for the wrong we did before You by speaking ill of
other people.

For the wrong we did before You in our work;
And for the wrong we did before You in the foods we eat
and the amount we drink.

For the wrong we did before You by refusing to be
generous;
And for the wrong we did before you by being proud and
haughty.

For the wrong we did before You in rejecting Your
authority;
And for the wrong we did before You in making harsh
judgments on other people.

וְעַל כֻּלָּם, אֱלוֹהַּ סְלִיחוֹת, סְלַח לָנוּ, מְחַל לָנוּ, כַּפֶּר־
לָנוּ.

V'al kulam, Eloah s'lichot, s'lach lanu, m'chal lanu, kapper lanu.

For all these wrongs, O God of forgiveness, forgive us,
wipe the slate clean, grant us atonement.

עַל חֵטְא שֶׁחָטָאנוּ לְפָנֶיךָ בִּצְדִיַּת רָע.
וְעַל חֵטְא שֶׁחָטָאנוּ לְפָנֶיךָ בְּצָרוּת עָיִן:
עַל חֵטְא שֶׁחָטָאנוּ לְפָנֶיךָ בְּקַלּוּת רֹאשׁ.

For the wrong we did before You by plotting against
others;
And for the wrong we did before You by tormenting
others.

For the wrong we did before You by dismissing serious
matters with a joke;
And for the wrong we did before You by being obstinate.

For the wrong we did before You by running to do evil;
And for the wrong we did before You by gossiping.

For the wrong we did before You by swearing falsely;
And for the wrong we did before You by hating others
without cause.

For the wrong we did before You by betraying a trust;
And for the wrong we did before You out of confusion,
unaware of the significance of our actions.

וְעַל כֻּלָּם, אֱלוֹהַּ סְלִיחוֹת, סְלַח לָנוּ, מְחַל לָנוּ, כַּפֶּר־
לָנוּ.

V'al kulam, Eloah s'lichot, s'lach lanu, m'chal lanu, kapper lanu.

For all these wrongs, O God of forgiveness, forgive us,
wipe the slate clean, grant us atonement.

Kaddish Shalem

יִתְגַּדַּל וְיִתְקַדַּשׁ שְׁמֵהּ רַבָּא. בְּעָלְמָא דִי בְרָא
כִרְעוּתֵהּ. וְיַמְלִיךְ מַלְכוּתֵהּ בְּחַיֵּיכוֹן וּבְיוֹמֵיכוֹן וּבְחַיֵּי
דְכָל בֵּית יִשְׂרָאֵל בַּעֲגָלָא וּבִזְמַן קָרִיב וְאִמְרוּ. אָמֵן:

יְהֵא שְׁמֵהּ רַבָּא מְבָרַךְ לְעָלַם וּלְעָלְמֵי עָלְמַיָּא:

יִתְבָּרַךְ וְיִשְׁתַּבַּח וְיִתְפָּאַר וְיִתְרֹמַם וְיִתְנַשֵּׂא וְיִתְהַדָּר
וְיִתְעַלֶּה וְיִתְהַלַּל שְׁמֵהּ דְקוּדְשָׁא. בְּרִיךְ הוּא. לְעֵלָּא
וּלְעֵלָּא מִן כָּל בִּרְכָתָא וְשִׁירָתָא תֻּשְׁבְּחָתָא וְנֶחֱמָתָא
דַּאֲמִירָן בְּעָלְמָא וְאִמְרוּ. אָמֵן:

תִּתְקַבֵּל צְלוֹתְהוֹן וּבָעוּתְהוֹן דְּכָל בֵּית יִשְׂרָאֵל
קֳדָם אֲבוּהוֹן דִּי בִשְׁמַיָּא וְאִמְרוּ. אָמֵן:

יְהֵי שְׁלָמָא רַבָּא מִן שְׁמַיָּא וְחַיִּים עָלֵינוּ וְעַל כָּל
יִשְׂרָאֵל וְאִמְרוּ. אָמֵן:

עֹשֶׂה שָׁלוֹם בִּמְרוֹמָיו הוּא יַעֲשֶׂה שָׁלוֹם עָלֵינוּ וְעַל כָּל
יִשְׂרָאֵל וְאִמְרוּ. אָמֵן:

NE'ILAH SERVICE
FOR
YOM KIPPUR

NE'ILAH SERVICE FOR YOM KIPPUR

פִּתְחוּ לִי שַׁעֲרֵי צֶדֶק אָבֹא בָם אוֹדֶה יָה:

Pit'chu li sha'arei tzedek
ah-voh vahm oh-deh Yah.

Open for each of us the gates of righteousness;
then shall we enter, praising God.

פְּתַח לָנוּ שַׁעַר. בְּעֵת נְעִילַת שַׁעַר. כִּי פָנָה יוֹם:
הַיּוֹם יִפְנֶה. הַשֶּׁמֶשׁ יָבוֹא וְיִפְנֶה. נָבוֹאָה שְׁעָרֶיךָ:
אָנָּא אֵל נָא. שָׂא נָא. סְלַח־נָא. מְחַל־נָא.
חֲמָל־נָא. רַחֶם־נָא. כַּפֶּר־נָא. כְּבֹשׁ חֵטְא וְעָוֹן:

P'tach lanu sha-ar b'eyt ne'ilat sha-ar
ki fanah yom.
Hayom yifneh, hashemesh yavo v'yifneh,
navo-ah sh'areycha.
Ana el na, sa-na, s'lach-na, m'chal-na,
chamol-na, rachem-na, kaper-na,
k'vosh cheyt v'avon.

Open the gate for us now when the gates are closing.
For day is passing, day is passing.
The sun turns home.
Let us come into Your gates.
Please, God, spare . . .
Please forgive . . .
Please have mercy . . .
Please forget.
Please forbear.
And please absolve.
Help us overcome sin and wrong-doing.

*   *   *

The drama of this day draws near its climax
Our bodies weaken as the end appears.

437

As our flesh diminishes
The space for our soul expands
Yearning to close the distance from the Soul which gave it
  birth.

Hungry body, yearning soul
We now approach the Ne'ilah gates
Of pardon, purity, and peace.

Look around you.

Those who once were strangers,
Crowding the space we thought our bodies needed,
Have now, as evening falls, become familiars,
Each narrow body spreading wings
On which together we may rise beyond the gates
To join each soul to Soul
Each little space we struggle to preserve
To Space.

When the Shofar sounds and this exalting day withdraws
    behind the curtain of the night
We shall begin to miss each other's company,
We who crowded out each other's space,
We who filled each other's space with awe.

And so, in these last scenes before the night descends
Let us reach out to touch each other's souls,
That, like God before the lights came up
Upon the first creation,
We might hover over that new day,
That new and holy, pure and radiant, year
For which we hunger,
A year in which we have discovered in a room of strangers
Wings to God.

U'va L'tzion Go-eyl (An Interpretation)

To Zion shall Redeemer come
To those of Jacob's children who do tshuva for their sins.
This is my covenant with you, says God:

The breath with which I formed the world and Eve and
    Adam,
The breath on which I whispered words to Moses, my most
    intimate prophet,
That breath, those words, shall you breathe all your days,
My most intimate people.

Even when your days expire,
My breath will animate your children and their children
Until Redemption reunites them with you for eternity.

May it be Your will, God of our parents and our children,
To turn our souls, in this hour of their cleansing,
To Your Torah
To fill them with love and awe,
Able better to do Your will and serve You
With a heart at peace.

Help us follow Your mitzvot in this world
That we may be worthy to live and behold and embrace the
    goodness and blessing
Of the Redemption Yet to Come.

As we rise up once more
To the Amidah
For the last time on this awesome day,
Fill our breath with whispers of Your glory,
Let our lips be worthy vessels for Your praise.

מִסּוֹד חֲכָמִים וּנְבוֹנִים. וּמִלֶּמֶד דַּעַת מְבִינִים. אֶפְתְּחָה
פִּי בִּתְפִלָּה וּבְתַחֲנוּנִים. לְחַלּוֹת וּלְחַנֵּן פְּנֵי מֶלֶךְ מָלֵא
רַחֲמִים מוֹחֵל וְסוֹלֵחַ לַעֲוֹנִים:

*Misod chachamim un'vonim, umi-lemed
da-at m'vinim, eft'cha fi bit'filah
uv'ta-chanunim, l'chalot ul'chanen
p'ney melech maley rachamim mocheyl
v'soley-ach la'avonim.*

Piyyut: El Nora Alila

אֵל נוֹרָא עֲלִילָה, אֵל נוֹרָא עֲלִילָה,
הַמְצֵא לָֽנוּ מְחִילָה בִּשְׁעַת הַנְּעִילָה. אֵל נוֹרָא עֲלִילָה.

מְתֵי מִסְפָּר קְרוּאִים, לְךָ עַֽיִן נוֹשְׂאִים,
וּמְסַלְּדִים בְּחִילָה בִּשְׁעַת הַנְּעִילָה. אֵל נוֹרָא עֲלִילָה.

שׁוֹפְכִים לְךָ נַפְשָׁם, מְחֵה פִּשְׁעָם וְכַחֲשָׁם,
הַמְצִיאֵם מְחִילָה בִּשְׁעַת הַנְּעִילָה. אֵל נוֹרָא עֲלִילָה.

הֱיֵה לָהֶם לְסִתְרָה, וְחַלְּצֵם מִמְּאֵרָה,
וְחָתְמֵם לְהוֹד וּלְגִילָה בִּשְׁעַת הַנְּעִילָה. אֵל נוֹרָא עֲלִילָה.

חֹן אוֹתָם וְרַחֵם, וְכָל-לוֹחֵץ וְלוֹחֵם,
עֲשֵׂה בָהֶם פְּלִילָה בִּשְׁעַת הַנְּעִילָה. אֵל נוֹרָא עֲלִילָה.

זְכֹר צִדְקַת אֲבִיהֶם, וְחַדֵּשׁ אֶת-יְמֵיהֶם,
כְּקֶֽדֶם וּתְחִלָּה בִּשְׁעַת הַנְּעִילָה. אֵל נוֹרָא עֲלִילָה.

With the inspired words of the wise, and with knowledge derived from the discerning, I will open my lips in prayer and supplication to entreat and implore the presence of the Monarch who is full of compassion, who pardons and forgives iniquity.

(Rise for the Amidah, on pages 156 through 171)

Piyyut: El Nora Alila

O God of awesome acts,
O God of awesome acts,
Blot out our wrongful acts:
The gates are closing.

We who are so few
Lift up our eyes to you
In trembling prayers to You:
The gates are closing.

For You our souls do long
Wipe out our every wrong!
For pardon do we long:
The gates are closing.

All wicked plots please thwart
O promise Your support
In joy be our support:
The gates are closing.

Grant us pardon, God our Judge,
Do not from mercy budge,
And our oppressors judge:
The gates are closing.

Recall with kindly heart
Our forebears pure of heart
Grant us a fresh start:
The gates are closing.

קְרָא נָא שְׁנַת רָצוֹן, וְהָשֵׁב שְׁאֵרִית הַצֹּאן,
לְאָהֳלִיבָה וְאָהֳלָה בִּשְׁעַת הַנְּעִילָה. אֵל נוֹרָא עֲלִילָה.

El Melech Yoshev: The Thirteen Qualities of God

אֵל מֶלֶךְ יוֹשֵׁב עַל כִּסֵּא רַחֲמִים.
מִתְנַהֵג בַּחֲסִידוּת מוֹחֵל עֲוֹנוֹת עַמּוֹ.
מַעֲבִיר רִאשׁוֹן רִאשׁוֹן.
מַרְבֶּה מְחִילָה לְחַטָּאִים וּסְלִיחָה לְפוֹשְׁעִים.
עוֹשֶׂה צְדָקוֹת עִם כָּל־בָּשָׂר וָרוּחַ.
לֹא כְרָעָתָם תִּגְמוֹל.

אֵל הוֹרֵיתָ לָנוּ לוֹמַר שְׁלֹשׁ עֶשְׂרֵה.
זְכָר־לָנוּ הַיּוֹם בְּרִית שְׁלֹשׁ עֶשְׂרֵה.
כְּמוֹ שֶׁהוֹדַעְתָּ לֶעָנָו מִקֶּדֶם   כְּמוֹ שֶׁכָּתוּב.
וַיֵּרֶד יְיָ בֶּעָנָן וַיִּתְיַצֵּב עִמּוֹ שָׁם וַיִּקְרָא בְשֵׁם יְיָ:

וַיַּעֲבֹר יְיָ עַל־פָּנָיו וַיִּקְרָא.

יְיָ יְיָ אֵל רַחוּם וְחַנּוּן. אֶרֶךְ אַפַּיִם וְרַב־חֶסֶד   וֶאֱמֶת:
נֹצֵר חֶסֶד לָאֲלָפִים. נֹשֵׂא עָוֹן וָפֶשַׁע וְחַטָּאָה וְנַקֵּה:

Proclaim a fruitful year
Restore Your flock this year
Let Your land know peace this year:
The gates are closing.

El Melech Yoshev: The Thirteen Qualities of God

Majestic God
So far away on mercy's throne
Let the compassion with which You rule the world
Enter our lives like the softening light
      of this departing day
And fade our sins away into the darkness
One by one,
Sheltering us with Your pardon.

Grant everyone whose life began amid the darkness of the
      womb
The revelation of Your righteousness,
The obliteration of our wrongdoing.

O God who shaped Your nature into Thirteen Qualities
That we might appeal to Your infinite distance in intimate
      words,
Let the Thirteen appear now out of the shadows
As a covenant in force on this forgiving day,
Just as it was after Israel made the Golden Calf
And in the shadows of the rock
You revealed to Moses Your everlasting pardon:
      As Adonay descended in the cloud
      Moses stood there with God
      And called out the name of Adonay,
      And Adonay passed before his face and called out:

*Adonay, Adonay, El rachum v'chanun, erech apayim v'rav
chesed ve-emet;*

*notzer chesed la-alafim, nosey avon va-fesha v'chata-ah
v'nakey.*

וְסָלַחְתָּ לַעֲוֹנֵנוּ וּלְחַטָּאתֵנוּ וּנְחַלְתָּנוּ:

סְלַח־לָנוּ אָבִינוּ כִּי חָטָאנוּ. מְחַל־לָנוּ מַלְכֵּנוּ כִּי
פָשָׁעְנוּ:
כִּי אַתָּה אֲדֹנָי טוֹב וְסַלָּח וְרַב־חֶסֶד לְכָל קֹרְאֶיךָ:

Piyyut: Ki Anu Amecha

כִּי אָנוּ עַמֶּךָ וְאַתָּה אֱלֹהֵינוּ. אָנוּ בָנֶיךָ וְאַתָּה אָבִינוּ:
אָנוּ עֲבָדֶיךָ וְאַתָּה אֲדוֹנֵנוּ. אָנוּ קְהָלֶךָ וְאַתָּה חֶלְקֵנוּ:
אָנוּ נַחֲלָתֶךָ וְאַתָּה גוֹרָלֵנוּ. אָנוּ צֹאנֶךָ וְאַתָּה רוֹעֵנוּ:
אָנוּ כַרְמֶךָ וְאַתָּה נוֹטְרֵנוּ. אָנוּ פְעֻלָּתֶךָ וְאַתָּה יוֹצְרֵנוּ:
אָנוּ רַעְיָתֶךָ וְאַתָּה דוֹדֵנוּ. אָנוּ סְגֻלָּתֶךָ וְאַתָּה קְרוֹבֵנוּ:
אָנוּ עַמֶּךָ וְאַתָּה מַלְכֵּנוּ. אָנוּ מַאֲמִירֶיךָ וְאַתָּה
מַאֲמִירֵנוּ:

Adonay, Adonay, God filled with motherlove, slow to
anger, great in covenantal love and truth; keeping love for
the thousands within the covenant, forgiving perverse actions,
rebelliousness, and sin; and acquitting.

May You pardon us for our wrongdoing and our sinfulness, and
take us as Your own.

And God renewed the covenant with us:
Before all the people I shall do marvels
Such as the earth and its inhabitants have never known.
And all those in whose midst you live
Shall see the awesome work of God.
For I am giving you the gift of My mitzvot
The very gift I gave you before you made the calf.
The God who pardoned our forebears' grevious wrong
Promises pardon for our wrongs in the twilight of this day.

Pardon us, Avinu, for we have sinned; forgive us, Malkeynu,
for we have done wrong.
For You, Adonay, are goodness itself, the Source of pardon,
great in covenantal love to all who call out to You.

Piyyut: Ki Anu Amecha

Ki anu amecha v'atta Eloheynu, anu vanecha v'atta avinu.
Anu avadecha v'atta Adoneynu, anu k'halecha v'atta chelkeynu.
Anu nachalatecha v'atta goraleynu, anu tzonecha v'atta ro-eynu.
Anu charmecha v'atta notreynu, anu f'ulatecha v'atta yotzreynu.
Anu ra'yatecha v'atta dodeynu, anu s'gulatecha v'atta k'ro-veynu.
Anu amecha v'atta malkeynu, anu ma'amirecha v'atta ma'ami-reynu.

For we are Your people, and You our God.
We are Your children, and You the One who gave us life.

FINAL CONFESSION OF THE DAY

Preparation

אֱלֹהֵינוּ וֵאלֹהֵי אֲבוֹתֵינוּ (וֵאלֹהֵי אִמּוֹתֵינוּ) תָּבֹא לְפָנֶיךָ תְּפִלָּתֵנוּ, וְאַל תִּתְעַלַּם מִתְּחִנָּתֵנוּ; שֶׁאֵין אֲנַחְנוּ עַזֵּי פָנִים וּקְשֵׁי עֹרֶף לוֹמַר לְפָנֶיךָ, יְיָ אֱלֹהֵינוּ וֵאלֹהֵי אֲבוֹתֵינוּ (וֵאלֹהֵי אִמּוֹתֵינוּ), צַדִּיקִים אֲנַחְנוּ וְלֹא חָטָאנוּ; אֲבָל אֲנַחְנוּ חָטָאנוּ.

Ashamnu

אָשַׁמְנוּ, בָּגַדְנוּ, גָּזַלְנוּ, דִּבַּרְנוּ דְפִי; הֶעֱוִינוּ, וְהִרְשַׁעְנוּ, זַדְנוּ, חָמַסְנוּ, טָפַלְנוּ שֶׁקֶר; יָעַצְנוּ רָע, כִּזַּבְנוּ, לַצְנוּ, מָרַדְנוּ, נִאַצְנוּ, סָרַרְנוּ, עָוִינוּ, פָּשַׁעְנוּ, צָרַרְנוּ, קִשִּׁינוּ עֹרֶף; רָשַׁעְנוּ, שִׁחַתְנוּ, תִּעַבְנוּ, תָּעִינוּ, תִּעְתָּעְנוּ.

Atta Noteyn Yad: The Value of Our Lives

אַתָּה נוֹתֵן יָד לְפוֹשְׁעִים, וִימִינְךָ פְּשׁוּטָה לְקַבֵּל שָׁבִים. וַתְּלַמְּדֵנוּ, יְיָ אֱלֹהֵינוּ, לְהִתְוַדּוֹת לְפָנֶיךָ עַל כָּל־עֲוֹנוֹתֵינוּ, לְמַעַן נֶחְדַּל מֵעֹשֶׁק יָדֵינוּ, וּתְקַבְּלֵנוּ בִּתְשׁוּבָה שְׁלֵמָה לְפָנֶיךָ, לְמַעַן דְּבָרֶיךָ אֲשֶׁר אָמָרְתָּ.

We are Your servants, and You the One who acquires us.
We are Your congregation, and You our only One.
We are Your heritage, and You our Destiny.
We are Your flock, and You our Shepherd.
We are Your vineyard, and You our Protector.
We are Your creatures, and You our Creator.
We are Your companion, and You our Beloved.
We are Your treasure, and You the intimate who redeems us.
We are Your people, and You our Sovereign.
We have chosen You, and You have chosen us.

FINAL CONFESSION OF THE DAY

Preparation

God of those who sought You out in ages past
Let our prayer also come before You
And do not turn aside from our entreaty.
For we are not so obstinate and stubborn
As to say before You:
We are righteous, we have done no wrong.
For indeed, we have done wrong,
And we join, now as the gates are swinging shut,
In the last confession of Yom Kippur
Before You.

Ashamnu

Ashamnu, bagadnu, gazalnu, dibarnu dofi, he-evinu, v'hir-shanu, zadnu, chamasnu, tafalnu sheker, ya-atznu ra, kizavnu, latznu, maradnu, ni-atznu, sararnu, avinu, pashanu, tzararnu, kishinu oref, rashanu, shichatnu, ti-avnu, ta-inu, ti'ta'nu.

Atta Noteyn Yad: The Value of Our Lives

You reach out Your strong hand to wrongdoers,
You extend Your welcome to those returning in tshuvah.
It is You who taught us to confess all wrongs before You
That we might stop hurting other people,
That we might be welcomed in Your presence.

וְאַתָּה יוֹדֵעַ שֶׁאַחֲרִיתֵנוּ רִמָּה וְתוֹלֵעָה; לְפִיכָךְ הִרְבֵּיתָ
סְלִיחָתֵנוּ. מָה אָנוּ, מֶה חַיֵּינוּ, מֶה חַסְדֵּנוּ, מַה־צִּדְקֵנוּ,
מַה־יְשָׁעֵנוּ, מַה־כֹּחֵנוּ, מַה־גְּבוּרָתֵנוּ. מַה־נֹּאמַר
לְפָנֶיךָ, יְיָ אֱלֹהֵינוּ וֵאלֹהֵי אֲבוֹתֵינוּ (וֵאלֹהֵי אִמּוֹתֵינוּ).
הֲלֹא כָּל־הַגִּבּוֹרִים כְּאַיִן לְפָנֶיךָ, וְאַנְשֵׁי הַשֵּׁם כְּלֹא
הָיוּ, וַחֲכָמִים כִּבְלִי מַדָּע, וּנְבוֹנִים כִּבְלִי הַשְׂכֵּל.
כִּי רֹב מַעֲשֵׂיהֶם תֹּהוּ, וִימֵי חַיֵּיהֶם הֶבֶל לְפָנֶיךָ. וּמוֹתַר
הָאָדָם מִן הַבְּהֵמָה אָיִן, כִּי הַכֹּל הָבֶל.

אַתָּה הִבְדַּלְתָּ אֱנוֹשׁ מֵרֹאשׁ וַתַּכִּירֵהוּ לַעֲמוֹד לְפָנֶיךָ.
כִּי מִי יֹאמַר לְךָ מַה תִּפְעָל, וְאִם יִצְדַּק מַה יִּתֶּן־לָךְ.
וַתִּתֶּן־לָנוּ, יְיָ אֱלֹהֵינוּ, בְּאַהֲבָה אֶת־יוֹם [הַשַּׁבָּת הַזֶּה
וְאֶת יוֹם] הַכִּפּוּרִים הַזֶּה, קֵץ וּמְחִילָה וּסְלִיחָה עַל
כָּל־עֲוֹנוֹתֵינוּ, לְמַעַן נֶחְדַּל מֵעֹשֶׁק יָדֵינוּ, וְנָשׁוּב אֵלֶיךָ
לַעֲשׂוֹת חֻקֵּי רְצוֹנְךָ בְּלֵבָב שָׁלֵם.

וְאַתָּה בְּרַחֲמֶיךָ הָרַבִּים רַחֵם עָלֵינוּ. כִּי לֹא תַחְפּוֹץ
בְּהַשְׁחָתַת עוֹלָם. שֶׁנֶּאֱמַר. דִּרְשׁוּ יְיָ בְּהִמָּצְאוֹ קְרָאֻהוּ
בִּהְיוֹתוֹ קָרוֹב. וְנֶאֱמַר: יַעֲזֹב רָשָׁע דַּרְכּוֹ וְאִישׁ אָוֶן
מַחְשְׁבֹתָיו וְיָשֹׁב אֶל־יְיָ וִירַחֲמֵהוּ וְאֶל־אֱלֹהֵינוּ כִּי־
יַרְבֶּה לִסְלוֹחַ: וְאַתָּה אֱלוֹהַּ סְלִיחוֹת חַנּוּן וְרַחוּם אֶרֶךְ
אַפַּיִם וְרַב־חֶסֶד וֶאֱמֶת וּמַרְבֶּה לְהֵיטִיב. וְרוֹצֶה אַתָּה
בִּתְשׁוּבַת רְשָׁעִים וְאֵין אַתָּה חָפֵץ בְּמִיתָתָם שֶׁנֶּאֱמַר.
אֱמֹר אֲלֵיהֶם חַי־אָנִי נְאֻם אֲדֹנָי יֱהוִה אִם־אֶחְפֹּץ
בְּמוֹת הָרָשָׁע כִּי אִם־בְּשׁוּב רָשָׁע מִדַּרְכּוֹ וְחָיָה. שׁוּבוּ
שׁוּבוּ מִדַּרְכֵיכֶם הָרָעִים וְלָמָּה תָמוּתוּ בֵּית יִשְׂרָאֵל:
וְנֶאֱמַר. הֶחָפֹץ אֶחְפֹּץ מוֹת רָשָׁע נְאֻם אֲדֹנָי יֱהוִה
הֲלוֹא בְּשׁוּבוֹ מִדְּרָכָיו וְחָיָה: וְנֶאֱמַר. כִּי לֹא אֶחְפֹּץ
בְּמוֹת הַמֵּת נְאֻם אֲדֹנָי יֱהוִה וְהָשִׁיבוּ וִחְיוּ:

Because You know that only dust awaits us at the end
You are merciful to us,
You are bountiful in Your pardon.
What are we? Of what value is our life?
What is our goodness, our righteousness?
What help can we offer those in distress?
What is our strength, our might, our power?
What can we say before You, Adonay our God,
God of all our worthy forebears,
For in Your presence
Mighty men are as nothing,
Women of renown as though they had never been,
The wisest of the sages like the most ignorant.
In Your presence even their lives are but a vapor in the wind,
All humanity seem scarcely more than animals,
All passing vapors in the wind.

What are we? Of what value is our life?
You have shown us the answer:
Human beings are precious to You.
You singled us out at the beginning from all Creation.
Even though the righteous cannot give You anything
Which is not Yours already,
You have given something irreplaceable to us:
This (Shabbat and) Day of Atonement,
Soon to conclude with Your pardon for all our wrongs,
Enabling us to stop hurting other people,
To start turning to You,
Doing Your will with hearts undivided,
Knowing You will respond out of Your great compassion
With compassion for each one of us.
What are we?
We are the recipients of Your love.
What is our goodness?
It is the goodness You see in each of us.

"I do not want you to die in your wrongdoing,"
You have told us.
"Do tshuvah, that you may live."

Avinu Malkeynu: Our Forgiving Parent, Our Sovereign

אָבִינוּ מַלְכֵּנוּ חָטָאנוּ לְפָנֶיךָ:

אָבִינוּ מַלְכֵּנוּ אֵין לָנוּ מֶלֶךְ אֶלָּא אָתָּה:

אָבִינוּ מַלְכֵּנוּ חַדֵּשׁ עָלֵינוּ שָׁנָה טוֹבָה:

אָבִינוּ מַלְכֵּנוּ הָפֵר עֲצַת אוֹיְבֵינוּ:

אָבִינוּ מַלְכֵּנוּ כַּלֵּה דֶּבֶר וְחֶרֶב וְרָעָב וּשְׁבִי וּמַשְׁחִית מִבְּנֵי בְרִיתֶךָ:

אָבִינוּ מַלְכֵּנוּ סְלַח וּמְחַל לְכָל־עֲוֹנוֹתֵינוּ:

אָבִינוּ מַלְכֵּנוּ הַחֲזִירֵנוּ בִּתְשׁוּבָה שְׁלֵמָה לְפָנֶיךָ:

אָבִינוּ מַלְכֵּנוּ שְׁלַח רְפוּאָה שְׁלֵמָה לְחוֹלֵי עַמֶּךָ:

אָבִינוּ מַלְכֵּנוּ חָתְמֵנוּ בְּסֵפֶר חַיִּים טוֹבִים:

אָבִינוּ מַלְכֵּנוּ חָתְמֵנוּ בְּסֵפֶר פַּרְנָסָה וְכַלְכָּלָה:

אָבִינוּ מַלְכֵּנוּ חָתְמֵנוּ בְּסֵפֶר זְכֻיּוֹת:

אָבִינוּ מַלְכֵּנוּ חָתְמֵנוּ בְּסֵפֶר סְלִיחָה וּמְחִילָה:

אָבִינוּ מַלְכֵּנוּ חֲמוֹל עָלֵינוּ וְעַל עוֹלָלֵינוּ וְטַפֵּנוּ:

אָבִינוּ מַלְכֵּנוּ פְּתַח שַׁעֲרֵי שָׁמַיִם לִתְפִלָּתֵנוּ:

אָבִינוּ מַלְכֵּנוּ עֲשֵׂה לְמַעַן בָּאֵי בָאֵשׁ וּבַמַּיִם עַל־קִדּוּשׁ שְׁמֶךָ:

אָבִינוּ מַלְכֵּנוּ חָנֵּנוּ וַעֲנֵנוּ כִּי אֵין בָּנוּ מַעֲשִׂים עֲשֵׂה עִמָּנוּ צְדָקָה וָחֶסֶד וְהוֹשִׁיעֵנוּ:

Avinu Malkeynu: Our Forgiving Parent, Our Sovereign

Avinu Malkeynu, we have done wrong before You.

Avinu Malkeynu, we have no Sovereign except You.

Avinu Malkeynu, let this be a good year for us.

Avinu Malkeynu, destroy the power of every oppressor and adversary.

Avinu Malkeynu, remove from all Your children disease, war, famine, exile and destruction.

Avinu Malkeynu, forgive and pardon all our wrongdoing.

Avinu Malkeynu, may we return to You in earnest repentance.

Avinu Malkeynu, send healing to all who are sick.

Avinu Malkeynu, seal us in Your book for a life of goodness.

Avinu Malkeynu, seal us in the book of sustenance.

Avinu Malkeynu, seal us in the book of meritorious acts.

Avinu Malkeynu, seal us in the book of forgiveness and reconciliation.

Avinu Malkeynu, show mercy to us and to our children.

Avinu Malkeynu, open the gates of heaven to our prayer.

Avinu Malkeynu, do it for the sake of those who went through fire and water to honor Your Name.

Avinu Malkeynu, be gracious and respond to us, for we have too few good deeds; act toward us with justice tempered by love, and bring us salvation.

*Avinu Malkeynu chawneynu va'a-neinu ki ein banu ma'asim
Asey imanu tz'dakah va'chesed v'hoshi-eynu*

The night descends once more on the atoning sunlight of lives made more profound and thoughtful by the words and hours we have spent together. What opened when the moon last rose as an Atonement Day has become At-one-ment Day, in which we have come closer to our people, have become more trusting of ourselves, and have lost some of our fears of the God before whom we have stood in awe. The night descends, and we, strengthened and renewed, arise.

We have shared many words about ourselves this Atonement Day, confessing error, thoughtlessness, misdeed, and wrong. And yet the very act of confronting failings has enabled us to confront our virtue, and so what we must leave with each other this day is the conviction of our inner worth, the knowledge that no matter what we do we are the child of God, a valued and irreplaceable jewel in the crown that is God's universe.

Now the gates are closing in the heavens which have been the witness of our hearts on this afflicting, wearying, yet now exalting day. As the sun descends into the sea, we pray that it may take our misdeeds, thoughtlessness, and wrongs with it, that when the stars rise in the clear night sky there might rise with them the first and tender steps of a committed, thoughtful life, our soul awake to the brightness of possibilities that life can offer us, to enable us to shine among our cosmos as the full, bright Tishri moon that soon will glow above us in the Sukkot sky.

The night descends, and we—strengthened and renewed—arise.

ALEYNU

(May be said here)

May the time not be distant, O God,
When Your enduring rule shall be established in the midst
    of the earth;
When justice shall prevail in the land,
Evil destroyed,
And the strong shall no more oppress the weak;
May sin be taken away from everyone
And, heir to our people's royal covenant,
May we each exercise the just power that is our birthright
As a child of God.
In youth may we gain wisdom,
Overflowing like a river with understanding;
Our soul profound enough to cover the earth,
Loved, each of us,
For the peace we bring to others.
May our deeds exceed our speech,
And may we never lift up our hand
But to conquer fear and doubt and grave despair.
Rise up like the sun, O God, over all humanity,
Cause light to go forth over all the lands between the seas,
And light up the universe with the joy of wholeness, of
    freedom and of peace.

עָלֵינוּ לְשַׁבֵּחַ לַאֲדוֹן הַכֹּל, לָתֵת גְּדֻלָּה לְיוֹצֵר
בְּרֵאשִׁית שֶׁלֹּא עָשָׂנוּ כְּגוֹיֵי הָאֲרָצוֹת וְלֹא שָׂמָנוּ
כְּמִשְׁפְּחוֹת הָאֲדָמָה שֶׁלֹּא שָׂם חֶלְקֵנוּ כָּהֶם וְגֹרָלֵנוּ
כְּכָל הֲמוֹנָם:

וַאֲנַחְנוּ כּוֹרְעִים וּמִשְׁתַּחֲוִים וּמוֹדִים
לִפְנֵי מֶלֶךְ מַלְכֵי הַמְּלָכִים הַקָּדוֹשׁ בָּרוּךְ הוּא.
שֶׁהוּא נוֹטֶה שָׁמַיִם וְיוֹסֵד אָרֶץ וּמוֹשַׁב יְקָרוֹ בַּשָּׁמַיִם
מִמַּעַל וּשְׁכִינַת עֻזּוֹ בְּגָבְהֵי מְרוֹמִים: הוּא אֱלֹהֵינוּ אֵין
עוֹד. אֱמֶת מַלְכֵּנוּ אֶפֶס זוּלָתוֹ כַּכָּתוּב בְּתוֹרָתוֹ וְיָדַעְתָּ

הַיּוֹם וַהֲשֵׁבֹתָ אֶל לְבָבֶךָ כִּי יְהֹוָה הוּא הָאֱלֹהִים
בַּשָּׁמַיִם מִמַּעַל וְעַל־הָאָרֶץ מִתָּחַת אֵין עוֹד:

*A-ley-nu l'sha-be-ach la-a-don hakol, la-tet g'du-lah l'yo-
tzer b'rey-sheet, she-lo a-sa-nu k'goyey ha-a-ra-tzot, v'lo
sa-manu k'mish-p'chot ha-a-da-mah; she-lo sam chel-key-
nu ka-hem, v'go-ra-ley-nu k'chol ha-mo-nam.
Va-a-nach-nu ko-r-im u-mish-ta-cha-vim u-mo-dim lif-
ney me-lech mal-chey ha-m'la-chim, ha-ka-dosh ba-ruch
hu, she-hu no-teh sha-ma-yim v'yo-sed a-retz, u-mo-shav
y'ka-roh ba-sha-mayim mi-ma-al, u-shchi-nat u-zo b'gav-
hey m'ro-mim.
Hu E-lo-hey-nu, ein od.
E-met mal-key-nu e-fes zu-la-to, ka-ka-tuv b'to-rah-toh.
V'ya-da-tah ha-yom va-ha-shevo-tah el l'vav-e-cha ki
Adonay hu ha-E-lo-him ba-sha-ma-yim mi-ma-al v'al ha-a-
retz mi-ta-chat, ein od.*

It is incumbent upon us to praise the Source of all creatures, to attribute greatness to the molder of creation,
who did not make our lot like the nations, nor like the
other families of the earth: for we bow down in reverence
and thanksgiving before the Ruler of all earthly rulers, the
Holy One, whom we praise.

וְנֶאֱמַר וְהָיָה יְיָ לְמֶלֶךְ עַל כָּל הָאָרֶץ בַּיּוֹם הַהוּא יִהְיֶה
יְיָ אֶחָד וּשְׁמוֹ אֶחָד:

*V'ne-e-mar: v'ha-yah A-do-nay l'me-lech al kol ha-a-retz;
Ba-yom ha-hu
Yih-yeh A-do-nay e-chad
U-sh'mo e-chad.*

שְׁמַע יִשְׂרָאֵל יְיָ אֱלֹהֵינוּ יְיָ אֶחָד:

Shma Yisrael Adonay Eloheynu Adonay Echad

Hear, O Israel: Adonay our God, Adonay is One.

(three times)

בָּרוּךְ שֵׁם כְּבוֹד מַלְכוּתוֹ לְעוֹלָם וָעֶד:

Baruch shem k'vod mal'chu-to l'olam va-ed.

Praised be the Name whose glorious kingdom is forever
and ever.

(seven times)

יְיָ הוּא הָאֱלֹהִים:

Adonay Hu Ha-Elohim!

Adonay is God.

Kaddish Shalem

יִתְגַּדַּל וְיִתְקַדַּשׁ שְׁמֵהּ רַבָּא. בְּעָלְמָא דִי בְרָא
כִרְעוּתֵהּ. וְיַמְלִיךְ מַלְכוּתֵהּ בְּחַיֵּיכוֹן וּבְיוֹמֵיכוֹן וּבְחַיֵּי
דְכָל בֵּית יִשְׂרָאֵל בַּעֲגָלָא וּבִזְמַן קָרִיב וְאִמְרוּ. אָמֵן:

יְהֵא שְׁמֵהּ רַבָּא מְבָרַךְ לְעָלַם וּלְעָלְמֵי עָלְמַיָּא:

יִתְבָּרַךְ וְיִשְׁתַּבַּח וְיִתְפָּאַר וְיִתְרֹמַם וְיִתְנַשֵּׂא וְיִתְהַדָּר
וְיִתְעַלֶּה וְיִתְהַלָּל שְׁמֵהּ דְּקֻדְשָׁא. בְּרִיךְ הוּא. לְעֵלָּא
לְעֵלָּא מִן כָּל בִּרְכָתָא וְשִׁירָתָא תֻּשְׁבְּחָתָא וְנֶחֱמָתָא
דַּאֲמִירָן בְּעָלְמָא וְאִמְרוּ. אָמֵן:

תִּתְקַבֵּל צְלוֹתְהוֹן וּבָעוּתְהוֹן דְּכָל יִשְׂרָאֵל קֳדָם
אֲבוּהוֹן דִּי בִשְׁמַיָּא וְאִמְרוּ. אָמֵן:
יְהֵא שְׁלָמָא רַבָּא רַבָּא מִן שְׁמַיָּא וְחַיִּים עָלֵינוּ וְעַל כָּל
יִשְׂרָאֵל וְאִמְרוּ. אָמֵן:
עֹשֶׂה שָׁלוֹם בִּמְרוֹמָיו הוּא יַעֲשֶׂה שָׁלוֹם עָלֵינוּ וְעַל כָּל
יִשְׂרָאֵל וְאִמְרוּ. אָמֵן:

May God's great name be praised and sanctified in the
world! May Your Rule be established in our lifetime and
the lifetime of the House of Israel. God's great name is
blessed and praised far beyond all blessings and praises we
can ever say in the world. May the praises and prayers of
all Israel be accepted in heaven before You. May there be a
great peace from heaven and life for us and all Israel. May
the One who makes peace in the high places, make peace
for us and all Israel! *Amen.*

FINAL SOUNDING OF THE SHOFAR

תְּקִיעָה גְדוֹלָה

לַשָׁנָה הַבָּאָה בִּירוּשָׁלָיִם:

La-shana ha-ba-ah bee-ru-shalayim.

Next year in Jerusalem.
Next year may a new world dawn for us all.

SOURCES

Many English readings and translations in the Machzor, including translations of the Torah and Haftarah passages, are the work of the editor. Authors of other passages are listed below. (R) signifies those which have been revised by the editor.

Pages

2f.   *To everything* . . . Rabbi Jack Riemer.

8 –9   *You who love my soul* . . . Translations of Y'did Nefesh by Rabbi Zalman Schachter-Shalomi.

9f.   *In heaven and on earth* . . . Joanne Greenberg (R).

11f.   *You are praised* . . . Translation by Rabbi Moshe Adler and Dr. Rachel Adler (R).

20f.   *The Kabbalists tell us* . . . Dr. Rachel Adler (R).

33f.   *Our God and God of our ancestors* . . . Translation by Rabbi Moshe Adler and Dr. Rachel Adler (R).

34f.   *Adonay, Our people have called You* . . . by Rabbi Laura Geller.

43   *May the time not be distant* . . . Union Prayer Book (R).

46   *May we find the world* . . . Berachot 17a, translated by the editor.

57   *Baruch She-amar* . . . Transliteration is in accord with a musical rendition by Rabbi Neil Comess-Daniels.

91f.   *When we really begin* . . . adapted by Rabbi Shammai Kantor and Rabbi Jack Riemer, from Rabbi Stanley Rabinowitz.

99f.   *Our God and God of our ancestors* . . . See pp. 33–34.

145   *In the world of matter* . . . Rabbi Nachman of Bratzlav, interpreted by the editor.

155   *All the world* . . . Translation of anonymous piyyut, *V'ye-etayu,* by Israel Zangwill. Slightly revised by the editor.

157–171   *Traditional Silent Amidah* . . . Many of the English versions are based on translations of Rabbi Moshe Adler and Dr. Rachel Adler (R). Others are by the editor.

177–239   *Musaf Amidah* . . . Many of the English versions are based on translations of Rabbi Moshe Adler and Dr. Rachel Adler (R). Others are by the editor.

245   *By the authority* . . . Interpretation by Rabbi Dan Dorfman and Rabbi Neil Comess-Daniels (R).

247–248   *All the vows on our lips* . . . Dr. Zev Falk. Translation by Rabbi Stanley Schachter.

251   *Praise me, says God* . . . Aaron Zeitlin, translated by Rabbi Emanuel Goldsmith.

252f.   *You are praised* . . . See pp. 11f.

265–267   *On Doing Wrong* . . . Mishna Yoma 8:9; Hilchot Tshuvah (The Laws of Repentance) from Maimonides' *Mishneh Torah:* 2:3, 7:3, 7:4; Babylonian Talmud, Kiddushin 30b; Hilchot Tshuvah 5:1. Translated by the editor.

270f.   *This is my prayer* . . . Hillel Bavli, translated by Rabbi Norman Tarnor.

271f.   *I pray to You, O God* . . . Julian Tuwim, translated by W. Dynowska.

272f.   *Praised are You* . . . Huub Oosterhuis (R).

295.   *A reaching-up song* . . . Translated by Rabbi Moshe Adler and Dr. Rachel Adler.

295f.   *Levi Yitzchak* . . . Translator unknown.

296f.   *Ruler of the world* . . . Rabbi Nachman of Bratzlav. Translator unknown.

304.   *Baruch she-amar.* See p. 57.

319.   *In some special way* . . . Rabbi Judah Loew (the Maharal) of Prague.

319.   *The same stream* . . . Rabindranath Tagore.

321.   *God means* . . . Rabbi Abraham Joshua Heschel *(Man Is Not Alone),* slightly revised by the editor.

323f.   *If you will pay attention* . . . Translation by Rabbi Moshe Adler and Dr. Rachel Adler.

324.   *God spoke to Moses* . . . Translation by Rabbi Moshe Adler and Dr. Rachel Adler.

325.   *Time is the border* . . . Rabbi Abraham Joshua Heschel *(Man Is Not Alone).*

333.   *When we really begin* . . . See pp. 91f.

341.   *My God, before I was formed* . . . Interpretation of *Elohai ad she-lo notzarti,* by the editor.

380f.   *At the rising of the sun* . . . Rabbi Sylvan Kamens and Rabbi Jack Riemer.

381f.   *Your joy is your sorrow unmasked* . . . Kahlil Gibran *(The Prophet).*

382f.   *Life is not fair* . . . Rabbi Harold Kushner *(When Bad Things Happen to Good People).*

384f.   *Strangers' eyes don't see* . . . Jacob Glatstein, "Nightsong," translated by Ruth Whitman.

397f.   *When the great Rabbi Israel Baal Shem-Tov* . . . Quoted by Elie Wiesel in *The Gates of the Forest.* Last line *(Listen, God . . .)* by Rabbi Moshe Adler and Dr. Rachel Adler, who originally used the story to introduce his Avodah Service.

399–404. *Seven days before Yom Kippur* . . . Translation by Rabbi Moshe Adler and Dr. Rachel Adler.

404f.   *Since the destruction* . . . by Rabbi Abraham Joshua Heschel (from *Man's Quest for God*) (R).

406–409. *These will I remember* . . . Translation by Rabbi Moshe Adler and Dr. Rachel Adler. Slightly revised by the editor.

409f.   *In reading of these Ten Martyrs* . . . Dr. Max Arzt (from *Justice and Mercy*).

415ff.   *Interpretation of tum'ah* as "a time of endings and beginnings" reflects Dr. Rachel Adler's essay, "Tum'ah and Toharah: Ends and Beginnings," in *The Jewish Woman: An Anthology,* published by Response, © 1973. See also her essay on Torah and Toharah in *The First Jewish Catalog,* ed. Siegel, Strassfeld and Strassfeld, published by Jewish Publication Society © 1973.